Lecture Notes in Computer Science 16295

The series Lecture Notes in Computer Science (LNCS), including its subseries Lecture Notes in Artificial Intelligence (LNAI) and Lecture Notes in Bioinformatics (LNBI), has established itself as a medium for the publication of new developments in computer science and information technology research, teaching, and education.

LNCS enjoys close cooperation with the computer science R & D community, the series counts many renowned academics among its volume editors and paper authors, and collaborates with prestigious societies. Its mission is to serve this international community by providing an invaluable service, mainly focused on the publication of conference and workshop proceedings and postproceedings. LNCS commenced publication in 1973.

Kamel Adi · Nora Boulahia-Cuppens ·
David Espes · Natalia Stakhanova ·
Mawloud Omar · Omer Nguena Timo
Editors

Risks and Security of Internet and Systems

20th International Conference, CRiSIS 2025, Gatineau QC, Canada, October 22–24, 2025
Proceedings

Editors
Kamel Adi
University of Quebec in Outaouais
Gatineau, QC, Canada

Nora Boulahia-Cuppens
Polytechnique Montréal
Montréal, QC, Canada

David Espes
University of Brest
Brest, France

Natalia Stakhanova
University of Saskatchewan
Saskatoon, SK, Canada

Mawloud Omar
University of Southern Brittany
Lorient, France

Omer Nguena Timo
University of Quebec in Outaouais
Gatineau, QC, Canada

ISSN 0302-9743 ISSN 1611-3349 (electronic)
Lecture Notes in Computer Science
ISBN 978-3-032-20731-9 ISBN 978-3-032-20732-6 (eBook)
https://doi.org/10.1007/978-3-032-20732-6

This Springer imprint is published by the registered company Springer Nature Switzerland AG
The registered company address is: Gewerbestrasse 11, 6330 Cham, Switzerland

Preface

The 20th International Conference on Risks and Security of Internet and Systems (CRiSIS 2025) marked a new milestone in the ongoing effort to address the evolving security challenges surrounding Internet-based applications, networks, and systems. Over the years, CRiSIS has adapted to shifting global contexts while consistently fostering progress in cybersecurity research. Recent editions illustrate this trajectory: the 2024 conference at TheCamp in Aix-en-Provence, France, offered a dynamic space for researchers, professionals, and industry experts to exchange insights, following the 2023 meeting in Morocco and the 2022 gathering in Sousse, Tunisia, which celebrated a return to in-person participation with 18 presented papers. Earlier, the 2021 edition hosted from Ames, Iowa, USA, and the 2020 conference, originally planned for Paris, were held virtually during the COVID-Pandamic, maintaining strong engagement comparable to the 2019 event in Hammamet, Tunisia.

CRiSIS 2025 took place from October 22–24, 2025, at the Université du Québec en Outaouais (UQO) in Gatineau, Québec, Canada. Bringing together leading researchers, experienced practitioners, and key industry figures, this edition provided an exceptional forum for examining the shifting cybersecurity landscape and the protection of interconnected digital systems. The contributions collected in these proceedings reflect the conference's enduring commitment to innovation, interdisciplinary collaboration, and the exchange of cutting-edge knowledge in an era of increasingly sophisticated and pervasive cyber threats.

CRiSIS 2025 attracted 52 paper submissions from 16 countries. Of these, 28 papers were accepted, resulting in an acceptance rate of about 54\%. All submissions underwent a rigorous peer-review process. All papers received two or three evaluations, ensuring thorough assessments while maintaining a balanced workload for the program committee.

The accepted papers were organized into sessions covering diverse and pressing topics in cybersecurity:

- AI for Software Security: Covers papers leveraging AI and machine-learning to automatically detect, fix, prevent software vulnerabilities and flaws.
- Cyber Threats and Prediction: Focuses on forecasting and modelling cyber-attacks or threat evolutions through statistical, ML, analytic methods to anticipate risks.
- Distributed Systems and IoT Security: Covers security issues and protections in distributed architectures and Internet-of-Things (IoT), including embedded systems, edge/fog, and networked devices.
- Intrusion Detection Systems (IDS): Presents research on techniques to detect intrusions, anomalous behavior, attacks in networks or systems.
- Privacy and Digital Trust: Covers user privacy, anonymization, trust management, identity, and secure data sharing in digital environments.

- Vulnerabilities and Resilience: Covers system vulnerabilities and explores methods to enhance robustness, fault-tolerance, and recovery to strengthen resilience against attacks/failures.
- Privacy, Threat Analysis, and Explainable Cybersecurity: Combines privacy concerns with threat modelling, and aims to make security decisions and analyses transparent and explainable.
- Advanced Attacks and Strategic Detection: Focuses on sophisticated attack methods (e.g., novel exploit techniques) and strategic detection, improving detection beyond standard or known threats.
- Security Governance, Compliance, and Adaptive Systems: Looks at organizational, legal, and ethical aspects of security governance and how systems can adapt their security posture to meet compliance and evolving risks

The achievements of CRiSIS 2025 reflect the commitment of a broad community of contributors. We express our appreciation to the Program Committee and external reviewers, whose careful assessments and insightful recommendations shaped a program that captured both the diversity and the evolution of cybersecurity research. We also thank our invited speakers for offering thought-provoking perspectives that enriched discussions and encouraged participants to explore new lines of inquiry.

We are equally grateful to the authors and attendees whose active involvement animated this edition of the conference. Their exchanges, collaborations, and constructive debates contributed to an atmosphere conducive to scientific progress and community building. Our recognition extends to the local organizing team at UQO, along with the supporting institutions and volunteers, whose diligent efforts ensured a smooth and engaging event.

We hope the contributions gathered in these proceedings will continue to inspire innovative research and foster sustained collaboration, reinforcing the shared ambition to develop more secure, reliable, and trustworthy digital systems.

January 6, 2026

Kamel Adi
Nora Boulahia-Cuppens
David Espes
Natalia Stakhanova
Mawloud Omar
Omer Nguena Timo

Organization

General Chairs

Kamel Adi	Université du Québec en Outaouais, Canada
Nora Boulahia-Cuppens	Polytechnique Montréal, Canada

Program Committee Chairs

David Espes	University of Brest, France
Natalia Stakhanova	University of Saskatchewan, Canada

Publication Chairs

Mawloud Omar	University of Southern Brittany, France
Omer Nguena Timo	Université du Québec en Outaouais, Canada

Program Committee

Kamel Adi	Université du Québec en Outaouais, Canada
Irfan Ahmed	Virginia Commonwealth University, USA
Mohamed Aiche	Blida 1 Saad Dahlab University, Algeria
Samiha Ayed	University of Technology of Troyes, France
Esma Aïmeur	University of Montréal, Canada
Abdelhakim Baouya	University of Toulouse, France
Safa Ben-Ayed	Higher Institute of Management, Tunisia
Lotfi Ben-Othmane	University of North Texas, USA
Philippe Bon	Gustave Eiffel University, France
Mohammed Amine Boudouaia	CESI, France
Myria Bouhaddi	Université du Québec en Outaouais, Canada
Nora Boulahia-Cuppens	Polytechnique Montréal, Canada
Abderraouf Boussif	Gustave Eiffel University, France
Jordi Castellà-Roca	Universitat Rovira i Virgili, Spain
Kalinka Regina Castelo-Branco	Universidade de São Paulo, Brazil
Saoussen Cheikhrouhou	University of Sfax, Tunisia
Depeng Chen	Anhui University, China

Contents

Intrusion Detection Systems (IDS)

Privacy and Digital Trust

Vulnerabilities and Resilience

Privacy, Threat Analysis, and Explainable Cybersecurity

Advanced Attacks and Strategic Detection

Security Governance, Compliance, and Adaptive Systems

AI for Software Security

Improving the Accuracy of Embeddings for Matching Tasks in Cybersecurity Using Generated Dictionaries

Arian Soltani[1,2(✉)], Abir Bala[3], Djeff Kanda Nkashama[1,2], Pierre-Martin Tardif[1,2], Ayoub Bahnasse[3], Marc Frappier[1,2], and Froduald Kabanza[1,2]

[1] Université de Sherbrooke, Sherbrooke, QC J1K 2R1, Canada
{arian.soltani,djeff.kanda.nkashama,pierre-martin.tardif,marc.frappier, froduald.kabanza}@usherbrooke.ca
[2] Pôle d'expertises en cybersécurité, UdS, Sherbrooke, QC J1K 2R1, Canada
[3] ENSAM, Université Hasan II de Casablanca, Casablanca, Morocco
bala.abir@ensam-casa.ma
https://www.usherbrooke.ca/pole-cybersecurite/

Abstract. Language embedding models can be used to automate several tasks in Cybersecyrity, such as matching exposed vulnerabilities to possible attacks. During our experiments with this approach, we found that due to the rapid pace of language model development, a newer general-purpose (GP) model often outperforms slightly older fine-tuned models, even though they miss understanding of the domain and its jargon. This effect renders the fine-tuning process ineffective, prompting the question: *How can GP embedding models be empowered with domain knowledge without fine-tuning?* To address this problem, we use an automatically generated dictionary of technical words and inject their meanings into the text before calculating the embeddings. This method is tested for labeling CVE vulnerabilities and CTI reports' sentences with MITRE ATT&CK attack TTPs, two prominent tasks for testing automation in cybersecurity operations. This approach demonstrates a general uplift in the capability of GP embedding models for cybersecurity domain-specific tasks. Moreover, our experiments show that this method has the potential to push GP models above domain-specific models.

Keywords: Cybersecurity · Embedding models · Semantic Matching · MITRE ATT&CK · Cyber Threat Intelligence (CTI) · Common Vulnerabilities and Exposures (CVE)

1 Introduction

As the cybersecurity landscape continues to expand and evolve, analysts face an increasingly overwhelming volume and complexity of threats. The sheer volume and sophistication of cyber threats have significantly strained the resources of

K. Adi et al. (Eds.): CRiSIS 2025, LNCS 16295, pp. 3–18, 2026.
https://doi.org/10.1007/978-3-032-20732-6_1

cybersecurity analysts. Automation has emerged as a critical solution to address these challenges [40], with language embedding models playing a crucial role in streamlining cybersecurity operations. Specifically, connecting vulnerabilities and threat intelligence with attack definitions through embedding models offers a structured approach to enhance threat detection, prediction, and proactive defense.

In this regard, knowledge and information sources such as MITRE ATT&CK framework, Common Vulnerabilities and Exposures (CVE), and Cyber Threat Intelligence (CTI) reports are foundational components in modern cybersecurity operations. The MITRE ATT&CK framework is a comprehensive, globally accessible knowledge base that catalogs adversary tactics, techniques, and procedures (TTPs) observed in real-world cyberattacks. It provides a structured taxonomy for understanding how threat actors operate, enabling organizations to model threats, assess risks, and prioritize defensive measures based on observed adversarial behaviors [23,30]. CVE, on the other hand, is a standardized database of publicly disclosed cybersecurity vulnerabilities. Each CVE entry provides a unique identifier, a description of the vulnerability, and references to related advisories and patches, facilitating consistent sharing and tracking of vulnerabilities between tools and organizations [17]. CTI reports synthesize information about threat actors, campaigns, attack vectors, and indicators of compromise, offering contextual intelligence that informs detection, response, and strategic decision-making [2,6]. Examples of these crucial data sources is presented in Fig. 1. Connecting these resources—mapping CVEs and CTI findings to the ATT&CK framework—enables a unified view of the threat landscape. This integration enhances the analyst's ability to correlate vulnerabilities with adversary behaviors and actionable intelligence, thus improving threat prediction, incident response, and proactive defense.

This integration is achieved using semantic matching that leverages language model vectorized representations (embeddings) of text [15–17,31]. A distance function such as cosine similarity is applied to these vectors to find similar matches among all possible options, as used in many matching tasks in cybersecurity. As these models are trained to represent general (and not domain-specific) text, it is possible that domain-specific knowledge is not exploited and the representations lack quality for downstream tasks such as retrieval, classification, and Semantic Textual Similarity (STS).

Automated matching can facilitate many arduous tasks in cybersecurity analysts' workloads that require manual labeling. Specifically, this approach can label vulnerabilities with possible attacks that they can facilitate. Performance in this task can suffer greatly from unrecognized technical words since software evolution constantly introduces new vocabulary. Embedding models' understanding of words is bound by their training data, which contains limited domain-specific information. This issue constrains the quality of representation for words and phrases related to cybersecurity. Low-quality representations can stem from several reasons. First, a word can have several meanings, all using the same embedding. For example, the word "IP" can also refer to "intellectual property" or

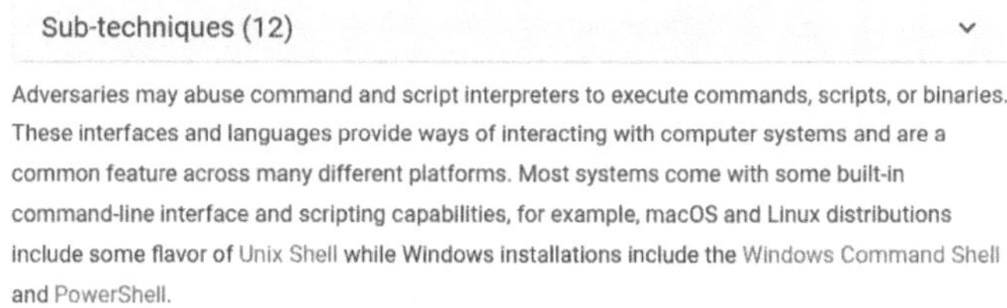
Command and Scripting Interpreter

Sub-techniques (12)

Adversaries may abuse command and script interpreters to execute commands, scripts, or binaries. These interfaces and languages provide ways of interacting with computer systems and are a common feature across many different platforms. Most systems come with some built-in command-line interface and scripting capabilities, for example, macOS and Linux distributions include some flavor of Unix Shell while Windows installations include the Windows Command Shell and PowerShell.

(a) ATT&CK Technique

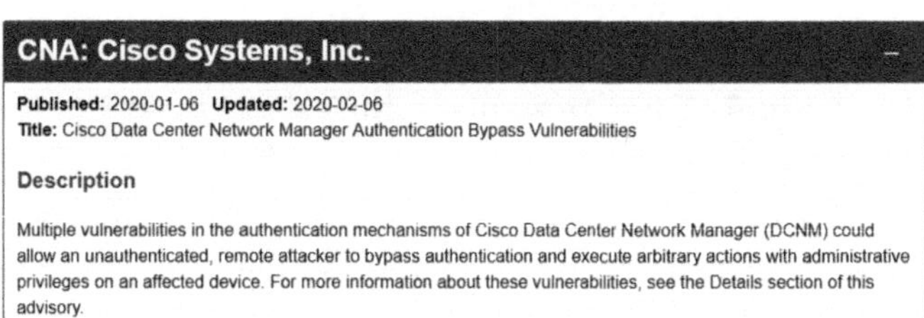
CNA: Cisco Systems, Inc.

Published: 2020-01-06 Updated: 2020-02-06
Title: Cisco Data Center Network Manager Authentication Bypass Vulnerabilities

Description

Multiple vulnerabilities in the authentication mechanisms of Cisco Data Center Network Manager (DCNM) could allow an unauthenticated, remote attacker to bypass authentication and execute arbitrary actions with administrative privileges on an affected device. For more information about these vulnerabilities, see the Details section of this advisory.

(b) CVE details

Fig. 1. Data source examples.

"imperial police", both of which are not related to cybersecurity and have a closer representation to "IP" compared to "internet protocol" or "internet location identifier" (Fig. 2). Another reason is that some acronyms do not represent their meaning close enough to their actual usage. The phrase secure shell (SSH) is far less representative for the meaning and purpose of this protocol than "Secret communication and command tunnel between computers". Mistokenization is another source of confusion for large language models (LLM) [27]. For example, the word "powershell" is tokenized as "powers" + "##hell", or "SSH" as "s" + "sh". Also in many cases, when the word is not recognized, it will be skipped entirely, causing much important context to be lost. This situation can be due to the scarcity of technical words in language models' training set or their nonexistence at the time of training the model, also known as the outdating issue, well known in the NLP literature [12].

Table 1. Generated word definitions examples

Word	Generated Definition
Botnet	internet malicious zombie computers
Spearphishing	tricking with fake emails
DNS	internet address book

In all these cases, it is possible to improve the matching ability of a language model by injecting context into the points where the aforementioned problems

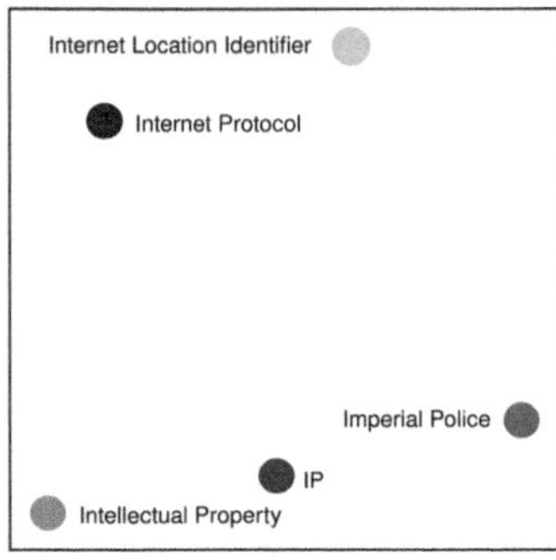

Fig. 2. Word Proximity in Embedding Space.

are likely to happen, i.e. words missing from the models' vocabulary. To find such words, we first identified the words in ATT&CK that language models struggle processing by tokenizing and reversing the tokenized word, and comparing it to the original word. Afterward, we utilized a pipeline using generative LLMs, providing context and examples for creating definitions for technical words. Table 1 provides examples of generated definitions. These definitions were then used to create better representations. Our experiments show that this simple approach can effectively improve the representation of cybersecurity attacks, vulnerabilities and threat intelligence texts.

This approach provides a solution for empowering GP embedding models with domain knowledge, making it beneficial from several aspects. First, it allows plug-and-play utilization of embedding models, effectively bridging the advancements in the natural language processing (NLP) domain to cybersecurity applications. Moreover, industry users of embedding models prefer using open-weight models due to privacy concerns and the cost of fine-tuning. Finally, this approach provides a real-time adaptation solution for emerging threats.

While previous work concerned with challenging the state-of-the-art in matching cybersecurity texts by customizing all the components of the pipeline, real-world conditions and limitations render such approaches impractical. In contrast, the goal of this research is to provide an effective yet easy-to-use method to improve the representation of cybersecurity texts, such as CVE vulnerabilities and CTI report snippets to MITRE ATT&CK.

In the following, we will first provide a background in NLP and review previous related works in Sect. 2, highlighting the shortcomings we aim to address. Next, in Sect. 3 we define our approach in detail, and demonstrate it by performing experiments, and discuss the results in Sect. 4.1. Finally, we review the progress and conclude with suggestions for future work.

2 Related Work

The goal of this research is to provide a plug-and-play solution to improve the ability of language embedding models. To this end, we will first introduce relevant definitions, terms, and techniques from NLP domain where these models and their applications originate. In the next section, a summary of works utilizing NLP tools for matching cybersecurity text will be presented, leading to idetifying the gaps where this research aims to fulfill.

2.1 Background

Natural language processing (NLP) encompasses a range of foundational tasks that enable machines to understand, process, and in some cases generate human language. Initial efforts in NLP focused on extracting and structuring meaningful information from raw text. For example, named entity recognition (NER) is concerned with identifying and classifying key entities in text into predefined categories such as Person, Organization, Location, Date, Quantity, etc. Text classification is another example of NLP tasks, which allows categorizing documents or sentences into predefined groups, such as labeling customer reviews as "positive" or "negative" for sentiment analysis or routing support tickets based on topic. As the number of tasks grew, researchers noticed that the similarity between different tasks allows training a GP model using masked language model (MLM) technique, capable of understanding language, and later finetuning them for downstream tasks [9]. More data, better computing power availability, and more sophisticated training methods allowed expanding the size of generative models, leading to the LLM revolution. These models only require natural language prompts to generate output, showing competitive capability in many tasks [7].

Text vectorization is a class of tasks in NLP focusing on generating vectorized representation of text (embeddings). Efforts in this direction started with word embedding models such as Word2Vec [22] and GloVe [26]. These methods were concerned with finding representations of words using end-to-end training. Word embeddings in the embedding space were observed to have several properties. For example, synonyms had closer points in the embedding space. Though word embeddings were a huge step for processing language, it was not able to capture complex meanings represented by sequences of words, i.e. sentences. This inspired the development of sentence embedding models [8,29]. Today, these models are used in many applications, including search engines that enable the retrieval of semantically close documents to a query rather than matching exact keywords in the query and the documents. Text vectorization methods allow general understanding of text achieving without needing training or finetuning [24]. This capability is called zero-shot ability, pointing out to the fact that the model requires zero iterations on the training data.

Text vectorization consists of many tasks including:

- **Multilabel Classification (MLC)** evaluates whether a model can correctly assign several different categories to one text sample (for example, labeling a single article as both "health" and "technology"). Unlike single-label classification, where only one tag is possible, multilabel classification allows for overlapping labels. The models' effectiveness is often measured by how well they rank the correct labels among all possible options, using metrics such as average precision.

- **Retrieval** assesses a model's ability to locate and rank the most relevant texts in response to a search query (such as matching a user's question to the most pertinent documents). Both the query and the candidate documents are converted into embeddings, and their similarity (often via cosine similarity) determines the ranking. The quality of the results typically measures the relevance of the top-ranked items.
- **Semantic Textual Similarity (STS)** examines how well a model can judge the degree of meaning shared between two pieces of text (for example, recognizing that "He went home" and "He returned to his house" are very similar in meaning). The model creates vector representations for each sentence, then calculates their closeness, usually with cosine similarity. The correlation between the model's scores and human ratings is measured using Spearman correlation to determine how closely the model's judgments match human understanding [24].

Inspired by similar tasks in NLP, we define the quality of text embeddings in the cybersecurity domain as their ability to correctly match information sources such as vulnerabilities (CVE) and threat reports (CTI).

2.2 Cybersecurity Text Matching

Since the introduction of NLP techniques for processing text, cybersecurity researchers have sought to specialize them for their purposes. Initial works in this regard use fundamental NLP techniques such as NER [14], MLM [3], and simple vectorization and similarity measurement methods such as Word2Vec, and TF-IDF [25].

CyBERT [28] and SecureBERT [3] trained and tested BERT-based models on cybersecurity text, and downstream tasks such as NER and MLM, demonstrating that domain knowledge can be taught to language models, paving the way for automating cybersecurity tasks. Labeling cybersecurity text with relevant attacks is one of these tasks. For instance in [17], the authors propose a Multi-Head Joint Embedding Neural Network model that automates the mapping process as a multi-label text classification task. They tackle the lack of labeled data through an unsupervised labeling technique, extracting relevant phrases from threat reports and ATT&CK descriptions, and initially process the text inputs using a word embedding model (Word2Vec [22]) trained on ATT&CK. The model is enriched with a curated knowledge base of attack scenarios and mitigation strategies, capturing both the attacker and the defender perspectives. In [11], the authors test various models, including several BERT-based architectures, finding SciBERT as the most capable model for the task with the highest F1-score.

Later works based on this approach started using Sentence Embedding models [8,32] instead of Word embedding models [5,22] to better capture the semantic meanings inside CVE and ATT&CK descriptions. [21] tested several neural network and deep learning multi-label classification methods on top of a sentence embedding model [8], concluding that LabelPowerSet combined with a Multi-layer Perceptron yields the best results.

Unsupervised training of a general purpose embedding model [32] on ATT&CK improves the state-of-the-art one step further [1]. Their fine-tuned embedding model (ATTACK BERT) was used to generate embeddings followed by a linear regression model to predict relationships. This method has shown promising results on CVE-ATT&CK and CTI-ATT&CK matching. Similar to [17], short phrases are extracted from texts for matching. Interestingly, this research found that Generative LLMs are not as capable as embedding-based methods in matching CVE and CTI to ATT&CK. Given the differences between the data used by previous works, [10] tries to reproduce and improve them, paving the way for future research. The results from many previous works were found to be irreproducible. In the cases where code repositories were available (such as [21]), significant improvements were achieved by using data augmentation and hyperparameter optimization of previous work.

In [4], the authors propose LADDER, a method to extract structured information from unstructured CTI reports, and label them with MITRE ATT&CK using a multistep algorithm. The algorithm consist of data collection, entity and relationship extraction using NER and RoBERTa [20], attack pattern extraction using SentenceBERT [29], and knowledge graph construction.

Although the role of domain-specific words is obviously clear for improving language model's understanding of the domain, few works have focused specifically on this issue. Bose et al. attempted keyphrase extraction from CVE/NVD and Twitter [6]. They introduce a hybrid system that combines deep learning transformers with novel tagging rules to improve key phrase sequence labeling for cyber-threat intelligence (CTI) tasks.

In [27], the authors state that the embedding models do not capture semantic relationships in cybersecurity contexts due to their reliance on individual words or n-grams. In this work, the authors touch on the problem of domain jargon, and try to alleviate this issue by creating embeddings for multi-word phrases (e.g., "password spraying") by identifying syntagmatic and paradigmatic relationships using part-of-speech tagging and a curated cybersecurity glossary. The method is evaluated on a dataset of connections between CTI reports and MITRE ATT&CK.

Notably, recent works have increasingly adopted GP models such as SentenceBERT [29], USE [8], and RoBERTa [20], reflecting a clear alignment with industry trends that favor open-weight, widely accepted models over narrowly fine-tuned alternatives. This shift highlights the valuable opportunity to enhance embedding models within these broadly applicable settings—a direction that has remained relatively underexplored.

The challenges mentioned in previous work include sensitivity to data and class imbalance [1,11,17]. Unlike previous works that utilize fine-tuning and training classifiers to address these issues, we propose an alternative zero-shot approach to improve the quality of the cybersecurity text representation within the same embedding space. This approach would allow plug-and-play utilization of newer and more advanced embedding models, effectively streamlining the use of advancements in the NLP domain. Moreover, it enables the improvement of DS matching tasks in private settings with customized software and configuration. These conditions are present in many industries where using data for training may cause numerous privacy concerns. Finally, it allows real-time adaptation to the newly introduced jargon. New vocabulary can be established by new feature development in software, zero-day vulnerabilities and attacks, etc. By simply recognizing and defining the new term, automated workflows have a better chance to deal with such novelties.

Table 2. Dictionary word selection and their counts

Source	Selected Words	Dictionary Hits
ATT&CK	217	3372
CVE	265	2175
CTI	251	14202

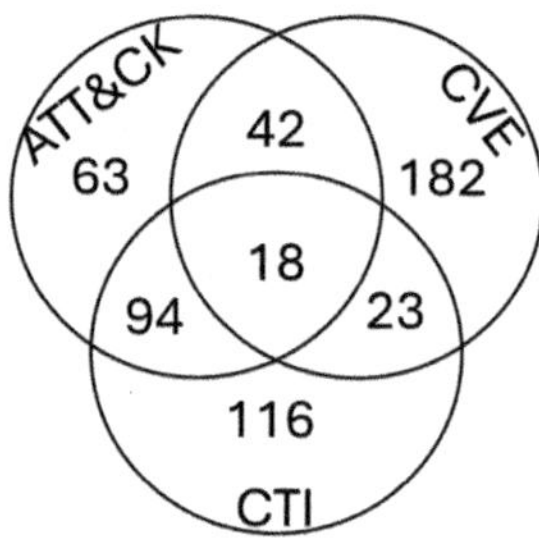

Fig. 3. Selected technical words' distribution in sources.

3 Methodology

Previous research shows that the performance of LLMs is largely dependent on providing relevant context [38], although this concept has not yet been examined for the integration of models. Our main goal is to develop a method that improves the matching ability of cybersecurity text embeddings with minimal effort and without training or finetuning. To this end, we isolate the points where more context is required and inject relevant context from a generated dictionary. Briefly, we first select words that might be misrepresented or skipped, generate definitions for them, and then measure the improvements over two prevalent cybersecurity matching tasks.

Dictionary Word Selection. To find technical and misrepresented words, the most frequent out-of-vocabulary (OOV) words were selected from each of the sources: MITRE ATT&CK, the CTI reports dataset and the CVE dataset. OOV words were selected by tokenizing the words, reversing the tokenization process and attempting to reconstruct the original word. Words that were not correctly reconstructed were labeled as OOV. After resolving overlaps and verification, 538 words remained. Most domain-specific words were frequent not only in entries, but also in between these sources, signaling that the approach will not be sensitive to introduction of new instances and sources. Figure 3 and Table 2 illustrate the distribution of words among sources. It is worth noting that the number of technical words specific to external sources (CTI and CVE) is large, suggesting that a predefined set of technical words will fall short as new vocabulary is introduced by the external sources (Fig. 4).

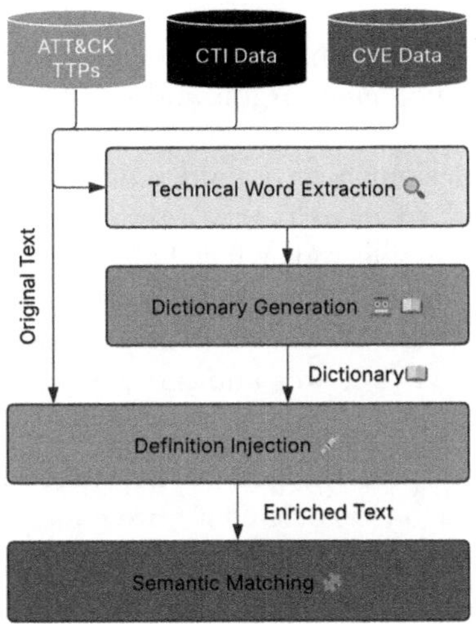

Fig. 4. Pipeline.

Constructing the Dictionary. After selecting the words for the dictionary, we use LLM prompting for automatically generating definitions. There exist technical difficulties for creating the dictionary:

- LLMs output structure and format does not solely depend on the prompt. Therefore their outputs could not always be processed. Some generated definitions needed to be manually edited.
- The generated definitions could still have complex and technical words. This problem could cause circular dependency in the injection phase. To address this issue, several prompts were tested, aiming to generate informative, yet simplistic definitions.

- The generated definitions could focus on a special use-case of a word. Providing context is often suggested to improve the quality of the output of Generative LLMs. Though for generating a dictionary, we observed that providing examples and external sources caused the definitions to lean towards a specifc use-case and lose generality.
- LLMs might mistakenly generate definitions that were not related to cybersecurity. For "rainbow" as in "rainbow tables" we repeatedly observed definitions related to being colorful or the LGBTQ+ flag.

Despite these technical issues, it is possible to generate acceptable and operational dictionaries with minimal manual verification and prompt customization. For example, one of the dictionary generation prompts that solved most of the mentioned problems is the following:

"*Explain the term [word] in the context of computers and cybersecurity to a teenager.*"

This prompt allows generating definitions that are technical enough to use the voabulary present in the embedding models (such as "linux" or "network"), but not so technical to introduce new jargon and cause the aforementioned dependency problem.

The quality of the dictionary profoundly depends on the selected LLM as well. Larger models tend to have better responses as demonstrated by LLM benchmarks [41]. Since we selected a few hundred frequent words, dictionary generation costs were minimal, though broadening the word selection policy might add cost considerations. We selected GPT3.5, a cheaper yet well-informed option to operate compared to newer and more expensive models.

Text Embeddings. The performance of the embedding models is quantified in [13] for comparison. For our experiments, we choose several models based on their popularity, and their performance in semantic matching tasks, similar to CVE-ATT&CK, and CTI-ATT&CK in our experiments. The chosen tasks are MLC, Retrieval, and STS, explained in Sect. 2.1.

These tasks are directly relevant to the applications of embeddings in security systems. For example, inspecting the information found about a given Indicator of Compromise (IoC) from a CTI report can be *classified* as one of the TTPs in ATT&CK. Another example would be the workflow of investigating existing system logs for evidence of an exploited vulnerability, where matching investigative queries and logs in the embedding space allows *semantic retrieval* rather than simply looking for exact matches. As such, the quality of embeddings for security systems is paramount in the functionality of Security Information and Event Management (SIEM).

The tokenization process of embedding models strips a lot of context and punctuation, leaving little room for variation in ways to inject definitions into the text. We did not observe any difference between several tested methods, hence the injection method is simply achieved by adding the definition in parentheses after the occurrence of a word. The only important note is to add the definition next to the word. This is due to the tendencies of the attention mechanism; one of the steps in the transformer architecture understands the relationship between the input sequence [35].

Matching in Embedding Space. The final step, semantic matching, is implemented similar to previous related work. Each CVE and CTI entry from the datasets and ATT&CK entry is translated into an embedding vector. After calculating the embeddings, several methods can be used to find matches between two sets of entries. The simplest yet most prominent method is to use cosine similarity between the two embedding vectors. Cosine similarity is invariant to the magnitude of the vectors. In this method, a lower angle (higher cosine value) indicates the degree of similarity between the two vectors in the embedding space. Specifically, a cosine similarity of 1 (corresponding to a 0° angle) indicates vectors with maximal similarity—they point in exactly the same direction. A cosine similarity of 0 (90° angle) means the vectors are unrelated or orthogonal. A cosine similarity of -1 (180° angle) reflects maximum dissimilarity, with the vectors pointing in perfectly opposite directions. The cosine similarity between A and B vectors is calculated as follows:

$$\cos(\theta) = \frac{\mathbf{A} \cdot \mathbf{B}}{\|\mathbf{A}\| \|\mathbf{B}\|} \tag{1}$$

Several works have suggested using custom classifiers in the final step of the pipeline to find similarity [1,17], however, since our goal is to measure the general uplift in the embedding quality without training or fine-tuning, additional customizations are omitted.

4 Experiments

To experiment the impact of generated dictionaries, we implemented the above-explained approach and selected several embedding models with varying properties and performances to test the approach. Embedding models were selected from the MTEB leaderboard [13], a general purpose benchmark for comparing embedding models for different related tasks. A summary of selected models can be found in Table 3. With each model, several relevant information is presented: name of the model, the variation available on Huggingface, the original source article, parameter size, dimensions of the output embedding vector, and its performance on three NLP tasks relevant to semantic matching: Multi-label Classification (MLC), Retrieval, and Semantic Textual Similarity (STS).

Experiments and measurements for this approach require credible data sources. For CVE-ATT&CK pairs, resources from "Mapping MITRE ATT&CK to CVEs for Impact" project [33] and the dataset provided by [1] were used. The accumulated dataset contains mapping of 840 CVEs to MITRE ATT&CK TTPs. For CTI-ATT&CK pairs, the dataset is provided by TRAM (Threat Report ATT&CK Mapper), containing 4,816 sentences extracted from CTI reports, along with their corresponding ATT&CK entry [34].

Table 3. Selected embedding models with their properties and performance

Name	Variation	Source	Size (M)	Dim's	MLC	Retrieval	STS
BGE Small	BAAI/bge-small-en-v1.5	[39]	33	512	17.01	37.51	60.26
BGE Base	BAAI/bge-base-en-v1.5	[39]	109	768	16.37	39.52	60.64
BGE Large	BAAI/bge-large-en-v1.5	[39]	335	1024	17.67	40.28	60.97
mxbai Xsmall	mxbai-embed-xsmall-v1	[18]	24	384	18.1	41.57	61.2
mxbai Large	mxbai-embed-large-v1	[18]	335	1024	N/A	N/A	N/A
GTE Small	thenlper/gte-small	[19]	33	384	16.27	36.72	63.48
GTE Base	thenlper/gte-base	[19]	109	768	16.15	36.84	63.89
GTE Large	thenlper/gte-large	[19]	335	1024	17.91	39.32	64.36
E5 Small	intfloat/e5-small-v2	[36]	33	384	15.14	46.6	60.15
E5 Base	intfloat/e5-base-v2	[36]	109	768	16.06	42	61.37
E5 Large	intfloat/e5-large-v2	[36]	335	1024	15.85	41.26	62.37
MiniLM12	all-MiniLM-L12-v2	[37]	33	384	3.56	40.6	63.44
MPNET	all-mpnet-base-v2	[32]	109	768	4.79	41.77	64.92
ATTACKBERT	basel/ATTACK-BERT	[1]	109	768	N/A	N/A	N/A

The measurements and comparisons between the results will be with recall@5 referring to the fraction of correct ground truth labels (ATT&CK techniques in this) that appear within the top five predictions made by the model for each example [1]. This metric evaluates how frequently the actual techniques are ranked among the top five by the model, with higher recall@5 scores meaning the embeddings were able to produce better matches in the pipeline.

4.1 Results

Results for matching CVE to ATT&CK entries are presented in Fig. 5aand results for matching CTI entries to ATT&CK entries are depicted in Fig. 5b

Generally, the results show an uplift in the quality of embeddings for matching. For matching CVEs to ATT&CK 11 of the 14 tested models demonstrated an average improvement of 14.71 %. GTE-large benefited the most from this approach with 35.9 % improvement. For matching CTI to ATT&CK, 12 of the 14 models had an average improvement of 1.64 %, reducing the error rate by an average of 4.4 %. Although this approach improved most models, it is worth noting that not all models benefited from this approach. In case of CVE-ATT&CK matching, MiniLM lost 13.43 %, and for CTI-ATT&CK matching, lost 2.34 % on average.

In case of CVE matching, we observe that not only the dictionary method has improved the general purpose models, it also improved the ATTACK-BERT domain-specific model. In the case of GTE-large, the dictionary method increased the matching performance beyond the domain-specific model ATTACKBERT. ATTACKBERT is a fine-tuned version of MPNET, originally

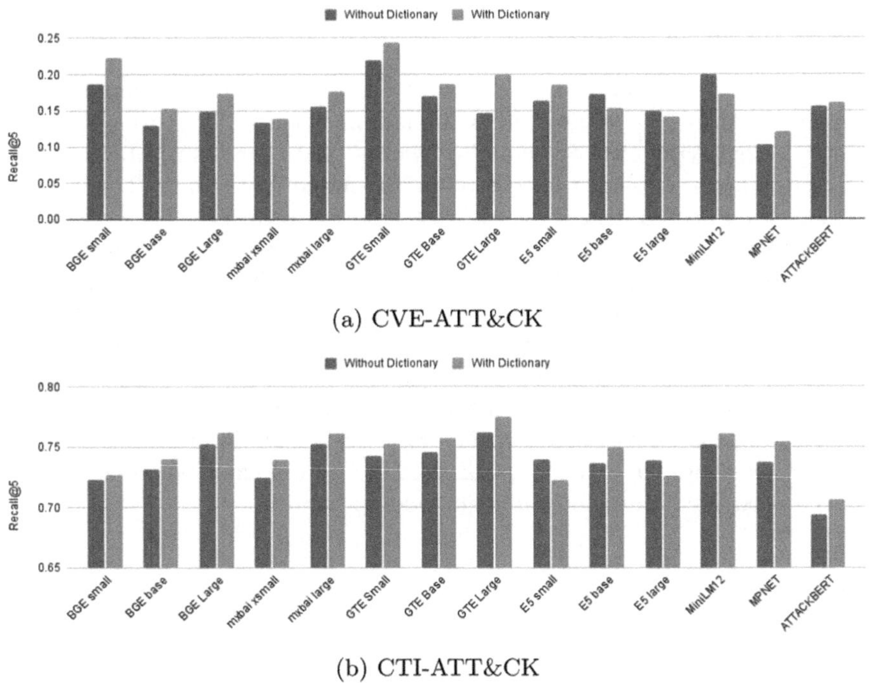

(a) CVE-ATT&CK

(b) CTI-ATT&CK

Fig. 5. Results on matching tasks.

targeting CVE-ATT&CK matching [1], and later models, even without the dictionary approach, demonstrate better performance for the same task. This supports the assumption that newer GP models tend to outperform previous fine-tuned models. These observations demonstrate the necessity and impact of zero-shot approaches to matching in cybersecurity.

It is also worth noting that even though the selected tasks from NLP are relevant, the measurements do not follow the same patterns. For example, in CVE-ATT&CK matching, as the number of the parameters (size of the models) grow in similar models (e.g. BGE small, base, large) do not follow the same tendencies as NLP task measurements represented in Table 3. This suggests that GP benchmarks do not necessarily provide relevant information for domain-specific performance [31].

Although this simple but effective approach improves the cybersecurity domain-specific performance of GP embedding models in general, more research is required to patch performance fluctuations of some models. Experimenting with the parameters of the word definition process such as definition length and peeking behind the intricacies of the attention mechanism would provide valuable insight into optimizing this approach and enabling it for real-world applications.

5 Conclusion

In this paper, we proposed a zero-shot method for enabling general purpose embedding models with cybersecurity domain knowledge. The proposed method consists of identifying out-of-vocabulary words, and then using LLMs to generate a dictionary to explain these words with simple vocabulary. The generated definitions are injected next to words' occurrences. To measure the effectiveness of this method on the quality of text embeddings, experminets were performed for two pivotal cybersecurity tasks: connecting vulnerabilities (CVE) and threat intelligence (CTI) to attacks (ATT&CK). Experiments show a general uplift in the quality of the embeddings for these tasks. This initial effort bridges NLP advancements in embedding models to cybersecurity domain, without constant requirement for costly training and fine-tuning. Further research is required to merge this approach with state-of-the-art CVE-ATT&CK and CTI-ATT&CK attribution methods, potentially leading to more intelligent labeling while foregoing the need to train or fine-tune embedding models.

References

1. Abdeen, B., Al-Shaer, E., Singhal, A., Khan, L., Hamlen, K.: SMET: semantic mapping of CVE to ATT&CK and its application to cybersecurity. In: IFIP Annual Conference on Data and Applications Security and Privacy, pp. 243–260. Springer (2023)
2. Abdeen, B., Al-Shaer, E., Singhal, A., Khan, L., Hamlen, K.W.: Smet: semantic mapping of cti reports and CVE to att&ck for advanced threat intelligence. J. Comput. Secur. (Preprint), 1–20 (2024)
3. Aghaei, E., Niu, X., Shadid, W., Al-Shaer, E.: SecureBERT: a domain-specific language model for cybersecurity. In: International Conference on Security and Privacy in Communication Systems, pp. 39–56. Springer (2022)
4. Alam, M.T., Bhusal, D., Park, Y., Rastogi, N.: Looking beyond iocs: automatically extracting attack patterns from external *CTI*. In: Proceedings of the 26th International Symposium on Research in Attacks, Intrusions and Defenses, pp. 92–108 (2023)
5. Beltagy, I., Lo, K., Cohan, A.: SciBERT: a pretrained language model for scientific text. arXiv preprint arXiv:1903.10676 (2019)
6. Bose, A., Yang, H., Shivers, M., Orazgeldiyev, A., Hsu, W.H.: Context-augmented key phrase extraction from short texts for cyber threat intelligence tasks. In: 2023 IEEE International Conference on Intelligence and Security Informatics (ISI), pp. 1–6. IEEE (2023)
7. Bubeck, S., et al.: Sparks of artificial general intelligence: early experiments with GPT-4. arXiv preprint arXiv:2303.12712 (2023)
8. Cer, D., et al.: Universal sentence encoder. arXiv preprint arXiv:1803.11175 (2018)
9. Devlin, J., Chang, M.W., Lee, K., Toutanova, K.: BERT: pre-training of deep bidirectional transformers for language understanding. arXiv preprint arXiv:1810.04805 (2018)
10. EL Jaouhari, S., Tamani, N., Jacob, R.I.: Improving ML-based solutions for linking of CVE to MITRE ATT &CK techniques. In: 2024 IEEE 48th Annual Computers, Software, and Applications Conference (COMPSAC), pp. 2442–2447. IEEE (2024)

11. Grigorescu, O., Nica, A., Dascalu, M., Rughinis, R.: CVE2ATT&CK: BERT-based mapping of CVEs to MITRE ATT&CK techniques. Algorithms **15**(9), 314 (2022)
12. Huang, J., Parthasarathi, P., Rezagholizadeh, M., Chandar, S.: Towards practical tool usage for continually learning LLMs. arXiv preprint arXiv:2404.09339 (2024)
13. Huggingface: MTEB Leaderboard. https://huggingface.co/spaces/mteb/leaderboard (2023) [. Accessed 1 Dec 2023]
14. Joshi, A., Lal, R., Finin, T., Joshi, A.: Extracting cybersecurity related linked data from text. In: 2013 IEEE Seventh International Conference on Semantic Computing, pp. 252–259. IEEE (2013)
15. Kanakogi, K., et al.: Tracing CVE vulnerability information to CAPEC attack patterns using natural language processing techniques. Information **12**(8), 298 (2021)
16. Kota, K., Manjunatha, A., et al.: CWE prediction using CVE description-the semantic similarity approach. Proc. Comput. Sci. **235**, 1167–1178 (2024)
17. Kuppa, A., Aouad, L., Le-Khac, N.A.: Linking CVE's to MITRE ATT&CK Techniques. In: Proceedings of the 16th International Conference on Availability, Reliability and Security, pp. 1–12 (2021)
18. Li, X., Li, J.: Angle-optimized text embeddings. arXiv preprint arXiv:2309.12871 (2023)
19. Li, Z., Zhang, X., Zhang, Y., Long, D., Xie, P., Zhang, M.: Towards general text embeddings with multi-stage contrastive learning. arXiv preprint arXiv:2308.03281 (2023)
20. Liu, Y., et al.: RoBERTa: a robustly optimized BERT pretraining approach. arXiv preprint arXiv:1907.11692 (2019)
21. Mendsaikhan, O., Hasegawa, H., Yamaguchi, Y., Shimada, H.: Automatic mapping of vulnerability information to adversary techniques. In: The Fourteenth International Conference on Emerging Security Information, Systems and Technologies SECUREWARE2020 (2020)
22. Mikolov, T., Chen, K., Corrado, G., Dean, J.: Efficient estimation of word representations in vector space. arXiv preprint arXiv:1301.3781 (2013)
23. MITRE Corporation: MITRE ATT&CK database. https://attack.mitre.org/ (2023). [Accessed 19 July 2023]
24. Muennighoff, N., Tazi, N., Magne, L., Reimers, N.: MTEB: massive text embedding benchmark. arXiv preprint arXiv:2210.07316 (2022)
25. Mumtaz, S., Rodriguez, C., Benatallah, B., Al-Banna, M., Zamanirad, S.: Learning word representation for the cyber security vulnerability domain. In: 2020 International Joint Conference on Neural Networks (IJCNN), pp. 1–8. IEEE (2020)
26. Pennington, J., Socher, R., Manning, C.D.: Glove: global vectors for word representation. In: Proceedings of the 2014 Conference on Empirical Methods in Natural Language Processing (EMNLP), pp. 1532–1543 (2014)
27. Purba, M.D., Chu, B., Al-Shaer, E.: From word embedding to cyber-phrase embedding: comparison of processing cybersecurity texts. In: 2020 IEEE International Conference on Intelligence and Security Informatics (ISI), pp. 1–6. IEEE (2020)
28. Ranade, P., Piplai, A., Joshi, A., Finin, T.: CyBERT: contextualized embeddings for the cybersecurity domain. In: 2021 IEEE International Conference on Big Data (Big Data), pp. 3334–3342. IEEE (2021)
29. Reimers, N., Gurevych, I.: Sentence-BERT: sentence embeddings using siamese BERT-networks. arXiv preprint arXiv:1908.10084 (2019)
30. Roy, S., Panaousis, E., Noakes, C., Laszka, A., Panda, S., Loukas, G.: SoK: the MITRE ATT&CK framework in research and practice. arXiv preprint arXiv:2304.07411 (2023)

31. Soltani, A., Nkashama, D.K., Masakuna, J.F., Frappier, M., Tardif, P.M., Kabanza, F.: Assessing language models for semantic textual similarity in cybersecurity. In: International Conference on Detection of Intrusions and Malware, and Vulnerability Assessment, pp. 370–380. Springer (2024)
32. Song, K., Tan, X., Qin, T., Lu, J., Liu, T.Y.: MPNet: masked and permuted pre-training for language understanding. Adv. Neural. Inf. Process. Syst. **33**, 16857–16867 (2020)
33. The Center for Threat-Informed Defense: Mapping MITRE ATT&CK®to CVEs for Impact. https://ctid.mitre.org/projects/mapping-attck-to-cve-for-impact/ (2021). Accessed 19 Sept 2024
34. The Center for Threat-Informed Defense: Threat Report ATT&CK Mapper (TRAM). https://ctid.mitre.org/projects/threat-report-attck-mapper-tram (2023). Accessed 19 Sept 2024
35. Vaswani, A., et al.: Attention is all you need. In: Advances in Neural Information Processing Systems, vol. 30 (2017)
36. Wang, L., et al.: Text embeddings by weakly-supervised contrastive pre-training. arXiv preprint arXiv:2212.03533 (2022)
37. Wang, W., Wei, F., Dong, L., Bao, H., Yang, N., Zhou, M.: MiniLM: deep self-attention distillation for task-agnostic compression of pre-trained transformers. Adv. Neural. Inf. Process. Syst. **33**, 5776–5788 (2020)
38. Wu, K., Wu, E., Zou, J.: ClashEval: quantifying the tug-of-war between an LLM's internal prior and external evidence (2024), https://arxiv.org/abs/2404.10198
39. Xiao, S., Liu, Z., Zhang, P., Muennighoff, N.: C-Pack: packaged resources to advance general Chinese embedding (2023)
40. Xu, H., et al.: Large language models for cyber security: a systematic literature review (2024). https://arxiv.org/abs/2405.04760
41. Yu, J., et al.: KoLA: carefully benchmarking world knowledge of large language models. arXiv preprint arXiv:2306.09296 (2023)

Beyond Detection: Evaluating LLMs' Semantic Understanding of Code Vulnerabilities

Charmant Nicolas Shangwe(✉), Alan Davoust, and Raphaël Khoury

Université du Québec en Outaouais, Gatineau, Canada
{shac04,alan.davoust,raphael.khoury}@uqo.ca

Abstract. As Large Language Models (LLMs) become increasingly integrated into software development and analysis workflows, a critical question arises: do these models truly understand the semantics of code, or do they merely excel at pattern matching? Our goal is to assess the extent to which LLMs can back their predictions in vulnerability detection by correctly attributing the identified vulnerabilities to the violation of particular rules as proof that their decision is based on actual code semantics understanding. We employed the SVEN dataset, composed of function-level code snippets, to conduct a series of experiments that evaluate both the model's ability to detect vulnerabilities and attribute predictions to the correct violated rule and measure LLMs' performance under varying experimental setups. Our findings reveal that while LLMs achieve reasonable accuracy in vulnerability detection, a significant drop in performance is observed when correct rule attribution is also required, exposing a gap between perceived accuracy and actual accuracy. The difference between actual and perceived accuracy offers critical insight into the depth of code semantics understanding of LLMs in vulnerability detection.

Keywords: Large Language Models (LLMs) · Code Semantics · Interpretability

1 Introduction

Software vulnerabilities pose serious threats to modern systems[1], which has given rise to extensive research in vulnerability detection and resulted in various techniques, including traditional approaches such as dynamic testing [2] and static analysis [6]. However, these techniques—particularly static analysis—struggle in practice with an immense number of false positives [5]. The limitations of traditional techniques prompted the exploration of machine learning-based methods, which achieved some degree of success but also faced drawbacks such as the need for high-quality training data and, above all, limited to no interpretability

[1] WhiteHouse: National cybersecurity strategy, 2023.

K. Adi et al. (Eds.): CRiSIS 2025, LNCS 16295, pp. 19–34, 2026.
https://doi.org/10.1007/978-3-032-20732-6_2

of predictions. Due to this lack of transparency in how machine learning-based techniques make decisions, they are often labeled as black boxes. Despite their success and widespread adoption for vulnerability detection, the basis of these models' decision-making remains unclear—whether they genuinely capture code semantics related to vulnerabilities or instead rely on unrelated features or factors [12].

The rise of Large Language Models, with their remarkable ability in various tasks, has led to the emergence of models and LLM powered services specifically tailored to code-related tasks, such as Github Copilot and Amazon's CodeWhisperer, these models have been used to detect security vulnerabilities [9,21,25,30], and various approaches have been explored to boost performance, including prompt engineering [27,28,32], fine-tuning [10,16,22,26], and others [12,20]. However, as with machine learning model approaches, the employment of LLMs for vulnerability detection remains a black box, in the sense that they provide a classification but aren't tested on their true understanding of code semantics. In a previous study by Du [12], LLMs have demonstrated elevated capability to differentiate function-level vulnerable code from non-vulnerable code compared to machine learning approaches, proving ideal for vulnerability detection; nevertheless, this does not entirely solve the challenge of understanding the basis of an LLM's decision to classify a given function-level code as vulnerable or not.

Study — To address this challenge, we designed a series of experiments to evaluate the ability of LLMs to detect vulnerabilities in function-level code while also backing the reasoning behind their classification decisions by referencing predefined rules. We began with the SVEN dataset [17], a manually labeled dataset containing 803 pairs of vulnerable and patched function-level code. From this dataset, we selected 7 CWEs that fall within the top 10 of the 2024 MITRE CWE Top 25 list. The MITRE Top 25 is updated annually and highlights the most dangerous software weaknesses based on real-world exploit data and potential impact. By focusing on these CWEs, our study emphasizes vulnerabilities that are both the most severe and the most widely recognized in software security research and practice. To guide our evaluation, we collected detailed descriptions of these CWEs from the official MITRE CWE website[2] and used the descriptions together with the analysis of fixes in the dataset to define rules applied in our experiments. Finally, we submitted the classification queries to two reasoning models (o4-mini, o3-mini) and two general-purpose LLMs (GPT-4o-mini, GPT-4.1-mini) and recorded their answers.

The rules associated with the different CWE are the following:

- **Rule 1 (CWE-22)**: The code must not construct a file pathname by concatenating external input (e.g., user-provided strings) into file operations (e.g., fopen, open, os.path) without validating or sanitizing the input to remove special elements (e.g., ../, ./, \) that could resolve the path outside the intended directory.

[2] http://cwe.mitre.org/.

- **Rule 2 (CWE-78)**: The code must not pass a string containing external input to OS command functions (e.g., system(), exec(), os.system(), subprocess.run()) without sanitizing the input to remove or escape command separators (e.g., ;, &, —) or special characters that could alter the command.
- **Rule 3 (CWE-89)**: The code must not construct an SQL query by concatenating external input into the query string unless the input is sanitized or parameterized (e.g., using prepared statements or parameterized queries).
- **Rule 4 (CWE-79)**: The code must not incorporate external input into web page output (e.g., HTML, JavaScript, or server-side templates) without encoding or sanitizing the input to neutralize special characters (e.g., <, >, ", ', &).
- **Rule 5 (CWE-125)**: The code must not read from a buffer using an index or pointer that exceeds the buffer's allocated bounds (e.g., past the end or before the start). The code must ensure all array or pointer accesses are within bounds using explicit checks.
- **Rule 6 (CWE-190)**: The code must not perform arithmetic operations (e.g., addition, multiplication) on integers without checking if the result exceeds the type's maximum or minimum value (e.g., INT_MAX, INT_MIN), which could cause overflow or wraparound.
- **Rule 7 (CWE-416)**: The code must not dereference or access a pointer after it has been freed (e.g., via free(), delete) unless the pointer is reassigned or set to NULL.

Overall, our paper makes the following contributions:

- We designed a set of explicit rules based on MITRE CWE descriptions to represent the semantic core of seven selected weakness types. These rules serve as structured criteria for interpreting LLM decisions.
- We propose a novel methodology based on a series of structured experiments and CWE-based rules to evaluate whether LLMs can not only detect vulnerabilities, but also base their predictions on specific violated rules, as a measure of semantic code understanding and interpretability.
- We proved that LLMs provide correct outcomes in vulnerability detection based on flawed reasoning, making them much less reliable than previously thought.

2 Background and Related Work

2.1 Common Weakness Enumeration (CWE)

CWE[2] is a community-driven classification system that provides a comprehensive catalog of known software weaknesses, developed and maintained by MITRE since 2005. CWE offers a standardized framework for identifying, describing, and mitigating common types of software vulnerabilities. Each entry in the CWE list represents a specific type of software flaw and is assigned a unique identifier (CWE-ID). These entries include rich metadata such as a description of the weakness, potential consequences, exploitation methods, likelihood of exploitation, and mitigation strategies. CWE also provides real-world examples with both vulnerable and corrected code snippets, making it an effective educational and evaluative resource.

2.2 Vulnerability Detection Using Machine Learning

Traditional vulnerability detection approaches, particularly static code analysis [6], rely on rule-based systems and heuristics to identify security flaws and programming errors. While effective in detecting well-defined patterns, these methods often suffer from high false positive rates [5] and limited generalization to unseen code structures.

To improve detection accuracy and scalability, researchers began integrating machine learning (ML) methods for vulnerability detection relying on manually defined quantitative code features – such as data structures, number of nested loops, and maximum count of control – which are then used in conjunction with traditional machine learning algorithms like Support Vector Machines (SVM) and K-Nearest Neighbors (KNN) [11]. Building on these foundations, the emergence of deep learning (DL) enabled automatic feature learning directly from raw code. Approaches such as VulDeePecker [19] and SySeVR employed BiLSTM [18] and BiGRU [7] networks to capture sequential token dependencies in function-level code.

More recent efforts have adopted graph-based methods, using Graph Neural Networks (GNNs) to model rich code structures including ASTs, DFGs, and PDGs, as seen in tools like Devign, ReVeal, and LineVD [4,31,35]. These models have shown promise in leveraging both the syntactic and semantic relationships within code for improved vulnerability detection. However, a critical limitation of nearly all prior ML and DL-based approaches is their lack of interpretability. These models, though often effective at classifying code as vulnerable or non-vulnerable, provide little to no insight into why a particular prediction was made. As a result, they operate largely as black boxes, which is particularly problematic where actionable explanations are essential for debugging. More importantly, it remains entirely possible that these models may produce correct classifications for the wrong reasons—for instance, relying on superficial patterns or irrelevant code features rather than truly understanding the underlying cause of a vulnerability,although recent work has sought to address the interpretability challenges of deep learning models for vulnerability detection, most of these efforts have been tailored specifically to Graph Neural Networks (GNNs) [8]. As for LLMs, it remains critical to know how and why LLMs arrive at their decisions—specifically, whether these decisions reflect any real semantic comprehension of code in the context of vulnerability detection. Our study addresses this gap by introducing a rule-based evaluation strategy designed to assess whether LLMs can not only correctly classify code as vulnerable or not, but also justify their predictions by connecting them to specific coding rules being violated or not.

2.3 General-Purpose Vs. Reasoning Models

Large language models (LLMs) can be distinguished into two broad categories: *general-purpose models*, which are designed for broad versatility, and *reasoning models*, which are optimized for multi-step inference and structured problem-solving [23]. This distinction is essential for understanding the scope of our evaluation and the rationale behind the models chosen for this study.

General-Purpose LLMs. General-purpose models aim to provide robust performance across a wide variety of tasks without explicit specialization in reasoning. They are pretrained on diverse corpora and optimized for broad coverage and adaptability. In this study, we included OpenAI's *GPT-4o-mini* and *GPT-4.1-mini* as representatives of this category.

Reasoning LLMs. Reasoning LLMs are explicitly designed or configured to enhance stepwise logical inference, mathematical reasoning, and complex problem-solving. They typically incorporate fine-tuning on reasoning traces or employ inference strategies such as chain-of-thought prompting or iterative self-refinement. In this study, we employed *OpenAI o4-mini* and *OpenAI o3-mini*, two models introduced as reasoning-focused variants in the o-series. These models are explicitly described by their provider as optimized for structured reasoning tasks, trading increased computational cost for improved multi-step performance. Their inclusion allows us to assess the degree to which reasoning-oriented adaptations provide measurable benefits compared to general-purpose models.

Model Selection Rationale. The choice of these four models was guided by the following principles:

- **Balanced representation.** We included two general-purpose LLMs (GPT-4.1-mini, GPT-4o-mini) and two reasoning-oriented LLMs (o4-mini, o3-mini), ensuring coverage of both categories central to the study.
- **Accessibility and reproducibility.** Each model is available via public APIs, ensuring that our experimental setup can be replicated.
- **Comparability across providers.** By including both general-purpose and reasoning-specialized OpenAI models, we ensure comparability across architectural design choices while minimizing confounds introduced by provider-specific differences.

2.4 Large Language Models for Vulnerability Detection

The rapid advancement of Large Language Models (LLMs) has transformed the landscape of AI, enabling remarkable performance across a wide spectrum of tasks, including code generation [34]. LLMs such as GPT-4, LLaMA, and Chinchilla [1,15,29] are built on transformer-based architectures and trained on massive corpora, equipping them with powerful capabilities in understanding and generating natural language as well as code. In the context of software security, a growing body of research has explored the use of LLMs for vulnerability detection. Early efforts used smaller, pre-trained models like CodeBERT, PLBART, and UniXcoder [14,24], while more recent studies have shifted attention to instructed and larger-scale LLMs, which demonstrate improved reasoning and code comprehension.

Several studies employing LLMs for vulnerability detection have justified their choice by highlighting the superior ability of LLMs to distinguish between vulnerable and non-vulnerable code, especially when compared to traditional machine learning approaches. This distinction is particularly notable given that vulnerable and patched functions often exhibit high textual similarity, making the task non-trivial [12]. There is a need for evaluation methods that go beyond surface-level classification to ensure that each prediction is grounded in a meaningful comprehension of the underlying vulnerability [33].

3 Dataset

Accurate and high-quality datasets are critical for evaluating models in vulnerability detection. However, many widely-used datasets in this space, such as BigVul [13], Devign [35], and CVEfixes [3], suffer from substantial data quality issues. These include inaccurate labels, data duplication, and automatic labeling methods that introduce noise—such as labeling all functions touched in a security-fixing commit as vulnerable, even when only a subset is truly affected. Manual evaluations have shown that label accuracy for these datasets ranges from only 24% to 60%, raising concerns about their suitability for training or evaluating models that aim to understand vulnerabilities in real-world contexts. In contrast, the SVEN dataset was selected for this study due to its high data quality and semantic relevance. SVEN is manually curated and achieves 94% label accuracy, the highest among benchmarked vulnerability datasets. It consists of 803 pairs of function-level code samples, where each pair includes a vulnerable function and its corresponding patched version, covering critical CWEs listed in MITRE top-25.SVEN's high-quality, CWE-labeled, pairwise format makes this level of comprehension-focused evaluation possible—something that most existing datasets cannot support.

4 Evaluation Metrics

Considering the multifaceted nature of our experiments—ranging from simple vulnerability detection to joint detection and rule attribution—multiple evaluation metrics were employed to provide a comprehensive view of LLM performance. Specifically, we used accuracy, precision, recall, and F1 score to evaluate overall performance. Additionally, in the advanced iterative approach, we measured the success rates of passing **Stage 1** (rule-specific evaluation) and **Stage**

2 (fallback prediction), providing deeper insight into the model's semantic reasoning process and ability to handle multi-step classification tasks.

The evaluation process was guided by the following key questions:

- **Vulnerability Detection:** Can the LLM correctly determine whether the code is vulnerable?
- **Rule Attribution:** If the code is indeed vulnerable, can the LLM identify the correct violated rule $R_k \in \{R_1, \ldots, R_7\}$?

To capture the nuanced outcomes of this joint task, we define classification categories as follows:

- **True Positive (TP):** The LLM correctly detects that the code is vulnerable *and* correctly identifies the violated rule.
- **False Negative (FN):** The LLM either fails to detect a vulnerability or detects it but attributes it to the wrong rule.
- **False Positive (FP):** The LLM wrongly identifies a non-vulnerable code as vulnerable for any reason(wrongly attributed rule).
- **True Negative (TN):** The LLM correctly classifies non-vulnerable code as safe and assigns "none" as the violated rule.

Table 1 summarizes how these categories map to prediction scenarios.

Table 1. Classification Definitions

Ground Truth	Vulnerability Detected	Rule Identified	Outcome
Vulnerable	Yes	Correct Rule	TP
Vulnerable	Yes	Incorrect Rule	FN
Vulnerable	No	–	FN
Non-Vulnerable	Yes	Any	FP
Non-Vulnerable	No	"None"	TN

- **Accuracy** measures the proportion of total correct predictions:

$$\text{Accuracy} = \frac{TP + TN}{TP + TN + FP + FN} \tag{1}$$

- **Precision** measures how many of the predicted positives are truly positive:

$$\text{Precision} = \frac{TP}{TP + FP} \tag{2}$$

- **Recall** (also known as sensitivity) measures how many of the actual positives were correctly predicted:

$$\text{Recall} = \frac{TP}{TP + FN} \tag{3}$$

- **F1 Score** is the harmonic mean of precision and recall:

$$\text{F1 Score} = 2 \cdot \frac{\text{Precision} \cdot \text{Recall}}{\text{Precision} + \text{Recall}} \tag{4}$$

5 Empirical Evaluation

The following experiments are designed to evaluate the extent to which Large Language Models (LLMs) understand code semantics in the context of vulnerability detection.

5.1 Experiment 1: Can LLMs Accurately Associate Each Function-Level Code Snippet to Its Corresponding Rule?

Before evaluating whether a Large Language Model (LLM) can justify vulnerability decisions through rule attribution, it is important to first assess whether LLMs can correctly associate each code snippet with its most semantically relevant rule. This step serves as a validation of our rule set: if the LLM consistently maps code instances to the appropriate rules, it suggests that the rules meaningfully capture distinguishable patterns in the code. To this end, we conducted a targeted experiment designed to test the model's capacity for rule association independently of any vulnerability status (see Fig. 1).

We constructed a balanced evaluation set by randomly selecting 20 function-level code snippets for each of the seven predefined CWE-based security rules, resulting in a total of 140 snippets. This sampling ensured equal representation across rules and avoided bias toward more frequent rule categories in the dataset. The LLM was then tasked with identifying the specific rule R_k from $\{R_1, R_2, \ldots, R_7\}$ to associate with each code snippet C_n. This setup constitutes a multi-class classification problem, in which each snippet must be assigned to exactly one corresponding rule. The best performance was observed with o3-mini, achieving an accuracy of 85%. While these results are modest, they are reasonable given the multiclass nature of the task. Notably, reasoning models outperformed general-purpose LLMs; the best performing general-purpose LLM, GPT-4.1-mini, reached 79% accuracy.

These findings presented in Table 2 provide a justified foundation for advancing to more complex experiments, specifically those evaluating whether LLMs can not only detect vulnerabilities but also explicitly attribute their predictions to the correct rule violations as an indication of code semantics understanding.

Table 2. Performance comparison of different LLMs on rule association task.

Model	Accuracy (%)	Precision (%)	Recall (%)	F1 Score (%)
o4-mini	82	83	79	78
o3-mini	85	88	82	83
GPT-4o-mini	75	72	70	66
GPT-4.1-mini	79	84	76	76

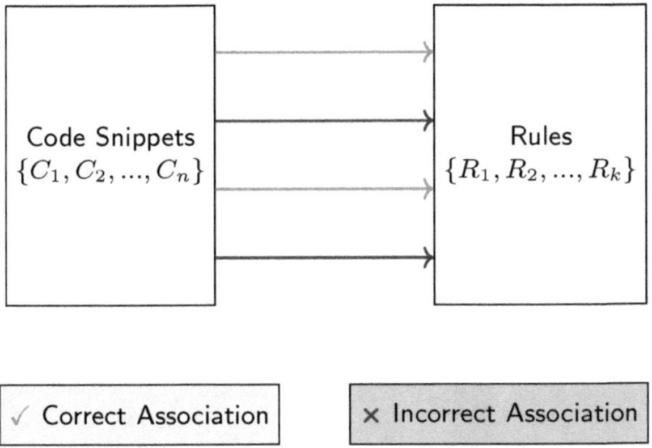

Fig. 1. Mapping code snippets C_n to rules R_k in Experiment 1, with validation of correct and incorrect matches.

5.2 Experiment 2: Do LLMs Detect Vulnerabilities for the Right Reasons?

In Experiment 1, we investigated whether LLMs could correctly associate code snippets with their most relevant predefined rules, independent of vulnerability status. This served as a prerequisite validation step, ensuring that the rule set was semantically meaningful and that the models were capable of working with it. Building on this foundation, Experiment 2 examines a more demanding question: when predicting vulnerabilities, can LLMs attribute their decisions to the correct rule violations? In other words, this experiment tests whether LLMs not only detect vulnerabilities but do so for the right reasons, thereby providing evidence of code semantic understanding beyond surface-level pattern recognition.

We carried out this experiment using the following approaches:

Pool Approach. In this approach (see Fig. 2), the LLM is presented with a function-level code snippet and tasked with two interrelated objectives: (1) Vulnerability Detection and (2) Rule Attribution. That is, the model must first judge the code snippet C_n as vulnerable or not vulnerable, and, if vulnerable, identify the violated rule R_k from a predefined pool of seven rules $\{R_1, R_2, \ldots, R_7\}$. If the code is deemed safe, the model returns "None." This setup simultaneously evaluates the LLM's ability to detect vulnerabilities and its capacity to map those vulnerabilities to specific semantic rules, as a sign of code semantics understanding.

We first analyze vulnerability detection performance in isolation, then extend the evaluation to require both correct vulnerability detection and correct rule attribution. Under this stricter criterion, performance drops substantially—accuracy, precision, and recall each decrease notably. This decline highlights a key distinction: while LLMs often succeed at flagging vulnerabilities, they do not always identify them for the correct semantic reasons. Consequently, part of the perceived detection success may be inflated by classifications that are not grounded in the correct logic.

Table 3 summarizes the LLMs performance under two evaluation settings: (1) vulnerability detection only, and (2) joint vulnerability detection with correct rule attribution.

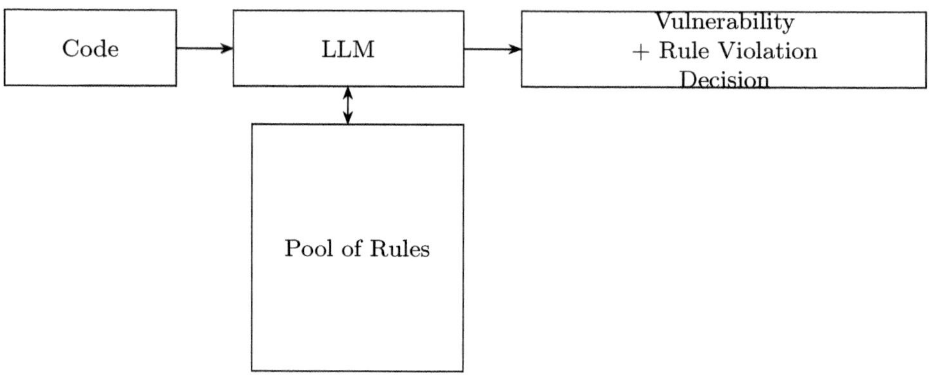

Fig. 2. Pool Approach.

Table 3. Performance Comparison under Two Evaluation Criteria

Model	Evaluation Criterion	Accuracy (%)	Precision (%)	Recall (%)	F1 Score (%)
o4 mini	Vulnerability Detection Only	71	72	71	71
	Detection + Attribution	66	66	66	66
GPT 4o mini	Vulnerability Detection Only	66	66	66	66
	Detection + Rule Attribution	62	62	62	62
o3 mini	Vulnerability Detection Only	70	71	70	69
	Detection + Rule Attribution	68	70	68	67
GPT 4.1 mini	Vulnerability Detection Only	66	67	66	65
	Detection + Rule Attribution	63	63	63	63

Notably, Reasoning models demonstrated superior performance in both tasks, namely *vulnerability detection* and *vulnerability detection with rule attribution.* Among them, *o3 mini* showed the smallest drop in accuracy, with only a 2% decline in the *vulnerability detection + rule attribution* task, indicating a comparatively stronger understanding of code semantics. In contrast, *o4 mini* experienced the steepest decline, with a 5% decrease in accuracy.

Advanced Iterative Approach. Building on the Pool Approach, which evaluated whether LLMs could detect vulnerabilities and attribute them to the correct rules, the Advanced Iterative Approach(see Fig. 3) probes a deeper question: can LLMs reason about code semantics in a manner similar to a human expert? In this experiment, the model is presented with a code snippet and a proposed violated rule, and must critically assess whether the proposed rule truly applies. If it does not, the model identifies the correct rule, effectively demonstrating mastery of the underlying code semantics. By structuring the evaluation as a multi-stage reasoning process, this approach provides a stricter and more informative test of the model's ability to ground vulnerability detection in meaningful semantic understanding, rather than relying on surface-level pattern recognition.

The experiment is divided into two reasoning stages:

- **Stage 1**: Each code instance C_n is evaluated iteratively against every predefined rule in the pool $\{R_1, R_2, ..., R_7\}$. If the model determines that C_n violates a particular rule R_k, it is immediately classified as vulnerable, and R_k is recorded as the violated rule.
- **Stage 2**: If a rule R_k is flagged as not violated during Stage 1, the model is then asked to emulate the behavior of a domain expert: it must examine the code and infer which rule—if any—best explains a potential vulnerability (Table 4). It selects the most likely violated rule $R_k \in \{R_1, ..., R_7\} \cup \{\texttt{none}\}$ and re-evaluates the pair (C_n, R_k). If the model confirms that C_n is vulnerable under R_k, this rule is accepted as the root cause. Otherwise, C_n is labeled as non-vulnerable and the violated rule is marked as `none`.

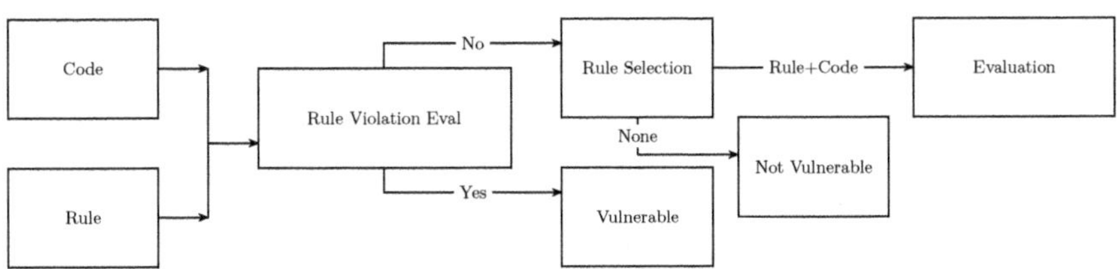

Fig. 3. Advanced Iterative Approach.

This experiment examines the internal decision-making process of LLMs by evaluating their performance across two reasoning stages. In **Stage 1**, the model is provided with a candidate rule R_k and asked to verify whether the code instance C_n violates it. Formally, Stage 1 outputs a binary decision

$$S_1(C_n, R_k) \in \{\texttt{violation}, \texttt{no violation}\}. \tag{5}$$

It is important to note that if $S_1(C_n, R_k) = \texttt{violation}$, we automatically consider **Stage 2** as passed, since the model has attributed the vulnerability

Table 4. Performance Comparison under Two Evaluation Criteria

Model	Evaluation Criterion	Accuracy (%)	Precision (%)	Recall (%)	F1 Score (%)
o4-mini	Vulnerability Detection Only	71	72	71	70
	Detection + Rule Attribution	68	69	68	68
GPT-4o-mini	Vulnerability Detection Only	52	55	52	45
	Detection + Rule Attribution	49	49	49	40
o3-mini	Vulnerability Detection Only	66	73	66	63
	Detection + Rule Attribution	64	71	64	61
GPT-4.1-mini	Vulnerability Detection Only	58	67	57	51
	Detection + Rule Attribution	56	65	58	48

to the correct rule R_k. Otherwise, if $S_1(C_n, R_k) = \texttt{no violation}$, the model proceeds to Stage 2 to identify the most likely violated rule (or none):

$$S_2(C_n) \in \{R_1, R_2, \ldots, R_7, \texttt{none}\}. \tag{6}$$

Success is therefore defined as both accurate vulnerability classification and correct rule attribution.

The dataset consists of function-level code pairs, each containing a vulnerable function and its patched counterpart. For each pair, we construct 14 evaluation cases by testing against all seven rules across both versions ($7 \times 2 = 14$).

For each LLM, we measure the average number of cases in which it completes: (i) Stage 1 alone, (ii) Stage 2 alone, and (iii) both stages correctly (referred to as *perfect cases*).Table 5 presents the procedural reasoning evaluation results.

Table 5. Procedural reasoning evaluation

Model	Stage 1	Stage 2	Perfect Cases
o4-mini	13	9	9
GPT-4o-mini	12	7	7
o3-mini	13	9	9
GPT-4.1-mini	13	6	6

As an illustrative example from the experiment, consider the evaluation of the function `dd_get_item_size`. When the vulnerable version of this function was tested against Rule 3 (see Fig. 4), GPT-4o mini correctly denied the violation at Stage 1 and proceeded to Stage 2, where it successfully identified Rule 1 as the actual rule being violated. In contrast, when the patched version of the same function was evaluated under the same conditions(see Fig. 5), the model once again rejected Rule 3 in Stage 1 but failed at Stage 2 by not recognizing that the added validation check `str_is_correct_filename` eliminated the vulnerability. This example illustrates a recurring pattern observed in the study and also noted in prior work: while the model can often detect vulnerabilities in code, it struggles to consistently recognize fixes once they are applied.

However, further analysis reveals discrepancies that go beyond simple rule attribution failures in some models. Specifically, an LLM may select a rule R_k

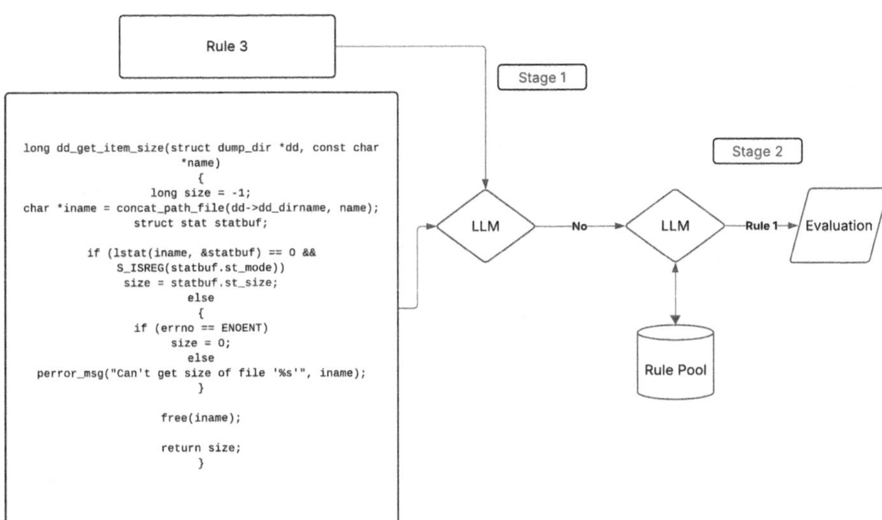

Fig. 4. Evaluation of the vulnerable version of `dd_get_item_size` by GPT-4o mini. The model correctly rejects Rule 3 at Stage 1 and identifies Rule 1 as the true violated rule in Stage 2.

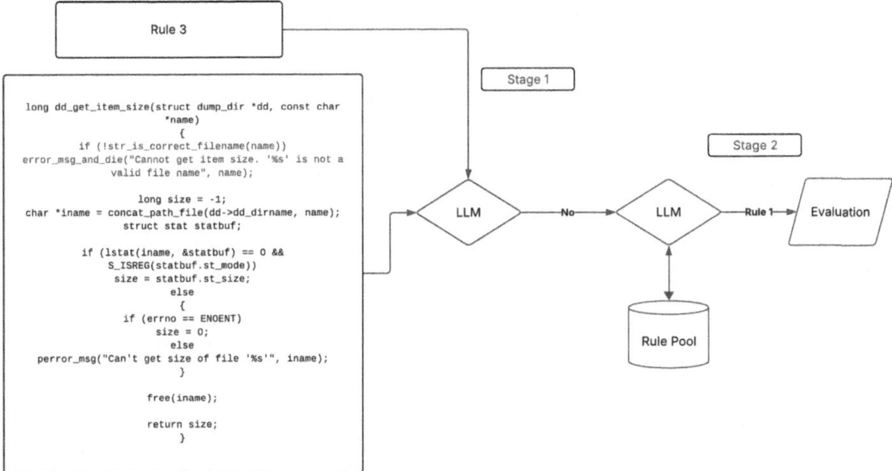

Fig. 5. Evaluation of the patched version of `dd_get_item_size` by GPT-4o mini. The model correctly rejects Rule 3 at Stage 1 but fails at Stage 2 to recognize that the added validation check `str_is_correct_filename` mitigates the vulnerability.

at Stage 2 as responsible for a vulnerability in C_n, yet during evaluation at the same stage classify the pair (C_n, R_k) as non-vulnerable. This inconsistency in the model's reasoning raises concerns about its semantic reliability, suggesting that its understanding of vulnerability patterns may be unstable or superficial. Further investigation of this issue is deferred to future work, as it falls beyond the scope of the current study.

6 Conclusion

This study set out to examine whether Large Language Models (LLMs) can go beyond surface-level vulnerability classification and demonstrate meaningful semantic understanding of code in the context of vulnerability detection. By leveraging a high-quality, manually labeled dataset and a series of structured evaluation experiments, we assessed LLMs' ability to identify not just that a vulnerability exists, but which underlying security rule has been violated from a predefined set of CWE-based rules as proof of semantic understanding of code in vulnerability detection.

Our results show that while LLMs such as `o4-mini` can achieve moderate accuracy in detecting vulnerabilities, their performance significantly declines when correct rule attribution is factored in—i.e., when correct rule attribution is required alongside detection. The drop in accuracy from 71% to 66% in the pool-based setting, and comparable outcomes in the advanced iterative setting, reveal a critical gap between perceived and actual model capability.

Although LLMs show promise in identifying insecure code patterns, their decision-making often lacks clear semantic grounding, limiting their reliability in high-stakes security applications. Our rule-based evaluation method not only exposes this shortfall but also provides a foundation for more rigorous testing of LLM code comprehension in future work.

At the same time, we also observe inconsistencies in how models justify their predictions: in some cases, they attribute a vulnerability to a specific rule but then fail to treat that same explanation as vulnerable when reevaluated directly,such contradictions point to instability in their reasoning processes, further underscoring the need for deeper investigation. A more thorough analysis of these discrepancies is left for future work, as addressing them lies beyond the scope of this study.

Disclosure of Interests. The authors declare that they have no competing interests.

References

1. Achiam, J., et al.: GPT-4 technical report. arXiv preprint arXiv:2303.08774 (2023)
2. Ball, T.: The concept of dynamic analysis. SIGSOFT Softw. Eng. Notes **24**(6), 216–234 (1999). https://doi.org/10.1145/318774.318944

3. Bhandari, G., Naseer, A., Moonen, L.: CVEFixes: automated collection of vulnerabilities and their fixes from open-source software. In: Proceedings of the 17th International Conference on Predictive Models and Data Analytics in Software Engineering, pp. 30–39 (2021)
4. Chakraborty, S., Krishna, R., Ding, Y., Ray, B.: Deep learning based vulnerability detection: are we there yet? IEEE Trans. Softw. ng. **48**(9), 3280–3296 (2021)
5. Chao, W., et al.: An android application vulnerability mining method based on static and dynamic analysis. In: 2020 IEEE 5th Information Technology and Mechatronics Engineering Conference (ITOEC), pp. 599–603 (2020)
6. Chess, B., McGraw, G.: Static analysis for security. IEEE Secur. Priv. **2**(6), 76–79 (2004)
7. Cho, K., et al.: Learning phrase representations using RNN encoder-decoder for statistical machine translation. arXiv preprint arXiv:1406.1078 (2014)
8. Chu, Z., et al.: Graph neural networks for vulnerability detection: a counterfactual explanation. In: Proceedings of the 33rd ACM SIGSOFT International Symposium on Software Testing and Analysis, pp. 389–401 (2024)
9. Ding, Y., et al.: Vulnerability detection with code language models: how far are we? arXiv preprint arXiv:2403.18624 (2024)
10. Du, X., et al.: Generalization-enhanced code vulnerability detection via multi-task instruction fine-tuning. arXiv preprint arXiv:2406.03718 (2024)
11. Du, X., et al.: Leopard: identifying vulnerable code for vulnerability assessment through program metrics. In: 2019 IEEE/ACM 41st International Conference on Software Engineering (ICSE), pp. 60–71. IEEE (2019)
12. Du, X., et al.: VUL-RAG: enhancing LLM-based vulnerability detection via knowledge-level RAG. arXiv preprint arXiv:2406.11147 (2024)
13. Fan, J., Li, Y., Wang, S., Nguyen, T.N.: A C/C++ code vulnerability dataset with code changes and CVE summaries. In: Proceedings of the 17th International Conference on Mining Software Repositories, pp. 508–512. MSR '20, Association for Computing Machinery (2020). https://doi.org/10.1145/3379597.3387501
14. Feng, Z., et al.: CodeBERT: a pre-trained model for programming and natural languages. arXiv preprint arXiv:2002.08155 (2020)
15. Finzi, M., et al.: Compute-optimal LLMs provably generalize better with scale. arXiv preprint arXiv:2504.15208 (2025)
16. Han, Z., Gao, C., Liu, J., Zhang, J., Zhang, S.Q.: Parameter-efficient fine-tuning for large models: a comprehensive survey. Trans. Mach. Learn. Res. (2024). https://openreview.net/forum?id=lIsCS8b6zj
17. He, J., Vechev, M.: Large language models for code: security hardening and adversarial testing. In: Proceedings of the 2023 ACM SIGSAC Conference on Computer and Communications Security, pp. 1865–1879. CCS '23, (2023). https://doi.org/10.1145/3576915.3623175
18. Li, Z., Zou, D., Xu, S., Jin, H., Zhu, Y., Chen, Z.: SySeVR: a framework for using deep learning to detect software vulnerabilities. IEEE Trans. Dependable Secure Comput. **19**(4), 2244–2258 (2021)
19. Li, Z., et al.: VulDeePecker: a deep learning-based system for vulnerability detection. arXiv preprint arXiv:1801.01681 (2018)
20. Li, Z., Dutta, S., Naik, M.: IRIS: LLM-assisted static analysis for detecting security vulnerabilities. arXiv preprint arXiv:2405.17238 (2024)
21. Ma, W., et al.: Combining fine-tuning and LLM-based agents for intuitive smart contract auditing with justifications. arXiv preprint arXiv:2403.16073 (2024)
22. Mao, Q., Li, Z., Hu, X., Liu, K., Xia, X., Sun, J.: Towards explainable vulnerability detection with large language models. IEEE Trans. Softw. Eng. **51**(10) (2025)

23. Qin, W., Suo, L., Li, L., Yang, F.: Advancing software vulnerability detection with reasoning LLMs: deepseek-R1's performance and insights. Appl. Sci. **15**(12) (2025). https://doi.org/10.3390/app15126651
24. Risse, N.: Detecting overfitting of machine learning techniques for automatic vulnerability detection. In: Proceedings of the 31st ACM Joint European Software Engineering Conference and Symposium on the Foundations of Software Engineering, pp. 2189–2191 (2023)
25. Sheng, Z., Chen, Z., Gu, S., Huang, H., Gu, G., Huang, J.: LLMs in software security: a survey of vulnerability detection techniques and insights. ACM Comput. Surv. (2025)
26. Shestov, A., et al.: Finetuning large language models for vulnerability detection. IEEE Access **13** (2025)
27. Steenhoek, B., Rahman, M.M., Roy, M.K., Alam, M.S., Barr, E.T., Le, W.: A comprehensive study of the capabilities of large language models for vulnerability detection (2024). arXiv preprint arXiv:2403.17218 (2024)
28. Tamberg, K., Bahsi, H.: Harnessing large language models for software vulnerability detection: a comprehensive benchmarking study. IEEE Access **13**, 29698–29717 (2025). https://doi.org/10.1109/ACCESS.2025.3541146
29. Touvron, H., et al.: Llama: open and efficient foundation language models. arXiv preprint arXiv:2302.13971 (2023)
30. Ullah, S., Han, M., Pujar, S., Pearce, H., Coskun, A., Stringhini, G.: LLMs cannot reliably identify and reason about security vulnerabilities (yet?): a comprehensive evaluation, framework, and benchmarks. In: 2024 IEEE Symposium on Security and Privacy (SP), pp. 862–880 (2024)
31. Viega, J., Bloch, J., Kohno, Y., McGraw, G.: ITS4: a static vulnerability scanner for C and C++ code. In: Proceedings 16th Annual Computer Security Applications Conference (ACSAC'00), pp. 257–267 (2000)
32. Yang, Y., et al.: DLAP: a deep learning augmented large language model prompting framework for software vulnerability detection. J. Syst. Softw. **219**, 112–234 (2025)
33. Zhang, C., Liu, H., Zeng, J., Yang, K., Li, Y., Li, H.: Prompt-enhanced software vulnerability detection using ChatGPT. In: Proceedings of the 2024 IEEE/ACM 46th International Conference on Software Engineering: Companion Proceedings, pp. 276–277 (2024)
34. Zhao, W.X., et al.: A survey of large language models. **1(2)** (2023)
35. Zhou, Y., Liu, S., Siow, J., Du, X., Liu, Y.: Devign: effective vulnerability identification by learning comprehensive program semantics via graph neural networks. In: Advances in Neural Information Processing Systems, vol. 32 (2019)

Cyber Threats and Prediction

A Hybrid Graph Neural Networks-Transformer Architecture for Enhanced Distributed Denial of Service Anomaly Detection in Cloud Network Data

Shiwam Keshri, Nidhi Sonkar, and Shiva Darshan Sasalu Lokesh(✉)

Department of Computer Science and Engineering, National Institute of Technology Warangal, Warangal, India
sk23csm2r21@student.nitw.ac.in, {nidhisonkar,shivadarshan}@nitw.ac.in

Abstract. Distributed Denial of Service (DDoS) detection in cloud environments requires high accuracy and real-time processing under constraints such as varying attack types and large-scale data. Traditional techniques based on Convolutional Neural Networks (CNNs) and Recurrent Neural Networks (RNNs) struggle to effectively capture spatial and temporal input, especially in complex cloud settings. This research introduces an effective hybrid model for DDoS detection that utilizes the encoder components of Graph Neural Networks (GNNs) and Transformers, leveraging the graph representation strengths of GNNs and the global attention mechanism of Transformers. This proposed methodology combines the relational learning capacity of GNN (GCN Encoders) with the contextual modeling advantages of Transformer encoders to achieve accurate and scalable DDoS detection for cloud networks. The model improves detection accuracy while being computationally efficient by utilizing a hybrid architecture designed for multiscale feature extraction and temporal correlation learning. Extensive studies on benchmark datasets show that our technique outperforms DDoS detection methods, demonstrating its effectiveness in protecting cloud-based systems.

Keywords: Cloud Security · DDoS Attacks · Graph Neural Networks · Transformers

1 Introduction

Detecting and mitigating DDoS attacks is crucial for cloud security. These attacks aim to overwhelm network resources [1]. These attacks disrupt essential systems by flooding them with malicious traffic, resulting in substantial downtime and financial losses for enterprises. DDoS detection requires examining complicated network traffic patterns to detect and forecast hostile activity, unlike simpler anomaly detection tasks [2]. DDoS detection plays a crucial role

K. Adi et al. (Eds.): CRiSIS 2025, LNCS 16295, pp. 37–53, 2026.
https://doi.org/10.1007/978-3-032-20732-6_3

in ensuring the availability and integrity of cloud services. DDoS detection prevents disturbances in cloud computing models such as Infrastructure as a Service (IaaS), Platform as a Service (PaaS), and Software as a Service (SaaS), ensuring uninterrupted access to cloud-hosted applications [3].

The rapidly increasing volume and complexity of network data, combined with the intelligence of modern DDoS attack methodologies, have presented considerable hurdles to existing detection approaches. These technologies, such as rule-based systems and machine learning classifiers, frequently analyze static features or specified criteria [4]. Although they have successfully detected simple attack patterns, they struggle to react to changing attack routes and large-scale traffic dynamics in real time. As attackers deploy increasingly sophisticated and diverse strategies, there is a growing demand for adaptable and intelligent systems that detect hidden patterns in high-dimensional network traffic data. Deep learning approaches have emerged as a viable solution to this problem, leveraging their ability to model complex, nonlinear relationships within data. Long-Short-Term Memory (LSTM) networks are commonly utilized for DDoS detection due to their ability to capture temporal dependencies in sequential data. However, LSTMs are computationally expensive and prone to overfitting, especially when dealing with imbalanced datasets, a prevalent problem in real-world network traffic scenarios [5].

Transformers [6] were created for natural language processing applications. They have recently gained popularity in DDoS detection due to their ability to represent long-range dependencies between sequences using self-attention methods. Transformers, unlike LSTMs, are better at understanding the correlations between all input features simultaneously, making them ideal for dealing with the complex and dynamic nature of network traffic. Furthermore, their scalability and ability to handle large datasets have made them increasingly desirable in cloud security applications, especially in resource-constrained contexts. Although these developments have significantly increased the accuracy and efficiency of intrusion detection systems, problems persist, notably in real-time DDoS detection within cloud environments. Existing models struggle with the dynamic and distributed nature of cloud systems, where traffic patterns can change quickly and attacks can adapt to evade standard detection measures. Furthermore, the scalability of these models remains a challenge, as cloud environments sometimes contain large volumes of data that must be processed and analyzed in real time.

Hybrid models leveraging the encoder modules of both Graph Neural Networks and Transformers have been developed to enhance the effectiveness of DDoS detection by capturing complex spatial and contextual patterns. GNNs can capture relational information in network traffic, such as the relationships between source and destination IPs or ports. In contrast, transformers give a global context by finding temporal and spatial correlations throughout the data. This complementary method enables hybrid models to examine local and real-time trends in network traffic, resulting in higher detection accuracy. Furthermore, these models are computationally efficient, making them appropriate for real-time applications in cloud settings. In recent years, the integration of GNNs and Transformers has shown great promise in overcoming the limitations of standalone techniques. GNNs excel at utilising the graph-like structure of network traffic, in which nodes represent entities (e.g., IP addresses) and edges reflect relationships (e.g., shared connections or temporal proximity). However, transformers improve this representation by capturing long-term dependencies and revealing global patterns that standard techniques often miss. This hybrid technique provides a robust solution to the challenges posed by developing DDoS attacks, with exceptional detection performance even in complex, large-scale datasets. The primary goal of this proposed work is to create and develop a hybrid GNN-Transformer model—utilizing only their encoder components—specifically for DDoS detection in cloud environments. The suggested architecture combines the relational modeling characteristics of GNNs with the temporal sequence analysis capabilities of Transformers to create a scalable and computationally efficient solution. This study describes the underlying approach, assesses the model's performance on benchmark datasets, and demonstrates its application to real-world cloud security scenarios involving large-scale network traffic.

The following sections of this paper are organized as follows: An overview of DDoS detection in cloud environments is presented in Sect. 1. Existing DDoS detection methods are reviewed in Sect. 2. Section 3 explains the proposed hybrid GNN-Transformer model for DDoS detection in cloud environments. The evaluation of the performance of the proposed model is discussed in Sect. 4. Section 5 concludes the study by summarizing the key findings and implications.

2 Related Works

DDoS attacks continue to be a persistent concern in cloud computing, prompting the development of effective detection techniques. Several research studies propose using deep learning, machine learning, and optimization strategies to mitigate DDoS attacks in cloud environments. Traditional techniques, which are based on static features and predefined criteria, are insufficient to address the complexity and volatility of new attack vectors. Researchers have developed innovative approaches to enhance detection performance.

Pandithurai et al. [7] developed a DDoS attack prediction model that combines a Honey Badger Optimization (HBO) feature selection algorithm [8] with Bi-LSTM in a cloud environment. Their approach focused on selecting ideal features to reduce computational time and improve classification accuracy, resulting in a 97% accuracy in predicting DDoS attacks. This technique outperformed traditional machine learning models (LSTM, DNN, and ANN) in accuracy, sensitivity, and precision. The study emphasized the problems of real-time DDoS detection, particularly in cloud systems. Optimizing features and managing missing data are critical to improving detection performance. Long et al. [9] presented a unique Transformer-based Network Intrusion Detection System (NIDS) for cloud environments. By utilizing the Transformer model's attention mechanism, their system demonstrated enhanced detection accuracy, particularly when examining complex interactions between network intrusion features. Their technique achieved a detection accuracy of more than 93%, which is comparable to

CNN-LSTM systems, demonstrating the efficacy of the Transformer in improving cloud security. The authors' approach addresses critical concerns, such as handling time-series data and the dynamic nature of cloud settings, proposing a more flexible solution to the evolving threat environment. David et al. [10] presented an information-theoretic strategy to detect DDoS attacks using time series models. Their system successfully predicted attack patterns by examining network traffic behaviour, overcoming hurdles such as prediction errors and unbalanced data. Their findings highlight the importance of utilizing advanced statistical models to improve detection rates in dynamic network environments. Batchu and Seetha [11] proposed an integrated technique to detect DDoS attacks by merging Deep Neural Networks (DNN) with sparse autoencoders for feature learning. Their technique efficiently distinguished DDoS traffic from regular network activity, decreasing overfitting and boosting detection performance. However, they acknowledged the difficulties of identifying real-time attacks, particularly with the standard of massive datasets in cloud environments. Agarwal et al. [12] applied deep learning models to detect DDoS attacks in cloud storage applications. They demonstrated the detection of DDoS attacks from regular traffic with excellent accuracy using deep learning algorithms. The model's capacity to scale with the increasing complexity of cloud networks is impressive; however, issues such as computing time and training data requirements have been identified. Velliangiri and Premalatha [13] developed an Intrusion Detection System (IDS) for DDoS attacks in cloud environments. Their research used statistical and machine learning techniques to identify attack patterns and prevent unauthorized entry. Despite their method's success in decreasing false positives, they underlined the importance of more efficient real-time detection systems as cloud computing scales. Phan and Park [14] suggested a protection strategy against DDoS attacks in SDN-based cloud settings. They successfully classified traffic and mitigated threats using a hybrid machine learning model that used self-organizing maps and support vector machines (SVM). However, their approach was limited in managing complicated, multivector DDoS attacks and scaling with big cloud networks. The range of these investigations highlights the ongoing advances in DDoS detection strategies. Traditional methods often fail against modern attack patterns, but hybrid models that combine deep learning and optimization algorithms have shown promise. The integration of GNNs and Transformers, as investigated in this research, represents the next step in addressing these challenges by leveraging both local and global patterns in network traffic to enhance detection performance.

3 Proposed Methodology

The overall architecture is depicted in Fig. 1 and forms the basis for the proposed method. The methodology integrates Graph Neural Networks (GCN Encoder) and Transformer Encoders to address the challenges of detecting DDoS attacks in network traffic. By leveraging the local feature extraction capabilities of GCNs and the global dependency modelling strength of Transformers, the hybrid architecture effectively captures topological and temporal relationships in network traffic data. This integration provides a robust solution to the evolving nature of DDoS attacks, which often requires sophisticated methods to distinguish between benign and malicious traffic patterns.

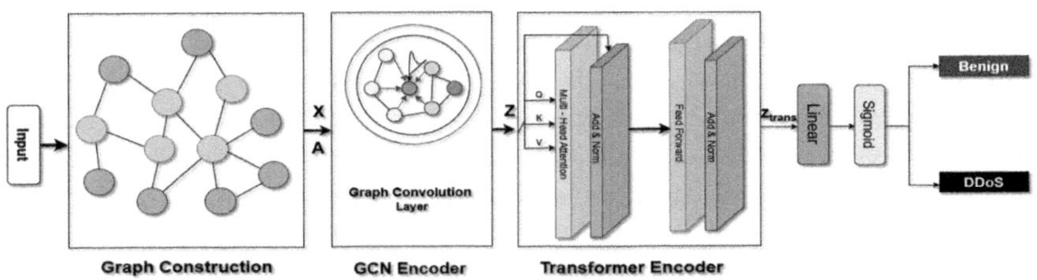

Fig. 1. Hybrid GNN-Transformer Model for DDoS Detection.

3.1 Input Layer: Data Representation and Graph Construction

Network traffic data is pre-processed and turned into a graph representation. Each traffic flow is represented as a node and the relationships between flows are depicted as edges. This hierarchical representation enables the model to use both local and global data effectively.

Dataset Preprocessing. The raw network traffic data set is pre-processed to facilitate high-quality feature extraction and effective model training. Initially, unnecessary columns such as ID and flow ID are eliminated from the dataset because they do not contribute to flow characterization.

Following that, categorical attributes are adequately handled. The Protocol field, which represents the transport protocol (e.g., TCP, UDP), is converted into numerical labels using Label Encoding. Furthermore, source and destination IP addresses (Src IP and Dst IP) are anonymized using SHA-256 cryptographic hashing, followed by modular reduction. This anonymization protects privacy while preserving a deterministic mapping suitable for downstream analysis without disclosing actual IP address information.

To prepare numerical attributes for graph learning, feature scaling is used. Flow duration, packet counts, byte counts, packet size statistics, inter-arrival times (IATs), and activity/inactivity periods are all normalized to the range $[0, 1]$ using Min-Max Normalization [15], which is described as shown in Eq. 1:

$$X' = \frac{X - X_{\min}}{X_{\max} - X_{\min}} \tag{1}$$

where X is the original feature value; $X_{\min}$ and $X_{\max}$ are the minimum and maximum values of the feature across the dataset; and X' represents the normalized value. This normalizing step keeps features with greater numeric ranges from dominating the learning process and encourages steady convergence during model training.

To address data quality concerns, infinite values resulting from anomalies are initially substituted with NaN values. Any missing values are then imputed using the median of the relevant feature columns, ensuring robustness against outliers. Additionally, the timestamp element, initially in Datetime format, is converted to Unix time (seconds) to efficiently record the temporal ordering of traffic flows, enabling the creation of a time-aware graph. Finally, the target variable (Label) is binarised, with flows labeled as "DDoS" receiving a value of one (representing attack traffic) and all other flows receiving a value of zero (indicating benign traffic). These systematic pretreatment methods produce a structured and clean dataset, allowing the generation of meaningful graph representations for effective graph-based learning.

Feature Matrix (X). Each node in the graph represents a network traffic flow, which is defined as a vector of attributes that capture various elements of flow behaviour. The feature set includes flow-specific attributes, such as Flow Duration, Total Forward Packets, Total Backward Packets, Total Length of Forward and Backwards Packets, encoded Protocol Identifiers, and higher-level statistical measurements, including packet size distributions, flow inter-arrival times (IATs), and activity/inactivity periods.

The destination port information is also included as a feature to detect any attacks targeting activities. Numerical characteristics are standardized to the range [0,1] using Min-Max Normalization, and categorical fields are encoded before graph generation. The feature matrix is formally defined as follows (see Eq. 2):

$$X = \{x_1, x_2, \ldots, x_F\} \tag{2}$$

where x_i denotes the ith normalized and encoded feature for a particular traffic flow. The graph neural network uses the feature matrix X as its primary input to learn node-level embeddings.

Adjacency Matrix (A). The adjacency matrix (A) represents the relationships between traffic flows in a graph. Edges between nodes are determined using spatial-temporal proximity criteria, which include destination IP addresses, ports, and timestamps. Two nodes (i, j) are deemed connected if their feature vectors (Dst.IP, Dst.Port, Timestamp) fall within a given radius in a multidimensional space.

A k-dimensional tree (KDTree) quickly determines neighboring flows, allowing fast neighbor searches based on combined spatial and temporal variables. The generation of edges is controlled by a radius threshold (r = 10) that connects flows within a specific radius. Self-loops are avoided by preventing a node from connecting to itself until no other neighbors are discovered; in that case, a dummy self-loop is added to ensure graph consistency.

This method captures both destination-based similarities and the temporal relationships inherent in network traffic. The adjacency matrix is defined as:

$$A_{ij} = \begin{cases} 1 & \text{if nodes } i \text{ and } j \text{ satisfy connectivity rules,} \\ 0 & \text{otherwise.} \end{cases}$$

Temporal Edge Formation. Temporal correlations are essential in detecting Distributed Denial of Service (DDoS) behaviors. A spatial-temporal proximity technique accurately represents network flow dependencies based on destination (static) and time (dynamic). Each flow is defined as a three-dimensional vector comprising the destination IP address, port, and timestamp.

Flows are considered connected if their spatial-temporal distance falls within a predetermined radius r, calculated using the Euclidean distance formula:

$$ED = \sqrt{(a)^2 + (b)^2 + (c)^2}$$

where a is $(DstIP_i - DstIP_j)$, b is $(DstPort_i - DstPort_j)$ and c is $(Timestamp_i - Timestamp_j)$. $DstIP_i$, $DstPort_i$, and $Timestamp_i$ indicate the destination IP, destination port, and timestamp of flow i, respectively. Using these combined attributes, a k-dimensional tree (KDTree) structure efficiently searches for neighbors.

Flows with identical destination information and near timestamps have a shorter spatial-temporal distance and are thus more likely to be connected; however, formal equality matching of destination IP and port is not required. Instead, spatial-temporal closeness is recorded holistically via a multidimensional proximity search. The resulting graph representation (X, A) successfully maintains the structural and dynamic behaviors of network traffic by integrating temporal relationships into the spatial neighbor search. This enhances the model's ability to detect temporally coordinated attacks, such as DDoS, while minimizing noise.

3.2 Graph Neural Network (GNN) Encoder

The GNN encoder extracts localized structural and feature correlations from the generated traffic flow graph. Each node updates its representation by aggregating feature information from nearby nodes through a graph connection.

Figure 1 shows the overall architecture and the sequential flow of information among the model's components: A Transformer encoder learns global dependencies and contextual embeddings throughout the graph after the initial node features are initially processed through a Graph Convolutional Network (GCN) layer to collect local structural information. Binary predictions are then generated by feeding the enhanced node representations into a fully connected classification head. The model may use both local and global patterns for precise node categorization because to its end-to-end architecture. Two approaches were used in light of the class imbalance in the CIC-IDS 2018 dataset, where benign traffic instances outnumber specific DDoS attack flows. During training, class-balanced sampling made sure that each batch contained a proportionate mix of benign and attack flows, and bias against minority classes was lessened by adapting the Binary Cross-Entropy loss function with class weights. Additionally, as they more accurately reflect model performance in unbalanced scenarios, evaluation metrics including precision, recall, F1-score, and ROC-AUC were given precedence above accuracy. Graph Convolution Network By combining the characteristics of a node's neighbors according to the weights of the adjacency matrix, the

GCN layer updates the node embeddings. A single GCN layer's function [16] is expressed as follows:

$$H^{(l+1)} = \sigma \left(\tilde{D}^{-1/2} \tilde{A} \tilde{D}^{-1/2} H^{(l)} W^{(l)} \right)$$

where: $\tilde{A} = A + I$: Adjacency matrix with self-loops added, $\tilde{D}$: Diagonal node degree matrix corresponding to $\tilde{A}$, $W^{(l)}$: Learnable weight matrix, $H^{(l)}$: Node embeddings at layer l, and σ: Activation function (ReLU).

Incorporating self-loops guarantees that every node preserves its identity across layers by incorporating its own characteristics during aggregation. By mitigating degree disparity, the normalization term $\tilde{D}^{-1/2}$ keeps strongly linked nodes from controlling the feature aggregation process.

With modular reduction, we used SHA-256 hashing to transform IP addresses into graph nodes. This method ensures the uniqueness and repeatability of node IDs, but it does not maintain topological or geographic closeness. Adjacency was constructed using the Euclidean distance metric using KD-Tree search, while connectedness was defined by the neighborhood radius parameter r. The model's robustness to this parameter choice was confirmed by a sensitivity analysis using $r \in \{5, 10, 15\}$, which showed steady performance (F1-score fluctuation within $\pm 0.8\%$). As a compromise between connectedness and graph sparsity, we chose $r = 10$.

Stacked GCN Layers. To capture higher-level information, two GCN layers are stacked. The first layer collects information from immediate neighbours, whereas the second layer broadens the receptive field to include information from two-hop neighbours. This stacking allows the model to learn patterns on several scales. The abstracted GCN update at each layer [16] is as follows:

$$H^{(l+1)} = \text{ReLU} \left(\text{GCNConv}(H^{(l)}, A) \right)$$

Internally, this corresponds to:

$$H^{(l+1)} = \sigma \left(\tilde{D}^{-1/2} \tilde{A} \tilde{D}^{-1/2} H^{(l)} W^{(l)} \right)$$

Output The GNN encoder outputs a node embedding matrix Z that stores the graph-aware [16] representations of all nodes after L layers of graph convolution, given by:

$$Z = H^{(L)}$$

Our approach uses two stacked GCN layers ($L = 2$) to aggregate information from neighbors of immediate and second order. These learned embeddings encode local topology and feature properties, serving as input to the Transformer encoder, which models higher-order and global dependencies.

3.3 Transformer Encoder

The Transformer encoder improves the ability of GNNs by simulating long-range dependencies and temporal correlations between traffic flows. While GCN layers efficiently gather local neighborhood information, the Transformer allows each node to attend to all other nodes in the graph, capturing global context through self-attention.

Input Transformation. The node embeddings $\mathbf{Z} \in \mathbb{R}^{n \times d}$ of the GNN are first modified to match the input dimension of the Transformer using a linear transformation (see Eq. 3).

$$Z_{\text{input}} = \text{Linear}(Z) \quad (3)$$

This transformation ensures that the node embeddings correspond to the input dimensionality specified by the Transformer's multihead self-attention mechanism.

Multi-head Self-attention To represent interactions between all node pairs, the Transformer employs multihead self-attention. The attention mechanism computes associations between all pairs of nodes, which allows the model to capture complex interactions. The queries, keys, and values of each attention head [17] are calculated as follows:

$$Q = ZW_Q, \quad K = ZW_K, \quad V = ZW_V$$

The attention output [17] is then calculated as follows:

$$\text{Attention}(Q, K, V) = \text{Softmax}\left(\frac{QK^\top}{\sqrt{d_k}}\right)$$

where: $Q = ZW_Q$: Query matrix, $K = ZW_K$: Key matrix, $V = ZW_V$: Value matrix, and d_k: Dimension of the key vectors.

The self-attention mechanism enhances the embeddings by allowing each node to attend to all other nodes in the graph. Multiple attention heads are concatenated and passed through a final linear layer. We used t-SNE dimensionality reduction on the latent feature space following the last Transformer encoder layer in order to gain a better understanding of the learnt embeddings. The capacity of the model to capture discriminative characteristics in the representation space was validated by the visualization, which showed a clear split between benign and DDoS traffic clusters.

Feed-Forward Layers. Following the attention mechanism, the output embeddings are refined using feedforward networks (FFNs) in position. Each FFN comprises two linear transformations with a non-linear activation function between. This enables the model to further transform the aggregated data from the attention stage, increasing its representational capacity. The feed-forward operation [17] is mathematically defined as follows:

$$\text{FFN}(x) = \sigma(xW_1 + b_1)W_2 + b_2$$

where σ is a nonlinear activation function (ReLU), W_1, W_2 are weight matrices and b_1, b_2 are bias terms. This component improves the learning of complex patterns seen in node representations.

Output The Transformer encoder outputs a contextual embedding matrix C that includes enriched and globally aware representations of nodes [18]. These embeddings are computed as follows:

$$C = \text{TransformerEncoder}(Z_{\text{input}})$$

where: $\mathbf{Z}_{\text{input}}$ is the linearly transformed node embedding matrix of the GNN, and $\mathbf{C} \in \mathbb{R}^{N \times d_{\text{model}}}$ is the contextual embedding matrix output by the transformer encoder, where N is the number of nodes and d_{model} is the output dimensionality.

These embeddings possess both local structure (from GCN) and long-range dependencies (from attention), making them ideal for downstream tasks. The matrix C serves as input for subsequent classification layers.

3.4 Classification Layers

The final stage of the architecture maps the contextual embeddings to binary-class predictions.

Fully Connected Layer The embeddings are projected to logits using a fully connected layer. Let $\mathbf{C} \in \mathbb{R}^{N \times d}$ be the contextual output embedding matrix of the Transformer encoder, where N is the number of nodes and d is the embedding dimension [19]. Each row $\mathbf{c}_i$ is passed through a linear projection to produce logits given by:

$$\hat{y}_i = \mathbf{W}^\top \mathbf{c}_i + b \quad \textit{or} \quad \hat{\mathbf{y}} = \text{Linear}(\mathbf{C}) = \mathbf{C}\mathbf{W} + \mathbf{b} \quad (\textit{matrix} \quad \textit{for} \quad \textit{all} \quad \textit{nodes})$$

where: $\hat{y}_i$: Logit value (scalar) for node i, calculated before applying sigmoid activation, $\mathbf{c}_i$: Contextual embedding vector for node i, obtained from the Transformer + GCN encoder, $\mathbf{W}$: Trainable weight matrix in the fully connected (linear) layer, b: Bias term added after the linear transformation, $\mathbf{C}$: Matrix of contextual embeddings for all nodes, where each row corresponds to $\mathbf{c}_i$, and $\hat{\mathbf{y}}$: Vector of predicted logits for all nodes.

Sigmoid Activation. The sigmoid function is used to turn each logit into a probability [20], given by:

$$P(y_i = 1 \mid \mathbf{x}_i) = \sigma(\hat{y}_i) = \frac{1}{1 + e^{-\hat{y}_i}}$$

where: $\sigma(\cdot)$: Sigmoid activation function, defined as $\sigma(z) = \frac{1}{1+e^{-z}}$, $P(y_i = 1 \mid \mathbf{x}_i)$: Predicted probability that the label y_i is 1, given the input $\mathbf{x}_i$, and $\mathbf{x}_i$: Input feature vector for node i (typically used in conditional notation; replaced by $\mathbf{c}_i$ post-encoding).

3.5 Training Objective

The model is trained using the Binary Cross-Entropy (BCE) loss, which is appropriate for binary classification [21]. The loss for N samples is defined as follows:

$$\mathcal{L} = -\frac{1}{N}\sum_{i=1}^{N}\left[y_i \log(\hat{y}_i) + (1 - y_i)\log(1 - \hat{y}_i)\right]$$

where: N: Number of samples, y_i: True label of sample i (0 or 1), and $\hat{y}_i$: Predicted probability for sample i after sigmoid.

This loss function optimizes the model by minimizing the difference between the predicted and actual labels, ensuring robust classification performance.

Figure 1 shows the overall architecture and the sequential flow of information among the model's components: Instead of being fed into a Transformer encoder, which learns global dependencies and contextual embeddings throughout the network, the initial node features are first processed through a graph convolutional layer (GCN) to collect local structure information. Binary predictions are then generated by feeding the enhanced node representations into a fully connected classification head. The model may use both local and global patterns for precise node categorization because to its end-to-end architecture. Two approaches were used in light of the class imbalance in the CIC-IDS 2018 dataset, where benign traffic instances outnumber specific DDoS attack flows. During training, class-balanced sampling made sure that each batch contained a proportionate mix of benign and attack flows, and bias against minority classes was lessened by adapting the Binary Cross-Entropy loss function with class weights. Additionally, as they more accurately reflect model performance in unbalanced scenarios, evaluation metrics including precision, recall, F1-score, and ROC-AUC were given precedence over accuracy.

Table 1. Parameter Configuration of the Model

Parameter	Value	Parameter	Value
Batch Size	1024	Heads of Attention	8
GCN Hidden Layer Size	64	Feedforward Dimension	512
GCN Output Layer Size	32	Dropout Rate	0.3
Embedding Dimension (d_{model})	80	Learning Rate	0.001
Transformer Encoder Layers	1	Optimizer	Adam
Loss Function	Binary Cross-Entropy		

4 Model Performance Evaluation

The proposed Hybrid GCN-Transformer model improves anomaly detection in network traffic data. The model uses Graph Convolutional Networks (GCN) to

Table 2. Model Performance Comparison

Model Name	Accuracy	Precision	Recall	F1-Score
Transformer Model	0.9476	0.6440	0.3943	0.4891
Bi-LSTM Model	0.9700	0.9400	–	–
Proposed Model	**0.9809**	**0.9798**	**0.9826**	**0.9812**

Table 3. Dataset Description

Aspect	Description	Aspect	Description
Dataset	CIC-IDS 2018	Attack Type	DDoS
Total Records	12,794,627	Label Types	DDoS, Benign
Number of Features	84	Feature Examples	Des-IP, Port, TS, PS, Flow Bytes/s

capture spatial interactions and Transformer layers to model long-term dependencies and patterns. The model is trained by the Binary Cross-Entropy (BCE) loss function Eq. 4, defined as:

$$L = -\frac{1}{N} \sum_{i=1}^{N} [y_i \log(\hat{y}_i) + (1 - y_i) \log(1 - \hat{y}_i)] \tag{4}$$

where: N: Number of samples, y_i: True label for the i-th sample, and $\hat{y}_i$: Predicted probability for the i-th sample.

This loss function reduces the difference between expected and actual labels by severely penalizing wrong predictions. By allocating a larger loss to confidently incorrect predictions and a smaller loss to accurate ones, the model is guided to acquire meaningful decision bounds. This enhances the model's ability to distinguish between regular and anomalous traffic, particularly in highly skewed or noisy datasets. To ensure there was no overlap with training or validation data, performance was assessed on the held-out test set. Accuracy, precision, recall, F1-score, and ROC-AUC are among the metrics that have been reported. To assure statistical reliability, we give the mean ± standard deviation for each experiment, which was conducted five times using different random seeds.

4.1 Experimental Settings

The evaluation method is divided into steps to ensure the transparency and reproducibility of the results. We begin by describing the experimental setup, which includes hardware configurations, a software environment, and hyperparameter settings, and then proceed to describe the datasets used in the study.

Experimental Environment and Parameter Configuration. The experiments were implemented using the Python programming language, leveraging the PyTorch deep learning framework along with the PyTorch Geometric (PyG) library for handling graph-structured data. All training and evaluation were conducted on a system equipped with an NVIDIA GPU for acceleration. The batch size is 1024 and dropout 0.3 were chosen to minimize overfitting and give consistent convergence. The eight attention heads in the Transformer layer allowed the model to learn a variety of interaction patterns across network traffic variables. The CIC-IDS 2018 dataset was divided into training, validation, and testing sets in a 70:15:15 ratio to ensure repeatability and avoid data leakage, with chronological splitting to preserve temporal ordering of traffic flows and prevent future information from being included during training. Model checkpoints, hyperparameter tuning, and early stopping were guided by the validation set, while the test set was held out until the final evaluation. Additionally, a five-fold cross-validation was conducted to confirm that the model's performance remained stable across different data partitions. The experimental configuration is summarized in Table 1.

After the dataset was divided into train, validation, and test subsets, all graph creation and preprocessing operations were carried out in order to rigorously prohibit data leakage. Each subset's graph adjacency was calculated separately to make sure that training was unaffected by test set information. This process ensures that splits are isolated both spatially and temporally. Training was conducted in a supervised learning environment. First, graph representations of each traffic flow were created, with nodes representing flow attributes and edges representing similarity measures. To address class imbalance, the GNN-Transformer architecture was trained end-to-end using weighted Binary Cross-Entropy loss. While keeping an eye on the validation F1-score, we implemented early halting with patience = 10 epochs. To reduce overfitting, L2 regularization and dropout layers (p = 0.3) were applied. Every instance of network traffic was represented as a node in order to create graphs from the CIC-IDS 2018 dataset. Cosine similarity between feature vectors was used to create edges, with a 0.7 cutoff to keep only significant relationships. As a result, nodes representing traffic flows with comparable statistical characteristics were guaranteed to be tightly connected. To increase scalability, each batch's adjacency matrix was created dynamically.

Dataset. The data set used for this experiment is the **CIC-IDS 2018** dataset, developed by the Communications Security Establishment (CSE) and the Canadian Institute of Cybersecurity (CIC) for the investigation of intrusion detection. The CIC-IDS 2018 dataset comprises regular network traffic and various attack scenarios, including Distributed Denial of Service (DDoS), resulting in a total of **12,794,627** records.

Each record in the data set contains **84 characteristic features** related to network flows, such as packet size, data stream length, duration, and data stream payload size. The detailed feature composition and attack types are described in the Table 3.

4.2 Evaluation Metrics

We evaluated the performance of the model using conventional classification metrics, including accuracy, precision, recall, F1-Score, and ROC-AUC. The definitions are as follows:

$$\text{Accuracy} = \frac{TP + TN}{TP + TN + FP + FN} \quad \text{Precision} = \frac{TP}{TP + FP}$$

$$\text{Recall} = \frac{TP}{TP + FN} \quad \text{F1-Score} = 2 \times \frac{\text{Precision} \times \text{Recall}}{\text{Precision} + \text{Recall}}$$

where: TP: True Positives, FP: False Positives, and FN: False Negatives.

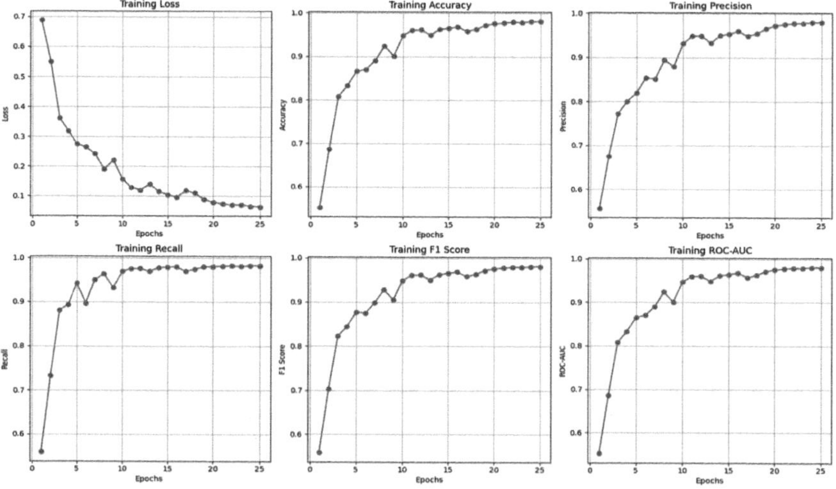

Fig. 2. Model Performance Over Epochs.

4.3 Experimental Results

The model's performance measures improved consistently throughout numerous epochs. Training performance metrics across epochs. The training results are summarized in the Table 2.

Latency. An NVIDIA RTX GPU was used to analyze inference latency in order to assess deployment viability. The Transformer-only model took 42 ms, the CNN-LSTM model took 51 ms, the GCN-only model took 47 ms, and the suggested GCNTransformer architecture took 55 ms to infer 10,000 flows on average. This is well within the real-time requirements for cloud-scale DDoS detection, with a throughput of around 181,000 flows per second. When compared to the separate baselines, the hybrid model has a little overhead, but the significant accuracy gains it offers overcome the additional expense.

We expanded our analysis to the NSL-KDD dataset, a popular intrusion detection benchmark, in order to evaluate generalizability. Our results on CIC-IDS 2018 are in line with our hybrid GCNTransformer's F1-score of 96.7% on NSL-KDD. The model's good generalization across various network contexts and attack distributions is demonstrated by this cross-dataset validation.

4.4 Training Metrics Visualization

Figure 2 illustrates the trend of various measures, including loss, accuracy, precision, recall, F1-score, and ROC-AUC, over 25 epochs during the training phase. Loss minimization and other performance indicators continually improve, showing that the model is learning effectively. The training loss reduces steadily and stabilizes around 0.05, indicating convergence. Accuracy shows a constant rising trend, approaching 0.98, reflecting the model's excellent correct prediction rate. Precision and recall exceed 0.95 in subsequent epochs, demonstrating the model's ability to identify abnormalities with few false positives and false negatives. The F1-score, a harmonic mean of precision and recall, is well-aligned and consistently above 0.95, indicating highly balanced performance. The ROC-AUC measure stabilizes above 0.98, indicating an outstanding capacity to discern between anomalous and regular classes. These patterns collectively show that the hybrid GCN-Transformer model generalizes well and performs consistently across epochs without overfitting.

5 Conclusion

In this study, we proposed a hybrid deep learning architecture for detecting Distributed Denial-of-Service (DDoS) in cloud environments that combines Graph Neural Networks (GNNs) with Transformer encoders. The GNN component successfully simulates spatial linkages between network flows by utilizing graph connectedness, whilst the Transformer captures long-range temporal dependencies using multi-head self-attention processes. The model was tested using the CIC-IDS 2018 dataset, which contains over 12 million traffic records and 84 flow-level variables. It was trained using Binary Cross-Entropy Loss and optimized with the Adam optimizer. Experimental results showed that the hybrid GCN-Transformer model consistently outperformed a baseline Transformer-only design regarding key metrics. The suggested model had a precision of 98.9%, recall of 97.98%, F1-score of 98.26%, and ROC-AUC of 98.12%, indicating a great capacity to recognize complex DDoS assault patterns with high accuracy and minimal false positives. These findings support the efficiency of combining graph-based spatial reasoning and sequence modeling for large-scale, high-dimensional traffic analysis in cloud-based intrusion detection systems.

References

1. Ahmad, Z., Khan, A.S., Shiang, C.W., Abdullah, J., Ahmad, F.: Network intrusion detection system: a systematic study of machine learning and deep learning approaches. Trans. Emerg. Telecommun. Technol. **32**(1), e4150 (2021)
2. Abdallah, A, M., et al.: Cloud network anomaly detection using machine and deep learning techniques—recent research advancements. IEEE Access **12**, 56749–56773 (2024)
3. Aldweesh, A., Derhab, A., Emam, A.Z.: Deep learning approaches for anomaly-based intrusion detection systems: a survey, taxonomy, and open issues. Knowl. Based Syst. **189**, 105124 (2020)
4. Fei, W., Li, T., Zhen, W., ShuLin, W., Xiao, C.Q.: Research on network intrusion detection technology based on machine learning. Int. J. Wireless Inf. Netw. **28**(3), 262–275 (2021)
5. Aydın, H., Orman, Z., Ali Aydın, M.: A long short-term memory (ISTM)-based distributed denial of service (DDos) detection and defense system design in public cloud network environment. Comput. Securi. **118**, 102725 (2022)
6. Vaswani, A., et al.: Attention is all you need. In: Advances in Neural Information Processing Systems, vol. 30 (2017)
7. Pandithurai, O., Venkataiah, C., Tiwari, S., Ramanjaneyulu, N.: DDos attack prediction using a honey badger optimization algorithm based feature selection and bi-LSTM in cloud environment. Expert Syst. Appl. **241**, 122544 (2024)
8. Mhawi, D.N., Aldallal, A., Hassan, S.: Advanced feature-selection-based hybrid ensemble learning algorithms for network intrusion detection systems. Symmetry **14**(7), 1461 (2022)
9. Long, Z., Yan, H., Shen, G., Zhang, X., He, H., Cheng, L.: A transformer-based network intrusion detection approach for cloud security. J. Cloud Comput. **13**(1), 5 (2024)
10. David, J., Thomas, C.: Detection of distributed denial of service attacks based on information theoretic approach in time series models. J. Info. Secur. Appl. **55**, 102621 (2020)
11. Raj Kumar Batchu and Hari Seetha: An integrated approach explaining the detection of distributed denial of service attacks. Comput. Netw. **216**, 109269 (2022)
12. Agarwal, A., Khari, M., Singh, R.: Detection of DDoS attack using deep learning model in cloud storage application. Wireless Pers. Commun., 1–21 (2022)
13. Velliangiri, S., Premalatha, J.: Intrusion detection of distributed denial of service attack in cloud. Clust. Comput. **22**(Suppl 5), 10615–10623 (2019)
14. Phan, T.V., Park, M.: Efficient distributed denial-of-service attack defense in SDN-based cloud. IEEE Access **7**, 18701–18714 (2019)
15. Henderi, H., Wahyuningsih, T., Rahwanto, E.: Comparison of min-max normalization and z-score normalization in the k-nearest neighbor (KNN) algorithm to test the accuracy of types of breast cancer. Int. J. Info. Info. Syst. **4**(1), 13–20 (2021)
16. Jiang, X., Zhu, R., Ji, P., Li, S.: Co-embedding of nodes and edges with graph neural networks. IEEE Trans. Pattern Anal. Mach. Intell. **45**(6), 7075–7086 (2020)
17. Lu, S., Wang, M., Liang, S., Lin, J., Wang, Z.: Hardware accelerator for multi-head attention and position-wise feed-forward in the transformer. In: 2020 IEEE 33rd International System-on-Chip Conference (SOCC), pp. 84–89. IEEE (2020)
18. Yang, J., et al.: GraphFormers: GNN-nested transformers for representation learning on textual graph. Adv. Neural. Inf. Process. Syst. **34**, 28798–28810 (2021)

19. Devlin, J., Chang, M., Lee, K., Toutanova, K.: BERT: pre-training of deep bidirectional transformers for language understanding. In: Proceedings of the 2019 Conference of the North American Chapter of the Association for Computational Linguistics: Human Language Technologies, vol. 1 (long and short papers), pp. 4171–4186 (2019)
20. Zaidi, A.: Mathematical justification on the origin of the sigmoid in logistic regression. Central Europ. Manag. J. **30**(4), 1327–1337 (2022)
21. Jurafsky, D.: Speech & Language Processing. Pearson Education India (2000)

A Data-Driven Framework for Performance Assessment of SIEM Solutions

Jason M. Green[1], Mahmoud N. Mahmoud[2], Abdolhossein Sarrafzadeh[3], and Ahmad Patooghy[1(✉)]

[1] North Carolina A&T State University, Greensboro, NC 27411, USA
apatooghy@ncat.edu
[2] University of Alabama, Tuscaloosa, AL 35487, USA
[3] Old Dominion University, Norfolk, VA 23529, USA

Abstract. Selecting the right Security Information and Event Management (SIEM) solution remains a critical yet often subjective decision for organizations facing ever-evolving cyber threats. Traditional evaluation approaches tend to rely on static benchmarks, vendor claims, or limited testing environments that fail to capture the complexity of real-world operations. To address this gap, we introduce a novel evaluation framework [4] (This work relates to Department of Navy award N00178-24-1-0012 issued by the Office of Naval Research.) designed to provide real-time, data-centric insights into SIEM performance. Unlike existing methods, our framework simulates realistic security environments with live data ingestion, dynamic threat injection, and continuous performance monitoring. This allows us to assess not only how well a SIEM tool performs under pressure, but how quickly and accurately it can detect and prioritize genuine threats across diverse network architectures. By focusing on operational metrics such as Mean Time to Detect (MTTD), False Positive Rate (FPR), Event Processing Speed (EPS), and Alert Correlation Accuracy, the framework offers a holistic, evidence-based methodology to identify the most effective SIEM solution for a given organizational context.

1 Introduction

Security Information Event Management (SIEM) platforms have become the cornerstone of Security Operations Centers (SOCs) [1]. SEIMs aggregate and analyze security related information from firewalls, endpoints, cloud services, and threat-intelligence feeds to offer continuous security monitoring services to network admins [2]. Concurrently, the SIEM market has expanded rapidly, with Gartner estimating a $4.5 billion market in 2023 driven by cloud-native and XDR integrations [3,4]. Yet many organizations struggle with complex deployments, inconsistent logs, and the challenge of tuning detection rules to manage alert volumes [5].

K. Adi et al. (Eds.): CRiSIS 2025, LNCS 16295, pp. 54–66, 2026.
https://doi.org/10.1007/978-3-032-20732-6_4

Traditional SIEM evaluations often rely on static feature checklists or retrospective analyses that overlook operational realities under production loads [1]. Industry frameworks such as the one proposed by ISACA [5,6], emphasize purpose-driven event logging and structured implementation processes to maximize SIEM value, but offer limited guidance on dynamic performance benchmarking. To address this, novel metrics have emerged: SIEM RADAR introduces compliance-focused measures for regulatory efficiency [7]; AI-assisted SIEM frameworks leverage machine learning to reduce alert fatigue and automate incident response workflows [8]. Evaluations of open-source SIEM solutions further underscore performance trade-offs between cost and throughput [1].

Despite these advances, a unified, real-time benchmarking methodology that can compare diverse SIEM platforms under realistic attack scenarios remains absent. In this paper, we propose a data-driven framework that simulates representative network traffic and multi-stage cyber-attacks, capturing key performance indicators, e.g., event throughput, detection latency, correlation fidelity, and alert prioritization accuracy. By providing objective, head-to-head comparisons, our framework aims to guide organizations in selecting and optimizing SIEM solutions that best align with their security requirements and operational constraints.

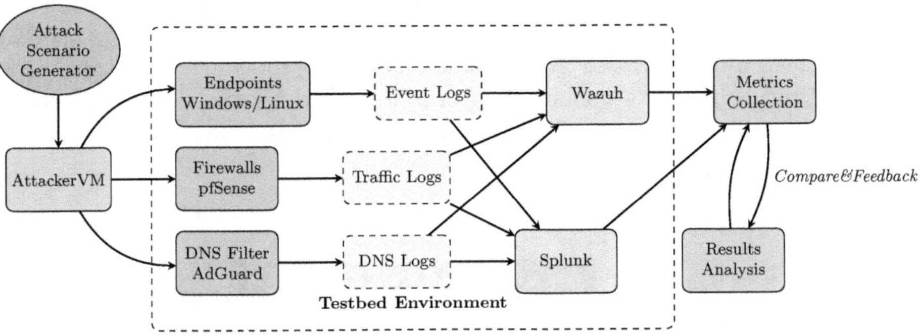

Fig. 1. Architecture diagram of the SIEM evaluation framework showing data flow from attack simulation through log collection to SIEM analysis. Color-coded components represent different system roles: attacker (red), data sources (blue), log streams (yellow), SIEM platforms (green), and analysis modules (purple). The dashed boundary encloses the testbed environment. (Color figure online)

2 Proposed Evaluation Framework

2.1 System Architecture

Figure 1 shows the proposed evaluation framework at a highgh level. At its core, the framework consists of five key color-coded layers: attack generation, data sources, log collection, SIEM processing, and analysis. The attack generation layer, represented by the Attack Scenario Generator and AttackerVM, provides a controlled environment for simulating various security threats. These attacks are directed against the data sources layer, which includes endpoints, firewalls, and DNS filters, each generating distinct types of security-relevant logs. The log collection layer aggregates these logs into three main streams: event logs from endpoints, traffic logs from firewalls, and DNS logs from the filtering service. These logs are then processed in parallel by both Wazuh and Splunk SIEM systems, allowing for direct comparison of their detection and analysis capabilities. Finally, the analysis layer, comprising metrics collection and results analysis, evaluates the performance of both SIEMs using standardized metrics and provides feedback for continuous improvement.

The evaluation environment uses a Proxmox Virtual Environment (PVE) cluster with high availability to simulate enterprise infrastructure. The cluster manages VMs for endpoints, servers, firewalls, and network appliances, with automated provisioning via Proxmox's REST API. Each VM runs appropriate logging agents (e.g., OSSEC, Windows Event Forwarding) to generate security logs. The network is segmented into corporate LAN, DMZ, and monitoring networks, with firewalls controlling inter-zone traffic. The DMZ hosts public services while endpoints reside in the corporate subnet, and a dedicated management VLAN isolates SIEM servers and logging infrastructure. Traffic injection combines scripted and automated methods: workload emulators generate benign activity (DNS queries, HTTP requests, logins), while tools like Metasploit inject attack scenarios (exploits, suspicious processes). All activities produce alerts and logs that flow through the network segments to the SIEM systems.

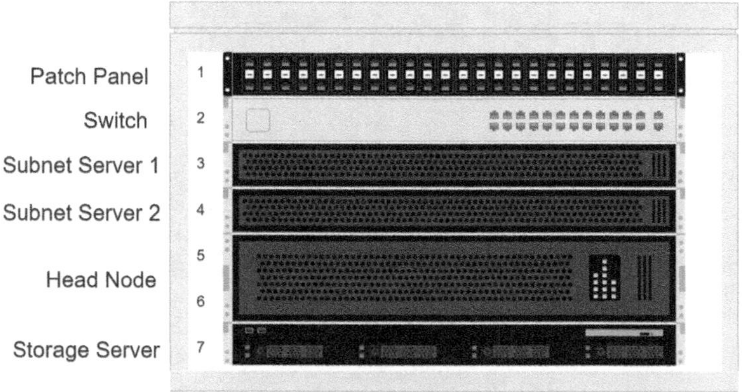

Fig. 2. System architecture of the SIEM evaluation testbed, showing network segmentation, key components, and data flow.

2.2 Testbed Architecture and Deployment

Physical Infrastructure and Virtualization The Proxmox cluster consisted of one primary **head node** and two **subnet nodes**, providing the computational isolation needed for simulating distinct network zones. The head node was a high-performance server (64 vCPUs, 64 GB RAM, 2 TB SSD storage) that acted as the core of the environment, while each subnet node was provisioned with 24 vCPUs, 64 GB RAM, and 2 TB storage. This distribution ensured that each SIEM tool could run on dedicated hardware of comparable capacity, supporting a fair performance evaluation. All three nodes were interconnected via Proxmox's virtual networking, allowing us to define custom networks and routing rules for the experiment. Using an enterprise-grade hypervisor like Proxmox facilitated reproducibility of the setup the entire configuration of virtual machines (VMs), networks, and storage can be exported or snapshotted for re-deployment, ensuring that other researchers could replicate the environment with minimal effort.

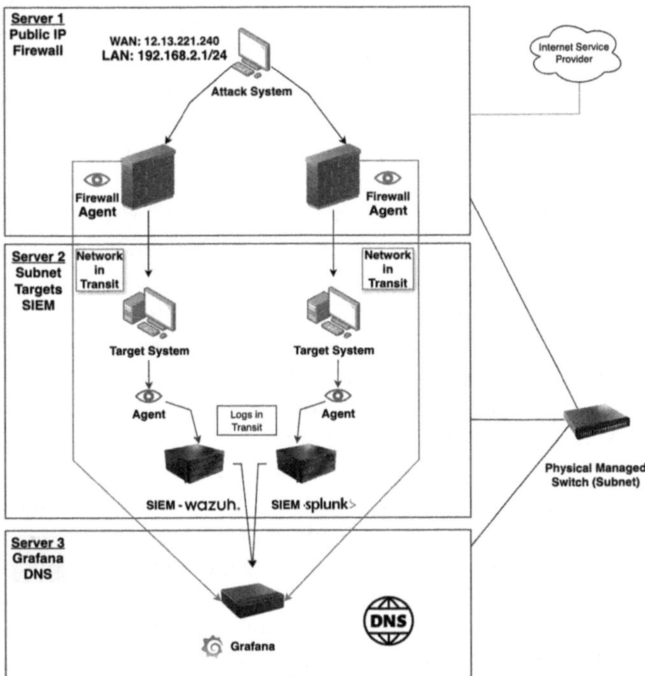

Fig. 3. Network flow of how the two SIEM solutions Wazuh & Splunk transmit logs for real time comparison.

Virtual Machines and Network Segmentation The lab architecture emulated a Security Operations Center (SOC) ecosystem through a multi-segment topology, as outlined in Fig. 2. The network design, shown in Fig. 3, consisted of two internal subnets (A and B), each protected by a pfSense firewall and hosting a Windows 11 endpoint alongside a SIEM server [9]. The attacker VM and monitoring/DNS VMs were deployed on the head node's network, connected to both pfSense firewalls' LAN interfaces to simulate either an enterprise core network or internet connection. This architecture mirrored real-world security environments with distinct zones for external threats, perimeter defense, and internal resources, enhancing the evaluation's external validity. The physical separation of SIEM solutions across different hosts and networks ensured independent event processing under identical conditions. The key components of the environment are as follows.

Attacker VM. A Kali Linux (with tools from Parrot OS) VM was used as the attack machine, simulating a rogue external adversary. This VM was connected to a **WAN network** facing the pfSense firewalls (described below), analogous to an external threat on the internet. It had access to a full suite of penetration testing tools and was the source of all simulated attacks.

Firewall VMs (pfSense). Two pfSense firewall appliances were deployed as virtual routers to segment the network. Each subnet node hosted one pfSense VM, creating two isolated internal networks (subnet A and subnet B). The pfSense instances served as gateways between the attacker (WAN side) and the internal resources (LAN side), enforcing network policies and logging traffic. This simulates a typical enterprise perimeter and internal firewall setup, with one pfSense protecting the Wazuh segment and the other protecting the Splunk segment.

Endpoint VMs (Windows 11). Two Windows 11 Pro VMs acted as endpoint hosts within each internal subnet (one per subnet). These mimic employee workstations or servers that generate realistic user and system activity. They were configured with default security tools (e.g., Windows Defender antivirus) and standard logging enabled. Each Windows VM produced event logs across multiple channels including Security, System, Application logs, and Microsoft Defender logs providing a rich set of telemetry for the SIEM tools.

SIEM VMs (Wazuh and Splunk). We deployed Wazuh and Splunk on separate dedicated VMs, one on each subnet node, to ensure they operated in parallel on comparable hardware. The Wazuh server (open-source SIEM) was installed on one VM in subnet A, and the **Splunk Enterprise** server on an identically sized VM in subnet B. Both SIEM VMs were allocated a generous share of their host resources (up to 24 vCPUs and 64 GB RAM each) to prevent resource bottlenecks from skewing the results. This isolated dual-SIEM setup allowed both tools to ingest the same log data simultaneously without interfering with each other's performance.

DNS Filtering VM (AdGuard). To emulate an internal DNS and web filtering service, an AdGuard Home instance was run in a VM on the head node. This provided DNS resolution for the endpoint VMs with the ability to block known malicious domains. The AdGuard VM generated its own query logs, which were also forwarded to the SIEMs. Including a DNS filtering component adds realism (many enterprises log DNS queries for security) and supplies another source of security data (e.g., alerts on blocked phishing domains).

Monitoring and Visualization VM. We set up a centralized monitoring server on the head node that hosted both InfluxDB and Grafana (via Docker containers). InfluxDB served as a time-series database to aggregate various metrics from the SIEMs and network devices, while Grafana was used to create real-time dashboards visualizing these metrics and event logs. This VM did not participate in the attacks or defenses directly; instead, it passively collected data (e.g., CPU usage, event throughput, alert counts) via APIs and agents from the other components for analysis.
Uptime Monitoring VM. Finally, an Uptime Kuma instance was deployed to continuously monitor the availability of critical services (SIEM endpoints, the Windows VMs, etc.). This ensured that all components remained operational throughout the tests and alerted us to any unexpected outages that could invalidate a test run. Although not directly related to security analysis, this service was important for maintaining a stable and reproducible experiment environment by quickly catching anomalies in the infrastructure itself.

2.3 Attack Scenarios and Execution

Simulated Threats for Evaluation. To thoroughly evaluate each SIEM's threat detection capabilities, we orchestrated a series of real-time attack scenarios using the Kali/Parrot attacker VM [10]. Three primary categories of attacks were conducted, each chosen to test different aspects of SIEM detection and analysis [11]:
Brute-Force Attack. We simulated rapid, repeated login attempts using incorrect credentials against a Windows 11 endpoint (via RDP or WinRM/SMB). This generated multiple authentication failure events in the Windows Security log, testing the SIEMs' ability to detect patterns of failed logins within a short time span. Both Wazuh (using built-in Windows authentication rules) and Splunk (via correlation search) were configured to trigger alerts when the attempt threshold was exceeded.
Distributed Denial-of-Service (DDoS) Simulation. Using 'hping3', the attacker VM generated a high-volume traffic flood (TCP/SYN flood and ICMP echo storms) targeting the pfSense firewalls and Windows host. This triggered hundreds of connection attempts and port scan alerts in the pfSense logs, while the Windows machine's performance logs recorded the network stress. The scenario tested both SIEMs' ability to handle log volume spikes while maintaining detection capabilities, as well as their throughput limits under burst conditions.
Reverse Shell Attack. We simulated a reverse shell attack by deploying a payload on the Windows host that attempted to establish a connection back to the attacker. The attack generated multiple detection points: Windows Defender alerts for malware detection, process creation events, and pfSense firewall logs for the outbound connection. This scenario tested both SIEMs' ability to detect host compromise through different mechanisms - Wazuh via its HIDS agent monitoring process events and Defender alerts, and Splunk through correlation of endpoint security alerts with unusual network connections. All attacks were

executed in a controlled environment using standard tools, with sufficient idle time between scenarios to establish baseline activity levels.

Automation and Timing for Fair Testing. To ensure consistent attack timing and conditions across both SIEMs, we automated the attack launch process using a custom script on the Kali/Parrot VM. All testbed components synchronized their clocks to a common NTP server (head node), maintaining timestamp consistency within milliseconds. The attack script initiated scenarios at precise intervals (e.g., at 10:31:00 if started at 10:30:45), establishing clear "ground truth" start times for accurate event alignment. The script executed scenarios in a fixed order with consistent parameters, enabling direct comparison across multiple trials regardless of timing or SIEM version. This automation improved reproducibility and allowed for easy framework extension with additional attack types. Both SIEMs operated autonomously during testing, generating alerts based on pre-configured rules without manual intervention. After each attack run, we collected raw logs, alert records, and Grafana metrics for post-analysis, facilitating straightforward computation of detection latency and false positive metrics.

2.4 Data Flow to SIEM

All data sources (endpoints, firewalls, DNS filters) send logs to both SIEM systems through mirrored streams. Endpoints use Wazuh agents or syslog forwarders to duplicate logs to both Wazuh manager and Splunk collector. Network devices forward logs similarly. All components are time-synchronized via NTP. Wazuh processes logs through its agent and syslog interfaces into Elasticsearch, while Splunk ingests via universal forwarders or syslog. This mirrored setup ensures identical event feeds for fair SIEM comparison.

2.5 Evaluation Methodology and Metrics

Our evaluation employs a comprehensive set of metrics that span technical, operational, and human dimensions of SIEM performance [12]. The study incorporates five key categories: detection and classification metrics that assess security effectiveness, performance metrics that quantify system efficiency, alert management metrics that evaluate threat intelligence capabilities, automation metrics that measure operational maturity, and analyst metrics that gauge human impact [13]. To ensure fair and consistent evaluation, we implemented our study using synchronized systems and identical data streams. The metrics were derived from established detection frameworks and contemporary SOC maturity models, providing a balanced assessment of both technical capabilities and operational impact. A detailed breakdown of all metrics can be found in Table 1.

In the metrics table, we use the following notation: N represents the total number of incidents, $t_{\text{detect},i}$ and $t_{\text{occurrence},i}$ are the detection and occurrence timestamps for incident i, TP (True Positives) and FP (False Positives) count

Table 1. Taxonomy of SIEM evaluation metrics, organized by functional category.

Category	Metric	Formula
Detection and Classification	Mean Time to Detect (MTTD)	$\frac{1}{N}\sum_{i=1}^{N}(t_{\text{detect},i} - t_{\text{occurrence},i})$
	Mean Time to Respond (MTTR)	$\frac{1}{N}\sum_{i=1}^{N}(t_{\text{remediate},i} - t_{\text{detect},i})$
	True Positive Rate (TPR)	$\frac{TP}{TP+FN}$
	False Positive Rate (FPR)	$\frac{FP}{FP+TN}$
	Precision (PREC)	$\frac{TP}{TP+FP}$
	Recall (REC)	$\frac{TP}{TP+FN}$
	Alert Classification Accuracy (ACA)	$\frac{TP+TN}{TP+TN+FP+FN}$
	False Negative Rate (FNR)	$\frac{FN}{TP+FN} = 1 - \text{TPR}$
Performance and Resources	Event Processing Speed (EPS)	$\frac{\text{Total Events}}{\text{Total Time (s)}}$
	Resource Utilization (RU)	$\mathbb{E}[U_{\text{CPU}}, U_{\text{MEM}}]$
	Processing Latency (PL)	$\mathbb{E}[t_{\text{process}} - t_{\text{ingest}}]$
	Degradation Rate (DR)	$\frac{dP(\lambda)}{d\lambda}$
Alert Management	Alert Correlation Accuracy (ACA)	$\frac{1}{m}\sum_{i=1}^{m}\delta(c_i, g_i)$
	Alert Prioritization Accuracy (APA)	$\rho(S(A), I)$
	Alert Enrichment Ratio (AER)	$\frac{\lvert\{a_i \in A \mid \text{ctx}(a_i) \neq \emptyset\}\rvert}{\lvert A\rvert}$
Automation and Maturity	Detection Time Improvement (DTI)	$\frac{\text{MTTD}_{\text{manual}} - \text{MTTD}_{\text{auto}}}{\text{MTTD}_{\text{manual}}} \times 100\%$
	Response Time Improvement (RTI)	$\frac{\text{MTTR}_{\text{manual}} - \text{MTTR}_{\text{auto}}}{\text{MTTR}_{\text{manual}}} \times 100\%$
	SOC Process Maturity (SPM)	$\mathbb{S} \in \{1, 2, 3, 4, 5\}$
Analyst Performance	Incident Throughput (IT)	$\frac{\text{Incidents}}{\text{Analyst Time Period}}$
	Investigation Accuracy (IA)	$\frac{\text{Correct Adjudications}}{\text{Total Adjudications}}$
	Workload Ratio (WR)	$\frac{\text{Alerts}}{\text{Analyst Capacity}}$

correct and incorrect alerts, while TN (True Negatives) and FN (False Negatives) represent correct and missed non-alerts. For correlation metrics, c_i and g_i denote computed and ground truth correlations, δ is the Kronecker delta function, ρ represents Spearman correlation, $S(A)$ is the alert severity score, I is the actual impact, and $\text{ctx}(a_i)$ represents the context of alert a_i. The degradation rate uses λ as the load parameter and P as the performance metric.

3 Results

Both SIEM solutions were evaluated side-by-side under identical conditions to ensure a fair comparison. Each tool ingested the same event streams on equal hardware resources, with attacks generated from a dedicated Kali Linux/Parrot OS attacker VM in a controlled testbed. All virtual machines were hosted on a Proxmox environment running on bare-metal hardware with an Intel Xeon Gold 6226R CPU and 128 GB DDR4 RAM.

The Splunk and Wazuh SIEM VMs were each allocated 8 vCPUs and 16 GB of RAM. The attacker VM (Kali/Parrot OS) was allocated 4 vCPUs and 8 GB of RAM, while the Grafana/InfluxDB monitoring node used 2 vCPUs and 4 GB RAM. This uniform provisioning ensured no unfair advantage in resource allocation during detection or processing.

Figure 4 summarizes the comparative outcomes for four representative attack scenarios—a brute-force login attack, a DDoS flood, a reverse shell exploit, and an SQL injection attempt—using key metrics: Mean Time to Detect (MTTD), False Positive Rate (FPR), Event Processing Speed (EPS), and Alert Correlation Accuracy (ACA). Overall, Splunk demonstrated faster detection and higher throughput, as expected for a commercial SIEM optimized for performance. Wazuh, in contrast, showed a modestly higher false positive rate, but its accuracy in correlating alerts was nearly on par with Splunk's, indicating comparable effectiveness in incident aggregation.

In the brute-force attack scenario (multiple rapid failed login attempts), Splunk achieved an MTTD of roughly 10.3 s, detecting the password attack faster than Wazuh's 13.7 s on average. This lower detection latency indicates Splunk's more efficient processing pipeline under moderate log volume. Splunk also generated fewer false alarms during this test, with an FPR of 2.5% compared to 4.0% for Wazuh, suggesting higher precision in distinguishing malicious events from benign background noise. Both SIEMs successfully correlated the stream of repeated login failures into a single concise alert: Splunk produced one aggregated brute-force incident (ACA ∼92%), and Wazuh similarly condensed the events with an ACA of about 87%, showing only a minor gap in correlation capability. The throughput demand in this scenario was relatively light; Splunk processed around 550 events per second at peak, slightly above Wazuh's ∼480 events/s, and neither showed signs of log loss or delay at this level of activity.

For the DDoS attack simulation (a high-volume traffic flood), Splunk again outpaced Wazuh in both detection speed and scalability. Splunk's mean time to

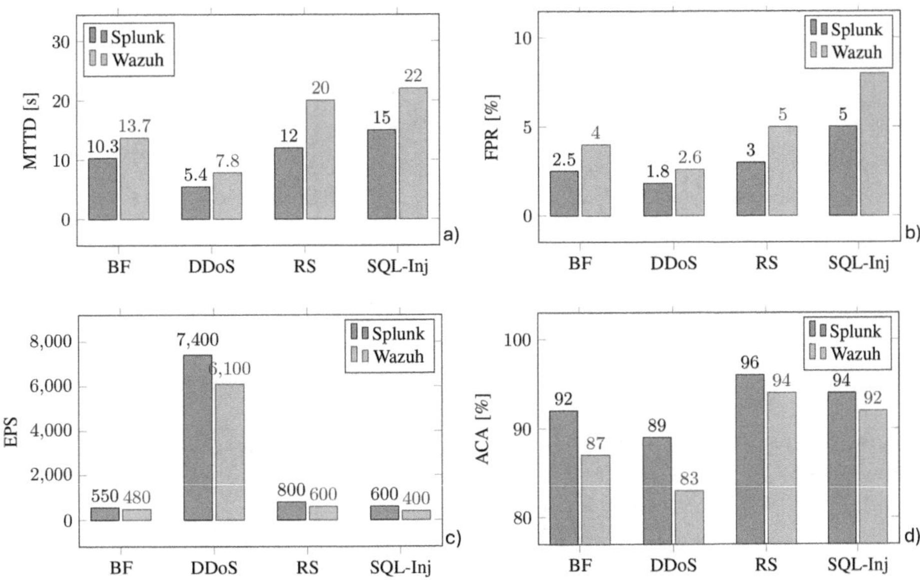

Fig. 4. Performance comparison between Splunk and Wazuh SIEM solutions across four simulated attack scenarios: Brute Force (BF), Distributed Denial of Service (DDoS), Reconnaissance Scan (RS), and SQL Injection (SQL-Inj): (a) compares the Mean Time to Detect (MTTD), (b) shows False Positive Rate (FPR), (c) Events Per Second (EPS), and (d) Attack Classification Accuracy (ACA).

detect the flooding attack was about 5.4 s, identifying the onset of the DDoS slightly ahead of Wazuh's 7.8 s. During the burst of log events generated by the flood, Splunk sustained a peak throughput of roughly 7,400 events per second, whereas Wazuh handled about 6,100 events/s before nearing saturation. Despite this extreme load, both platforms kept pace without dropping events, and they raised very few spurious alerts (the FPR remained low at ~1.8% for Splunk vs ~2.6% for Wazuh during the DDoS period). Notably, both SIEMs aggregated the distributed attack events into coherent incident reports: Splunk's correlation accuracy was ~89%, reflecting that it unified the flood of alerts into a single incident, while Wazuh reached ~83% ACA, only modestly lower. These findings highlight Splunk's advantage in high-throughput scenarios while demonstrating that Wazuh's performance, albeit slightly behind, remains within a practical range of effectiveness even under intense attack conditions.

The reverse shell attack introduced a multi-stage compromise, where the attacker established remote control over the internal endpoint. This attack was designed to test both SIEMs' host-level monitoring and their ability to correlate lateral movement indicators. Splunk maintained its detection advantage with an MTTD of 12.0 s, compared to Wazuh's 20.0 s. Splunk's EPS during this scenario was approximately 800 events per second, while Wazuh handled about 600. Both SIEMs maintained high alert correlation accuracy—96% for Splunk and 94% for

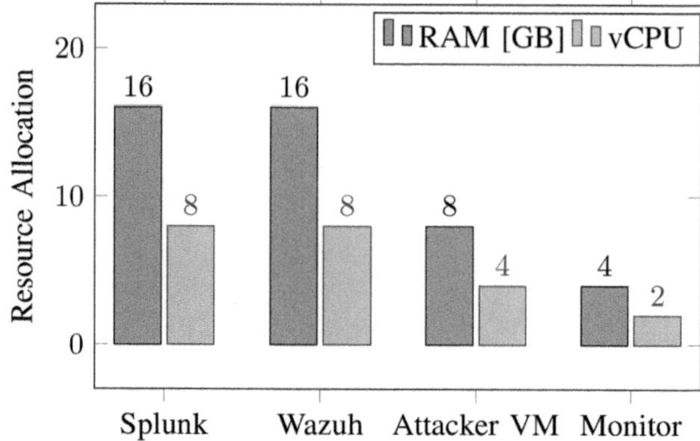

Fig. 5. Virtual machine resource usage for layers of the proposed SIEM evaluation framework.

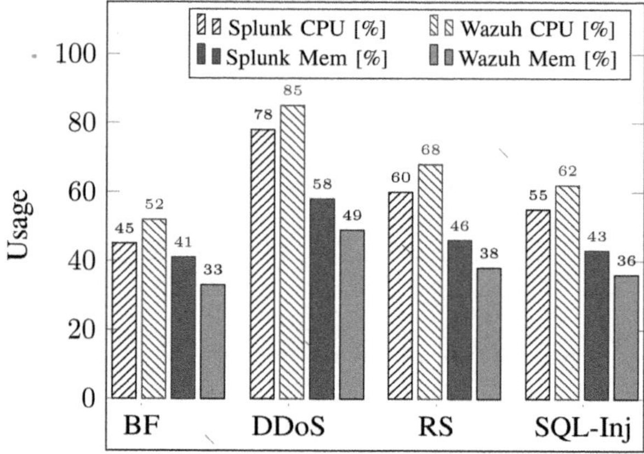

Fig. 6. Average CPU and Memory usage under simulated attack scenarios. Memory usage shown as percentage of the cap 16 GB allocated to each virtual machine.

Wazuh—demonstrating strong ability to connect disparate stages of the compromise. While Wazuh recorded a slightly higher FPR of 5.0% versus Splunk's 3.0%, both remained within acceptable bounds, underscoring effective differentiation between benign and malicious activity during complex host-based intrusions.

Finally, the SQL injection attack simulated a web-layer exploit targeting a vulnerable internal web application. The attack triggered both web server and application-level logs. Splunk detected the injection in 15.0 s, while Wazuh lagged slightly at 22.0 s. Splunk maintained a processing speed of 600 events per second during the test, compared to Wazuh's 400. The SQL injection test produced more noise in the log stream due to HTTP activity, reflected in a higher false positive rate for both systems: 5.0% for Splunk and 8.0% for Wazuh. Nevertheless, alert correlation remained strong, with ACA values of 94% and 92%, respectively.

These results confirm that both SIEM platforms are capable of accurately detecting and contextualizing multi-vector web application attacks, although Splunk consistently delivers faster and more scalable performance. Figure 5 and Figure 6, respectively, summarize the CPU/memory allocations (Fig. 5) and usage (Fig. 6) for each virtual machines involved in the evaluation.

4 Conclusion

In this study, we introduced the first comprehensive real-time evaluation framework for SIEM tools, marking a significant advancement in cybersecurity research and practice. Our framework was designed to operate within a realistic, multi-tiered SOC environment, allowing us to directly compare two prominent SIEM systems—Wazuh and Splunk—in real time. Through a series of meticulously simulated attack scenarios and continuous performance monitoring, we were able to obtain tangible, objective metrics such as Mean Time to Detect (MTTD), False Positive Rate (FPR), Event Processing Speed (EPS), and Alert Correlation Accuracy.

The comparative analysis between Wazuh and Splunk not only highlighted their respective strengths and weaknesses but also exposed the limitations of traditional evaluation methodologies that often rely on retrospective or static analyses. Our real-time approach cuts through the marketing fluff by providing concrete, performance-based evidence of each system's capability to detect, prioritize, and respond to threats under dynamic operational conditions. This level of detailed assessment is crucial for cybersecurity practitioners who must make informed decisions based on the actual performance of SIEM solutions, rather than solely on vendor claims or theoretical benchmarks.

Moreover, our framework represents a pioneering effort in the domain of SIEM evaluation. By incorporating realistic data generation, diverse attack simulations, and comprehensive performance monitoring, the framework sets a new standard for how SIEM tools should be tested and compared. Its application can significantly impact the cybersecurity community by guiding organizations in selecting the most effective SIEM solution tailored to their unique operational needs, ultimately enhancing overall security posture [14].

Looking ahead, the framework's adaptability allows for further refinement and expansion, such as integrating additional SIEM systems [15], incorporating machine learning-driven threat detection techniques, and exploring automated response mechanisms. As cyber threats continue to evolve in complexity, our work lays a solid foundation for ongoing innovation and continuous improvement in real-time cybersecurity evaluations.

References

1. Manzoor, E. A.: The path to choosing a SIEM system – a systematic literature review. FH Wedel (2024)

2. Scarfone, K., Mell, P.: Guide to intrusion detection and prevention systems (IDPS). NIST Special Publication 800-94 (2007). [Online]. Available: https://csrc.nist.gov/publications/detail/sp/800-94/final
3. Davies, A., González-Granadillo, G.: Magic quadrant for security information and event management. Gartner Research Note (2024). Accessed June (2024)
4. Magic quadrant for security information and event management (2024). Gartner Research Note. [Online]. Available: https://www.gartner.com
5. ISACA: A framework for SIEM implementation. ISACA J. **3** (2023)
6. Khraisat, A., Gondal, I., Vamplew, P., Kamruzzaman, J.: Survey of intrusion detection systems: techniques, datasets and challenges. Cybersecurity **2**(1), 1–22 (2019). https://doi.org/10.1186/s42400-019-0038-7
7. Akbaş, E.: Evaluating SIEM radar: a new metric for enhancing regulatory and compliance efficiency. In: European Conference on Cyber Warfare and Security (ECCWS) (2023)
8. Ban, T., Manadhata, P., Zomlot, L.: Breaking alert fatigue: AI-assisted SIEM framework for effective incident response. Appl. Sci. **13**(11), 6610 (2023)
9. Sommestad, T., Ekstedt, M., Holm, H.: The cyber security modeling language: evaluating the impact of SIEM configuration on threat detection. Comput. Sec. **39**, 93–110 (2013)
10. Cichonski, P., Millar, T., Grance, T., Scarfone, K.: Computer security incident handling guide. NIST Special Publication 800-61 Revision 2 (2012). [Online]. Available: https://csrc.nist.gov/publications/detail/sp/800-61/rev-2/final
11. MITRE: Mitre att&ck framework (2024). [Online]. Available: https://attack.mitre.org
12. McHugh, J.: Testing intrusion detection systems: a critique of the 1998 and 1999 DARPA intrusion detection system evaluations as performed by Lincoln laboratory. ACM Trans. Info. Syst. Sec. (TISSEC) **3**(4), 262–294 (2000)
13. Chandola, V., Banerjee, A., Kumar, V.: Anomaly detection: a survey. ACM comput. Surv. (CSUR) **41**(3), 15 (2009)
14. S. Inc., State of security report (2023). [Online]. Available: https://www.splunk.com/en_us/form/state-of-security.html
15. Cisco XDR and the future of SIEM: Bridging detection and response (2023). white Paper. [Online]. Available: https://www.cisco.com

Distributed Systems and IoT Security

External Entropy Supply for IoT Devices Employing a RISC-V Trusted Execution Environment

Arttu Paju[1(✉)], Juha Nurmi[1], Alejandro Cabrera Aldaya[1], Nicola Tuveri[1], Juha Savimäki[1,2], Marko Kivikangas[1], and Brian McGillion[3]

[1] Tampere University, Tampere, Finland
{arttu.paju,juha.nurmi,alejandro.cabreraaldaya,nicola.tuveri, juha.savimaki,marko.kivikangas}@tuni.fi
[2] Unikie Oy, Tampere, Finland
[3] Technology Innovation Institute (TII), Abu Dhabi, UAE
brian.mcgillion@tii.ae

Abstract. Entropy—a measure of randomness—is compulsory for the generation of secure cryptographic keys; however, Internet of Things (IoT) devices that are small or constrained often struggle to collect sufficient entropy. In this article, we solve the entropy provisioning problem for a fleet of IoT devices that can generate a limited amount of entropy. We employ a Trusted Execution Environment (TEE) based on RISC-V to create an external entropy service for a fleet of IoT devices. A small measure of true entropy or pre-installed keys can establish initial secure communication. Once connected, devices can request cryptographically strong entropy from a TEE-backed server. RISC-V offers True Random Number Generators (TRNGs) and a TEE for devices to attest that they are receiving reliable entropy. In addition, this solution can be expanded by adding IoT devices with sensors that produce high-quality entropy as additional entropy sources for the RISC-V entropy provider. Our open-source implementation shows that building trusted entropy infrastructure for IoT is both feasible and effective on open RISC-V platforms.

Keywords: RISC-V hardware · Entropy · Randomness · Trusted Execution Environment · Cryptography · Network protocols · IoT

1 Introduction

Entropy—a measure of randomness—is compulsory for the generation of secure cryptographic keys. Small or resource-constrained Internet of Things (IoT) devices often struggle to collect sufficient high-quality entropy for secure cryptographic operations. When constrained devices experience entropy starvation, it can result in predictable cryptographic outputs that undermine the security of keys and communications.

Previously, this problem was solved with (i) True Random Number Generators (TRNGs), which use inherently random physical processes like electronic

K. Adi et al. (Eds.): CRiSIS 2025, LNCS 16295, pp. 69–84, 2026.
https://doi.org/10.1007/978-3-032-20732-6_5

noise or photonic processes to provide a built-in entropy source, which is usually part of the device's main processor; (ii) Hybrid Entropy Sources, which use both software (pseudo-random) and hardware (true random) sources to produce random values; and (iii) Environmental Sources, which use IoT sensors, such as temperature, light, and motion sensors, can serve as sources of entropy if their readings are unpredictable; instability from oscillators or clock drift can also be a source of entropy. User interaction, i.e., a user touching buttons or moving the device as a source of entropy, is an extension of this concept.

However, it is important to take precautions to prevent adversaries from easily manipulating environmental data. If these options are unavailable or provide a limited amount of entropy, techniques such as whitening algorithms [1] can be used to derive longer keys from lower-entropy sources. Furthermore—using extractors such as cryptographic hash functions or key derivation functions—a small quantity of entropy that is available as a seed can be used to generate a larger, deterministic, but pseudo-random value [11,15,19]. However, these techniques may be computationally intensive for devices with limited resources.

Another option is to provide unique device certificates during manufacturing or configuration, but even if an IoT device begins with a strong key, that key must be periodically regenerated or re-seeded with new entropy to maintain security.

In this article, we solve the problem of entropy provisioning for a fleet of IoT devices that can generate a limited amount of entropy: A Trusted Execution Environment (TEE) based on RISC-V provides entropy for a fleet of devices. Initial secure communication can be established with a small measure of true entropy or with pre-installed keys. After establishing the channel, devices receive entropy from a reliable external source. RISC-V-based Secure Platform for ICT Systems Rooted at the Silicon Manufacturing Process (SPIRS) project provides TRNGs and TEE mechanisms for devices to attest to the provision of entropy. In addition, this solution can be expanded by adding IoT devices with sensors that produce entropy as additional entropy sources for the RISC-V entropy provider. TEE is used to enable a design with no Trusted Third Party (TTP) in our Entropy as a Service (EaaS) protocol.

We make the following novel contributions in this paper: (i) We design, develop, and publish a SPIRS TEE software development kit (SDK) that enables the development of Trusted Applications (TAs) for the RISC-V-based SPIRS platform—allowing open-source development of TAs for a RISC-V-based TEE. (ii) We design, develop, and publish an EaaS TA using the SPIRS TEE SDK—demonstrating how a RISC-V-based TEE can be used to create a secure external entropy service for a fleet of IoT devices.

2 Background

Entropy generates the desired randomness for security services. In practice, this randomness must be generated artificially. Achieving true randomness can be challenging and requires careful design. The aim of this research is to identify a solution to provide true entropy for a fleet of IoT devices that lack the resources to generate it themselves.

RISC-V is a reduced instruction set computer (RISC) architecture that is used to develop custom processors for many different purposes. TEE hardware is a high-level security solution to create a secure area for the central processing unit (CPU). This isolated security area aims to assure confidentiality and integrity. To achieve the aim of this research, RISC-V and TEE are both used within SPIRS. The SPIRS project is introduced more thoroughly in Sect. 2.1, Sect. 2.2, and Sect. 2.3.

2.1 Hardware: SPIRS Platform

The SPIRS [20] EU-funded project addresses innovative approaches to provide security and data privacy to Information and Communications Technology (ICT) elements. The project encompasses the complete design of a SPIRS platform, which integrates a dedicated hardware Root of Trust (RoT), a RISC-V processor core, and some peripherals. The SPIRS hardware platform (Fig. 1) includes three components:

- **CORE-V CVA6 Core:** The RISC-V processor in SPIRS is based on the open-source CORE-V CVA6 core, developed by the OpenHW group. The SPIRS project enhances the security of this core by addressing vulnerabilities identified in the PP84 protection profile of the Common Criteria [4]. Security countermeasures have been applied to ensure the processor operates securely, even in untrusted environments.
- **RoT:** The RoT is the foundational security element of the SPIRS platform, as it is the source of trust for the entire system built over it. The security of software components (execution environment, boot process, applications) relies on identifiers, random numbers, and cryptographic functions that are provided by the RoT. The RoT is modular and flexible, allowing for the addition or removal of components to optimize the system for specific applications. This flexibility ensures that the platform can adapt to new security threats by updating its RoT. The current version of the hardware RoT includes:
  - **Physical Unclonable Function (PUF)/TRNG:** A hardware-based mechanism, based on a Ring Oscillator architecture, which generates unique identifiers and random numbers for device authentication and security operations.
  - **AES-256:** A symmetric encryption engine for securing data.
  - **SHA-256:** A cryptographic hashing function used to ensure data integrity.
  - **Digital Signatures:** A hardware implementation of algorithms to accelerate and secure digital authentication.
- **Peripherals:** A collection of peripherals enables various use cases using the SPIRS platform.

  In addition to DDR3 memory, the platform includes Ethernet, UART, SPI, JTAG, Boot ROM, PLIC, and CLINT.

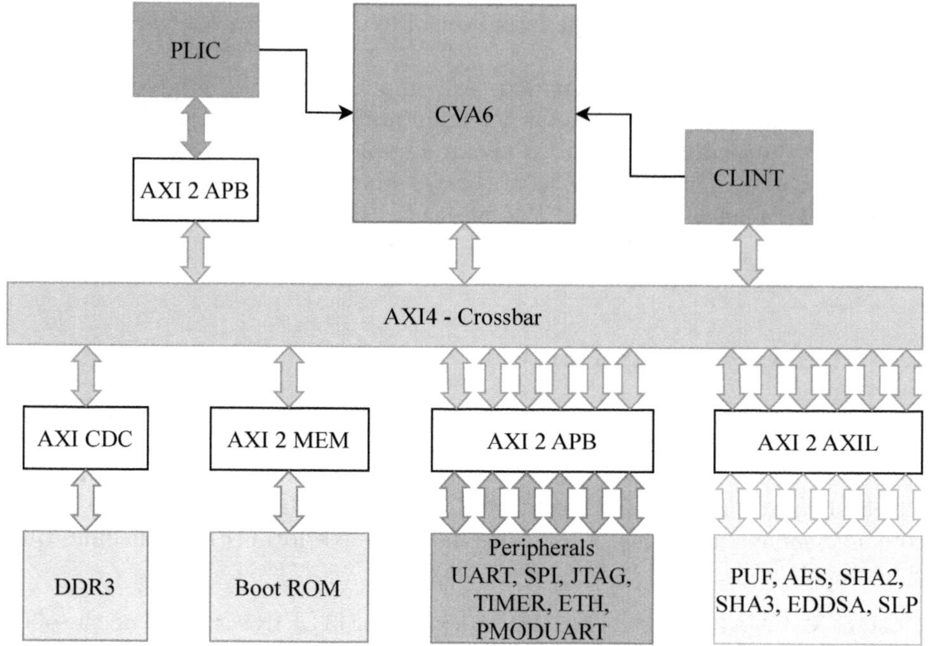

Fig. 1. SPIRS Hardware Platform

Prototype Platform Implementation. A prototype of the SPIRS platform integrates the above components, and demonstrates secure communication between the RISC-V processor, the RoT, and the High-Level Operating System (HLOS), mediated by the TEE.

To speed up and facilitate development, the SPIRS TEE SDK also includes a preconfigured virtualized environment, based on QEMU.

2.2 SPIRS TEE Platform

The TEE is a crucial element of the SPIRS platform. It enables secure execution of critical operations, isolating the trusted codebase from potentially compromised or untrusted components. Figure 2 visually summarizes the main components of the SPIRS TEE architecture and their interactions. The rest of this section, and the following one, provide more details about these components and how different actors interact with the SPIRS platform.

At the core of the TEE design is the **Security Monitor (SM)**, which has the highest execution privilege on the platform. The SM manages memory and device access, using Physical Memory Protection (PMP) [2, Section 3.7] for compartmentalization and leveraging the hardware RoT to ensure security. The SM also mediates communication between **TAs** running in the TEE and untrusted components, such as userspace **Client Applications (CAs)** within the HLOS.

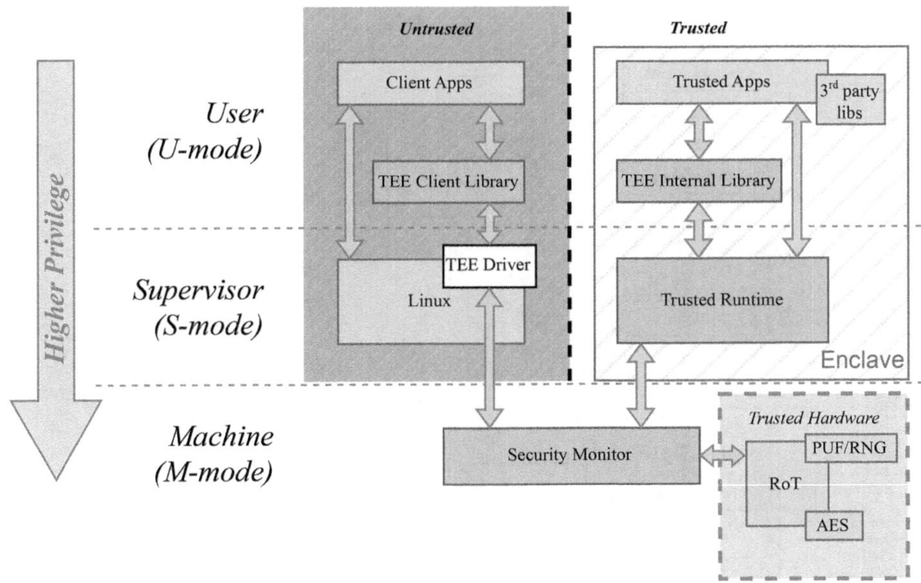

Fig. 2. Basic SPIRS TEE stack

TAs are lightweight applications running within the TEE, with minimal permissions to reduce the attack surface. These applications rely on the **SPIRS Trusted Runtime** for accessing RoT services and basic functionalities like memory management.

2.3 Software: SPIRS-TEE-SDK

The SPIRS TEE SDK simplifies the development, testing, and deployment of applications leveraging the SPIRS TEE. It is built upon a fork of the open-source Keystone framework [12], tailored specifically for RISC-V hardware platforms.

The SDK defines pairs of applications: CAs executing in the untrusted environment, and TAs running securely within the TEE. Communication between TAs and userspace CAs is mediated through dedicated **TEE Client** (`tee_client_api`) and internal (`tee_internal_api`) libraries, based on the GlobalPlatform (GP) TEE specifications [6–8].

Briefly, the typical workflow, depicted in Fig. 3 and detailed below, involves writing application logic for both the CA and TA, configuring build parameters (such as `APP_NAME` and a unique `TA_UUID`), and compiling them alongside the SPIRS Trusted Runtime into a single executable Keystone application package (`.ke`).

Figure 3 comprehensively depicts the different phases of a typical workflow when using the SPIRS TEE SDK:

Provisioning: The vendor of the SPIRS platform can provision specific boards, based on a description of the platform configuration ❶. This is processed by

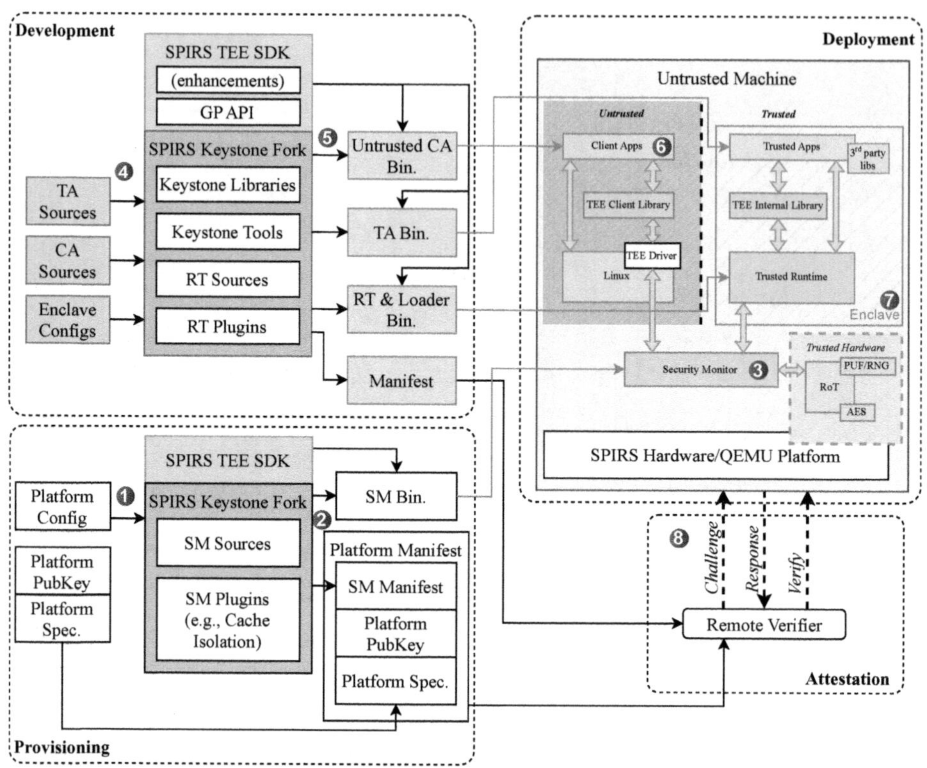

Fig. 3. SPIRS TEE SDK Workflow

the SPIRS fork of Keystone, augmented with further tweaks provided by the SPIRS SDK, to generate ❷ a trusted SM binary and a platform manifest, which embeds an SM manifest authenticating the binary, together with a public key and a specification related to the platform. Furthermore, this step is also used to initialize the SDK environment for development.

Development: Once the SDK environment is provisioned, developers can implement and maintain, for each of their TAs, the code base ❹ for the TA/CA pair, alongside the configuration tuning the enclave which will be spawned to run a specific TA in the SPIRS TEE (e.g., configuring memory boundaries and access to resources and peripherals, an `APP_NAME` and a unique `TA_UUID`). These will be processed through the SPIRS fork of Keystone, enhanced by tweaks and APIs provided by the SPIRS SDK, to generate ❺ executable binary artifacts for the CA and a single executable Keystone application package (`.ke`), which conveniently collects the TA binary artifact, the SPIRS Trusted Loader, the SPIRS Trusted Runtime (based on the Keystone Trusted Runtime *Eyrie*), and a manifest authenticating the bundle.
The SDK facilitates rapid prototyping and testing via integration with the QEMU virtualized environment, offering a practical alternative to physical

hardware during early development stages.
Additional capabilities include straightforward integration of third-party libraries via static linking, streamlined environment setup through provided scripts, and automated test execution within QEMU.

Deployment: The operator of the platform can install the SPIRS board where needed. They deploy on its storage, the SM binary output ❷ obtained through the *Provisioning*, their choice of a supported Linux kernel and filesystem (the SDK provisioning also produces these, although operators can optionally ship a different one, as needed), and on top of the filesystem they also install the *Development* artifacts ❺ for the CA and the executable Keystone application package.
At boot, the board uses the provisioned public key to authenticate the SM binary, before loading and executing it in memory ❸ to continue the Secure Boot process: the Linux kernel and filesystem are hashed before loading, and their values saved in dedicated security registers. The Linux Integrity Measurement Architecture (IMA) subsystem can read those values, and use additional security registers to record the digests of further loaded components.
Once boot is completed, a kernel driver allows userspace to interact with the SM to spawn an isolated TEE enclave ❼ to run the TA from the executable Keystone application package (`.ke`), as well as the associated CA ❻ in the *Untrusted* HLOS to interact with it.

Attestation: Finally, a Remote Attestation protocol ❽ based on Challenge/Response, allows a Remote Verifier to attest the authenticity of the hardware and software components of the platform, based on the Platform and TA manifests generated in *Provisioning* and *Development*. The attestation report can also leverage the Linux IMA subsystem and the secure registers, to let the SM generate a signed quote covering all the measured components.
The Remote Attestation mechanism integrated within the SPIRS TEE SDK extends the security properties of the established communication channels. On top of the confidentiality provided by protocols such as Transport Layer Security (TLS), upon successful completion of the Remote Attestation protocol, the communicating parties additionally gain *mutual authentication*, guaranteeing that each party's identity has been securely verified; *integrity*, ensuring not only the exchanged data but also the software state of the attested platform have not been tampered with, as well as proof of a genuine hardware configuration; and *freshness*, confirming that the attestation data reflects the current state rather than a replayed past state.
These extra security guarantees significantly reduce the threat surface protecting the communication channel against impersonation, replay, and tampering attacks, ultimately enhancing trust in the remotely attested execution environments.

3 Use Case: Entropy and IoT

True randomness, or entropy—a reliable measure of randomness—can be achieved with methods that can generate actual random data. This entropy is hard to achieve as it is not straightforward to identify methods for gathering truly random inputs or generating truly random data using specific input sources. The introduction describes a variety of previous methods for achieving entropy. However, these methods can call true randomness into question if the methods or inputs follow a pattern or the data can be manipulated.

Methods used for generating true randomness are known as TRNGs. TRNGs include, but are not limited to, chaos [21], electrical noise [21], free-running oscillators [21], quantum effects [21], and radioactive decay [23]. Chaos is addressed using methods like biosignals [3], multi-dimensional chaotic systems [5], and wind flow [10]. To explain further, radioactive decay is used to retrieve random signals to support creating true randomness [23]. TRNGs based on Ring Oscillators are a recent and well-known technique for achieving entropy in IoT systems [18].

In addition to TRNGs that use true randomness, there are also Pseudorandom Number Generators (PRNGs) which are algorithms that transform input seed values into longer and uniformly distributed deterministic bit streams, meaning that the same seed value will always result in the same output value. In order for a PRNG to be considered a Cryptographically Secure Pseudorandom Number Generator (CSPRNG), it must provide both forward and backward unpredictability.

Because of their limited resources, constrained IoT devices may encounter difficulty in producing the strong entropy necessary for cryptographically secure random numbers [9]. Furthermore, Petro and Cecil [17] identify numerous additional security issues with IoT Random Number Generators (RNGs), including (i) Lack of access to proper CSPRNG subsystems due to lack of modern OS; (ii) Developers frequently making incorrect calls to hardware TRNGs; (iii) The difficulty of handling hardware TRNG errors correctly; (iv) Inadequate documentation for bare-metal function calls; and (v) Flaws in the entropy distillation process that generate subpar quality hardware TRNG.

A way to solve the problem of limited entropy for IoT devices is to use EaaS [14], first introduced by Vassilev and Staples in 2016 [22]. In contrast to *Randomness Beacons* [13], in an EaaS system, a server only distributes secure and fresh entropy to clients that specifically request it, instead of broadcasting it in timed intervals. Previous research demonstrated that TEE offers security for diverse applications, and we are now broadening this research domain by introducing an external entropy provision service [16]. The entropy received from an EaaS server with secure TEE hardware is inherently suitable for cryptographic use, unlike the publicly known entropy provided by the more-researched Randomness Beacons.

4 EaaS Design

Our EaaS solution consists of three main components: (i) an IoT client; (ii) a Trusted Execution Server (TES); and (iii) entropy sources. The high-level idea is that a resource-constrained IoT device sends a Hypertext Transfer Protocol (HTTP) request to a server, which subsequently processes the request by fetching fresh entropy from the entropy sources, generates strong entropy by combining the entropy received from the entropy sources, and finally transmits the entropy to the IoT client. The protocol incorporates a verification function that validates both the digital signature generated by the TES and the freshness of the received entropy.

We employ a fleet of IoT devices in our implementation, each of which has a limited capacity to generate entropy. However, none of them has sufficient resources to independently generate strong and crypto-secure entropy. Thus, the IoT client is represented by one of the IoT devices in the fleet, while the remaining devices serve as the entropy sources.

Because the entropy fetching and generation portion of the protocol is executed within a TEE, the trust is placed in the TEE technology rather than a third-party entity (server operator). Thus, we refer to this server as a TES instead of a TTP server.

In order to use asymmetric encryption, we assume a key provisioning model which gets rid of the chicken-and-egg problem; i.e., we assume that the manufacturer has provided a strong initial key to the IoT client. Thus, the IoT client does not need to use EaaS for generating the strong key required for using the EaaS system in the first place. Additionally, we assume that the IoT client has previously obtained the public key of the TES (pk_{TES}).

When the IoT client wants to request entropy from the TES, it first generates a timestamp (t_1) and then sends a self-signed request to the TES that has been encrypted with the public key of the TES (pk_{TES}). The encrypted request contains the public key (pk_{IoT}), the quantity of entropy requested (ΔS), and a digital signature (σ_1).

After the TES receives the request, it fetches an amount ΔS of entropy from the entropy sources (denoted by ΔS_1 and ΔS_2), and then combines the entropy (denoted by S) and generates a timestamp (t_2). TES also creates a fixed-length symmetric session key ($sk_{session}$). To distribute the symmetric key to the IoT client, the TES encrypts the symmetric key $sk_{session}$ with the public key of the IoT client pk_{IoT}. This symmetric key $sk_{session}$ is used to encrypt the encapsulated message that contains both the generated entropy S and the timestamp t_2. Finally, TES signs both the encrypted symmetric session key and the encapsulated message with its secret key (sk_{TES}). The result is a digital signature (σ_2).

The response from TES to the IoT client is thus a message that contains: (i) a fixed-length symmetric session key $sk_{session}$, encrypted with the public key of the IoT client pk_{IoT}; (ii) an encapsulated response to the request for entropy. This response contains the generated entropy S and the timestamp t_2 and is encrypted with the fixed-length symmetric session key $sk_{session}$; (iii) a digital signature σ_2, signed with the secret key of TES sk_{TES}.

After decrypting the message, the IoT client verifies that: (i) the message contains the requested entropy S with the requested amount of entropy ΔS, the digital signature σ_2, and the timestamp of the entropy generation t_2; (ii) the freshness of the generated entropy ($t_2 > t_1$); and (iii) the digital signature σ_2 is valid. The protocol is depicted in Fig. 4.

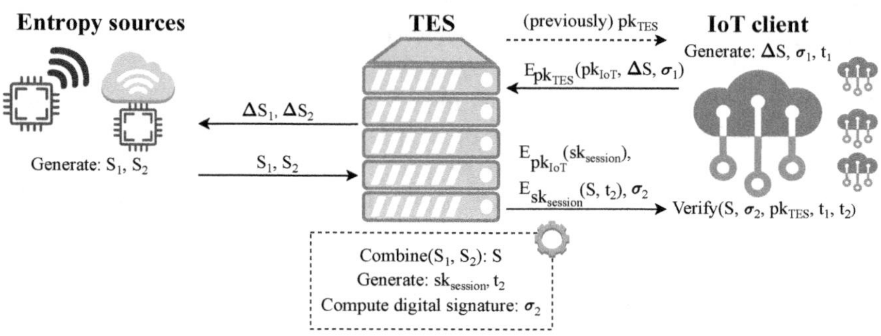

Fig. 4. EaaS Protocol

4.1 Security Considerations and Evaluations

TEE Provides Security Even if the Server Operator is Malicious. The TEE technology ensures the security of the EaaS system, even in the event of a malicious server operator, provided it functions properly. This justifies calling the server a TES rather than a TTP server. Side-channel attacks are a potential attack vector against the TEE technology that may undermine the security assumptions. While we are currently unaware of any side-channel attacks against the RISC-V-based TEE we use in our EaaS implementation, it is important to be aware of this potential attack vector.

Self-signing the Request for Entropy Protects Against a Malicious Actor on the Communication Link. We assume that there is a malicious actor on the link or that the link may have some corruption. Self-signing the request with the IoT device's private key binds the public and private keys, as well as the entropy quantity request for the transaction. Similar self-signing is used in Public-Key Infrastructure (PKI) with a Certificate Signing Request to certify a public key by a Certificate Authority. Without this self-signing, a malicious actor could perform a simple Denial of Service (DoS) attack by modifying the public key, preventing the requester from decrypting the response. Additionally, the malicious actor could alter the quantity of requested entropy, resulting in insufficient entropy for the requesting IoT client. Of course, a malicious actor can simply drop messages, but this only affects the requester. If the message is returned and rejected by the requester, it is likely that they will request it again. This could impact the TES, either by keeping it busy servicing constant messages or, in the worst-case scenario, by depleting the entropy source, which can affect all IoT nodes.

Throttling Requests from a Single Source Stops the Depletion of Entropy To avoid entropy depletion, we use a throttling mechanism on the TES to limit the number of requests from a single source. This protects the EaaS system from a bad actor who repeatedly makes valid requests to the TES with the goal of consuming all entropy. In addition to malicious actors, this will also offer protection against misconfigured or buggy networks/devices that repeatedly request entropy for non-malicious reasons. An alternative solution to fixing this problem would be to assume that the initial factory provisioning provides not only a key-pair but also a certificate that can be verified by the TES. However, this approach adds more overhead to the protocol and may not even be feasible on these constrained IoT devices. Thus, we instead implement a throttling mechanism.

A Symmetric Session Key is Used for Encrypting the TES Response Because of Public Key Encryption Data Size Limitations. The payload size for public key encryption is limited. For example, RSA can only perform one encryption step, which means it can only encrypt data up to the key size minus padding and header data. After removing padding, header data, timestamp, and signature data from our TES response, we are left with the data size available for the actual entropy payload. This means that either the requested amount of entropy must be less than this amount, or the protocol must support multiple messages in order to return all of the requested entropy in case the requested amount exceeds the available data size. Thus, to avoid unnecessary protocol overhead, we use fixed-length symmetric session keys to encrypt the TES response payload.

5 Software Implementation

We implemented our EaaS solution using the SPIRS TEE SDK with the QEMU virtualized environment. The software implementation was developed and tested on an Ubuntu 22.04.4 LTS machine. We used the QEMU platform instead of actual SPIRS hardware due to the ease of implementation and speed of development. The QEMU platform contains a RISC-V virtual machine image that includes bootloaders, SM, Linux kernel, and rootfs.

To provide developers with easy access to cryptographic functions, we used OpenSSL as a third-party library. In order to get the third-party library to work, we built a static OpenSSL library with a RISC-V musl toolchain and added it to the SPIRS TEE SDK build process.

We used a minimal Trusted Computing Base (TCB) design, running only the necessary components inside the TEE enclave (TA). In practice, only the code for obtaining and combining entropy, generating the keys, computing and verifying the digital signatures, and encrypting and decrypting the messages is run inside a TA. The rest of the code is executed on the CA.

Network Time Protocol (NTP) is used for timestamps. AES-128 is used for symmetric encryption and RSA-3072 is used for asymmetric encryption. We use a hybrid scheme: RSA-3072 for signatures and AES-128 for payload encryption.

The EaaS demo application serves as a functional Proof-of-Concept illustrating that the SPIRS TEE SDK is suitable for the practical development of useful TAs.

5.1 Limitations

A limitation of our work is that we are only using entropy gathered from the entropy sources, which in our case are the IoT devices in the fleet, all of which are based on the PUF/TRNG inside the hardware RoT of SPIRS devices. Therefore, any potential flaws with this PUF/TRNG implementation would also directly affect the quality of entropy generated by our EaaS system. To address this problem, our EaaS implementation could be modified to also use other trusted entropy sources. We recommend that real-world EaaS implementations use many trusted entropy sources that are based on different phenomena, so that any potential flaws in one method do not invalidate the quality of generated entropy. Since our EaaS design allows the easy addition of entropy sources, this is easily achievable in any real-world implementation based on our design.

The development happened on a virtualized QEMU environment instead of the actual SPIRS hardware. To get the software working on the actual SPIRS hardware, we would need to develop further mappings between the OpenSSL library and the trusted hardware implementations. However, since the cryptographic functions used in the software implementation are mostly the same functions that are supported by the trusted hardware components of the SPIRS TEE hardware platform, this should be straightforward to achieve. Future research should include hardware and performance benchmarking to assess the practicality and usability of our solution.

Our implementation relies on a single TES, creating a potential single point of failure. However, our design could be easily extended to include features such as load balancing for high availability in production environments where a single point of failure is not acceptable. The design could also be extended for a decentralized solution.

The threats posed by a future Cryptographically Relevant Quantum Computer (CRQC) inherently affect this project as well. In this work, we did not directly address Post-Quantum Cryptography (PQC) concerns, as the efforts for the PQC transition are orthogonal to our application. Nonetheless, it is worth remarking that as both confidentiality and authentication based on asymmetric cryptography are impacted by the quantum threats, real-world deployments of this work should select Post-Quantum/Traditional (PQ/T) hybrid algorithms to secure the communication channels against attacks such as Harvest-NowDecrypt-Later (HNDL). While threats to authentication do require an active attacker with access to a CRQC, the direct threat here does not need to be addressed as urgently as asymmetric encryption. Nonetheless, as we are well aware of the many challenges in any migration affecting the PKI, we remark on the urgency to address the PQC transition of the PKI to provide a sustainable migration path for devices and applications such as the ones described here. Finally, on a related note, we recognize that one limitation of the current implementation of the SPIRS platform is that its RoT does not embed support for PQC primitives: a natural evolution for the SPIRS project would consist in providing support in hardware and firmware to establish a chain of trust based on PQ/T hybrid algorithms.

6 Conclusion

In this paper, we presented a working EaaS demo application and its design that utilizes the SPIRS TEE SDK, demonstrating that developing useful TAs for an open-source RISC-V-based TEE is both feasible and effective. Our implementation highlights the potential of combining open hardware with secure software to address real-world challenges in IoT security.

EaaS Warrants Further Research. Our work showcases that designing and building a working EaaS implementation is practical and useful for IoT devices that lack sufficient resources to generate strong entropy by themselves. However, there is limited scientific research and practical applications for EaaS, as most of the attention seems to be on the somewhat-related Randomness Beacons. We believe our implementation illustrates that EaaS, particularly when backed by a TEE for a TES, offers distinct advantages in selective entropy delivery, remote attestation, and system scalability. EaaS ensures confidentiality, freshness, and trust in entropy distribution—making it a compelling direction for both academic inquiry and industrial adoption. We encourage future work to explore alternative entropy sources, multi-tenant TES infrastructures, and deployment in heterogeneous hardware ecosystems.

The SPIRS TEE SDK Allows Practical Development of TAs for Open-Source RISC-V Hardware. Our EaaS demo application demonstrates that the SPIRS TEE SDK enables practical development of TAs for the RISC-V-based SPIRS hardware platform. This application is a meaningful demonstration of how TAs can be developed on open-source RISC-V-based TEE hardware. The open-source toolchain, support for virtualization via QEMU, and integration of cryptographic primitives through trusted runtime components make the SDK suitable for rapid prototyping and academic experimentation. We anticipate that the SPIRS platform and SDK will lower the barrier to entry for developing new TAs in diverse domains, including embedded security, supply chain attestation, and privacy-preserving analytics.

Our Design Warrants Benchmarking and Comparison with Other Solutions. This paper presents our EaaS design and its simple QEMU-based implementation. The scope did not include performance or hardware measurements. Future research should measure the overhead of the EaaS implementation and evaluate its scalability for multiple concurrent IoT clients. Additionally, we recommend comparing our solution to other EaaS and Randomness Beacon systems.

7 Code Availability

As we fully support Open Science principles, we have published our code with an open-source (MIT) license. The code can be accessed through the following Git repository: https://gitlab.com/nisec/spirs-tee-sdk-eaastee-public-fork. The Git repository includes a detailed *README.md* file with a tutorial for using the SPIRS TEE SDK as well as running our demo EaaS application. The *README.md* file also explains the chosen algorithms and design choices in further detail.

Table 1. Contribution Table

Contributions	A.P.	J.N.	A.C.A.	N.T.	J.S.	M.K.	B.M.
Data curation	•	○	○	○	○	○	○
Formal Analysis	•	○	○	•	○	○	○
Funding acquisition	○	•	•	•	○	○	•
Investigation	•	•	○	•	•	○	○
Methodology	•	•	○	•	•	○	•
Project administration	•	•	•	○	○	○	○
Resources	○	○	•	○	○	○	○
Software	•	•	•	•	○	○	○
Supervision	•	•	•	○	○	○	○
Validation	○	○	○	•	○	○	○
Visualization	•	•	•	•	○	•	○
Writing—original draft	•	•	•	•	•	○	○
Writing—review & editing	•	•	○	○	○	○	•

8 Authorship Contributions

J.N., A.A., N.T., and B.M. acquired funding.
A.P. led the article writing and administration.
A.C.A. and N.T. designed the RISC-V SPIRS SDK.
A.P. and J.N. designed the entropy provision service.
J.S. analyzed the entropy provision protocol.
A.A., N.T., and B.M. validated and verified our work.
M.K. contributed to the visualization of diagrams.

A.P., J.N., and B.M. proofread the manuscript.
B.M., A.P., and J.N. edited the final version of the paper.
Contributor Roles Taxonomy (CRediT) statement of authorship contribution (Table 1).

Acknowledgments. This work was supported by the European Commission under the Horizon Europe funding programme, as part of the projects SafeHorizon (Grant Agreement 101168562) and QUBIP (Grant Agreement 101119746). Views and opinions expressed are, however, those of the author(s) only and do not necessarily reflect those of the European Union. Neither the European Union nor the granting authority can be held responsible for them. The authors declare no competing interests.

References

1. Amil, A., Gupta, S.: A universal whitening algorithm for commercial random number generators. CoRR abs/2208.11935 (2022). https://doi.org/10.48550/arXiv.2208.11935
2. Asanovic, K., et al.: The RISC-V instruction set manual. Volume II: Privileged Architecture. RISC-V International (2024). https://github.com/riscv/riscv-isa-manual/releases/tag/20240411, version 20240411
3. Clemente-López, D., de Jesus Rangel-Magdaleno, J., Muñoz-Pacheco, J.M.: A lightweight chaos-based encryption scheme for IoT healthcare systems. Internet of Things **25**, 101032 (2024). https://doi.org/10.1016/j.iot.2023.101032
4. EUROSMART: BSI-CC-PP-0084-2014: Security IC platform protection profile with augmentation packages. https://www.bsi.bund.de/SharedDocs/Zertifikate_CC/PP/aktuell/PP_0084.html (2014). Bundesamt für Sicherheit in der Informationstechnik (BSI). Accessed 4 June 2025
5. Fan, S., Wang, J.: Multi-dimension-precision chaotic encryption mechanism for Internet of Things. Internet of Things **26**, 101202 (2024). https://doi.org/10.1016/j.iot.2024.101202
6. GlobalPlatform Inc.: TEE client API specification v1.0. Tech. Rep. GPD_SPE_007, GlobalPlatform Inc. (2010). https://globalplatform.org/specs-library/tee-client-api-specification/
7. GlobalPlatform Inc.: TEE internal core API specification v1.1.2. Tech. Rep. GPD_SPE_010, GlobalPlatform Inc. (2016). https://globalplatform.org/specs-library/tee-internal-core-api-specification/
8. GlobalPlatform Inc.: GlobalPlatform TEE specification library (2025). https://globalplatform.org/specs-library/?filter-committee=tee. Accessed 4 June 2025
9. Kietzmann, P., Schmidt, T.C., Wählisch, M.: A guideline on Pseudorandom Number Generation (PRNG) in the IoT. ACM Comput. Surv. **54**(6), 112:1–112:38 (2021). https://doi.org/10.1145/3453159
10. Kim, M.S., Tcho, I.W., Choi, Y.K.: Cryptographic triboelectric random number generator with gentle breezes of an entropy source. Sci. Rep. **14**(1), 1358 (2024). https://doi.org/10.1038/s41598-024-51939-2
11. Krawczyk, H.: Cryptographic extraction and key derivation: the HKDF Scheme. In: Rabin, T. (ed.) CRYPTO 2010. LNCS, vol. 6223, pp. 631–648. Springer, Heidelberg (2010). https://doi.org/10.1007/978-3-642-14623-7_34

12. Lee, D., Kohlbrenner, D., Shinde, S., Asanovic, K., Song, D.: Keystone: an open framework for architecting trusted execution environments. In: EuroSys. ACM (2020). https://doi.org/10.1145/3342195.3387532
13. National Institute of Standards and Technology (NIST): Interoperable Randomness Beacons (2011). https://csrc.nist.gov/projects/interoperable-randomness-beacons. Accessed 4 June 2025
14. National Institute of Standards and Technology (NIST): Entropy as a Service (2016). https://csrc.nist.gov/Projects/Entropy-as-a-Service. Accessed 4 June 2025
15. von Neumann, J.: John von neumann collected works, vol. 5: Design of Computers, Theory of Automata and Numerical Analysis, chap. Various Techniques Used in Connection with Random Digits, pp. 768–770. Pergamon Press, Oxford, England (1961), notes by George E. Forsythe and reproduced from J. Res. Nat. Bus. Stand. Appl. Math. Series, vol. 3, pp. 36–38 (1955)
16. Paju, A., Javed, M.O., Nurmi, J., Savimäki, J., McGillion, B., Brumley, B.B.: SoK: a systematic review of TEE usage for developing trusted applications. In: Proceedings of the 18th International Conference on Availability, Reliability and Security, ARES 2023, Benevento, Italy, 29 August 2023–1 September 2023, pp. 34:1–34:15. ACM (2023). https://doi.org/10.1145/3600160.3600169
17. Petro, D., Cecil, A.: You're doing IoT RNG (2021). https://bishopfox.com/blog/youre-doing-iot-rng, DEF CON 29
18. Rojas-Muñoz, L.F., Sánchez-Solano, S., Martínez-Rodríguez, M.C., Brox, P.: True random number generator based on RO-PUF. In: 37th Conference on Design of Circuits and Integrated Systems, DCIS 2022, Pamplona, Spain, November 16–18, 2022, pp. 1–6. IEEE (2022). https://doi.org/10.1109/DCIS55711.2022.9970032
19. Santha, M., Vazirani, U.V.: Generating quasi-random sequences from slightly-random sources (extended abstract). In: 25th Annual Symposium on Foundations of Computer Science, West Palm Beach, Florida, USA, 24–26 October 1984, pp. 434–440. IEEE Computer Society (1984). https://doi.org/10.1109/SFCS.1984.715945
20. SPIRS: SPIRS homepage (2025). https://www.spirs-project.eu. Accessed 4 June 2025
21. Stipčević, M., Koç, Ç.K.: True random number generators. In: Koç, Ç.K. (ed.) Open Problems in Mathematics and Computational Science. LNCS, pp. 275–315. Springer, Cham (2014). https://doi.org/10.1007/978-3-319-10683-0_12
22. Vassilev, A., Staples, R.: Entropy as a service: unlocking cryptography's full potential. Computer **49**(9), 98–102 (2016). https://doi.org/10.1109/MC.2016.275
23. You, I., Youn, T.: Information Security Applications: 23rd International Conference, WISA 2022, Jeju Island, South Korea, August 24–26, 2022, Revised Selected Papers. Lecture Notes in Computer Science, Springer Nature Switzerland (2023). https://books.google.fi/books?id=K-irEAAAQBAJ

Adversarial Ensemble Framework: Leveraging GANs for Robust Intrusion Detection in IoT Networks

Abdoul Faycal Zoungrana, Hajar Moudoud(✉), Etienne Gael Tajeuna, and Kamel Adi

Computer Science and Engineering Department, Universite du Quebec en Outaouais, Gatineau, Canada
{zouf02,hajar.moudoud,etiennegael.tajeuna,Kamel.Adi}@uqo.ca

Abstract. The rapid expansion of Internet of Things (IoT) devices introduces complex security challenges that traditional intrusion detection systems struggle to address. This paper proposes an Adversarial Ensemble Framework using Generative Adversarial Networks (GANs) to improve the accuracy and resilience of intrusion detection in IoT environments. The framework tackles key issues such as class imbalance, concept drift, and adversarial attacks by employing multiple GAN variants such as Vanilla GAN, Conditional GAN (CGAN), and Wasserstein GAN (WGAN) to generate high-quality synthetic attack data. A dynamic ensemble learning mechanism selects the most effective model for each attack type based on performance metrics. Experiments on NSL-KDD and CIC-IDS2017 show that WGAN yields the most effective synthetic data, contributing to a detection rate of up to 96%. The approach proves particularly effective in identifying rare attacks, making it a scalable and adaptive solution for IoT security.

Keywords: Security · IoT Networks · Generative Adversarial Networks

1 Introduction

The IoT has introduced a paradigm shift in connectivity, enabling vast networks of devices to communicate across sectors such as healthcare, smart cities, industrial automation, and critical infrastructures. By 2025, the number of connected IoT devices is expected to be around 50 billion [1–3], creating a highly dynamic and heterogeneous digital ecosystem. However, this exponential growth also expands the attack surface, exposing IoT networks to a broad spectrum of cybersecurity threats. The heterogeneity of devices, limited computational resources, and decentralized architecture inherent to IoT environments undermine the effectiveness of traditional security approaches, which were originally designed for homogeneous and centralized networks. As a result, IoT systems

K. Adi et al. (Eds.): CRiSIS 2025, LNCS 16295, pp. 85–99, 2026.
https://doi.org/10.1007/978-3-032-20732-6_6

continue to face a broad spectrum of security threats, ranging from volumetric attacks, such as botnet-based DDoS attacks, to advanced persistent threats including data exfiltration.

Although Intrusion Detection Systems (IDS) remain a cornerstone of IoT security, their effectiveness remains highly limited today. This paper therefore aims to address the following fundamental challenges:

1. **Inability to detect rare and evolving threats:** signature-based IDS struggle to identify novel or polymorphic attacks, while anomaly-based IDS often suffer from high false positive rates due to behavioral variability in heterogeneous IoT devices [4,5].
2. **Severe data imbalance:** most publicly available IoT datasets are heavily skewed, with frequent attack types such as DoS dominating, and rare but critical classes like User-to-Root (U2R) or Advanced Persistent Threats (APTs) significantly underrepresented, leading to biased models with poor generalization [6,7].
3. **Underutilization of generative learning:** although Generative Adversarial Networks (GANs) [8] have shown promise in producing realistic synthetic data, their potential remains underexploited due to architectural limitations and the absence of dynamic mechanisms for selecting optimal detectors per attack type. Indeed, classical GAN architectures often suffer from unstable training, high susceptibility to mode collapse, and limited ability to generate diverse and representative data for complex attack scenarios.

To address these challenges, this paper introduces a novel Adversarial Ensemble Framework tailored for IoT networks. The proposed framework integrates multiple GAN variants for attack synthesis and incorporates a dynamic, rule-based ensemble mechanism to select the most effective detector per attack type.

The main contributions of this paper are as follows:

- We provide a comparative evaluation of Vanilla GAN, CGAN, and WGAN for generating synthetic IoT attack data, highlighting their impact on detection performance.
- We design a rule-based decision ensemble learning method that adaptively selects optimal models for each attack class based on real-time performance metrics.
- We validate our framework using the NSL-KDD and CIC-IDS2017 datasets, achieving enhanced detection rates, particularly for underrepresented attacks.

The remainder of this paper is structured as follows: Sect. 2 reviews the relevant literature; Sect. 3 details the proposed methodology; Sect. 4 presents the experimental setup and discusses the results. Finally, Sect. 5 concludes the paper and highlights potential directions for future research.

2 Related Works

Recent research has increasingly explored the use of GANs to enhance IDS, particularly to address data imbalance and improve detection of underrepresented attack classes. Zhao et al. [9] conducted a comprehensive evaluation of

Vanilla GAN, CTGAN, and WGAN on the CIC-IDS2017 dataset, restructuring the attack classes to simplify modeling complexity. Their approach integrated dimensionality reduction and employed a random forest classifier to assess performance. Although overall accuracy was improved, minority classes such as Botnet and Infiltration remained challenging to detect. They mitigated this by generating targeted synthetic samples, with Vanilla GAN and WGAN outperforming CTGAN in data fidelity. Similarly, Liu et al. [10] applied Conditional GANs (CGANs) to detect DDoS attacks in Software Defined Networks (SDN), leveraging five key flow-based features. The CGAN architecture enabled the generation of realistic flow data, enhancing detection robustness through adversarial training.

Beyond detection, generative AI technologies introduce novel security and privacy risks. Golda et al. [11] reviewed how models such as GAN and VAE, while beneficial in domains such as IoT and augmented reality, pose risks related to data ownership, interpretability, and adversarial susceptibility. Zhu et al. [12] extended this discussion by identifying GenAI-specific threats, referencing OWASP's top vulnerabilities in LLM-based systems. They emphasized mitigation strategies such as access control, behavior monitoring, and anonymization. In parallel, privacy-preserving approaches such as federated learning have been explored. Murmu et al. [13] introduced CusIAFL, a federated framework using Pix2Pix GANs for secure image transformation in distributed environments like 5G and healthcare. Their method improved classification performance while preserving data privacy, outperforming several baseline models.

Emerging applications of generative AI in security contexts further demonstrate both opportunities and challenges. Mohebbanaaz et al. [14] addressed fake image detection using CGANs, revealing the growing threat of realistic but manipulated media content on social platforms. However, despite these advances, notable research gaps remain. Existing studies seldom compare multiple GAN variants within a unified IDS framework tailored for IoT environments. Additionally, most ensemble detection approaches are static and lack adaptability to attack-specific behaviors. Our work responds to these gaps by proposing an adversarial ensemble framework that (i) evaluates Vanilla GAN, CGAN, and WGAN for IoT-specific attack generation, (ii) integrates a decision rule-based dynamic model selection mechanism, and (iii) demonstrates effectiveness using the NSL-KDD and CIC-IDS2017 datasets across diverse IoT attack scenarios.

3 Intrusion Detection Based GAN for IoT Networks

3.1 Generative Adversarial Networks (GANs)

GAN is a generative AI method that creates synthetic data that closely resembles real training data (see Fig. 1). It consists of two competing neural networks:

- Generator: creates fake data samples that mimic real data patterns (e.g., normal network traffic).
- Discriminator: attempts to distinguish between real and generated data.

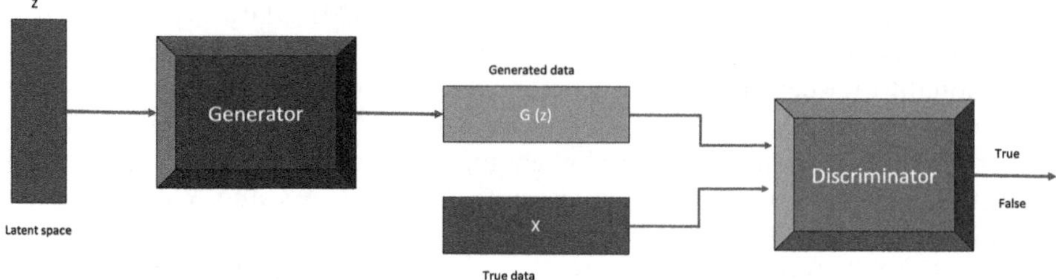

Fig. 1. GAN system architecture.

These models train simultaneously in an adversarial process where the generator tries to fool the discriminator while the discriminator works to detect fake data. Training continues until reaching equilibrium - the point where the discriminator can no longer reliably distinguish real from fake data and performs at near-random levels. This competitive training process enables GANs to generate highly realistic synthetic data by forcing the generator to continuously improve its ability to model complex data distributions.

3.2 System Model

To address the aforementioned challenges, we propose a comprehensive GAN-based intrusion detection framework that leverages three distinct GAN architectures: CGAN, WGAN, and Vanilla GAN. Each variant provides specific advantages for data augmentation in cybersecurity contexts. By integrating multiple GAN formulations, the proposed system effectively tackles the inherent issue of data imbalance, enhancing both the diversity and representativeness of synthetic attack samples.

Conditional GAN: The Conditional GAN integrates class label information directly into both the generator and discriminator during training. This conditioning mechanism enables the model to generate class-specific synthetic samples, which is particularly beneficial for addressing underrepresented attack categories.

The loss functions for the CGAN are defined as follows:

$$\mathcal{L}_D = -\mathbb{E}_{(x,y)\sim P_{\text{data}}}\left[\log D(x|y)\right] - \mathbb{E}_{z\sim P_z, y\sim P_y}\left[\log\left(1 - D(G(z|y)|y)\right)\right] \tag{1}$$

$$\mathcal{L}_G = -\mathbb{E}_{z\sim P_z, y\sim P_y}\left[\log\left(1 - D(G(z|y)|y)\right)\right] \tag{2}$$

Here, x denotes a real data sample, y is the corresponding class label, and z is a noise vector. $G(\cdot|y)$ and $D(\cdot|y)$ represent the conditional generator and discriminator, respectively.

Wasserstein GAN: To improve training stability and mitigate issues such as mode collapse, the WGAN employs the Wasserstein distance as its optimization criterion. Unlike CGAN, it removes the use of logarithmic loss and replaces it with a critic network trained under the Lipschitz constraint.

The WGAN architecture mirrors the CGAN in terms of structural parameters, but uses a linear activation in the output layer of the discriminator (critic). The generator and critic are trained using the following loss functions:

$$\mathcal{L}_D = -\mathbb{E}_{x\sim P_{\text{data}}}\left[D(x)\right] - \mathbb{E}_{z\sim P_z}\left[D(G(z))\right] \tag{3}$$

$$\mathcal{L}_G = -\mathbb{E}_{z\sim P_z}\left[D(G(z))\right] \tag{4}$$

In our proposed model, we consider that the generator receives a latent noise vector of size `latent_dim = 100` concatenated with label information, and passes it through a two-layer feedforward network with LeakyReLU activations and batch normalization. The critic network mirrors this structure with dropout layers to improve regularization. Training is conducted over 2000 epochs with weight clipping applied to maintain the Lipschitz condition.

Vanilla GAN: The Vanilla GAN serves as a baseline model, relying on the standard adversarial training framework. Unlike CGAN and WGAN, it generates synthetic samples solely from random noise vectors, without leveraging label information.

The discriminator outputs a probability using a sigmoid activation function and is optimized using binary cross-entropy loss. The objective functions are defined as:

$$\mathcal{L}_D = -\mathbb{E}_{x\sim P_{\text{data}}}\left[\log D(x)\right] - \mathbb{E}_{z\sim P_z}\left[\log\left(1 - D(G(z))\right)\right] \tag{5}$$

$$\mathcal{L}_G = -\mathbb{E}_{z\sim P_z}\left[\log D(G(z))\right] \tag{6}$$

The Vanilla GAN follows the same architectural parameters as the other variants but excludes label vectors from both generator and discriminator inputs. In our proposed model, we consider that the training is performed for 2000 epochs, and the model is evaluated based on generator/discriminator loss evolution and classification performance post-augmentation.

3.3 Model Selection Framework for IDS

We propose a model selection-based IDS that leverages GAN-driven data augmentation to train diverse classifiers. Instead of aggregating predictions through ensemble methods, our framework evaluates the performance of each classifier trained on data generated by a specific GAN variant—namely, CGAN, WGAN, and Vanilla GAN, and selects the best-performing model per attack class based on validation metrics. This strategy enhances detection accuracy, particularly in heterogeneous and class-imbalanced IoT network environments.

Let $\mathcal{D} = \{(x_i, y_i)\}_{i=1}^{N} \subset \mathbb{R}^d \times \mathcal{Y}$ be a labeled dataset, where $x_i \in \mathbb{R}^d$ is a feature vector and $y_i \in \mathcal{Y} = \{0, 1, \ldots, k\}$ represents the class label (0 for normal, $1 \ldots k$ for attack classes).

Each GAN architecture: CGAN, WGAN, and Vanilla GAN is used to generate synthetic data for underrepresented classes. The augmented datasets are then used to train three distinct classifiers:

$$\mathcal{B} = \{h_{\text{CGAN}}, h_{\text{WGAN}}, h_{\text{Vanilla}}\} \tag{7}$$

Each classifier h_j produces predictions as:

$$\hat{y}_i^{(j)} = h_j(x_i), \quad j \in \{\text{CGAN}, \text{WGAN}, \text{Vanilla}\} \tag{8}$$

Let $\mathbf{P} \in \mathbb{R}^{|\mathcal{Y}| \times 3}$ be the performance matrix, where $P_{y,j}$ denotes the evaluation score (e.g., class-wise F1-score or accuracy) of model h_j for class y.

The optimal model for each class $y \in \mathcal{Y}$ is selected as:

$$h_y^* = \arg\max_{j \in \{\text{CGAN}, \text{WGAN}, \text{Vanilla}\}} P_{y,j} \tag{9}$$

At inference time, given a new instance x, the final predicted class is obtained by:

$$\hat{y} = \arg\max_{y \in \mathcal{Y}} h_y^*(x) \tag{10}$$

This rule-based model selection framework dynamically routes each input through the classifier best suited for the predicted class. It provides fine-grained control and improves the robustness of the IDS by maximizing per-class performance rather than relying on a one-size-fits-all ensemble prediction.

Algorithm 1 outlines a four-phase process: GAN-based data augmentation, independent classifier training, per-class performance evaluation, and class-wise model selection. By leveraging CGAN, WGAN, and Vanilla GAN to enrich the training dataset, the system ensures diversity in learned decision boundaries.

4 Evaluation

The objective of this study is to assess whether the use of GANs improves the detection of attacks, particularly those underrepresented in datasets. We analyzed the effects of data augmentation using three GAN variants (CGAN, WGAN, and Vanilla GAN) on two datasets: NSL-KDD and CICIDS. Through this analysis, we were able to observe the advantages and limitations of each approach using standard performance metrics: Accuracy, Precision, Recall, and F1-Score.

Algorithm 1 Model Selection-Based Intrusion Detection Framework.

Require: Original training dataset $\mathcal{D}_{\text{orig}} = \{(x_i, y_i)\}_{i=1}^{N}$
Require: GAN variants: CGAN, WGAN, Vanilla GAN
Ensure: Trained classifiers $h_{\text{CGAN}}, h_{\text{WGAN}}, h_{\text{Vanilla}}$
Ensure: Class-wise selected model h_y^* for each $y \in \mathcal{Y}$
1: **Step 1: Data Augmentation**
2: **for** each GAN variant $G_j \in \{\text{CGAN}, \text{WGAN}, \text{Vanilla GAN}\}$ **do**
3: Train G_j on $\mathcal{D}_{\text{orig}}$ to generate synthetic samples for minority classes
4: Construct augmented dataset $\mathcal{D}_j = \mathcal{D}_{\text{orig}} \cup \mathcal{D}_{\text{synthetic}}^{(j)}$
5: **end for**
6: **Step 2: Classifier Training**
7: **for** each GAN variant $j \in \{\text{CGAN}, \text{WGAN}, \text{Vanilla}\}$ **do**
8: Train classifier h_j on augmented dataset $\mathcal{D}_j$
9: **end for**
10: **Step 3: Model Evaluation and Selection**
11: **for** each class $y \in \mathcal{Y}$ **do**
12: Evaluate each model h_j on validation set $\mathcal{D}_{\text{val}}$
13: Compute performance metric $P_{y,j}$ (e.g., F1-score)
14: Select best model for class y: $h_y^* = \arg\max_j P_{y,j}$
15: **end for**
16: **Step 4: Inference**
17: **for** each test instance $x \in \mathcal{D}_{\text{test}}$ **do**
18: Predict label: $\hat{y}_j = h_j(x)$ for all j
19: Final output: $\hat{y} = \arg\max_{y \in \mathcal{Y}} h_y^*(x)$
20: **end for**
21: **return** Class-wise best models $\{h_y^*\}_{y \in \mathcal{Y}}$

4.1 Experimental Setup

We implemented a custom neural network model composed of an initial dense layer of 128 ReLU-activated neurons, taking the input shape from `x_train`. This is followed by two dense layers with 64 neurons each, both using ReLU activation, then a dense layer with 32 neurons and ReLU activation as well. The final output layer is a dense layer with a number of neurons equal to the number of classes defined in the label mapping, using a Softmax activation function. The model is compiled with the Adam optimizer (learning rate = 0.0001), the sparse categorical cross-entropy loss function, and the accuracy metric. The training was conducted over 100 epochs with a batch size of 64, using `x_test` and `y_test` for validation.

Generator: the generator takes as input a noise vector with `latent_dim` set to 100 and a label of dimension `num_classes = 5`. These two inputs are concatenated and passed through a dense layer with 128 neurons, LeakyReLU activation (`alpha = 0.2`), and batch normalization (`momentum = 0.8`). The output then passes through a second dense layer with 256 neurons, also using LeakyReLU activation and batch normalization. The final output is produced by a dense layer with `data_dim` neurons and a `tanh` activation, generating synthetic data samples.

Discriminator: the discriminator receives as input a data vector of dimension `data_dim` and a label of dimension `num_classes`. These inputs are concatenated and passed through a dense layer with 256 neurons and LeakyReLU activation (`alpha = 0.2`), followed by another dense layer with 128 neurons and the same activation. The final output layer contains one neuron with a `sigmoid` activation function, which determines the validity of the input sample.

This model was trained for 2000 epochs, enabling us to monitor the generator and discriminator losses throughout the training process. Once training was complete, the GAN was used to augment the dataset, with a particular focus on the minority classes: `U2R` and `R2L`, which account for approximately 0% (52 instances) and 1% (995 instances) of the total dataset, respectively. The generator and discriminator loss histories during training are shown below.

We also define $\mathcal{M}(M)$, a performance metric (e.g., F1-score or Accuracy). Then the best model is selected by:

$$M^* = \arg\max_{M \in \mathcal{B} \cup \mathcal{E} \cup \{\mathrm{RL}\}} \mathcal{M}(M) \tag{11}$$

Macro Accuracy:

$$\text{Accuracy} = \frac{1}{N} \sum_{i=1}^{N} \mathbb{I}[M(x_i) = y_i] \tag{12}$$

Macro F1-score:

$$\text{F1}_{\text{macro}} = \frac{1}{|\mathcal{Y}|} \sum_{y \in \mathcal{Y}} \frac{2 \cdot \text{Precision}_y \cdot \text{Recall}_y}{\text{Precision}_y + \text{Recall}_y} \tag{13}$$

4.2 Experimental Results

This section presents the performance evaluation of the proposed GAN-based ensemble framework using the NSL-KDD and CICIDS2017 datasets. We focus on assessing the effect of CGAN, WGAN, and Vanilla GAN on the detection of rare and imbalanced attack classes.

Figure 2 shows the baseline confusion matrix on the NSL-KDD dataset prior to any data augmentation. It reveals strong detection for majority classes like DoS and Normal but demonstrates poor performance for rare classes such as U2R and R2L, which are almost entirely misclassified. This highlights the class imbalance issue that motivates the use of GAN-based augmentation. Prior to augmentation, the model achieved high overall accuracy but struggled to identify rare attacks like `u2r` due to severe class imbalance. After applying GAN-based data augmentation, notable improvements were observed.

Figure 3 displays the confusion matrices for the NSL-KDD dataset following data augmentation. The CGAN approach (Fig. 3a) demonstrated notable

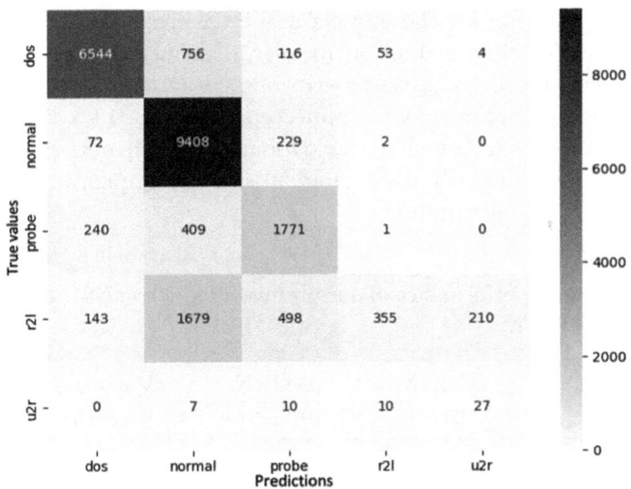

Fig. 2. Confusion matrix on NSL-KDD before data augmentation.

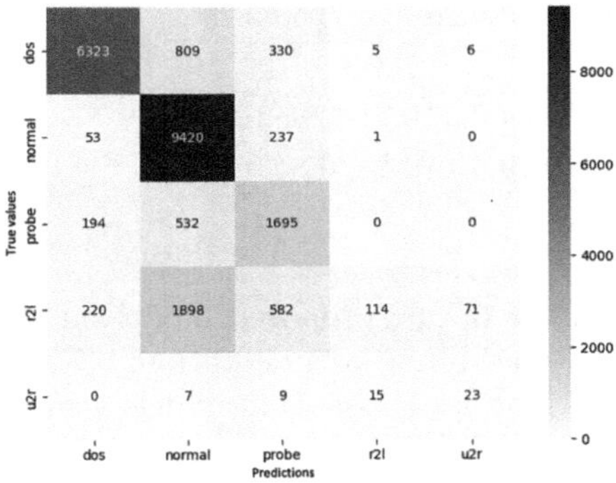

(a) CGAN

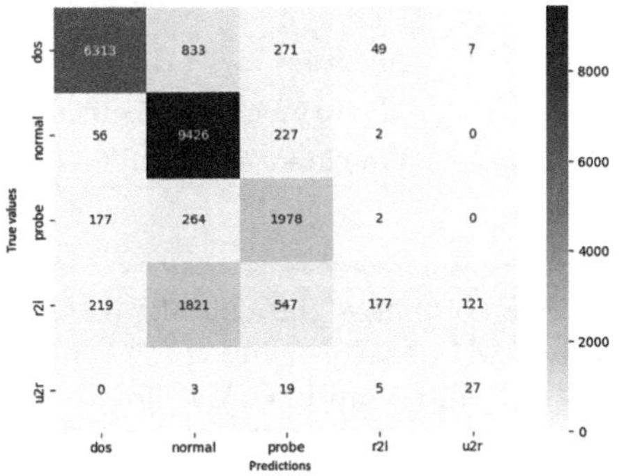

(b) WGAN

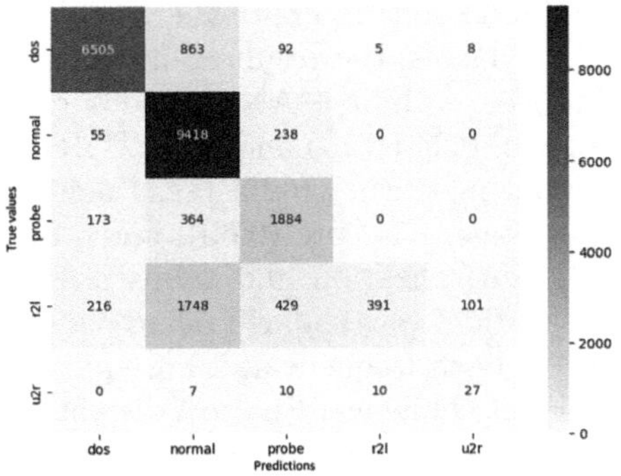

(c) Vanilla GAN

Fig. 3. Confusion matrices on NSL-KDD after data augmentation.

improvement in precision for the u2r class, increasing from 11% to 23%, though this came with a marginal reduction in overall accuracy. The WGAN method (Fig. 3b) produced more consistent performance across classes, achieving balanced enhancements particularly for underrepresented attack types. Meanwhile, the Vanilla GAN (Fig. 3c) yielded the strongest overall performance with 81% accuracy while simultaneously delivering substantial improvements in both r2l and u2r attack detection capabilities.

Table 1. Classification performance of our proposed model on NSL-KDD using CGAN, WGAN, and Vanilla GAN.

Class	CGAN			WGAN			Vanilla GAN		
	Prec.	Rec.	F1	Prec.	Rec.	F1	Prec.	Rec.	F1
DoS	0.93	0.85	0.89	0.93	0.84	0.89	0.94	0.87	0.90
Normal	0.74	0.97	0.84	0.76	0.97	0.85	0.76	0.97	0.85
Probe	0.59	0.70	0.64	0.65	0.82	0.72	0.71	0.78	0.74
R2L	0.84	0.04	0.08	0.75	0.06	0.11	0.96	0.14	0.24
U2R	0.23	0.43	0.30	0.17	0.50	0.26	0.20	0.50	0.28
Accuracy	0.78			0.79			0.81		
Macro Avg	0.67	0.60	0.55	0.65	0.64	0.57	0.71	0.65	0.60
Weighted Avg	0.80	0.78	0.74	0.80	0.79	0.76	0.84	0.81	0.78

Table 1 compares the classification performance of our proposed model on the NSL-KDD dataset using three types of GAN-based data augmentation: CGAN, WGAN, and Vanilla GAN. For the DoS and Normal classes, all models achieve high F1-scores (above 0.84), with Vanilla GAN slightly outperforming the others, especially in terms of precision and recall. The Probe class also shows improved performance with Vanilla GAN (F1 = 0.74), compared to CGAN (F1 = 0.64), highlighting the latter's limitations in capturing attack diversity. For the more challenging R2L and U2R classes, the results remain low across all models due to class imbalance. However, Vanilla GAN provides relative improvements in both cases, with F1-scores of 0.24 (R2L) and 0.28 (U2R), surpassing CGAN and WGAN. In terms of global metrics, Vanilla GAN achieves the highest overall accuracy (0.81), macro-average F1-score (0.60), and weighted-average F1-score (0.78), indicating better generalization and robustness. These results confirm that GAN-based augmentation, particularly using Vanilla GAN, enhances the classifier's ability to detect both frequent and infrequent attacks, although rare classes still pose a significant challenge. Figure 4 displays the confusion matrices for the CICIDS dataset following data augmentation. Results on CICIDS are more mixed due to its complexity and severe class imbalance.

Figure 5 presents the confusion matrices on the NSL-KDD dataset after data augmentation using CGAN (Fig. 5a), WGAN (Fig. 5b), and Vanilla GAN (Fig. 5c). The CGAN model exhibited improved detection for several classes

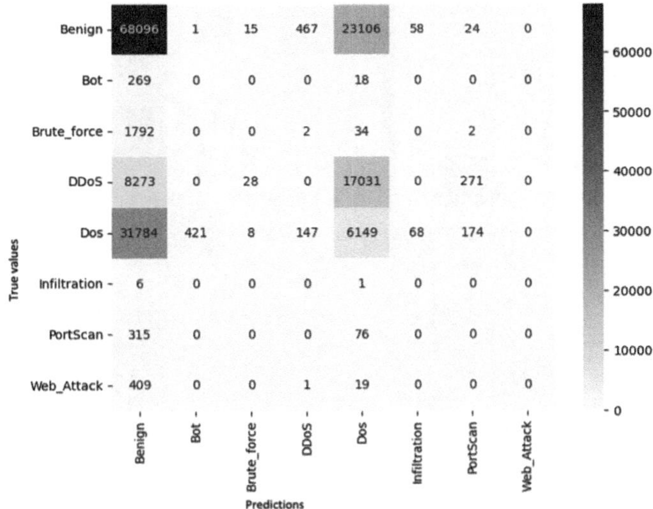

Fig. 4. Confusion matrix on CICIDS before data augmentation.

but showed considerable confusion between related attack types such as `brute_force`, `bot` and `infiltration`, leading to scattered misclassifications. The WGAN approach provided more balanced predictions, particularly reducing false positives in `portscan` and `web_attack` classes, though some overlap remained. In contrast, the Vanilla GAN model achieved the clearest separation between classes, significantly improving classification for `web_attack`, `brute_force`, and `infiltration` while maintaining high accuracy on frequent classes such as `dos`, `benign`, and `ddos`. These results further validate Vanilla GAN's effectiveness in learning discriminative features for both frequent and rare intrusion categories.

Table 2 compares the classification performance of our proposed model on the CISIDS dataset. The CICIDS dataset classification results show that CGAN, WGAN, and Vanilla GAN achieve similar modest performance with 41–43% accuracy, where all models perfectly detect DoS attacks (1.00 F1 score) but struggle significantly with most other attack types, showing low precision (0.25–0.31) and completely failing on DDoS detection (0.00 across all metrics). While WGAN performs slightly better overall, the consistently low macro averages (0.26–0.29) compared to weighted averages (0.32–0.36) reveal that all GAN-based approaches suffer from class imbalance issues and have difficulty distinguishing subtle attack patterns in network intrusion detection scenarios. Figures 6 and 7 summarize the multi-class classification results for GANs on NSLKDD and CISIDS, respectively.

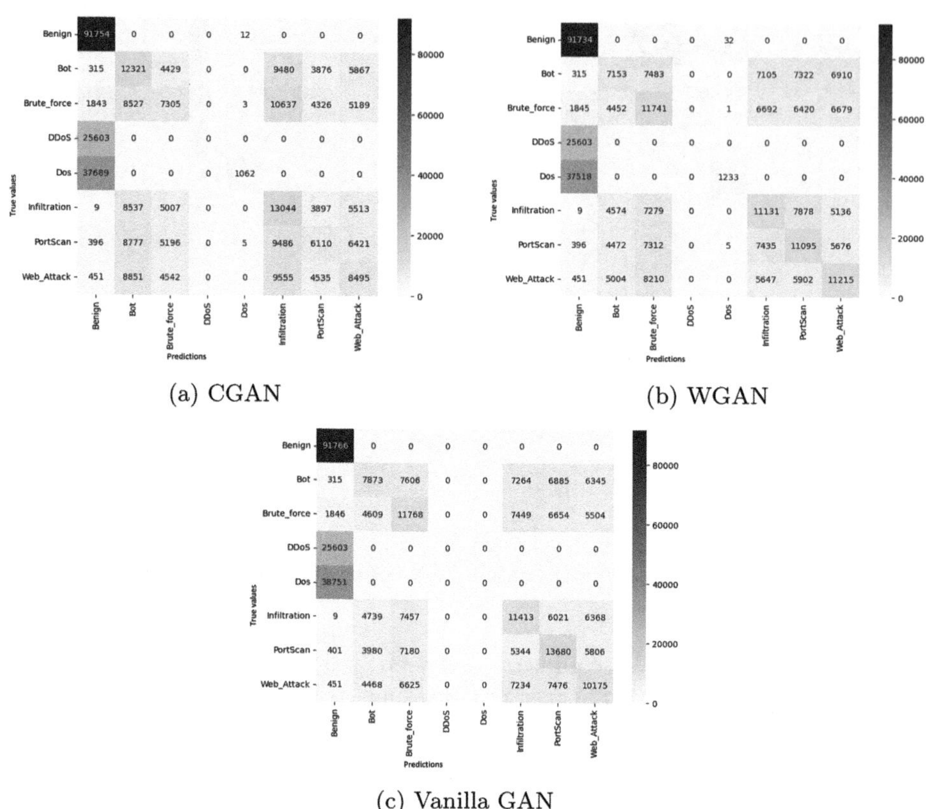

(a) CGAN

(b) WGAN

(c) Vanilla GAN

Fig. 5. Confusion matrices on CICIDS after data augmentation.

Table 2. Classification performance on CICIDS dataset using CGAN, WGAN, and Vanilla GAN.

Class	CGAN			WGAN			Vanilla GAN		
	Prec.	Rec.	F1	Prec.	Rec.	F1	Prec.	Rec.	F1
Benign	0.58	1.00	0.73	0.58	1.00	0.73	0.58	1.00	0.73
Bot	0.26	0.34	0.30	0.28	0.20	0.23	0.31	0.22	0.25
Brute Force	0.28	0.19	0.23	0.28	0.31	0.29	0.29	0.31	0.30
DDoS	0.00	0.00	0.00	0.00	0.00	0.00	0.00	0.00	0.00
DoS	0.98	0.03	0.05	0.97	0.03	0.06	0.00	0.00	0.00
Infiltration	0.25	0.36	0.30	0.29	0.31	0.30	0.29	0.32	0.31
PortScan	0.27	0.17	0.21	0.29	0.30	0.30	0.34	0.38	0.35
Web Attack	0.27	0.23	0.25	0.31	0.31	0.31	0.30	0.28	0.29
Accuracy	0.41			0.43			0.43		
Macro Avg	0.36	0.29	0.26	0.38	0.31	0.28	0.26	0.31	0.28
Weighted Avg	0.41	0.41	0.34	0.42	0.43	0.36	0.32	0.43	0.36

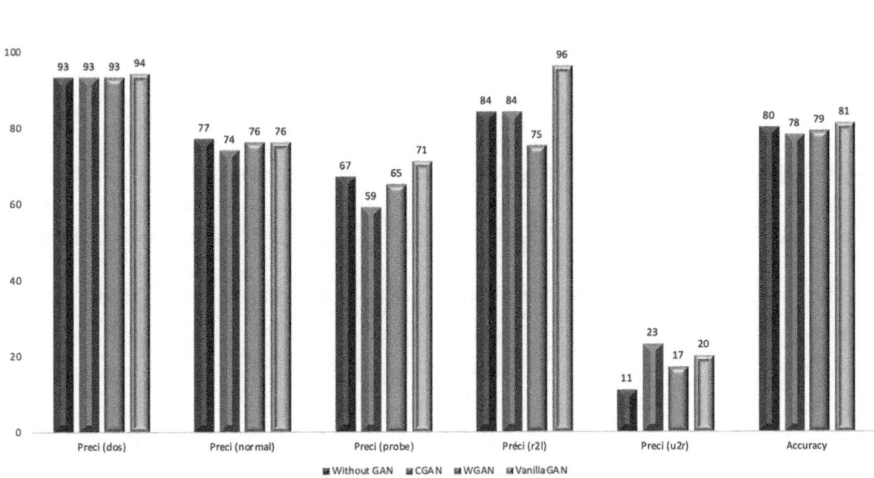

Fig. 6. Performance summary of each GAN type by attack category on NSL-KDD. Vanilla GAN achieved the best balance across classes.

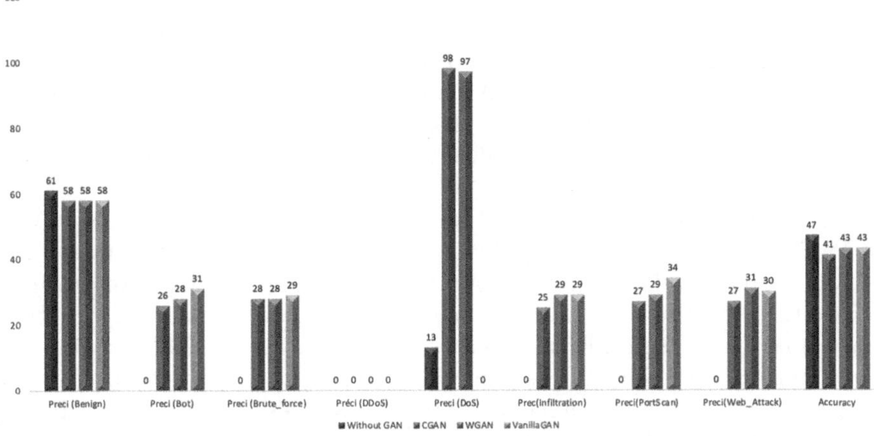

Fig. 7. Performance summary of each GAN type on CICIDS. WGAN and CGAN contributed most to rare class detection.

Tables 3 and 4 present a comparison of GAN models with our proposed system on NSL-KDD and CICIDS datasets, respectively, demonstrating that GAN-based augmentation effectively improved rare attack detection across both datasets. While Vanilla GAN achieved superior performance on NSL-KDD and CGAN/WGAN showed better improvements on CICIDS, the observed trade-off with overall accuracy emphasizes the critical need for attack-specific model selection, which our ensemble mechanism directly addresses.

Table 3. Comparison of GAN Types on NSL-KDD Dataset using model selection.

GAN Type	Prec. (DoS)	Prec. (Normal)	Prec. (Probe)	Prec. (R2L)	Prec. (U2R)	Accuracy
Without GAN	93%	77%	67%	84%	11%	80%
CGAN	93%	74%	59%	84%	23%	78%
WGAN	93%	76%	65%	75%	17%	79%
Vanilla GAN	94%	76%	71%	96%	20%	81%
EL-GAN (Our Proposal)	Vanilla GAN	Without GAN	Vanilla GAN	Vanilla GAN	CGAN	Vanilla GAN

Table 4. Comparison of GAN Types on CICIDS Dataset using model selection.

GAN Type	Prec. (Benign)	Prec. (Bot)	Prec. (Brute Force)	Prec. (DDoS)
Without GAN	61%	0%	0%	0%
CGAN	58%	26%	28%	0%
WGAN	58%	28%	28%	0%
Vanilla GAN	58%	31%	29%	0%
EL-GAN (Ours)	Without GAN	Vanilla GAN	Vanilla GAN	N/A

5 Conclusion

The rise of cyber threats and the increasing complexity of network environments, driven by the exponential evolution of technology, call for a reassessment of traditional intrusion detection systems. Although effective in classical contexts, these systems now show limitations when facing emerging attacks. In this context, approaches based on generative artificial intelligence, particularly GANs, offer a promising avenue.

This work evaluated the impact of three GAN variants (CGAN, WGAN, and Vanilla GAN) on intrusion detection using two widely used datasets: NSL-KDD and CICIDS. The results demonstrate that employing GANs can indeed improve the detection of certain underrepresented attack classes in the original data, notably u2r, r2l, Infiltration, and Brute force. For the NSL-KDD dataset, data augmentation using GANs sometimes led to an increase in overall accuracy (especially with the Vanilla GAN), while for the CICIDS dataset, although the overall accuracy decreased, the ability to detect rare attacks that were previously undetected significantly improved. Ensemble learning enables improved performance by leveraging the most appropriate GAN type according to the specific attack category. In future work, we intend to evaluate the scalability of the framework in large-scale, real-world IoT deployments, and to integrate continual learning mechanisms for adapting to emerging attack patterns without requiring complete retraining.

References

1. IDC: Worldwide global IoT connectivity forecast, 2023–2027 (2023), projects 41.6 billion IoT devices by 2025 (2023). https://www.idc.com/getdoc.jsp?containerId=prUS50446523

2. Statista: Number of internet of things (IoT) connected devices worldwide from 2019 to 2030. Statistical Report, 2024, estimates 29 billion IoT devices by 2030. https://www.statista.com/statistics/1183457/iot-connected-devices-worldwide/
3. Ericsson: Ericsson mobility report, forecasts 35 billion IoT connections by 2028. https://www.ericsson.com/en/reports-and-papers/mobility-report (2023)
4. Alsoufi, M.A., et al.: Anomaly-based intrusion detection systems in IoT using deep learning: a systematic literature review. Appl. Sci. **11**(18), 8383 (2021)
5. Arnaboldi, L., Morisset, C.: A review of intrusion detection systems and their evaluation in the IoT. arXiv preprint arXiv:2105.08096 (2021)
6. Abdelkhalek, A., Mashaly, M.: Addressing the class imbalance problem in network intrusion detection systems using data resampling and deep learning. J. Supercomput. **79**(10), 10611–10644 (2023)
7. Rani, M., Gagandeep: Effective network intrusion detection by addressing class imbalance with deep neural networks multimedia tools and applications. Multimedia Tools Appl. **81**(6), 8499–8518 (2022)
8. Goodfellow, I., et al.: Generative adversarial networks. Commun. ACM **63**(11), 139–144 (2020)
9. Zhao, X., Fok, K.W., Thing, V.L.L.: Enhancing network intrusion detection performance using generative adversarial networks (2024). https://arxiv.org/abs/2404.07464
10. Liu, L., Wang, J., Li, J.: A CGAN-based DDOS attack detection method in SDN. IEEE Trans. Netw. Serv. Manage., 1030–1034 (2021)
11. Golda, A., et al.:Privacy and security concerns in generative AI: a comprehensive survey. IEEE Access **12**, 48126–48144 (2024)
12. Zhu, B., Mu, N., Jiao, J., Wagner, D.: Generative AI Security: Challenges and Countermeasures (2024). https://arxiv.org/abs/2402.12617
13. Murmu, A., Kumar, P., Rao Moparthi, N., Namasudra, S., Lorenz, P.: Reliable federated learning with GAN model for robust and resilient future healthcare system. IEEE Trans. Netw. Serv. Manage. **21**(5), 5335–5346 (2024)
14. Mohebbanaaz, M., Jyothirmai, K., Mounika, E.S., Mounika, B.: Detection and identification of fake images using conditional generative adversarial networks (CGANS). IEEE Trans. Netw. Serv. Manage., 606–610 (2024)

Machine and Deep Learning for Indoor UWB Jammer Localization

Hamed Fard[1](✉), Mahsa Kholghi[2], Benedikt Groß[1], and Gerhard Wunder[1]

[1] Freie Universität Berlin, Berlin, Germany
{h.habibi.fard,benedikt.gross,g.wunder}@fu-berlin.de
[2] Ruhr Universität Bochum, Bochum, Germany
mahsa.kholghi@rub.de

Abstract. Ultra-wideband (UWB) localization delivers centimeter-scale accuracy but is vulnerable to jamming attacks, creating security risks for asset tracking and intrusion detection in smart buildings. Although ML and DL methods have improved tag localization, localizing malicious jammers within a single room and across changing indoor layouts remains largely unexplored. Two novel UWB datasets, collected under original and modified room configurations, are introduced to establish comprehensive ML/DL baselines. Performance is rigorously evaluated using a variety of classification and regression metrics. On the source dataset with the collected UWB features, Random Forest achieves the highest F1-macro score of 0.95 and XGBoost achieves the lowest mean Euclidean error of 20.16 cm. However, deploying these source-trained models in the modified room layout led to severe performance degradation, with XGBoost's mean Euclidean error increasing tenfold to 207.99 cm, demonstrating significant domain shift. To mitigate this degradation, a domain-adversarial ConvNeXt autoencoder (A-CNT) is proposed that leverages a gradient-reversal layer to align CIR-derived features across domains. The A-CNT framework restores localization performance by reducing the mean Euclidean error to 34.67 cm. This represents a 77% improvement over non-adversarial transfer learning and an 83% improvement over the best baseline, restoring the fraction of samples within 30 cm to 0.56. Overall, the results demonstrate that adversarial feature alignment enables robust and transferable indoor jammer localization despite environmental changes. Code and dataset available at https://github.com/afbf4c8996f/Jammer-Loc

Keywords: Jammer Localization · Deep Learning · Adversarial Domain Adaptation · Indoor UWB Jammer Dataset

1 Introduction

Ultra-wideband (UWB) ranging provides centimeter-scale accuracy for real-time positioning, yet its reliance on short-duration pulses and correlation-based

K. Adi et al. (Eds.): CRiSIS 2025, LNCS 16295, pp. 100–115, 2026.
https://doi.org/10.1007/978-3-032-20732-6_7

receivers makes it vulnerable to jamming attacks [20,27]. Robust and secure UWB localization is thus critical for applications such as asset tracking in restricted facilities and intrusion detection in smart buildings. Localization methods leveraging angle-of-arrival (AoA), time-of-flight (ToF), and received signal strength indicator (RSSI) have been extensively studied [1,6,28].

More recently, machine learning (ML) and deep learning (DL) approaches have been applied to UWB localization tasks, primarily focusing on classifying line-of-sight (LOS) vs non-line-of-sight (NLOS) conditions or regressing coordinates using features derived from channel impulse responses (CIR) [3,10]. However, these studies exhibit two critical limitations. First, existing research typically targets localization of legitimate tags rather than malicious jamming sources. Second, the challenge of maintaining model performance across varied physical environments has received relatively limited attention within these ML and DL frameworks. Consequently, robust and domain-invariant jammer localization has not been sufficiently explored.

This paper addresses these gaps through systematic investigation. First, performance baselines are established using ML and DL models trained on a newly collected source dataset, demonstrating strong results for both classification and regression. This initial benchmarking is critical, as models that do not achieve satisfactory performance in the source environment might lack the informative feature representations required for successful adaptation to different settings. Given the greater practical importance of accurate jammer localization, regression models are subsequently evaluated on a second dataset to formally quantify performance degradation caused by domain shift. To mitigate this degradation, a domain-adversarial neural network (DANN) framework [7] is adapted, utilizing a denoising ConvNeXt autoencoder [14] to learn compact CIR-derived feature representations and a gradient-reversal layer [7] to promote domain-invariant learning.

The main contributions of this work are:

1. Introduce two UWB datasets that include diagnostic features and raw CIR taps recorded in the same room on different days, initially and after changing the room setup.
2. Establish comprehensive classification and regression baselines using diagnostic features, supported by automated hyperparameter optimization and interpretability analyses (SHAP [16], mutual information, eta-squared (η^2)).
3. Adapt a domain-adversarial ConvNeXt autoencoder framework to align CIR-derived features across source and target domains, mitigating domain shift effects.
4. Compared the proposed domain-adversarial ConvNeXt autoencoder against its non-adversarial counterpart and two unsupervised domain adaptation baselines (CORAL [22] and MMD [15]) to quantify the benefits of adversarial alignment.

The remainder of this paper is organized as follows. Section 2 reviews related work. Section 3 describes the threat model and experimental setup. Section 4 presents the baseline methods, feature extraction, hyperparameter optimization, and the domain-adversarial framework. Section 5 reports experimental results. Section 6 concludes and outlines future work.

2 Related Work

Prior research on UWB jammer localization has concentrated on detecting and correcting jammed range measurements. For example, [11] addresses simulated jamming by classifying corrupted ranges with K-nearest neighbors and correcting them using neural networks. Similarly, [18] proposed a trustworthiness score derived from an autoencoder and evaluated robustness under jamming conditions using a publicly available UWB dataset released by those authors. These approaches, however, focus on mitigating specific interference scenarios without addressing generalization to unseen environments.

Domain adaptation techniques have also been explored to tackle distribution shifts between diverse environments or conditions in UWB localization. These methods address either regression tasks (estimating location parameters) or classification tasks (NLOS identification or location prediction). For regression, an adversarial bi-regressor network is utilized, leveraging multi-modal RF data, including UWB, to address layout changes through adversarial training [25]. In another domain generalization method, regression tasks such as ranging error and AoA estimation are performed by extracting domain-invariant features through domain adversarial training combined with mutual information estimation [26]. For classification tasks, a dual-domain MLP-Mixer framework is applied, employing domain alignment strategies achieved by minimizing a combined loss consisting of classification, weight regularization, and Maximum Mean Discrepancy (MMD) terms [12]. Additionally, CIR-based domain adaptive methods have been proposed for UWB NLOS classification (identification), wherein domain mappings are used to align source and target CIRs by jointly minimizing domain shifts, marginal distribution divergence, and conditional distribution divergence using the MMD criterion [17]. However, existing domain adaptation techniques in UWB localization primarily address the task of locating benign tags under distribution shifts or layout changes. To the best of our knowledge, robust localization of UWB jammers under such challenging conditions has not yet been specifically explored in existing literature.

3 Threat Model and Experimental Setup

3.1 Threat Model

The threat model assumes an attacker seeking to disrupt UWB-based localization. While UWB communication is often considered jamming-resistant due to its wide bandwidth, this assumption can be invalidated by practical hardware limitations. The DWM3001CDK development kits[1] used in this work, for example, support only UWB channels 5 and 9. An adversary aware that all anchor

[1] Documentation available at https://www.qorvo.com/products/p/DWM3001CDK#documents.

nodes operate on the 6.5 GHz front end (channel 5) can launch a highly effective, targeted jamming attack.

The adversary is assumed to employ a DW3000-series transceiver, identical to those of the receivers (anchors), configured to transmit continuous UWB frames at maximum regulatory power. This is implemented via a simple firmware loop in C using the Decawave API. The attacker gains knowledge of channel parameters, including data rate, preamble length, and synchronization codes, through a packet-sniffing algorithm as presented in [27]. The attacker possesses no specialized hardware advantages or advanced capabilities such as beamforming. Unlike conventional UWB-based tag localization, which assumes interference-free reception and relies on clean signals for position estimation, jammer localization is more challenging due to the reduced effective signal-to-noise ratio and the need to distinguish overlapping transmissions. Under these conditions, the goal of the localization system is to determine the jammer's two-dimensional position, given that each anchor node receives a superposition of legitimate tag pulses and continuous jamming frames.

3.2 Experimental Setup

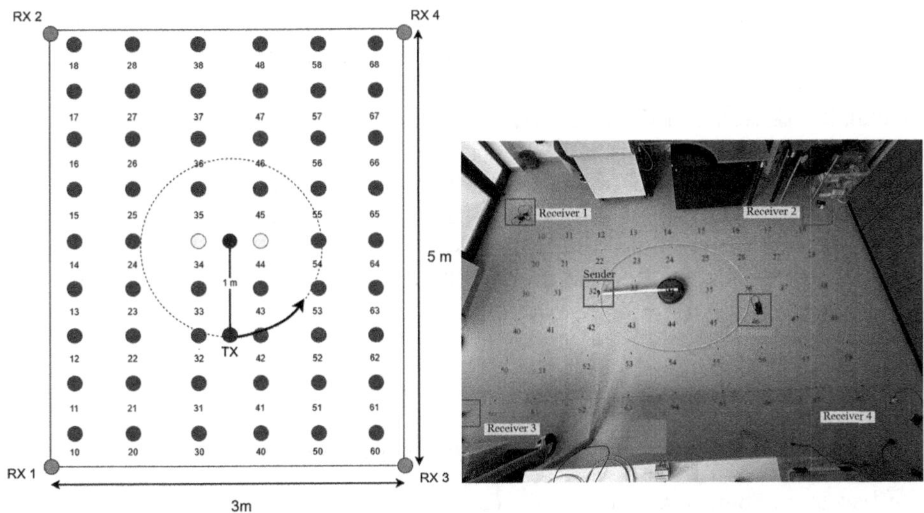

Fig. 1. Left: Schematic layout of the experimental environment showing the positions of the four UWB receivers (RX 1–4), the transmitter (TX) mounted on a TurtleBot robot with a 1 m extension arm, and the 52 distinct jammer positions (red dots) within a 3 m×5 m area. Right: The actual indoor setup, with the sender (TX), receivers (RX), and marked jammer locations on the floor corresponding to the schematic. (Color figure online)

Environment and Configurations. Experiments were conducted in an indoor laboratory over a 3 m × 5 m test grid. To study the effect of domain shift, data was collected in two distinct environmental configurations. The source domain consisted of the initial laboratory environment with standard furniture, where data was collected at 52 predefined jammer locations. For the target domain, the environment was perturbed by moving two desks, one chair, and several smaller objects outside the test grid. Data was then collected at 16 new, randomly selected jammer locations to simulate deployment in a different layout. The jammer positions for the source domain are illustrated in Fig. 1, while those for the target domain appear on the right side of Fig. 4.

Hardware Components. Four UWB receivers were positioned at the corners of the test grid. A legitimate UWB transmitter (tag) was mounted on a TurtleBot mobile robot via a 1 m extension arm. A separate DW3000-series transceiver, identical to the receivers, served as the interference source (jammer). Both the legitimate tag and the jammer operated in High Pulse Repetition (HPR) mode at standardized power levels.

Data Collection Protocol. The data collection followed a precise, automated protocol for each jammer position. First, the jammer was placed at a predefined (x, y) location on the grid and began transmitting continuously. Next, to simulate a dynamic operational environment with varying signal paths, the TurtleBot carrying the legitimate tag executed a full 360° rotation at the center of the grid while emitting packets at 10 ms intervals. During this rotation, each of the four receiver nodes recorded per-corner diagnostic readings from the DW3000 registers and the raw CIR taps. The collected measurements were subsequently annotated with the ground-truth (x, y) coordinates of the stationary jammer. This entire process was repeated for all 52 jammer positions in the source domain and all 16 positions in the target domain, resulting in two distinct datasets for training and evaluation. Data collection resulted in 461, 795 samples for the source domain and 28, 793 samples for the target domain. The dataset will be made publicly available.

4 Methodology

4.1 Feature Engineering and Data Preprocessing

For baseline experiments on the source dataset, numeric diagnostic features from the DW3000 transceivers (described in Table 1) were normalized using a standard scaler fitted to the training set. Scaler parameters from training were directly applied to validation, test, and target datasets. For the DANN pipeline, complex CIR samples were separately preprocessed. Each sample, originally comprising 300 taps, was converted into magnitude, sine phase, and cosine phase, truncated to the first 100 taps, and normalized using a standard scaler fitted jointly to source and target datasets. Truncation to 100 taps was applied after preliminary experiments indicated that tap sequences longer than 100 taps degraded model performance and introduced excessive noise. No other feature preprocessing techniques were applied beyond those described above, thereby preserving the generality of the pipeline.

Table 1. DW3000 Feature Descriptions

Feature	Description
PHE	Diagnostic reading for PHY-header error detection.
RSL	Diagnostic reading for Reed–Solomon decoding failures.
CRCG	Diagnostic reading for CRC/FCS integrity passes.
CRCB	Diagnostic reading for CRC/FCS integrity failures.
PREJ	Diagnostic reading for preamble rejection occurrences.
RSSI	Received signal strength (in dBm) as reported by the DW3000 diagnostics.
IpatovPeak	Amplitude of the strongest path detected in the channel impulse response.
IpatovPower	Total energy measured over the channel impulse response window.
IpatovF1	Early-time CIR energy measurement used to help locate the first-path.
IpatovF2	Mid-time CIR energy measurement used to refine the first-path timing estimate.
IpatovF3	Late-time CIR energy measurement used to further sharpen the first-path timing estimate.
CMPLX_CIR	Raw complex CIR vector of 300 taps.

4.2 Baseline Models: Machine and Deep Learning Approaches

Baseline models included Random Forest (RF), XGBoost (XGB), and K-Nearest Neighbors (KNN), as well as three deep learning models: SimpleNN (fully-connected residual network [9]), ConvMixer1D (CNN using depthwise convolutions [4] to mix channel-wise features), and Transformer Tabular (encoder-only transformer [23] without positional encoding). To ensure fair comparisons, hyperparameters for each ML and DL model were separately optimized for classification and regression tasks using Bayesian optimization with Optuna [2]. Optimal hyperparameters, such as learning rates, network size, number of epochs, and other training details, are determined by the code in our public repository.

4.3 Adversarial Domain Adaptation

Motivation. Domain shift refers to differences between source and target domain data distributions, which typically cause significant performance degradation when models trained in one domain are applied to another [5,21]. Such discrepancies challenge the robustness and generalization of deployed models. Unsupervised Domain Adaptation (UDA) methods tackle this issue by transferring knowledge from labeled source domain data to unlabeled or sparsely labeled target domain data [13,24]. Domain-adversarial approaches specifically aim at learning domain-invariant representations, improving model adaptability and generalization across domains [8]. A significant performance degradation was observed in this study when models trained and validated on the source dataset were evaluated on the target dataset, as will be shown in Sect. 5. To address this challenge, a domain-adversarial neural network (DANN) utilizing a denoising ConvNeXt autoencoder is employed. The autoencoder explicitly learns robust, domain-invariant representations, reducing domain discrepancy between source and target domains.

Model Architecture. The autoencoder is a compact, lightweight ConvNeXt-based architecture designed explicitly for processing CIR data. It takes as input 100 CIR taps with three channels (magnitude, sine phase, cosine phase). The encoder progressively compresses the input via three convolutional downsampling blocks, increasing channels from 3 to 128, with intermediate ConvNeXt residual blocks featuring layer normalization, depthwise convolutions, and GELU activations. Gaussian noise ($\sigma = 0.6$) is explicitly injected into encoder activations to promote robustness to input perturbations and prevent trivial identity mappings. The decoder symmetrically mirrors the encoder structure, utilizing transpose convolutional layers to restore the input dimensionality back to its original form. In total, the autoencoder comprises 782,211 parameters, making it efficient and suitable for resource-constrained scenarios.

Gradient Reversal Layer (GRL). The GRL [7] is inserted between the encoder and the domain classifier in the denoising ConvNeXt autoencoder pipeline. During the forward pass it passes the encoder's feature embeddings unchanged, but in backpropagation it multiplies the domain classifier's gradients by $-\lambda$. This gradient inversion encourages the encoder to learn features that are uninformative for domain discrimination, thereby aligning source and target feature distributions.

Domain Classifier. The domain classifier distinguishes source from target domain features, enabling adversarial alignment. Its architecture comprises two fully connected layers (128 and 64 units, respectively) with ReLU activations, followed by an output layer with sigmoid activation to predict domain labels.

Regression Head. The regression head predicts continuous target variables (i.e., coordinates). It is implemented as a single fully-connected linear layer that maps the shared encoder representation directly to the regression targets without intermediate activations.

Training Procedure. Training consists of three phases:

Autoencoder Pre-training. The ConvNeXt autoencoder is pre-trained exclusively on unlabeled source-domain data. This unsupervised training minimizes reconstruction loss between Gaussian-noise-injected inputs ($\sigma = 0.6$) and actual clean signals. Training occurs over 30 epochs with an initial learning rate of $1e-3$, progressively adjusted using linear warmup followed by cosine annealing.

Joint Adversarial Alignment. The pre-trained autoencoder undergoes adversarial alignment using data without class labels from both source and target domains, with domain labels used only for adversarial training. The model jointly minimizes reconstruction loss on target data and domain-classification loss via a gradient reversal layer, with the reversal strength parameter (λ) following a sigmoid schedule from 0.05 to 0.2 over 40 epochs. Domain-classifier performance is monitored using AUC, which initially increases to 0.66 and then gradually decreases as alignment progresses. Early stopping is triggered at epoch 18 based on AUC stagnation, with the score reaching 0.5145 and indicating convergence toward domain confusion, while reconstruction loss remains stable.

Fine-Tuning. Fine-tuning employs labeled target-domain data for supervised regression of spatial coordinates. Only the autoencoder's final encoder stage, decoder layers, final convolution layer, and the regression head are unfrozen. The domain classifier remains active during fine-tuning, acting as a regularizer to maintain domain-invariant feature representations. Training minimizes a combined loss composed of reconstruction loss, regression loss and adversarial domain loss. Over 200 epochs, hyperparameters α and λ_{ft} are progressively adjusted (from 0.5 to 0.1 and from 0.0 to 0.5, respectively), while β remains constant at 1.0. Cosine annealing schedulers are used for both the regression head and autoencoder learning rates. Training continues until performance plateaus, explicitly evaluated on a dedicated hold-out set for unbiased assessment of adaptation effectiveness. The key quantities described above for the fine-tuning phase are plotted in Fig. 2. In Fig. 2(a), the reconstruction loss L_{rec}, regression loss L_{reg} and adversarial domain loss L_{dom} are shown over 200 epochs to illustrate their evolution during fine-tuning. Figure 2(b) displays the annealing schedules for the reconstruction weight α and adversarial weight λ_{ft}.

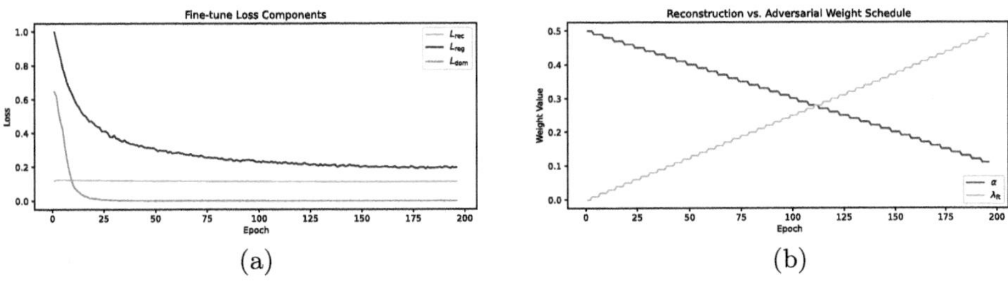

Fig. 2. Fine-tuning convergence over 200 epochs: (a) loss components L_{rec}, L_{reg}, L_{dom}; (b) weight schedules for α and λ_{ft}

Formalization of Loss Components. To summarize the losses utilized at each training phase mathematically, the following equations define reconstruction, regression, and adversarial losses employed (Eqs. 1-7). In these equations, x_i^t denotes unlabeled samples from the target domain, x_j^s denotes unlabeled samples from the source domain, and x_i denotes labeled target-domain samples used for supervised fine-tuning. The terms N_t, N_s, and N_c represent the respective number of samples in these sets. $AE_\theta(\cdot)$ is the ConvNeXt autoencoder, and $f_\theta(\cdot)$ indicates the autoencoder's learned feature extractor (bottleneck representation). $D_\phi(\cdot)$ represents the domain classifier, while $R_\psi(\cdot)$ is the regression head predicting spatial coordinates. Finally, $\mathrm{GRL}_\lambda(\cdot)$ denotes the Gradient Reversal Layer, which acts as an identity function during forward propagation and reverses gradients scaled by $-\lambda$ during backpropagation.

$$\mathcal{L}_{\text{rec}} = \frac{1}{N_t}\sum_{i=1}^{N_t}\left\|AE_\theta(x_i^t) - x_i^t\right\|_2^2, \tag{1}$$

$$\mathcal{L}_{\text{dom}} = \frac{1}{N_s + N_t}\left[\sum_{j=1}^{N_s}\mathrm{BCE}\big(D_\phi(\mathrm{GRL}_\lambda(f_\theta(x_j^s))), 0\big) + \sum_{i=1}^{N_t}\mathrm{BCE}\big(D_\phi(\mathrm{GRL}_\lambda(f_\theta(x_i^t))), 1\big)\right], \tag{2}$$

$$\mathcal{L}_{\text{adapt}} = \mathcal{L}_{\text{rec}} + \lambda\,\mathcal{L}_{\text{dom}}, \tag{3}$$

$$\mathcal{L}_{\text{rec}}^{\text{ft}} = \frac{1}{N_c}\sum_{i=1}^{N_c}\left\|AE_\theta(x_i) - x_i\right\|_2^2, \tag{4}$$

$$\mathcal{L}_{\text{reg}} = \frac{1}{N_c}\sum_{i=1}^{N_c}\left\|R_\psi(f_\theta(x_i)) - y_i\right\|_2^2, \tag{5}$$

$$\mathcal{L}_{\text{dom}}^{\text{ft}} = \frac{1}{N_c}\sum_{i=1}^{N_c}\mathrm{BCE}\big(D_\phi(\mathrm{GRL}_{\lambda_{\text{ft}}}(f_\theta(x_i))), 0\big), \tag{6}$$

$$\mathcal{L}_{\text{ft}} = \alpha\,\mathcal{L}_{\text{rec}}^{\text{ft}} + \beta\,\mathcal{L}_{\text{reg}} + \lambda_{\text{ft}}\,\mathcal{L}_{\text{dom}}^{\text{ft}}. \tag{7}$$

Evaluation Metrics. Experiments report total runtime in minutes (Time) and the following regression performance metrics: mean, median, and 90th percentile (P90) of Euclidean distance errors between predicted and actual spatial coordinates (in centimeters), the fraction of predictions within 30 cm ($F_{\leq 30\text{cm}}$), and root mean squared error (rmse), mean absolute error (mae), and coefficient of determination (R^2) computed separately for each spatial axis (x, y) to quantify anisotropic prediction quality.

4.4 Implementation and Computational Resources

Experiments ran on a 64-bit Debian GNU/Linux 12 workstation with an Intel Core i9-10980XE CPU, 32 GB RAM, and an NVIDIA RTX A5500 GPU (24 GB VRAM), using PyTorch.

5 Experiments and Results

Classification on Source Dataset. The goal of this experiment is to evaluate the classification performance of various ML and DL models when trained, validated, and tested solely on the source dataset. Table 2 shows that RF achieved an accuracy of 0.95 and an F1-macro of 0.95 in under 3 min, followed by XGB with 0.94 accuracy and F1-macro in the same time frame. The Transformer model reached 0.93 accuracy in 34 minutes, S_NN obtained 0.91 in 11 minutes, and CM1D reached 0.78 in 13 minutes. By contrast, KNN achieved only 0.50 accuracy, likely because the large number of classes (52) dilutes neighbor density in the feature space. The close agreement between F1-macro and F1-weighted scores indicates balanced performance across all classes. These results demonstrate that classical ML models achieve competitive classification performance with substantially lower computational cost. Furthermore, the high and balanced scores confirm the utility of the diagnostic features for this task. Figure 3 shows the confusion matrices for the three DL models.

Table 2. Classification performance of models on source dataset (52 classes).

Model	Accuracy	F1-macro	F1-weighted	Precision	Recall	Time
CM1D	0.7797	0.7800	0.7797	0.7877	0.7803	13
S_NN	0.9144	0.9146	0.9143	0.9163	0.9142	11
Trans	0.9310	0.9313	0.9310	0.9318	0.9312	34
XGB	0.9381	0.9383	0.9380	0.9385	0.9383	**3.00**
RF	**0.95**	**0.95**	**0.95**	**0.95**	**0.95**	**3.00**
KNN	0.5041	0.5046	0.5044	0.5056	0.5040	6.00

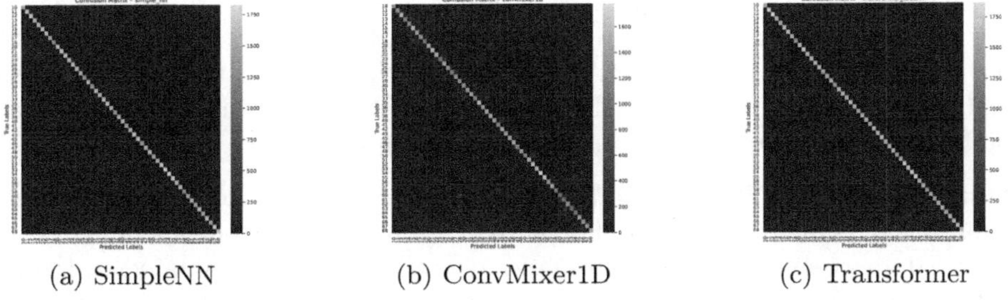

(a) SimpleNN (b) ConvMixer1D (c) Transformer

Fig. 3. Confusion matrices of the three deep learning models evaluated on the source dataset (52 classes).

Regression on Source Dataset. The goal of this experiment is to assess the regression performance of various ML and DL models for spatial localization when trained, validated, and tested solely on the source dataset. Table 3 shows that XGB achieved the lowest mean error (20.16 cm) and median error (10.54 cm) with $F_{\leq 30\text{cm}} = 0.80$ in 2 minutes. CM1D and S_NN both incurred mean errors near 28 cm and $F_{\leq 30\text{cm}} < 0.75$, indicating only moderate localization accuracy from these DL architectures. RF exhibited unbalanced axis errors with $\text{rmse}_X = 3.23$ cm and $\text{rmse}_Y = 59.90$ cm leading to a mean error of 43.15 cm and $F_{\leq 30\text{cm}} = 0.48$. The 90th-percentile error (P90) further underscores XGB's robustness (50.84 cm) compared to RF (100.60 cm) and the DL baselines. Across all models, $R^2_X \geq 0.99$ confirms a strong fit along the X axis whereas lower R^2_Y values reflect greater variance along the Y axis. These results suggest that in the source domain classical ML models, particularly XGB, outperform the deep architectures in both accuracy and robustness to outliers and do so with comparable or lower training times.

Table 3. Regression performance metrics for localization on the source dataset.

Model	rmse_X	rmse_Y	mae_X	mae_Y	R^2_X	R^2_Y	mean	med	P90	$F_{\leq 30\text{cm}}$	Time
CM1D	7.40	45.31	4.04	27.81	**0.99**	0.87	28.79	15.74	73.04	0.71	10
S_NN	16.80	45.40	5.97	26.08	0.96	0.87	28.23	13.37	73.35	0.74	4
Trans	15.83	46.60	7.14	29.48	0.96	0.87	31.86	17.92	76.46	0.68	17
XGB	4.51	**33.50**	2.43	**19.52**	**0.99**	**0.93**	**20.16**	**10.54**	**50.84**	**0.80**	**2**
RF	**3.23**	59.90	**0.73**	43.10	**0.99**	0.78	43.15	31.34	100.60	0.48	**2**

Feature Interpretability. The goal of this analysis is to identify which diagnostic readings influence localization error. Table 4 gives four importance measures: SHAP, XGBoost gain, mutual information and eta-squared. A mean rank across these measures shows the consensus ordering. The top four features in this ranking are RSL, PHE, PREJ and CRCB. The Ipatov-derived features and RSSI have lower importance. These results confirm the value of the core diagnostic features for localization. They also suggest that the lower ranking features could be removed in future work to reduce model complexity.

Domain Shift on Target Dataset. In this section, the robustness of source-trained models is evaluated under the new room layout. Models trained on the source dataset suffer severe performance degradation when evaluated on the target dataset after the room layout is changed. This domain shift is also visualized in Fig. 5 in the Appendix, where per-tap differences between source and target features are measured using the Wasserstein distance [19] and the absolute difference in normalized means. Table 5 shows that XGB's mean error rose from 20.16 cm to 207.99 cm and $F_{\leq 30\text{cm}}$ fell from 0.80 to 0.03. CM1D and S_NN exhibited similar failures with mean errors above 200 cm and negative axis-wise R^2

Table 4. Feature-level importance metrics for the XGBoost regressor predicting Euclidean distance. Lower mean-rank indicates higher feature importance.

Feature	SHAP	XGB Imp.	Mutual Info	Eta	Mean Rank
RSL	39.72	0.415	2.410	0.366	1.00
PHE	26.20	0.232	2.197	0.268	2.25
PREJ	27.34	0.124	1.297	0.148	3.25
CRCB	8.03	0.209	1.080	0.250	3.50
CRCG	3.90	0.009	0.082	0.066	5.00
RSSI	0.95	0.006	0.009	0.017	7.00
IpatovPeak	0.45	0.001	0.010	0.045	7.25
IpatovF3	0.35	0.002	0.002	0.024	8.00
IpatovPower	0.29	0.001	0.002	0.018	9.00
IpatovF1	0.30	0.001	0.007	0.013	9.00
IpatovF2	0.19	0.001	0.002	0.016	10.75

Table 5. Localization performance on the target dataset for models trained exclusively on the source domain and for those employing domain adaptation.

Model	$rmse_X$	$rmse_Y$	mae_X	mae_Y	R^2_X	R^2_Y	mean	med	P90	$F_{\leq 30cm}$
CM1D	127.18	200.91	101.56	165.20	−1.24	−1.37	208.95	199.14	376.82	0.02
S-NN	140.04	223.63	117.62	194.18	−1.71	−1.94	241.75	243.29	393.52	0.02
Trans	142.08	208.93	116.01	174.42	−1.79	−1.57	225.22	221.44	381.16	0.03
XGB	128.16	193.96	103.90	161.15	−1.27	−1.21	207.99	193.57	361.27	0.03
RF	125.86	169.46	102.69	139.26	−1.19	−0.69	188.35	175.14	344.50	0.00
Coral	102.34	165.33	84.44	137.40	−0.45	−0.61	173.90	166.55	300.60	0.02
MMD	100.39	163.37	82.69	135.71	−0.39	−0.57	171.59	163.27	296.43	0.02
CNT	85.51	140.38	74.25	117.41	−0.01	−0.16	148.02	142.61	249.05	0.03
A-CNT	**24.74**	**38.63**	**16.60**	**27.54**	**0.92**	**0.91**	**34.67**	**26.62**	**69.03**	**0.56**

values indicating performance below that of a constant-mean predictor. These results confirm the severity of the domain shift induced by layout change.

Domain Adaptation. To compare adaptation strategies using CIR features, classical UDA methods (CORAL and MMD) were compared against a non-adversarial method (CNT) and its adversarial variant (A-CNT). While all four methods shared the same encoder, their overall architectures differed: CORAL and MMD used encoder-only models with feature alignment, whereas CNT and A-CNT employed the same autoencoder architecture. The only distinction between CNT and A-CNT was the use of gradient reversal for adversarial alignment in the latter. CORAL and MMD reduced mean error relative to source-only training (e.g., to 173.90 cm with CORAL), while CNT achieved further improvement with 148.02 cm. This suggests that the compact representations learned by the autoencoder may generalize better across domains than shallow feature alignment alone. A-CNT achieved the best performance, with a mean error of 34.67 cm and R^2 scores of 0.92 and 0.91. These results indicate that classical UDA methods offer benefits over source-only training, but adversarial domain alignment yields significantly greater gains. Furthermore, to qualitatively assess the effect of adversarial domain adaptation, t-SNE plots are provided in the appendix (Fig. 6), visualizing the A-CNT model's feature representations both before and after applying the GRL.

To assess whether the domain-adversarially aligned feature representations truly capture the underlying spatial structure of jammer activity, the pooled bottleneck embeddings of the 3,000 hold-out samples were first partitioned into five zones by K-means clustering on their ground-truth (x, y) coordinates. A logistic regression classifier was then trained and evaluated using only these held-out embeddings, with 5-fold cross-validation to eliminate any bias from model adaptation. Across folds, the logistic regression achieved an average ROC-AUC of 0.9937 and an accuracy of 0.9283. In Fig. 4, the "×" markers denote the true centroids of each zone and marker size scales with the number of visits at that location. These results confirm that a simple linear decision boundary suffices to separate spatial regions in feature space and demonstrate that the learned representations not only align across domains but also preserve fine-grained spatial discriminability.

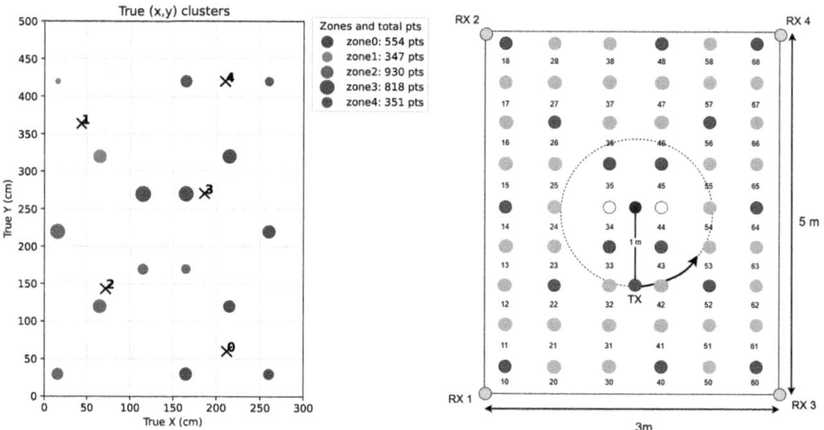

Fig. 4. Left: K-means clustering of the 3000 hold-out ground-truth (x, y) points into five spatial zones. Marker "×" shows each zone centroid and area is proportional to visit count. Right: Schematic of the modified experimental layout with four UWB receivers (RX 1–4), the TurtleBot-mounted transmitter (TX) on a 1 m arm, and the 16 jammer positions (red dots) in a 3 m×5 m area.

6 Conclusion

The challenge of UWB jammer localization in dynamic indoor environments was addressed in this study. It was demonstrated that traditional machine learning models, while effective in a static setting (achieving a mean Euclidean error of 20.16 cm), suffered catastrophic performance degradation when the room layout was altered, with errors increasing tenfold to 207.99 cm. This highlighted the severe impact of domain shift on UWB localization. To overcome this, a domain-adversarial ConvNeXt autoencoder (A-CNT) was proposed. This model was shown to effectively mitigate domain shift by aligning features across different environments. A localization error of 34.67 cm was achieved in the new environment, representing a significant 83 % improvement over the best source-trained baseline. Furthermore, it was shown that while other UDA methods offered benefits over source-only training, adversarial domain alignment yielded significantly greater gains. These findings underscored the necessity of adversarial learning for robust and transferable localization in dynamic, real-world settings. Future work should explore the extension of this research to 3D layouts, multiple rooms, and continuous domain adaptation.

Acknowledgments. HF and GW were supported by the Federal Ministry of Education and Research of Germany (BMBF) within "6G-RIC: 6G Research and Innovation Cluster", under project identification number 16KISK025, and the BMBF joint project "UltraSec: Security Architecture for UWB-based Application Platform", project identification number 16KIS1682. GW was supported by the German Science Foundation (DFG) within priority program SPP 2378: "ResNets: Resilience in Connected Worlds" under grant WU 598/12-1.

A Appendix

A.1 Domain Shift Visualization

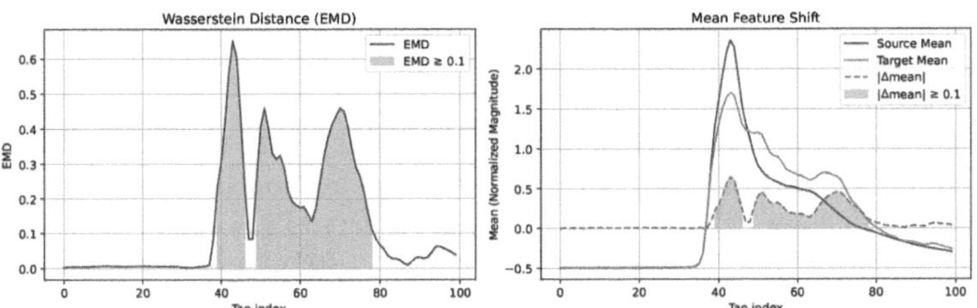

Fig. 5. Side-by-side visualization of domain shift across taps. Left: Per-tap Wasserstein distance (EMD), with shaded regions indicating multiple intervals where EMD ≥ 0.1. Right: Mean feature values for source and target domains, with shaded regions where the absolute difference $|\Delta\text{mean}| \geq 0.1$. A dashed green curve shows $|\Delta\text{mean}|$ per tap. Shaded areas are bounded by the actual metric values for visual fidelity.

A.2 t-SNE Visualization of Feature Alignment

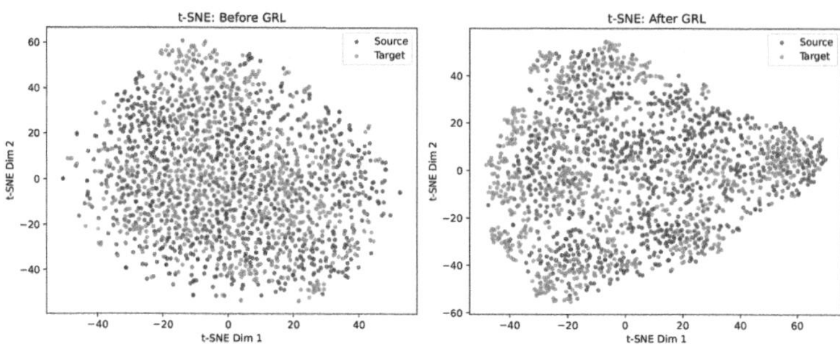

Fig. 6. t-SNE visualization of feature representations before and after adversarial domain adaptation. Pretraining results in initial domain overlap, while GRL reshapes the feature space to promote domain confusion. Although overlap in the projected space is reduced after adaptation, the learned representation leads to improved target generalization, demonstrating that improved generalization can occur even as feature distributions diverge in projection.

References

1. Aditya, S., Molisch, A.F., Behairy, H.M.: A survey on the impact of multipath on wideband time-of-arrival based localization. Proc. IEEE **106**(7), 1183–1203 (2018)
2. Akiba, T., Sano, S., Yanase, T., Ohta, T., Koyama, M.: OPTUNA: a next-generation hyperparameter optimization framework. In: Proceedings of the 25th ACM SIGKDD International Conference on Knowledge Discovery & Data Mining, pp. 2623–2631 (2019)
3. Bregar, K., Mohorčič, M.: Improving indoor localization using convolutional neural networks on computationally restricted devices. IEEE Access **6**, 17429–17441 (2018)
4. Chollet, F.: Xception: Deep learning with depthwise separable convolutions. In: Proceedings of the IEEE Conference on Computer Vision and Pattern Recognition, pp. 1251–1258 (2017)
5. Farahani, A., Voghoei, S., Rasheed, K., Arabnia, H.R.: A brief review of domain adaptation. In: Advances in Data Science and Information Engineering: Proceedings from ICDATA 2020 and IKE 2020, pp. 877–894 (2021)
6. Fischer, G.K., et al.: A systematic survey and comparative analysis of angular-based indoor localization and positioning technologies. IEEE Commun. Surv. Tutorials (2025)
7. Ganin, Y., et al.: Domain-adversarial training of neural networks. J. Mach. Learn. Res. **17**(59), 1–35 (2016)
8. HassanPour Zonoozi, M., Seydi, V.: A survey on adversarial domain adaptation. Neural Process. Lett. **55**(3), 2429–2469 (2023)
9. He, K., Zhang, X., Ren, S., Sun, J.: Deep residual learning for image recognition. In: Proceedings of the IEEE Conference on Computer Vision and Pattern Recognition, pp. 770–778 (2016)

10. Jiang, C., Shen, J., Chen, S., Chen, Y., Liu, D., Bo, Y.: UWB NLOS/LOS classification using deep learning method. IEEE Commun. Lett. **24**(10), 2226–2230 (2020)
11. Jun, L., Ruizhi, Z., Xiaofeng, S.: Precise positioning method of UWB in signal jamming. In: 2022 19th International Computer Conference on Wavelet Active Media Technology and Information Processing (ICCWAMTIP), pp. 1–4. IEEE (2022)
12. Li, L., Xing, Z., Guo, X., Zheng, H.: D-2MLOC: dual-domain MLP-mixer framework for CSI-fingerprinting indoor localization. IEEE Trans. Cognit. Commun. Netw. (2025)
13. Liu, X., et al.: Deep unsupervised domain adaptation: a review of recent advances and perspectives. APSIPA Trans. Sig. Inf. Process. **11**(1) (2022)
14. Liu, Z., Mao, H., Wu, C.Y., Feichtenhofer, C., Darrell, T., Xie, S.: A convnet for the 2020s. In: Proceedings of the IEEE/CVF Conference on Computer Vision and Pattern Recognition, pp. 11976–11986 (2022)
15. Long, M., Cao, Y., Wang, J., Jordan, M.: Learning transferable features with deep adaptation networks. In: International Conference on Machine Learning, pp. 97–105. PMLR (2015)
16. Lundberg, S.M., Lee, S.I.: A unified approach to interpreting model predictions. In: Advances in Neural Information Processing Systems, vol. 30 (2017)
17. Nkrow, R.E., Boshoff, D., Silva, B., Hancke, G.P.: Adalos: a domain adaptive UWB NLOS identification for dynamic settings. IEEE Internet Things J. (2025)
18. Peterseil, P., Etzlinger, B., Khanzadeh, R., Springer, A.: Trustworthiness score for UWB indoor localization. In: GLOBECOM 2023-2023 IEEE Global Communications Conference, pp. 189–194. IEEE (2023)
19. Peyré, G., Cuturi, M., et al.: Computational optimal transport: with applications to data science. Found. Trends® Mach. Learn. **11**(5-6), 355–607 (2019)
20. Poturalski, M., Flury, M., Papadimitratos, P., Hubaux, J.P., Le Boudec, J.Y.: The cicada attack: degradation and denial of service in IR ranging. In: 2010 IEEE International Conference on Ultra-Wideband, vol. 2, pp. 1–4. IEEE (2010)
21. Singhal, P., Walambe, R., Ramanna, S., Kotecha, K.: Domain adaptation: challenges, methods, datasets, and applications. IEEE Access **11**, 6973–7020 (2023)
22. Sun, B., Feng, J., Saenko, K.: Return of frustratingly easy domain adaptation. In: Proceedings of the AAAI Conference on Artificial Intelligence, vol. 30 (2016)
23. Vaswani, A., et al.: Attention is all you need. In: Advances in Neural Information Processing Systems, vol. 30 (2017)
24. Wilson, G., Cook, D.J.: A survey of unsupervised deep domain adaptation. ACM Trans. Intell. Syst. Technol. (TIST) **11**(5), 1–46 (2020)
25. Xia, H., Wang, P.P., Koike-Akino, T., Wang, Y., Orlik, P., Ding, Z.: Adversarial bi-regressor network for domain adaptive regression. arXiv preprint arXiv:2209.09943 (2022)
26. Xue, M., Xu, Z., Zhang, J., Wang, H., Shen, Y.: A generalization method for indoor localization via domain-invariant feature learning. IEEE Commun. Lett. (2025)
27. Yang, Y., et al.: UWBAD: towards effective and imperceptible jamming attacks against UWB ranging systems with cots chips. In: Proceedings of the 2024 on ACM SIGSAC Conference on Computer and Communications Security, pp. 3376–3390 (2024)
28. Yang, Z., Zhou, Z., Liu, Y.: From RSSI to CSI: Indoor localization via channel response. ACM Comput. Surv. (CSUR) **46**(2), 1–32 (2013)

Intrusion Detection Systems (IDS)

CAGAID: Context-Aware Gait Anomaly-Based Intrusion Detection

Youssef Yamout[1(✉)], Shahrear Iqbal[2], and Mohammad Zulkernine[1]

[1] Queen's University, Kingston, ON, Canada
21yhy@queensu.ca, mz@queensu.ca
[2] National Research Council, Fredericton, NB, Canada
shahrear.iqbal@nrc-cnrc.gc.ca

Abstract. Gait-based intrusion detection systems detect deviations from an authenticated user's baseline gait pattern to identify unauthorized access or data tampering attempts. Failure to detect these intrusions can lead to data breaches, unauthorized system access, and malicious system lockouts crippling critical operations. Existing approaches often produce false positives due to their inability to differentiate between security threats and benign gait variations. We introduce (CAGAID), a Context-Aware Gait Anomaly-Based Intrusion Detection System that captures sudden changes in gait signals and provides additional information to validate them by modeling temporal dependencies. This work utilizes environmental context (terrain slope variations and multi-point sensor placement), sensor context (accelerometer/gyroscope positioning), and user context (individual baseline patterns), to minimize false positives by enabling the system to account for natural gait variations under varying conditions. Contextual understanding ensures the detection system minimizes unnecessary security alerts while maintaining high sensitivity to genuine threats. For instance, the system can distinguish between normal gait variations caused by environmental factors and potential data tampering attempts. The experimental results demonstrate CAGAID's effectiveness and potential for dual use in security and health monitoring applications. The enhanced detection capability enables more reliable authentication, thereby mitigating security vulnerabilities while minimizing operational disruptions caused by false alarms.

Keywords: Gait Anomaly Detection · Attack Detection · Security Monitoring · Context-Aware Intrusion Detection

1 Introduction

Gait-based intrusion detection systems leverage an individual's walking style for continuous authentication and security monitoring [3]. When these systems fail to detect intrusions accurately, malicious actors can remotely lock residents out of their homes and tamper with security systems. A key challenge is differentiating between genuine security threats and benign gait variations that occur

K. Adi et al. (Eds.): CRiSIS 2025, LNCS 16295, pp. 119–135, 2026.
https://doi.org/10.1007/978-3-032-20732-6_8

naturally due to environmental factors or health-related conditions [1]. Gait's reliability as a biometric measure stems from its unique and complex pattern specific to each person, making it difficult to spoof [7,9]. However, the effectiveness of gait-based authentication systems depends heavily on the gait data collection and analysis method. Current approaches are classified into non-wearable [11] and wearable methods [13]. Non-wearable methods rely on external systems like cameras or floor sensors and offer passive detection but often require specific setups and are vulnerable to environmental tampering. In contrast, wearable methods utilize inertial sensors comprising accelerometers and gyroscopes, providing direct, continuous monitoring and enhanced security through proximity verification, though they may be susceptible to sensor-level attacks [19]. While researchers have traditionally focused on feature extraction and optimization using Inertial Measurement Unit (IMU) sensors, the complex nature of sensor data makes conventional feature estimation susceptible to adversarial manipulation [18]. These modern approaches show promise in addressing security concerns and the need for context-aware detection to distinguish between security intrusions and legitimate gait variations.

This paper introduces a Context-Aware Gait Anomaly-Based Intrusion Detection System (CAGAID) based on BiDirectional Long-Short-Term Memory (BiLSTM) networks and Convolutional Neural Networks (CNNs). CAGAID analyzes three-dimensional accelerometers and gyroscope data, commonly available in wearable devices like smartphones, smartwatches, and sensor bands. Unlike traditional methods that rely on manually extracted features vulnerable to manipulation, CAGAID employs deep learning to capture spatial and temporal dependencies in gait patterns. Unlike existing CNN-LSTM approaches that focus solely on pattern recognition, CAGAID introduces adaptive context-aware thresholding that dynamically adjusts detection sensitivity based on environmental conditions. The system integrates environmental and sensor context to generate accurate security alerts while minimizing false positives. Experimental results using open-source inertial gait datasets demonstrated that CAGAID achieved significantly higher attack detection rates when incorporating context awareness, particularly in identifying sensor manipulation attempts.

The rest of the paper is organized as follows. Section 2 reviews the related work across security, health, and dual-purpose systems. Section 3 presents the methodology by introducing CAGAID's architecture with its core components and implementing the detection and classification mechanisms. Section 4 describes the datasets utilized, the data preprocessing methods applied, and the approach for generating the attack dataset. Section 5 presents the experimental evaluation, and Sect. 6 summarizes the proposed work and outlines future research directions.

2 Related Work

Recent gait analysis systems primarily focus on security authentication [15, 17], health monitoring [2,14], or emerging dual-purpose applications [4,8].

Security-focused approaches demonstrate feasible real-time authentication and resource-efficient implementations but lack contextual awareness for distinguishing legitimate variations from attacks. Health-focused research emphasizes movement disorder detection through phase-specific analysis [14] and device-free monitoring [2] with no context. CAGAID addresses key limitations in existing works by combining security and health monitoring capabilities with comprehensive context awareness. Unlike previous approaches that focus on single applications, CAGAID follows a four-stage workflow: (1) continuous sensor data are segmented using sliding windows, (2) spatial-temporal features are extracted via a CNN-BiLSTM model with attention weighting, (3) context analysis assesses both environmental and sensor conditions, and (4) adaptive thresholding is applied to classify anomalies as either security threats or health-related events.

3 Methodology

CAGAID introduces a novel approach to detect security-related intrusions and health-related anomalies through several core components, as illustrated in Fig. 1. Data windowing segments the continuous input gait data into overlapping windows. The windows collection component aggregates these segments for processing. A training phase follows, establishing the model parameters and detection thresholds. The trained model feeds into the anomaly detection component, which works with context analysis. The context analysis incorporates three key factors: environmental context (terrain and location), historical patterns of previous behaviors, and user baseline profiles. These components form a feedback loop, continuously adapting the system to different scenarios. This section details the architectural components and the implementation of detection and classification mechanisms.

3.1 Architecture

CAGAID's architecture consists of four major components that work in sequence to process and analyze gait data. These components are described in detail below.

Data Windowing. Data windowing is an essential technique used in time-series analysis and plays a significant role in processing and analyzing gait data using accelerometer and gyroscope signals. A sliding data window is a fixed-size or dynamically adjusted segment that slides across time series data and captures snapshots of the signal data within a specified time frame. Sliding data windows often overlap and create overlapping segments of data for analysis. For instance, a window size of 1 s with a 50% overlap will move the window forward by half a second each time. Gait patterns, like most human activities, are continuous and complex. They consist of varying phases that reveal unique movement characteristics. Data windowing helps break down these complex patterns into identifiable segments.

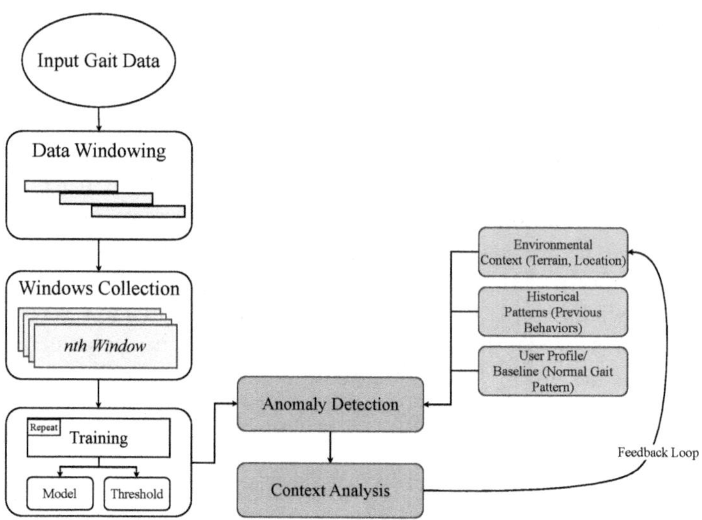

Fig. 1. Context aware gait anomaly-based intrusion detection architecture

Windows Collection. The Windows Collection Component gathers segmented data created through the data windowing component. Once the sliding windows are applied to the raw accelerometer and gyroscope signals, the corresponding segments are extracted and stored for further processing. These segments serve as the fundamental building blocks for subsequent analysis, enabling the detection of key gait features and anomalies. To preserve contextual information, the component labels each window with metadata, such as timestamps or activity identifiers.

Anomaly Detection. The Anomaly Detection Component employs a hybrid neural network architecture with CNN-BiLSTM and an attention mechanism. CNN layers extract spatial features, while BiLSTM captures temporal dependencies. This component works with context analysis to help with the decision-making process of reducing false positives for attack detection and fall detection while maintaining detection sensitivity.

Context Analysis. The Context Analysis Component processes three context types: sensor context (placement and type), environmental context (ground conditions and movement types), and user context (baseline patterns). These factors generate a context score influencing the anomaly detection decision threshold, enabling adaptive sensitivity based on current conditions.

3.2 Implementation: Detection and Classification

CAGAID relies on a neural network for feature extraction, an attention mechanism for pattern identification, and a decision framework for context-aware classification. These components work together to classify anomalies as security intrusions or health-related events.

Neural Network Architecture. CAGAID utilizes a hybrid neural network to capture spatial and temporal patterns. The input data consists of 6 channels representing accelerometer and gyroscope readings (3 axes each) from the IMU sensors placed at the body's center, left, and right positions. Data flows through the network sequentially, with each component processing and transforming the data before passing it to the next. The network entails a 1D Convolutional Neural Network comprising two sequential blocks. Each block uses convolutional layers (32 and 64 filters) to extract multi-scale features, followed by batch normalization and ReLU activation. A dropout rate of 0.2 prevents overfitting and maintains feature richness. The spatial features feed into a bidirectional LSTM network with two layers, each containing 64 units. This layer creates a comprehensive temporal representation $h_t = [\overrightarrow{h_t}, \overleftarrow{h_t}]$ that captures both past and future dependencies. Table 1 shows the neural network architecture.

Table 1. Neural Network Architecture

Layer	Configuration	Output Shape
Input	6 Channels (Accelerometer + Gyroscope)	(Batch, 50, 6)
Conv1D	32 filters, kernel size 5, ReLU	(Batch, 46, 32)
BatchNorm1D	Applied to Conv1D output	(Batch, 46, 32)
Conv1D	64 filters, kernel size 3, ReLU	(Batch, 44, 64)
BatchNorm1D	Applied to Conv1D output	(Batch, 44, 64)
Dropout	p=0.2	(Batch, 44, 64)
BiLSTM	2 layers, 64 units per layer	(Batch, 44, 128)
Attention	Self-attention mechanism	(Batch, 128)
Fully Connected	Dense layer, 64 units, ReLU	(Batch, 64)
Output	Softmax (Classification)	(Batch, 2)

Attention Mechanism. CAGAID employs a self-attention mechanism that focuses on detecting gait pattern changes. The attention module computes importance weights across different timestamps. The system processes data in overlapping windows to maintain temporal continuity and integrates multiple observed context channels through Eq. 1 below:

$$\omega = f(a, s, e) \tag{1}$$

where ω is the aggregated context, a is the attention weight calculated from the sensor time series data, s represents sensor-specific information observed in the dataset (such as sensor placement), and e captures environmental context variables directly measured during data collection (such as walking slope conditions). The attention-weighted context a captures the temporal patterns in the gait data by assigning important weights to different time points. The attention mechanism hence provides temporal focus maps that highlight which time segments most influence anomaly classifications, enabling security analysts to examine specific movement phases that triggered alerts manually.

Decision Framework. The CAGAID decision framework is formalized in Algorithm 1, and it implements a two-phase decision-making process for intrusion detection. The first phase performs feature extraction with attention weights for anomaly detection, while the second phase analyzes these features to characterize sudden anomalies. The attention mechanism adjusts feature importance, helping identify critical movement patterns and sensor contributions. DetectAnomaly(F, α) computes deviation scores by comparing attention-weighted feature representations against predefined baseline thresholds. CharacterizePattern(F, α) distinguishes between sudden and gradual anomalies using temporal gradient analysis. The algorithm then evaluates the context η and sensor coverage patterns σ, where AnalyzeContext(C) assesses environmental factors and AnalyzeSensors(S) verifies sensor placement consistency. Confidence scoring γ enables reliable differentiation between health-related anomalies and security intrusions.

4 Data Preprocessing and Attack Dataset Generation

This section details the datasets, preprocessing steps, and attack dataset generation process utilized in this study. Two complementary datasets are employed: one establishes baseline gait patterns for evaluating security intrusions, while the other focuses on detecting health-related anomalies. The data preprocessing methodology is described, incorporating data augmentation and scaling techniques specifically designed to address the distinctive features of sensor-based gait data. Additionally, the approach used for generating the attack dataset is explained.

4.1 Datasets

The Anomaly Detection Falling People Dataset provides health-related anomaly validation data for CAGAID, particularly for fall detection [5]. This dataset is modified from UCI's Localization Data for Person Activity dataset [20] and contains three-axis accelerometer data from 25 individuals in a smart home environment. The OU-ISIR Gait Database [12] serves as our baseline gait dataset. It enables security intrusion detection evaluation through modeled acoustic attacks. It uses three waist-mounted (left, right, and center) IMUZ sensors (accelerometer and gyroscope) to record gait from 744 subjects 100 Hz, capturing both level and slope walking conditions.

Algorithm 1: Context-Aware Sudden Gait Anomaly Detection Algorithm

```
Input: Sensor data S, context C
Output: Anomaly classification A, confidence γ
1  /* Phase 1: Feature Extraction and Anomaly Detection */
2  Extract features F = {f_1, ..., f_T} and attention weights α = Attention(F);
3  Deviation score δ = DetectAnomaly(F, α);
4  if δ < threshold then
5  |  return (NORMAL, 1.0);
6  end
7  /* Phase 2: Sudden Pattern Analysis and Context-Aware Classification
     */
8  Pattern ρ = CharacterizePattern(F, α);
9  if ρ = SUDDEN then
10 |  Context η = AnalyzeContext(C), Sensor σ = AnalyzeSensors(S);
11 |  if η.normal ∧ σ.global ∧ VerifyPhysicalConstraints(F) then
12 |  |  return (HEALTH, η.confidence);
13 |  else
14 |  |  γ = max(η.confidence, σ.confidence);
15 |  |  return (SECURITY, γ);
16 |  end
17 else
18 |  return (NORMAL, 1.0);
19 end
```

4.2 Data Preprocessing

We applied a preprocessing step in both datasets by sampling in fixed-width sliding windows of one second with a 50% overlap. The choice to consider a fixed-width sliding window rather than an exact window fitted on a movement cycle depends on the hardness of recognizing an exact cycle for each user behavior. Moreover, different behaviors can have different-length cycles, which can deteriorate the sample, reduce the information, or add noise through normalization.

Data Augmentation. Data augmentation enhances model robustness and generalization by applying controlled transformations to the original sensor data while preserving its physiological meaning. This approach combines random translation sampling within $[-0.2, 0.2]$ with three additional transformations designed explicitly for wearable sensor data: temporal permutation, which introduces controlled randomization in movement timing; magnitude scaling through random scalar multiplication $(0.8 - 1.2)$; and jittering via additive Gaussian noise to simulate sensor artifacts. These transformations address real-world sensor data variations caused by placement inconsistencies, movement timing differences, and environmental noise.

Data Scaling. Gait data typically comprises measurements from multiple sensor types, including accelerometers (measuring in m/s^2) and gyroscopes (measuring in degrees/second). These diverse measurement units create inherent scale disparities that significantly impact model performance. For instance, typical accelerometer readings might range from -20 to $+20\,m/s^2$, while gyroscope readings might span from -180 to $+180°/s$. Standard scaling, or standardization, transforms each feature independently by centering it around zero and scaling it to unit variance.

4.3 Attack Dataset Generation

We generate acoustic attacks on gait data to evaluate potential interference effects in real-world scenarios, which impact the integrity and reliability of gait analysis systems. Acoustic transduction is vulnerable in MEMS-based IMUs due to their mechanical resonance properties [16,19,19]. We generated interference patterns by applying Gaussian noise to model both resonant frequency patterns ($\pm 4\%$ amplitude deviation) and low-frequency modulation ($\pm 5\%$ amplitude deviation), as seen in Fig. 2. These deviations align with typical MEMS sensor vulnerabilities in the 2.5–25 kHz range, consistent with vulnerability profiles identified in previous research [6]. The resultant effects are captured on sensor-proof masses. These remote attacks remain significant as they can operate across air gaps, allowing adversaries to manipulate sensors without physical contact [16]. The attack model follows $X_{attacked} = X_{original} + \mathcal{N}(0, \sigma^2)$, where σ controls the deviation magnitude. The attack generation implements controlled noise distributions, with controlled scenarios applying continuous 0.1–0.2 s bursts of acoustic interference. The noise magnitude is amplified by a factor of 2.0 relative to the standard deviation of the original signal (2σ), creating significant but plausible deviations in sensor readings that mirror real-world attack scenarios [19].

From a topological perspective, we assume a remote adversary capable of generating targeted acoustic waves without physical sensor access. The attack probability of 0.5 simulates a scenario where the attacker strategically chooses when to initiate interference rather than maintaining continuous disruption, which could be more easily detected [10]. The primary objective is to induce targeted misclassification by masking genuine health anomalies (false negatives) or corrupting legitimate authentication patterns (false positives). Each modified sequence is paired with its original version and includes precise attack sample labeling for evaluation. We carefully monitored the distribution of attack instances to ensure a balanced representation of attack samples across the dataset splits.

The training set contained 9.37% attack samples, the validation set contained 13.87% attack samples, and the test set contained 12.5% attack samples. This slight imbalance was intentionally preserved to reflect real-world scenarios where attacks occur less frequently than normal behaviors. The final augmented dataset is split into training, validation, and test sets with a 70/15/15 split ratio. This distribution provided sufficient data for model training while reserving adequate samples for validation and testing.

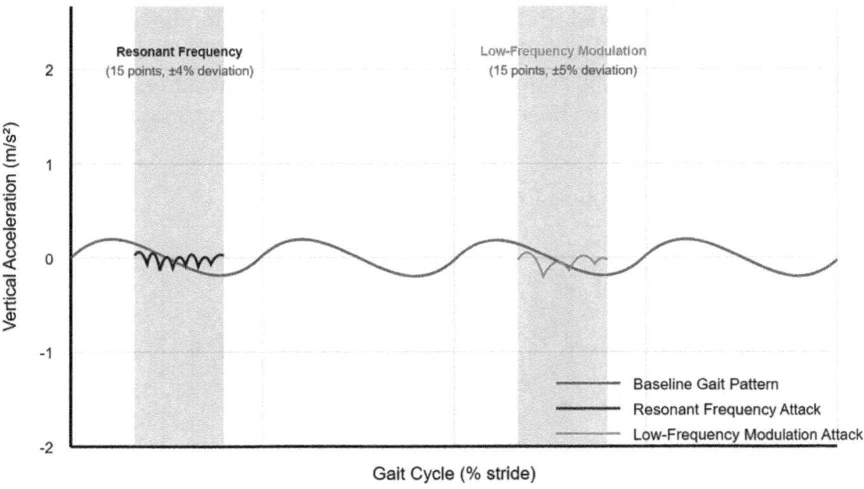

Fig. 2. MEMS Sensor Acoustic Interference During Gait Analysis

5 Experimental Evaluation

This section presents the experimental evaluation of CAGAID. We evaluate the system's performance through detection capabilities and analyze its effectiveness in identifying acoustic transduction attacks and health-related events, mainly falls. We also provide a detailed discussion on the impact of integrating context information on attack detection accuracy and conduct a comparative analysis against traditional detection methods. We also analyze the impact of window size selection on detection performance and discuss some of our work's limitations.

5.1 Performance Analysis

We evaluate CAGAID's detection effectiveness in security and health-related scenarios, focusing on acoustic attack detection and fall recognition across various contexts and sensor configurations.

Security-Related Detection. CAGAID's effectiveness in detecting security-related anomalies focuses on its robustness against acoustic transduction attacks. To systematically evaluate our approach, we tested three model configurations: a base model, a model with attention mechanisms, and the full model with attention and context awareness. The progressive improvement in detection capabilities with each architectural enhancement is visualized in Fig. 3. Key findings from the acoustic attack detection experiments include an improved recall by 7.62% with the addition of attention mechanisms. This improvement suggests the attention mechanism's effectiveness in identifying subtle attack patterns that traditional approaches might miss. Context awareness enhanced precision by 10.63%

compared to the base model, indicating better discrimination between legitimate gait variations and actual attacks. The complete model achieved an F1-score of 81.00%, representing a 6.66% improvement over the attention-only model, highlighting the complementary benefits of attention and context in attack detection.

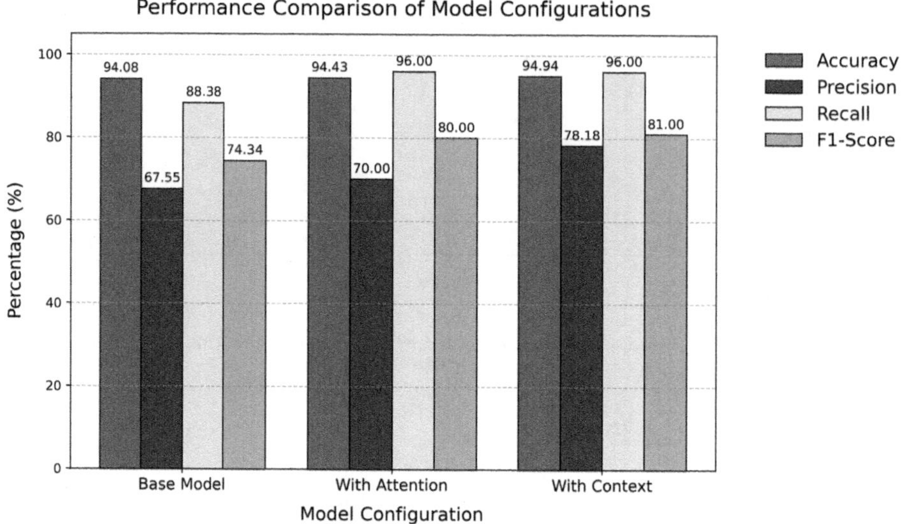

Fig. 3. Performance comparison of different model configurations for acoustic attack detection. The context-aware model shows consistent improvements across all metrics, particularly in precision and F1-score.

Health-Related Detection. The fall detection system demonstrated varied performance across different contexts and sensor configurations, as shown in Table 2. The training analysis reveals the significant impact of incorporating different contextual elements into the fall detection system. The training curves are illustrated in Fig. 4, demonstrate how the model's learning behavior evolves as more contextual information is added. Starting with sensor placement integration, we observed a 2.0% improvement in overall accuracy, suggesting that understanding the physical positioning of sensors helps the model better interpret movement patterns. When adding activity context, precision increased by an additional 4.0%. This improvement indicates that knowing the type of activity being performed helps the model make more accurate distinctions. The combination of sensor placement and activity context ultimately led to the highest F1-score of 92.0%, demonstrating that these contextual elements work together to improve detection performance.

The training curves in Fig. 4. visually support these findings, showing smoother convergence and more stable learning patterns as additional context

Table 2. Performance Metrics for Fall Detection

Context Type	Accuracy ↑	Precision ↑	Recall ↑	F1-Score ↑
No Context	92.0	92.0	84.0	88.0
Sensor Placement	94.0	91.0	**93.0**	89.0
Sensor Placement, Activity	**94.6**	**95.0**	89.0	**92.0**

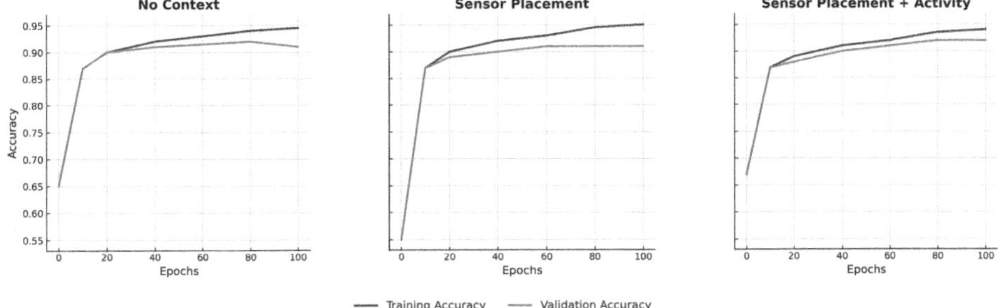

Fig. 4. Training and validation accuracy curves for fall detection across different context configurations. The plots demonstrate how incorporating additional contextual information (sensor placement and activity data) affects model convergence and final performance.

is incorporated. These results validate our approach of progressively integrating different types of contextual information, showing how each layer of context contributes to building a more robust and accurate fall detection system.

5.2 Context Analysis

While our primary work focused on integrating context awareness into gait anomaly detection, this section explores contextual factors and their impact on detection performance within our experimental framework. An analysis of context availability also provides further insights into CAGAID's effectiveness.

Contextual Factor Analysis. The initial implementation incorporated two primary contextual elements: environmental conditions (slope) and sensor placement (left, right, and center waist positions). Further analysis of the OU-ISIR dataset reveals additional contextual factors that can be leveraged to improve detection performance:

- **Walking Speed Variations:** The dataset contains natural variations in walking speed among subjects. We extracted walking pace as an additional contextual factor by analyzing step frequency from the accelerometer data.
- **Direction Changes:** By analyzing gyroscope data, we identified segments containing direction changes versus straight-line walking, representing different contextual authentication scenarios.

Table 3 summarizes the extracted contextual factors and their representation within the dataset.

Table 3. Contextual Factors Extracted from Experimental Data

Contextual Factor	Extraction Method	Representation
Slope Condition	Directly available	Categorical
Sensor Placement	Directly available	Categorical
Walking Speed	Frequency analysis	Continuous
Direction Changes	Pattern analysis	Binary

Impact of Contextual Integration. We conducted an ablation study to quantify different contextual factors' individual and combined impact on attack detection performance. The ablation study revealed several key insights about contextual integration:

Sensor Placement Context: Consistent with our main findings, sensor placement information provided the most substantial individual improvement (5.2% F1-score increase), likely due to its direct relevance to attack differentiation. By understanding sensor placement, the system can better identify when signals from a specific position exhibit anomalous patterns inconsistent with the user's typical movement characteristics.

Walking Speed Context: Incorporating walking speed as a contextual factor improved the F1-score by an additional 3.1%. This improvement stems from the system's enhanced ability to establish appropriate baseline expectations for sensor readings at different walking velocities, reducing false positives during natural speed variations.

Complementary Effects: The combination of all contextual factors achieved a 10.7% improvement in the F1-score over the no-context baseline, demonstrating complementary effects that exceed the sum of individual contributions (8.3%). This synergistic effect suggests that the relationships between contextual factors provide additional discriminative power.

Weighted Context Integration: Based on our analysis, we implemented a weighted context integration approach that assigns greater importance to the most discriminative contextual factors. This weighted approach achieved a 1.8% higher F1-score compared to uniform context weighting.

Context Availability Analysis. Not all contextual information may be consistently available in real-world deployments. We analyzed detection performance under scenarios with partial context availability, as might occur in practical

Table 4. Attack Detection Performance Under Partial Context Availability

Context	Precision ↑	Recall ↑	F1-Score ↑
Full Context	**78.18**	**96.0**	**81.0**
Sensor Placement	74.5	93.8	78.2
Environmental	71.3	94.2	75.4
No Context	67.6	88.4	74.3

applications. Table 4 presents detection performance metrics for various context availability scenarios.

This analysis demonstrates CAGAID's graceful performance degradation when contextual information is limited. Even with partial context availability (such as sensor placement only), the system maintains significantly better performance than no-context baselines, with only a 2.8% reduction in F1-score compared to full context operation.

Our findings from this enhanced context analysis reinforce the value of contextual integration in gait-based intrusion detection and provide practical insights for implementations where contextual data may be limited or unavailable.

5.3 Comparative Analysis

To evaluate CAGAID's effectiveness against traditional approaches, we compared performance metrics comprehensively, as shown in Table 5. The system incorporating context awareness and the hybrid neural architecture achieves the highest accuracy at 94.94% and F1-score at 81.00%. This represents a notable improvement over the base system without context awareness (94.08% accuracy, 74.34% F1-score). The increase in F1-score while maintaining high accuracy demonstrates that context awareness effectively reduces false positives without compromising detection capability. The traditional CNN approach (92.30% accuracy, 72.00% F1-score) shows limitations in capturing temporal dependencies, while the LSTM-only approach performs slightly better (93.10% accuracy, 73.00% F1-score) due to its temporal analysis capabilities. These results demonstrate that CAGAID's hybrid architecture successfully combines the spatial feature extraction capabilities of CNNs with the temporal modeling of LSTMs, while context awareness further enhances its discriminative power.

5.4 Window Size Analysis

Different window sizes reveal performance trade-offs in attack detection shown in Table 6. A larger window of 100 samples achieves high recall (96%) and F1-score (81%), but it increases detection latency and misses brief attack bursts. We tested various window sizes to find the optimal detection accuracy, as the attacks may manifest as short bursts or longer ones. The precision curve reveals an

Table 5. Comparison with Partial and Non-Context Aware Approaches

Approach	Accuracy ↑	F1-Score ↑	Context-Aware
CAGAID	**94.94**	**81.00**	**Yes**
CNN-LSTM	94.08	74.34	No
Traditional CNN	92.30	72.00	No
LSTM-only	93.10	73.00	Partial

interesting pattern where smaller window sizes (10 samples) achieved very high precision (96.31%) but extremely low recall (13.66%). When utilizing a window size closer to the attack burst length, the model becomes very conservative and highly confident in its attack classifications (hence high precision). As the window size increases, the model gains additional context about the traffic patterns, allowing it to detect more subtle attacks. The trade-off is visible when moving from a window size of 10 to 40, where precision drops from 96.31% to 73.23% while recall significantly improves from 13.66% to 42.95%. Dynamic window sizing based on traffic patterns and attack signatures, combined with rate-based features, could better adapt to the varying nature of acoustic attacks while maintaining detection efficiency. Implementing ensemble detection methods that combine predictions from multiple window sizes could provide a more robust solution, leveraging the high precision of smaller windows and the high recall of larger ones while mitigating their individual weaknesses.

Table 6. Performance metrics for selected window sizes in attack detection

Window Size	Accuracy ↑	Precision ↑	Recall ↑	F1 ↑
10	89.20	**96.31**	13.66	23.92
20	89.26	88.87	17.68	29.50
40	90.59	73.23	42.95	54.14
60	91.63	75.12	53.27	62.34
80	92.92	74.27	63.92	68.71
100	**94.94**	78.18	**96.00**	**81.00**

5.5 Limitations

We identify some limitations despite the results achieved.

- **Computational overhead from the attention mechanism:** The self-attention layer introduces significant computational complexity, scaling quadratically with sequence length $O(n^2)$ for input sequences of length n. In our implementation with 1-s windows 100 Hz sampling rate, this results in

attention computations over 100×100 matrices for each window. While manageable for offline analysis, this overhead becomes particularly challenging for real-time monitoring on resource-constrained wearable devices.
- **Limited evaluation of cross-sensor attack scenarios:** While our evaluation demonstrates robust performance for single-sensor attacks, we have not fully explored sophisticated multi-sensor attack scenarios. Coordinated attacks that simultaneously target multiple sensors with different interference patterns might exploit potential vulnerabilities in our context-aware decision-making. The current evaluation also doesn't address scenarios where attackers might adaptively modify their attack patterns based on sensor placement and environmental conditions.

6 Conclusion

The ability to detect security intrusions and health-related anomalies in gait analysis systems is crucial for maintaining effective authentication and preventing malicious system lockouts crippling critical operations while ensuring user safety. This paper presents CAGAID, a context-aware gait anomaly-based intrusion detection system that reduces false security alarms by leveraging environmental context awareness, including terrain conditions and sensor placement. Experimental results validate CAGAID's effectiveness across both security and health monitoring applications. In security scenarios, the system achieves 94.94% accuracy in detecting acoustic attacks with an F1-score of 81.00%, demonstrating robust protection against data tampering attempts. CAGAID shows strong performance with 94.6% accuracy and an F1-score of 92.0% in fall detection. The enhanced detection capability allows for robust authentication systems, reducing security vulnerabilities while minimizing operational disturbances from false alarms.

While these results are promising, we identify several directions for future work. The attention mechanism's computational efficiency needs optimization for resource-constrained devices. Also, investigating more sophisticated multi-sensor attack scenarios would enhance the system's security robustness. These enhancements would further strengthen CAGAID's applicability in environments where reliable authentication and health monitoring are essential for maintaining system integrity while minimizing operational disruptions.

Acknowledgments. This project was partially supported by collaborative research funding from the National Research Council of Canada's Aging in Place Challenge Program.

References

1. Cola, G., Avvenuti, M., Vecchio, A., Yang, G.Z., Lo, B.: An unsupervised approach for gait-based authentication. In: 2015 IEEE 12th International Conference on Wearable and Implantable Body Sensor Networks (BSN), pp. 1–6 (2015)

2. Dong, Y., Kim, S.E., Schadl, K., Huang, P., Ding, W., Rose, J., Noh, H.Y.: In-home gait abnormality detection through footstep-induced floor vibration sensing and person-invariant contrastive learning. IEEE J. Biomedical Health Inform. (2024)
3. Hagoort, I., Vuillerme, N., Hortobágyi, T., Lamoth, C.J.: Age and walking conditions differently affect domains of gait. Hum. Mov. Sci. **89**, 103075 (2023)
4. Rostovski, J., Ahmadilivani, M.H., Krivošei, A., Kuusik, A., Alam, M.M.: Real-Time Gait Anomaly Detection Using 1D-CNN and LSTM. In: Särestöniemi, M., et al. (eds.) NCDHWS 2024. CCIS, vol. 2084, pp. 260–278. Springer, Cham (2024). https://doi.org/10.1007/978-3-031-59091-7_17
5. Jorekai: Anomaly Detection Falling People Events (2024). https://www.kaggle.com/datasets/jorekai/anomaly-detection-falling-people-events. Accessed 03 Nov 2024
6. Khazaaleh, S., Korkmaz, A., Khurshid, A.: Vulnerability assessment of MEMS gyroscopes to acoustic attacks. IEEE Trans. Instrum. Meas. **68**(8), 2768–2777 (2019)
7. Kumar, A., Jain, S., Kumar, M.: Face and gait biometrics authentication system based on simplified deep neural networks. Int. J. Inf. Technol. **15**(2), 1005–1014 (2023)
8. Lee, M.C., Lin, J.C., Katsikas, S.: GAD: a real-time gait anomaly detection system with online adaptive learning. In: Pitropakis, N., Katsikas, S., Furnell, S., Markantonakis, K. (eds.) SEC 2024. IFIP AICT, vol. 710, pp. 308–322. Springer, Cham (2024). https://doi.org/10.1007/978-3-031-65175-5_22
9. Liang, Y., Samtani, S., Guo, B., Yu, Z., Member, S.: Behavioral biometrics for continuous authentication in the internet-of-things era: an artificial intelligence perspective. IEEE Internet Things J. **7** (2020)
10. Manshaei, M.H., Zhu, Q., Alpcan, T., Bacşar, T., Hubaux, J.P.: Game theory meets network security and privacy. ACM Comput. Surv. **45**(3) (2013)
11. Martini, E., et al.: Pressure-sensitive insoles for real-time gait-related applications. Sensors **20**(5), 1448 (2020)
12. Ngo, T.T., Makihara, Y., Nagahara, H., Mukaigawa, Y., Yagi, Y.: The largest inertial sensor-based gait database and performance evaluation of gait-based personal authentication. Pattern Recogn. **47**(1), 228–237 (2014)
13. Prasanth, H., et al.: Wearable sensor-based real-time gait detection: a systematic review. Sensors **21**(8), 2727 (2021)
14. Rostovski, J., Krivošei, A., Kuusik, A., Alam, M.M., Ahmadov, U.: Real-Time Gait Anomaly Detection Using SVM Time Series Classification, pp. 1389–1394. Institute of Electrical and Electronics Engineers Inc. (2023)
15. Shakya, S., Taparugssanagorn, A., Silpasuwanchai, C.: Convolutional neural network-based low-powered wearable smart device for gait abnormality detection. Internet Things **4**, 57–77 (2023)
16. Son, Y., et al.: Rocking drones with intentional sound noise on gyroscopic sensors. In: 24th USENIX Security Symposium, pp. 881–896 (2015)
17. Song, W., et al.: Pistis: replay attack and liveness detection for gait-based user authentication system on wearable devices using vibration. IEEE Internet Things J. **10**, 8155–8171 (2023)

18. Tay, N.C., Connie, T., Ong, T.S., Teoh, A.B.J., Teh, P.S.: A review of abnormal behavior detection in activities of daily living. IEEE Access **11**, 5069–5088 (2023)
19. Trippel, T., Weisse, O., Xu, W., Honeyman, P., Fu, K.: WALNUT: waging doubt on the integrity of MEMS accelerometers with acoustic injection attacks. In: 2017 IEEE European Symposium on Security and Privacy (EuroS&P), pp. 3–18 (2017)
20. Vidulin, Vedrana, L.M.K.B.P.R., Krivec, J.: Localization Data for Person Activity. UCI Machine Learning Repository (2010)

Federated Intrusion Detection System Based on Unsupervised Machine Learning

Maxime Gourceyraud, Rim Ben Salem(✉), Christopher Neal, Frédéric Cuppens, and Nora Boulahia-Cuppens

Polytechnique Montréal, Montréal, Canada
{maxime.gourceyraud,rim.ben-salem,christopher.neal,frederic.cuppens, nora.boulahia-cuppens}@polymtl.ca

Abstract. Recent research on Intrusion Detection Systems (IDS) has increasingly adopted machine learning techniques. However, the majority of these systems rely on supervised learning methods, which require fully labeled training datasets, an often impractical and resource-intensive demand. Moreover, traditional centralized IDS present significant barriers to inter-organizational knowledge sharing, as collaboration would necessitate the disclosure of sensitive data.

To address these challenges, we propose an IDS that leverages unsupervised learning to minimize the need for labeled data. We further enable collaborative learning through the integration of a federated learning framework, which preserves data privacy across participating clients. To enhance privacy beyond existing federated clustering models, a novel federated K-means++ initialization technique is introduced. Additionally, a method for computing the simplified silhouette score in a federated setting is proposed. Our findings indicate that transitioning from a centralized to a federated architecture does not significantly compromise performance.

Keywords: Federated Intrusion Detection · Federated K-Means++ · Federated Silhouette · Unsupervised Learning

1 Introduction

Cybercrime has become a major global concern, posing serious economic challenges. In fact, the World Trade Organization (WTO) estimates that the cost of cybercrime reached $8,150 billion USD in 2023, and could escalate to $13,820 billion USD by 2028 [1]. For organizations worldwide, detecting cyberattacks in real time is crucial to mitigating their impact. With the increasing frequency of attacks and the growing volume of data handled by companies and organizations alike, automating the detection process through Intrusion Detection System (IDS) software has become essential. Traditionally, intrusion detection relies on signature-based methods, where the IDS maintains a database of known attacks and compares incoming data against this repository. A match with any

K. Adi et al. (Eds.): CRiSIS 2025, LNCS 16295, pp. 136–152, 2026.
https://doi.org/10.1007/978-3-032-20732-6_9

known attack results in the data being labeled accordingly. While effective at identifying known threats, this method depends on static rules and is insufficient for adapting to new, evolving attacks. However, with advances in Machine Learning (ML), IDS are increasingly capable of identifying previously unseen threats, enhancing their ability to respond to the dynamic nature of cyberattacks.

In recent years, ML-based IDS have predominantly utilized supervised learning algorithms to learn attack patterns by analyzing labeled data. However, the sheer volume of data generated by an organization's normal operations is too vast to label exhaustively, making the process labor-intensive and resource-demanding. To circumvent this issue, unsupervised ML algorithms, which do not require extensive data labeling, can be employed. For instance, clustering algorithms group data into partitions, or clusters, without prior knowledge of class labels. A popular algorithm for data clustering is the K-Means algorithm, introduced by Lloyd [2], which creates clusters based on the proximity of data points to cluster centroids.

Furthermore, IDS can significantly benefit from shared insights among organizations facing similar threats. However, two major challenges hinder effective inter-organizational collaboration: data heterogeneity and the need for centralized data aggregation. Traditional machine learning frameworks rely on centralized architectures, requiring data to be collected at a single location. This introduces privacy risks and creates a single point of failure. For instance, compromising a central server that stores data from multiple participants could lead to the exposure of extensive sensitive information. In contrast, decentralized data storage, whether across departments or organizations, requires an attacker to breach each entity individually, thereby substantially reducing the overall risk. Federated Learning (FL), introduced by McMahan et al. [3], addresses these concerns by enabling local model training at the client level and secure model aggregation at the server side. This approach preserves data locality and enhances privacy.

This paper presents a novel privacy-preserving IDS that integrates unsupervised learning with federated learning, enabling effective collaboration across organizations while maintaining data confidentiality. We validate this approach with experiments using the UNSW-NB15 [4] and CIC-IDS2017 [5] datasets. We summarize the contributions of this work as follows:

- Proposing an IDS architecture that integrates clustering algorithms and is compatible with federated learning.
- Introducing a federated k-means++ initialization that is mathematically equivalent to its centralized counterpart.
- Presenting a method for computing a simplified silhouette score for clustering model selection within a federated framework.

The remainder of the paper is organized as follows. Section 2 presents a review of related work. The proposed methodology is detailed in Sect. 3, followed by the experimental results in Sect. 4. Section 5 discusses the findings, and Sect. 6 concludes the paper.

2 Related Work

This section provides an overview of clustering algorithms suitable for Federated Learning environments, followed by a presentation of relevant centralized and federated IDS frameworks.

2.1 Clustering Algorithms

Client Clustering. This approach groups clients during the aggregation step to enhance the performance of a supervised model. For example, CADIS [6] utilizes the penultimate layer of locally trained deep learning models to compute a client similarity matrix. By leveraging a layer of the model trained on the client side, it is possible to infer the data distribution indirectly, without accessing the raw data itself. During model aggregation at the server, the updates from each client are weighted based on two factors: the size of the client's local dataset and the inverse of the number of similar clients. As a result, clients belonging to larger clusters receive lower weights, while those in smaller clusters are given higher weights, ensuring that unique or underrepresented data distributions have a stronger influence on the global model.

Federated Clustering. Throughout this paper, this term is reserved to algorithms that cluster clients' data, rather than the clients themselves. One of the earliest algorithms introduced in this category is K-FED [7], which is based on K-Means clustering. In K-FED, clients execute the clustering algorithm proposed by Aswathi et al. [8], while the server aggregates the centroids using Lloyd's algorithm [2]. Notably, K-FED operates in a single round of communication. If there are k clusters overall, each client must not have more than $\sqrt{k}$ clusters locally.

Two other federated clustering algorithms were introduced around the same time. First, Garst and Reinders [9] propose K-Means++ initialization [10] at the client level. The server then aggregates the centroids by applying Lloyd's algorithm, where each centroid is weighted by the size of the cluster it represents. Clients refine the model by performing one iteration of Lloyd's algorithm on their local data using the global centroids. A new communication round begins after the server re-aggregates the updated centroids from clients. The algorithm terminates after a fixed number of communication rounds. Second, the algorithm of Holzer et al. [11] is similar but does not require all clients to participate in the protocol at the same time. Each selected client updates the global centroids by performing one step of Lloyd's algorithm. The server aggregates the updated centroids using a weighted average, cluster by cluster. The weight of each centroid is the size of its corresponding cluster on the client side.

2.2 Unsupervised IDS

This section reviews related IDS research that applies unsupervised learning within centralized or federated learning frameworks. Emphasis is placed on studies that utilize the same benchmark datasets as this work: UNSW-NB15 and

CIC-IDS2017 to ensure a fair and consistent basis for comparison. A summary of the key findings from these studies is presented in Table 1.

Centralized IDS. Prasad et al. [12] introduce a clustering approach that initializes cluster centers using sets of semi-identical instances. These instances represent dense regions in the data space, effectively minimizing the influence of outliers during initialization. Their method outperforms traditional clustering techniques by requiring fewer iterations to converge and achieving higher clustering accuracy. The authors validate their approach using the CICIDS-2017 dataset. The proposed method achieves superior performance metrics, including a detection rate of 88%, precision of 88.57%, and an F-measure of 88.28%, surpassing other unsupervised methods such as standard K-means and New K-means.

The model proposed by Yang et al. [13] is developed by training an autoencoder, a representative unsupervised deep learning architecture, exclusively on normal network traffic data. To detect anomalies, the model computes an anomaly score by combining the reconstruction loss with the Mahalanobis distances derived from each layer's output of the trained autoencoder. By applying a predefined threshold to this score, anomalous network traffic can be effectively identified. The model's performance is evaluated using the UNSW-NB15 dataset and reports an accuracy of 0.85 ± 0.01 and an F_1 score of 0.84 ± 0.01.

On the other hand, Geng et al. [14] propose DUdetector, an unsupervised algorithm using Transformer and CM&RC-AE for dual-granularity learning. Their approach is designed to overcome the struggle of the existing network intrusion detection methods facing unknown attacks. Another approach that tackles one of the challenges of IDS is proposed by Abudurexiti et al. [15], namely the limited availability of labeled data and the lack of interpretability in existing methods. The authors propose an unsupervised framework using time series data analysis, combining Time Convolutional Network (TCN) and Kolmogorov–Arnold Network (KAN)-based Variational Auto-Encoder (VAE) to detect anomalies and capture long-term dependencies. The impact of hyperparameter tuning on the effectiveness of IDS is examined by Iturbe-Araya et al. [16] in the specific context of smart homes. Four models (Elliptic Envelope, Isolation Forest, Local Outlier Factor, and One-class SVM) were applied to four datasets (Bot-IoT, IoTID20, N-baiot, and Ton-IoT), showing significant performance improvements with hyperparameter optimization.

Federated IDS. Md Tayeen et al. [17] propose a federated learning algorithm using FedAvg [3]. They train an auto-encoder in a federated manner on normal data and then perform anomaly detection. However, the only parameters sent to clients are the weights of the layer preceding the latent space and those of the layer following it. Strictly speaking, federated training only concerns the latent space. The F_1 score obtained on UNSW-NB15 is 0.91 ± 0.003.

Aouedi et al. [18] introduce a supervised IDS enhanced with unsupervised learning. They train an auto-encoder in a federated way. Following this, on the server side, they train a neural network with little labeled data. This is not exactly an unsupervised model, but we consider this work important to highlight as the intrusion detection literature in this domain is sparse.

Table 1. Summary of the performances relevant work

Reference	Dataset	Setup	Accuracy	F_1
Prasaad et al. [12]	CIC-IDS2017	Centralized	0.8860	0.8828
Sirisha et al. [19] (k-means)	CIC-IDS2017	Centralized	0.79	0.88
Sirisha et al. [19] (IForests)	CIC-IDS2017	Centralized	0.37	0.91
Yang et al. [13]	UNSW-NB15	Centralized	0.85	0.84
Md Tayeen et al. [17]	UNSW-NB15	Federated	/	0.91
Aouedi et al. [18]	UNSW-NB15	Federated	0.8432	/

3 Methodology

3.1 IDS Architecture

The proposed IDS architecture, illustrated in Fig. 1, consists of two main components: clustering and classification. Initially, unlabeled data is processed and clustered locally by each client in the federated setup. Each client performs clustering on its own dataset using a federated K-Means approach, ensuring data privacy. Once clusters are formed, clients apply their domain expertise to label them based on the characteristics of the data they observe. This labeling process is conducted independently by each client under an "honest but curious" assumption. The server then aggregates the labeled cluster information to build a global model. Finally, new data is classified according to the label of the cluster it belongs to. The following sections detail each component of this architecture.

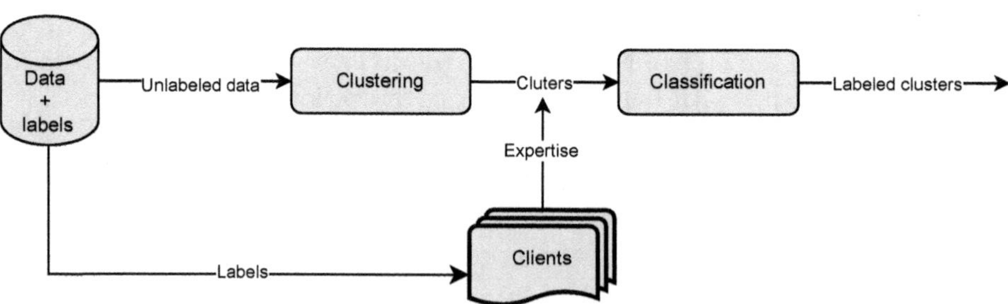

Fig. 1. Representation of the proposed IDS

3.2 Federated Clustering

Our approach uses Federated K-Means clustering as proposed by Garst and Reinders [9]. We also perform clustering in a centralized setup based on K-Means [2] in order to use it as a baseline for our system. The initialization of the Federated K-Means clustering of Garst and Reinders [9] requires that every client participating in the protocol sends to the server the results of the k-means++ initialization [20] on their data. Let $k \in \mathbb{N}^*$ be the number of clusters required for the clustering and $N \in \mathbb{N}^*$ be the number of clients. The protocol introduced by Garst and Reinders requires that the clients disclose a total of kN entries. While our federated K-Means++ initialization builds upon their approach, our contribution lies in reformulating the probability distributions to avoid data leakage and improve privacy preservation. In this section, we propose the federated k-means++ initialization to enhance the privacy of the clustering algorithm. Table 2 lists the symbols that will be referred to and used throughout the remainder of the paper, along with their definition.

Table 2. Symbols and their definitions

Symbol	Definition
X_j	Dataset of client j
C_j	Client j
$n_{i,j}$	Size of cluster i in client j
$p_{i,j}$	Proportion of benign data in cluster i of client j
S_{C_j}	Average silhouette score of client j

K-Means Properties. Before introducing the Federated K-means++ initialization, we need to reformulate the probability distributions used in K-Means++ [20]. Let $(X_j)_{j\in\{1,\dots,N\}}$ be the datasets of the clients $(\mathcal{C}_j)_{j\in\{1,\dots,N\}}$ and $X = \bigcup_{j=1}^{N} X_j$ the total dataset. Suppose that each $x \in X$ is either unique or there is a way to distinguish every entries with the same values. For each $x \in X$, we have:

$$P_{\mathcal{U}}(x) = \frac{1}{|X|} = \frac{|X_j|}{|X|} \times \frac{1}{|X_j|} = P_{\mathcal{U}}(C_j)P_{\mathcal{U}}(x|C_j) \tag{1}$$

Equation 1 shows that the uniform distribution on a dataset X can be equivalently expressed as a choice of a client C_j that then realizes the uniform sampling on its own data. Similarly, the D^2 distribution introduced for the k-means++ initialization [20] can be expressed as choice of a client and this client samples its data with a local D^2 distribution. This is shown by Eq. 2. Let c be the set of centroids at any moment. Let for all $j, Z_j = \sum_{x\in X_j} d(x,c)$ with

$d(x,c) = \min_{i \in \{1,...,|c|\}} (||x - c_i||_2^2)$ and $Z = \sum_{j=1}^{N} Z_j = \sum_{x \in X} d(x,c)$. The D^2 probability distribution can be written as:

$$P_{\mathcal{D}^2}(x) = \frac{d(x,c)}{Z} = P(C_j) P_{\mathcal{D}^2}(x|C_j) = \frac{Z_j}{Z} \times \frac{d(x,c)}{Z_j} \quad (2)$$

The probability distributions employed in the K-means++ initialization can be reformulated in a decentralized manner, accommodating any data distribution across clients. Notably, this formulation ensures that the server does not require direct access to the clients' local data, thereby preserving data privacy.

Federated K-Means++ Initialization. Algorithm 1 uses the properties discussed above to create a federated version of the K-Means++ algorithm equivalent to its centralized counterpart. With this algorithm, the server only accesses the centroids selected by the clients, and does not access to the rest of their data.

Algorithm 1 Federated K-Means++ Initialization

Require: k, $\mathcal{C} = (\mathcal{C}_j)_j$, $(X_j)_j$
1: The clients send the size of their datasets to the server.
2: The server samples a client $\mathcal{C}_j$ in $\mathcal{C}$ with $P(\mathcal{C}_j) = \frac{|X_j|}{|X|}$
3: The client $\mathcal{C}_j$ samples the first centroid c_1 uniformly on X_j
4: $c \leftarrow \{c_1\}$
5: **for** $i \in \{2, ..., k\}$ **do**
6: The server samples a client $\mathcal{C}_{i'}$ in $\mathcal{C}$ with $\forall j, P(\mathcal{C}_j) = \frac{Z_j}{Z}$
7: The client $\mathcal{C}_{i'}$ samples c_i where $P(c_i|\mathcal{C}_{i'}) = \frac{d(c_i,c)}{Z_{i'}}$
8: $c \leftarrow c \cup \{c_i\}$
return c

Algorithm 2 describes the Federated K-Means clustering process that incorporates the Federated K-Means++ initialization (Algorithm 1) into Garst and Reinders' approach. It outlines how the clustering is performed collaboratively across multiple clients without sharing raw data, while still allowing iterative refinement of cluster centroids. c^j are the centroids of the j-th client and C^j are the clusters associated with them. n^j is the size of the clusters of the j-th client and c^g the global centroids. The client ignores centroids with no associated data, thus removing empty clusters from consideration.

3.3 Federated Simplified Silhouette

K-Means clustering has two main issues: the initialization and the choice of the number of clusters k. We cover the issue of initialization in Sect. 3.2. Since clustering is used an unsupervised set of techniques, metrics such as accuracies are other performance metrics cannot be used. Thus, we introduce the notion of federated simplified silhouette score. The silhouette score [21] is a metric to

Algorithm 2 Federated K-Means with Federated K-Means++ initialization

Require: k
  # Federated k-means++ initialization
  $c_g \leftarrow$ federated_kmeans++$(k, \mathcal{C}, (X_j)_j,)$
  for round r **do**
    For each client $\mathcal{C}_j \in \mathcal{C}$ **:**
      $c^j \leftarrow c^g$
      Determine n^j
      # The client $\mathcal{C}_j$ ignores the centroids without data associated with.
      $n^j \leftarrow C^j[s! = 0 \text{ for } n \text{ in } n^j]$
      $k_j \leftarrow$ size(n_j)
      # The clients compute one step of Lloyd's algorithm
      # Lloyd's algorithm is applied with c^j as intial centroids.
      $n^j, c^j \leftarrow$ kmeans$(X_j, k_j,$ init $= c^j)$
      Send n^j, c^j to the server.
    At the server :
      # Centroids and size of clusters are concatenated.
      # It creates a dataset on which the server applies k-means.
      $c \leftarrow [c^1|c^2|...|c^N]$
      $s \leftarrow [s^1|s^2|...|s^N]$
      # Aggregation step. Lloyd's algorithm weighted by the clusters' size.
      $c^g \leftarrow$ kmeans$(c, k,$ weights $= s)$
      Send c^g to the clients.

estimate how good a clustering is for each data point. To reduce the computation cost, Hruschka et al. [10] proposed a simplified version of this metric. For each $x \in X$, let us note $c(x)$ the centroid associated with x. Let c be the set of centroids and d be the distance between x and $c(x)$. The simplified silhouette score $s(x)$ is computed as follows:

$$\begin{cases} a(x)= & d(x, c(x)) \\ b(x)= & \min_{i \in \{1,\dots,k\}, c_i \neq c(x)} d(x, c_i) \\ s(x)= & \frac{b(x)-a(x)}{max(a(x),b(x))} \end{cases}$$

We adapt the formula of s to a federated setup. For each client $\mathcal{C}_j$, the average silhouette score is $\overline{S_{C_j}}$ and can be obtained as follows:

$$\overline{S_{C_j}} = \frac{1}{|X_j|} \sum_{x \in X_j} s(x) \tag{3}$$

The server then aggregates the individual scores by taking a weighted average, where the weights correspond to the size of each client's dataset across the network.

$$
\begin{aligned}
S &= \frac{1}{\sum_{j=1}^{N} |X_j|} \sum_{j=1}^{N} |X_j| \overline{S_{C_j}} \\
&= \frac{1}{\sum_{j=1}^{N} |X_j|} \sum_{j=1}^{N} \sum_{x \in X_j} s(x) \qquad (4) \\
S &= \frac{1}{|X|} \sum_{x \in X} s(x)
\end{aligned}
$$

Consequently, the average silhouette score S, derived using Formula 4 effectively mirrors the result that would be obtained if the server had direct access to all client data, without actually requiring such access. This score is referred to as the average federated simplified silhouette score. The objective remains to identify the optimal number of clusters k by maximizing this score, following the same principle as in centralized clustering. Throughout this paper, we use the terms federated silhouette and federated simplified silhouette interchangeably.

3.4 Binary Classification

Once the clusters are formed, the IDS needs the clients to estimate the proportion of benign communications in each cluster. For each client j and cluster i, the estimated proportion of benign communications is denoted as $p_{i,j}$. Additionally, clients report the size of each cluster, with the size of cluster i from client j represented as $n_{i,j}$. The server aggregates this information to compute the overall proportion of benign communications for each cluster i across the entire network.

$$
P_i = \frac{\sum_j p_{i,j} \times n_{i,j}}{\sum_j n_{i,j}} \qquad (5)
$$

In a centralized setup, the data owner directly estimates P_i. Once P_i is computed, the classification rule applied is straightforward: cluster i is labeled as benign if $P_i > 0.5$, and as an attack cluster if $P_i \leq 0.5$. After classification, all data points within the cluster inherit the corresponding label, either benign or attack.

To evaluate the performance of the models, we designate the attack class as the positive class, as detecting malicious activity is the primary objective. We employ standard evaluation metrics, including accuracy, precision, recall, and F_1 score, to assess the effectiveness of the classification.

3.5 Datasets

To assess the effectiveness of the proposed federated IDS, we utilize two widely adopted benchmark datasets in intrusion detection: UNSW-NB15 and CIC-IDS2017. As both datasets are originally centralized, we partitioned them to simulate a federated learning environment. The methodology for this partitioning is detailed in the following section.

UNSW-NB15. The UNSW-NB15 dataset was developed by the University of New South Wales to address limitations found in earlier intrusion detection datasets [4]. It was specifically designed to capture realistic and diverse normal behaviors alongside contemporary attack scenarios. Widely adopted in the intrusion detection research community, this dataset includes both relatively straightforward attacks, such as Distributed Denial of Service (DDoS), and more sophisticated threats like exploitation-based attacks.

To construct a federated version of the UNSW-NB15 dataset, we partitioned the data based on the values of a specific categorical variable. In this setup, each client is assigned data corresponding to a single class. For example, one client contains only normal communications, while another consists exclusively of DDoS attack samples, and so on. While this approach does not reflect an ideal scenario with independently and identically distributed (IID) samples across clients, it serves as a practical compromise for simulating a federated learning environment using the UNSW-NB15 dataset.

CIC-IDS2017. The CIC-IDS2017 [5] dataset was developed by the University of New Brunswick with the goal of simulating realistic network traffic alongside modern cyberattacks. To achieve this, the creators incorporated a diverse range of protocols, devices, and operating systems, ensuring a comprehensive and representative dataset. Since the network environment was fully controlled during data collection, every communication instance was accurately labeled. Normal traffic is categorized as benign, while malicious activities are labeled according to their specific attack types, such as DDoS, Web-based attacks, and others.

To generate a federated version of the CIC-IDS2017 dataset, we grouped the data based on the destination IP address of each communication. In this configuration, each client represents a distinct receiver within the network, thereby simulating a more realistic federated environment. This approach reflects practical deployment scenarios where individual devices or endpoints receive specific subsets of network traffic, making the setup more representative of real-world conditions.

Data Preprocessing. Before applying our approach, we perform a series of preprocessing steps to prepare the data. First, we remove any entries containing missing values. Next, infinite values are replaced with the minimum or maximum of the corresponding variable, depending on context. Categorical variables are transformed into binary (one-hot encoded) representations. Each numerical variable is then normalized to fall within the interval $[0;1]$. We further apply unsupervised variable selection based on value frequency, as proposed by Prasad et al. [12], to reduce dimensionality and enhance model performance. Redundant data entries are also eliminated. Finally, the dataset is randomly shuffled and split into a training set comprising 80%. of the data and a test set comprising the remaining 20%.

3.6 Overview of Experimental Approach

In this section, we present the training procedure for our federated IDS based on unsupervised learning. The process consists of the following key steps:

1. The algorithm is trained using a range of cluster numbers k, from 1 to 300 for the CIC-IDS2017 dataset and from 1 to 70 for the UNSW-NB15 dataset. Additionally, the number of communication rounds r is varied across the values 0, 5 and 10 to evaluate the impact of federated interactions on clustering performance.
2. The value of the communication rounds parameter r is selected as the smallest value for which the silhouette score curve reaches a global or local maximum, indicating optimal clustering quality with minimal communication overhead.
3. The optimal number of clusters k is selected as the value corresponding to the global or a local maximum of the simplified silhouette score curve, ensuring well-separated and meaningful cluster structures.
4. Each client participates in a voting process to determine the composition of its local clusters, as previously described. The server then aggregates the votes from all clients to establish a global consensus on cluster composition.
5. The final class label of each cluster, attack or benign, is determined based on the selected voting strategy, which aggregates the individual client assessments of cluster composition.
6. Each communication instance is assigned the label of its corresponding cluster, thereby completing the classification process based on the unsupervised clustering and federated aggregation.

4 Results

4.1 Model Selection

Figure 2 illustrates the variation of the silhouette score as a function of the number of clusters for both the UNSW-NB15 and CIC-IDS2017 datasets. In these figures, the blue curves represent the silhouette scores obtained using the centralized k-means algorithm. The remaining curves depict the evolution of the silhouette score with respect to r, the number of communication rounds between clients and the server.

UNSW-NB15. For UNSW-NB15 (Fig. 2a), the centralized k-means curve and the curves for $r = 5$ and $r = 10$ share the same shape. In contrast, the curve for $r = 0$ appears flat. We tested the centralized version of k-means++ on the same data, and it generated a curve similar to the one with $r = 0$. Therefore, the flat shape is not an error of the federated k-means++. Even though the first three curves share the same shape, their maxima occur at different values of k, the number of clusters. Specifically, the curves for $r = 5$ and $r = 10$ have a maximum around $k = 30$, whereas the centralized k-means curve reaches its maximum at $k = 9$. This indicates that the federated models tend to shift the maximum

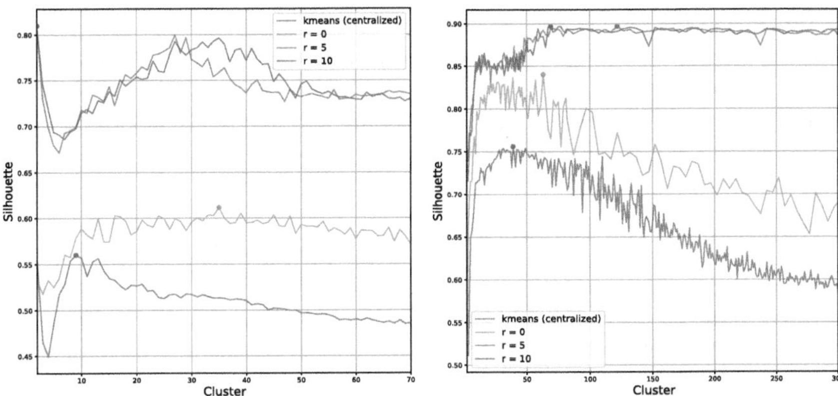

(a) Evolution of the average silhouette score on UNSW-NB15 dataset

(b) Evolution of the average silhouette score on CIC-IDS2017 dataset

Fig. 2. Evolution of the average silhouette score as a function of the number of clusters (fed. K-Means with fed. K-Means++ init.).

silhouette score toward higher values of k. The curve with $r = 0$ shows no clear maximum, so we selected the number of communication rounds that produces a curve with a distinct maximum. In this case, we chose $r = 5$, and then selected the maximum of the curve, which occurs at $k = 27$.

CIC-IDS2017. For CIC-IDS2017 (Fig. 2b), we observe that the silhouette curves for the centralized k-means and the federated k-means++ ($r = 0$) share a similar shape. In contrast to UNSW-NB15, the curves for $r = 5$ and $r = 10$ differ significantly from the centralized curve and do not exhibit a clear maximum. The only federated curve resembling the centralized one corresponds to $r = 0$. Therefore, we selected this number of communication rounds and chose the maximum of this curve, which occurs at $k = 63$.

Model Selection. We can see in Fig. 2 that as r increases, the silhouette score also increases. This may suggest an improvement in clustering quality, since the silhouette score is a measure of cluster cohesion and separation. However, the shapes of the curves in Fig. 2b for $r > 0$ are clearly not as expected. Typically, a silhouette curve should exhibit at least one local maximum and then decrease as k increases. Here, this pattern is absent, even for $r = 0$ and in the centralized setup, although the centralized curves do show a maximum before $k = 300$. This indicates that the federated iterations do not behave as anticipated. A similar suboptimality is observed for the UNSW-NB15 dataset, where the maxima of the curves for $r > 0$ are shifted toward higher values of k compared to the centralized setup. From these observations, we conclude that the federated models studied produce suboptimal results with respect to the silhouette score. While the initialization we proposed is equivalent to its centralized counterpart, there is no *a priori* guarantee that the aggregation function from Garst and Reinders [9], which we employed, is equivalent to the update step in Lloyd's algorithm. This discrepancy may explain why the results are less satisfactory than those obtained in the centralized setting.

4.2 Evolution of Performance Metrics

Figure 3 illustrates the evolution of the F_1 score as a function of the number of clusters. Similar to Fig. 2, this figure shows the variation of the F_1 score for different values of r in the federated K-Means algorithm with federated K-Means++ initialization.

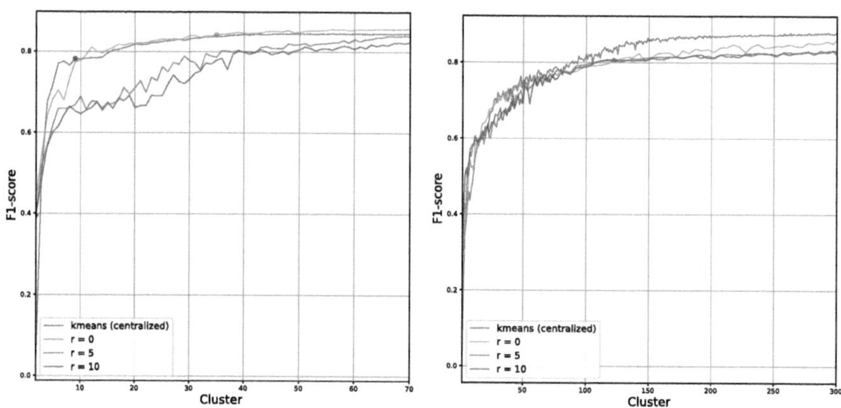

(a) Evolution of F_1 score on UNSW-NB15 dataset

(b) Evolution of F_1 score on CIC-IDS2017 dataset

Fig. 3. Evolution of the average F_1 score as a function of the number of clusters (fed. K-Means with fed. K-Means++ init.).

UNSW-NB15. For UNSW-NB15 (Fig. 3a), all curves exhibit an increasing trend as k grows. Two distinct groups of curves can be observed. The first group consists of the centralized algorithm and the federated version with $r = 0$, both demonstrating superior performance. The second group includes the curves for $r = 5$ and $r = 10$. Although these curves gradually approach the performance of the first group as k increases, they remain consistently lower across most values of k.

CIC-IDS2017. For CIC-IDS2017 (Fig. 3b), all curves exhibit an increasing trend, similar to UNSW-NB15. However, unlike UNSW-NB15, the federated curves for CIC-IDS2017 are closer to each other, while the centralized curve remains clearly above the others starting from $k = 50$. The curve for $r = 0$ outperforms the other two federated curves between $k = 20$ and $k = 70$, and again after $k = 160$.

Summary of Performance Evolution. For both datasets, the performance of the centralized k-means algorithm is generally superior to that of the federated versions for a fixed k. This suggests that increasing the number of clusters improves performance. However, a larger number of clusters also requires greater expertise from the clients. If this expertise is provided by cybersecurity analysts, labeling numerous clusters can become tedious. Moreover, since we employed unsupervised learning to reduce the burden of manual labeling, participants should be aware of this trade-off before deploying the proposed IDS. We also observe that the performance for $r = 0$ is equivalent to or better than that of the other two federated scenarios. From a performance perspective, it is preferable to keep r as low as possible. Therefore, iterating on the centroids after the federated k-means++ initialization does not yield performance benefits. This finding aligns with the suboptimality of the aggregation function highlighted in Sect. 4.1.

4.3 Performance Comparison

Table 3 and 4 compare the performance of the K-Means algorithm, federated K-Means [9], and federated K-Means with the proposed federated K-Means++ initialization. The results are computed using UNSW-NB15 and CIC-IDS2017, respectively.

UNSW-NB15 Dataset. As shown in Table 3, the federated models achieve higher accuracy and precision compared to the centralized model, indicating fewer false positives. However, both federated models exhibit lower recall, meaning they produce more false negatives. The performance of these federated models should also be considered in relation to the number of clusters required, as both federated algorithms demand significantly more clusters than the centralized approach.

Table 3. Performance comparison between the models with selected hyperparameters (UNSW-NB15)

Model	Accuracy	Precision	Recall	F_1	k	r
k-means (centralized)	0.7659	0.6640	0.9500	0.7817	9	/
Garst&Reinders	0.7706	0.6904	0.9201	0.7889	15	0
Fed. k-means & fed. k-means++	0.7743	0.7121	0.8456	0.7731	27	5

CIC-IDS2017 Dataset. Table 4 indicates that the federated models achieve comparable or better accuracy, recall, and F_1 scores than the classical centralized model. However, they exhibit lower precision and require more clusters. It is also observed that the selected r value is 0 for both federated algorithms. As discussed in Sects. 4.1 and 4.2, choosing $r > 0$ is not always relevant. In this study, $r = 0$ for the federated K-Means of Garst and Reinders indicates that there is only one aggregation step after the local K-Means++ initialization.

Table 4. Performance comparison between the models with selected hyperparameters (CIC-IDS2017)

Model	Accuracy	Precision	Recall	F_1	k	r
k-means (centralized)	0.8958	0.7505	0.6969	0.7227	39	/
Garst&Reinders	0.9121	0.7041	0.9554	0.8107	83	0
Fed. k-means & fed. k-means++	0.8947	0.6765	0.8613	0.7578	63	0

5 Discussion

In Sects. 4.1 and 4.2, we observe a suboptimality in the aggregation process: the model's performance deteriorates as the number of rounds increases. Nevertheless, the studied models outperform the clustering algorithms presented in Table 1 in terms of accuracy.

Although additional communication rounds do not improve model performance, the results obtained in both centralized and federated setups are similar or better overall. Federated models, however, require more clusters to achieve comparable performance, making them less efficient. This inefficiency is tempered by the accuracy gains discussed earlier. While some single-IDF approaches slightly outperform our proposed system, they introduce privacy risks and create a single point of failure. The slight reduction in performance is therefore offset by improved security and opens avenues for future research on balancing these trade-offs.

Since the model successfully detects attacks, it demonstrates effective collaboration among clients during training. For instance, in UNSW-NB15, one client contains only normal communications, yet with centroids learned across the network, it can detect attacks previously unseen. Similarly, in the federated dataset created for CIC-IDS2017, 203 out of 212 datasets consist solely of normal communications, yet the learning process still identifies attacks.

6 Conclusion

In this paper, we proposed an IDS architecture leveraging clustering algorithms in both centralized and federated settings. Our approach improves client data privacy compared to the federated K-Means of Garst and Reinders by introducing a federated K-Means++ initialization, without any overall loss in performance. Furthermore, the IDS and learning process described enable collaboration among clients without sharing datasets with the server. To guide the selection of federated clustering models, we introduced an average federated simplified silhouette score and demonstrated its equivalence to the centralized version.

Future research should focus on refining aggregation techniques to enhance the performance of federated models, paving the way for more robust and scalable cybersecurity solutions in decentralized networks. This direction not only promises improvements in IDS efficacy but also expands opportunities for cross-organizational collaboration without compromising sensitive information. Additionally, we plan to evaluate our system on datasets beyond UNSW-NB15 and CIC-IDS2017 to further validate its generalizability.

References

1. World Trade Organization: 2023 was a big year for cybercrime – here's how we can make our systems safer (2024)
2. Lloyd, S.: Least squares quantization in PCM. IEEE Trans. Inf. Theory **28**(2), 129–137 (1982)
3. McMahan, B., Moore, A., Ramage, D., Hampson, S., y Arcas, B.A.: Communication-efficient learning of deep networks from decentralized data. In: Proceedings of the 20th International Conference on Artificial Intelligence and Statistics, vol. 54, pp. 1273–1282. PMLR (2017)
4. Moustafa, N., Slay, J.: UNSW-NB15: a comprehensive data set for network intrusion detection systems (UNSW-NB15 network data set). In: 2015 Military Communications and Information Systems Conference (MilCIS). IEEE (2015)
5. Sharafaldin, I., Lashkari, A.H., Ghorbani, A.A.: Toward generating a new intrusion detection dataset and intrusion traffic characterization. In: 4th International Conference on Information Systems Security and Privacy (ICISSP), pp. 108–116, Portugal, 01–04 November 2018
6. Nguyen, N.H., et al.: Cadis: handling cluster-skewed non-IID data in federated learning with clustered aggregation and knowledge distilled regularization. In: 2023 IEEE/ACM 23rd International Symposium on Cluster, Cloud and Internet Computing, pp. 249+ (2023)
7. Dennis, D.K., Li, T., Smith, V.: Heterogeneity for the win: one-shot federated clustering. In: Proceedings of International Conference on Machine Learning (ICML), vol. 139, Electr Network, 18–24 July 2021 (2021)
8. Awasthi, P., Sheffet, O.: Improved spectral-norm bounds for clustering. In: Gupta, A., Jansen, K., Rolim, J., Servedio, R. (eds.) APPROX/RANDOM -2012. LNCS, vol. 7408, pp. 37–49. Springer, Heidelberg (2012). https://doi.org/10.1007/978-3-642-32512-0_4
9. Garst, S., de Reinders, M.: Federated k-means clustering. arXiv, October 2023
10. Hruschka, E.R., de Castro, L.N., Campello, R.J.G.B.: Evolutionary algorithms for clustering gene-expression data. In: Fourth IEEE International Conference on Data Mining (ICDM'04), pp. 403–403, Brighton, UK, 01–04 November 2004
11. Holzer, P., Jacob, S.: Dynamically weighted federated k-means. arXiv, November 2023

12. Prasad, M., Tripathi, S., Dahal, K.: Unsupervised feature selection and cluster center initialization based arbitrary shaped clusters for intrusion detection. Comput. Secur. **99**, 102062 (2020)
13. Yang, D., Hwang, M.: Unsupervised and ensemble-based anomaly detection method for network security. In: 2022 14th International Conference on Knowledge and Smart Technology (KST), pp. 75–79 (2022)
14. Geng, H., Ma, Q., Chi, H., Zhang, Z., Yang, J., Yin, X.: Dudetector: a dual-granularity unsupervised model for network anomaly detection. Comput. Netw. **257**, 110937 (2025)
15. Abudurexiti, Y., Han, G., Zhang, F., Liu, L.: An explainable unsupervised anomaly detection framework for industrial internet of things. Comput. Secur. **148**, 104130 (2025)
16. Iturbe-Araya, J.I., Rifà-Pous, H.: Enhancing unsupervised anomaly-based cyberattacks detection in smart homes through hyperparameter optimization. Int. J. Inf. Secur. **24**(1) (2024)
17. Tayeen, A.S.M.: Misra, S., Cao, H., Harikumar, J.: Cafnet: compressed autoencoder-based federated network for anomaly detection. In: MILCOM 2023 - 2023 IEEE Military Communications Conference (MILCOM), pp. 325–330 (2023)
18. Aouedi, O., Piamrat, K., Muller, G., Singh, K.: Intrusion detection for softwarized networks with semi-supervised federated learning. In: ICC 2022 - IEEE International Conference on Communications, pp. 5244–5249 (2022)
19. Sirisha, A., Chaitanya, K., Krishna, K., Kanumalli, S.: Intrusion detection models using supervised and unsupervised algorithms - a comparative estimation. Int. J. Saf. Secur. Eng. **11**, 51–58 (2021)
20. Arthur, D., Vassilvitskii, S.: k-means++: The advantages of careful seeding. In: Proceedings of the Eighteenth Annual ACM-SIAM Symposium on Discrete Algorithms, pp. 1027–1035. PA, USA (2007)
21. Rousseew, P.J.: Silhouettes: a graphical aid to the interpretation and validation of cluster analysis. J. Comput. Appl. Math. **20**, 53–65 (1987)

Domain Adversarial Neural Networks with Adversarial Robustness Evaluation for Intrusion Detection Systems

Ines Guerziz[1,2](✉), Tiago Falk[1,2], Long Bao Le[1], and Zakaria Abou El Houda[1,2]

[1] INRS-EMT Center on Energy, Materials and Telecommunications, University of Quebec, Montreal, QC, Canada
{tiago.falk,long.le,zakaria.abouelhouda}@inrs.ca
[2] INRS-UQO Joint Research Unit on Cybersecurity and Digital Trust, Gatineau, QC, Canada
ines.guerziz@inrs.ca

Abstract. Modern Network Intrusion Detection Systems (NIDS) face the dual challenge of maintaining performance across diverse network environments while resisting adversarial manipulations. This paper investigates the intersection of domain adaptation and adversarial robustness in NIDS, a topic that has not been extensively studied. We implement a Domain-Adversarial Neural Network (DANN) with dynamic gradient reversal to adapt models from NSL-KDD to UNSW-NB15. To evaluate security, we assess the model under Fast Gradient Sign Method (FGSM) and Projected Gradient Descent (PGD) attacks. Additionally, we introduce FGSM-based adversarial training to enhance robustness. Our results show that while domain adaptation improves cross-domain detection, it also increases susceptibility to adversarial attacks. Incorporating adversarial training mitigates this vulnerability, improving resilience without compromising performance on clean data. These findings provide key insights for designing adaptive and secure intrusion detection systems.

Keywords: Domain Adaptation · Adversarial Neural Networks · Adversarial Attacks · FGSM · PGD · Intrusion Detection Systems · Attack Resilience

1 Introduction

With the continuous evolution of network technologies such as 5G, IoT, and edge computing, the landscape for cybersecurity is becoming increasingly complex. Network Intrusion Detection Systems are critical for detecting malicious activities within these dynamic and heterogeneous environments. However, the performance of traditional machine learning-based NIDS is often compromised when there is a significant domain shift between the source (training) and target

K. Adi et al. (Eds.): CRiSIS 2025, LNCS 16295, pp. 153–165, 2026.
https://doi.org/10.1007/978-3-032-20732-6_10

(deployment) environments. Domain shift occurs when the distribution of features in the source domain differs from the target domain, leading to degradation in model accuracy and performance. This is particularly challenging in modern networks where environments can vary dynamically, creating discrepancies in network traffic characteristics, user behavior, and attack patterns [1].

Recent advancements in domain adaptation techniques, such as DANN [2], have shown promise in addressing these challenges. DANN uses a gradient reversal layer to learn domain-invariant features that generalize better across different domains. These models aim to minimize the discrepancy between the source and target domain distributions, making NIDS more adaptable to various network environments.

1.1 Adversarial Attacks on Network Intrusion Detection Systems

While domain adaptation helps to address the challenges of domain shift, NIDS are also increasingly susceptible to adversarial attacks. These attacks involve crafting input data that is intentionally designed to mislead machine learning models into making incorrect predictions. The adversarial perturbations are often imperceptible to human observers, yet they can cause significant misclassifications, potentially allowing malicious activities to bypass detection [3]. In the context of NIDS, attackers can exploit these vulnerabilities to evade detection systems that rely on machine learning models.

There are two primary types of adversarial attacks commonly applied to NIDS: the Fast Gradient Sign Method [4] and the Projected Gradient Descent [5]. FGSM is a single-step attack that uses the gradient of the loss function to generate adversarial examples by perturbing the input in the direction of the gradient's sign. PGD, on the other hand, is an iterative method that refines adversarial perturbations over multiple steps, increasing the potency of the attack. These methods have been shown to be effective in fooling machine learning models in controlled, single-domain settings [6]. However, their effectiveness in the context of domain-adapted NIDS remains underexplored. This paper aims to fill this gap by investigating how adversarial examples, crafted in the source domain, transfer to the adapted target domain, thereby exploring the intersection of domain adaptation and adversarial robustness.

1.2 The Intersection of Domain Adaptation and Adversarial Attacks

The intersection of domain adaptation and adversarial attacks creates a complex challenge for the robustness of NIDS. On one hand, domain adaptation techniques like DANN can improve the generalization of models to new domains by learning domain-invariant features. On the other hand, these same adaptations can inadvertently reduce the model's robustness to adversarial perturbations. Our work specifically investigates how the learning of domain-invariant features may affect the vulnerability of NIDS to adversarial attacks, as well as how adversarial examples might transfer between domains, which has not been adequately addressed in prior research [7].

We hypothesize that the domain-invariant representations learned by DANN models may exhibit lower adversarial margins, making them more susceptible to attacks. Additionally, adversarial examples crafted for a source domain, such as NSL-KDD [8], may still be effective against domain-adapted models in the target domain, such as UNSW-NB15 [9]. This phenomenon of attack transferability across domains remains largely unexplored in the context of NIDS. Through a series of experiments involving FGSM and PGD attacks, we demonstrate that the effectiveness of adversarial examples increases by up to 22% after domain adaptation, highlighting a significant vulnerability in domain-adapted NIDS. We further show that incorporating FGSM-based adversarial training mitigates this vulnerability, improving robustness against attacks while maintaining high accuracy on clean data.

2 Related Works

The effectiveness of Network Intrusion Detection Systems depends heavily on the quality and representativeness of the data used during training. However, in real-world applications, network environments are dynamic and heterogeneous, leading to significant domain shifts between training (source) and deployment (target) environments. Traditional supervised learning approaches often fail under these conditions, necessitating research into domain adaptation methods to enhance NIDS generalization across diverse network settings.

Domain adaptation techniques have gained prominence in recent years as a means to address domain shift. A seminal contribution in this area is the DANN, which introduces a Gradient Reversal Layer (GRL) to promote the learning of domain-invariant features. Extensions to DANN have explored minimizing distribution discrepancies using measures such as Maximum Mean Discrepancy (MMD) [10] and Correlation Alignment (CORAL) [11], as well as adversarial feature learning [12]. In the context of cybersecurity, domain-adaptive NIDS have demonstrated improved performance in cross-network intrusion detection scenarios, yet most existing methods employ static adaptation parameters, limiting their flexibility in rapidly evolving network environments.

In parallel, adversarial machine learning has revealed significant vulnerabilities in deep learning-based NIDS. Studies have shown that adversarial attacks, which involve small perturbations crafted to evade detection, can drastically reduce NIDS accuracy [13,14]. This has raised concerns about the robustness of both traditional and domain-adapted models. Techniques such as the Fast Gradient Sign Method and Projected Gradient Descent have been widely used to generate adversarial examples, exposing the need for defense mechanisms that can withstand such perturbations. While adversarial training has been adopted in various security-critical applications to improve model robustness [15], few works have combined adversarial robustness with domain adaptation strategies in NIDS.

Moreover, our implementation follows the original DANN framework, where the gradient reversal strength is dynamically adjusted during training. This scheduling strategy gradually increases the adaptation strength, ensuring a smoother and more effective domain alignment as training progresses. Although dynamic adjustment is part of the standard DANN methodology and not a novel contribution, it helps stabilize the learning of domain-invariant features. In our work, we specifically apply the DANN architecture to network intrusion detection systems (IDS) rather than the image classification tasks originally explored in prior research. Our primary focus is on assessing how domain adaptation impacts the robustness of models against adversarial attacks, and on showing how adversarial training can alleviate these vulnerabilities, offering guidance for developing more resilient and adaptable NIDS.

3 Methodology

The first step in our methodology involves preparing and preprocessing the data from the source and target datasets. This section outlines the key steps taken to clean, balance, and extract relevant features from the raw datasets prior to the domain adaptation stage. The following process was employed:

3.1 Dataset Description

In this study, we utilized two publicly available network intrusion detection datasets: NSL-KDD and UNSW-NB15.

- NSL-KDD: The dataset is an improved version of the widely used KDD Cup 1999 dataset, containing network traffic data labeled as benign or malicious. It is commonly used for evaluating the performance of intrusion detection systems (IDS) and includes various types of attacks such as DoS, Probe, and U2R.
- UNSW-NB15: The dataset was designed to address the shortcomings of older datasets like KDD. It includes a diverse set of attack types, such as DDoS, Exploits, and Generic Attacks, and is more representative of modern network traffic compared to older datasets.

The datasets were chosen to serve as the source and target domains in a domain adaptation context. The source domain represents one network environment (NSL-KDD), while the target domain represents another, potentially more challenging environment (UNSW-NB15).

3.2 Data Preprocessing

In our methodology, several data preprocessing steps were employed to prepare the datasets for model training:

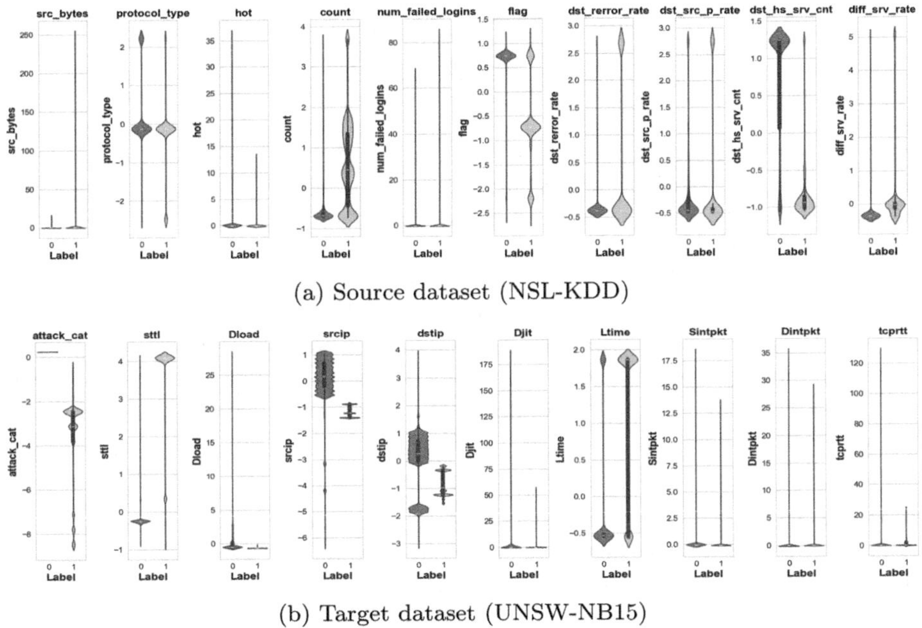

(a) Source dataset (NSL-KDD)

(b) Target dataset (UNSW-NB15)

Fig. 1. Violin plots showing the distribution of selected features in the source dataset (NSL KDD) and target dataset (UNSW-NB 15). (a) Source dataset, (b) Target dataset.

Label Encoding: Categorical features, such as protocol types and service names, were encoded using the LabelEncoder. This conversion of non-numeric labels into numeric values ensures compatibility with machine learning models.

Handling Missing and Infinite Values: To address missing or infinite values in the datasets, these were replaced with the median of the respective columns. This approach prevents missing or infinite data from disrupting the model training process.

Binary Label Mapping: The target labels were transformed into binary values, where a label of 0 indicates benign traffic and 1 represents attack traffic. This binary encoding simplifies the classification task by clearly distinguishing between benign and malicious network activities.

Feature Selection: To identify the most relevant features for classification, an XGBoost model was trained separately on both the source and target datasets. The model's embedded feature importance mechanism was employed to compute an importance score for each feature $\mathbf{x}_j \in \mathbf{X}$, defined as:

$$G_j = \frac{1}{T} \sum_{t=1}^{T} \sum_{i \in I_t} \frac{\partial^2 \mathcal{L}}{\partial x_j^2} \quad (1)$$

where G_j denotes the average second-order gradient (Hessian) with respect to feature x_j, $\mathcal{L}$ represents the loss function optimized by XGBoost, I_t is the set of samples at tree t, and T is the total number of trees. Based on these scores, the top 10 features from each dataset were selected, ensuring that only the most informative features were retained for subsequent analysis.

Figure 1 shows the violin plots for the selected features, illustrating their distribution across the two classes (benign and attack) in both the source and target datasets. These plots provide a visual representation of how each feature varies across different classes, further aiding in the selection of the most discriminative features for model training.

Feature Scaling. Numerical features were standardized using StandardScaler, which normalizes all features to have a mean of zero and a standard deviation of one. This scaling step ensures that all features contribute equally to the model, improving model performance and convergence.

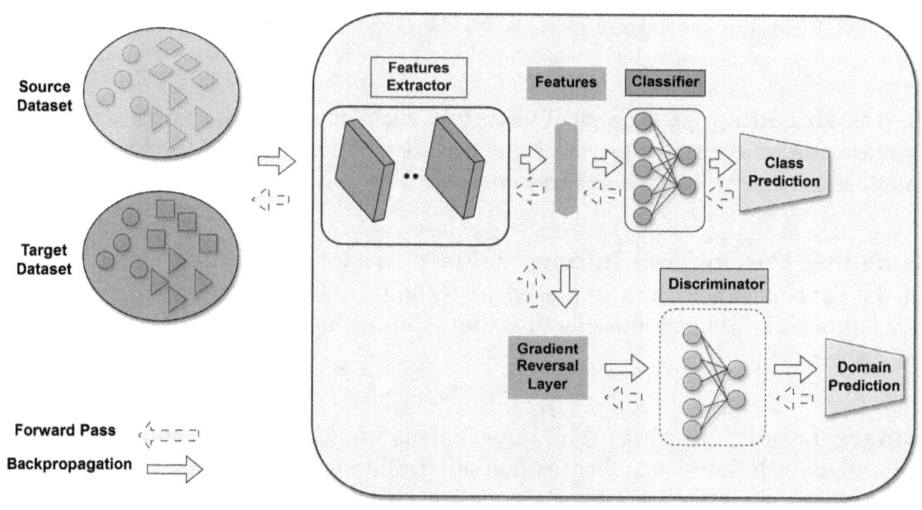

Fig. 2. Domain Adaptation Technique for Intrusion Detection System

3.3 DANN Model

As illustrated in Fig. 2, our Domain-Adversarial Neural Network consists of three main components:

The model architecture is composed of three main components: a feature extractor, a classifier, and a domain classifier. **The feature extractor**, which is shared by both subsequent components, consists of two linear layers with batch normalization, ReLU activations, and dropout, transforming the raw input into a meaningful hidden representation. **The classifier** uses this representation to perform the final intrusion detection, predicting whether an instance belongs to a normal or abnormal class. In parallel, **the domain classifier** aims to distinguish between source and target domains. To ensure that the learned features are domain-invariant, a Gradient Reversal Layer is placed between the feature extractor and the domain classifier. During backpropagation, the GRL reverses the gradients flowing to the feature extractor, encouraging it to learn representations that are useful for classification while being indistinguishable across domains.

3.4 Training Objective

The DANN training objective consists of two terms:

Classification Loss (L_{class}): This term ensures that the model performs well on the source domain classification task.

$$L_{\text{class}} = -\sum_{i=1}^{C} y_i \log(\hat{y}_i) \tag{2}$$

Domain Loss (L_{domain}): This term ensures that the feature extractor learns domain-invariant features. It encourages the feature extractor to learn representations that confuse the domain classifier, thereby making the features domain-agnostic.

$$L_{\text{domain}} = -\sum_{i=1}^{2} d_i \log(\hat{d}_i) \tag{3}$$

Thus, the total loss L_{total} is a weighted sum of the classification and domain losses:

$$L_{\text{total}} = L_{\text{class}} + \lambda \cdot L_{\text{domain}} \tag{4}$$

where λ is a hyperparameter that controls the weight of the domain loss relative to the classification loss.

3.5 Adversarial Attacks

The goal of adversarial attacks is to evaluate the robustness of machine learning models by introducing small perturbations to input data that mislead the model.

FGSM (Fast Gradient Sign Method). FGSM is a gradient-based attack that uses the sign of the gradient of the loss function with respect to the input data. The formula for FGSM is:

$$\mathbf{x}_{\text{adv}} = \mathbf{x} + \epsilon \cdot \text{sign}\left(\nabla_{\mathbf{x}} \mathcal{L}(\theta, \mathbf{x}, y)\right) \tag{5}$$

where $\mathbf{x}$ represents the original input, $\mathcal{L}$ denotes the loss function used for training, and y is the true class label. The symbol $\nabla_{\mathbf{x}}$ refers to the gradient of the loss with respect to the input $\mathbf{x}$. The perturbation is scaled by ϵ, a hyperparameter that controls the strength of the adversarial attack.

PGD (Projected Gradient Descent). PGD is an iterative extension of FGSM. It performs multiple iterations of FGSM with small steps, projecting the perturbed input back into the valid input space after each iteration. The formula for PGD is:

$$\mathbf{x}_{t+1} = \text{clip}_{\mathbf{x},\epsilon}\left(\mathbf{x}_t + \alpha \cdot \text{sign}\left(\nabla_{\mathbf{x}} \mathcal{L}(\theta, \mathbf{x}_t, y)\right)\right) \tag{6}$$

Here, α denotes the step size used in each iteration of the attack. The variable $\mathbf{x}_t$ represents the perturbed input at iteration t. The function $\text{clip}_{\mathbf{x},\epsilon}(\cdot)$ ensures that the resulting perturbation remains within an ϵ-ball around the original input $\mathbf{x}$.

3.6 Defense Baseline: Adversarial Training

As described in the previous subsection, adversarial attacks such as FGSM and PGD are typically used to evaluate the robustness of machine learning models. In addition to using these attacks for evaluation, we also employ them during training to establish a defense baseline through *adversarial training* [16]. This strategy exposes the model to both clean and adversarially perturbed samples, forcing it to learn feature representations that are not only domain-invariant but also more resilient to adversarial perturbations.

Specifically, we adopt the Fast Gradient Sign Method as illustrated in Eq. 5 to generate adversarial examples on-the-fly during training. For each batch of source samples (x_s, y_s), a corresponding adversarial batch (x_s^{adv}, y_s) is generated. The model is then trained on the combined set of clean and adversarial samples.

The resulting training objective becomes:

$$L_{total} = L_{class}(x_s, y_s) + L_{class}(x_s^{adv}, y_s) + \lambda \cdot L_{domain}(x_s, x_t) \tag{7}$$

where L_{class} represents the classification loss applied to both clean and adversarial samples, and L_{domain} is the domain loss that promotes domain-invariant feature learning. By jointly minimizing these terms, the model is encouraged to perform well on the primary classification task, maintain generalization across domains, and improve robustness against adversarial perturbations.

4 Evaluation and Results

We evaluate the proposal on a Windows system with a 13th Gen Intel® Core^{TM} i7-13620H processor (2.40 GHz), 454 GB of memory, and an Nvidia GeForce RTX 4050 GPU. The learning rate is set to 0.001, with a batch size of 64 and a maximum of 20 epochs. To assess performance, we measure the accuracy of the network intrusion system.

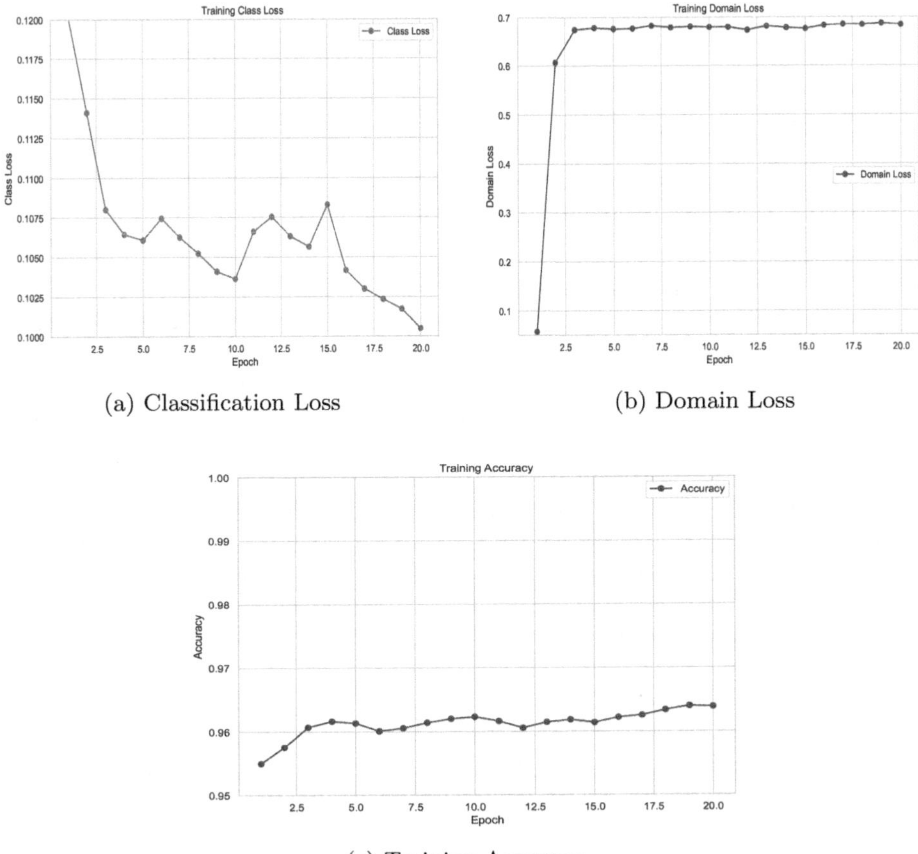

(a) Classification Loss

(b) Domain Loss

(c) Training Accuracy

Fig. 3. Training performance: (a) Classification Loss, (b) Domain Loss, (c) Training Accuracy.

4.1 Training Performance

The training dynamics of the Domain-Adversarial Neural Network (DANN) model were closely monitored as shown in Fig. 3 through three key metrics:

- **Classification Loss:** The classification loss consistently decreases over the course of training, starting from approximately 0.12 and reducing to about 0.105 (plot a). This decline demonstrates that the feature extractor is successfully learning discriminative features for the classification task on the source domain.
- **Domain Loss:**The domain loss shows an initial sharp decline during the first few epochs and then stabilizes around 0.6 (plot b). In DANN, domain loss is associated with the domain classifier's ability to distinguish between source and target domain features. The stabilization suggests that the adversarial training has reached a balance: the feature extractor is learning domain-invariant features, making it harder for the domain classifier to distinguish between source and target domains.
- **Classification Accuracy:** The classification accuracy improves steadily from about 95.7% to approximately 96.2% (plot c). This increase indicates that even while optimizing for domain invariance, the model preserves and enhances its predictive power on the primary classification task.

Overall, these results suggest successful adversarial domain adaptation: the model maintains high classification performance while simultaneously minimizing domain discrepancy, achieving better generalization to the target domain.

We evaluate the model's robustness against adversarial attacks using the Fast Gradient Sign Method and Projected Gradient Descent under varying perturbation magnitudes (ϵ). The results are summarized in Fig. 4, where the model's performance under attack is compared to its performance on clean (unperturbed) data. Without any adversarial perturbation, the model achieves an accuracy on the target domain of 43.43%. As ϵ increases, the model's accuracy consistently drops for both FGSM and PGD attacks, confirming that larger perturbations cause more misclassifications. PGD generally results in lower accuracies compared to FGSM at the same ϵ, reflecting PGD's stronger, iterative nature in crafting more effective adversarial examples.

Even at a very small perturbation level ($\epsilon = 0.010$), there is a noticeable decline in accuracy, suggesting that the model is moderately vulnerable even to minimal adversarial noise. At higher perturbations ($\epsilon = 0.200$), the model accuracy drops to approximately 31% (FGSM) and 28% (PGD), demonstrating that without specific adversarial training, the model struggles significantly against crafted attacks.

4.2 Adversarial Training Results

To assess the effectiveness of adversarial training as a defense mechanism, we trained an additional DANN model using the FGSM-based adversarial training procedure described in Sect. 3.6. The goal was to evaluate whether exposing the model to adversarial perturbations during training improves its robustness against unseen adversarial examples at test time.

Figure 5 compares the performance of the baseline DANN model with the adversarially trained DANN in both FGSM and PGD attacks at different perturbation strengths. On clean (unperturbed) samples, the adversarially trained

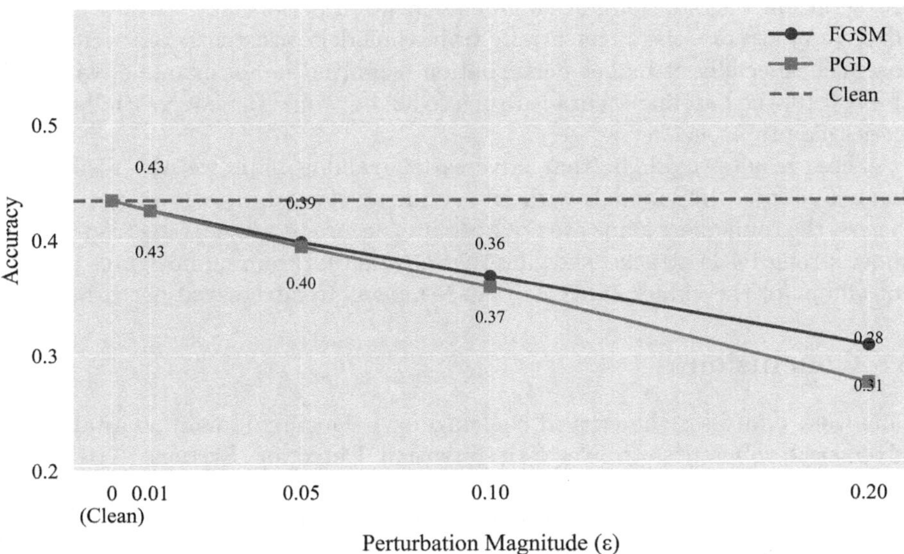

Fig. 4. Adversarial Robustness Analysis: Accuracy under FGSM (blue line) and PGD (red line) attacks at varying perturbation magnitudes. The green dashed line indicates performance on clean data. (Color figure online)

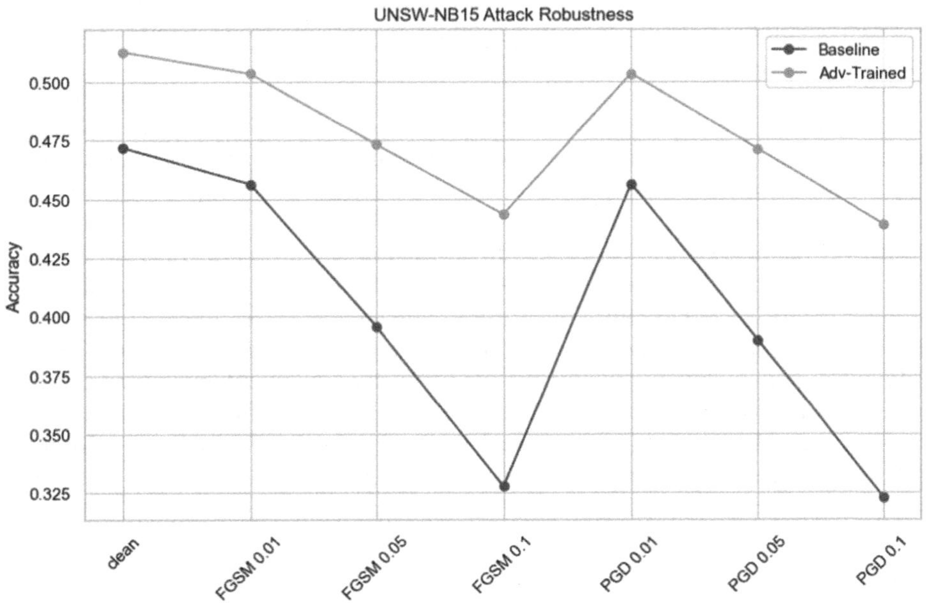

Fig. 5. Comparison of baseline and adversarially trained DANN models under FGSM and PGD attacks with varying perturbation magnitudes.

model achieves accuracy comparable to the baseline, indicating that there is no significant degradation in benign classification performance. However, under adversarial attacks, the adversarially trained model consistently outperforms the baseline, especially at higher perturbation magnitudes. For example, with PGD at $\epsilon = 0.10$, the baseline accuracy drops to 32.4%, while the adversarially trained model maintains 44.0%.

These results highlight that adversarial training improves the resilience of domain-adapted IDS models without sacrificing clean-data performance. Nevertheless, the robustness gains are not absolute: accuracy still degrades significantly under strong PGD attacks, showing that adversarial training mitigates but does not eliminate the vulnerability of DANN models to adversarial perturbations.

5 Conclusion

This work addresses the critical challenge of balancing domain adaptation and adversarial robustness in Network Intrusion Detection Systems (NIDS). We implemented a Domain Adversarial Neural Network (DANN) to improve the adaptability of NIDS across diverse network environments, focusing on knowledge transfer from the NSL-KDD to the UNSW-NB15 dataset. The DANN effectively learns domain-invariant features, enabling better generalization to unseen domains.

Our experiments revealed a fundamental trade-off, while domain adaptation enhances cross-domain performance, it also introduces new vulnerabilities to adversarial attacks. The baseline DANN model, without adversarial training, showed a significant drop in accuracy under FGSM and PGD attacks, even with small perturbations causing noticeable misclassifications.

To mitigate this, we incorporate FGSM-based adversarial training as a defense baseline. The results demonstrate that adversarially trained DANN models maintain performance on clean data while significantly improving robustness against both FGSM and PGD attacks. For example, at higher perturbation levels, the adversarially trained model consistently outperforms the baseline, indicating the effectiveness of joint domain adaptation and adversarial training.

These findings highlight that integrating adversarial defense mechanisms into domain-adaptive NIDS can substantially enhance their reliability and security. However, robustness is not an absolute strength, and iterative attacks such as PGD still reduce accuracy, emphasizing the need for further research. Future work should explore advanced hybrid approaches that combine domain adaptation, adversarial training, and other defense strategies, with the aim of building NIDS that are adaptive to new network environments and resilient to evolving adversarial threats.

References

1. Mainuddin, M., Duan, Z., Dong, Y.: Network traffic characteristics of IoT devices in smart homes. In: 2021 International Conference on Computer Communications and Networks (ICCCN), pp. 1–11. IEEE (2021)

2. Ganin, Y., et al.: Domain-adversarial training of neural networks. J. Mach. Learn. Res. **17**(59), 1–35 (2016)
3. Papernot, N., McDaniel, P., Goodfellow, I., Jha, S., Celik, Z.B., Swami, A.: Practical black-box attacks against machine learning. In: Proceedings of the 2017 ACM on Asia Conference on Computer and Communications Security, pp. 506–519 (2017)
4. Goodfellow, I.J., Shlens, J., Szegedy, C.: Explaining and harnessing adversarial examples. arXiv preprint arXiv:1412.6572 (2014)
5. Madry, A., Makelov, A., Schmidt, L., Tsipras, D., Vladu, A.: Towards deep learning models resistant to adversarial attacks. arXiv preprint arXiv:1706.06083 (2017)
6. Wang, M., Yang, N., Gunasinghe, D.H., Weng, N.: On the robustness of ml-based network intrusion detection systems: an adversarial and distribution shift perspective. Computers **12**(10), 209 (2023)
7. Yan, H., et al.: Automatic evasion of machine learning-based network intrusion detection systems. IEEE Trans. Dependable Secure Comput. **21**(1), 153–167 (2023)
8. Tavallaee, M., Bagheri, E., Lu, W., Ghorbani, A.A.: A detailed analysis of the KDD CUP 99 data set. In: 2009 IEEE Symposium on Computational Intelligence for Security and Defense Applications, pp. 1–6. IEEE (2009)
9. Jatti, S., Sontif, V.K.: UNSW-NB15: a comprehensive data set for network intrusion detection systems. Int. J. Recent Technol. Eng. (2019)
10. Long, M., Zhu, H., Wang, J., Jordan, M.I.: Deep transfer learning with joint adaptation networks. In: International Conference on Machine Learning, pp. 2208–2217. PMLR (2017)
11. Sun, B., Saenko, K.: Deep CORAL: correlation alignment for deep domain adaptation. In: Hua, G., Jégou, H. (eds.) ECCV 2016. LNCS, vol. 9915, pp. 443–450. Springer, Cham (2016). https://doi.org/10.1007/978-3-319-49409-8_35
12. Tzeng, E., Hoffman, J., Saenko, K., Darrell, T.: Adversarial discriminative domain adaptation. In: Proceedings of the IEEE Conference on Computer Vision and Pattern Recognition, pp. 7167–7176 (2017)
13. Hu, W., Tan, Y.: Generating adversarial malware examples for black-box attacks based on GAN. In: International Conference on Data Mining and Big Data, pp. 409–423. Springer (2022). https://doi.org/10.1007/978-981-19-8991-9_29
14. Rigaki, M., Garcia, S.: Bringing a GAN to a knife-fight: adapting malware communication to avoid detection. In: 2018 IEEE Security and Privacy Workshops (SPW), pp. 70–75. IEEE (2018)
15. Carlini, N., Wagner, D.: Defensive distillation is not robust to adversarial examples. arXiv preprint arXiv:1607.04311 (2016)
16. Shafahi, A., et al.: Adversarial training for free! In: Advances in Neural Information Processing Systems, vol. 32 (2019)

Privacy and Digital Trust

Transparent Consent Tracking in Child-Oriented LLM Applications via Smart Contracts

Masoud Barati[1(✉)], Chen Zhou[1], Nafiseh Kahani[2], Diana Rogachova[1], Diana Addae[2], and Raymond Xiao[1]

[1] School of Information Technology, Carleton University, Ottawa, Canada
masoud.barati@carleton.ca,
{chenzhou4,dianarogachova,raymondxiao}@cmail.carleton.ca

[2] Department of Systems and Computer Engineering, Carleton University, Ottawa, Canada
kahani@sce.carleton.ca, dianaaddae@cmail.carleton.ca

Abstract. As Large Language Models (LLMs) are increasingly used in applications designed for children, concerns around data privacy and informed consent have grown more urgent. Many existing consent systems are opaque, hard to verify, and prone to misuse, making it difficult to meet privacy requirements such as those outlined in Canada's Personal Information Protection and Electronic Documents Act (PIPEDA), which governs the collection, use, and disclosure of personal information by private-sector organizations. In this paper, we present a blockchain-based approach that uses smart contracts to securely capture, verify, and track parental or child consent over time. By combining blockchain's transparency and immutability with automated compliance checks, our solution helps ensure that consent is both traceable and enforceable throughout system interactions. We also propose an architecture that integrates this model into LLM-based applications, providing a more secure and accountable framework for managing consent. To evaluate our approach, we implement a prototype and test it on a local blockchain. The results show that our system runs efficiently, with low overhead and affordable gas costs, making it a promising solution for privacy protection in Internet-connected AI applications.

Keywords: Large language models · PIPEDA · Consent management · Blockchain and smart contract · Data privacy

1 Introduction

Large Language Models (LLMs) are considered a groundbreaking advancement in Artificial Intelligence (AI) [7]. These models can generate human-like text and, more recently, create and process other forms of media, including voice and video. Their capabilities have transformed industries and reshaped how individuals interact with technology in everyday life [7,15]. Children are among those

K. Adi et al. (Eds.): CRiSIS 2025, LNCS 16295, pp. 169–185, 2026.
https://doi.org/10.1007/978-3-032-20732-6_11

most impacted by these advancements, as generative AI becomes increasingly integrated into educational and entertainment tools [18]. For instance, LLM-powered educational applications, such as adaptive and personalized learning systems, are being developed for use in schools and universities [23]. Beyond formal education, children also explore and experiment with these technologies on their own, even when the tools are primarily designed for adult users [18]. While LLMs offer valuable educational opportunities, they also raise serious ethical concerns, particularly around data privacy [17]. Many LLM applications collect personal and sensitive data, including information from children [17,24]. Given the sensitive nature of children's data and their limited ability to fully understand online privacy risks [6], it is crucial to implement automated mechanisms that provide parents and guardians with clear, meaningful insights into data collection, usage, and sharing practices. Furthermore, obtaining parental consent through a traceable and tamper-proof platform is essential for promoting transparency and accountability.

Recent advances in consent management allow users to dynamically grant, revoke, or modify consent, increasing control over personal data [5,20]. Regulations like Canada's PIPEDA require explicit consent before collecting or using personal information [14,31]. However, challenges such as organizational complexity and fragmented data practices make robust consent management difficult [4,20]. Blockchain, with its decentralized and immutable design, offers a promising solution [1]. Research has explored blockchain-based consent systems in healthcare [2,3] to improve trust and user control. Similar efforts extend to IoT [21,27], identity management [10], and data storage [19,30].

While usage of blockchain for consent management has been studied in several areas, its application in AI-driven systems is relatively new [28], particularly in LLM-based applications for children. In fact, one of the main challenges is the privacy risks of children's interactions with LLMs and the need for meaningful consent based on clear, transparent, and understandable privacy policies. Another challenge is automatically detecting violations of consent principles in LLM applications with respect to existing privacy regulations (e.g., PIPEDA and Children's Online Privacy Protection Act (COPPA) [11]).

In order to address these challenges, this paper presents the design and implementation of an automated, transparent consent management solution for LLM-based applications targeting children, using blockchain and smart contract technologies. We begin by formally defining the privacy policies of LLM-based services, along with the processes for obtaining and withdrawing user consent. These policy elements and consent procedures are then encoded into algorithms to enable their implementation through smart contracts. The paper also proposes a new architecture that shows how smart contracts can be integrated into LLM applications to submit and verify consent evidence within a blockchain network. Our main contributions include:

- modeling the lifecycle of data processing, policy enforcement, and consent handling in LLM applications using formal descriptions;

- designing an architectural model for integrating blockchain and decentralized application (DApp) into LLM-based applications;
- proposing a set of smart contracts for obtaining consent and verifying age, recording data processing logs, and detecting consent violations;
- developing a prototype to evaluate the proposed blockchain-based solution in terms of cost, CPU usage, and overhead.

The paper is structured as follows. Section 2 reviews related work. Section 3 presents a data handling scenario in LLM applications for children and defines relevant policies and consent functions. Section 4 introduces our blockchain-based model and proposes the consent protocol. Section 5 presents the experimental results, and finally Sect. 6 concludes the paper.

2 Related Work

The use of blockchain for consent management in LLM-based applications for children is a new and largely unexplored area. However, existing research highlights blockchain's potential for enhancing consent and privacy management in fields such as healthcare [2,29], IoT ecosystem [21,27,32], identity management [10], and data storage auditing [19,25,30]. In healthcare, blockchain frameworks use smart contracts to encode patients' access policies, enabling secure, real-time consent enforcement without intermediaries [9,13,16,22]. For instance, Philippe et al. [13] proposed a blockchain-based solution for managing patient consent in e-health environments. In IoT, blockchain addresses privacy and security issues by enforcing user-defined consent policies across distributed devices. Rantos et al. [26] introduced ADvoCATE, an Ethereum-based platform incorporating a policy analyzer and consent notary to support secure and transparent data sharing. Blockchain has also been applied to decentralized identity (DID) systems. Faber et al. [10] proposed BPDIMS, a user-centric identity management framework that emphasizes consent, transparency, and data control. For data storage, blockchain enables users to manage consent securely and track usage transparently. Truong et al. [30] and Kaaniche et al. [19] proposed systems for regulatory compliant consent handling and tamper-proof auditing, using smart contracts and hierarchical encryption to preserve privacy and control access.

Kakarlapudi and Mahmoud [20] surveyed existing work on blockchain integrated data privacy and consent management. Garcia et al. [12] examined privacy-preserving mechanisms, consent strategies, and identity management approaches. The surveys reveal current challenges in integration and regulatory compliance, highlighting the benefits of blockchain's transparency, immutability, and decentralization. One suggested future research direction is improved security and decentralized privacy.

While blockchain has been applied to consent management in domains like healthcare, IoT, and identity systems, its use in managing consent for children's interactions with LLMs remains unexplored. This paper presents the first blockchain-based framework that enables automated, transparent, and regulation-compliant parental consent in LLM-based applications for children.

By formally modeling consent policies and embedding them into smart contracts, our approach introduces a novel mechanism for consent verification and violation detection in generative AI systems involving minors.

3 Our Data Processing Lifecycle Model in LLM Applications

This section begins by presenting a scenario that illustrates data handling processes within LLM-based applications designed for children. It then introduces a formal framework to describe data processing and consent management throughout the application lifecycle.

3.1 The Scenario of Data Processing in LLM Applications

LLM-based applications for children (e.g., PinwheelGPT, Chat Kids [8]) typically process personal data through a lifecycle starting with data collection at account registration. Parents first create accounts by providing personal details such as name, address, birthdate, gender, and email. Afterward, children enter their own information, including name, birthdate, school, parent's email, and password. This data enables the application to deliver and manage age-appropriate personalized experiences, such as tailored child-level learning content. Personal data also helps communicate updates to parents and improves the LLM by analyzing how children interact with the application. Throughout the lifecycle, personal data may be accessed by employees, contractors, or service providers for support purposes. Some third-party LLM tools process interaction data to generate responses but are strictly prohibited from using it for independent purposes like advertising or profiling. Data may also be disclosed to authorities when legally required, such as in child safety investigations.

Parental consent is central to this process. Parents act as gatekeepers, approving data collection and monitoring their children's application use. So, clear consent mechanisms are significant to uphold the ethical and legal standards of processing children's data in these applications.

3.2 A Formal Description of Data Processing in LLM

As outlined in Sect. 3.1, various processors (e.g., contractors, providers) may handle children's and parents' data, such as data access, transfer, or profiling during an LLM application's lifecycle. Privacy laws (e.g., PIPEDA) require meaningful consent before any collection or use of personal data (Sect. 6.1 [14]). This consent must be based on clear understanding of processing purposes.

To support transparent and automated consent management in LLM-based applications, we formally model workflows involving personal data and define representation of positive and negative consents. These formalizations enhance clarity around data flows, roles, and interactions related to consent handling.

Definition 1. The lifecycle of processing activities on personal data within an LLM application is formally expressed as a tuple $L = \langle P, O, D, R \rangle$, where P is a set of data processors, O is a set of data processing operations, D is a set of personal data items, and $R \subseteq P \times O \times D$ is a relation set such that each relation specifies which processor performs which operation on which personal data item.

Notably, the processing operations in this definition encompass a broad range of actions executed on user data, including collection, reading, organization, structuring, storage, adaptation, alteration, retrieval, use, consultation, profiling, transfer, dissemination, and data erasure.

After defining the lifecycle model (Definition 1) for data handling in LLM applications, the following steps ensure PIPEDA compliance. First, privacy policies must align with PIPEDA, ensuring personal data is not collected or used for unspecified purposes (Schedule1, Clause 4.3.2 [14]). Processors must also obtain user consent before data access, as per Sect. 6.1. Second, the model must include a privacy policy, explicitly governing data collection and usage. Third, Implementation must follow the lifecycle model, allowing only consented operations and flagging any without consent as violations.

These steps imply that privacy policies must clearly state the purpose of data collection and use by processors in an LLM application. Accordingly, we define privacy policies formally as follows:

Definition 2. Let $L = \langle P, O, D, R \rangle$ represent the model of data processing lifecycle in an LLM-based application, and S be a set of data processing purposes. A set of privacy policies $\mathcal{P}$ on the relation $\mathcal{R} \subseteq R \times S$ is defined as a collection of statements of the form: "p `performs` o `on` d `for the purpose of` s", where $p \in P$, $o \in O$, $d \in D$ and $s \in S$.

Informally, each statement in the privacy policy specifies the processing operation being performed, the data processor responsible, the data items involved, and the purpose for which the processing operation occurs. This definition can bridge the formal model with human-friendly policy statements, as demonstrated in the following example.

Example 1. Given Definition 2 and the scenario in Sect. 3.1, assume that $p \in P$ is the application provider, $o \in O$ is data sharing operation, $d \in D$ is a data item that includes parental email, and $s \in S$ represents the purpose of communicating updates to parents. A privacy policy $\pi \in \mathcal{P}$ could be a statement: "*the application provider* (p) `performs` *data sharing* (o) `on` *parental email* (d) `for the purpose of` *communicating updates* (s)".

Users (parents or children) must provide consent before any data processor (actor) collects or uses their personal data, in accordance with PIPEDA's principles of consent and accountability. When the privacy policy is formally defined (as in Definition 2), a user's consent – whether positive or negative – can be formally represented as the following function.

Definition 3. Let $\mathcal{P}$ be the set of all possible privacy policies, and let T represent time instances. We define a Boolean function $C : \mathcal{P} \times T \rightarrow \{\top, \bot\}$ that models user consent for a given privacy policy π at time t:

$$C(\pi, t) = \begin{cases} \top, & \text{if } \exists\, t' \leq t \text{ such that } U(\pi, t') = \top, \\ & \text{and } \forall\, t'' \in (t', t], U(\pi, t'') \neq \bot, \\ \bot, & \text{otherwise.} \end{cases}$$

To track changes over time, we introduce an update function $U : \mathcal{P} \times T \rightarrow \{\top, \bot\}$, where:

$$U(\pi, t) = \begin{cases} \top, & \text{if the user grants consent at time } t, \\ \bot, & \text{if the user withdraws consent at time } t. \end{cases}$$

Informally, this definition means the LLM application tracks consent over time: if a user grants consent and has not withdrawn it since, the consent remains active. If withdrawn, it is marked as such. The application checks consent status by ensuring no withdrawals occurred from the last grant till now.

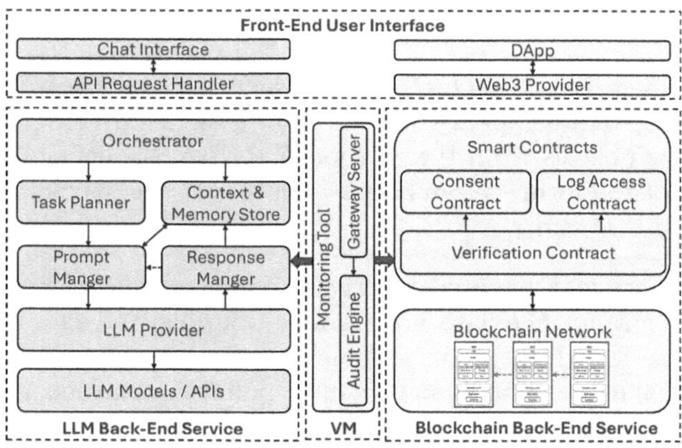

Fig. 1. A blockchain-based model for consent acquisition and verification in LLM

4 Implementation Model

This section introduces a blockchain-based solution for obtaining and verifying consent in LLM applications. Using smart contracts and a public blockchain, we ensure transparent, tamper-proof recording of parental or child consent. Our approach automates compliance checks for LLM providers, supporting PIPEDA's consent requirements. As shown in Fig. 1, the proposed architecture integrates

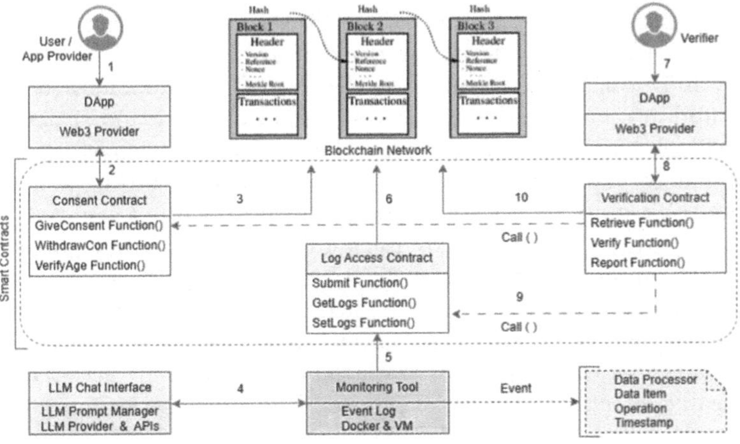

Fig. 2. A consent management protocol in an LLM application using blockchain

blockchain to manage consent and detect violations. While it includes a monitoring tool for data events, we assume these events are available and focus on smart contract-based consent and verification.

As seen from the figure, the model contains three parts: (i) LLM front-end and back-end services, (ii) blockchain front-end and back-end service, and (iii) a monitoring tool in the middle hosted on a virtual machine. The front-end user interface in our model involves a *chat interface* for receiving user queries submitted to the LLM and a *decentralized application (DApp)* for securely transmitting user consent to privacy policies on a blockchain. These policies are determined by the provider of the LLM application. The *API request handler* manages requests from the chat interface, facilitating text generation from the LLM while logging data access events and forwarding them to the monitoring tool. The *web3 provider* in the user interface provides a bridge between the DApp and the blockchain network. It allows the DApp to interact with our proposed smart contracts, send transactions, and retrieve blockchain data.

Regarding the LLM back-end service in our proposed model, the *orchestrator* manages the flow of requests between the LLM, memory store, and the API request handler for the aim of efficient execution, fault tolerance, and load balancing. It also handles task scheduling and resource allocation in order to optimize system performance. The *task planner* decomposes the user's request into structured subtasks, dynamically refining, expanding, or pruning them as the user progresses for adaptive and goal-oriented execution. The *context and memory store* provides relevant, real-time data for each prompt by retrieving semantically related information from both current context data and previous interactions. The *prompt manager* structures and optimizes prompts to include the necessary context or memory. It helps the LLM receive the right inputs and leads to the quality and relevance of responses while reducing possible errors. The *response manager* refines the LLM's output, which makes it align with the intended goals, accuracy, tone, and format for the user's request. Finally, the role of the *LLM provider* is to offer the infrastructure, model access, and support for deploying and using LLM. It manages the model's development (e.g., GPT-4), training, updates, and maintains the system's availability and scalability.

In the blockchain back-end service, we have a factory of smart contracts and a blockchain network for deploying the contracts and recording some verifiable information. We implement a smart contract, called *consent contract*, to capture the positive or negative consents of user for determined privacy policies. The *log access smart contract* is invoked by the monitoring tool to store a set of event log, each conveys what processing operation (e.g., access) was executed by an LLM actor on user data. The *verification smart contract* contains opcodes for retrieving information recorded by both the consent and log access contracts. It automatically detects privacy violations and flags them for visibility to a trusted verifier (e.g., a privacy commissioner).

The monitoring tool in our model can be implemented using different technologies (e.g., container, WebAssembly, OpenTelemetry). Its main responsibility is tracking any access and data manipulation by LLM actors on users personal data and creating events that contain such information. The tool can have two core components, called *gateway server* and *audit engine*. The former is responsible for collecting, processing, and forwarding data from the API request handler and other components within the LLM back-end service to the audit engine in the monitoring system. The role of the audit engine is creating the events based on the information received from the gateway server and calling the log access contract to send the events into the blockchain. Each event records details pertinent to a data processor (e.g., an LLM provider) who performed an operation on the user's data, including the time it occurred.

4.1 Realizing Consent Management and Verification Protocols

This section details the implementation of the consent management protocol using blockchain and smart contracts. It presents the steps for users (parents, guardians) to submit consents on the blockchain and the automated verification of operations based on consent legal principles through smart contracts.

Figure 2 illustrates the protocol governing interactions among entities and components in our model to enable both recording consent and its legal verification. In this protocol, parents, application providers, and the trusted verifier are assumed to have blockchain accounts or wallet IDs, which allow them to connect to the blockchain and execute smart contracts. Moreover, the assumption is that the application provider has clearly defined the privacy policies off-chain and submitted a copy to the blockchain in the format specified in Definition 2. Given these assumptions, we can follow a sequence of processing steps in our proposed protocol. As shown in Fig. 2, users can access the *consent contract* through the DApp (Fig. 2-step 1), implemented in the front-end interface of the LLM application, and retrieve the policies defined by the application provider (Fig. 2-step 2). They can then give their votes as positive or negative consent and submit them to the blockchain via the smart contract (Fig. 2-step 3).

Algorithm 1 Consent contract

```
1: Initialize: C ← ∅
2: function VerifyAge(u)
3:     return true if GetAge(u) ≥ legal_age, else false
4: end function
5: function GiveConsent(u, p, 𝒫)
6:     while 𝒫 ≠ ∅ do                                ▷ While there exists a policy
7:         Select π from 𝒫
8:         if VerifyAge(u) then
9:             C ← C ∪ {⟨u, p, π, ⊤, Now(), GetAge(u)⟩}
10:        end if
11:        Remove π from 𝒫
12:    end while
13: end function
14: function WithdrawConsent(u, π)
15:    if ∃⟨u, p, π, c, t, a⟩ ∈ C then
16:        Update c ← ⊥, t ← Now()
17:    end if
18: end function
19: function GetUserConsent(u, π)
20:    return latest ⟨u, p, π, c, t, a⟩ ∈ C
21: end function
```

Algorithm 1 presents the implementation of the consent contract over a set of policies $\mathcal{P}$. The set C stores consent records, where each record includes an anonymized user ID u, a data processor p, a policy $\pi \in \mathcal{P}$, and the timestamp t. The policies are described by the structure $\langle p, o, d, s \rangle$, as defined in Definition 2, which specifies the components of a policy (i.e., processor, operation, data item, and processing purpose). The algorithm verifies the user's anonymized age a before granting consent to each policy, so that only users meeting the legal age requirement (e.g., minimum 13 years old in PIPEDA) can provide consent. The age is anonymized using generalization (e.g., age range groups). With the anonymity of blockchain user identity, this generalized age information is unlikely to reveal user identity. Once consent is granted, the contract records the consent along with the current timestamp and the anonymized user age. Users can later withdraw their consent, and the corresponding consent record will be updated to reflect so. The contract can also provide the latest consent status for a given policy for future verification.

After the user consents to the application provider's policies, the monitoring tool begins tracking data processing operations (e.g., access, transfer) performed by LLM actors (e.g., LLM provider, administrator) on user data (Fig. 2-step 4). Simultaneously, it automatically deploys the *log access contract* (Fig. 2-step 5) and executes the `Submit` function to record events on blockchain. These events correspond to the relation set $R \subseteq P \times O \times D$ from Definition 1, where each event $\langle p, o, d \rangle$ represents an operation o executed by actor p on data item d. Moreover, the contract logs the timestamp of each access event.

Algorithm 2 Log access contract

```
 1: Initialize:
 2:     ℒ ← ∅                                   ▷ Event log: set of tuples ⟨p, o, d, t⟩
 3: function SUBMIT(p, o, d)                                  ▷ Log access event
 4:     t ← getCurrentTimestamp()
 5:     ℰ ← ⟨p, o, d, t⟩
 6:     ℒ ← ℒ ∪ {ℰ}                                        ▷ Append event to log
 7:     storeOnBlockchain(ℰ)
 8: end function
 9: function GETLOGS
10:     return ℒ
11: end function
```

Algorithm 2 represents the implementation of the log access contract. The algorithm records data processing operations and verifies data access events using the blockchain. It stores an event log $\mathcal{L}$ with the form of $\langle p, o, d, t\rangle$ and the timestamp t. The `Submit` function logs access events and stores them on the blockchain. The `GetLogs` function serves recorded events from the blockchain.

To verify user consents and check the compliance of data processors with them, a trusted verifier (e.g., privacy commissioner) using the DApp can connect to the blockchain (Fig. 2-step 7) upon the user's request to automatically detect violations. Precisely, the verifier invokes the *verification contract* (Fig. 2-step 8) to determine whether a processing operation was executed on personal data without the user's consent. The contract internally calls both the consent and log access contracts to retrieve logs and consents (Fig. 2-step 9) and flag possible violations for the verifier (Fig. 2-step 10).

Algorithm 3 Verification contract

```
 1: Initialize: 𝒱 ← ∅                                  ▷ Set of detected violations
 2: function VERIFY(u, p, o, d, t_exec)
 3:     ⟨u, p, π, c, t_c, a⟩ ← arg max_{⟨u,p,π,c,t_c,a⟩∈C} t_c   ▷ Retrieve latest consent for (u, p)
 4:     if c = ⊥ or ⟨u, p, π, c, t_c, a⟩ ∉ C then                 ▷ No valid consent
 5:         𝒱 ← 𝒱 ∪ {⟨u, p, o, d, t_exec⟩}
 6:         return false
 7:     else if t_c > t_exec then                    ▷ Consent was given after operation
 8:         𝒱 ← 𝒱 ∪ {⟨u, p, o, d, t_exec⟩}
 9:         return false
10:     else
11:         return true                                              ▷ Valid operation
12:     end if
13: end function
14: function REPORTVIOLATIONS
15:     for all ⟨p, o, d, t_exec⟩ ∈ ℒ do
16:         u ← GetUser(p)                      ▷ Get user associated with processor p
17:         if VERIFY(u, p, o, d, t_exec) = false then
18:             Report Consent Violation(p, o, d, t_exec)
19:         end if
20:     end for
21: end function
```

Algorithm 3 implements the verification smart contract, ensuring that all data processing events logged in the access contract align with prior user consent. It retrieves the most recent consent record and verifies each operation against it. If no valid consent is found, or if the operation occurred before consent was granted, the action is flagged as a privacy violation. The algorithm reviews all events, checks compliance, and logs violations for further review by the verifier. Definitions of the notations used are provided in Appendix A.

5 Experimental Results

To assess the performance and overhead of our proposed approach, we developed prototype smart contracts using Solidity and conducted benchmarking. We assumed that each user-application pair exclusively uses a dedicated set of smart contracts, which simplifies data structures and avoids state contention. The prototypes were deployed on a local Ethereum Proof-of-Stake (PoS) test network with hardware consisting of a 4-core 3.20 GHz CPU, 8 GB RAM, running Ubuntu 20.04. The test network comprised one Geth execution client, one Lighthouse consensus client, and one Lighthouse validator, with CPU allocations of 2, 1, and 1 cores respectively. Benchmarking was performed using the Hyperledger Caliper tool. The main functions evaluated were `GiveConsent` in the consent contract, `SubmitLog` in the log access contract, and `Verify` in the verification contract. The `WithdrawConsent` is integrated as a Boolean parameter "allow" within `GiveConsent`; setting it to False effectively withdraws consent. The detailed benchmark results are presented in the following subsections.

5.1 The Cost of Smart Contracts

Gas cost reflects the computational effort required for Ethereum blockchain transactions and is commonly used to measure smart contract execution expenses. Before benchmarking, contracts were manually deployed and executed to record their Gas usage, as shown in Table 1. Estimated fees are based on Ethereum's average Gas and Ether prices on March 24, 2025. Deploying the consent, log access, and verification contracts used 724149, 760261, and 905877 Gas, respectively. The `GiveConsent` function used 192439 Gas for new consent and 171562 for updates or withdrawals. `SubmitLog` required 164657 Gas for the first record and 143998 for subsequent ones. Unlike others, the `Verify` function is read-only with no transaction cost; its Gas usage, roughly $52211 + 13626n$ ($\approx$65837 for $n = 1$), is shown for comparison, where n is the number of prior consent actions. These measured gas costs reveal the non-negligible overhead of trust. In practice, alternative blockchain platforms may balance trust and cost.

Table 1. The Cost of Prototype Smart Contracts

Smart Contract Transaction/Call	Used Gas (Wei)	Estimated Fee (Ether)	Estimated Fee (USD)
Consent contract deployment	724149	0.00151	3.15
GiveConsent function (new consent)	192439	0.000402	0.84
GiveConsent function (update/withdraw)	171562	0.000402	0.84
Log access contract deployment	760261	0.00159	3.30
SubmitLog function (the first record)	164657	0.000344	0.72
SubmitLog function (the subsequent record)	143998	0.000344	0.72
Verification contract deployment	905877	0.00189	3.94
Verify function	≈65837	0	0

5.2 The Performance of Contract Functions

Three functions in our proposed smart contracts are critical in performance. The `GiveConsent` function latency determines the user experience when giving and withdrawing consents. The `SubmitLog` function throughput affects the operational fluency in personal data processing. The `Verify` function throughput determines the validation efficiency of verifiers.

The GiveConsent benchmark tested fixed send rates from 2 to 10 TPS over 300 s per round. It reached a maximum throughput of 7.9 TPS and average latency of 11.3 s (Fig. 3a). Throughput increased with send rate up to 8 TPS, but latency spiked at 10 TPS due to transaction backlog. The main bottleneck was the Ethereum testnet, where PoS consensus allows one block every 12 s with a 30 million Gas limit – yielding a theoretical max of about 14.5 TPS. With EIP-1559, the effective block gas target is 50%, halving the throughput to 7.9 TPS. When a high gas price was forced, the throughput hit 14 TPS, matching the theoretical limit. Thus, the blockchain mechanics and GiveConsent's gas cost together decide the throughput ceiling.

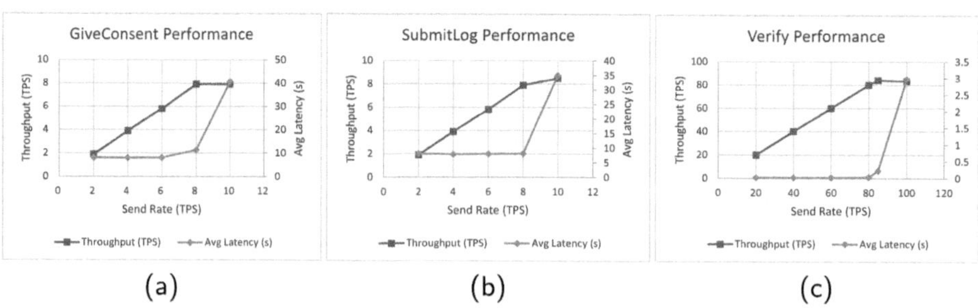

Fig. 3. Smart contract performance (a) GiveConsent throughput and avg latency, (b) SubmitLog throughput and avg latency, (c) Verify throughput and avg latency

The SubmitLog benchmark tested fixed send rates from 2 to 10 TPS over 300 s. With similar gas costs, its throughput and latency closely matched GiveConsent (Fig. 3b), peaking at 8.5 TPS. High latency at 10 TPS was due to transaction backlog. Like GiveConsent, SubmitLog's bottleneck is the blockchain's block gas limit and EIP-1559, which limit the total gas per block.

The Verify function benchmark differs since it is read-only, using calls instead of transactions at rates from 20 to 100 TPS. Pre-generated 300 consent records and 3,000 log records simulate typical application loads. Throughput rose from 20 to 84 TPS, plateauing afterward, with latency spiking at 85 and 100 TPS (Fig. 3c). Without transactions, blockchain limits do not apply; throughput depends on the Geth client's ability to process Verify operations over the data.

5.3 The Overhead of Contract Functions

Besides throughput and latency, resource use of blockchain components was tracked during benchmarks. Memory, disk I/O, and network traffic were minimal: about 200 MB memory for the execution and consensus clients, 30 MB for the validator; disk I/O in hundreds of KB; and under 5 MB total traffic per 300-second round. CPU usage was more revealing and matched throughput trends. Figure 4 shows CPU use. In the GiveConsent benchmark, execution client CPU rose linearly with throughput, while consensus client and validator usage stayed steady, since PoS consensus creates blocks independently of transactions. Total CPU stayed low (under 10% of a core), aligning with blockchain throughput limits. SubmitLog showed similar patterns, with minor consensus and validator CPU fluctuations unrelated to workload. For Verify, a CPU-heavy task, execution client CPU grew linearly to 165% of a core at max throughput.

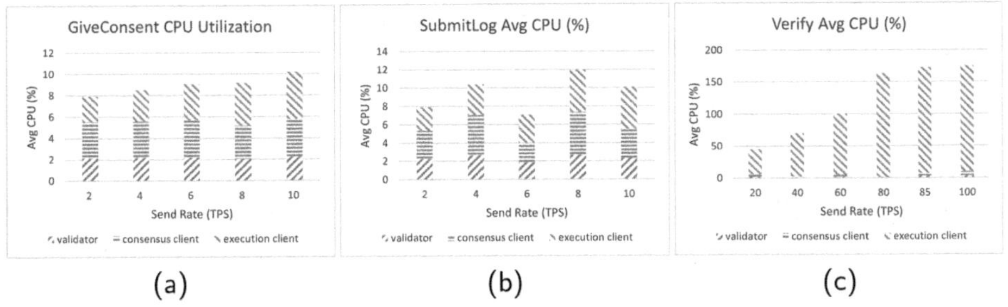

Fig. 4. Blockchain CPU utilization: (a) Avg CPU utilization for GiveConsent, (b) Avg CPU utilization for SubmitLog, (c) Avg CPU utilization for Verify

6 Conclusion

This paper proposed a blockchain-based architecture for LLM applications designed for children. By defining the data processing lifecycle within these applications, we provided formal descriptions of privacy policies and consent mechanisms to support their implementation in a tamper-proof and verifiable manner. We introduced a consent management protocol that allows parents and guardians to review and approve data processing purposes involving their children's information in advance. Moreover, the protocol enables trusted verifiers to detect and be notified of violations of non-consented data processing. We implemented the protocol and evaluated its cost and performance via benchmarks. The results confirm that the solution is viable for child-oriented LLM applications.

Some challenges are not addressed in the design but can be resolved by integrating other techniques. For example, cost delegation to service providers can shift transaction costs from users; alternative blockchain can improve performance and reduce costs. Along with such techniques, our model can balance transparency, regulatory compliance, and real-world feasibility, providing a meaningful step toward secure and trustworthy consent management in sensitive AI applications involving children.

Future work will focus on implementing the monitoring tool proposed in our architecture. We also plan to explore a general framework for identifying the types of processing operations performed by LLM actors on children's data. In addition, enhancing data protection through secure and distributed file systems will be a key area of continued research.

Acknowledgments. This paper was made possible in-part through the support of the National Cybersecurity Consortium and the Government of Canada (CSIN). Also, the authors would like to thank the Natural Sciences and Engineering Research Council of Canada (NSERC) for their financial support.

A Used Notations

Table 2 provides the descriptions of the notations and symbols used in the paper.

Table 2. Glossary of Notations

Symbol	Definition
P	A set of data processors
O	A set of data processing operations
D	A set of personal data items
$\mathcal{P}$	A set of privacy policies
R	A relation set relating processor, operation and data
$C(\pi, t)$	Consent function on policy π in time t
$U(\pi, t)$	Update function for consent
T	Time instances
S	A set of data processing purposes
$\mathcal{L}$	A set of event logs
$\mathcal{V}$	A set of detected violations
L	The lifecycle model for data processing activities
u	An anonymized user ID
a	An anonymized version of user age
d	A personal data item
t_{exec}	The timestamp when a data operation was executed

References

1. Abu-Dabaseh, F., et al.: Enhancing privacy and security in decentralized social systems: blockchain-based approach. In: 2024 2nd International Conference on Cyber Resilience (ICCR), pp. 1–6 (2024)
2. Albanese, G., Calbimonte, J.-P., Schumacher, M., Calvaresi, D.: Dynamic consent management for clinical trials via private blockchain technology. J. Ambient. Intell. Humaniz. Comput. **11**(11), 4909–4926 (2020). https://doi.org/10.1007/s12652-020-01761-1
3. Barati, M., Buchanan, W.J., Lo, O., Rana, O.: A privacy-preserving distributed platform for COVID-19 vaccine passports. In: Proceedings of the 14th IEEE/ACM International Conference on Utility and Cloud Computing Companion, pp. 1–6. ACM, Leicester, United Kingdom (2022)
4. Barati, M., Rana, O., Petri, I., Theodorakopoulos, G.: GDPR compliance verification in internet of things. IEEE ACCESS **8**, 119697–119709 (2020)
5. Barati, M., Theodorakopoulos, G., Rana, O.: Automating GDPR compliance verification for cloud-hosted services. In: 2020 International Symposium on Networks, Computers and Communications (ISNCC), pp. 1–6. IEEE (2020)
6. Bioglio, L., Capecchi, S., Peiretti, F., Sayed, D., Torasso, A., Pensa, R.G.: A social network simulation game to raise awareness of privacy among school children. IEEE Trans. Learn. Technol. **12**(4), 456–469 (2018)
7. Chkirbene, Z., Hamila, R., Gouissem, A., Devrim, U.: Large language models (LLM) in industry: a survey of applications, challenges, and trends. In: 2024 IEEE 21st International Conference on Smart Communities: Improving Quality of Life using AI, Robotics and IoT (HONET), pp. 229–234 (2024)

8. Choice Internet Brands, Inc.: Kids ChatGPT: Learn, Play & Talk with A.I. Made for Kids (2025). https://kidschatgpt.com/. Accessed 21 May 2025
9. Ekblaw, A., Azaria, A., Halamka, J.D., Lippman, A.: A case study for blockchain in healthcare: MedRec prototype for electronic health records and medical research data. In: Proceedings of IEEE Open and Big Data Conference, vol. 13, p. 13. Vienna, Austria (2016)
10. Faber, B., Michelet, G., Weidmann, N., Mukkamala, R.R., Vatrapu, R.: BPDIMS: a blockchain-based personal data and identity management system. In: The 52nd Hawaii International Conference on System Sciences, pp. 6855–6864 (2019)
11. Federal Trade Commission (FTC): Children's online privacy protection act (coppa) (2024). https://www.ftc.gov/legal-library/browse/rules/childrens-online-privacy-protection-rule-coppa. Accessed May 2025
12. Garcia, R.D., et al.: A survey of blockchain-based privacy applications: an analysis of consent management and self-sovereign identity approaches. arXiv preprint arXiv:2411.16404 (2024)
13. Genestier, P., et al.: Blockchain for consent management in the eHealth environment: a nugget for privacy and security challenges. J. Int. Soc. Telemed. eHealth **5**, e9–e24 (2017)
14. Government of Canada: Personal information protection and electronic documents act (pipeda) (2024). https://laws-lois.justice.gc.ca/eng/acts/P-8.6/. Accessed May 2025
15. Haque, M.A., Li, S.: Exploring ChatGPT and its impact on society. AI and Ethics, pp. 1–13 (2024)
16. Hu, C., et al.: CrowdMed-II: a blockchain-based framework for efficient consent management in health data sharing. World Wide Web **25**(3), 1489–1515 (2022)
17. Huang, L.: Ethics of artificial intelligence in education: student privacy and data protection. Sci. Insights Educ. Front. **16**(2), 2577–2587 (2023)
18. Irwin, J., Dharamshi, A., Zon, N.: Children's privacy in the age of artificial intelligence. Canadian Standards Association (2021)
19. Kaaniche, N., Laurent, M.: A blockchain-based data usage auditing architecture with enhanced privacy and availability. In: 2017 IEEE 16th International Symposium on Network Computing and Applications (NCA), pp. 1–5. IEEE (2017)
20. Kakarlapudi, P.V., Mahmoud, Q.H.: A systematic review of blockchain for consent management. In: Healthcare, vol. 9, p. 137. MDPI (2021)
21. Khatiwada, P., Yang, B., Lin, J.C., Mugurusi, G., Underbekken, S.: A reference design model to manage consent in data subjects-centered internet of things devices. IoT **5**(1), 100–122 (2024)
22. Khatoon, A.: A blockchain-based smart contract system for healthcare management. Electronics **9**(1), 94 (2020)
23. Miao, F., Holmes, W., Huang, R., Zhang, H., et al.: AI and education: a guidance for policymakers. UNESCO Publishing (2021)
24. Mooradian, N., Franks, P.C., Srivastav, A.: The impact of artificial intelligence on data privacy: a risk management perspective. Rec. Manag. J. **35**(1) (2025)
25. Neisse, R., Steri, G., Nai-Fovino, I.: A blockchain-based approach for data accountability and provenance tracking. In: Proceedings of the 12th International Conference on Availability, Reliability and Security. ARES '17. Association for Computing Machinery, New York, NY, USA (2017)

26. Rantos, K., Drosatos, G., Demertzis, K., Ilioudis, C., Papanikolaou, A., Kritsas, A.: ADvoCATE: a consent management platform for personal data processing in the IoT using blockchain technology. In: Lanet, J.-L., Toma, C. (eds.) SECITC 2018. LNCS, vol. 11359, pp. 300–313. Springer, Cham (2019). https://doi.org/10.1007/978-3-030-12942-2_23
27. Rantos, K., Drosatos, G., Kritsas, A., Ilioudis, C., Papanikolaou, A., Filippidis, A.P.: A blockchain-based platform for consent management of personal data processing in the IoT ecosystem. Secur. Commun. Netw. **2019**(1), 1431578 (2019)
28. Shinde, R., Patil, S., Kotecha, K., Potdar, V., Selvachandran, G., Abraham, A.: Securing AI-based healthcare systems using blockchain technology: a state-of-the-art systematic literature review and future research directions. Trans. Emerg. Telecommun. Technol. **35**(1), e4884 (2024)
29. Tith, D., et al.: Patient consent management by a purpose-based consent model for electronic health record based on blockchain technology. Healthc. Inform. Res. **26**(4), 265–273 (2020)
30. Truong, N.B., Sun, K., Lee, G.M., Guo, Y.: GDPR-compliant personal data management: a blockchain-based solution. IEEE Trans. Inf. Forensics Secur. **15**, 1746–1761 (2019)
31. Walters, N.: Privacy law issues in blockchains: an analysis of PIPEDA, the GDPR, and proposals for compliance. Can. J. Law. Technol. **17**(2), 1–44 (2019)
32. Zhou, C., Barati, M., Shafiq, O.: A compliance-based architecture for supporting GDPR accountability in cloud computing. Futur. Gener. Comput. Syst. **145**, 104–120 (2023)

Interpreting Differential Privacy: Linking Privacy Budget to Disclosure Risk

Mahboobeh Dorafshanian(✉), Mohamed Mejri, and Djedjiga Mouheb

Department of Computer Science and Software Engineering, Laval University, Quebec City, Canada
{mador146,momej,djmou7}@ulaval.ca

Abstract. Differential Privacy (DP) has become a standard method for safeguarding individual data in statistical and machine learning systems. However, its core parameter, the privacy budget ε, remains abstract and difficult to interpret, especially with respect to the risk of disclosure in the real world. This paper explores the link between ε and the Risk of Data Disclosure (RoD), aiming to provide both theoretical and practical clarity. We begin by reviewing existing research linking DP with RoD and highlight the limitations of current models in helping practitioners understand or manage risk. Next, we present a detailed empirical evaluation using synthetic health data, measuring how changes in ε influence both RoD and utility, evaluated using the Mean Squared Error (MSE). Our results show a clear trade-off: smaller ε enhances privacy but decreases accuracy, while larger ε offers better utility at the expense of increased disclosure risk. These insights offer practical guidance for choosing ε in real-world settings and support more interpretable and responsible DP implementations.

Keywords: Differential Privacy · Risk · Data privacy · Security · Big Data · Privacy Budget · Risk of Data Disclosure

1 Introduction

Today, the risk of information disclosure is increasing, and, particularly in Canada, this risk has increased drastically 160% year over year [22]. With the California Consumer Privacy Act (CCPA) [19] effective on January 1, 2020, and the General Data Protection Regulation (GDPR) [45] applied in the EU from May 2018, there is a compelling demand to provide rigorous privacy guarantees to users when analyzing and collecting their data.

The concept of Differential Privacy is motivated by the assumption that attackers have arbitrary background knowledge [15]. Differential Privacy aims to limit the ability of an attacker, who can only learn information from the release of a dataset, within a multiplicative factor ε, regardless of the background knowledge the attacker possesses.

Despite the publication of hundreds of papers on Differential Privacy models and mechanisms and their application in various fields such as machine learning

K. Adi et al. (Eds.): CRiSIS 2025, LNCS 16295, pp. 186–201, 2026.
https://doi.org/10.1007/978-3-032-20732-6_12

[1,24], database [47,52], and security, several critical challenges remain unresolved.

Central to DP is the privacy parameter ε, often referred to as the privacy budget. Despite its mathematical rigor, ε remains difficult to interpret in practice [10]. How much privacy does a specific value of ε provide? What is the real risk of re-identification or disclosure when using a given ε? These questions are crucial not only for data scientists but also for legal advisors, policy makers, and end-users. However, the gap between the theoretical definition of DP and its practical implications - especially in terms of the *Risk of Data Disclosure (RoD)*—has not been adequately addressed.

Motivated by this gap, our paper investigates the relationship between ε and RoD in both theoretical and empirical terms. We aim to answer the following questions:

- How can the privacy guarantee provided by ε-DP be translated into a more intuitive and quantifiable risk of data disclosure?
- How do changes in ε affect both privacy (as measured by RoD) and utility (as measured by accuracy loss)?

To address these questions, we present a comprehensive study that includes the following.

1. A structured review of the literature on Differential Privacy and risk quantification, highlighting gaps in how current models relate ε to disclosure risk.
2. A practical framework for understanding how the privacy budget affects real-world risks, using illustrative examples.
3. An empirical evaluation using synthetic health data to quantify the relationship between ε, risk of disclosure (RoD), and utility (measured via Mean Squared Error (MSE)).

Our findings demonstrate how varying the values of ε leads to measurable and predictable changes in RoD and precision. By providing this bridge between formal definitions and practical consequences, we offer actionable insights for practitioners, researchers, and policymakers who must choose privacy settings in real-world deployments.

1.1 Motivating Example

Suppose that we have a hospital database. In this database, we have private information about patients, such as height, weight, and HIV. In the Differential Privacy domain, we imagine that the attacker has unbounded background information. Without applying the Differential Privacy mechanisms, the risk of data disclosure is high (nearly 100%), and an attacker can obtain any information from the database. But how can we reduce this risk? How can we measure and control the risk of data disclosure by privacy budget ε? We will discuss these questions during our study to find the appropriate answers and come back to explain more about this example in Section IV.B.

The remainder of this paper is organized as follows. Section 2 introduces the main notation and the foundational concepts related to Differential Privacy. Section 3 presents a structured review of recent literature addressing Differential Privacy and data disclosure risk, highlighting key contributions and gaps. Section 4 develops the core context and methodology of the study, including a practical example and an empirical evaluation of how variations in the privacy budget ε affect both risk and utility. Finally, Sect. 5 concludes the paper and outlines directions for future research.

2 Preliminaries

2.1 Differential Privacy Framework

'Differential privacy (DP) [54] is a tool to broadly share information about a dataset by describing the patterns of groups within the dataset while preserving individual data in the dataset.'

To better understand this definition, consider a survey on people's average monthly income. Definitely, many might not want to say the exact amount. How can privacy be preserved in such cases? In the DP approach, we asked each individual to choose a random value (noise) in an interval of +100 to −100, add it to their average salary, and give us the result of the sum. For example, if one's income is 4000$, by adding a random number −100 to it, he gives us the result 3900$ in this case. Thus, he preserves his privacy. Generally, DP adds noise (a random number) to the data (input or output) to make it more private and secure.

By Cynthia Dwork [16]: "Differential Privacy describes a promise made by a data holder or curator to a data owner (individuals) and the promise is like this: "if individuals allow their information to be used in any study or analysis, they will not be adversely affected, no matter that other datasets, studies or information sources are available now or in the future"". The key query for Differential Privacy is "if we remove or add a person to the dataset and the query result does not change, then the person's privacy is completely protected". Using the differential privacy framework, as illustrated in Fig. 1, we can assess the guarantees provided by the algorithm designed to protect privacy.

To check this, suppose that we have the original database D with N entries, we create a parallel database D' with $N-1$ entries. We have binary data in our database, and we want to have a 'Sum query'. Thus, we should add all 1's and give the result. When we run the "Sum query" in each database, if the $S(D) \neq S(D')$, it means non-zero sensitivity, because the outputs are different, and this query is conditioned on the individual's data in the database.

Differential Privacy can address many limitations of previous works, such as randomization [50,53], k-anonymity [35], t-closeness [32], and l-diversity [44,56]. In fact, we randomize part of the mechanism's behavior to provide privacy. The key to randomness is to make it hard to tell which result came from randomness and which came from real data. Without randomization, we can ask such a question: "What parameters does the algorithm choose when we apply it to

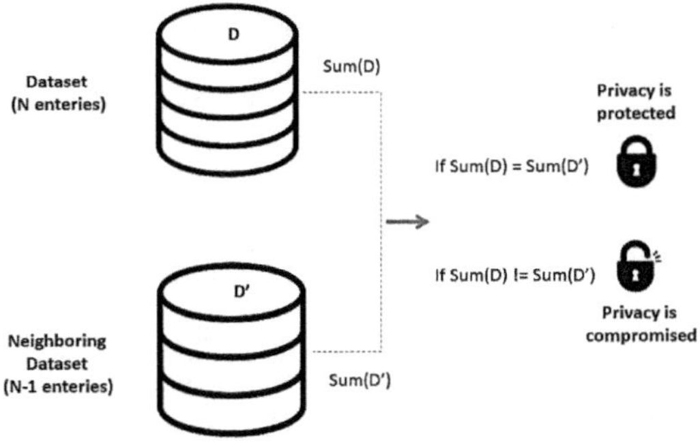

Fig. 1. Differential Privacy framework.

the database?" By applying randomness to the algorithm, we would be able to ask: "What is the probability that the algorithm chooses parameters in the set of possible parameters, when we apply it to the database?" We introduce this probability as the privacy budget (ε) in the Differential Privacy domain. A smaller privacy budget provides stronger privacy guarantees. Intuitively, in Differential Privacy, we can measure how much the output can change if we change the information of a single person in the database. It is worth mentioning again that Differential Privacy is a definition, not an algorithm. For a given value of ε and a given query (q), there are many differentially private algorithms to achieve a good result for q. Some will guarantee better privacy and accuracy than others [34,48]. In Table 1, we summarize the notation used in our paper.

Table 1. Important notations used throughout the paper.

Notion	Description
$\mathcal{M}$	Privacy mechanism (probabilistic)
$\mathcal{X}$	Universe Set of data types
$\mathbb{N}$	Set of all non-negative integers
$x \in \mathbb{N}^{\|\mathcal{X}\|}$	Dataset in the possible datasets(we also use D, D', y, ...)
$\mathcal{M}(x)$	The distribution of the outputs of $\mathcal{M}$ given input x
$Range(\mathcal{M})$	Set of possible outputs of the mechanism
$\mathcal{S} \subseteq Range(\mathcal{M})$	Subset of possible outputs
ε	The maximum distance between the result of a query on database (x) and database (y)
δ	The probability of data leakage
$\|\|x - y\|\|_1$	L_1 norm measures how many records are different between x and y

2.2 Formal Definition Of Differential Privacy

According to Cynthia Dwork's book [16]: A randomized algorithm $\mathcal{M}$ with domain $\mathbb{N}^{|\mathcal{X}|}$ is (ε,δ)–differential private if for all $\mathcal{S} \subseteq Range(\mathcal{M})$ and for all $x, y \in \mathbb{N}^{|\mathcal{X}|}$ such that $\|x - y\|_1 \leq 1$:

$$Pr[\mathcal{M}(x) \in \mathcal{S}] \leq exp(\varepsilon)Pr[\mathcal{M}(y) \in \mathcal{S}] + \delta \tag{1}$$

This is a formal definition of Differential Privacy, which guarantees that the manner of a randomized algorithm on similar input databases is likely the same. $\mathcal{M}$ is a random algorithm. We have two models for applying $\mathcal{M}$. First, send the query to the original dataset and then add the noise to the result (i.e., query(D)+ *noise*). Second, we add the noise to the dataset and then send the query to the synthetic dataset (i.e., query ($D + noise$)). $\mathcal{S}$ is a set of all possible outputs of $\mathcal{M}$ that could be predicted. x is the entries in the database (that is, N). y is the entries in the parallel database (that is, $N - 1$). The epsilon (ε) is the maximum distance between the result of a query in the database (x) and the same query in the database (y). Delta (δ) is the probability of data leakage. It is worth noting that this definition does not create DP. It is just measuring how much privacy is granted by a query. Moreover, it compares the result of a query $\mathcal{M}$ in the database (x) and in a parallel database (y), which has a lower entry. The probability of random distribution can differ between the database (x) and the adjacent database (y) by epsilon (ε) and delta (δ).

Epsilon (ε), which is also known as the privacy parameter or the privacy budget. It is a metric of privacy loss by adding or removing one entry. When ε is small, (ε,δ)-Differential Privacy states that for all pairs of neighbor databases x, y and all outputs $\mathcal{M}$, an attacker cannot find which is the true database by observing the output. Practically, the value of ε is less than 1, such as 0.01, 0.1, 0.5, and 0.8. Small epsilons have quite similar behavior, so they guarantee similar privacy. When ε is large, for example, (10, δ)-differentially private mechanism, it shows that the ratio of probabilities of observing $\mathcal{M}$ conditioned on the database x or y, is large. Thus, by a smaller ε we have better privacy, but a less accurate result. Delta (δ) is another parameter in DP. When $\delta = 0$, we say that the mechanism is ε-differentially private. Delta is the probability that the data will accidentally leak. In practice, the value of δ, which is less than the inverse of any polynomial in the size of the database, is more useful. We can see that ε is independent of the size of the database, while δ is dependent on it. So, which one is better? ε-Differential Privacy or (ε, δ)-Differential Privacy?

ε-Differential Privacy or (ε,0)-Differential Privacy states that when we run the mechanism $\mathcal{M}$ on the databases x and the adjacent database y, the outputs are (almost) equally likely to be the same. While (ε, δ)-Differential Privacy asserts that for all adjacent databases x and y, the output value of $\mathcal{M}$ will be generated extremely unlikely, much more or much less when the database is x or y. It ensures that for every pair of neighboring databases x, y, with probability at least 1-δ, the absolute value of the privacy loss is bounded by ε. In other words, in ε-Differential Privacy, when the probability of data leak is zero, differentially private datasets have very similar output (with distance of one or less).

We use (ε, δ)-Differential Privacy in the case of large databases when the probability of data leakage and sensitivity are high.

2.3 Global Sensitivity (Δf)

To calibrate noise, we define the **global sensitivity** of a function f as [1]:

$$\Delta f = \max_{\|x-y\|_1 \leq 1} \|f(x) - f(y)\|_1$$

This is the maximum amount of data that can change the query result for a single individual. The Laplace mechanism adds noise proportional to $\frac{\Delta f}{\varepsilon}$.

2.4 Laplace Mechanism

Given a function f, the Laplace mechanism is defined as [16]:

$$M(x) = f(x) + \text{Lap}\left(\frac{\Delta f}{\varepsilon}\right)$$

This ensures ε-Differential Privacy by spreading the output distribution enough to obscure the effect of any individual record.

3 Literature Review

Differential Privacy (DP) has emerged as a foundational technique for protecting individual privacy in data analysis across diverse domains, including healthcare [4,29,49], genomics data sharing [6], and location privacy [2,11,20,25,26,43,55]. While extensive research has advanced DP techniques, this section focuses on studies specifically addressing the risk of data disclosure (RoD) and the interplay between privacy guarantees and practical privacy risks. For foundational background on DP concepts and mechanisms, we refer readers to the seminal works and comprehensive surveys by Dwork [15,16], which provide in-depth theoretical foundations [14,17] and detailed analyses of DP mechanisms [27].

3.1 Practical Tools and Frameworks for Differential Privacy

To bridge the gap between theory and practice, several tools and libraries have been developed to facilitate the implementation and adoption of DP. Notably, the GRAM-DP library by Aitsam *et al.*. [3,12] offers a user-friendly platform that simplifies DP application by enabling users to configure privacy parameters and assess their impact on data disclosure risk. This framework includes illustrative use cases that demonstrate DP's practical utility. However, GRAM-DP's scope is limited in that it does not incorporate different adjacency definitions or advanced composition theorems, which are critical for a comprehensive risk assessment and privacy accounting.

3.2 Privacy Budget Selection and Theoretical Risk Modeling

Selecting an appropriate privacy budget ε remains a central challenge in DP deployment, as it directly governs the privacy-utility trade-off and risk exposure. Lee and Clifton [31] provide a detailed theoretical analysis linking ε to RoD. Their model assumes an adversary with arbitrary background knowledge except uncertainty about an individual's participation in a dataset D'. By evaluating the adversary's posterior belief updates upon observing a DP mechanism's output, they rigorously show how ε constrains information leakage. This enables obtaining bounds on ε to maintain changes in adversarial belief within acceptable thresholds. While pioneering, their analysis focuses exclusively on background knowledge attacks, omitting other attack vectors such as linkage attacks.

Recent contributions have strengthened the link between ε, risk, and usability. Zhu and Fernandez [58] introduce a *Relative Disclosure Risk* (RDR) metric that makes ε's effect on individual risk within the dataset transparent, supported by practical algorithms and a user study aimed at helping the selection of privacy budgets. Kazan and Reiter [28] propose a Bayesian framework aligning ε with acceptable posterior disclosure probabilities, enabling data stewards to calibrate privacy release based on quantifiable risk thresholds.

3.3 Contextual Risk and Multi-Consumer Privacy Models

Several studies have explored modeling privacy risk in more complex contextual settings. Bkakria *et al.*. [7] introduce a three-dimensional framework that captures contextual risk in DP by considering data utilization contexts and data consumer characteristics. They aim to optimally allocate the privacy budget across multiple data consumers, though they acknowledge the inherent NP-hardness of measuring privacy budget accurately in complex scenarios.

Dankar and Badgi [11] address limitations in biomedical data sharing, proposing a risk-aware system that models privacy risk through four factors: purpose of data access, data sensitivity, user risk profile, and user location. Although providing valuable insights into contextual privacy risk, their work does not specifically address risk quantification within the DP framework.

3.4 Empirical Evaluations and Comparative Tool Analysis

Zhang *et al.*. [57] conduct a comprehensive evaluation of open-source DP tools, assessing their impact on different functionalities and quantifying privacy-utility trade-offs. Their work offers practical guidelines for selecting DP tools tailored to user privacy and utility requirements, and they make their evaluation framework publicly available for reproducibility.

Hayes *et al.*. [21] investigate the interaction between adversarial risk and DP-induced noise, examining how DP mechanisms affect model robustness and generalization. Their analysis shows that choices such as clipping norms and adversarial perturbation sizes influence privacy risks and optimization performance.

Drechsler and Bailie [13] examine the challenges of applying DP to complex survey data, including weighting, sampling, and imputation strategies, and how these affect RoD in practice.

3.5 Risk of Data Disclosure and Related Models

McClure *et al.* [36] study the relationship between prior and posterior beliefs in synthetic binary data generated under DP, highlighting challenges in extending their analysis beyond simple binary or numerical datasets.

Naldi and Giuseppe [39] propose a notion of RoD linked to noise pollution in the count of queries, offering a method to select ε by measuring the output deviation. However, their approach is limited to counting queries and does not extend to joint distributions.

Zaeem *et al.* [33] present a graphical Bayesian model called the Identity Ecosystem to represent and analyze the risks of exposure to correlated personal attributes. Their framework predicts the future risk and losses associated with identity exposure, addressing complex interdependencies that are often overlooked in traditional DP analyzes. Jarmin *et al.* [23] advocate for formal criteria in the evaluation of disclosure risk, evaluating the counterfactual risk methodology of DP, and comparing it with absolute risk frameworks.

3.6 Comparative Analysis of Privacy Techniques

Table 2 summarizes a comparative evaluation of common privacy-preserving techniques along with Differential Privacy. The comparison highlights their relative robustness against linkage and background knowledge attacks, compatibility with various types of database, and primary challenges.

Table 2. Comparison of Privacy Techniques

Technique	Linkage Attack	Background Knowledge Attack	Database Compatibility	Challenges
Randomization [53]	High	High	Yes	Adds noise to non-sensitive data
K-Anonymity [9]	Medium	High	Yes	Vulnerable to homogeneity and other attacks; NP-hard
T-Closeness [32]	Medium	Medium	Yes	Insufficient privacy guarantees
L-Diversity [35]	Medium	Medium	Yes	Vulnerable to skewness and similarity attacks
DP [17]	None	None	No	Some mechanisms require modified data servers

Table 3 further compares Differential Privacy techniques based on data server types, privacy budget management, risk of disclosure considerations, and impact of information disclosure on risk management.

Table 3. Comparison of Differential Privacy Techniques

Technique	Data Server Type	Privacy Budget Management	RoD Consideration	Impact of Disclosure on Risk Management
FLEX [26]	Trusted compatible	No	No	No
Chorus [40]	Untrusted compatible	No	No	No
WPINQ/PINQ [37,42]	Untrusted modified	No	No	No
Sample &Aggregate [41]	Trusted modified	No	No	No
Airavat [46]	Trusted modified	No	No	No
GUPT [38]	Untrusted modified	No	No	No
Tsou *et al.* [51]	Trusted compatible	Yes	Yes	No
Kohli *et al.* [30]	Trusted compatible	Yes	Yes	No
Barthe *et al.* [5]	Trusted compatible	Yes	No	No
Fioretto *et al.* [18]	Trusted compatible	Yes	No	No
GRAM-DP [3,12]	Trusted compatible	Yes	Yes	Yes

Our review reveals that while many works adopt fixed or predetermined privacy budgets without explicitly quantifying RoD, only a few studies rigorously address risk from multiple perspectives. To the best of our knowledge, none comprehensively evaluates how information disclosure impacts overall risk management. This gap motivates the need for more holistic and practical approaches, which our work aims to contribute.

4 Context and Method

4.1 The Relationship Between ε and the ROD

In [8], Tsou *et al.* used a non-interactive mechanism to guarantee data privacy and to evaluate the Risk of Data disclosure (RoD) using maximal noise estimation. The targeted dataset is protected with k-anonymization under the quantity of noise defined in Differential Privacy.

In their recent work, Tsou *et al.* [51] proposed a method for evaluating RoD based on noise estimation for a multidimensional counting query in a dataset with independent numerical attributes. They proposed this definition [51]: A randomized function $\mathcal{M}$ is ε–differential private if for any datasets D_1, D_2 with at most one different record and any possible outputs $\mathcal{S} \subseteq Range(\mathcal{M})$,

$$Pr[\mathcal{M}(D_1) \in \mathcal{S}] Pr[\mathcal{M}(D_2) \in \mathcal{S}] \leq e^{\varepsilon} \tag{2}$$

where the probability Pr depends on $\mathcal{M}$ randomness.

Differential Privacy can be implemented by adding Laplace noise to the output of the query or the original dataset to perturb the sensitive data. In the dataset, the maximal effect of a record on the output of a query function is global sensitivity. For any query q, the stochastic function $\mathcal{M}$,

$$\mathcal{M}(D) = q(D) + \{Lap_1(\frac{1}{\lambda}), Lap_2(\frac{1}{\lambda}), \ldots, Lap_n(\frac{1}{\lambda})\} \tag{3}$$

satisfies ε–Differential Privacy, that $Lap_i(\frac{1}{\lambda})$ are i.i.d. Laplace variables with $\lambda = \frac{\varepsilon}{\Delta q}$ [51]. Adding Laplace noise to individuals' records can guarantee their privacy.

If $A(j)$ is the real numerical value of the j-th individual's data in the original dataset D, by adding Laplace noise to it: $A'(j) = A(j) + Lap_j(\frac{1}{\lambda})$. Due to the value of Laplace noise $Lap_j(\frac{1}{\lambda})$, we have the variation in the value of $A'(j)$. So, the actual value $A(j)$ would be in the interval $[A'(j) - Lap_j(\frac{1}{\lambda}), A'(j) + Lap_j(\frac{1}{\lambda})]$. The parameter $\frac{1}{\lambda}$ generates the noise which is from $-\infty$ to $+\infty$.

The value of Laplace noise is selected randomly and unboundedly, but we can estimate the maximal value of noise $\max(Lap(\frac{1}{\lambda}))$. The detail of this estimation is described in [51]. The $\max(Lap(\frac{1}{\lambda}))$ is the maximum value of noise related to the value of ε. The maximum value of the noise is equivalent to $-\frac{\varepsilon * ln(2-2\gamma)}{\Delta q}$. Now we can define the RoD according to the maximum value of the noise. By applying the Laplace noise, the actual value of $A(j)$ would be hidden in the interval $R = [A'(j) - Lap_j(\frac{1}{\lambda}), A'(j) + Lap_j(\frac{1}{\lambda})]$. So, if there are ξ_j values which fall into R, the RoD for the actual value $A(j)$ is equal to $\frac{1}{\xi_j}$ ($\frac{1}{\xi_j}$ is the estimated probability for the actual value $A(j)$).

4.2 An Example for Evaluating RoD

Here, we give an example of using certain statistical attributes and evaluating the ROD for the assigned sensitive attribute. Suppose that we have a hospital database that includes private and sensitive information about patients. This information includes height, weight, and the status of HIV.

In Fig. 2, we suppose that an adversary has the background information about the patient, such as an individual's weight (65kg) and height (157cm), and wants to determine whether this person has HIV or not. In the case that we do not

Original Database (D)		
Attributes		
Height (cm)	Weight (kg)	HIV (Y/N)
149	65	0
148	60	0
152	90	0
155	72	0
159	83	0
157	65	1
163	85	1
166	62	0
174	79	0
167	97	0

Synthetic Database (D′)		
Attributes		
Height (cm)	Weight (kg)	HIV (Y/N)
155	59	0
149	68	0
155	100	0
155	53	1
150	68	1
167	72	0
175	95	1
155	46	0
175	83	0
179	93	0

Fig. 2. Example for evaluating the RoD for the assigned sensitive attribute of HIV.

use the Differential Privacy approach, the target person can directly identify themselves (as shown in the left column of the table), and the risk of data disclosure is equal to 1.

Next, we use the Differential Privacy mechanism and perturb the output by adding this noise. In the previous section, we added the noise to the actual data; the actual values of individuals' information will be hidden within an interval. In our example, the maximum value of noise is 20 for weight, 10 for height, and 1 for HIV to release the synthetic dataset. In the right column (the synthetic dataset that we add noise to), we have 5 rows that can be matched to the adversary information. So, the risk of data disclosure for weight (65 kg) and height (157 cm) is $\frac{1}{5}$, and the risk of data disclosure for the sensitive attribute HIV is $\frac{2}{5}$. Consequently, by applying Differential Privacy, the risk of data disclosure to determine one's sensitive attribute is reduced from 1 to $\frac{2}{5}$. By this simple example, we show how using Differential Privacy and adding noise can influence the risk of data disclosure. In practice, we know that many factors should be considered for computing the appropriate value of noise, such as the mechanism, the sensitivity of queries, and the model of the Differential Privacy algorithm (Global or local Differential Privacy).

4.3 Empirical Evaluation of ε, RoD, and Accuracy

The simple example above illustrates the effect of applying Differential Privacy on the risk of disclosure of individual records. To better understand how ε affects the wider trade-off between privacy and utility, we now provide an empirical evaluation using synthetic data for two attributes: weight and height. This complements the theoretical analysis and illustrates how the risk of disclosure and accuracy loss evolve with varying values of ε.

We generate a synthetic dataset that contains 1,000 individuals, each with two normally distributed attributes:

- **Weight (kg)**: $\mu = 70$, $\sigma = 10$
- **Height (cm)**: $\mu = 170$, $\sigma = 8$

To simulate Differential Privacy, we applied the *Laplace mechanism*, which adds calibrated random noise to each record:

$$x' = x + \text{Lap}(0, b) \quad \text{where} \quad b = \frac{1}{\varepsilon}$$

We varied ε across the following values:

$$\varepsilon \in \{0.01, 0.1, 0.5, 1.0, 2.0\}$$

with global sensitivity $\Delta q = 1$ for both attributes.

We evaluated two key metrics:

1. **Mean Squared Error (MSE)**: Measures the degradation of data utility: $\text{MSE} = \frac{1}{n}\sum_{i=1}^{n}(x_i - x_i')^2$
2. **Risk of Disclosure (RoD)**: Estimated by the inverse of the number of similar values (within noise scale b): $\text{RoD}_i = \frac{1}{|\{j:|x_j' - x_i'| < b\}|}$ The average RoD is computed across all records.

As we observe in Fig. 3 and Table 4:

- With $\varepsilon = 0.01$, the noise is large, making the original data almost unrecoverable. MSE is high (> 10 for weight), but RoD is very low, reflecting strong privacy.
- With $\varepsilon = 2.0$, the added noise is minimal, resulting in low MSE. However, RoD increases, indicating weaker privacy guarantees.

Table 4. RoD and MSE for Varying ε Values

ε	Weight MSE	Height MSE	Weight RoD	Height RoD
0.01	10.1	9.2	0.055	0.059
0.1	1.21	1.07	0.13	0.14
0.5	0.24	0.22	0.21	0.22
1.0	0.11	0.09	0.29	0.31
2.0	0.06	0.05	0.38	0.42

These results empirically confirm the *privacy-utility trade-off* inherent in Differential Privacy. Lower ε values provide stronger privacy, reducing RoD, but

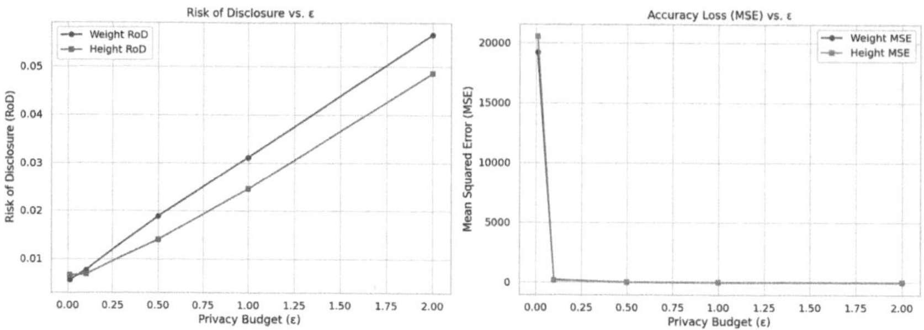

Fig. 3. Trade-off Between Privacy Budget (ε), Risk of Disclosure (RoD), and Mean Squared Error (MSE) for Weight and Height.

increase noise and degrade utility. Larger ε values improve accuracy but increase disclosure risk. In real-world scenarios, the selection of ε should be context-dependent. Attributes like weight may allow a higher ε (e.g., 1.0), while sensitive information such as HIV status may require a stricter setting (e.g., 0.1). This empirical study complements the theoretical perspective and aids stakeholders in selecting meaningful and defensible privacy parameters based on measured outcomes.

5 Conclusion

Differential privacy is a powerful framework for protecting individual information, yet its practical implementation depends on the interpretability of its parameters, particularly the privacy budget ε. In this paper, we have addressed the longstanding challenge of understanding how ε relates to the risk of data disclosure (RoD) and data utility.

We first provided a formal grounding of ε and global sensitivity, followed by a structured review of the existing literature linking DP to disclosure risk. To bridge theory with practice, we introduced an empirical evaluation using synthetic health data, where we measured how varying ε impacts both RoD and accuracy loss (via MSE) on different attributes. Our results demonstrate a consistent and measurable trade-off: Lower ε leads to stronger privacy but higher noise, while larger ε improves utility at the expense of increased disclosure risk.

By quantifying this relationship, our findings help demystify the abstract nature of ε and support more informed and context-sensitive parameter selection in privacy-preserving data analysis. Practitioners can use such insights to calibrate ε according to both privacy regulations and acceptable levels of accuracy degradation.

Future work may explore real-world datasets, alternative mechanisms such as Gaussian noise, and the combined effects of multiple privacy parameters in federated or correlated environments.

References

1. Abadi, M., et al.: Deep learning with differential privacy. In: Proceedings of the 2016 ACM SIGSAC Conference on Computer and Communications Security, pp. 308–318 (2016)
2. Abowd, J.M.: Protecting the confidentiality of America's statistics: adopting modern disclosure avoidance methods at the census bureau. Research Matters, Census Blogs (2018)
3. Aitsam, M.: Differential privacy made easy. In: 2022 International Conference on Emerging Trends in Electrical, Control, and Telecommunication Engineering (ETECTE), pp. 1–7. IEEE (2022)
4. Azencott, C.A.: Machine learning and genomics: precision medicine versus patient privacy. Philos. Trans. Roy. Soc. A Math. Phys. Eng. Sci. **376**(2128), 20170350 (2018)
5. Barthe, G., Chadha, R., Krogmeier, P., Sistla, A.P., Viswanathan, M.: Deciding accuracy of differential privacy schemes. Proc. ACM Program. Lang. **5**(POPL), 1–30 (2021)
6. Berger, B., Cho, H.: Emerging technologies towards enhancing privacy in genomic data sharing (2019)
7. Bkakria, A., Tasidou, A., Cuppens-Boulahia, N., Cuppens, F., Bouattour, F., Ben Fredj, F.: Optimal distribution of privacy budget in differential privacy. In: International Conference on Risks and Security of Internet and Systems, pp. 222–236. Springer (2018)
8. Chen, H.L., et al.: Evaluating the risk of data disclosure using noise estimation for differential privacy, pp. 339–347 (2017)
9. Chester, S., Kapron, B.M., Srinivasan, V., Srivastava, G., Thomo, A.: Anonymization and deanonymization of social network data (2014)
10. Cuppens, F., Bouattour, F., Fredj, F.B.: Optimal distribution of privacy budget in differential privacy. In: Risks and Security of Internet and Systems: 13th International Conference, CRiSIS 2018, Arcachon, France, October 16–18, 2018, Revised Selected Papers, vol. 11391, p. 222. Springer (2019)
11. Dankar, F.K., Badji, R.: A risk-based framework for biomedical data sharing. J. Biomed. Inform. **66**, 231–240 (2017)
12. Dorafshanian, M., Mejri, M.: Differential privacy: toward a better tuning of the privacy budget (ε) based on risk. In: ICISSP, pp. 783–792 (2023)
13. Drechsler, J., Bailie, J.: The complexities of differential privacy for survey data (2024). https://arxiv.org/abs/2408.07006
14. Dwork, C., Lei, J.: Differential privacy and robust statistics. In: Proceedings of the Forty-First Annual ACM Symposium on Theory of Computing, pp. 371–380 (2009)
15. Dwork, C., McSherry, F., Nissim, K., Smith, A.: Calibrating noise to sensitivity in private data analysis. In: Halevi, S., Rabin, T. (eds.) TCC 2006. LNCS, vol. 3876, pp. 265–284. Springer, Heidelberg (2006). https://doi.org/10.1007/11681878_14
16. Dwork, C., Roth, A.: The algorithmic foundations of differential privacy. Found. Trends Theor. Comput. Sci. **9**(3–4), 211–407 (2014)
17. Dwork, C., Smith, A.: Differential privacy for statistics: What we know and what we want to learn. J. Privacy Confidentiality **1**(2) (2010)
18. Fioretto, F., Van Hentenryck, P., Zhu, K.: Differential privacy of hierarchical census data: an optimization approach. Artif. Intell. **296**, 103475 (2021)

19. Goldman, E.: An introduction to the California consumer privacy act (CCPA). Santa Clara Univ, Legal Studies Research Paper (2020)
20. Hawes, M.: Differential privacy and the 2020 decennial census. In: APHA's 2020 VIRTUAL Annual Meeting and Expo (Oct. 24-28). APHA (2020)
21. Hayes, J., Balle, B., Kumar, M.P.: Learning to be adversarially robust and differentially private. arXiv preprint arXiv:2201.02265 (2022)
22. HouseofCommons (2016). https://ourcommons.ca/Reports/RP8587799/ethirp04-e.pdf
23. Jarmin, R.S., et al.: An in-depth examination of requirements for disclosure risk assessment. Proc. Natl. Acad. Sci. **120**(43), October 2023. https://doi.org/10.1073/pnas.2220558120, http://dx.doi.org/10.1073/pnas.2220558120
24. Ji, Z., Lipton, Z.C., Elkan, C.: Differential privacy and machine learning: a survey and review. arXiv preprint arXiv:1412.7584 (2014)
25. Jiang, Y., Wang, C., Wu, Z., Du, X., Wang, S.: Privacy-preserving biomedical data dissemination via a hybrid approach. In: AMIA Annual Symposium Proceedings, vol. 2018, p. 1176. American Medical Informatics Association (2018)
26. Johnson, N., Near, J.P., Song, D.: Towards practical differential privacy for SQL queries. Proc. VLDB Endowment **11**(5), 526–539 (2018)
27. Kasiviswanathan, S.P., Nissim, K., Raskhodnikova, S., Smith, A.: Analyzing graphs with node differential privacy. In: Theory of Cryptography Conference, pp. 457–476. Springer (2013)
28. Kazan, Z., Reiter, J.P.: Prior-itizing privacy: A bayesian approach to setting the privacy budget in differential privacy (2024). https://arxiv.org/abs/2306.13214
29. Kim, J.W., Jang, B., Yoo, H.: Privacy-preserving aggregation of personal health data streams. PLoS ONE **13**(11), e0207639 (2018)
30. Kohli, N., Laskowski, P.: Epsilon voting: mechanism design for parameter selection in differential privacy, pp. 19–30 (2018)
31. Lee, J., Clifton, C.: How much is enough? Choosing epsilon for differential privacy, pp. 325–340 (2011)
32. Li, N., Li, T., Venkatasubramanian, S.: t-closeness: privacy beyond k-anonymity and l-diversity. In: 2007 IEEE 23rd International Conference on Data Engineering, pp. 106–115. IEEE (2007)
33. Liau, D., Zaeem, R.N., Barber, K.S.: Evaluation framework for future privacy protection systems: a dynamic identity ecosystem approach. In: 2019 17th International Conference on Privacy, Security and Trust (PST), pp. 1–3 (2019). https://doi.org/10.1109/PST47121.2019.8949059
34. Ligett, K., Neel, S., Roth, A., Waggoner, B., Wu, S.Z.: Accuracy first: Selecting a differential privacy level for accuracy constrained ERM. Advances in Neural Information Processing Systems **30** (2017)
35. Machanavajjhala, A., Kifer, D., Gehrke, J., Venkitasubramaniam, M.: l-diversity: Privacy beyond k-anonymity. ACM Trans. Knowl. Discovery Data (TKDD) **1**(1), 3–es (2007)
36. McClure, D., Reiter, J.P.: Differential privacy and statistical disclosure risk measures: an investigation with binary synthetic data. Trans. Data Priv. **5**(3), 535–552 (2012)
37. McSherry, F.D.: Privacy integrated queries: an extensible platform for privacy-preserving data analysis. In: Proceedings of the 2009 ACM SIGMOD International Conference on Management of Data, pp. 19–30 (2009)
38. Mohan, P., Thakurta, A., Shi, E., Song, D., Culler, D.: Gupt: privacy preserving data analysis made easy. In: Proceedings of the 2012 ACM SIGMOD International Conference on Management of Data, pp. 349–360 (2012)

39. Naldi, M., D'Acquisto, G.: Differential privacy: An estimation theory-based method for choosing epsilon. arXiv preprint arXiv:1510.00917 (2015)
40. Near, J.: https://github.com/uvm-plaid/chorus (2020)
41. Nissim, K., Raskhodnikova, S., Smith, A.: Smooth sensitivity and sampling in private data analysis. In: Proceedings of the Thirty-Ninth Annual ACM Symposium on Theory of Computing, pp. 75–84 (2007)
42. Proserpio, D., Goldberg, S., McSherry, F.: Calibrating data to sensitivity in private data analysis: a platform for differentially-private analysis of weighted datasets. Proc. VLDB Endowment **7**(8), 637–648 (2014)
43. Quinton, S., Reynolds, N.: Characteristics of digital data (2018)
44. Rajendran, K., Jayabalan, M., Rana, M.E.: A study on k-anonymity, l-diversity, and t-closeness techniques. IJCSNS **17**(12), 172 (2017)
45. Regulation, G.D.P.: General data protection regulation (GDPR). Intersoft Consulting, Accessed in October 24(1) (2018)
46. Roy, I., Setty, S.T., Kilzer, A., Shmatikov, V., Witchel, E.: Airavat: Security and privacy for mapreduce. In: NSDI, vol. 10, pp. 297–312 (2010)
47. Shankar, A.G., Babu, V.J.: Differential privacy preserving in big data analytics for body area networks
48. Soria-Comas, J., Domingo-Ferrer, J., Sánchez, D., Megías, D.: Individual differential privacy: a utility-preserving formulation of differential privacy guarantees. IEEE Trans. Inf. Forensics Secur. **12**(6), 1418–1429 (2017)
49. Subramanian, R.: Applications of differential privacy to healthcare. Available at SSRN 4005908 (2022)
50. Tian, G.L.: A new non-randomized response model: the parallel model. Stat. Neerl. **68**(4), 293–323 (2014)
51. Tsou, Y.T., Chen, H.L., Chang, Y.H.: Rod: Evaluating the risk of data disclosure using noise estimation for differential privacy. IEEE Trans. Big Data (2019)
52. Ul Hassan, M., Rehmani, M.H., Rehan, M., Chen, J.: Differential privacy in cognitive radio networks: a comprehensive survey. Cognitive Computation, pp. 1–36 (2022)
53. Warner, S.L.: Randomized response: a survey technique for eliminating evasive answer bias. J. Am. Stat. Assoc. **60**(309), 63–69 (1965)
54. Wikipedia (2021). https://en.wikipedia.org/wiki/DifferentialprivacyRobustnesstopost-processing
55. Winslett, M., Yang, Y., Zhang, Z.: Demonstration of damson: Differential privacy for analysis of large data. In: 2012 IEEE 18th International Conference on Parallel and Distributed Systems, pp. 840–844. IEEE (2012)
56. Yang, G., Li, J., Zhang, S., Yu, L.: An enhanced l-diversity privacy preservation. In: 2013 10th International Conference on Fuzzy Systems and Knowledge Discovery (FSKD), pp. 1115–1120. IEEE (2013)
57. Zhang, S., Hagermalm, A., Slavnic, S.: An evaluation of open-source tools for the provision of differential privacy. arXiv preprint arXiv:2202.09587 (2022)
58. Zhu, Z., Fernandez, R.C.: Within-dataset disclosure risk for differential privacy (2025). https://arxiv.org/abs/2310.13104

Privacy in ERP Systems: Behavioral Models of Developers and Consultants

Alicia Pang[1], Katsiaryna Labunets[2], and Olga Gadyatskaya[1(✉)]

[1] Leiden University, Leiden, The Netherlands
o.gadyatskaya@liacs.leidenuniv.nl
[2] Utrecht University, Utrecht, The Netherlands
k.labunets@uu.nl

Abstract. Applications like Enterprise Resource Planning (ERP) systems have become an indispensable part of the corporate digital infrastructure. These systems store sensitive data about customers, suppliers, and employees, and thus companies have to process these data in accordance with applicable regulations like the GDPR (the EU General Data Protection Regulation). This can be challenging due to a variety of reasons. For example, prior research has shown that developers sometimes lack knowledge about privacy.

In this work, we focus on privacy in ERP systems in the context of an international consultancy firm. We investigate the privacy awareness regarding privacy-by-design and data minimization of two important populations: developers of ERP systems and managers and consultants responsible for services related to ERP systems. Applying thematic analysis, we elicit privacy behavioral models of these two populations using Fogg's Behavioral Model (FBM) framework. Our findings provide a means to stimulate more adequate privacy-related behaviors for developers and consultants.

Keywords: Usable privacy · ERP systems · Data minimization · Privacy-by-design

1 Introduction

Due to fast-paced technology developments, companies around the world collect and share large amounts of personal data. However, technological developments also provide new opportunities for cyberattacks, such as identity theft or data breaches [38]. As a result, protecting the privacy of personal data has become extremely important to protect individuals [14]. To better protect personal data, in 2018 the EU introduced the General Data Protection Regulation (GDPR), which is applicable to the personal data of all EU residents, even if the processing company is based overseas. However, not all companies are aware of the importance of data protection and the challenges that the GDPR brings [6,11].

K. Adi et al. (Eds.): CRiSIS 2025, LNCS 16295, pp. 202–217, 2026.
https://doi.org/10.1007/978-3-032-20732-6_13

The GDPR is underpinned by several important principles such as *data minimization* and *privacy-by-design* (PbD). Integrating privacy into the structure of the organization is one way to change people's behavior. As a result, PbD is treated as a core strategy for the entire organization [10]. However, there are still some challenges to overcome when implementing it: this concept has been characterized as "vague", leaving many unanswered concerns relating to how to apply it in system design [30,35]. Researchers and engineers tend to associate the PbD concept with certain privacy-enhancing technologies (PETS) [16]. On the other hand, privacy-by-design cannot be reduced to a set of rules or the use of a specific technology, as it is a process that involves a variety of technological and organizational measures that enforce privacy and data protection principles through the use of appropriate and adequate technical and organizational methods, including PETS [9].

It has emerged that key stakeholders in organizations like developers and managers do not yet have a clear understanding of privacy, implications of GDPR, or what the concepts of privacy-by-design and data minimization mean for their work [6,16,19,23,30]. In our research, we study *perceptions and behaviors regarding these important concepts and the GDPR in general* of two populations: *developers* who develop and maintain ERP systems (which includes creating specific functionalities based on customer requirements and solving technological problems) and *consultants and managers* who actually support the customers and help to set up ERP systems. In addition, managers and consultants are responsible for privacy protection and ensuring the confidentiality of personal data[1]. This study was done at a multi-national consultancy company in the Netherlands. We focus on ERP systems because this is an important type of system ubiquitously used by enterprises to handle sensitive data.

We performed a qualitative study and collected data via 16 semi-structured interviews with the target populations. We analyzed the data using thematic analysis and we mapped the identified concepts and themes to BJ Fogg's Behavioral Model [15]. In this way, we discovered the key perceptions, motivations, ability factors and triggers that make it (im)possible for our study groups to perform data minimization, PbD, and other privacy-related tasks in their jobs. Our study sheds light on the factors that affect the implementation of privacy protection for ERP systems.

2 Background

GDPR and Related Principles. The General Data Protection Regulation (GDPR), also known as Regulation (EU) 2016/679, is a privacy law introduced by the European Parliament that aims to give European residents more control over their personal information [14]. To protect personal data, the GDPR establishes seven principles that must be followed when collecting, processing,

[1] In this study, the only difference between a manager and a consultant is that a manager can manage a consulting project independently, whereas a consultant is supported by a (senior) manager. Thus, we group people in these roles.

or controlling personal data. These principles are *lawfulness, fairness and transparency*; *collection for a specified and legitimate purpose*; *data minimization* (collected data is relevant, adequate and limited); *accuracy*; *limited retention*; *secure processing*; and *accountability* [14]. Software systems, such as ERP systems, process personal data and therefore must adhere to these principles to comply with the GDPR.

The enactment of the GDPR created many challenges for organizations, as the existing data processing procedures had to be modified or re-developed, with new roles and tasks introduced into existing business processes. Additionally, the GDPR specifies the principles but does not mandate how they should be implemented technically, leading to doubts and loopholes [22]. For example, Art. 25 of GDPR stipulates that organizations must follow *privacy-by-design* (PbD) and *privacy-by-default* paradigms when processing personal data – but it refrains from suggesting concrete technical implementation measures, except pseudonymization, which is provided as an example.

Given the complexity of GDPR, in this research, we focus only on the two core GDPR concepts – *data minimization* and *privacy-by-design* – and we investigate how these principles are understood and operationalized by professionals (developers and consultants) in a large service company.

Data minimization (DM) is a principle that advises minimizing the use of personal data in software systems [32]. Although it appears to be straightforward, the DM principle can present a challenge, as, for example, it can be in conflict with the business needs, as, for example, collecting as much customer data as possible can enable better marketing strategies [2].

Privacy-by-design (PbD) refers to a technical and strategic management approach that commits to choosing and implementing governance controls to reduce the privacy risks of information systems [35] and implies that privacy must be considered throughout the whole design process [10].

Enterprise Resource Planning (ERP). ERP systems are business information systems designed to manage all resources, information, and relevant tasks for the entire business operations. Nowadays, even small and medium-sized businesses use ERPs [17]. These systems are available from different vendors, with Microsoft, SAP, and Oracle being the most popular. Common ERP systems integrate modules such as production planning, purchasing, supply chain, inventory management, human resources, accounting, marketing, and finance.

A software solution such as an ERP system that collects, saves, and analyzes personal data (e.g., customer data) obviously needs to comply with data protection laws, including the GDPR. Personal data is often not marked explicitly as such, making it difficult to find it among hundreds of tables in the ERP system. It can take a lot of time and effort to find and manage personal data in systems of this scale and complexity [3].

Behavior Models. Theories of behavior change and behavioral models have been put forward to help develop interventions to promote good habits and minimize harmful behaviors. In an attempt to explain behavior change, each behavioral change theory or model focuses on different aspects. The social cognitive theory, theories of reasoned action, the trans-theoretical model of behavior change, the health action process model, the COM-B model [25], and BJ Fogg's Behavior Model (FBM) [15] are among the most common frameworks [36].

In this study, we use FBM to investigate the privacy behaviors of developers and consultants. According to FBM [15], human behavior is the result of three factors: *motivation*, *ability*, and *trigger*. In short, behavior occurs when someone wants to do something (motivation), is able to do it easily (ability), and there is something that drives the action (trigger or prompt) [15].

3 Research Approach

In this study, we collected data via semi-structured interviews with the target populations. All interviews were conducted online via Microsoft Teams; the average duration of an interview was about 1 h. The interviews were recorded and then transcribed. Some interviews (when both parties were native Dutch speakers) were conducted in Dutch; transcripts of these interviews were then translated into English for analysis.

Our interview protocol contained 3 segments. In the first segment, demographic information of the interviewee was collected, and their suitability as a participant was confirmed. In the second segment, the interviewees were asked questions related to their understanding of privacy, DM, and PbD, and their responsibilities related to data protection. In the final segment, we asked questions focused on the privacy challenges for ERP systems, the participants' experience, and responsibilities related to implementing DM and PbD in ERP systems, and what challenges they had in that respect.

Participants. This research was conducted within an EU office of a multinational consulting company that provides, among others, consulting services on setting up and managing ERP systems to various organizations.

Recruitment. We used convenience sampling to recruit study participants at the consultancy firm. We sent an e-mail to a potential interviewee in a relevant role, informing them about the study and asking when they would be available for an interview. An invitation to the interview and a consent form were sent to the respondents who replied positively. The consent form contained further information regarding the study and asked for the respondent's consent to participate and for us to record the interview for transcription purposes. No remuneration was provided for participation.

Demographics. We recruited and interviewed 9 consultants/managers and 7 developers (16 people in total). We checked with them that they qualified as participants in our study based on their position (role), experience in working with ERP systems, involvement in privacy-related decisions, and level of education. The demographic information of the participants is summarized in Table 1. In the remainder of the paper, participants in the developer role have IDs starting

Table 1. Summary of participants' demographics.

Level of education			Role			Work experience		
	C/M ($n = 9$)	**D** ($n = 7$)		**C/M** ($n = 9$)	**D** ($n = 7$)		**C/M** ($n = 9$)	**D** ($n = 7$)
BSc	3 (33%)	4 (57%)	ERP developer	–	3 (43%)	Min	2 years	2 years
MSc	6 (67%)	3 (43%)	Software architect	–	2 (29%)	Median	10 years	9 years
			Data engineer	–	1 (14%)	Max	31 year	14 years
			Internal advisor	1 (11%)	–			
			Legal council	1 (11%)	–			
			(Senior) consultant	2 (22%)	–			
			(Senior) manager	5 (56%)	1 (14%)			

Note: C/M - Consultant/Manager; D - Developer

with *D* (e.g., D1), consultants have IDs starting with *C*, and managers have IDs starting with *M*.

Data Analysis. To analyze the data for this research, three researchers first conducted a five-phase thematic analysis following Braun and Clarke [8]. In the first phase, *familiarization with the data*, three researchers read the transcripts to understand their content. In the second phase, *generation of initial codes*, one coder systematically analyzed the transcripts and inductively coded them, forming the initial codebook, which was reviewed by two independent researchers. In the third phase, *searching for themes*, the three researchers identified recurring concepts and patterns in the data, grouped codes, and named the found themes. In the fourth phase *reviewing themes*, the themes were examined for being coherent and relevant, and refined. In the fifth phase *defining and naming themes*, the specifics of each theme were further refined, and themes were clearly defined. During these phases, the researchers met frequently to discuss the codebook and the themes, and all disagreements were resolved. To ensure the quality and reliability of the final codebook, one of the researchers (not the original coder) used the final codebook to code two randomly selected transcripts. This resulted in Krippendorff's α equal to 0.971, indicating a very high agreement [4].

Once the codebook was finalized and the themes were defined, these were then analyzed by the three researchers together and deductively labeled into *motivations*, *ability*, and *triggers* following FBM [15], as explained in Sect. 5. We used the `Atlas.ti` software for coding the data (without the AI features).

Ethical Considerations. The study design was approved by the Science Ethics Committee at Leiden University. All participants were informed about the goals of the study and the data we collected, and consented to participation prior to the interview. Participants were not remunerated.

Limitations. There are limitations to this study that need to be discussed. First, our sample is limited, as we only interviewed employees from a single consultancy service company in a single EU country. Culture and business practices within the company and the national regulatory and cultural landscape may affect our findings. Furthermore, as we used convenience sampling, our participants were motivated to participate, and they might be more privacy-aware or consider it more important than other employees. Future research replicating this study across various organizations and countries could address this limitation. Social desirability bias is another potential limitation of this study. We rely on self-reported behaviors and perceptions of our respondents, and they might have been provoked by the interview setting to inflate the importance of privacy and security in their job. We tried to calibrate for that by also asking questions about factual knowledge (e.g., their own definitions of data minimization and privacy by design) and asking for clarifications and examples, where possible.

4 Results

The Role of GDPR in the Work of Developers and Consultants: For some of our respondents, the role of GDPR is quite significant. Some developers stated that they had to develop extra functionalities in the ERP system to ensure the application was GDPR-compliant. Another developer stated that they and their colleagues take GDPR very seriously and must abide by it: "*If one of our developers doesn't abide by GDPR, they might end up losing their job. Or there will be strict actions taken against them. So the data protection is very key. And we all, as a developer, as a consultant, we abide by it, and we have to follow it*" (D4). GDPR was also a major driver for privacy management in ERP systems: "*I have never bothered about privacy [before GDPR]. Because nobody told me that it was important in ERP. I didn't know this*" (D4).

However, there is an alternative opinion that GDPR does not directly impact developers' work, but there is more awareness about protecting data confidentiality in general. Similarly, managers and consultants noted that the GDPR influenced their work by *increasing privacy awareness* to some extent:

"*I will not say that there is a very strict follow-up, and the awareness is not quite there yet. When this law was not yet in place, employee data and suchlike were handled more senselessly. But now it's more sensitive*" (C8).

Despite the fact that GDPR is mandatory and that it has created awareness, GDPR is not high on the priority list, and doing a training on it does not sound exciting, as one developer put it: "*I have other business to do and no time for that. The GDPR will be the lowest priority on my list. It's not the most exciting thing either*" (D2).

Developers and consultants working with major vendors and existing ERP platforms noticed that many of the suppliers showcase the compliance and trustworthiness of their products with privacy and data protection certifications: "*Microsoft themselves give the system with a full privacy and data protection certificate. So that comes with the tool*"(M4). As a result, developers and managers do not need to worry much about GDPR compliance in their ERP systems. They consider it to be GDPR-compliant by default because privacy comes "*out of the box*" in the available ERP frameworks: "*The ERP system is already compliant. So you don't have to be mindful of the GDPR part*" (M1).

ERP Privacy Challenges: Our participants shared several privacy/GDPR-related challenges for the ERP systems. Firstly, access control is perceived as a data management challenge, but this task is a shared responsibility for all ERP system stakeholders, as developer D1 stated: *"the challenge for us is to classify those roles so they don't see more information than they need. That's an exercise everybody does."* However, this participant perceives it as imposed by GDPR: *"GDPR is the reason that we have the challenge. Nobody would have been bothered about that."*

One of the managers stated that one of their responsibilities is to manage access data rights for specific users: "*When I design an authorization, certain people are allowed to see specific data. But also ensure that this data is not visible to everyone*" (M2).

Yet, ultimately it is the customer, not the consultant, who decides which roles have access to which data. The consultant advises and supports the customer in the implementation and technical aspects. However, it is the customer who uses the system and is ultimately responsible for what they put into the system: "*The use of the system is by the client and also their responsibility with what they put in or not* " (C8).

However, our participants observed a number of malpractices among their customers regarding data handling. One of the consultants received an email with an Excel file containing all the employees' salaries from their customer. Another developer received a database from the customer with all the (personal) data. The developer asked the customer for a test database, but this does not always happen in practice: "*During development, we get files, for example, the payroll interface. So we can see all the wages of companies for that month. Then I always ask for a test file, but the customer does not provide it in practice. They fail, and we get an actual file with that data. It's not OK*" (D3).

Managers emphasized the importance of data privacy frameworks and organizational privacy policies, which are designed to protect privacy and minimize data-related malpractices: *"it becomes very important for me to follow the guidelines and principles and work on such projects"* (M1). Another challenge that most consultants or managers experience is the system integration when personal data from one system gets consumed by another system.

Data Minimization (DM): The data minimization concept is relatively familiar to developers: most of our developer participants provided similar definitions of it: *"less mandatory fields are possible [...] if you don't need that, you don't need that"* (D1). Similarly, more than half of the consultants/managers were familiar with the *data minimization* concept. However, some participants did not know or were unsure of the exact meaning of DM, as it played a minimal role in their function.

Privacy-by-Design (PbD) is a somewhat familiar concept for developers and consultants, yet some developers could not explain what PbD means: they had never heard of it and had no (direct) experience with it. Some consultants and managers were also unaware of what it entails and had no prior experience with PbD. This observation aligns with van Rest et al. [30], who noted that

PbD remains a vague concept among managers, with its exact meaning often unclear. Meanwhile, some consultants were aware of this term but remarked that they neither work with it nor have any hands-on experience. Despite this, both developers and managers describe the concept of PbD in a similar way: *"In my view, privacy-by-design is already taking privacy into account when implementing or configuring a system"* (M2).

Impediments: Developers and consultants frequently see *privacy as a security problem.* Regarding the privacy goals of the ERP system, the developers were more focused on securing information and restricting access to it than protecting privacy: "*The ERP system is mainly used within companies. From the outside [...] you effectively have all the tools to detect if a certain subset of data is sent out. There is also an extensive roles system with security. [...] So it's all pretty watertight* " (D2).

Furthermore, there is often a conflict between business needs and privacy regulations. According to a developer, customer requirements can be challenging, e.g., a client may request specific data, such as date of birth, raising concerns about GDPR compliance. This increases the workload for developers and consultants when designing and configuring ERP systems.

To conclude, not all developers, consultants, and managers are familiar with privacy concepts like data minimization and PbD. This lack of knowledge makes it challenging to implement these concepts in an ERP system. One key reason for this gap is insufficient training in privacy-related practices: *"No, I haven't seen people [learn] about data minimization much"* (M4).

Strategies and Techniques for Implementing DM and PbD: Due to their lack of knowledge, developers and consultants are unfamiliar with the techniques and strategies for implementing PbD and DM in ERP systems, which aligns with the findings by Oetzel et al. [27]. However, privacy protection techniques have already been implemented in ERP systems, as mentioned earlier. As a result, developers and consultants often perceive that they do not have to think about or implement PbD or DM: "*But in the ERP system, as I said, these are standard screens that are globally accepted and agreed upon. I don't have to put anything specific to achieve this privacy-by-design*" (M1).

Among the mentioned strategies and methods, we can mention *data retention and deletion policies:* As a developer explained, data is retained in the system for a specified period and then automatically deleted after a certain number of years. The developer's only responsibility is to define the retention rule, and the system handles the rest.

Moreover, *external support* can play a role: consultants explained that whenever a project involves processing a lot of personal data in the ERP system, a data migration team or a dedicated compliance team can be brought in to help. Other common security controls the developers use to safeguard privacy are *multi-factor authentication*, *logs auditing* and *role-based access control.*

Two managers stated that there are *templates/blueprints* available within their consultancy firm. These blueprints explain what the organization thinks about the PbD or DM concepts. Sometimes the blueprints are presented to the customer to check whether this approach is suitable for them.

5 Behavior Model

Based on the results from the previous section, we now discuss the behavior of developers, consultants, and managers. The BJ Fogg Model is used to understand behavior, using the formula: $behavior = motivation + ability + triggers$. We deductively assigned labels related to *motivation*, *ability*, *trigger*, and *general* to the codes in our codebook to identify the aspects of behavior. The resulting behavioral model of developers is illustrated in Fig. 1, while Fig. 2 shows the behavioral model of the consultants and managers. For the lack of space, we only discuss some of the most interesting aspects of these models.

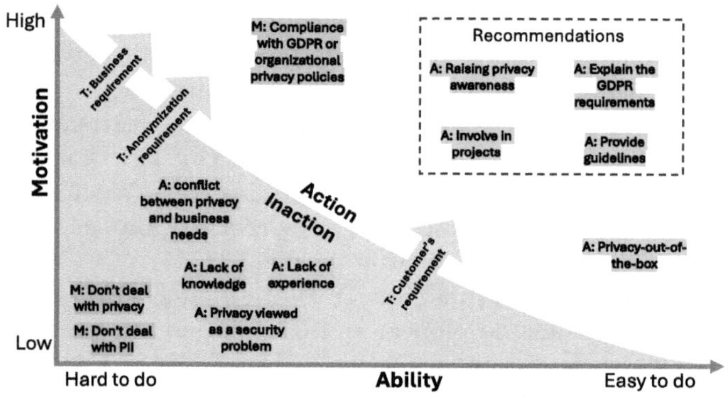

Fig. 1. Privacy behavior model for developers. Light blue stands for motivations (M); yellow for ability (A), and pink for triggers (T). (Color figure online)

Concepts. **Motivation:** Motivation can be described as how much the person is driven to do something or against it. There must be a reason why a specific behavior is being performed. A question that can be asked to gauge whether it is related to motivation is "am I willing to do this?" [15]. For example, when an interviewee mentions GDPR compliance or the need to follow some instructions, this motivates them to implement privacy into the system.

Ability: Ability refers to how easy or hard it is for someone to perform something at a particular time. We consider that, for example, when an interviewee mentions that they have no knowledge about data minimization, implementing data minimization in the system will be difficult for them. Another example of ability is when an interviewee mentions some system functionality that makes it easier for them to protect privacy.

Triggers: A trigger is an event that starts the process. There are different triggers that have been described in the literature, such as social, forced, and

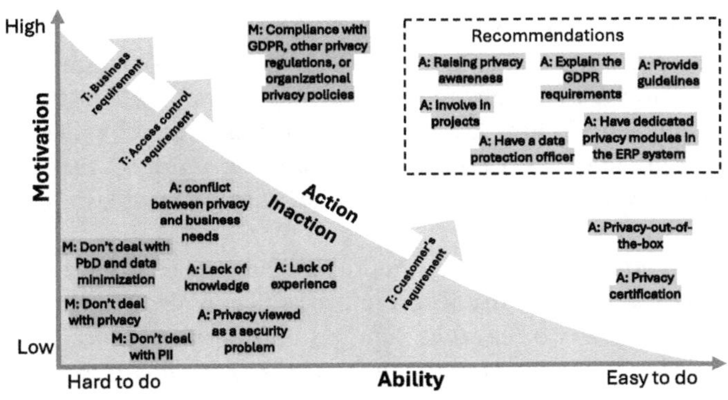

Fig. 2. Privacy behavior model of consultants and managers. Light blue stands for motivations (M); yellow for ability (A), and pink for triggers (T). (Color figure online)

proactive triggers [12]. For example, when an interviewee mentions business or customer requirements, this effectively serves as a trigger to perform a privacy-related task.

Developers' Behavior. **GDPR compliance** and **the organization's privacy policies** are notable motivations for developers to follow the GDPR requirements. If they do not follow the GDPR requirements, there are consequences for their job. Therefore, they are "*highly*" driven to follow the GDPR and other policy requirements.

In some ERP systems, little personal information is kept, so developers **do not deal with or work with personal information in the ERP system.** In that case, the motivation to implement privacy techniques to protect this personal information can be very low. Another (de)motivation can be that the developer (perceives that they) *do not deal with privacy*: their motivation is then low. This is how D2 expresses their thoughts on privacy: *"No, you don't think about privacy at that moment"*.

A **conflict between privacy and business needs** can affect the developer's ability. While the business needs something like creating a function where they can access everything in the system, this can conflict with privacy laws. This makes the developer's ability "*obstructed*".

Mixing different privacy concepts and a general **lack of knowledge** can also hinder the developer's ability. Furthermore, the ability can be obstructed because developers see **privacy as a security problem**. Not having the appropriate expertise can make implementing privacy techniques hard. This is how D1 answered the question whether privacy-by-design is essential for the ERP system: "*It's not like public domain data. It is a private network where only people in the organization can see the data. And with a certain level of clearance.*"

However, **privacy out of the box** makes the developers' work more accessible. When ERP providers implement privacy frameworks in the system, developers have less work to do.

The behavior also has to be triggered. An example trigger for a developer can be a **requirement**. These can be business- or customer-related. **Business requirements** focus more on operational needs such as system performance, cost, and storage. This is how D2 explains that, based on a business requirement, they need to apply DM: "*Not because of privacy but more because of the database size. The storage is minimized and additional storage also costs more money for the customer*" (D2).

Customer requirements focus more on what the customer demands. Moreover, **the customer being involved** in projects can also trigger the developer's behavior: "*You want to process that data, and also give a choice to the customers or the people who give you the data to have a say in how it is managed or how it is stored or how it is shared*" (D1).

Improvements of Behavior. In FBM, improvement of behavior means increasing the ability or motivation, or adding a trigger, what facilitates moving across the action line. One of the recommendations is to have **general guidelines**. This may be classified as a motivation or ability for the developer. According to one of the developers, it can be demotivating and annoying if there are no general guidelines or if those are not clear: "*D7*But having your procedures in place, and simple procedures, not too much complication. When you make things more complicated, it's just becoming annoying".

According to one of the developers, getting **involved in a project** can increase the ability: "*D6*That I'm getting involved in. [...] Everyone is getting a little bit involved in, 'Hey, we made this and this choice, for example. [...]' So that you get a detailed description of how it happens, take people in there and tell them why choices were made".

Raising privacy awareness by, for instance, following training, presentations or workshops can change the developer's ability: "*By having training, having a mandatory boot camp, just to give you the policies of the company. So explain, based on the rule on what they will have, what they need to do*" (D1).

Consultants and Managers' Behavior. Consultants and managers are motivated by **the GDPR compliance**: "*C9*You must be compliant, and of course, Microsoft must also comply with the package" . Another motivation for the consultants and managers can be the **organization's privacy policy**. For example, one of the managers explained that it is essential to follow the guidelines and principles that come from the GDPR. Therefore, it is a "*high*" motivation because the manager sees it necessary to follow: "*So becomes very important for me to follow the guidelines and principles and work on such projects*" (M1).

However, it can also be that the consultants and managers are not motivated, e.g., if they **do not deal with data minimization, privacy-by-design, privacy, or personal information.** Consultants or managers do not deal with DM or PbD because it is not part of their responsibility. This is how one of the managers put this: "*I don't have any specific deal with this data minimization or privacy by design in my day-to-day life*" (M2).

The ability of consultants and managers is also impeded by **conflicting interests between privacy and business needs.** For example, M1 explains that the business wants to test with real-life data, which is not necessarily allowed under the GDPR because it contains personal information. This obstacle for the manager results in low ability ("*hard to do*").

The lack of knowledge and the mixing of different privacy concepts also obstruct the ability of the managers and consultants to implement privacy techniques in the ERP system. Moreover, the ability to implement privacy techniques in the ERP system can also be impeded if consultants and managers **see privacy as a security problem.** This is how manager M4 explained what their responsibility is related to privacy: "*M4*'And from my side, it's about keeping the system secure in terms of proper security authorizations. And of course, on the technical side, Microsoft already gives a certificate. ".

Furthermore, consultants and managers sometimes have **no experience with PbD and DM in the ERP system**. Thus, the ability to implement these privacy techniques can be low: "*My experience is that I don't have much experience.*" (M2) However, **privacy out of the box** makes the consultants' and managers' behavior "*easier*". This way, consultants and managers perceive that they do not have to implement privacy concepts themselves and think about whether the system is GDPR-compliant. "*Like I said, the ERP system is already compliant. So you don't have to be mindful of the GDPR part*" (M1).

Consultants and managers are triggered to perform certain behaviors. **Customer involvement** and **customer requirements** can be important triggers because the customer gives input on what data should be in the system together with the consultant: "*Requirements are collected from the customer. The customer must say that these are our requirements in the field of privacy. We do not want everyone to be able to view the data of others. If they're going to use the HR module within the ERP system, all your details are listed there, so their address and bank details. Sometimes the salary is also paid via the ERP system. Then the customer will undoubtedly have requirements regarding privacy*" (M2).

As mentioned earlier, an **organization's privacy policy** motivates consultants and managers, but it can also be a trigger for consultants and managers to think about how to manage sensitive information in the system.

Improvements of Behavior. A variety of recommendations given by managers and consultants can help to improve this behavior. One of the recommendations is to appoint a **data protection officer (DPO)** for a project. This recommendation makes the consultants' and managers' behavior "*easier*": "*The first thing I would say is [...] do you have a data protection officer or data controller as part of your projects? That is the most important or the first question*" (M1). Another recommendation is establishing a **GDPR checklist** to make the consultants' and managers' work more accessible. This checklist ensures that every release within a project complies with GDPR, which makes thinking about GDPR during the project much more manageable. Having **general guidelines** can be sufficient for the managers or consultants to increase their ability: "*And if I have the general guidelines on how this data should be handled, I think that is sufficient for us*" (M1).

The ability of consultants or managers can also be improved or made more accessible by providing privacy modules in the ERP system. M6 explained that implementing privacy modules manually takes a lot of time and effort: "*M6* And it would be good if in the future, from Salesforce or SAP, they would already take that into account. So look at what is the law and regulations? What is privacy? And then offer modules so you don't have to create all that by hand".

Raising privacy awareness is also a recommendation to improve the ability of the consultants and managers. This will increase the knowledge, and as a result, the consultants and managers will be able to implement privacy techniques more easily and without problems.

The last recommendation that can improve the ability of consultants and managers is to **involve everyone** during the project. For example, M2 explained that it is wise to bring developers, consultants, and everyone involved in a project together and talk to them to solve privacy problems: "*Another thing that is also important is that consultants and developers sit together. Then we can discuss what the challenges are in this area and how we can solve them, what we can and cannot do during the implementation*" (M2).

6 Discussion

Developers, consultants, and managers behave almost the same way when it comes to privacy in ERP systems. Ultimately, their behaviors can be improved following the given recommendations. We note that consultants and managers provided more recommendations to improve behavior compared to developers. For example, managers suggested hiring a data protection officer for a project and implementing privacy modules in the ERP system.

It is known that PbD is not a very well-known concept for managers [30]. The literature also shows that DM is a challenging concept for developers because they are not attuned to the privacy risks posed by the collected data and users' concerns about their privacy [31]. Our research shows that these observations are still relevant when considering how managers and developers behave regarding privacy techniques in the ERP system. The literature proposes a DM methodology for software systems [33]. However, our findings show that neither developers nor consultants adhere to this methodology. Moreover, *Privacy Impact Assessment* (PIA) provides clear privacy objectives and specifies a means to achieve them. It is also known as a "*milestone towards privacy-by-design*" [13]. However, PIA was not mentioned by our interviewees as a solution for implementing PbD.

7 Related Work

While security and privacy perceptions and behaviors of developers, security professionals, and other stakeholders are an active research area [5,7,21,26,37, 39], to the best of our knowledge, no research has been done on identifying consultants' and developers' behavioral models related to ERP system privacy.

Developers' Privacy Perceptions. Developers often believe that anonymizing data is more effective than privacy laws and practices in minimizing privacy concerns, and are often more prepared, compared to users, to give up privacy in return for better system functionality [34]. They also might not always agree on what constitutes personal information [24] and overestimate their privacy inclinations and collect more data than their privacy attitudes might indicate [23]. Furthermore, it has been previously reported that developers frequently view privacy from a data security perspective and focus on technical solutions against data-related threats (access control, encryption, and anonymization) [16,19,28,29]. This is consistent with our findings. Studies [16,19] also found that the developers' work environment, namely the company's privacy culture, influences their privacy perceptions and beliefs. Thus, organizations can affect developers' behavior regarding privacy engineering by creating and facilitating a privacy culture [20]. Privacy regulations like GDPR positively affected developers' behaviors and organizations' privacy cultures [19]. This is consistent with our findings.

Other Stakeholders. To the best of our knowledge, there is limited literature research about the privacy perceptions of managers or consultants. Henderson et al. [18] focuses on the actions an information system (IS) manager needs to take if there is a privacy concern within a system, but not on how the managers perceive privacy afforded by an IS system. Abomhara et al. [1] studied the perspectives and attitudes of stakeholders engaged in national identification systems, reporting that there was a negative correlation between knowledge about PbD techniques and attitude towards it, explained by the perceived complexity. Closest to our work, Dalela et al. [11] conducted a study of security and privacy practices in Danish companies, which included both managers and developers as participants. They found that managers and developers alike require better awareness about privacy practices and that GDPR was an important push towards improved data collection and protection methods.

8 Conclusions

In this study, we investigated the behavior of developers and consultants regarding GDPR compliance of ERP systems, and specifically their knowledge and perceptions regarding privacy-by-design and data minimization in the ERP system. We conducted semi-structured interviews and applied thematic analysis to discern developers' and consultants' perceptions and behavior following Fogg's Behavioral Model. We found that, while the enactment of GDPR had a major influence on privacy practices, there are still knowledge gaps and limited ability, motivation, and triggers to follow GDPR in ERP systems.

Acknowledgments. This research has been partially supported by the Dutch Research Council (NWO) under the project NWA.1215.18.008 Cyber Security by Integrated Design (C-SIDe).

References

1. Abomhara, M., Nweke, L.O., Yayilgan, S.Y., Comparin, D., Teyras, K., de Labriolle, S.: Enhancing privacy protections in national identification systems: an examination of stakeholders' knowledge, attitudes, and practices of privacy by design. Int. J. Inf. Secur., 1–25 (2024)
2. Andrew, J., Baker, M.: The general data protection regulation in the age of surveillance capitalism. J. Bus. Ethics **168**, 565–578 (2021)
3. Arachchi, S.M., Chong, S.C., Madhushani, A.: Quality assurance and quality control in ERP systems implementation. Am. Sci. Research J. Eng. Tech. Sci. **11**(1), 70–83 (2015)
4. Atlas.ti: Inter-coder agreement analysis (2020)
5. Binkhorst, V., Fiebig, T., Krombholz, K., Pieters, W., Labunets, K.: Security at the end of the tunnel: the anatomy of VPN mental models among experts and non-experts in a corporate context. In: Proceedings of USENIX Security'22, pp. 3433–3450 (2022)
6. Birrell, E., Rodolitz, J., Ding, A., Lee, J., McReynolds, E., Hutson, J., Lerner, A.: SoK: technical implementation and human impact of internet privacy regulations. In: Proceedings of S&P'24, pp. 673–696. IEEE (2024)
7. Boteju, M., Ranbaduge, T., Vatsalan, D., Arachchilage, N.A.G.: SoK: demystifying privacy enhancing technologies through the lens of software developers. arXiv preprint arXiv:2401.00879 (2023)
8. Braun, V., Clarke, V.: Using thematic analysis in psychology. Qual. Res. Psychol. **3**(2), 77–101 (2006)
9. Castelluccia, C., et al.: Data protection engineering: from theory to practice (2022)
10. Cavoukian, A., et al.: Privacy by design: the 7 foundational principles. Inf. Privacy Commissioner Ontario, Canada **5**, 12 (2009)
11. Dalela, A., Giallorenzo, S., Kulyk, O., Mauro, J., Paja, E.: A mixed-method study on security and privacy practices in Danish companies. arXiv preprint arXiv:2104.04030 (2021)
12. Das, S., Dabbish, L.A., Hong, J.I.: A typology of perceived triggers for end-user security and privacy behaviors. In: Proceedings of SOUPS'19, pp. 97–115 (2019)
13. European Data Protection Supervisor: Opinion 5/2018 – preliminary opinion on privacy by design (2018). https://edps.europa.eu/sites/edp/files/publication/18-05-31_preliminary_opinion_on_privacy_by_design_en_0.pdf
14. European Union: Regulation (EU) 2016/679 on the protection of natural persons with regard to the processing of personal data and on the free movement of such data (General Data Protection Regulation) (2016). https://eur-lex.europa.eu/eli/reg/2016/679/oj/eng
15. Fogg, B.J.: A behavior model for persuasive design. In: Persuasive Technology, pp. 1–7 (2009)
16. Hadar, I., Hasson, T., Ayalon, O., Toch, E., Birnhack, M., Sherman, S., Balissa, A.: Privacy by designers: software developers' privacy mindset. Empir. Softw. Eng. **23**, 259–289 (2018)
17. Hasan, M.T.: Impact of ERP system in business management. Int. J. Manag. Stud. **5**(4), 4 (2018)
18. Henderson, S.C., Snyder, C.A.: Personal information privacy: implications for mis managers. Inf. Manage. **36**(4), 213–220 (1999)
19. Iwaya, L.H., Babar, M.A., Rashid, A.: Privacy engineering in the wild: understanding the practitioners' mindset, organisational aspects, and current practices. IEEE Trans. Softw. Eng. (2023)

20. Iwaya, L.H., Iwaya, G.H., Fischer-H"ubner, S., Steil, A.V.: Organisational privacy culture and climate: a scoping review. IEEE Access **10**, 73907–73930 (2022)
21. Kudriavtseva, A., Hotak, N.A., Gadyatskaya, O.: My code is less secure with Gen AI: surveying developers' perceptions of the impact of code generation tools on security. In: Proceedings of SAC'25, pp. 1637–1646. ACM (2025)
22. Kutyłowski, M., Lauks-Dutka, A., Yung, M.: GDPR–challenges for reconciling legal rules with technical reality. In: Proceedings of ESORICS'20, pp. 736–755. Springer (2020)
23. van der Linden, D., Hadar, I., Edwards, M., Rashid, A.: Data, data, everywhere: quantifying software developers' privacy attitudes. In: Proceedings of STAST'19, pp. 47–65. Springer (2021)
24. Ma, X., Gurjar, A., Chaora, A., Camp, L.J.: Programmer's perception of sensitive information in code. In: Proceedings of USEC'24 (2024)
25. Michie, S., Van Stralen, M.M., West, R.: The behaviour change wheel: a new method for characterising and designing behaviour change interventions. Implement. Sci. **6**(1), 1–12 (2011)
26. Nurgalieva, L., Frik, A., Doherty, G.: A narrative review of factors affecting the implementation of privacy and security practices in software development. ACM Comput. Surv. **55**(14s), 1–27 (2023)
27. Oetzel, M.C., Spiekermann, S.: A systematic methodology for privacy impact assessments: a design science approach. Eur. J. Inf. Syst. **23**(2), 126–150 (2014)
28. Peixoto, M., Ferreira, D., Cavalcanti, M., Silva, C., Vilela, J., Ara'ujo, J., Gorschek, T.: The perspective of Brazilian software developers on data privacy. J. Syst. Softw. **195**, 111523 (2023)
29. Prybylo, M., Haghighi, S., Peddinti, S.T., Ghanavati, S.: Evaluating privacy perceptions, experience, and behavior of software development teams. arXiv preprint arXiv:2404.01283 (2024)
30. van Rest, J., Boonstra, D., Everts, M., van Rijn, M., van Paassen, R.: Designing privacy-by-design. In: Annual Privacy Forum, pp. 55–72. Springer (2014)
31. Schiffner, S., et al.: Towards a roadmap for privacy technologies and the general data protection regulation: a transatlantic initiative. In: Proceedings of APF'18, pp. 24–42. Springer (2018)
32. Senarath, A., Arachchilage, N.A.G.: Understanding software developers' approach towards implementing data minimization. arXiv preprint arXiv:1808.01479 (2018)
33. Senarath, A., Arachchilage, N.A.G.: A data minimization model for embedding privacy into software systems. Comput. Secur. **87**, 101605 (2019)
34. Sheth, S., Kaiser, G., Maalej, W.: Us and them: a study of privacy requirements across North America, Asia, and Europe. In: Proceedings of ICSE'14, pp. 859–870 (2014)
35. Spiekermann, S.: The challenges of privacy by design. CACM **55**(7), 38–40 (2012)
36. Taj, F., Klein, M.C., van Halteren, A.: Digital health behavior change technology: bibliometric and scoping review of two decades of research. JMIR Mhealth Uhealth **7**(12), e13311 (2019)
37. Van Acken, J.P., Jansen, F., Jansen, S., Labunets, K.: Who is the IT department anyway: an evaluative case study of shadow IT mindsets among corporate employees. In: Proceedings of USENIX SOUPS'24, pp. 527–545 (2024)
38. Verizon: 2025 Data Breach Investigations Report (2025)
39. Wee, A., Kudriavtseva, A., Gadyatskaya, O.: "I have heard of it": A study with practitioners on adoption of secure software development frameworks. In: Proceedings of EuroS&PW'24, pp. 626–633. IEEE (2024)

Vulnerabilities and Resilience

Analysis of the eBPF Vulnerabilities in the Linux Kernel

Rosario Rizza(✉), Riccardo Sisto, and Fulvio Valenza

DAUIN, Politecnico di Torino, Turin, Italy
{rosario.rizza,riccardo.sisto,fulvio.valenza}@polito.it

Abstract. eBPF has become a fundamental part of modern Linux, offering in-kernel programmability for networking, observability, and security tasks. Its rapid expansion, however, has enlarged the kernel's attack surface—particularly in security-critical components such as the verifier—where frequent vulnerabilities have been reported. These flaws pose significant risks to kernel stability and security. This paper conducts a study of 249 eBPF-related Common Vulnerabilities and Exposures (CVE) records published between 2014 and April 2025, considering Common Weakness Enumeration (CWE) tags, Common Vulnerability Scoring System (CVSS) severity metrics, kernel-version mappings, timing, and more, enabling a comprehensive view of long-term trends. Our investigation focuses on the temporal evolution of eBPF-related vulnerabilities, how long they remain unpatched, where they occur within the eBPF subsystem, what coding flaws cause them, and how severe and impactful they are.

Keywords: eBPF · CVE · Linux Kernel · Security · Vulnerability Analysis · Verifier

1 Introduction

The extended Berkeley Packet Filter (eBPF) has rapidly evolved from a packet filtering mechanism into a general-purpose execution environment embedded within the Linux kernel. It powers applications ranging from low-level observability tools (e.g., `bcc`, `bpftrace`) to security frameworks (e.g., seccomp filtering) and high-performance networking (e.g., XDP, Cilium). Its versatility, performance, and low-level integration with the kernel have favored widespread adoption and increased its popularity.

However, the increasing programmability of the kernel comes at a cost: a broader attack surface. Despite significant engineering efforts to harden the eBPF runtime, vulnerabilities continue to be discovered regularly. A better understanding of where, why, and how these bugs occur is essential for improving the security of the kernel as a whole. The eBPF community is quite active in the security field, and numerous papers have been published to describe the vulnerabilities of eBPF. However, although the analysis of Common Vulnerabilities and Exposures (CVEs) database records is known to be useful to provide insights into

K. Adi et al. (Eds.): CRiSIS 2025, LNCS 16295, pp. 221–236, 2026.
https://doi.org/10.1007/978-3-032-20732-6_14

specific classes of security issues, this kind of analysis has been done only to a limited extent for eBPF-related vulnerabilities: Mohamed *et al.* [14] studied eBPF-related CVEs published in a limited time range to justify the development of a fuzzer.

This paper performs a more thorough analysis of the 249 eBPF-related CVEs reported between 2014 and April 2025. Section 2 situates our work within the existing literature; Sect. 3 summarizes essential background; Sect. 5 outlines our data-collection and analysis methodology; Sect. 4 introduces the research questions, and Sect. 6 addresses them, by providing insights into the temporal and structural behavior of eBPF vulnerabilities; Sect. 7 concludes and summarizes the results obtained.

2 Related Work

The analysis of CVE records (e.g. [15,16]) is a common practice to get insights about specific security issues. To our knowledge, in the field of eBPF security, a paper by Mohamed *et al.* [14] presented the only prior study on eBPF-related CVEs. They classified 18 eBPF-related CVEs published in the two years preceding their 2023 publication and showed that the eBPF verifier is the eBPF module most frequently compromised. This study was used to motivate the development of a fuzzer to detect new vulnerabilities affecting the eBPF verifier. It is quite limited because it just considers a few of the many eBPF-related vulnerabilities published as CVEs and a few aspects.

Our study broadens the previous one in several ways. First, it enlarges the analysis time range, spanning the entire public history of eBPF CVEs (2014âĂŠApril 2025). Secondly, it considers richer metadata such as CWE category, CVSS severity, vulnerable kernel versions, and more, and related statistics. Such extra data lets us observe long-term trends and gives a complete view of the history of the eBPF subsystem's security.

Our study follows an increasing research interest in eBPF security, including eBPF-focused fuzzers, such as [7,18], proposals for hardening the eBPF subsystem, such as [6,21], and proof-of-concept exploits of eBPF system vulnerabilities, such as [9,11].

Prior work has mined CVE and NVD data to build large-scale datasets of real-world vulnerabilities. Examples include Big-Vul, which links thousands of C/C++ vulnerabilities from GitHub projects to their CVE records [4], curated datasets of Java vulnerabilities and fixing commits used in industrial settings [15], and CVEfixes, an automated and continuously updated collection covering more than 5,000 CVEs across open-source projects [1]. Beyond traditional software ecosystems, large-scale CVE-based analyses have also been applied to IoT firmware, highlighting the prevalence of memory-related threats [16]. Together, these efforts demonstrate how systematic CVE mining can uncover domain-specific security insights—an approach we extend to the eBPF subsystem.

3 Background

3.1 eBPF

eBPF (extended Berkeley Packet Filter) [19] is a lightweight, in-kernel technology that allows user-defined bytecode to be executed within the Linux kernel. Originally introduced for packet filtering, eBPF has evolved into a general-purpose subsystem that supports a wide range of use cases, including tracing, security enforcement, and high-performance networking.

Architecture Overview An eBPF program is typically loaded from user space via the `bpf()` system call. Upon loading, the program is verified by the eBPF verifier, which ensures safe and secure execution properties such as memory safety, bounded loops, and safe access to kernel data. Once verified, the program may be interpreted and executed by the eBPF virtual machine, or compiled to native code by a JIT compiler, depending on the architecture and system configuration. Programs interact with kernel subsystems through a restricted set of helper functions, which serve as an API boundary between eBPF code and kernel internals. In order to interact with the user space, special data structures, called maps, are used.

Security Model. The eBPF verifier enforces a strict set of rules to guarantee that programs cannot crash the kernel, access invalid memory, or perform unauthorized privileged operations. However, due to the complexity of static verification and the evolving nature of eBPF features, the verifier and related components have become a recurring source of security vulnerabilities. In some cases, flaws in the verifier or helper functions have allowed unprivileged users to escalate privileges or corrupt kernel memory [11].

In order to run eBPF, the Linux capability `CAP_BPF` is required, with additional capabilities such as `CAP_NET_ADMIN` for networking hooks or `CAP_PERFMON` for performance tracing; while unprivileged eBPF mode exists, it is disabled by default on most mainstream distributions [3].

3.2 CVEs

Modern vulnerability tracking relies on a layered taxonomy maintained by MITRE. At the root sits the *Common Vulnerabilities and Exposures* (**CVE**) list, which assigns a unique identifier to every publicly disclosed security flaw, ensuring that vendors, researchers, and tooling refer to the same issue unambiguously [13]. Each CVE record is then often enriched by two companion schemes. The *Common Platform Enumeration* (**CPE**) catalog provides a structured name for every affected product or version, allowing a CVE to specify its exact impact range (e.g. `cpe:/o:linux:linux_kernel:5.15`) [12]. Meanwhile, the *Common Weakness Enumeration* (**CWE**) classifies the underlying programming fault—such as `CWE-119` *"Improper Memory Bounds Restriction"*—so that analysts can discuss root causes independently of any particular platform [2]. In addition, the *Exploit Prediction Scoring System* (**EPSS**) provides a probabilistic score indicating the likelihood that a given vulnerability will be exploited in the wild within the next 30 days. This allows security teams to prioritize remediation based on exploitation risk rather than just technical severity [5].

Linux Kernel CVE's Management. The Linux kernel community integrates this into a defined disclosure workflow [20]. New kernel issues are first reported—often under embargo—to the private `linux-distros` mailing list, giving major vendors time to prepare patches. The kernel security team then requests or reuses a CVE identifier and announces the vulnerability on `linux-cve-announce` once a patch is available. Stable-branch maintainers back-port the patch to all supported releases, while distributors map the CVE to their package versions through CPE names and publish advisories that reference the relevant CWE category.

4 Research Questions

To guide our analysis of eBPF-related vulnerabilities, we formulate a set of targeted research questions in order to examine when vulnerabilities appear, how they evolve across successive kernel releases, and how long they remain unpatched—thus outlining a timeline of exposure and remediation. In parallel, we analyze eBPF vulnerabilities from three complementary perspectives: *where* they occur within the subsystem, *what* kinds of coding errors cause them, and *how* severe or exploitable they tend to be.

- **RQ1:** What is the temporal distribution of eBPF-related CVEs?
- **RQ2**: What is the trend of the number of eBPF-related CVEs affecting each Linux kernel minor version?
- **RQ3**: How long do eBPF-related vulnerabilities remain latent in the Linux kernel before being patched?
- **RQ4:** Which eBPF modules are most affected by eBPF-related CVEs?
- **RQ5:** What are the most frequent CWE categories among eBPF-related CVEs?
- **RQ6:** How severe are eBPF-related vulnerabilities and what do CVSS vector metrics reveal about their exploitation characteristics?
- **RQ7:** How exploitable are eBPF-related CVEs?

5 Methodology

5.1 Data Acquisition

The first step of our analysis consisted of downloading the entire archive of publicly disclosed CVEs from the National Vulnerability Database (NVD), maintained by the National Institute of Standards and Technology (NIST) [17].

The dataset used was retrieved on April 29, 2025, hence it contained all the CVEs registered up to that date with the latest updates. We paired this data with the Linux official git repository metadata [10], specifically with the commit history to extrapolate the commit date and the files that were involved.

5.2 Data Classification and Refinement

To identify eBPF-related vulnerabilities, we first performed a keyword-based filtering by selecting all entries containing the substring `bpf`, which yielded a total of 401 CVEs. This raw subset was refined through manual inspection, classifying each entry as *included*, *external*, or *excluded*. *External* refers to vulnerabilities affecting eBPF-related software outside the Linux kernel itself, such as user-space tools like Cilium; a total of 63 of these CVEs were found in the database. The *excluded* category includes cases where the term `bpf` appears only incidentally, but not connected to BPF, or where eBPF is merely used as a vector to trigger or exploit other vulnerabilities not inherent to eBPF internals. Only the entries classified as *included* were retained, resulting in a final dataset of 249 CVEs for analysis.

6 Results and Discussion

In this section, we present the results of our analysis and provide answers to the research questions introduced in the previous section. Each answer to the questions contains a note on the methodology used to extract the dimension needed for calculating the result, and the analysis of the output.

6.1 RQ1: What Is the Temporal Distribution of eBPF-Related CVEs?

Methodology. To analyze the temporal evolution of eBPF-related CVEs, we relied on their official publication dates as recorded in public vulnerability databases. For consistency and to capture trends at a suitable granularity, we aggregated CVEs into fixed four-month intervals. This grouping ensures regular spacing across the timeline and accommodates the most recent disclosures, including those from the first third of 2025. We compared the eBPF-related CVEs publishing to the trend of the totality of the CVE published for the same time period.

Analysis. The resulting distribution reveals a general upward trend over the years, punctuated by a few early anomalies (Fig. 1). An initial bump appears around 2017, followed by relatively low but persistent activity. A more noticeable increase occurs between 2021 and 2022, and from late 2023 onward, the number of CVEs more than doubles compared to previous intervals, culminating in a peak in the first third of 2024, with over 60 new vulnerabilities reported.

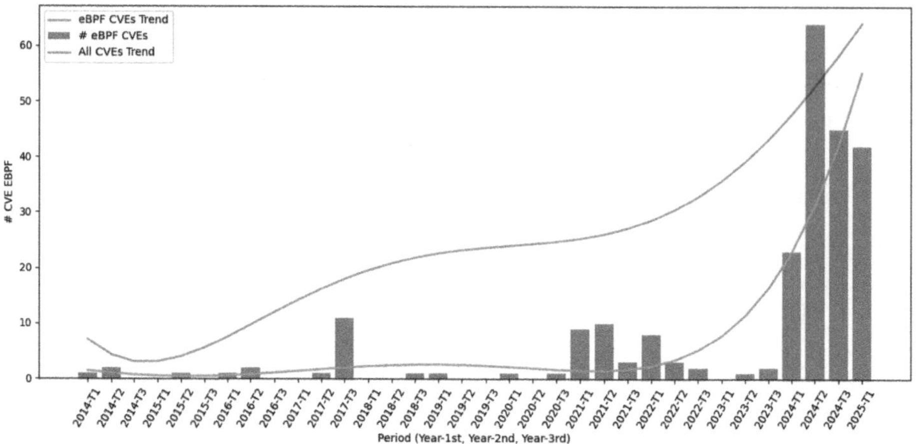

Fig. 1. Temporal distribution of eBPF-related CVEs compared to all CVE trend, aggregated by four-month intervals.

To better understand the long-term trend beyond short-term fluctuations, we applied a smoothed interpolation technique. The resulting curve shows a non-linear, but clearly upward trajectory, with minor local fluctuations—including a slight rise around 2019—before accelerating more steeply in recent intervals. This trend supports the interpretation that eBPF has become an increasingly critical and exposed component in the Linux kernel. The sharp increase in the number of vulnerabilities reported in the past year may also be linked to the concurrent development and publication of new fuzzing-based techniques for systematic vulnerability discovery, such as [7] [18], as well as to the growing complexity of the verifier [8]. However, comparing the trend of the eBPF-related CVEs with the trend of the totality of published CVEs, we notice that they have a high positive correlation (0.723), which suggests that the eBPF-related CVEs follow the general trend of all published CVEs. Nevertheless, the steeper slope of the eBPF curve shows that their number has been rising at a much higher pace.

6.2 RQ2: What Is Trend of the Number of eBPF-Related CVEs Affecting Each Linux Kernel Minor Version?

Methodology. For each CVE we extracted the list of affected kernel versions—encoded in the CVE record through CPE strings—and mapped those CPE tuples to the corresponding minorâĂŘrelease numbers. After this step, we obtained, for the first release (and for each patch) of every Linux kernel minor version, the total number of CVEs affecting it. In Fig. 2, we plot the number of CVEs affecting the first release of every Linux Kernel minor version.

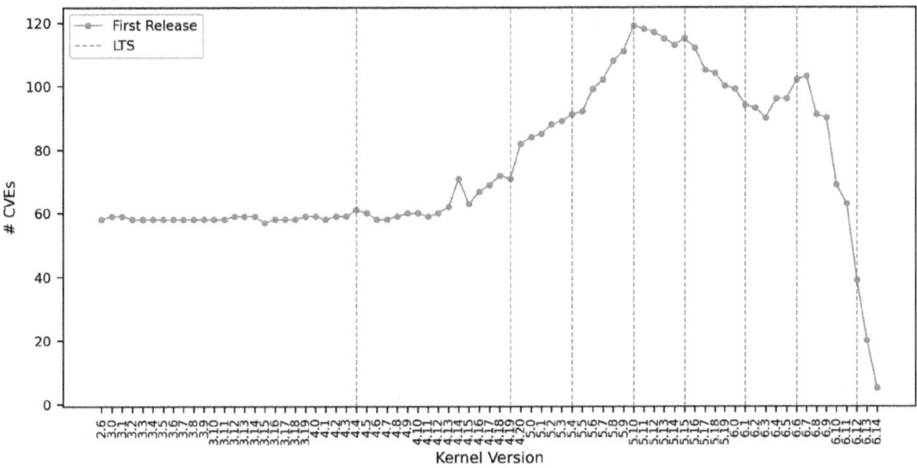

Fig. 2. eBPF-related CVEs affecting the first release of each kernel minor version.

Analysis. Beginning with version 4.14, the count of eBPF-related CVEs affecting the first release of the version increases steadily, peaking at just over 100 in kernel 5.10, which is an LTS. The increasing trend might be favored by a growing interest and a consequent faster development in the eBPF subsystem. The most recent minor versions exhibit lower counts, probably just because they have had less time in the field for vulnerabilities to be discovered and reported. LTS versions often appear as local maxima, reflecting more active development and backporting efforts compared to adjacent non-LTS releases.

6.3 RQ3: How Long Do eBPF-Related Vulnerabilities Remain Latent in the Linux Kernel Before Being Patched?

Methodology. For each CVE in our dataset we identified the first kernel release reported as vulnerable (from CVE metadata) and the commit that introduced the corresponding patch (from the mainline Git history). We then computed the latency, in days, between the release date of the affected version and the date the fix was merged. Descriptive statistics were produced for 70% of CVEs, i.e., the ones for which this information is available.

Analysis. Across the complete set, the mean time-to-fix is 1037.6 days and the median is 737 days, with a maximum of 7744 days. Removing the two longest delays reduces the mean slightly to 995 days while leaving the median unchanged, suggesting that most vulnerabilities are characterized by a broadly similar exposure window and that extreme cases have limited influence on the central tendency. No temporal pattern is apparent: both older and more recent kernel versions show a mix of vulnerabilities uncovered within weeks and others persisting for several years. The large standard deviation (about 1060 days), almost equal to the mean, confirms this wide dispersion—there is no single "typical" discovery delay, but rather a broad spectrum of latency times across the entire history of eBPF development. Moreover, there is no significant correlation between the patch latency and the CVE severity (the computed correlation is 0.06), which is concerning given the potential impact of delayed remediation for serious vulnerabilities. Among the 32 vulnerabilities with a severity score of at least 7, only 10 were fixed within the first year, and 15 within two years—meaning that more than half (17 vulnerabilities) remained unpatched for over two years after their initial release. Overall, eBPF-related vulnerabilities tend to persist in the kernel for roughly two to three years before a corrective patch is merged. This long persistence, associated with the high occurrence rate and the absence of correlation with severity, raises a warning, showing that the eBPF system could be a significant catchment area for zero-day vulnerabilities.

6.4 RQ4: Which eBPF Modules Are Most Affected by eBPF-Related CVEs?

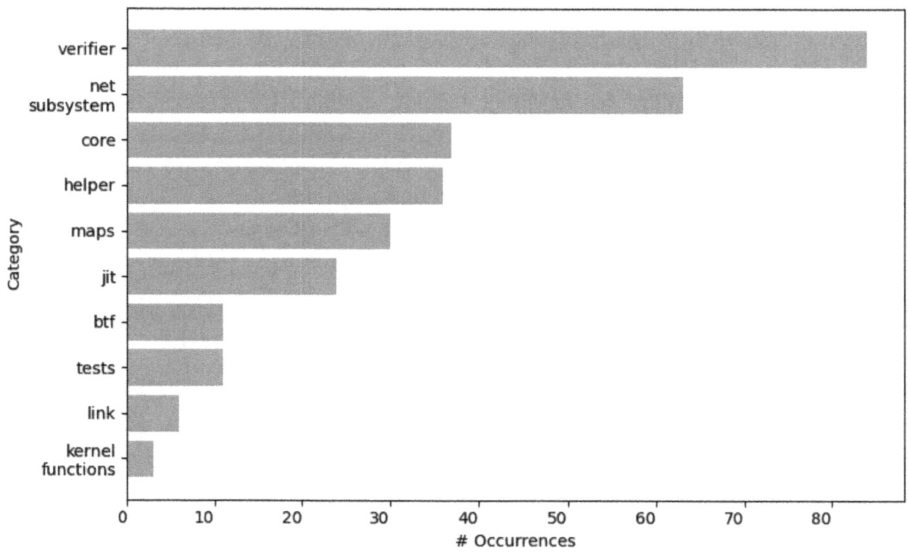

Fig. 3. Top 10 eBPF subsystem modules affected by CVEs.

Methodology. To identify which components of the eBPF subsystem are most frequently affected by security vulnerabilities, we first performed a manual classification of all eBPF-related CVEs. Each CVE was analyzed and assigned to one or

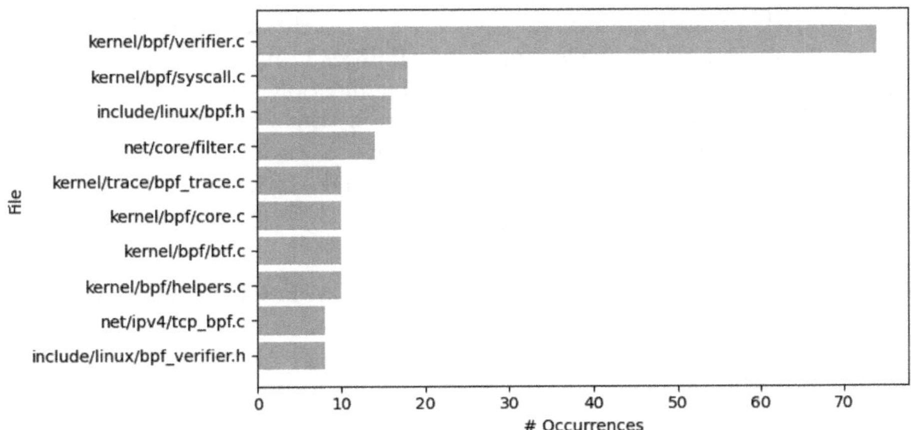

Fig. 4. Top 10 files most frequently modified in commits addressing eBPF-related CVEs.

more functional modules, depending on the nature of the vulnerability. The categories include: *verifier* (responsible for validating eBPF programs before execution), *core* (handling the internal logic, system calls, and virtual machine behavior), *maps* (managing eBPF maps), *helpers* (covering helper functions), *kernel functions* (kfuncs), *JIT compiler* (just-in-time translation to native instructions), *BTF* (providing compatibility and internal structure management), *self-tests* (internal testing infrastructure), and various *subsystems* (e.g., networking, tracing, and performance hooks).

Importantly, this categorization is not mutually exclusive: a single CVE may span multiple modules. For instance, a verifier flaw that fails to correctly validate access to a helper function is associated with both the *verifier* and *helpers* categories.

To complement this logical classification with a source-level perspective, we further analyzed the code changes applied to fix each vulnerability. For every CVE with an associated public fix, we extracted the commit(s) from the mainline Linux kernel repository and recorded the modified source files. Even if the patched files may not always indicate the origin of the vulnerability, the two analyses yielded similar results.

Analysis. The manual classification, shown in Fig. 3, reveals that the *verifier* is the most impacted module by a significant margin, followed by the *networking subsystem*, the *core*, and the *helpers* and *maps* modules. This distribution confirms the eBPF verifier's central role and its historical fragility in handling complex or edge-case program logic [14]. The file-level analysis shown in Fig. 4 further reinforces these findings. The most frequently modified file in CVE-related commits is `verifier.c`, which alone appears in nearly 70 commits—over three times more than the next file, `syscall.c`. Additional verifier-related files, such as `bpf_verifier.h`, also rank in the top 10. The top modified files are overwhelmingly located within `kernel/bpf/`, with a few exceptions in `include/linux/` and `net/core/`, the latter reflecting vulnerabilities in networking integration.

Overall, both the logical module-based classification and the physical source-level analysis converge on the same conclusion: the eBPF verifier represents the most vulnerable and maintenance-intensive part of the eBPF subsystem. Its complexity, central role in enforcing safety, and ongoing evolution make it a persistent source of security challenges.

6.5 RQ5: What Are the Most Frequent CWE Categories Among eBPF-Related CVEs?

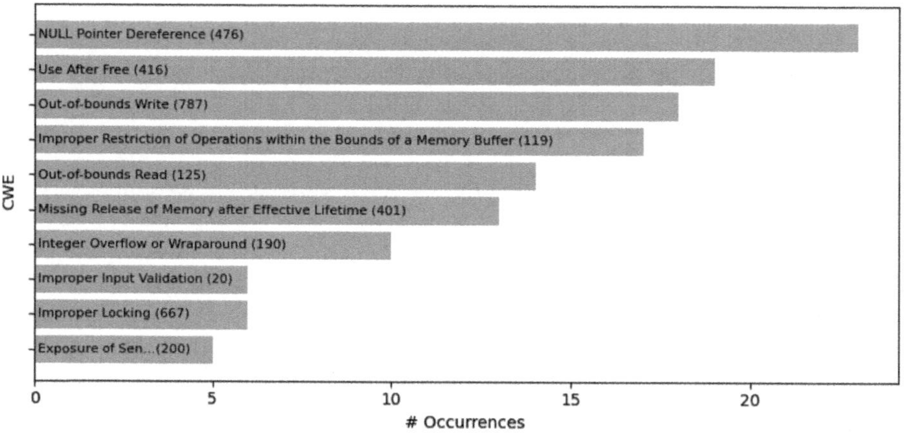

Fig. 5. Top 10 CWE categories found among CVEs related to eBPF.

Methodology. To determine the most common root causes of eBPF-related vulnerabilities, we collected the Common Weakness Enumeration (CWE) identifiers associated with each CVE having this data available (around 41% of the dataset). Each CWE provides a standardized description of the underlying coding issue that led to the vulnerability. This analysis allows us to reason not only about where vulnerabilities occur, but also about why they occur—offering insights into recurring programming patterns that compromise eBPF's security.

Analysis. Among the top 10 CWE categories identified in eBPF-related CVEs, we observe a clear predominance of memory-related issues. The most frequent category is `CWE-476` (NULL Pointer Dereference). Other critical entries include `CWE-125` (Out-of-bounds Read) and `CWE-787` (Out-of-bounds Write). If considered together, these categories account for a significant portion of all eBPF-related CVEs, indicating that memory access remains a central source of risk. Figure 5

These results highlight the difficulty of safe low-level memory handling in eBPF's performance-critical C code. Although C remains viable, memory safety is still the subsystem's chief challenge. Strengthening design, testing, and tooling— or adopting safer language features—could lead to a smaller eBPF's vulnerability rate [8].

6.6 RQ6: How Severe Are eBPF-Related Vulnerabilities and What Do CVSS Vector Metrics Reveal About Their Exploitation Characteristics?

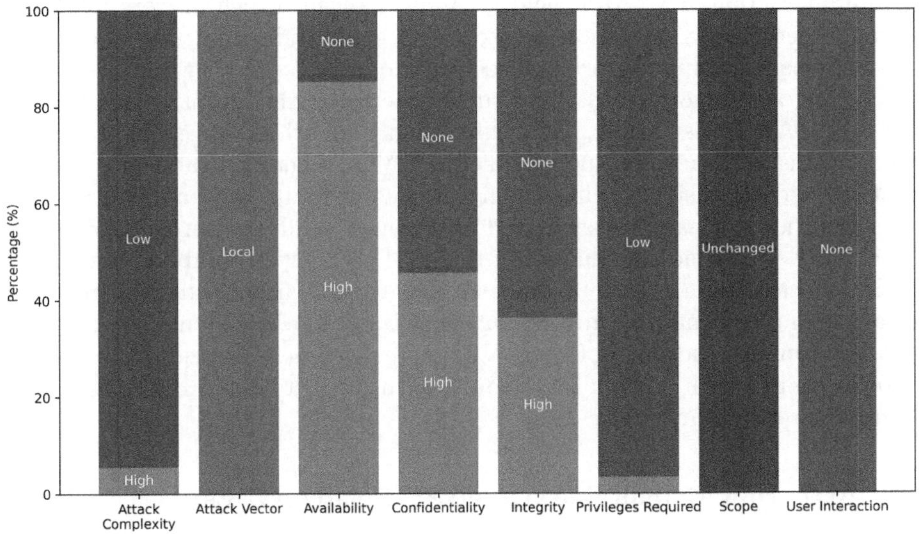

Fig. 6. Percentage Distribution of CVSS Values per Metric.

Methodology. We collected base severity scores for all eBPF-related CVEs from the NVD, along with the highest available score including third-party advisories, to account for cases where the NVD score was missing or a third-party assessment provided a differing evaluation. However,a significant part of the CVE's had no evaluation (30%). Basic descriptive statistics (mean, median, min, max) were computed on the final score to understand tendency and extremes. For a finer-grained view, we extracted CVSS v3.0 and CVSS v3.1 vector components both from NVD's evaluation and the corresponding vector of the highest score assigned including third-party advisory, and studied the distribution of any possible value for each dimension of the vector. To contextualize these results, we also compared them with the distribution of CVSS scores across Linux kernel CVEs, providing a baseline to assess whether eBPF vulnerabilities differ significantly from kernel vulnerabilities in general.

Analysis. The CVSS vector analysis, shown in Fig. 6, paints a clear picture of how eBPF-related vulnerabilities are typically scored. The attack vector is always classified as *Local* by the NVD, although one occurrence was classified as *Network* by a third-party advisor, with overall low impact. This pattern is largely consistent with kernel CVEs in general, which are also mostly local, though they include a broader variety of cases reaching network and even physical vectors. Exploits are generally rated with *Low* attack complexity, in line with the kernel as a whole where the same trend dominates. The majority of eBPF CVEs require only *Low* privileges, whereas kernel vulnerabilities more often allow for no privileges at all, compliant with the need for `CAP_BPF` in eBPF execution. User interaction is almost always marked *None*, and similarly kernel CVEs rarely require interaction. The *Scope* field is rarely changed, which mirrors the kernel overall, where scope escalation is also exceptional, indicating that the impact usually remains within the original security domain.

Looking at impacts, availability suffers the most: the majority of CVEs are scored *High* for this metric, although roughly one-third have no availability impact. This is broadly in line with kernel CVEs, where availability is also the most affected dimension. Confidentiality impact is evenly split; about half of the vulnerabilities can expose sensitive data through arbitrary kernel reads, while the remainder pose no confidentiality threat. This is again comparable to kernel CVEs, which show a similar balance though with a slightly stronger tendency toward high confidentiality impact. Integrity is not affected by many vulnerabilities, yet roughly one-third of the CVEs score *High* here as well. Kernel CVEs follow a comparable distribution, though with integrity compromise appearing slightly more frequently (Fig. 7).

6.7 RQ7: How Exploitable Are eBPF-Related CVEs?

Methodology. To assess the exploitability of vulnerabilities in the eBPF subsystem, we collected Exploit Prediction Scoring System (EPSS) values for all CVEs in our dataset using the official EPSS API. The EPSS score estimates the probability that a CVE will be exploited in the wild within the next 30 days [5]. We computed basic descriptive statistics (mean, median, minimum, maximum) to capture the overall exploitability landscape. Additionally, a manual search by student researchers identified 12 eBPF-related CVEs for which public exploit code exists and has been executed with varying degrees of success.

Analysis. The EPSS distribution of eBPF-related CVEs is concentrated at very low values, around $2 \cdot 10^{-4}$, roughly resembling a normal distribution. Descriptive statistics confirm this skew: the mean EPSS is $6.2 \cdot 10^{-3}$, while the median is $3.8 \cdot 10^{-4}$. However, a few outliers exhibit substantially higher scores, up to 0.83021, orders of magnitude above the majority. At the same time, the overall probability of exploitation for these vulnerabilities appears low, with only a handful of outliers exhibiting substantially higher risk.

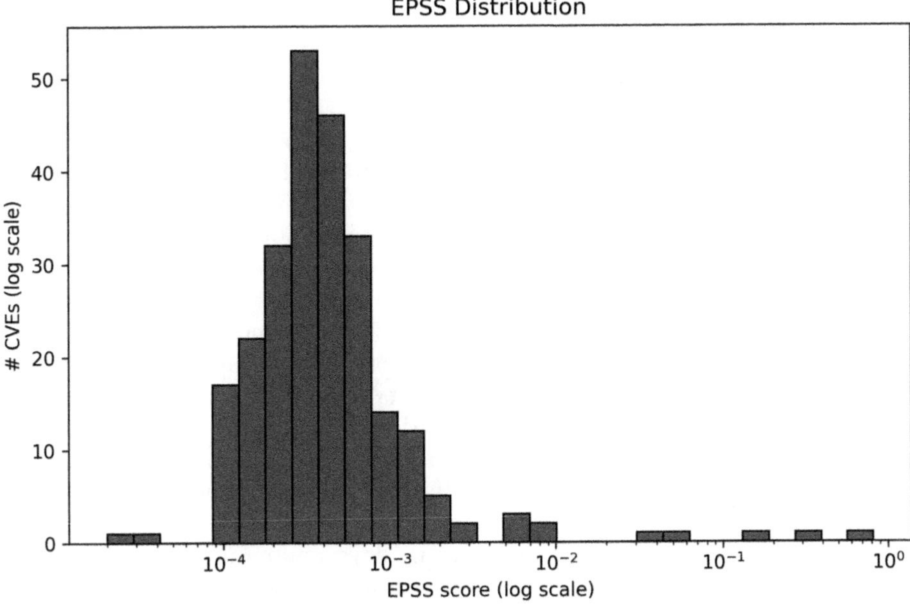

Fig. 7. Distribution of EPSS scores for eBPF-related CVEs.

Manual exploit testing revealed that the 12 identified CVEs could be leveraged for various attacks, predominantly privilege escalation. Other outcomes include memory address disclosure, denial-of-service (kernel crashes), and additional undefined behavior. It is worth noting that most modern distributions disable unprivileged eBPF by default [3], significantly limiting the practical exposure. Nevertheless, these exploits demonstrate that privileged eBPF execution remains a high-risk vector when memory safety flaws exist. This distribution fits well with the relatively small number of practical exploits observed in testing.

It should also be considered that the generally low likelihood of exploitation may be influenced by the fact that EPSS scores were retrieved at the time of data collection. As a result, it is plausible that many of the affected kernel versions had already been patched or were no longer widely deployed, potentially contributing to the reduced probability of exploitation.

7 Conclusions

Our investigation of 249 eBPF-related CVEs (2014âĂŞApril 2025) reveals three salient patterns. First, the annual volume of disclosures is steadily increasing, underscoring the growing attack surface exposed by eBPF's rapid evolution. Second, vulnerabilities persist for a long time: half remain hidden for more than two years before a fix lands, signaling the need for earlier detection and coordinated patching. Third, structural analysis pinpoints the verifier as the subsystem's primary weakness, with memory-safety flaws accounting for most reported issues; typical exploits are local, low-complexity and yield medium-to-high impact scores. Putting all the findings together raises an important warning about the eBPF system's exposure to security risk. Vulnerabilities related to eBPF are becoming more and more frequent, a significant part of them are high-severity, and the average time-to-fix is in the order of years, without apparent correlation with severity. These results suggest that even severe vulnerabilities remain unpatched for a long time before becoming public, as more than half of the high-severity cases took over two years to be fixed, implying a significant risk of being discovered independently and exploited as zero-day vulnerabilities.

In practice, most proof-of-concept exploits found online target privilege escalation; however, since recent Linux distributions disable unprivileged eBPF by default [3], the actual impact of such exploits is relatively reduced in contemporary environments. However, this limitation might result in programs being granted excessive privileges they should not have. In addition, recent advances such as *Agni* [21], which enables partial formal verification of the verifier logic, and *Brf* [7], a fuzzing-based approach to accelerate vulnerability discovery, represent promising directions to mitigate future flaws and reduce the delay in CVE discovery, which emerged as a major concern in our analysis.

Future work will map known proof-of-concept exploits to the CVEs identified here and assess how much risk propagates to user-space projects that embed or depend on eBPF functionality.

Acknowledgment. This paper has received funding by the Smart Networks and Services Joint Undertaking (SNS JU) under the European Union's Horizon Europe research and innovation programme under Grant Agreement No 101139067 (ELASTIC). Views and opinions expressed are however those of the author(s) only and do not necessarily reflect those of the European Union. Neither the European Union nor the granting authority can be held responsible for them.

References

1. Bhandari, G., Naseer, A., Moonen, L.: Cvefixes: automated collection of vulnerabilities and their fixes from open-source software. In: Proceedings of the 17th International Conference on Predictive Models and Data Analytics in Software Engineering, pp. 30–39. PROMISE 2021. Association for Computing Machinery, New York (2021). https://doi.org/10.1145/3475960.3475985, https://doi.org/10.1145/3475960.3475985
2. Corporation, M.: Common weakness enumeration (cwe). https://cwe.mitre.org (2025), https://cwe.mitre.org
3. Edge, J.: Bpf and security (2023). https://lwn.net/Articles/946389/. Accessed 17 Sept 2025
4. Fan, J., Li, Y., Wang, S., Nguyen, T.N.: A c/c++ code vulnerability dataset with code changes and cve summaries. In: Proceedings of the 17th International Conference on Mining Software Repositories, pp. 508–512. MSR '20, Association for Computing Machinery, New York (2020).https://doi.org/10.1145/3379597.3387501, https://doi.org/10.1145/3379597.3387501

5. Forum of Incident Response and Security Teams (FIRST): The epss model. https://www.first.org/epss/model (2025). Accessed 17 Sept 2025
6. Gershuni, E., Amit, N., Gurfinkel, A., Narodytska, N., Navas, J.A., Rinetzky, N., Ryzhyk, L., Sagiv, M.: Simple and precise static analysis of untrusted linux kernel extensions. In: Proceedings of the 40th ACM SIGPLAN Conference on Programming Language Design and Implementation, pp. 1069–1084. PLDI 2019. Association for Computing Machinery, New York (2019).https://doi.org/10.1145/3314221.3314590, https://doi.org/10.1145/3314221.3314590
7. Hung, H.W., Amiri Sani, A.: Brf: Fuzzing the ebpf runtime. Proc. ACM Softw. Eng. **1**(FSE) (Jul 2024). https://doi.org/10.1145/3643778
8. Jia, J., Sahu, R., Oswald, A., Williams, D., Le, M.V., Xu, T.: Kernel extension verification is untenable. In: Proceedings of the 19th Workshop on Hot Topics in Operating Systems, pp. 150–157. HOTOS '23, Association for Computing Machinery, New York (2023). https://doi.org/10.1145/3593856.3595892, https://doi.org/10.1145/3593856.3595892
9. Jin, D., Atlidakis, V., Kemerlis, V.P.: EPF: Evil packet filter. In: 2023 USENIX Annual Technical Conference (USENIX ATC 23), pp. 735–751. USENIX Association, Boston, MA (Jul 2023). https://www.usenix.org/conference/atc23/presentation/jin
10. Linus Torvalds: Linux kernel source repository. https://git.kernel.org/pub/scm/linux/kernel/git/torvalds/linux.git. Accessed 18 May 2025
11. Liu, Q., Shen, W., Zhou, J., Zhang, Z., Hu, J., Ni, S., Lu, K., Chang, R.: Interp-flow hijacking: Launching non-control data attack via hijacking ebpf interpretation flow. In: Garcia-Alfaro, J., Kozik, R., Choraś, M., Katsikas, S. (eds.) Computer Security - ESORICS 2024, pp. 194–214. Springer Nature Switzerland, Cham (2024)
12. MITRE Corporation: Common platform enumeration (cpe). https://cpe.mitre.org/. Accessed 19 May 2025
13. MITRE Corporation: Cve - common vulnerabilities and exposures. https://www.cve.org/. Accessed 19 May 2025
14. Mohamed, M.H.N., Wang, X., Ravindran, B.: Understanding the security of linux ebpf subsystem. In: Proceedings of the 14th ACM SIGOPS Asia-Pacific Workshop on Systems, pp. 87–92. APSys '23. Association for Computing Machinery, New York (2023). https://doi.org/10.1145/3609510.3609822
15. Ponta, S.E., Plate, H., Sabetta, A., Bezzi, M., Dangremont, C.: A manually-curated dataset of fixes to vulnerabilities of open-source software. In: Proceedings of the 16th International Conference on Mining Software Repositories, pp. 383–387. MSR '19, IEEE Press (2019).https://doi.org/10.1109/MSR.2019.00064
16. Safronov, V., Bostan, I., Allott, N., Martin, A.: How memory-safe is iot? assessing the impact of memory-protection solutions for securing wireless gateways. In: Proceedings of the 14th International Conference on the Internet of Things, pp. 261–266. IoT 2024. Association for Computing Machinery, New York (2025). https://doi.org/10.1145/3703790.3703820, https://doi.org/10.1145/3703790.3703820
17. of Standards, N.I., Technology: National vulnerability database. https://nvd.nist.gov (2025). https://nvd.nist.gov
18. Sun, H., Xu, Y., Liu, J., Shen, Y., Guan, N., Jiang, Y.: Finding correctness bugs in ebpf verifier with structured and sanitized program. In: Proceedings of the Nineteenth European Conference on Computer Systems. pp. 689–703. EuroSys '24. Association for Computing Machinery, New York (2024). https://doi.org/10.1145/3627703.3629562
19. The Linux Kernel Archives: Bpf - linux kernel documentation. https://docs.kernel.org/bpf/. Accessed 2025 19 May

20. The Linux Kernel Archives: Using cves to track security vulnerabilities in the linux kernel. https://docs.kernel.org/process/cve.html. Accessed 19 May 2025
21. Vishwanathan, H., Shachnai, M., Narayana, S., Nagarakatte, S.: Verifying the verifier: ebpf range analysis verification. In: Enea, C., Lal, A. (eds.) Computer Aided Verification, pp. 226–251. Springer, Cham (2023)

Revealing Unreported OT Vulnerabilities from Public Discussions

Arslane Fawzi Halilou(✉) and Natalia Stakhanova(✉)

Department of Computer Science, University of Saskatchewan, Saskatoon, Canada
kjc705@usask.ca, natalia@cs.usask.ca

Abstract. The convergence of Information Technology (IT) and Operational Technology (OT) has transformed industrial systems into interconnected, data-driven environments. While this shift enhanced real-time monitoring, automation, and decision-making, it has also expanded the attack surface of Industrial Control Systems (ICS), exposing them to significant cybersecurity risks. Although official databases such as MITRE's CVE and the NVD encompass large numbers of known vulnerabilities, evidence shows that vulnerabilities are often discussed in public sources (e.g., social media, blogs, forums) before their official disclosure. This lag poses a critical risk for OT systems, where applying patches is challenging due to legacy hardware and operational constraints. To address this, we propose a predictive framework that identifies undisclosed OT-related vulnerabilities by monitoring online sources such as mailing lists, news websites, and security podcasts. Our proposed framework filters content using device specifications and protocol information to isolate OT-relevant discussions. It then uses linguistic patterns from known vulnerabilities to detect vulnerability indicators. Experimental results demonstrate high accuracy for the proposed framework ranging from 86% to 99% in detecting signals of OT vulnerabilities in public discussions across multiple sources.

1 Introduction

No software is free of vulnerabilities. To identify these security flaws, traditional approaches rely on expert analysis and systematic examination of the software. Once a vulnerability is discovered, the first step is to confirm that it is a genuine security flaw and assess its impact to evaluate the severity of the vulnerability and its potential consequences. If the vulnerability is confirmed, it is documented and reported. Ideally, after responsible disclosure process, all software vulnerabilities should be officially documented and registered in authoritative databases such as the National Vulnerability Database (NVD) and the Common Vulnerabilities and Exposures (CVE) database. Unfortunately, the reality is different. Many vulnerabilities remain undisclosed, underreported, or are shared informally through public forums, news outlets, or technical discussions before they appear in official records. As a result, monitoring online public and unofficial sources to uncover vulnerabilities not present in official databases has become increasingly important.

K. Adi et al. (Eds.): CRiSIS 2025, LNCS 16295, pp. 237–253, 2026.
https://doi.org/10.1007/978-3-032-20732-6_15

The existing studies have focused on social media platforms, GitHub, cybersecurity blogs, and dark web forums to address the limitations of official vulnerability databases. The majority of these studies demonstrate that such public sources can serve as effective early warning systems for rapidly spreading cyberattacks [3,13,18,22,25–27]. Typically, these approaches rely on a precompiled dictionary of terms describing known attacks (e.g., malware, trojan) and emphasize the use of social media platforms to provide early alerts, assess the scale of attacks, and identify affected geolocations. A few efforts have also attempted to detect signs of undisclosed vulnerabilities using a predefined ontology indicative of vulnerabilities [21]. However, the robustness of these methods for detecting vulnerabilities not officially reported remains limited.

In this work, *we explore the potential of public sources to reveal undisclosed or underreported vulnerabilities*. This is particularly relevant in the operational technology (OT) domain, where the critical nature of systems, combined with challenges such as legacy hardware and strict operational constraints, makes patching particularly difficult.

We propose a framework that proactively monitors online sources to identify OT-related vulnerabilities, leveraging features derived from OT device specifications and linguistic patterns extracted using topic modeling techniques, i.e., BERTopic and Latent Dirichlet Allocation (LDA), commonly found in known vulnerability descriptions from official databases. We evaluate the robustness of the proposed framework across several online sources, including the Full Disclosure mailing list, the Ars Technica news site, and transcripts of the Security Now podcast, using a dataset of over 125,000 messages, articles, and podcast episodes.

Experimental results demonstrate high accuracy for the proposed ensemble-based framework, ranging from 86% to 99% across all three datasets. Precision and recall were particularly strong on the Full Disclosure dataset, reaching 87% and 83% respectively, highlighting the framework's effectiveness in detecting vulnerable OT content. Performance on the SecurityNow and Ars Technica datasets remained solid but showed a noticeable drop in precision, recorded at 56% and 67% respectively. A decline in recall was also observed for Ars Technica (46%) compared to SecurityNow (80%). While the lower performance on SecurityNow is expected due to its informal language, unstructured format, and frequent topic shifts, the relatively weaker results on Ars Technica are more surprising given its structured text. Further analysis of false positives revealed that Ars Technica articles often reference vulnerabilities indirectly or as part of broader discussions, which complicates the classification task.

These findings suggest that, regardless of the content source or the level of textual structure, similar language is consistently used to describe vulnerabilities. This linguistic consistency enables the model to effectively identify indicators of officially undisclosed vulnerabilities across diverse sources.

The rest of this paper is organized as follows. Section 3 gives an overview of related works and our contribution. In Sect. 4, we explain our proposed approach.

Section 5 describes the experimental results obtained for the proposed model. Finally, this work is concluded in Sect. 6.

2 Background

Traditionally, the vulnerability discovery process aims to identify security flaws in software systems. Once a vulnerability is discovered, the first step is verification, where the issue is tested to confirm that it is a genuine security flaw rather than a false positive. If the vulnerability is confirmed, an impact assessment is conducted to evaluate the severity of the vulnerability and its potential consequences. After this assessment, the vulnerability is documented and reported either internally, to the software vendor, or to public vulnerability databases, depending on the disclosure policy. Developers then work to create and test a patch that resolves the issue without introducing new problems. Once the fix is validated, it is deployed across affected systems. Finally, if appropriate, the vulnerability and its resolution are publicly disclosed, with an official CVE identifier and a CVSS (Common Vulnerability Scoring System) score.

Disclosure Policy. A vulnerability can be disclosed following a responsible disclosure policy, full disclosure, or private disclosure, depending on the context, the discoverer's intent, and the affected organization's practices. If *responsible disclosure* (also known as coordinated disclosure) policy is followed, the researcher privately notifies the affected vendor and allows time for a fix before making the details public. In contrast, *full disclosure* involves publicly revealing the vulnerability shortly after discovery, regardless of whether a patch is available. *Private disclosure* occurs when the information is shared only with the vendor and never made public, while *non-disclosure* refers to situations where the vulnerability is not reported at all, sometimes due to legal concerns, lack of incentives, or malicious intent.

3 Related Work

Software vulnerabilities have been at the center of research for decades. The vulnerability discovery process is actively studied. In this paper, we focus on related work related to existing vulnerabilities that were discovered through traditional means but were never officially disclosed.

Vulnerability as Early Warning System. Public online sources have been widely examined to predict rapidly spreading cyberattacks [3,13,18,22,25–27]. Typically, these studies rely on official vulnerability repositories such as CVE or a precompiled dictionary of terms describing known attacks.

Many of these efforts leverage messages on the Twitter platform. For instance, Le et al. [17] proposed a model to collect tweets related to existing vulnerabilities. Quentin et al. [18] introduced an automated framework for the real-time detection and geolocation of ongoing security incidents, based on a predefined taxonomy of cybersecurity-related terms. Sabottke et al. [24] explored the use of Twitter platform for early detection of exploits against known vulnerabilities contained in NVD database.

A similar approach was taken by Mittal et al. [21], who introduced Cyber-Twitter, a real-time monitoring system that analyzes the Twitter stream to extract information about emerging threats and vulnerabilities. Their system relies on a security ontology and is tailored to the organization's custom system profile. Another Twitter-based monitoring system, SYNAPSE, was proposed by Alves et al. [3]. Unlike broader approaches, SYNAPSE collects tweets exclusively from selected security-related accounts and filters the content to extract intelligence relevant to the assets of the monitored infrastructure. The potential of the Twitter platform for zero-day vulnerability detection was explored by Sauerwein et al. [26]. The study mapped tweets to different phases of the vulnerability lifecycle showing that vulnerabilities are discussed on Twitter before their official public disclosure. Alevizopoulou et al. analyzed Twitter platform for collection of IoT device relevant security tweets [1]. While Twitter proves valuable for early cybersecurity insights, its character limit presents a challenge for conveying detailed technical information [7].

Beyond Twitter, existing approaches such as DISCOVER [25] leveraged multiple sources including Twitter, blogs, and dark web forums to monitor terms potentially indicative of cyber threats (attacks) for early warning generation.

Several studies explored the possibility of assessing the likelihood of known software vulnerability exploitation based on data in public sources such as rating of vulnerabilities by Common Vulnerability Scoring System (CVSS) [6], dark web [2], CVE and Twitter [14].

Numerous studies also examined methods for predicting the severity of already discovered vulnerabilities as an alternative to manual severity assessments [10,11,19,28,30,31]. More recent work explores the use of large language models (LLMs) for CVSS classification [20,23].

Unlike these studies that rely on officially known vulnerabilities to determine their exploitability or access the scope of the exploitation, we propose a framework that proactively scans public sources to identify undisclosed and therefore not officially registered OT vulnerabilities.

Inconsistencies in Vulnerability Databases. The vast majority of vulnerability-related studies rely on official vulnerability repositories. However, numerous inconsistencies have been identified in these data sources. These include discrepancies in severity scores and vulnerability types [4], mismatches in software names and versions between the standardized NVD database and the unstructured CVE descriptions [9], differences in CVSS base metrics assigned by different organizations [15], inconsistencies between identical or semantically similar NVD entries [32], and inconsistencies in NVD's CPE tags [29].

4 Proposed Approach

The ultimate goal of our approach is to predict whether a public discussion includes an indication of a security vulnerability. Accurate identification of public discussions that are likely to lead to official vulnerabilities is critical for a timely system response. To facilitate early identification of vulnerabilities specific to OT devices, we propose a framework that (1) identifies OT device-related content and (2) determines whether it describes a security vulnerability. Figure 1 illustrates the general flow of the proposed framework that consists of three main stages: data preprocessing, feature modelling, and vulnerability identification.

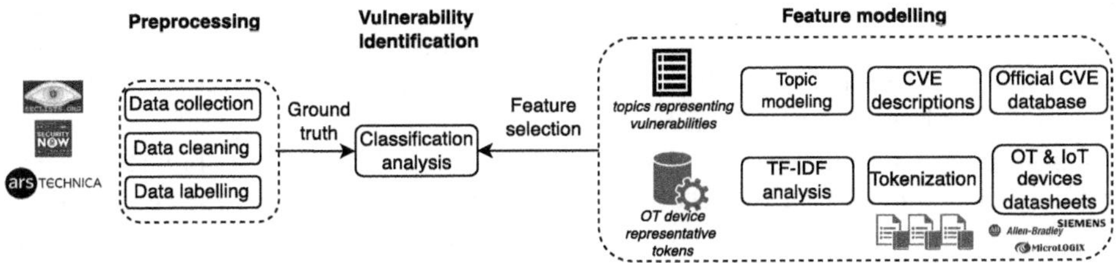

Fig. 1. Flow of the proposed framework.

4.1 Preprocessing

Data Collection. Collecting data from various sources is essential for effectively identifying potential vulnerabilities in OT devices. Public discussions related to cybersecurity can occur across a wide range of platforms, including social media, technical forums, security podcasts, research publications, vulnerability databases, and news sites. Each source offers unique perspectives, levels of technical detail, and timeliness. By aggregating information from diverse channels, the framework can capture a broader and more representative view of emerging threats, reduce blind spots, and improve the accuracy of both device-related content identification and vulnerability recognition.

For our analysis, we leveraged three sources of information: FullDisclosure mail list (from 2002 to 2024), Ars Technica news site (from 2006 to 2025), and SecurityNow podcast (from 2005 to 2025). To collect information across multiple sources, we designed custom crawlers to collect all available messages from mail list, all news articles (including those not related to security), and all public episodes of the podcast. The period wherein the data was collected differed according to the source: 27 dec 2024 to 6 Jan 2025 for FullDisclosure, 22 April 2025 to 25 April 2025 for Ars Technica, and 25 April 2025 for SecurityNow.

Data Cleaning. Once the data was collected, it was preprocessed to remove duplicate entries, unparseable characters, and HTML tags. However, punctuation was intentionally preserved, as removing it could alter critical versioning information such as product versions, firmware identifiers, and hardware model numbers (e.g., CPU types) that are commonly associated with vulnerabilities.

For example, removing punctuation from the following article excerpt *"...the attacks targeted iPhones running iOS versions 15.7 through 16.0.3..."* would fragment the software version numbers into arbitrary digits that could be misinterpreted as unrelated data, e.g., dates.

Data Labelling. To establish ground truth, we labelled the extracted datasets. Labelling of OT-related content was done based on a precompiled dictionary of keywords known to indicate industrial OT devices, such as programmable logic controllers (PLCs), remote terminal units (RTUs), and supervisory control and data acquisition (SCADA) systems. The labelled data was manually verified afterwards to ensure its relevance.

Vulnerable content, on the other hand, was labeled based on the presence of an official CVE identifier in the text. A CVE identifier is a standardized string referring to a unique, officially disclosed vulnerability, formatted as CVE-Year-UniqueID, where the unique ID is typically four digits or more. The presence of such a string in messages, emails, or articles strongly suggests that the content refers to a vulnerability. Based on this criterion, any extracted content containing a CVE identifier was labeled as vulnerable; otherwise, it was labelled as not vulnerable. As with OT-related content, we manually reviewed the labeled data to avoid misclassifications particularly in Ars Technica articles, which sometimes mention CVE strings in contexts unrelated to actual vulnerabilities.

4.2 Feature Modelling

A critical step in identifying vulnerable content is constructing a set of features that are representative of OT devices and their associated vulnerabilities. Since the descriptions we collected from the three sources may contain subjective language and may not consistently indicate vulnerabilities, we aimed to derive features that are more broadly representative of vulnerable OT content.

To achieve this, we leveraged two primary sources: specification documentation for OT devices and the CVE database.

To derive *features that can identify OT-related content* beyond device names, we collected datasheets and manuals for 65 devices used in industrial automation and process control. To ensure diversity and coverage, we selected devices from 12 of the top 50 global industrial automation companies, as ranked by Emerson [5]. Since OT devices share some functionalities with IoT devices, it is important to distinguish between the two to avoid overlap. Therefore, we also collected datasheets for 150 IoT devices not used in industrial settings, but commonly found in home, health, and fitness applications (e.g., smart lock, wearable devices, remote patient monitoring devices). The collected datasheets were converted to plain text. The resulting text was tokenized using whitespace as the delimiter, producing two sets of tokens for IoT and OT datasheets. To improve the quality of analysis, we filtered out tokens that were present in both sets, only retaining tokens exclusive to OT domain.

To assess the importance of tokens indicative of OT devices, we further employed Term FrequencyInverse Document Frequency (TF-IDF) analysis, a widely used technique in natural language processing for evaluating the significance of terms across datasheets [16]. This technique combines the term frequency (TF) and the inverse document frequency (IDF).

Term Frequency (TF): is used to calculate the occurrence of the word in a datasheet. For a word t in a datasheet d, let $f_{t,d}$ be the number of times t

appears in d and $\sum_{t' \in d} f_{t',d}$ the total number of terms in datasheet d.

$$\mathrm{TF}(t,d) = \frac{f_{t,d}}{\sum_{t' \in d} f_{t',d}}$$

The Inverse Document Frequency (IDF): reflect the importance of a word across multiple datasheets by calculating its occurrence across the entire corpus. For term t in a corpus D, let N be total number of datasheets in the corpus and n_t be the number of datasheets wherein term t appears. The number *1* in the denominator is used to avoid division by zero.

$$\mathrm{IDF}(t,D) = \log\left(\frac{N}{1+n_t}\right)$$

Term FrequencyInverse Document Frequency (TF-IDF): combines both TF and IDF to determine the significance of a word across a corpus.

$$\text{TF-IDF}(t,d,D) = \mathrm{TF}(t,d) \times \mathrm{IDF}(t,D)$$

Based on the TF-IDF scores, we selected the top 500, 1000, and 2000 tokens as candidate feature sets describing only OT devices.

To derive *features describing vulnerabilities*, we leveraged the CVE database, the official source of disclosed vulnerabilities. Since vulnerability descriptions in such databases are typically very brief (averaging at 42 words), we chose not to use TF-IDF for feature extraction. We employed topic modelling techniques: BERTopic and Latent Dirichlet Allocation (LDA). Topic modelling techniques are unsupervised, meaning they do not require labelled data to guide the analysis. These methods operate under the assumption that by uncovering hidden patterns in the data, they can identify semantically relevant words, which can then be used to annotate new texts. In our context, these techniques can help derive a set of distinguishing features representing descriptions of vulnerabilities.

For this analysis, we extracted all available CVE entries from the official CVE repository spanning the years 1999 to 2024. The descriptions of these CVEs were used to extract features that could help distinguish vulnerable content from benign. We deliberately chose not to restrict the scope to only OT-related CVE descriptions, both to compensate for the limited coverage of OT vulnerabilities in the CVE database and to enable the detection of vulnerabilities affecting OT devices beyond those explicitly disclosed.

For each CVE description, we removed common linking words (e.g., 'and', 'also', 'furthermore', 'moreover', 'but', 'however', 'although', 'so'), then tokenized the text using space as the token separator. This formed the full set of tokens. We refer to this set of tokens as 'All'. We then conducted topic modeling analysis using BERTopic and Latent Dirichlet Allocation (LDA) on this set.

4.3 Identification of Vulnerability Description

To enable the identification of OT-related vulnerable content, our proposed system combines two sets of features: one derived from OT device documentation

Table 1. Model parameters for XGBoost and Random Forest algorithms

Parameter	XGBoost	Random Forest
n_estimators	100	150
max_depth	5	10
class_weight	–	`balanced_subsample`
scale_pos_weight	N/P	–
random_state	42	42
n_jobs	Default (None)	-1 (all processors)

and the other from official vulnerability descriptions in the CVE database. These features are then used to train machine learning classifiers. In this work, we explore two classification algorithms: Random Forest and XGBoost.

Random Forest (RF) [12] is an ensemble learning method that constructs multiple decision trees during training and outputs the class selected by the majority of trees during inference. It is robust to overfitting and performs well with high-dimensional feature spaces. XGBoost (Extreme Gradient Boosting) [8] is a scalable and efficient gradient boosting framework that builds decision trees sequentially. Each new tree attempts to correct the errors made by the previous ones, and the model is optimized using a gradient descent algorithm. XGBoost is known for its high performance on classification tasks, especially in structured data settings.

To build a robust predictive model, we combine RF and XGBoost using a soft voting ensemble approach. RF reduces variance by averaging the predictions of multiple deep decision trees trained on bootstrapped subsets of the data, while XGBoost reduces bias through gradient boosting, iteratively improving performance by focusing on errors made by previous models.

The ensemble approach aggregates the predicted class probabilities from each model and selects the class with the highest average probability. Instead of selecting the final class based on the majority vote of predicted labels (as in hard voting), soft voting averages the predicted probabilities for each class across both models and selects the class with the highest average probability. The soft voting ensemble produced more stable, reliable, and generalizable results by compensating for the individual errors of each model, ultimately enhancing overall robustness.

5 Experimental Results

5.1 Experimental Setup

The framework was implemented using Python programming language with the following libraries: Py2pdf for conversion of datasheets to plain text, Scikit-learn for TF-IDF scores calculation, NLTK (Natural Language Toolkit) for BERTopic, LDA topic modeling and stop words removal, and finally Pandas and Pyarrow for

Table 2. Data summary

Source	# of documents	# unique documents	# unique related to OT devices	# unique with CVE
Full Disclosure	100,757	100,569 (99.8%)	855 (0.9%)	14,843 (14.6%)
Ars Technica	25,276	24,924 (98.6%)	7,567 (29.9%)	460 (1.8%)
Security Now	1,028	1,016 (98.8%)	935 (92%)	169 (16.4%)
Total	127,061	126,509 (99.6%)	9,357 (7.4%)	1,5472 (12.2%)

data processing. All experiments were conducted using 10-fold cross validation. Table 1 states the parameters used for classification algorithms.

All experiments were conducted on a Linux machine running Pop OS, equipped with 134 GB of RAM, 20 CPU cores, and an MSI GeForce RTX 2060 GPU.

5.2 Overview of Collected Data

Table 2 gives an overview of collected data. Overall, we collected 127,061 messages across three sources. Most of them are unique. Among them, 12.2% contain CVE identifiers, and 7.4% are OT device-related. Of all three sets, Full disclosure dominates in volume with the least proportion of content with CVE mention (0.9%). Ars Technica, on the other hand, has minimal vulnerability coverage (1.7%) and moderate focus on OT related content (30%). Security Now podcast, unlike the other datasets, has the highest rates in terms of contents describing vulnerabilities and OT devices, despite its small size (which can be explained by the nature of the source).

Vulnerability-Related Features. The feature sets extracted using BERTopic and LDA techniques from CVE descriptions are presented in Table 3. Overall, we obtained 281,206 CVE entries from the official CVE repository. From this corpus, three sets of tokens were identified as the most relevant for detecting vulnerability-related content in text with 13,688, 1,679, and 206 tokens in All, BERTopic, and LDA sets. Interestingly, these token sets primarily consist of alphabetic characters, with alphanumerical characters only appearing in the set "All", and no presence of numeric characters across the three sets.

OT-Related Features. The results of the device datasheet analysis are presented in Tables 4 and 5. We collected a total of 200 manuals, evenly split between OT and IoT devices. OT device datasheets were generally longer, with the majority exceeding 5 pages in length (80.5%), whereas IoT datasheets were typically shorter, with 55.5% containing fewer than 5 pages. This is likely because OT device datasheets tend to include more detailed information and operational guidelines, as they are primarily intended for industrial use, unlike consumer IoT devices, which typically require simpler documentation. This richer content increases the likelihood of successfully distinguishing OT-related content from IoT-specific content.

Table 3. Feature sets extracted by topic modelling techniques on CVE descriptions. Only alphabetic and alphanumerical tokens are present in these sets.

Features	Total tokens	Alphabetic tokens	Alphanumerical tokens
BERTopic	1,679	1,679 (100.00%)	0 (0%)
LDA	206	206 (100.00%)	0(0%)
All	13,688	11,174 (81.63%)	2514 (18.37%)

Table 4. Overview of extracted datasheets

Device category	# of documents	Documents (<5 pages)	Documents (5-15 pages)	Documents (> 15 pages)	Unparseable	# of tokens
OT	200	27 (13.5%)	45 (22.5%)	116 (58.0%)	12 (6.0%)	281,058
IoT	200	111 (55.5%)	36 (18%)	53 (26.5%)	0 (0%)	107,295
Total	400	138 (34.5%)	81 (20.2%)	169 (42.2%)	12 (3%)	669,411

Out of the 281,058 tokens collected from OT documents, 261,445 were found exclusively in OT sources. We retain this feature set for our experiments.

5.3 Vulnerability Identification Results

To evaluate the framework, we conduct 3 sets of experiments: ① evaluation of OT-related features, ② evaluation of features for vulnerability content, ③ evaluation of ensemble approach for identifying potential vulnerability descriptions in OT products with a unified feature set.

Classification of OT-Related Content. Table 6 describes the performance of classifiers across three datasets (Full Disclosure, Ars Technica, SecurityNow).

Based on the results, both models performed similarly well overall, particularly on the Ars Technica and Full Disclosure datasets, achieving 9698% accuracy. The Random Forest classifier outperformed XGBoost on less structured and noisier sources, namely Full Disclosure and SecurityNow, which aligns with RF's known robustness to noise. XGBoost, on the other hand, showed better performance than Random Forest when evaluated on the Ars Technica dataset.

Performance on the SecurityNow dataset was comparatively low, with RF achieving 92% accuracy and XGBoost ranging between 89% and 93%. This result is likely due to the nature of the data, as it consists of podcast transcripts where the text is less structured and speakers often use informal or ambiguous language, unlike the more formal writing found in the other sources.

Despite variations in model performance across datasets, the results support our initial hypothesis that *the inherent capabilities and specifications of OT devices can be effectively used to detect text describing industrial control systems.*

Table 5. Description of tokens per datasheets.

Document Length	Total tokens	OT tokens	IoT tokens	Tokens only in OT set	Common tokens
<5 pages	27,653	4,963 (17.9%)	17,727 (64.1%)	3,083 (11.2%)	1,880 (6.8%)
5-15 pages	55,661	20,531 (36.9%)	14,599 (26.3%)	16,203 (29.1%)	4,328 (7.8%)
>15 pages	586,097	255,564 (43.6%)	74,969 (12.8%)	242,159 (43.1%)	13,405 (2.3%)
Total	**669,411**	**281,058** (42%)	**107,295** (16%)	**261,445** (39.1%)	**19,613** (2.9%)

Table 6. Experimental results for OT related content.

Source	Number of	Random Forest			XGBoost		
	Features	Accuracy	Precision	Recall	Accuracy	Precision	Recall
Full disclosure	500	**0.989**	**0.913**	**0.953**	0.970	0.723	0.987
	1000	0.987	0.894	0.941	0.976	0.766	0.987
	2000	0.984	0.875	0.930	**0.979**	**0.790**	**0.987**
Ars Technica	500	**0.992**	**0.996**	**0.976**	0.998	0.999	0.994
	1000	0.985	0.989	0.961	0.998	1.000	0.994
	2000	0.982	0.985	0.950	**0.998**	**1.000**	**0.994**
SecurityNow	500	0.920	0.920	1.000	0.892	0.935	0.948
	1000	0.920	0.920	1.000	0.904	0.933	0.965
	2000	**0.925**	**0.925**	**1.000**	**0.934**	**0.952**	**0.978**

Classification of Vulnerable Content. Table 7 presents evaluation results on features derived by topic modelling techniques on CVE dataset.

As the results indicate, a different trend compared to the previous analysis is observed in this set of experiments. The XGBoost classifier generally outperformed RF on most datasets, particularly in terms of accuracy. However, the performance varied significantly across feature sets.

For the Full Disclosure dataset, XGBoost achieved the highest accuracy (94.65%) with the full token set, followed by BERTopic-derived features (92.61%) and LDA-derived features (89.33%). This aligns with the observation that larger feature sets (e.g., the full 13,688 tokens) yielded better performance compared to the reduced feature sets from LDA (206 tokens) and BERTopic.

Interestingly, the RF classifier exhibited different trend on Ars Technica and SecurityNow datasets. In Ars Technica, RF achieved higher accuracy than XGBoost (95.61% with LDA vs. 96.98% for XGBoost), but its precision was notably low (0.2815 for RF vs. 0.3529 for XGBoost with LDA). Similarly, in SecurityNow, RF struggled with recall (12.72% with the 'All' token set).

For Ars Technica, the RF classifier's low precision indicates a high rate of false positives, where benign articles were incorrectly flagged as vulnerable. Manual investigation showed that articles discussing CVEs in broader contexts (e.g., economics or politics) were commonly misclassified. For example, the article discussing spear-phishing campaigns targeting both the Trump and Biden presiden-

Table 7. Experimental results for vulnerable content.

Source	Features	Random Forest			XGBoost		
		Accuracy	Precision	Recall	Accuracy	Precision	Recall
Full disclosure	All	**0.908**	**0.626**	**0.905**	**0.947**	**0.749**	**0.948**
	BERTopic	0.895	0.589	0.904	0.926	0.678	0.933
	LDA	0.859	0.507	0.912	0.893	0.584	0.911
Ars Technica	All	0.934	0.207	0.907	**0.985**	**0.571**	**0.757**
	BERTopic	0.942	0.232	0.913	0.976	0.425	0.767
	LDA	**0.956**	**0.282**	**0.874**	0.970	0.353	0.744
SecurityNow	All	0.843	0.615	0.127	**0.871**	**0.640**	**0.544**
	BERTopic	**0.855**	**0.667**	**0.229**	0.863	0.602	0.572
	LDA	0.830	0.498	0.472	0.814	0.441	0.458

tial campaigns was falsely identified as describing a vulnerability. This ambiguity arises from the mixed signals in such articles terms associated with vulnerabilities may co-occur with unrelated topic specific language, confusing the model.

In SecurityNow, the RF classifier's low recall reveals a failure to detect actual vulnerable content, likely due to the dataset's informal structure (e.g., irregular grammar, abrupt topic shifts). Such noise disrupts RF's reliance on static, hierarchical decision boundaries.

XGBoost, while not perfect, demonstrated more balanced precision-recall trade-offs in these cases. It's superior performance in these cases stems from its iterative error correction and gradient-based optimization, which better handles sparse signals and nonlinear feature interactions. For instance, in SecurityNow, XGBoost achieved a recall of 54.38% (vs. RF's 12.72%) with 'All' token set, demonstrating its adaptability to noisy data.

Beyond performance comparison, the results reveal that regardless of the source of content or the level of text structure, *similar language is consistently adopted to describe vulnerabilities.*

The Ensemble Approach. The final set of experiments focused on evaluating the framework assembled based on the conclusions drawn from previous analyses.

According to the results, the performance of the classification models for OT related content varied across Full disclosure, Ars Technica, and SecurityNow on different number of features without a clear optimal configuration. The classification of vulnerable content showed that 'All' and BERTopic features give comparable overall results across all three datasets. Since both feature sets involve trade-offs, we retained both for comparison purposes. The full vulnerability-related feature set is considerably larger than the set selected by the BERTopic modeling technique (13,688 vs. 1,679 features), suggesting that while topic modeling effectively reduces dimensionality, it may also exclude terms that contribute to improved detection performance in broader contexts. Based on these findings,

Table 8. Experimental results for the proposed model.

Source	Feature sets		Ensemble			Random Forest			XGBoost		
	Vuln.	OT	Accuracy	Precision	Recall	Accuracy	Precision	Recall	Accuracy	Precision	Recall
Full Disclosure	All	500	0.996	0.848	0.833	0.986	0.465	0.489	0.996	0.835	0.859
		1000	**0.996**	**0.872**	**0.812**	0.986	0.487	0.472	**0.996**	**0.862**	**0.836**
		2000	0.992	0.828	0.802	**0.985**	**0.687**	**0.618**	0.993	0.878	0.813
	BERTopic	500	0.995	0.833	0.816	0.988	0.567	0.538	0.996	0.841	0.813
		1000	**0.996**	**0.859**	**0.812**	0.989	0.583	0.508	**0.996**	**0.857**	**0.824**
		2000	0.991	0.831	0.771	**0.986**	**0.687**	**0.659**	0.993	0.867	0.784
SecurityNow	All	500	**0.873**	**0.598**	**0.769**	**0.878**	**0.605**	**0.743**	**0.856**	**0.550**	**0.803**
		1000	0.864	0.556	0.760	0.866	0.570	0.764	0.850	0.538	0.752
		2000	0.861	0.556	0.802	0.864	0.579	0.805	0.860	0.566	0.776
	BERTopic	500	0.859	0.554	0.757	0.862	0.565	0.742	0.861	0.561	0.719
		1000	0.855	0.526	0.773	**0.861**	**0.572**	**0.765**	0.845	0.507	0.762
		2000	**0.871**	**0.569**	**0.772**	0.858	0.544	0.801	**0.860**	**0.559**	**0.750**
Ars Technica	All	500	0.992	0.270	0.400	0.993	0.259	0.339	0.992	0.227	0.365
		1000	0.993	0.235	0.370	0.995	0.304	0.260	0.990	0.204	0.408
		2000	**0.995**	**0.524**	**0.468**	**0.992**	**0.319**	**0.441**	**0.996**	**0.505**	**0.521**
	BERTopic	500	0.991	0.212	0.389	0.993	0.289	0.322	0.990	0.230	0.394
		1000	0.990	0.225	0.418	0.991	0.215	0.378	0.991	0.260	0.372
		2000	**0.996**	**0.677**	**0.452**	**0.994**	**0.482**	**0.387**	**0.996**	**0.655**	**0.471**

we included the full set of features from the previous classifications to better evaluate the final model.

Table 8 illustrates the results obtained for the ensemble model. The results of the model show strong overall performance, particularly on the Full Disclosure dataset, where both precision and recall reach high values across all classifiers. The ensemble model consistently performs best, slightly outperforming XGBoost, while Random Forest tends to lag behind, lowering the overall performance of the ensemble in some cases.

For Security Now dataset, the model performed moderately well with a noticeable decrease in performance compared to Full Disclosure, specifically in precision results. This drop is likely due to the highly unstructured nature of the text in this dataset, which makes it more difficult for the model to accurately identify vulnerable content.

Interestingly, all models struggled to identify vulnerable OT content in Ars Technica despite being a more structured source. Classification models exhibited low precision and recall on this dataset, with average precision around 25% and recall around 39%.

These results suggest that the articles in structured news discuss vulnerability related content in a broader topic, introducing thereby unwanted noise. This eventually affects the results obtained for the models.

The pattern in Ars Technica is further illustrated in the results obtained from BERTopic-based features. While BERTopic helps structure noisy CVE descriptions into more coherent topics, it does not significantly improve detection of operational technology (OT) related vulnerabilities in Ars Technica.

The trend for Ars Technica, however, changes when 2000 tokens of the OT relted feature set is used. For this particular set, we noticed a much improved results but still lower than those of Full Disclosure even with the more formal structure of text used in Ars Technica. This suggests that a richer feature set allows better detection of vulnerable OT content within this dataset. The results also indicate that OT related content tends to often appear in the context of vulnerability discussions.

The ensemble model generally achieved a more consistent balance between precision and recall compared to both Random Forest and XGBoost across most datasets and feature sets. While XGBoost occasionally produced higher recall (notably on the Ars Technica dataset), the ensemble model consistently maintained superior or comparable performance in both metrics. Random Forest, on the other hand, exhibited notably lower precision, especially on noisier datasets which affected its reliability in detecting vulnerable OT-related content. These results suggest that the ensemble approach effectively mitigates individual model weaknesses and enhances robustness in vulnerability detection tasks.

Despite challenges for Ars Techncia dataset, the model shows promise. Its strong performance on unstructured sources like Full Disclosure and Security Now indicates its robustness in noisy environments.

6 Conclusion

The increasing convergence of IT and OT networks has introduced significant cybersecurity challenges, exposing OT Systems to previously unforeseen threats. Traditional vulnerability databases often fail to timely capture these emerging risks which necessitate proactive approaches to identify undisclosed OT vulnerabilities. Our framework addresses this gap by monitoring unofficial online sources such as news websites, mailing lists, and security podcasts while leveraging device specifications to filter OT-relevant discussions. By analyzing linguistic patterns against known vulnerability descriptions, we distinguish actual vulnerabilities from benign content. Our experimental results demonstrate the effectiveness of this approach across diverse datasets, including structured and unstructured sources. The Random Forest classifier exhibited superior robustness in noisy, less structured environments (i.e., Full Disclosure and Security Now), while XGBoost performed better in more organized contexts (i.e., Arstechnica). Notably, utilizing all CVE-derived features significantly improved detection accuracy, reinforcing the importance of comprehensive linguistic analysis in identifying vulnerability discussions. These findings also validate our hypothesis that OT device specifications based filtering can effectively isolate OT related vulnerabilities in public sources. Moreover, they highlight the consistency in vulnerability descriptions across different sources, regardless of their structure. By bridging the intelligence gap in OT security, our framework enables prediction of potential risks, enhancing thereby resilience of critical infrastructure against cyber threats that could compromise safety, operations, and environmental integrity.

References

1. Alevizopoulou, S., Koloveas, P., Tryfonopoulos, C., Raftopoulou, P.: Social media monitoring for iot cyber-threats. In: 2021 IEEE International Conference on Cyber Security and Resilience (CSR), pp. 436–441 (2021)
2. Almukaynizi, M., Grimm, A., Nunes, E., Shakarian, J., Shakarian, P.: Predicting cyber threats through hacker social networks in darkweb and deepweb forums. In: Proceedings of the 2017 International Conference of The Computational Social Science Society of the Americas. CSS 2017. Association for Computing Machinery, New York (2017)
3. Alves, F., Bettini, A., Ferreira, P.M., Bessani, A.: Processing tweets for cybersecurity threat awareness. Inf. Syst. **95**, 101586 (2021)
4. Anwar, A., Abusnaina, A., Chen, S., Li, F., Mohaisen, D.: Cleaning the NVD: comprehensive quality assessment, improvements, and analyses. IEEE Trans. Dependable Secure Comput. **19**(6), 4255–4269 (2022)
5. Boyes, W., O'Brien, L.: The 50 largest automation companies around the world keep on keepin' on despite the recession. Control Magazine, December 2009
6. Bozorgi, M., Saul, L.K., Savage, S., Voelker, G.M.: Beyond heuristics: learning to classify vulnerabilities and predict exploits. In: Proceedings of the 16th ACM SIGKDD International Conference on Knowledge Discovery and Data Mining, KDD '10, pp. 105–114. Association for Computing Machinery, New York (2010)
7. Burnap, P., Javed, A., Rana, O.F., Awan, M.S.: Real-time classification of malicious urls on twitter using machine activity data. In: 2015 IEEE/ACM International Conference on Advances in Social Networks Analysis and Mining (ASONAM), pp. 970–977 (2015)
8. Chen, T., Guestrin, C.: Xgboost: A scalable tree boosting system. In: Proceedings of the 22nd ACM SIGKDD International Conference on Knowledge Discovery and Data Mining, KDD '16, pp. 785–794. Association for Computing Machinery, New York (2016)
9. Dong, Y., Guo, W., Chen, Y., Xing, X., Zhang, Y., Wang, G.: Towards the detection of inconsistencies in public security vulnerability reports. In: 28th USENIX Security Symposium (USENIX Security 19), pp. 869–885. USENIX Association, Santa Clara, August 2019. https://www.usenix.org/conference/usenixsecurity19/presentation/dong
10. Edkrantz, M., Said, A.: Predicting cyber vulnerability exploits with machine learning. In: Scandinavian Conference on AI (2015). https://api.semanticscholar.org/CorpusID:12126104
11. Elbaz, C., Rilling, L., Morin, C.: Fighting n-day vulnerabilities with automated CVSS vector prediction at disclosure. In: Proceedings of the 15th International Conference on Availability, Reliability and Security, ARES '20. Association for Computing Machinery, New York (2020)
12. Ho, T.K.: Random decision forests. In: Proceedings of 3rd International Conference on Document Analysis and Recognition, vol. 1, pp. 278–282. IEEE (1995)
13. Horawalavithana, S., Bhattacharjee, A., Liu, R., Choudhury, N., O. Hall, L., Iamnitchi, A.: Mentions of security vulnerabilities on reddit, twitter and github. In: IEEE/WIC/ACM International Conference on Web Intelligence, WI '19, pp. 200–207. Association for Computing Machinery, New York (2019)
14. Huang, S.Y., Ban, T.: Monitoring social media for vulnerability-threat prediction and topic analysis. In: 2020 IEEE 19th International Conference on Trust, Security and Privacy in Computing and Communications (TrustCom), pp. 1771–1776 (2020)

15. Jiang, Y., Atif, Y.: Towards automatic discovery and assessment of vulnerability severity in cyber–physical systems. Array **15**, 100209 (2022)
16. Kadhim, A.I.: Term weighting for feature extraction on twitter: a comparison between bm25 and tf-idf. In: 2019 International Conference on Advanced Science and Engineering (ICOASE), pp. 124–128 (2019). https://doi.org/10.1109/ICOASE.2019.8723825
17. Le, B.D., Wang, G., Nasim, M., Babar, M.A.: Gathering cyber threat intelligence from twitter using novelty classification. In: 2019 International Conference on Cyberworlds (CW), pp. 316–323 (2019)
18. Le Sceller, Q., Karbab, E.B., Debbabi, M., Iqbal, F.: Sonar: automatic detection of cyber security events over the twitter stream. In: Proceedings of the 12th International Conference on Availability, Reliability and Security. ARES '17. Association for Computing Machinery, New York (2017)
19. Manai, E., Mejri, M., Fattahi, J.: Helping cnas generate cvss scores faster and more confidently using XAI. Appl. Sci. **14**(20) (2024). https://www.mdpi.com/2076-3417/14/20/9231
20. Miranda, L., et al.: Learning CNA-oriented CVSS scores. In: 2024 IEEE 13th International Conference on Cloud Networking (CloudNet), pp. 1–5 (2024)
21. Mittal, S., Das, P.K., Mulwad, V., Joshi, A., Finin, T.: Cybertwitter: Using twitter to generate alerts for cybersecurity threats and vulnerabilities. In: 2016 IEEE/ACM International Conference on Advances in Social Networks Analysis and Mining (ASONAM), pp. 860–867 (2016)
22. Nunes, E., et al.: Darknet and deepnet mining for proactive cybersecurity threat intelligence. In: 2016 IEEE Conference on Intelligence and Security Informatics (ISI), pp. 7–12 (2016)
23. Qin, Y., Xiao, Y., Liao, X.: Vulnerability intelligence alignment via masked graph attention networks. In: Proceedings of the 2023 ACM SIGSAC Conference on Computer and Communications Security, CCS '23, pp. 2202–2216. Association for Computing Machinery, New York (2023)
24. Sabottke, C., Suciu, O., Dumitraş, T.: Vulnerability disclosure in the age of social media: exploiting twitter for predicting real-world exploits. In: Proceedings of the 24th USENIX Conference on Security Symposium, SEC'15, pp. 1041–1056. USENIX Association, USA (2015)
25. Sapienza, A., Ernala, S.K., Bessi, A., Lerman, K., Ferrara, E.: Discover: mining online chatter for emerging cyber threats. In: Companion Proceedings of the The Web Conference 2018, WWW '18, p. 983–990. International World Wide Web Conferences Steering Committee, Republic and Canton of Geneva, CHE (2018)
26. Sauerwein, C., Sillaber, C., Huber, M.M., Mussmann, A., Breu, R.: The tweet advantage: an empirical analysis of 0-day vulnerability information shared on twitter. In: Janczewski, L.J., Kutyłowski, M. (eds.) ICT Systems Security and Privacy Protection, pp. 201–215. Springer, Cham (2018)
27. Shah, S., Madisetti, V.K.: MAD-CTI: cyber threat intelligence analysis of the dark web using a multi-agent framework. IEEE Access **13**, 40158–40168 (2025)
28. Shahid, M.R., Debar, H.: Cvss-bert: Explainable natural language processing to determine the severity of a computer security vulnerability from its description. In: 2021 20th IEEE International Conference on Machine Learning and Applications (ICMLA), pp. 1600–1607 (2021)

29. Thomas, R.J., Gardiner, J., Chothia, T., Samanis, E., Perrett, J., Rashid, A.: Catch me if you can: an in-depth study of cve discovery time and inconsistencies for managing risks in critical infrastructures. In: Proceedings of the 2020 Joint Workshop on CPS&IoT Security and Privacy, pp. 49–60. CPSIOTSEC'20. Association for Computing Machinery, New York (2020)
30. Yamamoto, Y., Miyamoto, D., Nakayama, M.: Text-mining approach for estimating vulnerability score. In: 2015 4th International Workshop on Building Analysis Datasets and Gathering Experience Returns for Security (BADGERS), pp. 67–73 (2015)
31. Yin, J., Tang, M., Cao, J., Wang, H.: Apply transfer learning to cybersecurity: predicting exploitability of vulnerabilities by description. Knowl.-Based Syst. **210**, 106529 (2020)
32. Zhang, S., Cai, M., Zhang, M., Zhao, L., de Carnavalet, X.d.C.: The flaw within: Identifying CVSS score discrepancies in the NVD. In: 2023 IEEE International Conference on Cloud Computing Technology and Science (CloudCom), pp. 185–192 (2023)

Strengthening Maritime Cyber Resilience: The Imperative Need for a Global and Cooperative MOOC Initiative

Yvon Kermarrec(✉), Rodrigue N'Goran, and Patrick Erard

Lab-STICC - IMT Atlantique - Technopole de l'Iroise, Brest 29200, France
yvon.kermarrec@imt-atlantique.fr

Abstract. The maritime industry, increasingly reliant on interconnected digital systems for navigation, communication, and operations, faces a growing challenge with numerous cyber threats. From GPS spoofing and electronic chart manipulation to ransomware attacks on port infrastructure through basics security challenges, the potential for disruption, economic loss, and even environmental disasters are very significant. This makes mandatory and comprehensive cybersecurity training for all maritime personnel; it is not just beneficial, but very critical for all the stakeholders involved in the maritime domain.

In the context of an EU project (EDIH call), we have decided to develop a MOOC to raise awareness on maritime cyber security. Such a MOOC's benefits are accessibility at any time, scalability and updates to integrate new threads and innovation to a high level that involves innovation and r&d. Such a product is not yet already available (to the best of our knowledge). We, as authors and initiators of the project, would like to deliberate emphasis on the development of a MOOC on cyber maritime cyber security with a collaborative nature, calling for multi-stakeholder contributions and with research contributors.

Keywords: Maritime Cybersecurity · Cyber Awareness · Education

1 Introduction: The Digital Transformation of the Maritime Industry

Modern shipping industry has undergone a dramatic and major digital transformation over the past decades. Today's vessels are essentially floating factories, equipped with sophisticated information systems (e.g. ; ECDIS, integrated navigation systems), high quality Man Machine Interfaces (MMI) to control various systems of a more global system-of systems (SoS), integrated bridge management systems, complex OT systems and decision aided systems. Shore-based operations and harbor infrastructures have similarly evolved to meet new efficiency and safety requirements and operations, with port management systems, cargo tracking platforms, and supply chain networks all interconnected through complex digital infrastructures.

K. Adi et al. (Eds.): CRiSIS 2025, LNCS 16295, pp. 254–265, 2026.
https://doi.org/10.1007/978-3-032-20732-6_16

This digitization has brought unprecedented efficiency and safety improvements. Real-time weather routing optimizes fuel consumption and voyage planning, while predictive maintenance systems prevent costly breakdowns at sea and enhances global reliability. However, this same connectivity that enables these benefits also creates multiple entry points for malicious actors seeking to exploit vulnerabilities in maritime systems. As usual in other related IT systems, innovation and internet /interoperability needs have increased the attack surface.

As already mentioned by BIMCO, EU ENISA, the French ANSSI, the US Coast Guards and similar security agencies, training and education are one way to avoid blocked situations and attacks. Awareness presents a higher challenge for the maritime industry as « all -and each - are in the same boat ». Such training should empower crew members, shore staff and related stakeholders to recognize and respond to potential threats, transforming them from potential vulnerabilities into the pillars of the first line of defense. It fosters a culture of security awareness, ensuring best practices are fulfilled among the board, from secure password management to identifying phishing etc. to a comprehension of the consequences of each of their « digital actions ». Without this vital investment in human capital, even the most advanced technological defenses can be undermined by human error or lack of awareness. Ultimately, robust cybersecurity training safeguards not only the vessels and their cargo, but also the lives of seafarers and the sustainability of this major means of trade between countries.

In the context of EDIH EU Project, our objective is to build a MOOC that can be used directly and at various levels by the seafarers and on a larger scale by the (military or commercial) stakeholders. We have already investigated and build a post-grad curriculum at IMT Atlantique but the MOOC presents a unique opportunity to wider the audience. Moreover, as an addition to the learning materials, we would like to create a dynamic community to produce more contents so to address issues to what we proposed in the initial version of the MOOC.

Moreover, maritime domains present specificities and constraints that are unique. Cybersecurity tool providers intend to reuse and adapt their existing offer, but the very specific nature of the maritime domain requires dedicated solutions and R&D investigations. The French Navy chair that I supervised for 7 years had these concerns with 2 major leaders of the French industry. In this context, 14 PhD degrees have been obtained on diverse topics that are of interest for the French Navy, academics and the industry. We claim that this fruitful cooperation be developed and extended. This MOOC has also been designed so to that academics may discover new investigation and applications domains, industry can identify potential markets and the maritime industry can benefit of the research outcomes.

We have organized this paper in 5 major sections. In the first chapter, we recall the challenges of the transformation and the digitalization of the maritime sector. In the second section, we present our objectives for the development of this MOOC and its very structure and contents. We call then in Sect. 4 for the creation a dynamic community of academics, industry and maritime stakeholders to meet the challenges of maritime cybersecurity: one expert cannot address alone cybersecurity as it is a transversal topic and evolves at an extremely high tempo. We finally conclude and draw perspectives on new opportunities to assess and credit the dedication of seafarers to maritime security awareness.

2 The Digital Transformation of the Maritime Sector

The maritime industry undergoes, currently, an unprecedented digital transformation, harnessing cutting-edge technologies such as the Internet of Things (IoT), big data analytics, artificial intelligence (AI) and autonomous systems. This technological revolution paves the way for noticeable efficiency gains, optimization of shipping routes, proactive prediction of maintenance, and rationalization/efficiency of port operations by anticipating the "orchestral" organization of associated logistics with the arrival or departure of a giant ship of the seas.

Digital innovations transform traditional operational practices: 'just in time' operations, real-time remote monitoring of ships, precise tracking of cargo throughout its journey, and substantial improvements in communications between the various stakeholders of the maritime supply chain. These advances show significant reductions in operating costs and offer shipowners and port managers unprecedented perspectives for optimizing their strategic decisions for their critical harbor infrastructures.

The emergence of autonomous vessels represents one of the most spectacular developments in this very "traditional" sector. These intelligent and autonomous vessels, which can navigate without direct human intervention, promise to build a major milestone in the maritime transport by offering high levels of availability, safety and energy efficiency. They could also reduce human error, one of the main causes of maritime accidents in busy harbors.

However, this accelerated and unprecedented digitalization raises considerable challenges that require special attention. The colossal volume of data generated by interconnected systems demands extremely robust management and analysis infrastructures and the imperative need of reliable, secured and high-speed networks. Maritime companies need to invest heavily in data centers, real-time processing systems and dedicated teams capable of exploiting and "mining" this strategic information, while defending their valuable asset whether at sea or on shore from acyber attacks or related events.

The integration of legacy systems with new digital platforms raises critical challenges of consistency and interoperability. This technological cohabitation frequently generates compatibility issues, operational disruptions, substantial transition costs or even failure or holes in the protection mechanisms. Stakeholders must « navigate » between the need to modernize their equipment (software, hardware or even OT) and the imperative of maintaining continuity of service through cost effectiveness.

Cyber-attacks on the maritime industry can take particularly severe forms. The disruption of navigation and communication systems can lead to catastrophic collisions, groundings or positioning errors, endangering the lives of crews and impacting the marine environment. Manipulation/alteration of cargo manifests and financial transactions can result in considerable economic losses, compromising confidence in the global supply chains as seen with the Maersk cyber event. The Admiral database (valuable from France Cyber Maritime web site) highlights the most recent and public cyber events with an ever increasingly high impact and inspiration of the attackers.

Ransomware attacks represent a particularly pernicious and low-cost threat, capable of instantly paralyzing port operations and creating bottlenecks in international supply chains. These disruptions can have cascading repercussions on the global economy, as demonstrated by the Suez Canal blockage or the geopolitical uncertainties by the red Sea or the Persian Gulf. These disruptions may also have severe impacts on countries and food chains as we saw with the blockage of the Black Sea during the conflict between Ukraine and Russia.

Data integrity, the foundation of modern maritime decision-making, is a national security issue. Corruption or falsification of critical information (e.g., maritime charts, AIS positions) can lead to dangerous operations, massive commercial fraud or violations of environmental regulations. Alterations of custom declarations can be organized at a wide scale by "narcos" and even AIS cargo position can be used by them to load/unload their illegal cargoes in a discrete manner.

Faced with these challenges, the maritime industry needs to develop a proactive and global approach to cybersecurity, engaging all and each of the stakeholders at their level. This involves implementing advanced intrusion detection systems, specialized training for crews in digital best practices, establishing incident response protocols and teams, and international collaboration to combat international threats and share common experiences. The maritime industry needs also specific methods and tools to protect, detect and react to cyber events when they occur. This requires a new "deal" where researchers and stakeholders upfront can be mobilized: the academics to discover the maritime specificities and the maritime stakeholders to integrate the new paradigms of cybersecurity. Innovation is a key response to address ever changing challenges and attacks.

The maritime sector also faces a critical digital skills deficit in its workforce. Seafarers, engineers and technicians trained in traditional methods need to acquire new technological skills to adapt to digital environments. Whereas classic IT people should get acquainted with the specificities of the maritime context. This transition requires intensive training programs, considerable investment in human resource development, and an overhaul of maritime educational curricula. The curricula should at least give rationale (at the right level for each) for the expected security measure so to be applied and to engage stakeholders.

3 Why a MOOC?

Massive Open Online Courses (MOOCs) represent a transformative shift in the accessibility of training. They offer unparalleled flexibility, enabling students to learn at their own convenience: anywhere and anytime. This makes them an ideal solution for balancing training with personal and professional commitments. Their « open » nature, often accompanied by free or low-cost certification options, democratizes access to high-quality content, sometimes provided by well-known institutions and expert lecturers through experience reports and interviews. This democratization effectively eliminates geographical and financial barriers enhance the global level of competences. MOOCs facilitate the acquisition of new professional skills, which are crucial for employability and career transitions. They also foster personal development, encourage the exploration of new subjects, and promote lifelong learning. The interactivity of MOOC platforms, often featuring forums and learning communities, facilitates knowledge sharing and networking. In essence, MOOCs serve as a powerful tool for self-training, enabling individuals to update their knowledge and enrich their professional competences.

In the context of the EDIH framework, IMT Atlantique ensures the development of 3 MOOCs: one on digital law, a 2nd one on critical infrastructures with a focus on IoT and cybersecurity for the Industry 4.0, and the 3rd one to raise awareness on maritime cybersecurity. As former chair of a research group under the aegis of the French Navy and COMCYBER (the cyber commandant of the French Department of Defence), I undergo the challenge of producing this new learning materials by capitalizing on my experience as chair leader, the supervision of 8 PhD students, and my concerns to an international opening – which in my view the ONLY way to tackle this cyberattack frenzies we encounter at a global level. Moreover, in the specific context of the well-established lack of competencies of IT and cybersecurity among seafarers, a MOOC and its validation could constitute an extremely valuable certification of the competences acquired by an individual. This learning effort and commitment could then be valued by the employers with the assignment of new responsibilities and a salary increase. Thus, motivating more stakeholder to engage with this new training.

As indicated above, this course material targets at least three audiences:

- Academics involved in technical domains (network, computer science, cyber security...) so that they can discover the maritime domain,
- Maritime leaders (harbor directors, shipping companies...) so that they can identify new research trends and propose further investigations,
- Seafarers to make them aware of cybersecurity and their individual and collective responsibilities.

4 Our Proposed MOOC Framework: Structure and Content Pillars for Education

This MOOC-style online training course is a self-paced course (without a tutor provided) consisting of approximately 30 h of learning plus additional materials. The French version will be delivered online on the FUN (France Université Numérique) MOOC platform and the English version on Coursera.

4.1 Description

The MOOC addresses the issue of cybersecurity specific to maritime infrastructure (ships and ports, in particular) and its various stakeholders. It explains to learners that cybersecurity is a cross-disciplinary topic that concerns not only technical aspects (networks, sophisticated hardware components, advanced IT, etc.) but also regulatory and legal aspects (particularly French, European, and international), as well as organizational and human aspects.

The MOOC objectives are the following:

- To introduce the specific features of the maritime cyber domain to beginners, enabling them to understand the context and challenges of this field.
- To engage the various participants in the MOOC in identifying and proposing actions to ensure the security of these infrastructures.
- To draw the attention of decision-makers to the importance of an action plan and training for crews and other stakeholders in a maritime infrastructure context.

4.2 Teaching Approaches

The course is divided into learning sequences to facilitate knowledge acquisition. It will be supplemented by video lessons explaining the theory, video interviews with experts in the field to illustrate the concepts and notions covered in the lectures, case studies, and quiz-based assessments. The MOOC will be initially released as a self-learning and consistent asset with an adequate pedagogy to embrace a wide audience. If needed, we could extend it and include support, focus groups and interactions with academics. We may also release certificate of success to assess the gain of new skills and competences.

4.3 MOOC Content

The definition of this curriculum is also built on our experience of developing a full year post graduate academic program, extensive talks and interviews with maritime stakeholders to address their specific needs, letter of mission from the French Navy and expert committees to assess the quality of the learning contents and deliver the national degree (French "mastere spécialisé"). The course I proposed for this MOOC is so far organized in 7 major modules; 5 of them are complete. The learning materials are done, and we plan to include in the next weeks interviews from experts and demos.

Module 1: "Introduction to Maritime Cybersecurity" with the Following Learning Objectives

- Understand the specific challenges of cybersecurity in the maritime sector.
- Identify the main threats and impacts.
- Present some major events to outline the issues and challenges.

Module 2: "Review of Cybersecurity Basics" with the Following Learning Objectives

- Review the fundamental concepts of cybersecurity and introduce the terminology that will be used throughout the MOOC.
- Cybersecurity and its challenges in our world.
- Understand the main attack and defense techniques.

Module 3: "Maritime Systems Architecture" with the Following Learning Objectives

- Understand the critical technologies used in the maritime sector
- Identify vulnerabilities specific to maritime systems.

Module 4: "Maritime Cybersecurity Risk Management" with the Following Learning Objectives

- Learn to identify, assess, and manage cybersecurity risks in the maritime context.
- Identify an action plan to address various threats.

Module 5: "Cybersecurity Basics Applied Onboard" with the Following Learning Objectives

- Discover the ANSSI, ENISA and US Coast Guards documents and manifestoes.
- Adapt cybersecurity fundamentals to the specific needs of ships and ports
- Present onboard recommendations and best practices based on ANSSI and ENISA documentation on these maritime topics.

Module 6: "Human Factors and Impacts in Maritime Cybersecurity" with the Following Learning Objectives

- Understand the specificities of these factors in the life of a ship and how they are taken into account in decision-making.
- Why are these human factors different in the case of a ship?

Module 7: "Legal Aspects – Digital Law and Maritime Law" with the Following Learning Objectives

- Understand the specificities of these laws and their relationship
- Understand the challenges and impacts of transitions between the various applicable laws, both national and international.

5 A Research Showcase

As research coordinator of the cyber defense chair of the French Navy, I have supervised directly 5 PhD students, supported and advised 8 more, and forged with the French Navy and the academics a research program that was later approved by the industrials.

The current directions that I identified are the following:

- Designing and anticipating future software and system architectures to handle and contain cyber-erosion. This last theme presents a specificity as a ship duration (around 40 to 50 years) overcome technology improvements. Software and hardware upgrades, end of support from vendors for outdated software versions, integration of new components will challenge the original design that was made when the ship was created. Minor and major upgrades are needed, without compromising the whole stability and consistency and integrating upgrades that are needed throughout the ship life duration.
- Increasing confidence in AI for knowledge, command support and cyber crisis management. On a ship in the middle of the oceans, seafarers may face situations they are not trained to indent nor respond. Moreover, on a commercial ship, ICT functions may be managed by a more knowledgeable seafarer and experts may be reached from the shore stations through satellite communications. We believe that some of the data collection and initial analyses of a cyber event could be tracked and analyzed by a computer system, initial reactions may be identified by a computer decision-aided system before solicitation the actions of the remote expert.
- Communications and resilience of systems and organizations. Attacks have occurred and will occur... but an impacted ship should provide resilience, (reduced) continuity of services except for the critical functions.

We can identify research trends in cybersecurity but when applied to the maritime domain these subjects may raise attention when they are presented clearly and in the applied maritime context. The research outcomes of the chair consisted in numerous contributions in conferences, journals, demonstrators and proofs of concept. Some of them have been made operational and are now deployed on ships, to enhance the detection of cyber events. For the research outcomes and prospective investigation, we have decided to integrate interviews and demos into the MOOC directly. They provide additional learning materials for those interested and also constitute a bridge between the academics, the industrials and the state agencies.

6 A Collaborative Endeavor: Call for Multi-stakeholder Contribution

6.1 The Imperatives for Collaboration

This production of this MOOC is at an initial stage, has not been released yet and therefore there is no direct evaluation so far. Nevertheless, through the early phases, I can assert the necessity for a global effort because:

- No single entity can tackle this challenge alone.
- There is a requirement to leverage diverse expertise and resources.
- I feel a need to ensuring relevance, credibility, quality and widespread adoption.
- I believe in an international creation and cooperation with both academic, military and civilian bodies, equipment providers, shipping companies to name a few.

6.2 Specific Roles for Key Stakeholders

We have built a short, but what I think is a complete and coherent, program to raise awareness in the maritime cybersecurity domains and to present recent advances on innovation needs. Nevertheless, the intended audience should come with different origins and expectations, specific training requirements and needs. I have identified so far these potentials users:

- Shipping companies and ship owners may want to have a more succinct technical view but a stronger section on their responsibilities in case of a cyber event.
- Port authorities and operators may need a specific focus on securing networks and access when the ship is on the quay
- Technology providers so that they can discover the very specific features of the maritime domain which is rather unique due to its very nature: a ship operates in a remote area with low communication facilities and ICT people are not always there to respond to a specific request from the equipment provided
- Classification societies and regulatory bodies to share a common framework and terminology.
- Academia and research institutions because the maritime industry needs innovation, applied research to tackle ever changing contexts.
- Cybersecurity experts and consultancies because there is a huge and an unexplored demand from this maritime industry to assess and determine a work agenda to secure maritime operations from the very early stages of the ship design to its operations at sea through the required maintenance and updates a ship will depart from the harbor.

6.3 Mechanisms for Contribution

So far, I have identified the following activities to engage the various interested parties and develop the MOOC content

- Content development workshops with a mix of academics, equipment providers, national agencies, ship builders,...
- Expert review panels to assess the quality and adequacy of the learning materials

- Financial sponsorship and in-kind contributions to secure the pedagogical development
- Marketing and outreach partnerships
- Joint research initiatives for MOOC content enhancement.
- International actions through EU, IMO (International Maritime Organization) or bilateral academic actions.

7 The Vision: A Globally Resilient Maritime Ecosystem

The maritime industry is involved in a forced movement to integrate new technologies. Without entering into the details, this industry has made the emergence of key actors, but their supremacy and leadership might be challenged by new players at any time. There is still a fierce competition among them, but concentration should occur due to the US new tariffs policies or the geostrategic instability in the Near and Middle East. The occurrence of severe incidents would alter the reputation of a so-called victim with immediate impacts from its clients, national bodies (which may restrict the ship movement or remove the navigability credits), and most importantly insurers (who may frown their eye line when dealing with costs of negligence or inexplicable competences lacks). There is also a wide opportunity for academics to develop and credit expertise for those who can follow with success the continuous learning track on maritime cybersecurity. Such a certificate could be mandated, for example, in the near future when entering the EU seas to accommodate new secure trade policies.

Finally, I would like to highlight the collective benefits of a well-informed and well-trained workforce. This would also create opportunities for seafarers to advance their careers.

8 Conclusion and Perspectives

In an increasingly interconnected world, maritime cybersecurity is of critical importance to the global security of the oceans and contribute to international trade. Modern ships, smart ports, autonomous ships, and navigation systems depend massively on digital technologies, which in turn introduce and create new vulnerabilities that require immediate and coordinated attention.

In the face of these emerging challenges, an MOOC devoted to maritime cybersecurity represents a particularly suitable and scalable solution. This pedagogical approach offers unique advantages for meeting large-scale maritime cybersecurity training needs. Accessibility is the first major advantage of MOOCs. They enable thousands of learners to be reached simultaneously across the globe, without geographical constraints or capacity limitations. Maritime professionals, wherever they are, can access adequate training to enhance their competences and skills. Flexibility is another decisive advantage and ease of reach through an internet browser.

At this time (June 2025), this initial version of the MOOC is completed at 80 per cent and I still need to include additional learning materials and interviews from experts to develop the awareness and interest of the learners. The curriculum I followed relies directly from my experience as the chairman of an R&D research team under the aegis of the French Navy with a specific attention to academic knowledge dissemination. However, the effectiveness of this approach depends on a mobilization and contributions by all players in the maritime sector. Shipowners, port managers, regulatory authorities, training organizations and cybersecurity experts must join forces to create a coherent and comprehensive training ecosystem.

This collaboration can also be the root for more formalized cooperation under EU programs (such as Erasmus and capacity building frameworks). I would call thus for a global initiative to make sea safer and to contribute somehow to new forms of sharing of cyber experiences, competences and skills.

References

1. Oruc A.: Cyber security of the integrated navigation system (INS). PhD dissertation - Trondheim: Norwegian University of Science and Technology. NTNU (2024)
2. Jacq, O.: Détection, analyse contextuelle et visualisation de cyber-attaques en temps réel : élaboration de la Cyber Situational Awareness du monde maritime. PhD dissertation. NNT : 2021IMTA0228. tel-03145173 (2021)
3. Amro, A., Oruc, A., Gkioulos, V., Katsikas, S.: Navigation data anomaly analysis and detection. Information **13**(3), 104 (2022). https://doi.org/10.3390/info13030104
4. Amro, A., Gkioulos, V., Katsikas, S.: Communication Architecture for Autonomous Passenger Ship. Proc. Inst. Mech. Eng. Part O J, Risk Reliab (2021)
5. Oruc, A., Chowdhury, N., Gkioulos, V.: A modular cyber security training programme for the maritime domain. Int. J. Inf. Secur. **23**, 1477–1512 (2024). https://doi.org/10.1007/s10207-023-00799-4
6. Kavallieratos, G., Katsikas, S., Gkioulos, V.: Cyber-attacks against the autonomous ship. In: Katsikas, S.K., et al., (eds.) SECPRE/CyberICPS -2018. LNCS, vol. 11387, pp. 20–36. Springer, Cham (2019). https://doi.org/10.1007/978-3-030-12786-2_2
7. Jacq, O., Kermarrec, Y., Simonin, J.: Cyber attacks real time detection: towards a cyber situational awareness for naval systems. In: Proceedings of the 2019 International Conference on Cyber Situational Awareness, (Cyber SA), Oxford, UK, 3–4 June 2019
8. Boudehenn, C.: Génération de données pour l'analyse et la détection d'anomalies dans les systèmes cybernétiques navals. PhD dissertation, IMT Atlantique 2022. NNT : 2022IMTA0336. tel-04007599
9. Kabore, R., Kouassi, A., N'goran, R., Asseu, O., Kermarrec, Y., et al.: Review of anomaly detection systems in industrial control systems using deep feature learning approach. Engineering, **13** (1), 30–44 (2021). https://doi.org/10.4236/eng.2021.131003.hal-03174461
10. D. Naouar, J.E. Hachem, J.-L. Voirin, J.F., Kermarrec, Y.: Towards the integration of cybersecurity risk assessment into model-based requirements engineering: In: IEEE 29th International Requirements Engineering Conference (RE). Notre Dame, IN, USA 2021, pp. 334–344 (2021). https://doi.org/10.1109/RE51729.2021.00037

11. Androjna, A., Satler, T.B., Srše, J.: An overview of maritime cyber security challenges. In: 19th International Conference on Transport Science (2020)
12. BIMCO The guidelines on cyber security onboard ships (2020). https://www.ics-shipping.org/wp-content/uploads/2021/02/2021-Cyber-Security-Guidelines.pdf
13. Chiprianov, V., Kermarrec, Y., Rouvrais, S.: Meta-tools for software language engineering : a flexible collaborative modeling language for efficient telecommunications service design In: Proceedings FlexiTools'2010 : Workshop on Flexible Modeling Tools (in Conjonction with the 32nd ACM/IEEE ICSE Intelligence Conference on Software Engineering), Cape Town, South Africa (2010)
14. N'goran, R., Tetchueng, J.-L., Pandry, G., Kermarrec, Y., Asseu, O.O.: Trust assessment model based on a zero trust strategy in a community cloud environment Engineering, vol. 14, no. 11, pp. 479–496 (2022). https://doi.org/10.4236/eng.2022.1411036
15. Jacq, O., Kermarrec, Y., et al.: The Cyber-MAR Project: first results and perspectives on the use of hybrid cyber ranges for port cyber risk assessment. In: 2021 IEEE International Conference on Cyber Security and Resilience (CSR), pp. 409–414 (2021). https://doi.org/10.1109/CSR51186.2021.9527968
16. Larsen, M.H., Lund, M.S.: Cyber risk perception in the maritime domain: a systematic literature review. IEEE Access **9**, 144895–144905 (2021). https://doi.org/10.1109/ACCESS.2021.3122433
17. Haugli-Sandvik, M., Lund, M., Bjørneseth, F.B.: Maritime decision-makers and cyber security: deck officers' perception of cyber risks towards IT and OT systems. Int. J. Inf. Secur. **23**, 1–19 (2024)
18. Becmeur, T., et al.: A platform for raising awareness on cyber security in a maritime context 2017 In: International Conference on Computational Science and Computational Intelligence (CSCI), pp. 103–108 (2017). https://doi.org/10.1109/CSCI.2017.17
19. ANSSI. Best practices for cyber security on board ships. Report from ANSSI agency, France (2016)

Improving Hyperledger Indy With Post-quantum and Optimal Credential Attributes Selection Agents

Saha Fobougong Pierre[1](✉), Badran Nancy[2], Mejri Mohamed[1], and Adi Kamel[2]

[1] Department of computer science and software engineering, Laval University, 2325, rue de l'université, Québec (Québec) G1V 0A6, Canada
{pisaf1,momej}@ulaval.ca

[2] Computer Security Research Laboratory, Université du Québec à Outaouais, Québec, Canada
{badn04,kamel.adi}@uqo.ca

Abstract. Self-Sovereign Identity (SSI) systems offer a decentralized and secure approach to digital identity management. However, these systems still face significant challenges, particularly vulnerabilities to future quantum computing threats and inefficiencies in the selection of Verifiable Presentations (VPs). In this paper, we propose a novel architecture that addresses both these issues by the introduction of two complementary agents: a Post-Quantum Cryptographic (PQC) Agent and an Optimal Credential Attributes Selection Agent. The PQC Agent integrates quantum-resistant cryptographic mechanisms, specifically Dilithium2 signatures and Kyber/AES hybrid encryption, to significantly enhance the security of credentials and verifiable presentations against quantum capable adversaries. Simultaneously, the optimisation agent leverages the power of Satisfiability Modulo Theories (SMT) to determine the optimal subset of identity attributes required for service access, while preserving the user's privacy. We present the design, implementation, and evaluation of this integrated architecture for Indy SSI framework. Experimental results demonstrate that our architecture not only improves resilience to quantum threats, but also enhances privacy by limiting attribute disclosure to the minimum necessary for service access.

Keywords: Self-sovereign Identity · Indy · Post-Quantum Cryptography · SMT · Selective Disclosure

1 Introduction

Self-Sovereign Identity (SSI) systems have established as a cornerstone in rethinking of digital identity operation, enabling a user-centric management of individual credentials, selective imparting of identity properties and cryptographic proof of origin. SSIs are made possible through Decentralized Identifiers (DIDs), Verifiable Credentials (VCs), and Verifiable Presentations (VPs),

K. Adi et al. (Eds.): CRiSIS 2025, LNCS 16295, pp. 266–281, 2026.
https://doi.org/10.1007/978-3-032-20732-6_17

operationalized by systems such as Hyperledger Indy, Sovrin, IOTA Identity. Nevertheless, the continued use of these systems with classical cryptographic primitives (like RSA, ECDSA, Ed25519, BLS) makes them vulnerable to future attacks, most notably scalable quantum computing [14]. Shor's algorithm breaks contemporary asymmetric primitives in polynomial time, whereas Grover's algorithm degrades symmetric encryption, meaning that larger key sizes and stronger resilience strategies are required [19]. Meanwhile, current SSI systems do not have a mechanism of advising users about what subset of identity attributes should be revealed by a user in a credential presentation. Existing solutions utilize static templates or full-credential reveals in selective disclosure scenario with an increased leakage in personal data. This lack of expressiveness and precision is at odds with data minimization and privacy-by-design principles in current digital identity frameworks and regulations such as the GDPR.

This work puts forth a new SSI architecture featuring two orthogonal agents to bridge this gap: a Post-Quantum Cryptography (PQC) Agent and an SMT-Based Attribute Selection Agent. Identity messages such as credential offers, requests, and verifiable presentations are cryptographically secure using post-quantum digital signatures, hybrid encryption, and key encapsulation methods. This extends and generalizes the hybrid PQ/T approach introduced in [19] by considering not only issuer-side signature layers, but also holder-side presentation protocols and verifier-side signature verification.

The SMT Agent, however, produces the verifier's policy as a satisfiability problem and solves it within the bounds of costs incurred which are a function of how sensitive the user is towards each attribute. By using a formal optimisation process to decide what subset of attributes are essential and minimally risky to release, we guarantee that only minimal and necessary attributes are made available, a privacy-by-design approach, and provide a more principled counterpart to existing selective disclosure schemes.

Our proposed architecture is built on open standards and cryptographic libraries like liboqs and Z3 Solver, and is capable of being integrated with other DID methods and credential formats. It is based on recommendations from NIST's post-quantum transition roadmap and follows the hybrid signature recommendations from the IETF PQC working groups.

1.1 Contributions

In this study, we present a novel self-sovereign identity (SSI) architecture that incorporates post-quantum cryptographic primitives alongside logic-based privacy optimisation throughout the identity credential lifecycle. Our solution is designed to ensure quantum-resilient authenticity, confidentiality, and data minimization, while maintaining compatibility with established SSI frameworks such as Hyperledger Indy. The primary contributions of this work are summarized as follows:

- **A modular and Post-Quantum Secure SSI architecture:** We have developed an SSI architecture that integrates post-quantum digital signatures

(Dilithium2), key encapsulation mechanisms (Kyber512), and secure credential flows. This architecture ensures end-to-end resistance to quantum threats while maintaining interoperability with traditional SSI infrastructures.
- **Formal privacy optimisation through SMT-Based integration:** We proposed an SMT-based attribute selection agent that considers selective disclosure as a constrained optimisation problem. By applying logical rules to evaluate which identity attributes are strictly necessary, the agent automatically selects the minimal subset required to satisfy a verifier's request, effectively reducing unnecessary exposure of personal data.
- **End-to-end Post-Quantum security of credential Flows:** The proposed design guarantees cryptographic protection across all phases of the schema lifecycle and credential exchange, including schema definition, credential offer, request, and presentation. Each message is digitally signed using Dilithium2, while sensitive data is secured through hybrid Kyber-AES encryption, effectively mitigating the risk of future quantum-enabled decryption attacks.
- **A Complete and Evaluated Prototype Implementation:** As proof of concept, we implemented and made available the proposed architecture, including the PQC and SMT-based optimisation agents. Experimental results demonstrate the design's feasibility and efficiency, showing low cryptographic latency while enabling real-time execution of SSI workflows.

1.2 Outline

In Sect. 2, we introduce Hyperledger Indy and, in addition, we provide preliminaries on PQC and Verifiable Presentation Optimisation approaches. Section 3 highlights related work while in Sect. 4, we describe our proposed architecture and the different identity management processes. Section 5 presents the proof-of-concept implementation. The performance measurements of proposed solutions are presented in Sect. 6 and Sect. 7 concludes our paper.

2 Preliminary Background

2.1 Hyperledger Indy

Hyperledger Indy[1] is a permissioned distributed ledger designed for decentralized identity. Unlike universal blockchains, it has in-built identity primitives such as Decentralized Identifiers (DID), schemas, and verifiable credentials (VC) as per W3C standards at its core. Based on the Plenum Byzantine Fault Tolerant protocol, Indy guarantees low latency, auditability, and a record of tampering for its operation. It supports selective disclosure and zero-knowledge proofs through the Anoncreds format, allowing you to comply with privacy regulations, such as GDPR. User data stays off-ledger and in the custody and control of users, where public components are written in an immutable way. However, Indy has scalability issues and it leverages classical cryptography which would suffer from quantum computer attack in future [8].

[1] https://lf-hyperledger.atlassian.net/wiki/spaces/indy/overview.

2.2 Post-quantum Cryptography

Quantum computing will subvert the ground of classical public-key cryptography where RSA, Diffie-Hellman, and ECC—related computations based on factorization and discrete logarithms—can be solved by Shor's algorithm on a quantum computer [6,15]. In order to counter this, Post Quantum Cryptography (PQC) offers alternatives based on problems thought to be both resistant to classical and quantum attacks.

PQC consists of five classes of algorithmic families: code-based, lattice-based, hash-based, multivariate, and isogeny-based cryptography [6]. The most prevalent candidate is based on lattice problems, because they are both well-established theoretically and efficient. In particular, lattice-based NIST recommendations, e.g., CRYSTALS-Kyber (KEM) [1] and CRYSTALS-Dilithium (digital signatures) [7], are based on hard lattice problems like Shortest Vector Problem (SVP) and Learning With Errors (LWE) which are NP-hard, and offer worst-case to average-case reduction.

These lattice-based primitives realize key generation, encapsulation, and decapsulation. KYBER provides IND-CCA security which can be used for secure communication in DID frameworks, DILITHIUM achieves EUF-CMA security for digital signatures [6]. Both are multi-security level (128, 192, 256 bits), whose performances are comparable, versus resistance to cryptanalysis of future computers [2].

2.3 VP Optimisation in SSI

Selective Disclosure of Attributes (SDA) is the pivotal mechanism by which SSI systems fulfill the data-minimization principle while preserving credential interoperability. A recent systematic review by [3] reports that almost 70 % of new SSI research addresses SDA directly, underscoring its centrality in both European (European Union Digital Identity) and North-American initiatives. The latest ETSI (European Telecommunications Standards Institute) technical report further notes that regulatory imperatives—eIDAS 2 and the GDPR in particular—are driving the adoption of cryptographic schemes that guarantee both non-correlation and zero-knowledge proofs.

Early SSI deployments relied on Camenisch–Lysyanskaya (CL) signatures as implemented in Idemix [5], whose zero-knowledge proofs already supported range and inequality predicates. Nevertheless, the signature size and holder-side computation make them challenging for constrained mobile wallets, as the ETSI cryptographic analysis points out. To overcome these limitations, the community is converging on BBS+ signatures [20], whose constant size enables natively unlinkable proofs. The W3C Candidate Recommendation Data Integrity BBS Cryptosuites v1.0 formalises this approach with primitives for statement detachment and holder binding. [12] extend it by specifying an anonymous-credential system that combines privacy-preserving revocation with hardware anchoring (TPM/SE), demonstrating industrial-grade feasibility.

Within widely adopted JSON-based token formats, the IETF OAuth group is standardising Selective Disclosure JWT (SD-JWT); draft-22 (May 2025) introduces holder-key binding and replay protection. [4] propose CSD-JWT, which compresses proofs via a cryptographic accumulator, reducing presentation size by 27%–93% and making SDA practical on low-bandwidth devices. In a complementary vein, [3] combine Merkle trees, BLS signatures and Bulletproofs (BLS-MT-ZKP) to disclose attribute sets drawn from multiple credentials while supporting multi-issuer aggregation; performance measurements show negligible verification overhead compared with equivalent BBS+ solutions.

Although contemporary cryptographic schemes give holders the technical power to hide or reveal their attributes, they provide no compass for deciding which elements to disclose; so the risk of over-sharing persists. [18] fills this very gap by assigning a risk score to each identity attribute and recasting the task of selecting a subset that satisfies the verifier's request as a Max-Weighted SMT problem solved by SMT solver. In this paper, we exploit this approach to propose an SMT agent that automatically optimises the presentation and recommends to the holder the set of attributes that both meets the verifier request and minimises overall exposure.

3 Related Work

Recent work [10,11,17] confirms that a "cryptographically-relevant" quantum computer would break the RSA and elliptic-curve primitives that anchor today's Self Sovereign Identity (SSI) ecosystems. The work in [9] emphasises that Verifiable-Credential (VC) frameworks such as Camenisch–Lysyanskaya and BBS+, still dominant in Hyperledger Indy and many W3C deployments, lean on strong-RSA or discrete-log assumptions and must therefore be replaced or redesigned before a harvest - now - decrypt - later adversary materialises. Their tutorial shows how a lattice-based signature (Jeudy – Roux - Langlois – Sander) can substitute the classical building blocks, yet flags three open research problems—selective disclosure, non-interactive renewal and scalable revocation—that remain unsolved for post-quantum ZKP credentials. Where a full swap-out seems premature, hybridisation offers a pragmatic bridge, [16] outline a PQ/T hybrid SSI in which each credential and its presentation carry a combined proof containing both an Ed25519/BBS+ signature and its Dilithium counterpart; legacy verifiers ignore the PQC component while quantum-ready verifiers check both. This design preserves backward compatibility yet doubles message size and verification cost, illustrating the tension between security and efficiency that pervades the transition phase.

Authors in [22] advocate reinforcing SSI by augmenting cryptography with quantum-resistant key distribution. They couple Quantum-Key Distribution (QKD) links with a blockchain-based SSI controller for 6G networks; QKD supplies forward-secure keys while the ledger enforces decentralised control over identifiers. Although immune to Shor-style attacks, their architecture inherits

QKD's high infrastructure cost and limited reach, highlighting that physical-layer quantum techniques mitigate, but do not replace, the need for algorithmic PQC.

At protocol level, Yao et al. [21] demonstrate that key-encapsulation mechanisms (KEMs) can act as authenticators within the SPDM device - identity handshake, outperforming Dilithium - based signatures and illustrating how post - quantum KEM authentication could harden transport layers that deliver SSI payloads. Their benchmark shows reduced handshake latency, but the authors acknowledge deployment hurdles such as certificate-chain tooling and hybrid - mode governance. Zhukabayeva et al. [23] integrate hash-based signatures into Hyperledger Fabric to protect electronic health-record credentials; discrete-event simulation confirms that the resulting throughput penalty is acceptable for permissioned settings. Their analysis underlines that ledger throughput and storage blow-up are the main bottlenecks once key and signature sizes exceed a few kilobytes.

Collectively, these studies converge on three strategic options for hardening SSI against quantum adversaries. First, direct substitution—e.g., lattice signatures for DID/VC signing—delivers strong forward secrecy but demands new standards for proof size and revocation. Second, hybrid proofs provide an incremental path yet incur operational overhead and double-stack complexity. Third, adjunct defences (QKD channels, KEM-based handshakes, ledger-level PQC pilots) mitigate discrete vulnerabilities but do not by themselves guarantee end-to-end quantum safety.

4 Proposed Architecture

4.1 Architecture Overview

Our proposed'quantum-resilient" SSI architecture (Fig. 1) preserves Hyperledger Indy while layering post-quantum security and privacy controls on top. Each traditional SSI role—Issuer, Holder, Verifier and the VDR (here Indy ledger)—keeps its standard Indy, but is paired with a dedicated PQC Agent that manages quantum-safe keys and signatures. The Holder hosts an additional SMT Agent that enforces privacy by filtering proof-requests to reveal only the least-sensitive attributes needed. For every new identifier, the Issuer's PQC Agent generates a Dilithium key pairs, integrates it with the classical Ed25519 DID and publishes it. All public PQC artifacts including Dilithium public keys, PQC credential schemas, revocation data and SMT policies are stored immutably. The corresponding CIDs are referenced in Indy transactions, allowing any party to retreive the latest parameters without bloating the ledger.

When a credential is issued, the Issuer signs it twice—Ed25519 (Indy) and Dilithium (PQC)—resulting a hybrid VC. Upon receiving a proof-request, the Holder's SMT Agent minimizes attribute disclosure. The Wallet then creates a classical presentation which the Holder's PQC Agent re-signs in Dilithium, yielding a hybrid VP. The Verifier's PQC Agent obtains the Dilithium key via the CID stored in Indy/IPFS, verifies both signatures, and accepts the proof only if Ed25519 and Dilithium checks pass. Communication between entities is secured with Kyber KEM followed by AES-256. Therefore, the system remains interoperable with legacy Indy agents (they can ignore the PQC layer) while providing immediate quantum resilience and privacy minimization for upgraded participants.

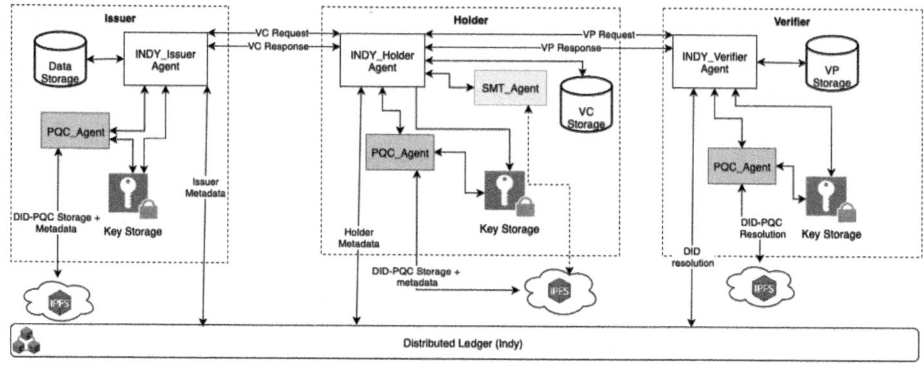

Fig. 1. Enhanced SSI Post Quantum Architecture Overview

4.2 Post-quantum Agent

Let $\mathcal{D} = \{\text{did}_1, \text{did}_2, \ldots, \text{did}_n\}$ be the set of decentralized identifiers (DIDs). For each did $\in \mathcal{D}$, the agent maintains the following:

- **Signature Keys :** $(\text{pk}_{\text{sig}}^{\text{did}}, \text{sk}_{\text{sig}}^{\text{did}}) \in \{0,1\}^* \times \{0,1\}^*$ where $(\text{pk}_{\text{sig}}^{\text{did}}, \text{sk}_{\text{sig}}^{\text{did}}) \leftarrow$ `Dilithium2.KeyGen()`
- **KEM Keys:**$(\text{pk}_{\text{kem}}^{\text{did}}, \text{sk}_{\text{kem}}^{\text{did}}) \in \{0,1\}^* \times \{0,1\}^*$ where $(\text{pk}_{\text{kem}}^{\text{did}}, \text{sk}_{\text{kem}}^{\text{did}}) \leftarrow$ `Kyber512.KeyGen()`
  The agent maintains a function: $\mathcal{K} : \mathcal{D} \rightarrow (\text{pk}_{\text{sig}}, \text{sk}_{\text{sig}}, \text{pk}_{\text{kem}}, \text{sk}_{\text{kem}})$ and store the following JSON object locally or in their key vaults.

```
{
  "did": {
    "dilithium_public_key": "...", "dilithium_private_key": "...",
    "kyber_public_key": "...", "kyber_private_key": "..."
  }
}
```

- **Signature:** $\sigma \leftarrow \texttt{Sign}_{\text{sk}_{\text{sig}}^{\text{did}}}(m)$
- **Signature verification:** $\texttt{Verify}_{\text{pk}_{\text{sig}}^{\text{did}}}(m, \sigma) \in \{\texttt{true}, \texttt{false}\}$
- **Encryption:** Given $m \in \{0,1\}^*$ and recipient's $\text{pk}_{\text{kem}}^{\text{did}}$:
  - Encapsulation: $(c\_kem, k) \leftarrow \texttt{Encaps}(\text{pk}_{\text{kem}}^{\text{did}})$
  - Symmetric encryption using AES-GCM: $\text{c\_data} \leftarrow \texttt{AESGCM.Encrypt}_k(n, m)$ where $n \in \{0,1\}^{96}$ is a nonce.

  - Output: (c_kem, c_data, n)
- **Decryption :**
  - Decapsulation: $k \leftarrow \texttt{Decaps}(c\_kem, \mathrm{sk}_{\mathrm{kem}}^{\mathrm{did}})$
  - Decryption: $m \leftarrow \texttt{AESGCM.Decrypt}_k(n, \mathrm{c\_data})$

4.3 VP Optimisation Agent

The SMT agent used in our architecture is based on the work of [18]. This work proposes a formal chain—spanning the modelling of verifiable credentials (VCs) to fully-automated optimisation—that helps users decide *what* to disclose when a service requests proof of identity. The formal model blends *product-family algebra, propositional logic, and SMT optimisation* to decide, prove, and optimise identity presentations—paving the way for digital wallets capable of negotiating, in real time, an optimal balance between access and privacy. In concrete terms, each attribute (or attribute–value pair) is treated as a *feature*; a coherent set of features forms a *product*, and the ensemble of all possible products constitutes a *product family*. A translation function encodes any product family as a Boolean formula in disjunctive normal form (DNF), and its inverse recovers the original "product" representation. To focus solely on attribute presence, the authors introduce the operator $\langle\!\cdot\!\rangle^+$, which removes negative literals from the resulting formula.

On this basis, conformance between what the user holds (VC family) and what the service requires (Request - R family) is captured by a hierarchy of relations: standard refinement ($\sqsubseteq$) [13], partial refinement ($\sqsubseteq_{\mathcal{P}}$), and refinement with substitution ($\sqsubseteq_{\Gamma}$), the latter searching for suitable values of attributes still unknown to the verifier. After logical translation, checking whether a user can authenticate reduces to testing the satisfiability of the implication $\langle VC\rangle^+ \Rightarrow \langle R\rangle^+$, a task delegated to the Z3 SMT solver, which instantly returns a verdict and, when applicable, a model indicating which values to assign.

To minimise disclosure, each attribute receives a risk score. The authors define an ordering $\preceq^r$ on product families: one family is preferred if its total risk is lower. Finding the "just-sufficient" presentation thus becomes a *Max-Weighted SMT* optimisation problem: the constraint $\langle VC\rangle^+ \Rightarrow \langle R\rangle^+$ is enforced while the cost function

$$\sum_i \mathrm{risk}(a_i) \times \mathrm{val}(a_i)$$

is minimised (Where a_i is an attribute and $\mathrm{val}(a_i)$ indicating whether a_i is selected or not). Consequently, Z3 solver automatically returns the attribute set that is both compliant and of minimal risk.

4.4 Architecture Processes

In this section, we present some of the processes implemented by the proposed architecture.

Registration. As shown in Fig. 2, once the entity's DID has been created, the entity calls the Post-quantum agent to create the post-quantum parameters associated with the DID. The entity creates a schema that defines the structure of a Verifiable Credential (VC), i.e., the list of attributes it contains. This schema is published to the ledger. The issuer then creates a credential definition linked to that schema, specifying how the VC will be signed and whether revocation is supported. This definition is also written to the ledger.

In this process, the PQC agent acts as a cryptographic companion that provides post-quantum security. It generates a Dilithium2 signature key pair and a Kyber512 encryption key pair for each DID. The PQC agent allows issuers to sign critical objects (schemas, credential definitions) with quantum-resistant digital signatures. Because post-quantum signatures are often large, the PQC agent stores these signatures off-ledger (e.g., on IPFS) and embeds their fingerprint (CID) into schema or credential metadata.

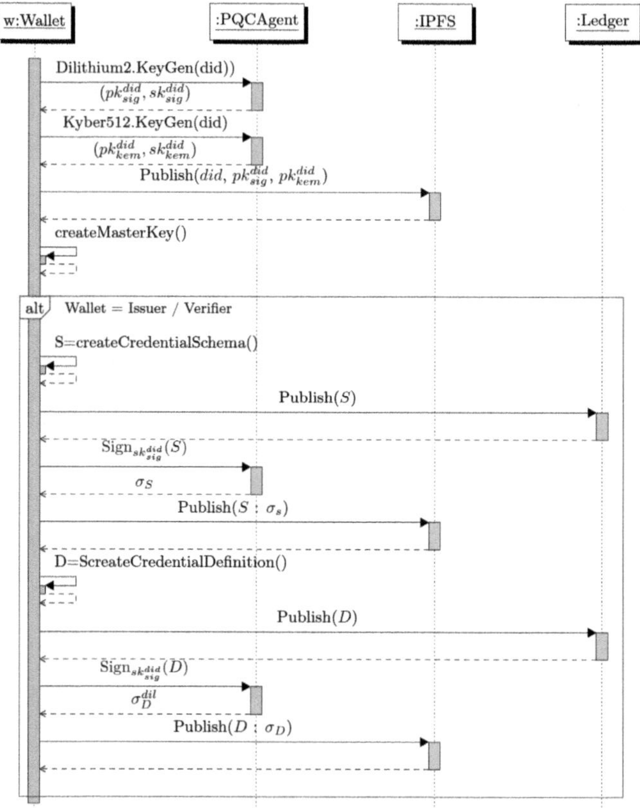

Fig. 2. Entities registration process

Verifiable Credential Issuance. This process (Fig. 3) begins when the issuer constructs a credential offer, which includes the identifiers of the schema and the credential definition, along with metadata for issuance. Before sending the offer, the issuer's PQC agent signs it using a post-quantum private key. This signature is either directly attached to the offer or stored on IPFS (in the case of large size) and referenced via a Content Identifier (CID) embedded in the metadata. The holder can then verify the authenticity of the offer by retrieving the issuer's public post-quantum key from the IPFS.

In response, the holder prepares a credential request containing cryptographic commitments derived from their master secret. This request includes critical fields such as *blinded_ms* and *blinded_ms_correctness_proof*, which encapsulate a blinded version of the master secret. To ensure their confidentiality against quantum-capable adversaries, these fields are encrypted by the holder's PQC agent using AES-256, itself encapsulated with Kyber512. This encryption ensures that the issuer cannot reconstruct or infer the master secret, thereby preserving the integrity of the Anoncreds model under post-quantum threat models. Additionally, the PQC agent signs the credential request with the holder's Dilithium2 private key, enabling the issuer to verify its authenticity using a public key retrieved from the IPFS.

Once validated, the issuer generates the credential by signing the provided attributes using a classical key (e.g., Ed25519 or BLS). A post-quantum signature is applied, either embedded or referenced via a CID if stored externally. The completed VC is then encrypted (using Kyber-AES) and sent to the holder, who decrypts and verifies its cryptographic integrity, including the post-quantum signature, and stores it in their SSI wallet. This overall process ensures VC issuance that is compliant with current SSI standards while anticipating future vulnerabilities introduced by quantum computing.

Verifiable Presentation Submission. This process (Fig. 4) begins with the verifier constructing a proof request that specifies the attribute requirements for verification. This request may define logical combinations (e.g., *name AND (degree OR work_experience)*) or include multiple alternative schemas. Before transmission, the verifier's PQC agent signs the proof request using its private Dilithium2 key. The signature is either embedded directly in the request or referenced via a content identifier (CID) on IPFS. The holder, upon receiving the request, uses the verifier's public key—retrieved from IPFS—to verify the authenticity of the proof request.

The verified proof request is then processed by the SMT Agent, which plays a central role in ensuring minimal data disclosure. This agent evaluates the attributes available in the holder's wallet and the logical structure of the verifier's request. It also considers the privacy cost assigned to each attribute by the holder. Using formal constraint-solving (e.g., Z3 SMT), the agent identifies the minimal subset of attributes that satisfies the request while minimizing the cumulative cost of disclosure. This ensures that the holder discloses no more information than strictly necessary.

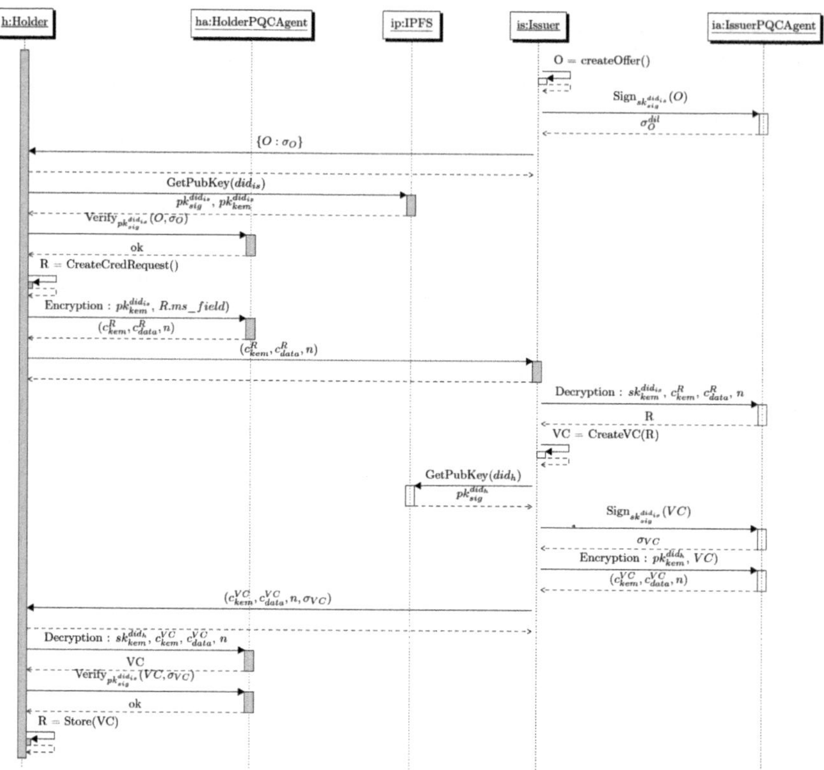

Fig. 3. Verifiable Credential issuance process

The holder then, constructs the Verifiable Presentation using the Anoncreds protocol. The presentation includes cryptographic proofs for the selected attributes and preserves zero-knowledge if needed. Before sending the VP, the PQC agent performs a final post-quantum digital signature using the holder's Dilithium2 private key. The resulting signed presentation is then fully encrypted using the verifier's Kyber process.

Upon receipt, the verifier decrypts the VP using their Kyber private key, verifies the Dilithium2 signature using the holder's public key (obtained from the IPFS), and then processes the Anoncreds proof to ensure the validity of the attributes. If all verifications succeed, the VP is accepted as valid.

5 Proof-of-Concept Implementation

5.1 Technical Stack and Environment

These experiments were performed on a virtual machine (Intel(R) x86_64 CORE(TM) i5-6200U CPU @2.30 GHZ, 4 GB RAM, Ubuntu 22.04) using

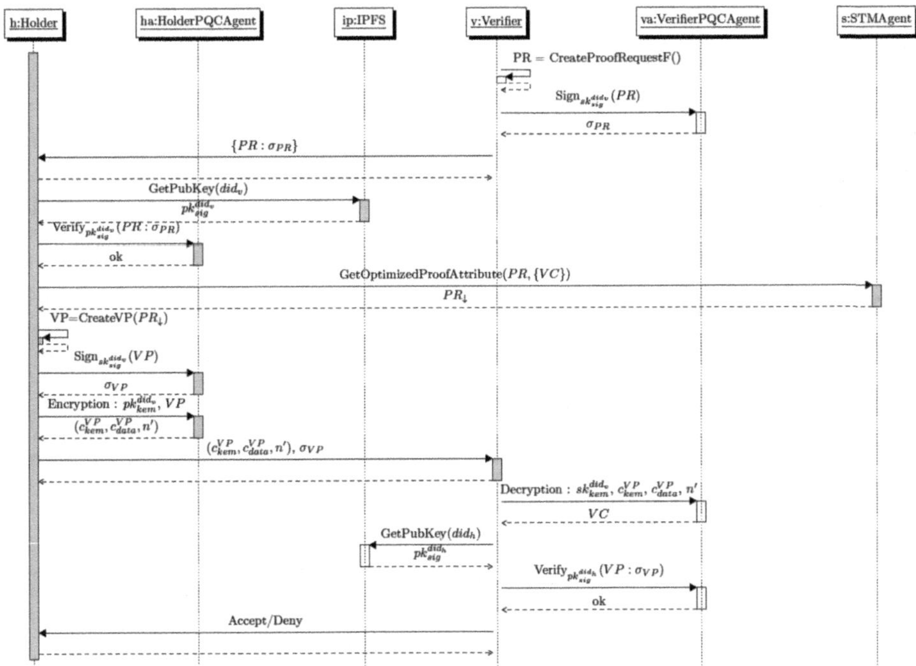

Fig. 4. Verifiable presentation submission process

a Python-based implementation that integrates the liboqs library for post-quantum cryptography and the Z3 solver for logical optimisation. The python code can be downloaded here: https://github.com/crisis2025/Proof-Of-Concept.

A local Hyperledger Indy network is containerised with Docker to provide a self-contained SSI ledger that supports DID creation, schema and credential-definition publication, and verifiable-credential issuance. All identity operations are orchestrated through the Indy SDK, preserving selective disclosure and secure storage semantics. To avoid bloating the ledger with large, non-native objects, post-quantum signatures and auxiliary metadata are stored off-chain in IPFS. Post-quantum security is supplied by the Open Quantum Safe project's liboqs library, whose Dilithium-2 and Kyber-512 primitives are invoked via Python ctypes to sign credentials and encrypt sensitive artifacts. The entire architecture is coded in Python, and each SSI agent is exposed as a lightweight asynchronous REST service via FastAPI.

5.2 Experimental Results

We carried out a set of experiments targeting two key dimensions: the computational overhead, introduced by post-quantum cryptographic operations (signatures and encryption), and the efficiency of the SMT-based attribute selection agent. The simulation results are available at the following address: https://github.com/crisis2025/Proof-Of-Concept/blob/main/simulatedoutput.txt.

PQC Cryptographic Performance. Results showed that Dilithium2 key generation, signing, and verification are completed in approximately 0.175 ms, 0.318 ms, and 0.232 ms respectively, while Kyber512 key generation, encapsulation, and decapsulation each take around $0.069ms$, $0.093ms$ and $0.119ms$. Encryption and decryption operations take approximately 0.038 ms and 0.047 ms. These results demonstrate that post-quantum cryptographic primitives can be executed efficiently on standard hardware, introducing minimal latency and making them suitable for real-time use in SSI workflows, particularly for signing credentials and securely exchanging keys.

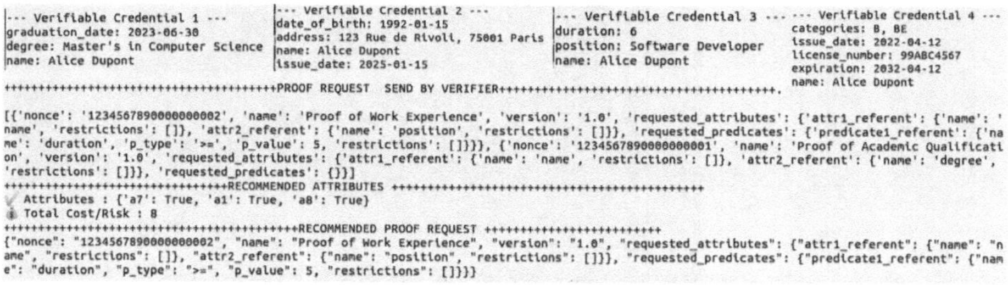

```
--- Verifiable Credential 1 ---
graduation_date: 2023-06-30
degree: Master's in Computer Science
name: Alice Dupont

--- Verifiable Credential 2 ---
date_of_birth: 1992-01-15
address: 123 Rue de Rivoli, 75001 Paris
name: Alice Dupont
issue_date: 2025-01-15

--- Verifiable Credential 3 ---
duration: 6
position: Software Developer
name: Alice Dupont

--- Verifiable Credential 4 ---
categories: B, BE
issue_date: 2022-04-12
license_number: 99ABC4567
expiration: 2032-04-12
name: Alice Dupont

++++++++++++++++++++++++++++++++++++++++PROOF REQUEST  SEND BY VERIFIER++++++++++++++++++++++++++++++++++++++++.

[{'nonce': '1234567890000000002', 'name': 'Proof of Work Experience', 'version': '1.0', 'requested_attributes': {'attr1_referent': {'name': 'name', 'restrictions': []}, 'attr2_referent': {'name': 'position', 'restrictions': []}}, 'requested_predicates': {'predicate1_referent': {'name': 'duration', 'p_type': '>=', 'p_value': 5, 'restrictions': []}}}, {'nonce': '1234567890000000001', 'name': 'Proof of Academic Qualification', 'version': '1.0', 'requested_attributes': {'attr1_referent': {'name': 'name', 'restrictions': []}, 'attr2_referent': {'name': 'degree', 'restrictions': []}}, 'requested_predicates': {}}]
++++++++++++++++++++++++++++++++++++RECOMMENDED ATTRIBUTES ++++++++++++++++++++++++++++++++++++++++++++++++
 Attributes : {'a7': True, 'a1': True, 'a8': True}
 Total Cost/Risk : 8
++++++++++++++++++++++++++++++++++++++++++++++RECOMMENDED PROOF REQUEST ++++++++++++++++++++++++++
{"nonce": "1234567890000000002", "name": "Proof of Work Experience", "version": "1.0", "requested_attributes": {"attr1_referent": {"name": "name", "restrictions": []}, "attr2_referent": {"name": "position", "restrictions": []}}, "requested_predicates": {"predicate1_referent": {"name": "duration", "p_type": ">=", "p_value": 5, "restrictions": []}}}
```

Fig. 5. SMT AGENT Selection

Table 1. Performance of SMT-based attribute selection

Sc.	VCs	Attr/VC	Req. Sets	Attr/Req	Time (ms)	Selected Attr.
S1	2	3	1	2	0.2–0.5	a1, a2
S2	4	3	2	2–3	3–12	a7, a1, a8

SMT-Based Attribute Selection. Figure 5 illustrates, for example, that by assigning the values *{"name": 3, "date_of_birth": 7, "degree": 6, "graduation_date": 3, "address": 3, "issue_date": 3, "license_number": 3, "categories": 3, "license_issue_date": 3, "expiration": 3, "position": 2, "duration": 3}* to wallet attributes of a holder who has received four VCs from different issuer, and wishes to access a service that offers two access possibilities, the SMTAGENT recommends the one generating the minimum risk/cost.

Table 1 presents the results of two experimental scenarios: S1 and S2. From left to right, we report: the number of credential families available in the holder's wallet; the average number of attributes per credential; the number of request families defined by the verifier (i.e., logical alternatives); the average number of attributes required per request; the solving time in milliseconds for the SMT optimizer to select an attribute subset; and an example of the selected attributes returned by the solver. In both scenarios, the SMT Agent successfully computed an optimal and satisfiable attribute within a reasonable time. Scenario S1 represents a basic case where the request aligns directly with one available VC, while Scenario S2 (same results as Fig. 5) includes multiple overlapping credential families and multiple request patterns. This demonstrates that the optimisation process remains fast and effective under moderate wallet, making it viable for real-time identity presentations. However, it is worth noting that as the number of credentials and the logical depth of verifier requests increase, solving time may grow non-linearly.

6 Discussion

As shown in Table 2, our architecture positions itself midway between the three main lines of post-quantum research on SSI. At one extreme, [9] advocate a full lattice-based replacement of all classical signatures and zero-knowledge credentials, an approach that guarantees post-quantum soundness but inflates every credential to hundreds of kilobytes and forces a global ledger refactor. At the other extreme, [22] secure the communication layer with quantum-key distribution, sidestepping application changes but leaving credentials themselves exposed to Shor-class attacks. Between these poles, [16] propose a dual-signature hybrid in which each VC carries both an Ed25519 (or BBS+) and a Dilithium proof; while this satisfies backward compatibility, it doubles message size and complicates wallet governance.

Our design borrows the compatibility advantage of [16] and avoids their systematic overhead by restricting the Dilithium add-on to the handful of Indy transactions, schema publication and credential issuance—leaving day-to-day

Table 2. Comparison of the main post-quantum integration strategies for SSI. ✓ = criterion fully satisfied; △= partially; ✗= not satisfied; "N/A" = criterion not applicable.

Lead reference	Backward compat.	Ledger change	Payload growth	Deploy. effort	Long-term PQ safety	Decision-level selective disclosure
[9]	✗	High	High	High	✓	△
[16]	✓	Medium	Medium	Medium	✓	△
[22]	N/A	High	None	Very High	✓ †	✗
[23]	△	Medium	Low	Medium	△	△
This work	✓	**None**	**Low**	**Low–Med.**	✓	✓

† Secures only the communication channel; credential layer remains classical unless combined with PQ signatures.

DIDComm traffic untouched. In doing so, we keep the global payload growth low and spare the ledger from any structural change, a difficulty highlighted by [23] when they graft post-quantum certificates into Hyperledger Fabric. Because the SMT Agent operates locally, it also preserves the existing disclosure wizard that helps holders choose the minimal attribute set; contrast this with the full-substitution prototypes of [9], whose bulky lattice proofs currently lack user-friendly disclosure tooling.

7 Conclusion and Future Work

The evolution of Self-Sovereign Identity (SSI) architectures toward post-quantum cryptography (PQC) is both a necessary and timely response to the threat posed by quantum computing. Current SSI frameworks rely on classical digital signatures that are vulnerable to quantum attacks, notably through Shor's algorithm. To address this, the proposed architecture integrates quantum-resistant cryptographic primitives (Dilithium for signatures and Kyber for encryption), an SMT-based agent for optimizing attribute disclosure, and a secure presentation protocol that ensures end-to-end PQC-protected interactions.

From a research standpoint, this work opens several promising avenues. First, replacing classical credentials with post-quantum zero-knowledge schemes (ZK-PQC), such as lattice or hash-based alternatives to CL-signatures (e.g., BBS+), would enable full quantum-resistant selective disclosure. Second, introducing autonomous, intelligent agents that merge SMT solvers with machine learning could enhance adaptive privacy control by adjusting disclosure costs based on context and verifier behavior. Finally, expanding the architecture to support multi-ledger interoperability would require a federated post-quantum identity resolution mechanism, enabling credential validation and DID operations across heterogeneous blockchain environments.

References

1. Avanzi, R., et al.: Crystals-kyber algorithm specifications and supporting documentation. NIST PQC Round **2**(4), 1–43 (2019)
2. Bavdekar, R., Chopde, E.J., Agrawal, A., Bhatia, A., Tiwari, K.: Post quantum cryptography: a review of techniques, challenges and standardizations. In: 2023 International Conference on Information Networking (ICOIN), pp. 146–151. IEEE (2023)
3. Bećirović Ramić, Š, et al.: Selective disclosure in digital credentials. ICT Express **10**(4), 916–934 (2024)
4. Buldini, A., Mazzocca, C., Montanari, R., Uluagac, S.: Compact and selective disclosure for verifiable credentials. arXiv preprint arXiv:2506.00262 (2025)
5. Camenisch, J., Van Herreweghen, E.: Design and implementation of the idemix anonymous credential system. In: Proceedings of the 9th ACM Conference on Computer and Communications Security, pp. 21–30 (2002)

6. Chen, L., et al.: Report on post-quantum cryptography, vol. 12. US Department of Commerce, National Institute of Standards and Technology (NIST) (2016)
7. Ducas, L., et al.: Crystals-dilithium: algorithm specifications and supporting documentation. Round-2 submission to the NIST PQC project **35** (2019)
8. Dunphy, P.: A note on the blockchain trilemma for decentralized identity: learning from experiments with hyperledger indy. arXiv preprint (2022), https://arxiv.org/abs/2204.05784
9. Dutto, S., Margaria, D., Sanna, C., Vesco, A.: Toward a post-quantum zero-knowledge verifiable credential system for self-sovereign identity. Cryptology ePrint Archive (2022)
10. Gidney, C.: How to factor 2048 bit RSA integers with less than a million noisy qubits. arXiv preprint arXiv:2505.15917 (2025)
11. Gouzien, É., Sangouard, N.: Factoring 2048-bit RSA integers in 177 days with 13 436 qubits and a multimode memory. Phys. Rev. Lett. **127**(14), 140503 (2021)
12. Graebnitz, C., Buchmann, N., Seiffert, M., Margraf, M.: A specification of an anonymous credential system using bbs+ signatures with privacy-preserving revocation and device binding. Cryptology ePrint Archive (2025)
13. Höfner, P., Khedri, R., Möller, B.: An algebra of product families. Software Syst. Model. **10**(2), 161–182 (2011)
14. Krul, E., Paik, H.y., Ruj, S., Kanhere, S.S.: SOK: trusting self-sovereign identity. arXiv preprint arXiv:2404.06729 (2024)
15. Mosca, M.: Cybersecurity in an era with quantum computers: Will we be ready? IEEE Secur. Privacy **16**(5), 38–41 (2018)
16. Pino, A., Margaria, D., Vesco, A.: On PQ/T hybrid verifiable credentials and presentations to build trust in IoT systems. In: 2024 9th International Conference on Smart and Sustainable Technologies (SpliTech), pp. 1–6. IEEE (2024)
17. Roetteler, M., Naehrig, M., Svore, K.M., Lauter, K.: Quantum resource estimates for computing elliptic curve discrete logarithms (2017). https://arxiv.org/abs/1706.06752
18. Saha, P.F., Mejri, M., Adi, K.: Toward the foundation of digital identity theory. In: Proceedings of the 21st International Conference on Security and Cryptography, vol. 12172, pp. 812–819 (2024). https://doi.org/10.5220/0012838100003767
19. Solavagione, A., Vesco, A.: Transition of self-sovereign identity to post-quantum cryptography. In: 2025 International Conference on Quantum Communications, Networking, and Computing (QCNC), pp. 174–181. IEEE (2025)
20. Tessaro, S., Zhu, C.: Revisiting BBS signatures. In: Hazay, C., Stam, M. (eds.) EUROCRYPT 2023. LNCS, vol. 14008, pp. 691–721. Springer, Cham (2023). https://doi.org/10.1007/978-3-031-30589-4_24
21. Yao, J., Hlayhel, A., Matusiewicz, K.: Postquantum KEM authentication in SPDM for secure session establishment. IEEE Des. Test **41**(5), 17–26 (2023)
22. Zeydan, E., et al.: Enhanced security with quantum key distribution and blockchain for digital identities. In: 2024 IEEE International Mediterranean Conference on Communications and Networking (MeditCom), pp. 489–494. IEEE (2024)
23. Zhukabayeva, T., Ur Rehman, A., Tariq, N., Benkhelifa, E.: Hyperledger fabric based post quantum cryptography healthcare application using discrete event simulation. IEEE Access (2024)

Privacy, Threat Analysis, and Explainable Cybersecurity

Adaptive Noise Injection Guided by Feature Importance for Membership Privacy in MLaaS

Radia Kassa[1,2](✉), Kamel Adi[1], and Abdelkamel Tari[2]

[1] Computer Security Research Laboratory, University of Quebec in Outaouais, Gatineau, QC, Canada
kamel.adi@uqo.ca

[2] Laboratoire LITAN, École supérieure en Sciences et Technologies de l'Informatique et du Numérique, Bejaia, Algérie
{kassa,tari}@estin.dz

Abstract. The growing adoption of Machine Learning as a Service (MLaaS) has raised serious concerns about privacy breaches, particularly through Membership Inference Attacks (MIAs). In such attacks, an adversary attempts to determine whether a specific data sample was part of the training dataset by exploiting differences in model behavior through limited API access. To address this challenge, we propose an adaptive inference-time defense that perturbs queries using a constrained optimization framework. The injected noise is modulated on the basis of the importance of the input feature, introducing controlled uncertainty into the model predictions. This uncertainty limits information leakage while preserving output quality. Experiments on benchmark datasets show that our method reduces MIAs success rates to around 50%, making them no more effective than random guessing, while maintaining high classification accuracy.

Keywords: Machine Learning as a Service · Membership Inference Attacks · Inference-Time Defense · Adaptive Noise Injection · Feature Importance · Query Perturbation · Constrained Optimization · Privacy-Preserving Machine Learning

1 Introduction

In recent years, Machine Learning as a Service (MLaaS) has emerged as a widely adopted paradigm, enabling users to leverage powerful ML models hosted in the cloud without the need for local computation or training. Major providers, including Google Cloud AI, Amazon SageMaker and Microsoft Azure, offer APIs that expose pre-trained models for a variety of tasks such as image classification, fraud detection, and personalized recommendations. Although scalable and easily accessible, publicly deployed ML models face significant privacy risks. Frequently trained on sensitive data, these models may unintentionally memorize

K. Adi et al. (Eds.): CRiSIS 2025, LNCS 16295, pp. 285–301, 2026.
https://doi.org/10.1007/978-3-032-20732-6_18

aspects of their training sets, especially due to overfitting, thereby exposing themselves to sophisticated extraction attacks. Among the most critical threats are Membership Inference Attacks (MIAs), in which adversaries seek to determine whether a specific data point was part of the training set by analyzing subtle patterns in the model output, such as prediction vectors. MIAs exploit the fact that models tend to produce overly confident predictions for training examples compared to unseen data. Such discrepancies create exploitable weaknesses, allowing attackers to distinguish between members and non-members, often with alarming accuracy. The consequences of these attacks are particularly severe when models are trained on highly sensitive information, such as medical records. The National Institute of Standards and Technology [18] classifies such incidents as direct privacy violations, which conflict with data protection regulations such as the General Data Protection Regulation [21]. Shokri *et al.* [15] were the first to demonstrate the effectiveness of MIAs on widely used black-box MLaaS platforms. Their foundational work showed that an attacker could infer information about the training data solely from the model's outputs. They formalized MIAs as a binary classification task, leveraging shadow models to distinguish members from non-members of the training set. Since then, increasingly sophisticated MIAs variants have been proposed to target different model architectures and data types. In response to these attacks, a variety of defense strategies have been proposed which can be broadly classified into three main categories: regularization, knowledge distillation, and information perturbation. However, despite their apparent effectiveness, these defenses have significant limitations against sophisticated attacks and do not always ensure an effective trade-off between privacy and utility. This highlights the urgent need for new defense mechanisms capable of balancing privacy and utility effectively without degrading model performance.

To achieve this goal, we propose a new inference-time defense mechanism that adaptively perturbs incoming queries based on the importance of the feature. A carefully designed and controlled noise vector is injected directly into the inputs before prediction, to protect the model's outputs from any information leakage. The perturbation is computed through a constrained optimization problem with two main objectives:

1. Reducing overconfidence in model predictions by introducing a controlled uncertainty into the outputs.
2. Preserving the utility of the model by adapting the perturbation according to feature importance.

By combining these objectives, our defense introduces uncertainty in a controlled manner that preserves the predictive performance of the model. This targeted perturbation strategy effectively mitigates privacy risks without degrading accuracy. The key novelty of our approach, unlike prior defenses, is that perturbations are applied at the input level during inference and are adaptively guided by feature importance, rather than being uniform or restricted to model outputs. We evaluated the effectiveness of our method on benchmark datasets, showing that it reduces black-box MIAs success rates to approximately 50% %, thus confirming its ability to achieve a robust and practical trade-off between privacy and utility.

2 Related Work

We provide a comprehensive overview of MIAs and the corresponding defense mechanisms.

2.1 Membership Inference Attacks

Membership inference attacks target various ML deployment settings, including black-box scenarios in which only model predictions are accessible to the adversary. In such cases, a typical strategy involves training a binary classifier that distinguishes between members and non-members by exploiting the model's tendency to generate more confident output for training data than for unseen inputs. The seminal work by Shokri *et al.* [15] introduced the shadow model technique, in which the adversary trains multiple shadow models on datasets drawn from the same distribution as the target model's training data. These shadow models mimic the behavior of the target, and their output vectors are used to train an attack classifier that is then applied to the target model to infer the membership status of new samples. Later, Salem *et al.* [13] relaxed many of the assumptions of [15]. They demonstrated that a single shadow model is sufficient and it does not need to share the same architecture or data distribution as the target model. They also proposed a data transfer attack, in which the attacker can build an effective attack model using unrelated public datasets. Meanwhile, Nasr *et al.* [12] improved the accuracy of the attack by incorporating additional features, such as class labels. Other researchers proposed metric-based binary classifiers that directly determine the membership of a record based on predefined thresholds, including prediction confidences, entropy, or modified entropy. This approach was introduced by Yeom *et al.* [23] and was further studied by Salem *et al.* [13]. Subsequently, Song *et al.* [16] summarized and improved these works and also proposed a state-of-the-art metric-based attack called the privacy risk score. Furthermore, Carlini *et al.* [3] introduced LiRA (Likelihood Ratio Attack), a state-of-the-art metric-based method that uses a likelihood ratio test to compare the model output when a sample is included in training versus when it is excluded. By fitting Gaussian distributions to the confidence scores under both conditions, LiRA achieves highly accurate membership inference with a remarkably low false positive rate. The authors also proposed using the True Positive Rate (TPR) and very low False Positive Rates (FPR) as a robust evaluation metric, which has since become standard in recent membership inference research [2,4,5,20,22,24].

2.2 Defenses Against MIAs

Various defense techniques have been proposed to mitigate MIAs by reducing the statistical gap between training and non-training data. Key strategies include information perturbation, regularization, and knowledge distillation, each providing a different trade-off between privacy and model utility.

Information perturbation aims to protect sensitive data by injecting personalized noise or altering the information exposed by the model, thereby obscuring the signals typically exploited by MIAs and reducing privacy leakage. Among the prominent approaches, Differential Privacy (DP) stands out for introducing noise during training to prevent leakage of individual data. Techniques such as DP-SGD [1] clip gradient norms and add gaussian noise at each optimization step. Despite offering strong privacy guarantees, these methods often lead to a significant degradation in model accuracy. Another line of defense involves modifying the model's output after inference. Shokri *et al.* [15] proposed two simple techniques: returning only the top-k confidence scores or the predicted label. Although this reduces the information available to adversaries, models remain vulnerable to MIAs. A more sophisticated method, called MemGuard, was introduced by Jia *et al.* [7] to defend against MIAs by injecting adversarial noise directly into prediction vectors after inference. This carefully crafted perturbation transforms outputs into adversarial examples intended to mislead the attacker's classifier. Although this approach preserves model accuracy and does not require retraining, Song and Mittal [16] have shown that it remains vulnerable to metric-based membership inference attacks. Another form of information perturbation operates directly on the training data by injecting noise into input features to obscure membership-related signals. Zhang *et al.* [25] introduced a fuzzy function that adds random noise to the training data and generates augmented samples to enrich the dataset. Although data perturbation can effectively conceal sensitive information, it requires careful tuning to avoid significant degradation in model utility. Subsequently, Kassa *et al.* [8] proposed a defense framework based on optimal injection of noise into training data, formulated as a constrained optimization problem guided by shapley values, with the aim of preserving important features while enhancing privacy.

Regularization techniques aim to mitigate model overfitting and improve generalization capabilities. Many works [9,13,15] have demonstrated that overfitting is a key factor contributing to the effectiveness of MIAs. In this context, Shokri *et al.* [15] highlighted that L2 regularization can effectively reduce the success rate of MIAs. Subsequently, various regularization methods have been explored to counter these attacks, including dropout [17], model stacking [13], and early stopping [16]. Nasr *et al.* [12] proposed adversarial regularization, an optimization framework formulated as a min-max game between the defense mechanism and the inference attacker. This approach integrates an adversarial regularizer into the loss function with the objective of simultaneously minimizing the prediction error and maximizing membership privacy. Subsequently, Li *et al.* [10] introduced a defense method that combines Mixup with Maximum Mean Discrepancy (MMD) to reduce the generalization gap between members and non-members. Their approach interpolates between pairs of training samples using Mixup, and incorporates MMD-based regularization to align the distributions of prediction outputs for member and non-member data.

Knowledge distillation is used to train a student model using the soft output of a teacher model, with the aim of preserving accuracy while protecting sensitive data. Initial approaches, like that of Shejwalkar and Houmansadr [14], rely on public unlabeled datasets, but their effectiveness is limited by data availability. To address this, other methods such as complementary [26] and cross-distillation [6] have been developed to apply distillation directly on private data. More recently, self-distillation techniques like SELENA [19] and SEDMA [11] have emerged, allowing a single model to improve privacy and performance by leveraging its own predictions as pseudo-labels.

Despite the progress made, current defenses against MIAs still have limitations, and the privacy-utility trade-off remains a major challenge. It is therefore essential to develop more adaptive and lightweight defenses capable of ensuring an optimal privacy-utility trade-off.

3 Preliminaries and Problem Formulation

In this section, we present the key concepts and their associated notation used throughout this paper, followed by the formulation of the problem.

3.1 Preliminaries and Notation

Supervised ML. In this paper, we study supervised ML for classification tasks. We consider a classification model, denoted by $f : \mathbb{R}^d \rightarrow \mathbb{R}^k$, where $x = (x_1, \ldots, x_d) \in \mathbb{R}^d$ represents an input feature vector and $f(x) \in \mathbb{R}^k$ corresponds to a predicted probability distribution over the k possible classes. The model, parameterized by θ, is trained on a dataset $\mathcal{D}_{\text{tr}} = \{(x^{(n)}, y^{(n)})\}_{n=1}^{|\mathcal{D}_{\text{tr}}|}$, where $x^{(n)} \in \mathbb{R}^d$ denotes an input feature vector and $y^{(n)}$ is the corresponding ground truth label. The training objective is to minimize the average prediction loss over $\mathcal{D}_{\text{tr}}$:

$$\min_{\theta} \frac{1}{|\mathcal{D}_{\text{tr}}|} \sum_{n=1}^{|\mathcal{D}_{\text{tr}}|} \mathcal{L}\big(f_\theta(x^{(n)}), y^{(n)}\big) \tag{1}$$

where $|\mathcal{D}_{\text{tr}}|$ denotes the size of the training set and $\mathcal{L}$ is the prediction loss function (e.g., cross-entropy loss) measuring the discrepancy between the model's output and the ground truth labels. The model's output $f(x) \in \mathbb{R}^k$ satisfies $\sum_{j=1}^{k} f(x)_j = 1$, meaning it represents a valid probability distribution over the k possible classes. The predicted label is then obtained as $\hat{y} = \arg\max_j f(x)_j$.

Integrated Gradients is an attribution method used to estimate the contribution of each input feature x_i to the prediction of a model. It addresses the limitations of local gradient methods by integrating the gradients along a continuous path from a baseline input x' to the actual input x. Let f be a differentiable function representing the model, which maps an input $x = (x_1, x_2, ..., x_d) \in \mathbb{R}^d$ to an output $f(x)$. The integrated gradient of feature x_i is defined as:

$$\mathrm{IG}_i(x) = (x_i - x_i') \cdot \int_{\alpha=0}^{1} \frac{\partial f(x' + \alpha(x - x'))}{\partial x_i} \, d\alpha \tag{2}$$

here, x' is a baseline input, typically chosen as a zero vector or an average over the dataset, and $\alpha \in [0, 1]$ is a parameter that traces a straight-line path between the baseline and the actual input. The term $(x_i - x_i')$ represents the difference between the input feature and its baseline value. The integral $\int_0^1 \frac{\partial f(\cdot)}{\partial x_i} \, d\alpha$ computes the average gradient of the model output with respect to x_i along this path. The integrated gradient thus measures the cumulative effect of the feature x_i on the model output, accounting for its progressive impact from the baseline to the actual input.

A high value of $\mathrm{IG}_i(x)$ indicates a strong influence of x_i on the output $f(x)$, while a value close to zero suggests a weak or negligible contribution. Integrated gradients satisfy important theoretical properties such as *completeness* and *sensitivity*, making them a reliable tool for interpreting the predictions of neural networks.

3.2 Problem Formulation

We consider a setting with three main actors: the model provider, the attacker, and the defender.

Model Provider. We consider a machine learning service provider that owns a private training dataset D, potentially containing sensitive information. The provider trains a target classifier f, which we assume to be a neural network in this work. To simplify, we refer to the model provider's classifier as the *target classifier*. The model is then deployed as a cloud service or integrated into client-side applications (e.g., mobile or IoT apps), allowing users to query the model and obtain predictions for their own input samples x. The provider grants only black-box access to the model via a public API: users submit a query x and receive a prediction vector v, representing the posterior probability distribution over the possible classes. Formally, this interaction is defined as follows.

$$f : \boldsymbol{x} \longrightarrow \boldsymbol{v}$$

where $v_j \in v$ denotes the predicted probability that the input sample x belongs to the class j, and the prediction corresponds to the class with the highest probability, that is, $\arg\max_j v_j$.

Only the API interface is exposed to users, while the internal structure of the model f and the training dataset D remain private. As a result, users and potential attackers can interact with the model solely through its observable output, maintaining a black-box interaction framework.

Attacker. We consider a black-box adversary whose goal is to uncover information about the private training dataset D of the model provider. The attacker has only query access to the target classifier f through a public API, meaning they can submit input samples x and receive their associated prediction vectors $\boldsymbol{v} = f(x)$. To achieve their objective, the attacker leverages black-box MIAs [12,13,15]. In such attacks, the adversary trains a separate binary classifier, referred to as *attack classifier* $\mathcal{A}$, which takes as input the prediction vector $\boldsymbol{v}$ and estimates the membership status of the queried sample. Formally, the attack classifier is defined as follows:

$$\mathcal{A}(f(x)) \rightarrow [0, 1]$$

where an output close to 1 indicates that x probably belongs to the target model's training dataset, whereas a value close to 0 suggests non-membership.

To consider a strong threat model and a powerful adversary, we assume that the attacker has access to a subset of the training data of the target model. The attacker also has knowledge of the model architecture, the training algorithm and general functioning of the deployed defense mechanism. These assumptions allow us to model an informed attacker capable of training auxiliary models that mimic the behavior of the target model, thereby enabling a rigorous evaluation of our defense framework against realistic and advanced threats. We will discuss more details on how the attacker could train its attack classifier in Sect. 5.

Defender. The defender can be either the model provider or a trusted third party aiming to protect the confidentiality of training data against black-box MIAs. Unlike traditional methods that perturb the model outputs, our approach directly perturbs the input samples x before inference. Specifically, for each incoming query, a carefully optimized noise vector η is added to the input:

$$x' = x + \eta$$

where η is computed by solving a constrained optimization problem. The perturbed input x' is then used to obtain the prediction of the model. The perturbation η is designed to achieve two main objectives:

- Reducing the effectiveness of attacks: making the attack classifier inaccurate in distinguishing between members and non-members, thus protecting the confidentiality of the training set.
- Preserving model utility: ensuring that the added noise does not significantly degrade the predictive accuracy of the target model, maintaining performance close to the original model.

4 Our Defense Framework

We propose a defense framework to counter MIAs by injecting carefully controlled perturbations η into input queries during inference. The objective is to obscure exploitable patterns in the model behavior that could reveal training membership information, while preserving the predictive performance of the model. This balance between privacy and utility is achieved through a constrained optimization framework that governs the noise generation process. An overview of our defense mechanism is illustrated in Fig. 1. By increasing the uncertainty in the output of the model, the defense reduces the attacker's ability to distinguish members from non-members, while preserving the model's reliability through dedicated *security* and *utility* constraints.

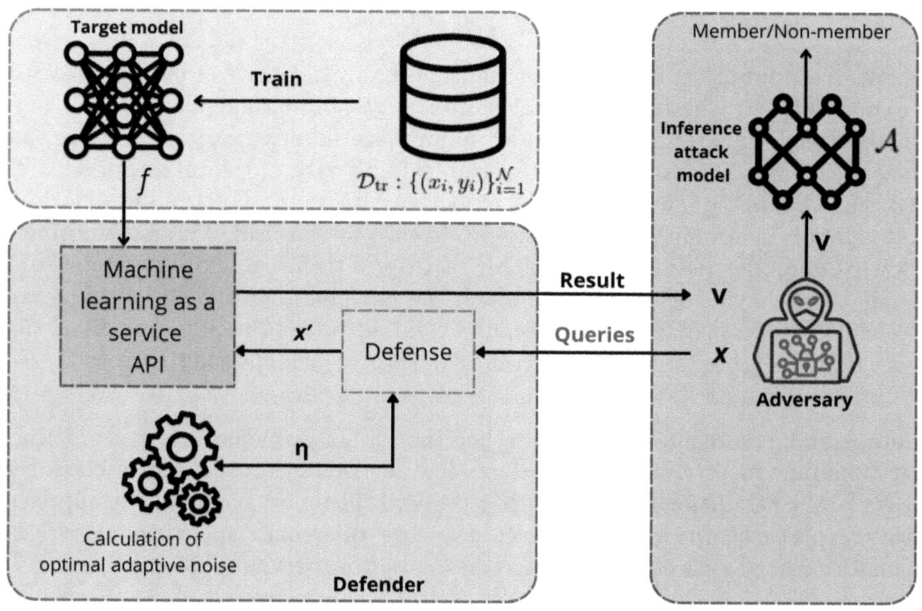

Fig. 1. Overview of the Proposed Defense Framework Against Black-Box Membership Inference Attacks in MLaaS.

The *security constraint* ensures that the injected noise reduces the model's overconfidence by limiting the probability assigned to the correct class. This limitation is critical, as highly confident predictions are typically characteristic of training samples, making their membership more easily detectable. By enforcing an upper bound on the predicted probability for the correct class, the defense introduces controlled uncertainty that obscures membership-revealing signals. This constraint is formalized as follows:

$$f(x + \eta)_y \leq \gamma \tag{3}$$

where $f(x+\eta)_y$ is the probability assigned to the correct class after perturbation, and $\gamma > 0$ is a threshold that limits the maximum allowable confidence. By preventing the emergence of sharp confidence peaks, this constraint weakens the signals exploitable by MIAs, particularly when the correct class strongly dominates the others.

However, regulating this value alone is not sufficient. Even if the true-class probability is capped, the gap between this class and the competing classes may still remain excessively large. Such a wide margin is itself a strong membership indicator, since member samples typically produce much sharper prediction gaps than non-members. To address this issue, we introduce a second constraint that explicitly limits the difference between the probability of the true class and that of the most competitive incorrect class. This constraint is defined as:

$$f(x+\eta)_y - \max_{j \neq y} f(x+\eta)_j \leq \delta \tag{4}$$

where $\delta > 0$ denotes the maximum allowed margin. This condition prevents the model from producing an abnormally large separation between the correct class and the others, thereby enforcing a more moderate and less exploitable prediction profile.

Together, these two security constraints keep the model's predictions in a regime of controlled ambiguity. By simultaneously limiting the true-class probability and preventing excessive separation between classes, they make member and non-member outputs more indistinguishable, significantly reducing the distinctive signals exploited by membership inference attacks.

To ensure *utility*, we impose a constraint that maintains the consistency of the prediction of the model before and after perturbation. Specifically, the perturbed input must still be classified into the same category as the original input, thereby preventing the perturbation from causing the sample to cross the decision boundary. This constraint is formalized as:

$$\arg\max_j f(x+\eta)_j = \arg\max_j f(x)_j \tag{5}$$

where arg max returns the predicted class with the highest probability. By preserving the decision boundary for perturbed samples, the model retains its classification accuracy despite the injected perturbation. However, the arg max function is not differentiable, making this constraint incompatible with differentiable optimization methods used to compute the optimal noise. To resolve this issue, we refine the constraint by using *integrated gradients* to guide the allocation of noise between features according to their relative importance to the prediction of the model. The underlying idea is that the features do not contribute equally: perturbing highly influential features could significantly alter the decision of the model, while perturbing the less critical ones introduces uncertainty without substantially affecting the accuracy of the classification. Let $\eta = (\eta_1, \ldots, \eta_d)$ be the perturbation vector to be applied to $x = (x_1, \ldots, x_d)$, we formulate the constraint as follows:

$$|\eta_i| \leq \epsilon \cdot \left(1 - \beta \cdot \frac{|\mathrm{IG}_i(x)|}{\max_j |\mathrm{IG}_j(x)|}\right) \tag{6}$$

where $\epsilon > 0$ is a noise budget, $\beta > 0$ is a weighting parameter, and $\mathrm{IG}_i(x)$ denotes the integrated gradients of the feature i. This design ensures that only minimal noise is added to the features most critical to the model's output, preserving the decision boundary, while allowing greater perturbations on less important features to strengthen privacy protection.

Furthermore, for samples located near the decision boundary, even small perturbations may alter the predicted label. To address this, we introduce an additional constraint based on the *local robustness* of the model, limiting the magnitude of the general perturbation according to the local sensitivity and confidence margin of the model. we formulate the constraint as follows:

$$||\eta||_2 \leq \frac{\Delta f(x)}{||\nabla f(x)||_2} \tag{7}$$

where $\Delta f(x)$ represents the difference in score between the two most probable classes, and $||\nabla f(x)||_2$ denotes the norm of the input gradient, reflecting the local sensitivity of the model. To prevent prediction shifts, this constraint limits perturbations in cases of high model sensitivity or tight decision boundaries.

These two utility constraints jointly ensure that the perturbed input remains correctly classified. By minimizing noise in critical features and bounding the overall perturbation using local robustness, the defense preserves the decision boundary and prevents misclassifications.

Combining all elements, the overall objective is to minimize the magnitude of the perturbation while ensuring compliance with both security and utility constraints.

$$\begin{aligned} \min_{\eta} \quad & ||\eta||_2 \\ \text{s.t.} \quad & f(x+\eta)_y \leq \gamma \\ & f(x+\eta)_y - \max_{j \neq y} f(x+\eta)_j \leq \delta \\ & |\eta_i| \leq \epsilon \cdot \left(1 - \beta \cdot \frac{|\mathrm{IG}_i(x)|}{\max_j |\mathrm{IG}_j(x)|}\right), \quad \forall i = 1, \ldots, d \\ & ||\eta||_2 \leq \frac{\Delta f(x)}{||\nabla f(x)||_2} \end{aligned} \tag{8}$$

This formulation ensures minimal perturbation while maintaining both privacy guaranties and model performance. The perturbation procedure is summarized in Algorithm 1.

Algorithm 1. Inference-Time Perturbation Strategy

Require: Incoming query x, trained model f
Ensure: Protected prediction on perturbed input $f(x')$

1: Compute Integrated Gradients: $\mathrm{IG}(x)$
2: Compute prediction margin: $\Delta f(x)$
3: Compute gradient norm: $\|\nabla f(x)\|_2$
4: Solve the constrained optimization problem to obtain optimized perturbation η
5: Perturb input: $x' \leftarrow x + \eta$
6: **return** protected prediction: $f(x')$

5 Experimentation

In this section, we present an experimental evaluation of our proposed defense mechanism. We first describe the experimental setup and the evaluation metrics used to assess the privacyâĂŞutility trade-off. Then, we analyze the experimental results to demonstrate the effectiveness of our approach in mitigating MIAs.

5.1 Experimental Setup

Datasets. We perform experiments on three widely used benchmark datasets for MIAs: Purchase100, Texas100 and CIFAR100

Purchase100. Consists of 197,324 customer purchase records, each with 600 binary features that indicate whether a specific item was purchased. The classification task is to predict customer shopping patterns in 100 classes.

Texas100. Contains 67,330 hospital discharge records, each with 6,170 binary characteristics that represent the presence or absence of specific symptoms. The goal is to predict the medical procedure assigned to the patient among 100 classes.

CIFAR100. Is an image classification dataset that has 60,000 images in 100 object classes. Each image has a size of 32×32×3.

Target Model. We use a fully connected neural network as the target model for the Purchase100 and Texas100 datasets. The architecture includes four hidden layers with sizes [1024, 512, 256, 128]. Each hidden layer uses the ReLU activation function, while the output layer applies a softmax function to predict the probabilities of more than 100 classes. The models are trained using the Adam optimizer, with the cross-entropy loss function, a learning rate of 0.001, over 100 epochs. For the CIFAR100 dataset, we employ a ResNet-18 architecture as the target model. Training is performed using the SGD optimizer with a learning rate of 0.1, momentum of 0.9, and the cross-entropy loss function, over 200 epochs. The datasets used in our experiments are summarized in Table 1.

Table 1. Dataset splits used in our experiments. "Train" refers to the data used to train the target model, while "Test" denotes the data used to evaluate its accuracy. "Known" represents the portion of the training data accessible to the adversary for constructing the attack model. "Target" corresponds to the data used to evaluate membership inference attacks, comprising an equal number of member and non-member.

Dataset	Train	Test	Known	Target
Purchase100	20,000	20,000	10,000	10,000
Texas100	20,000	10,000	5,000	5,000
CIFAR100	30,000	10,000	5,000	5,000

Inference Attack Model. In our evaluation, we adopt a black-box MIAs strategy. A shadow model is first trained using half of the target model's training data, along with a set of non-member samples drawn from the same distribution as the training data. The purpose of this model is to replicate the behavior of the target model and generate the output required to train a binary attack model, which aims to determine whether a given sample is a member or not of the target model's training set. The attack model consists of three fully connected subnets, each operating on the prediction vector, the one-hot encoded label, and their concatenation. Each subnetwork uses a ReLU activation function, with weights initialized from a normal distribution $\mathcal{N}(0, 0.01)$ and biases initialized to zero. The model is trained using the Adam optimizer, with a learning rate of 0.001 for 100 epochs, with the cross-entropy loss function. The final output is a membership probability that indicates the likelihood that a given sample belongs to the target model's training data.

We consider two attack models. The standard attack model is trained on the raw outputs of the shadow model, while the adaptive attack model assumes knowledge of the deployed inference-time defense. In this case, the adversary reproduces the perturbation locally on its auxiliary examples, collects the defended shadow output, and trains the classifier on these defended vectors. This setup allows the attacker to better approximate the behavior of the defended target model and to evaluate whether privacy gains persist under stronger adversares.

Evaluation Metrics. To evaluate our defense, we assess both the utility of the model and the protection of privacy using the following metrics:

Inference accuracy and *Attack AUC (Area Under the ROC Curve):* measure the attack model's ability to distinguish members from non-members. Inference Accuracy uses a fixed threshold of 0.5, while Attack AUC evaluates performance across all thresholds using the ROC curve, which plots the TPR against the FPR. Values close to 0.5 indicate low attack effectiveness and strong privacy protection.

Classification accuracy: measures the proportion of samples correctly classified by the model on an evaluation set, reflecting its overall performance.

Utility loss: refers to the degradation in classification accuracy introduced by the defense, measured as the difference in accuracy between the undefended and defended models. A smaller value indicates a minimal impact on performance.

5.2 Experimental Results

We evaluate the effectiveness of our proposed defense mechanism against black-box MIAs. To this end, we conducted a comparative study involving four models under the same training and attack configurations: an undefended model, trained without any privacy-preserving mechanism and serving as the baseline; a DP-SGD model, where noise is directly injected during the training process to ensure differential privacy; a uniform noise mechanism, an inference-time defense where a fixed amount of noise is added uniformly to each query, regardless of feature importance; and our adaptive noise mechanism, an inference-time defense that perturbs queries through a constrained optimization framework, with injected noise adaptively modulated based on the importance of input features.

To assess the privacy guarantees of each defense strategy, we report the attack AUC, which quantifies the effectiveness of MIAs across all decision thresholds. As illustrated in Fig. 2, the undefended model exhibits high AUC scores, indicating strong susceptibility to MIAs. The uniform noise mechanism reduces the AUC to 58%. In contrast, our adaptive noise mechanism significantly reduces the AUC on the Purchase100 and CIFAR100 datasets, reaching the optimal value of 50%—equivalent to random guessing—thus indicating strong privacy protection. On the Texas100 dataset, DP-SGD proves to be the most effective, reducing the AUC to 51% and demonstrating its relative strength in this setting.

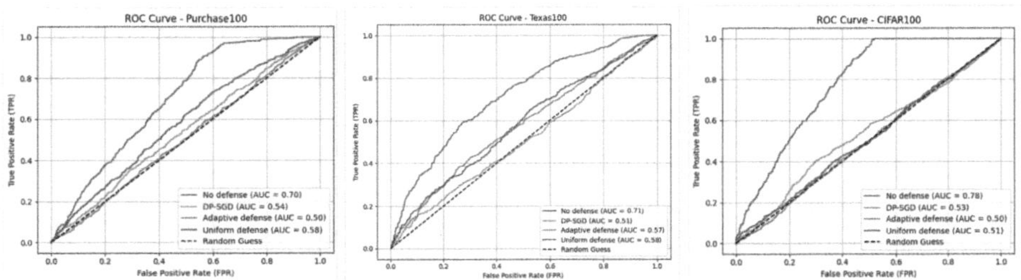

Fig. 2. Attack AUC Under Different Strategies.

Then, we evaluate the utility of each model by assessing their classification performance on an evaluation dataset. As illustrated in Fig. 3, the adaptive noise mechanism maintains a high classification accuracy, very close to that of the undefended model across all three datasets. In contrast, the uniform noise mechanism significantly degrades utility on both the Texas100 and CIFAR100 datasets, while DP-SGD severely impacts performance on Texas100 and performs less effectively on the others. This indicates that our method effectively preserves classification accuracy.

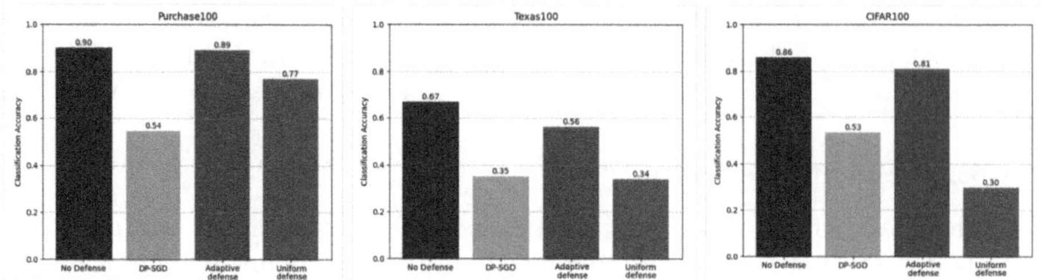

Fig. 3. Classification Accuracy under Different Defense Strategies.

Finally, to better understand the privacy-utility trade-off, we analyze the relationship between inference attack accuracy and utility loss. As shown in Fig. 4, the undefended models exhibit both high inference accuracy and zero utility loss, confirming their vulnerability to MIAs. In contrast, our adaptive noise mechanism achieves the most favorable balance, simultaneously minimizing the attack success rate and maintaining minimal utility loss. The uniform noise mechanism shows moderate effectiveness, reducing inference accuracy to some extent but at the cost of significant utility loss, particularly on the CIFAR100 and Texas100 datasets. However, DP-SGD achieves relatively low inference accuracy, especially on Texas100, but leads to a degradation in utility, thus indicating a suboptimal trade-off between privacy and performance.

These results confirm that our adaptive noise mechanism provides the best trade-off between privacy protection and model performance. Moreover, our defense, evaluated in both standard and adaptive attack scenarios, achieves the same AUC and inference accuracy results in each case, demonstrating that it effectively reduces the statistical gap between the output distributions of member and non-member samples and limits any advantage an adaptive attacker could gain.

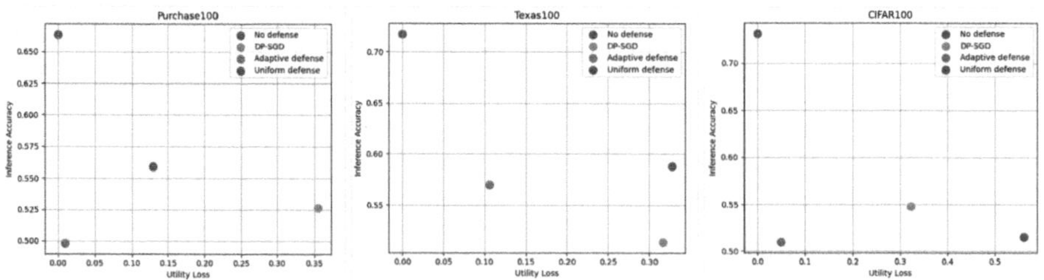

Fig. 4. Privacy-Utility Trade-off: Inference Accuracy Vs. Utility Loss.

6 Conclusion

In this paper, we present a novel defense against black-box membership inference attacks based on adaptive noise injection guided by feature importance. The originality of our approach lies in perturbing input queries during the inference phase, adjusted according to the relevance of each feature, thereby enhancing privacy protection while preserving prediction utility. The method operates directly at inference time, requires no retraining, and can be seamlessly integrated into MLaaS systems.

Our framework is built on two complementary pillars. On one hand, a security constraint aims to reduce the model's overconfidence by capping the probability assigned to the correct class and by enforcing a maximum allowable margin over the alternatives, thereby introducing controlled uncertainty. On the other hand, a utility constraint leverages integrated gradients and local robustness to limit the impact of noise on the most influential features, while controlling its overall magnitude to prevent misclassifications.

Experimental results on the benchmark datasets Purchase100, Texas100 and CIFAR100 demonstrate that our method significantly reduces the success rate of black-box MIAs without compromising classification performance. These results highlight the effectiveness of our adaptive perturbation strategy in achieving a practical trade-off between privacy protection and model utility.

In future work, we plan to refine and lighten the current optimization constraints to reduce computational overhead while maintaining robustness. Additionally, we intend to integrate a dynamic query filtering mechanism, designed to trigger perturbation only for inputs deemed high-risk, thus avoiding costly and often unnecessary systematic application. We also aim to extend our framework to other attack scenarios and evaluate its scalability across various model architectures and application domains.

References

1. Abadi, M., et al.: Deep learning with differential privacy. In: Proceedings of the 2016 ACM SIGSAC Conference on Computer and Communications Security, pp. 308–318 (2016)
2. Bertran, M., Tang, S., Roth, A., Kearns, M.J., Morgenstern, J.H., Wu, S.Z.: Scalable membership inference attacks via quantile regression. In: Advances in Neural Information Processing Systems, vol. 36, pp. 314–330 (2023)
3. Carlini, N., Chien, S., Nasr, M., Song, S., Terzis, A., Tramèr, F.: Membership inference attacks from first principles. In: 2022 IEEE Symposium on Security and Privacy (SP), pp. 1897–1914. IEEE (2022)
4. Chen, Z., Pattabiraman, K.: A method to facilitate membership inference attacks in deep learning models (2024). arXiv preprint, https://arxiv.org/abs/2407.01919
5. Chen, Z., Pattabiraman, K.: Overconfidence is a dangerous thing: Mitigating membership inference attacks by enforcing less confident prediction. In: Proceedings of the NDSS Symposium (2024)

6. Chourasia, R., Enkhtaivan, B., Ito, K., Mori, J., Teranishi, I., Tsuchida, H.: Knowledge cross-distillation for membership privacy (2021). arXiv preprint. https://arxiv.org/abs/2111.01363
7. Jia, J., Salem, A., Backes, M., Zhang, Y., Gong, N.Z.: Memguard: defending against black-box membership inference attacks via adversarial examples. In: Proceedings of the 2019 ACM SIGSAC Conference on Computer and Communications Security, pp. 259–274 (2019)
8. Kassa, R., Adi, K., Bouhaddi, M.: Optimal noise injection on training data: a defense against membership inference attacks. In: Proceedings of the 22nd International Conference on Security and Cryptography - Volume 1: SECRYPT, pp. 531–538. INSTICC, SciTePress (2025). https://doi.org/10.5220/0013639300003979
9. Leino, K., Fredrikson, M.: Stolen memories: leveraging model memorization for calibrated White-Box membership inference. In: Proceedings of the 29th USENIX Security Symposium (USENIX Security 20), pp. 1605–1622 (2020)
10. Li, J., Li, N., Ribeiro, B.: Membership inference attacks and defenses in classification models. In: Proceedings of the Eleventh ACM Conference on Data and Application Security and Privacy, pp. 5–16 (2021)
11. Nakai, T., Wang, Y., Yoshida, K., Fujino, T.: SEDMA: self-distillation with model aggregation for membership privacy. In: Proceedings on Privacy Enhancing Technologies (2024)
12. Nasr, M., Shokri, R., Houmansadr, A.: Machine learning with membership privacy using adversarial regularization. In: Proceedings of the 2018 ACM SIGSAC Conference on Computer and Communications Security, pp. 634–646 (2018)
13. Salem, A., Zhang, Y., Humbert, M., Berrang, P., Fritz, M., Backes, M.: ML-leaks: model and data independent membership inference attacks and defenses on machine learning models (2018). arXiv preprint. https://arxiv.org/abs/1806.01246
14. Shejwalkar, V., Houmansadr, A.: Membership privacy for machine learning models through knowledge transfer. In: Proceedings of the AAAI Conference on Artificial Intelligence, pp. 9549–9557 (2021)
15. Shokri, R., Stronati, M., Song, C., Shmatikov, V.: Membership inference attacks against machine learning models. In: 2017 IEEE Symposium on Security and Privacy (SP), pp. 3–18. IEEE (2017)
16. Song, L., Mittal, P.: Systematic evaluation of privacy risks of machine learning models. In: 30th USENIX Security Symposium (USENIX Security 21), pp. 2615–2632. USENIX (2021)
17. Srivastava, N., Hinton, G., Krizhevsky, A., Sutskever, I., Salakhutdinov, R.: Dropout: a simple way to prevent neural networks from overfitting. J. Mach. Learn. Res. **15**(1), 1929–1958 (2014)
18. Tabassi, E., Burns, K.J., Hadjimichael, M., Molina-Markham, A.D., Sexton, J.T.: A taxonomy and terminology of adversarial machine learning. Interagency or internal report, National Institute of Standards and Technology (2019). https://doi.org/10.6028/NIST.IR.8269-draft
19. Tang, X., Mahloujifar, S., Song, L., Shejwalkar, V., Nasr, M., Houmansadr, A.: Mitigating membership inference attacks by Self-Distillation through a novel ensemble architecture. In: Proceedings of the 31st USENIX Security Symposium (USENIX Security 22), pp. 1433–1450 (2022)
20. Wen, Y., et al.: Canary in a coalmine: better membership inference with ensembled adversarial queries (2022). arXiv preprint. https://arxiv.org/abs/2210.10750
21. Wikipedia contributors: General Data Protection Regulation (2021)

22. Ye, J., Maddi, A., Murakonda, S.K., Bindschaedler, V., Shokri, R.: Enhanced membership inference attacks against machine learning models. In: Proceedings of the 2022 ACM SIGSAC Conference on Computer and Communications Security, pp. 3093–3106. ACM (2022)
23. Yeom, S., Giacomelli, I., Fredrikson, M., Jha, S.: Privacy risk in machine learning: analyzing the connection to overfitting. In: 2018 IEEE 31st Computer Security Foundations Symposium (CSF), pp. 268–282. IEEE (2018)
24. Zarifzadeh, S., Liu, P., Shokri, R.: Low-cost high-power membership inference attacks (2024). arXiv preprint. https://arxiv.org/abs/2312.03262
25. Zhang, T., He, Z., Lee, R.B.: Privacy-preserving machine learning through data obfuscation (2018). arXiv preprint. https://arxiv.org/abs/1807.01860
26. Zheng, J., Cao, Y., Wang, H.: Resisting membership inference attacks through knowledge distillation. Neurocomputing **452**, 114–126 (2021)

Generating Causal Logs to Explain Attacks

Viet-Huy Ha(✉), Vincent Gauthier, and Eric Totel

SAMOVAR, Télécom SudParis, Institut Polytechnique de Paris, 91120 Palaiseau, France
viet-huy.ha@telecom-sudparis.eu

Abstract. The growing complexity and volume of cyber threats demand more efficient methods for intrusion detection and incident analysis. Traditional Security Information and Event Management (SIEM) systems often struggle with multi-step attacks, as they lack explicit causal links among individual events. To address this limitation, we propose a causal log generation framework that leverages extended Berkeley Packet Filter (eBPF) technology to intercept system calls in real time. By assigning vector timestamps to relevant events, our method dynamically constructs causal graphs, enabling precise reconstruction of an attack's progression across system boundaries. We evaluate our approach against the real-world attack scenario, such as Command and Control (C&C) backdoor activities, demonstrating that causal logs greatly improve traceability and forensic insight compared to conventional SIEM-based correlation. We further discuss the scalability challenges of large-scale deployments and how causal logging may transform threat hunting and incident response.

Keywords: intrusion detection · attack explanation · causal logs · causality graphs

1 Introduction

Intrusion detection and threat analysis are usually restricted by the inherent complexity of large-scale systems and the sophistication of modern cyberattacks. Security Information and Event Management (SIEM) solutions aim to address these challenges by gathering data from diverse sources (system logs, network traffic, application events, and more) and applying various correlation rules or anomaly detection algorithms. Although SIEMs play a critical role in centralizing and organizing security data, correlating multi-step attacks remains a significant hurdle. Typical logs record discrete events without capturing the deeper, causal relationships that connect them. As a result, reconstructing an incident (or even detecting one in progress) can be error-prone and time-consuming.

Recent advances in kernel instrumentation, notably eBPF (extended Berkeley Packet Filter), have paved the way for finer-grained visibility into system

K. Adi et al. (Eds.): CRiSIS 2025, LNCS 16295, pp. 302–318, 2026.
https://doi.org/10.1007/978-3-032-20732-6_19

activities. By intercepting system calls and associating them with corresponding processes, files, and network sockets, eBPF provides an opportunity to generate more nuanced logging data. Instead of simply recording an event, a causal log explicitly encodes how one event leads to another via a series of causal chains, thus creating a clearer narrative of how an attacker moves through the system.

In this paper, we introduce a new framework for generating and analyzing causal logs in real time. Specifically, we describe how eBPF can be used to monitor relevant system calls in a lightweight manner, how vector timestamps can capture the partial ordering of concurrent events, and how these enhanced logs can be translated into causality graphs. We then demonstrate the efficacy of our approach by applying it to the common attack scenario: Command and Control (C&C) backdoor compromises. Through this example, we show how capturing causal links facilitates more accurate attack explanation and assists security analysts in piecing together even highly stealthy, multi-step intrusions. Finally, we discuss the broader benefits and practical considerations surrounding large-scale deployments of causal logging.

2 State of the Art

2.1 Causal Logs

Causal logs have been referenced in various studies [1,3], but there is no widely accepted definition of the term. Most existing methodologies retrospectively infer causality from conventional logs, analyzing past system activities to reconstruct event sequences. This retrospective approach suffers from inherent limitations, such as insufficient granularity, noise, and difficulty distinguishing genuine causal relationships from coincidental correlations. Thus, threat detection and forensic investigations remain inefficient, as analysts must manually infer attack pathways from disparate log entries.

Unlike conventional logs, an explicitly causal log would inherently record causal relationships at event occurrence time, significantly enhancing accuracy and reducing the manual effort needed during forensic analyses. Systematically embedding causality into logs provides an improved basis for swiftly reconstructing multi-step attack scenarios.

2.2 Causality

In distributed systems, causality denotes how events affect each other, guiding the logical order of operations critical for maintaining consistency, debugging, and enhancing security [2]. Distributed causality is traditionally divided into:

- *Internal Causality*: Sequential dependencies within a single process.
- *External Causality*: Dependencies across processes mediated through communication (e.g., message passing or shared resources).

Lamport's Logical Clocks [2] provide a foundational approach to capturing causality, utilizing monotonically increasing scalar timestamps. Despite their effectiveness in sequencing events, scalar clocks do not fully capture concurrent events across different processes.

Advanced frameworks by D'Ausbourg [6] and Xosanavongsa [5] further refine causal dependency models by incorporating object states and contextual factors. These models effectively handle heterogeneous systems involving complex interactions among diverse objects and contexts, essential for accurately mapping multi-stage security incidents (Fig. 1).

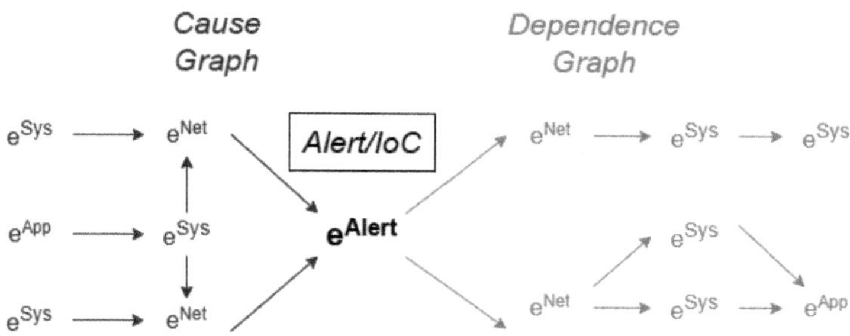

Fig. 1. Xosanavongsa's causal dependency frameworks [5].

3 Xosanavongsa's Model

Addressing limitations of traditional causal frameworks, Xosanavongsa's model integrates Lamport's "happened-before" relation and D'Ausbourg's object-based dependencies, enriched by runtime context [4,5]. This contextual approach is particularly beneficial for tracing intricate, multi-object interactions in security breaches.

3.1 Contextual Action and Sessions

A contextual action $(a, (o, t))$ is an operation performed by an object o at a specific state (o, t). Objects are categorized as either active (processes, interfaces) or passive (files, pipes), clearly pinpointing each action's context. Sessions group sequences of causally linked actions within an object, formally defined as consecutive contextual actions without causal overlaps:

$$Session_n(o) = \{(a_i, (o, t_i)/(o, t_i) \rightarrow (o, t_{i+1})\}$$

This session-based grouping aids in isolating coherent causal sequences within objects, crucial for detailed attack reconstruction.

3.2 Contextual Action Causal Dependency

Xosanavongsa introduces a contextual causal dependency operator ($\mapsto$), extending Lamport and D'Ausbourg frameworks to comprehensively cover both internal (within-object) and external (cross-object) interactions:

- Same-object dependency occurs within continuous sessions, following chronological order.
- Cross-object dependency emerges through information flow or explicit message exchanges between distinct objects or processes.

By explicitly distinguishing between session-based dependencies and cross-object interactions, Xosanavongsa's framework accurately captures both local and global causalities.

3.3 Contextual Events

A contextual event (e, o, t_e) pairs an observable logged event with its object and timestamp. Observations from contextual actions generate sets of logged events that facilitate establishing event-level causal dependencies. Events are causally dependent if their underlying contextual actions share defined causal relationships:

$$(e_1, o_1, t_{e_1}) \rightharpoonup (e_2, o_2, t_{e_2}) \text{ if and only if } (a_1, (o_1, t1)) \mapsto (a_2, (o_2, t2))$$

Thus, the event-level causal dependency directly inherits the causal structure from contextual actions, ensuring comprehensive causality capture within the generated logs. This approach precisely reflects the true system dynamics, significantly enhancing the accuracy of forensic analysis and threat detection.

4 Generating Causal Logs

4.1 Computing Causality with Vector Clocks

Capturing accurate causal relationships among events in a distributed system is challenging due to the lack of a global clock and the possibility of concurrent operations. Early work by Lamport introduced logical (scalar) clocks, which assign monotonically increasing integers to events while preserving a "happened-before" ordering [2] (Fig. 2). However, Lamport's scalar clocks do not fully capture concurrency: if two events occur in parallel in different processes, scalar timestamps alone can erroneously place one before the other.

Definitions and Update Rules. Let $p_i \in \mathbf{P}$ be a set of processes. We denote the vector clock for process $p_i \in \mathbf{P}$ as V_{p_i} with size $|\mathbf{P}|$. For instance, the entry k in the vector V_{p_i} tracks p_i's current knowledge logical time about the process p_k. The following rules describe how vector clocks are updated:

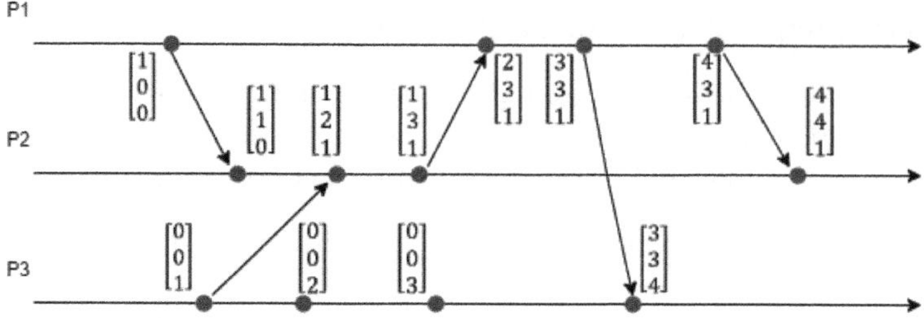

Fig. 2. Lamport Vector clock.

- *Internal Event in p_i* (e.g., a system call within the process): $V_{p_i}[i] \leftarrow V_{p_i}[i]+1$ This increments the local clock entry whenever an internal event occurs in process p_i.
- *Send event occurs in p_i* (e.g., sending data via a socket or pipe):
  - Increment the local entry: $V_{p_i}[i] \leftarrow V_{p_i}[i]+1$
  - Attach the updated vector clock V_{p_i} to the outgoing message.
- *p_i receives message from p_j* (e.g., reading from a socket, pipe, or file where causal data originated)
  - Upon receipt of a vector V_{p_j} from sender p_j:
    $V_{p_i}[j] \leftarrow max(V_{p_i}[j], V_{p_j}[j])$;
  - Then, increment the local clock entry: $V_{p_i}[i] \leftarrow V_{p_i}[i]+1$

These operations ensure that for any two events a and b in the system, a "happened-before" b (denoted $a \rightarrow b$) implies $V(a) < V(b)$ elementwise (i.e., $V(a) \neq V(b)$ and $V(a)[k] \leq V(b)[k]$ for all k, with at least one strict inequality).

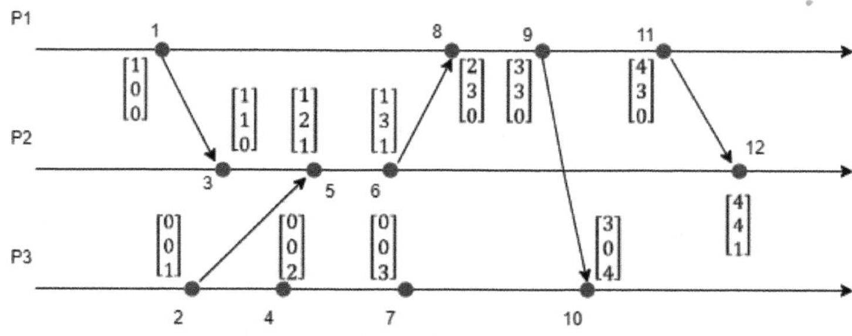

Fig. 3. Event-Based Vector Clocks.

Direct-Dependency Optimization. While vector clocks faithfully capture causal ordering, maintaining or merging full vector clocks for every single system event can be expensive. Fowler and Zwaenepoel [7] proposed a direct-dependency technique, wherein each process tracks only the event identifiers on which it directly depends instead of carrying a full vector of size N. This smaller structure is sometimes called a "dependency vector" or "DDD" (direct dependency descriptor). Whenever a process receives an event from another process, it merges just the relevant direct-dependency information; at the end of execution—or when constructing a global view—these direct dependencies can be expanded back into full vector clocks [9]. This approach often reduces overhead significantly and works especially well if the number of active processes N is large or if system calls are frequent. The mechanism of Direct-Dependency is presented as follows:

1. *Dependency Vector*: Each process p_i maintains a dependency vector D_i which record the latest event from each process that directly influences p_i. Initially, each element of D_i is set to zero.
2. *Internal Events*: When an event occurs at p_i, the corresponding entry in the dependency vector is incremented: $D_i[i] := D_i[i] + 1$
3. *Sending Message*: When p_i sends a message to P_j, it piggybacks the updated value of its dependency vector related to p_i (i.e., $D_i[i]$)
4. *Receiving Messages*: Upon receiving a message from p_i, process P_j updates its dependency vector as follows: $D_i[j] = max(D_i[j], D_j[j])$ This operation ensures that P_j's dependency vector reflects the most recent events from p_i that directly influence P_j.

4.2 Generating Vector Clock

Building on the foundational concepts of Lamport vector clocks [2], direct vector clocks [7] and direct dependency [8], we propose an event-centric approach to maintaining vector clock in Fig. 3. Rather than simply updating a single vector clock per process, we assign a dedicated vector clock to each security-relevant event (i.e., each captured system call). By doing so, we capture the causal state precisely at the moment the event is triggered, making it much easier to resolve interactions among multiple processes. By assigning individual indexes to events, it becomes easier to track their respective vector timestamps, facilitating efficient updates and queries. This refined approach enhances the precision of causal relationship tracking, improving the system's capability to identify intricate event sequences and detect multi-step attacks with greater accuracy.

Motivation for Event-Based Vector Clock. Traditional process-level vector clocks increment and merge timestamps whenever a process sends or receives data. While effective, this approach can become less granular when dealing with frequent, concurrent events. In practice, multi-step attacks often hinge on very specific system calls (for instance, a `write()` that plants malicious data, or a `clone()` that spawns a new thread of execution). Maintaining a process-wide vector clock alone risks obscuring these discrete causal "handoffs".

By contrast, event-based vector clocks reflect the system's causal state at the precise moment an event occurs. That distinction is crucial for:

- Fine-Grained Causal Links: If multiple sends occur concurrently, each send event can be assigned a distinct timestamp. Subsequent receive events can then determine the specific send event(s) they are causally dependent on.
- Direct Dependencies: Inspired by the Fowler and Zwaenepoel approach [7], we store only the minimal set of dependency pointers or timestamps needed for each event. This prevents vector-clock inflation and can reduce overhead in systems where the number of processes is large.

Event-Based Vector Clock Technique. Our method expands on the Direct Dependency model proposed in [7]. The essence of this technique is to record, for each event e, only the vector clock (or partial vector) that pertains to the processes directly influencing e. Formally:

- *Initialization*:
  - *Event Set* $\mathbf{E}$:
    Define a set of events $\mathbf{E}$ with $|\mathbf{E}|$ indicating the total number of events.
  - *Process Identifiers* δ:
    Create an array or structure δ of size $|\mathbf{E}|$, used to record which process generated each event. In other words, $\delta[e]$ identifies the process to which event e belongs.
  - *Processes Set* $\mathbf{P}$:
    Let $\mathbf{P}$ be a set of processes, with $|\mathbf{P}|$ denoting the total number of processes.
  - *Process Vector Clocks*:
    For each process $p_i \in \mathbf{P}$, initialize a vector clock V_{p_i} of length $|\mathbf{P}|$. Set all entries of V_{p_i} to 0, including the local entry $V_{p_i}[i]$: $V_{p_i}[k] \leftarrow 0$ for $\forall k \in [1..|\mathbf{P}|]$
  - *Event Vector Clocks*:
    We initialize a vector clock $\mathcal{V}_e$ of size $|\mathbf{P}|$ for each event in $\mathbf{E}$:
    $\mathcal{V}_e[k] \leftarrow 0$ for $\forall k \in [1..|\mathbf{P}|]$
  - *Sequence Number* $\mathcal{K}$:
    Define a global sequence number $\mathcal{K} = 0$. Each time a new event is generated, $\mathcal{K}$ is incremented. This variable serves both as a running total of all events and as the unique sequence number assigned to each new event.
- *Event Creation*: Whenever an event e occurs (e.g., a system call in process p_i):
  - Assign $\mathbf{E}_e = \mathcal{K}$.
  - Increment the local process vector entry $V_{p_i}[i]$ by 1.
  - Increment the global event counter $\mathcal{K}$ by 1.
  - Assign $\delta_e = p_i$ to record that process p_i is the owner of event e.
  - Calculate vector clock of e:
    - $\mathcal{V}_e[p_i] = V_{p_i}[i]$
    - If $V_{p_i}[i] \geq 2$, let $k = V_{p_i}[i] - 1$ (denotes the previous event of e in p_i), we have $\mathcal{V}_e[p]{=}\mathcal{V}_k[p]$ for $\forall p \in \mathbf{P}$ $(p \neq p_i)$.

- *External Merges*: If this event corresponds to receiving data from event e' in another process p_j (e.g., via `read()`, `recv()`, or a file operation that another process wrote), we update $\mathcal{V}_e$ by $\mathcal{V}_e[j] = \mathcal{V}_{e'}[j]$.
- *Dependency Linking*: Because each event e explicitly stores its vector $\mathcal{V}_e$, it is straightforward to reconstruct a global partial order or to convert partial vectors to a full vector clock if needed.

This event-level logging approach precisely captures causal relationships by assigning a dedicated vector timestamp to each system event at the exact time of its occurrence, rather than maintaining a single clock per process. Consequently, we can directly reconstruct accurate causal dependencies between events, enabling detailed visualization and analysis through causal dependency graphs.

Constructing the Full Vector Clock. Once each event e is annotated with its own vector clock V_e, we can construct a process-level or global-level timeline. Techniques such as those described by Baldy et al. [9] allow us to "inflate" or expand these direct-dependency vectors into full-fledged vector clocks for all events in a system. In brief:

1. We collect all events $\mathbf{E} = \{e_1, e_2, ..., e_k\}$.
2. For each event $e_i \in \mathbf{E}$ we retrieve partial vector $\mathcal{V}_{e_i}$.
3. We perform incremental merges across events that share direct dependencies, ensuring that every transitive relationship is accounted for.
4. The result is a consistent vector-time assignment that respects Lamport's happened-before relation while preserving concurrency where no causal link exists.

The main advantage is that we do not carry a large vector for every operation upfront. Instead, we store the smaller direct dependencies at each event. Only if a full system-level view is required (e.g., for a forensic timeline or an offline correlation step) do we synthesize the final vector clocks.

4.3 Using eBPF to Intercept System Calls

The Extended Berkeley Packet Filter (eBPF) is a innovative Linux kernel framework that offers an efficient and adaptable means of monitoring system calls, making it well-suited to capturing the causal links across diverse system events. Through carefully sandboxed execution of custom programs within the kernel, eBPF delivers real-time tracing functionality (without requiring any modifications to kernel source code), thereby enabling in-depth analysis and seamless correlation of events as they unfold.

Capturing System Calls with eBPF. System calls act as the fundamental interface between user processes and the kernel, making them pivotal in deciphering how a system behaves. By leveraging eBPF, these calls can be instrumented in real time to collect details such as process identifiers, arguments, and return values. Armed with this data, it becomes feasible to uncover how individual events are linked, thereby constructing the causal dependencies that reveal the underlying interactions and flow of execution within the system.

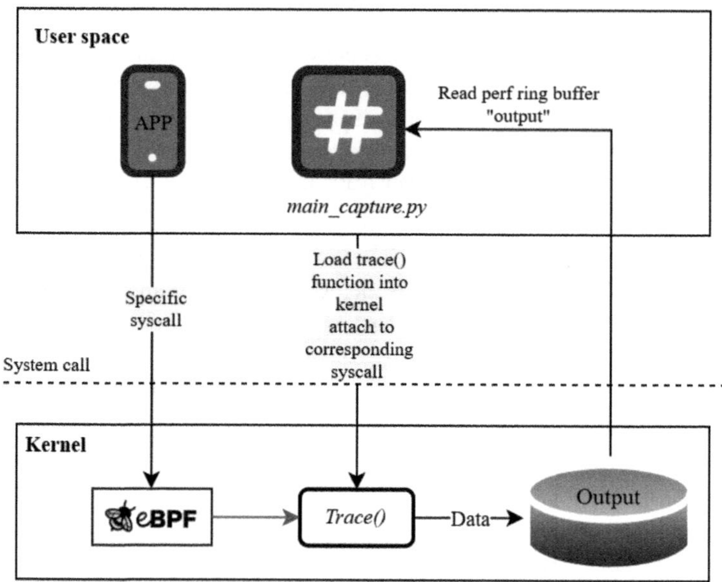

Fig. 4. EBPF Implementation.

Figure 4 depicts an eBPF tracing configuration that links user space with the Linux kernel in order to record syscall occurrences. In user space, an application (*APP*) initiates system calls, which are intercepted by a Python script (*main_capture.py*) that dynamically injects a *trace*() function into the kernel. Once deployed, the eBPF program attaches itself to specified syscalls, tracking parameters such as call arguments and return values any time those syscalls run. The trace function then writes the gathered information into a kernel ring buffer, which the Python script regularly reads. Ultimately, this data is stored in an output destination, enabling developers to review or analyze syscall events for generating causality graph. By capturing calls at the kernel level, the approach delivers granular insights into application operations (spawned syscalls), all without having to rebuild the kernel or change existing user programs.

Constructing Causal Dependencies. Prior investigations [2,5,6] have demonstrated that causal dependencies among system calls can be reliably detected and documented in causal logs by examining event interactions. Within a single process, Lamport's "happened-before" relationship [2] serves to determine causality. For external events spanning multiple processes, D'Ausbourg's

Table 1. Syscalls list

Syscall	Causality property
`clone()`	Since the child process is almost identical to the parent, the `clone()` call can be considered a preceding event, impacting the child's first event.
`pipe2()`	The `pipe2()` system call creates a communication channel between processes, establishing a causal dependency. Tracking all pipefd instances and linking them with other system calls is crucial for identifying these dependencies.
`read()` and `write()`	The `read()` system call establishes causal dependencies in both PIPE and FILE communications. In PIPE communication, it depends on prior `write()` calls to the same PIPE, where processes using the corresponding"write_fd" are considered preceding events. In FILE communication, `read()` links to earlier `write()` calls on the same file, aiding in tracking event sequences and dependencies.
`send()` and `recv()`	The `send()` system calls create a causal link by transmitting data from one socket to another, while the `recv()` system calls establish a corresponding dependency chain by receiving this data, linking the sending and receiving processes.
`copy_file_range()`	The `copy_file_range()` system call creates a causal dependency between file objects by transferring data directly between file descriptors within the kernel. Since the data copied from fd_in affects the content of fd_out, any process that previously wrote to fd_in or subsequently reads from fd_out establishes a causal relationship with the `copy_file_range()` call.
`accept()`	The `accept()` system call creates a new socket file descriptor for an incoming connection. While it doesn't directly establish a causal dependency, it sets up the communication channel that enables subsequent operations (like `send()`, `recv()`, `read()`, `write()`,...) to create causal links between processes.
`connect()`	The `connect()` system call initiates a connection from the client to a server endpoint by binding the client's socket file descriptor. Although this call does not directly establish a causal dependency, it creates the communication channel through which subsequent operations, such as `send()`, `recv()`, `read()`, `write()`,..., can build causal relationships between processes.

framework [6] and Xosanavongsa's model [5] offer robust methods for constructing causal links. Taken together, these approaches yield a thorough representation of both internal and cross-process causal relationships. Below are illustrative examples:

- *Process Creation*: Calls like `fork()` and `clone()` create causal links between parent and child processes.

- *Message Passing*: Communication via `pipe2()` or `socket()` generates dependencies between `send()` (sender) and `recv()` (receiver).
- *File Operations*: Writing and subsequent reading from a file establish causal chains among processes.

As illustrated in Table 1, we provide an explanation of the causality properties associated with several key system calls that play a significant role in establishing causal relationships.

4.4 Result Logs

To gather enough information for comprehensive analysis and causal graph construction, we employ two complementary logging formats: Causal logs and Raw logs. By capturing system events in these distinct ways, we ensure that we have both a higher-level overview of event flows and a granular, low-level record of each event's context and parameters.

```
(11, [b'', b'apache2', 1, 5825, 2453715366127, 0, 12, 0, 0])
(13, [b'', b'apache2', 326, 5825, 2453716012816, 20924, 12, 13, 0])
(16, [b'', b'apache2', 0, 5825, 2453716020025, 0, 12, 0, 0])
(18, [b'', b'apache2', 0, 1835, 2455017349965, 0, 12, 0, 0])
(20, [b'', b'apache2', 0, 1835, 2455018720692, 0, 13, 0, 0])
(22, [b'', b'apache2', 293, 1835, 2458718285741, 0, 12, 13, 0])
(23, [b'', b'apache2', 33, 6128, 2458718440246, 1, 13, 1, 0])
(24, [b'/bin/sh', b'apache2', 59, 6128, 2458718444698, 0, 1835, 0, 0])
(25, [b'', b'apache2', 435, 1835, 2458718628901, 0, 6128, 0, 0])
(26, [b'', b'apache2', 3, 1835, 2458718648761, 0, 13, 0, 0])
(27, [b'', b'sh', 0, 6128, 2458719490982, 0, 3, 0, 0])
```

Fig. 5. Raw syscall logs.

```
11,5825,write,2453715366127,[9],{5825: 5},1c4f8f27-1739-4c80-9270-04e1c9afa44d
13,5825,copy_file_range,2453716012816,[11],{5825: 6},c18f0deb-ff77-4a99-9b72-48b3a8901205
16,5825,read,2453716020025,[13],{5825: 7},0fc20eae-5f43-4a08-a2a7-737e36177d79
18,1835,read,2455017349965,[],{1835: 1},b55e2c75-d2a1-46bb-904f-0c0a65850351
20,1835,read,2455018720692,[18],{1835: 2},0d069fde-52f1-440b-942f-12d88880a52e
22,1835,pipe2,2458718285741,[20],{1835: 3},54d1d9bf-dade-478d-9965-fa9d8d1d6a95
23,6128,dup2,2458718440246,[25],{6128: 1},a0342b92-cae5-4498-89e6-e6d51e4483ab
24,6128,execve,2458718444698,[23],{6128: 2},ad676ba0-0d60-4b50-bb1f-71a13706576b
25,1835,clone3,2458718628901,[22],{1835: 4},06cce493-4aa7-4654-8135-f8e5a4d5636e
```

Fig. 6. Causal logs.

Raw syscall logs (Fig. 5). Originating directly from the eBPF tracing function within the kernel, Raw Logs contain a broader set of fields (such as process names, PIDs, timestamps, and possibly more granular details like syscall arguments or return values). By using this data for processing, we obtain causal logs to calculate causal dependencies among the events.
Causal logs (Fig. 6). These logs are generated by a user-space program that processes event data received from the kernel. Each entry contains columns for ID, PID, SYSCALL, TIME, PREV_NODE, VECTOR_TIME, and UUID, offering a concise yet robust snapshot of system call activity.

- ID provides a unique identifier for each event, making it straightforward to refer to individual actions.
- PID indicates the process where the event occurred.
- SYSCALL labels which system call was invoked (e.g., `write()`, `read()`, or `fork()`).
- TIME captures the timestamp, allowing chronological ordering of events.
- The fields PREV_NODE and VECTOR_TIME enable us to trace dependencies between events, which is essential for mapping causal relationships among processes and threads. Additionally, we leverage this data to perform backward calculations, reconstructing the complete vector clock and establishing a detailed causality framework.
- UUID serves as a globally unique reference that can correlate the event with additional logs or external data sources.

By focusing on these key fields, Causal Logs provide a streamlined perspective on the most pertinent event details. They are particularly helpful when visually mapping out how different processes interact, since each event can be connected to its predecessor in the causal chain.

4.5 Result Graphs

After gathering the causal logs and computing vector timestamps, we merge that information to build the causality-dependency graph. As shown in Fig. 7, each system call is plotted as an event (a point) on its process line. Periods in which no direct system call is invoked (such as reading a file without generating an observable event) are denoted $e_{\emptyset}$. An arrow between two events indicates their causal relationship. These relationships can be understood as follows:

- Within Each Process: Internal events are connected based on the order in which they occur, reflecting their inherent sequencing.
- Socket Communication ($P1 \leftrightarrow P3$): Calls to `send()` and `recv()` establish a direct causal link between Process $P1$ and Process $P3$.
- File I/O ($P1 \leftrightarrow P2$): An indirect dependency arises between P1 and P2 when data is written to and then read from a file (these `write()` and `read()` calls form a causal chain across the $FILE$ object).
- Process Creation ($P2 \leftrightarrow P3$): When $P2$ creates $P3$ (via `clone()`), it introduces a parent–child relationship. $P2$'s `clone()` call precedes P3's first observable event.

This causal graph provides a clear visual representation of how the system's events are chained together through both direct and indirect dependencies. By observing which nodes connect and in what order, it is possible to piece together the narrative of a complex multi-stage attack. Investigators can, for example, start at a suspicious event (anomalous write or newly spawned process) and follow the backward arrows to see how the malicious action was initiated, or track forward to see its impact on subsequent events. Such a causal view is

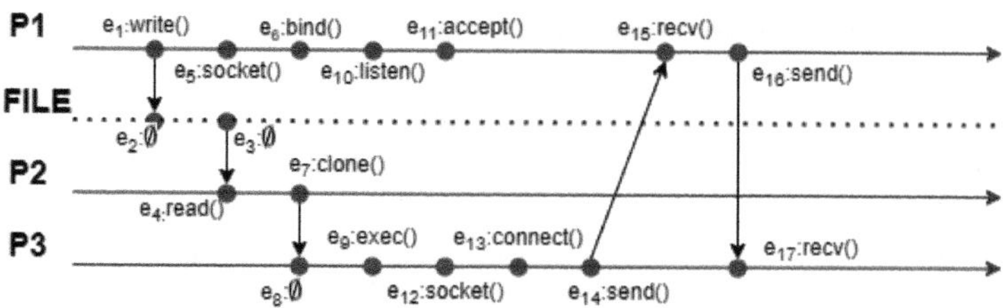

Fig. 7. Result graph illustration.

particularly valuable when performing forensic analysis, since it reveals not just what happened, but why it happened (i.e., which specific actions triggered or enabled each subsequent step).

5 Explaining Attacks

In this section, we demonstrate how causal logs explain real-world cyberattacks by deconstructing a specific Backdoor / Command and Control (C&C) Attack. This multi-stage intrusion serves as our case study because its complexity and prevalence make it an ideal example for showcasing how our framework reconstructs an attack's progression.

Our analysis begins by defining the Threat Model and Attack Scenario, which outlines the adversary's capabilities, the target environment, and the entry point for exploitation. We then use the causal logs and the corresponding graph generated by our framework to trace the attack from initial compromise to final impact.

The subsequent "Attack Explanation" uses causal diagrams to visualize these event connections. This allows security analysts to pinpoint the critical steps, such as privilege escalation or lateral movement, that enabled the attacker to achieve their goals. This level of visibility into multi-process interactions and complex pivot steps is difficult to achieve using conventional logging methods.

5.1 Backdoor Command and Control (C&C) Attack

Threat Model and Attack Scenarios: As illustrated in Fig. 8, a Command and Control (C&C) attack scenario presumes that an adversary has already deployed a backdoor (often via malware infection or a compromised account) on the target host. Once this backdoor is active, it attempts to establish an outbound connection (e.g., reverse shell, HTTP-based beacon, or custom TCP protocol) to an attacker-controlled C&C server. This model relies on the fact that most internal networks allow outbound traffic more freely than inbound traffic, making it easier for the attacker to maintain a hidden channel. There are some common objectives of a C&C attacker:

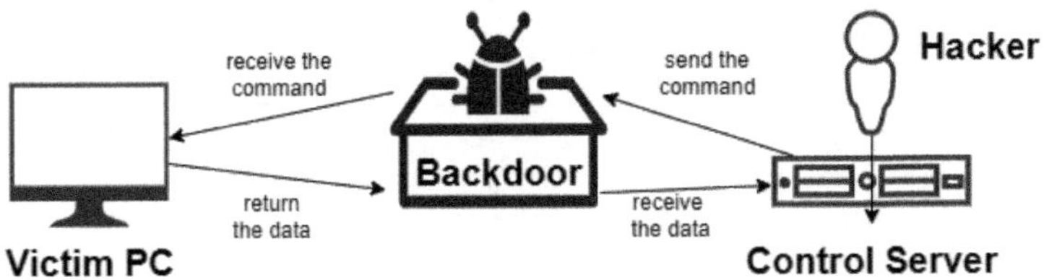

Fig. 8. Command and Control (C&C) - Threat Model.

- *Maintaining Persistent Access*: The backdoor re-connects or remains dormant until commanded by the attacker.
- *Network Reconnaissance and Lateral Movement*: The attacker uses the compromised host as a foothold to scan the environment, harvest credentials, or pivot to high-value targets.
- *Data Exfiltration or Further Exploits*: Once entrenched, the attacker exfiltrates sensitive data, deploys ransomware, or sets up additional persistence mechanisms.

A typical attack unfolds in stages:

1. *Backdoor Installation*: The attacker drops or installs a malicious agent on the target system (could be part of a phishing campaign, exploit kit, or via stolen credentials).
2. *Outbound Beaconing*: The backdoor attempts periodic communication to the remote C&C server, often disguising traffic as legitimate.
3. *Remote Commands and Lateral Movement*: The attacker issues commands, enumerates the network, and escalates privileges using the compromised system as a launch point.
4. *Data Exfiltration or Final Impact*: Sensitive data is transferred out, or further disruptive actions (like encrypting files or destroying logs) are triggered.

Explaining the Attack. Figure 9 depicts a Backdoor-based C&C attack in which a malicious agent (the "backdoor") has already been placed on the target system. Two primary command-execution flows appear in parallel, shown with green arrows labeled `(1a) to (4a)` and yellow arrows labeled `(1b) to (4b)`. A thick red arrow labeled `(5)` marks the final "exit" command from the attacker that ends the session. Below is a step-by-step explanation of these labeled transitions and what they signify in the causal logs:

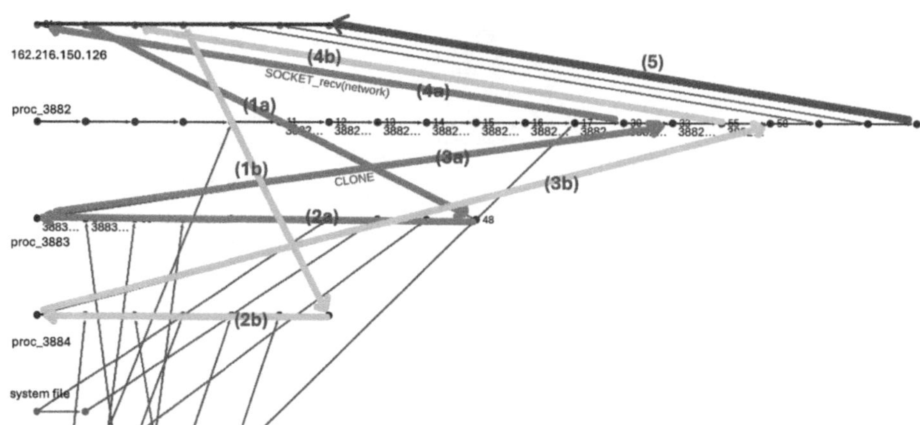

Fig. 9. Command and Control (C&C) - Causality Graph.

- `Arrow (5):`
  The attacker issues an `exit` or similar termination command from a remote server (e.g., `162.216.150.126`) to shut down the existing control channel. We can typically see a final `recv()` call in `proc_3882` (the main backdoor process), capturing the termination command. Immediately afterward, the process may invoke system calls like `close()` or `shutdown()` on the socket to end the session.
- `Arrow (4a) and Arrow (4b):`
  Prior to exiting, the attacker transmits multiple commands via the C&C channel to direct the compromised host (such as enumerating processes, reading files, or scanning ports). In the logs, each new command is indicated by a `recv()` call in `proc_3882`, which reads data from the attacker's socket. Shortly afterward, a corresponding `send()` may appear if the backdoor acknowledges receipt or prepares a response.
- `Arrow (3a) and Arrow (3b):`
  Upon receiving a new command, `proc_3882` clones a child process (e.g., `proc_3883 or proc_3884`) to execute the attacker's request in isolation. This design allows the main backdoor to remain free to handle further commands without blocking. In the logs, these spawns appear as `clone()` (or `fork()`) calls within `proc_3882`. Immediately following that, the child process sets up any necessary file descriptors or pipes, linking back to its parent so that output can be routed back to the attacker.
- `Arrow (2a) and Arrow (2b):`
  The newly spawned child processes carry out the attacker's requests (running binaries, collecting system data, or attempting privilege escalation). Causal logs often show `execve()` for command execution, `open()` and `read()` for file operations, or `setuid()` if privilege changes are attempted. These calls follow shortly after the child is cloned, forming clear evidence of malicious behavior and highlighting which specific resources are accessed or modified.

- `Arrow (1a) and Arrow (1b)`:
  Once the child completes its assigned task, it transmits any output (e.g., command results, file contents) to control server `162.216.150.126` over the established network connection, captured in the logs as a final `send()` to the attacker's IP and port. This chain of events (command in, child execution, output returning) reveals precisely how reconnaissance or exfiltration occurs in real time.

By examining each arrow in reverse, from the "exit" command (`Arrow 5`) back through the child processes (`Arrows 2a/2b and 3a/3b`) and the commands they executed (`Arrows 4a/4b`), analysts can reconstruct the entire life cycle of the C&C attack. This provides a transparent view of how the attacker maintained remote control: receiving commands, spawning helper processes, executing malicious actions, and returning data to the attacker's server. Armed with these causal insights, defenders gain the clarity needed to pinpoint when and how the system was compromised, block the offending IP addresses or processes, and implement better egress filters and host protections to mitigate future incidents.

6 Conclusion and Future Work

We presented a novel framework leveraging eBPF to generate causal logs, significantly enhancing the detection and analysis of Command and Control (C&C) backdoor activities. Our method explicitly traces causal relationships between system calls at the kernel level, improving the interpretability and traceability of complex threats compared to traditional SIEM-based techniques.

Despite these advances, several challenges remain. The fine-grained tracing introduces overhead, particularly in resource-limited environments or high-volume systems. Scaling causal logging for distributed and cloud-native architectures also poses significant complexity. Moreover, enriching causal logs by integrating diverse data sources (e.g., network traffic, application logs) could further enhance threat detection capabilities.

Future work will focus on optimizing performance by exploring lightweight tracing and hardware-assisted monitoring to minimize overhead; enhancing scalability through efficient aggregation of causal logs across distributed systems for a comprehensive global perspective; advancing detection via graph-based machine learning, such as Graph Neural Networks, to automatically identify suspicious patterns; and incorporating additional data sources, including network and user activity logs, to achieve a more holistic view and stronger threat correlation.

By addressing these challenges, we aim to refine and extend our causal logging framework into a comprehensive threat analysis solution. Ultimately, the goal is to combine high-fidelity, causally rich data with scalable analytics and machine learning techniques, thereby enhancing the effectiveness of security monitoring systems and enabling more proactive defenses against sophisticated cyber threats.

Acknowledgment. This work has been partially supported by the French National Research Agency under the France 2030 label (Superviz ANR-22-PECY-0008). The views reflected herein do not necessarily reflect the opinion of the French government.

References

1. Kobayashi, S., Fukuda, K., Esaki, H.: Mining causes of network events in log data with causal inference. In 2017 IFIP/IEEE Symposium on Integrated Network and Service Management (IM), pp. 45–53. IEEE (2017)
2. Lamport, L.: Time, clocks, and the ordering of events in a distributed system. In Concurrency: The Works of Leslie Lamport, pp. 179–196 (2019)
3. Markakis, M., et al.: From logs to causal inference: diagnosing large systems (2024)
4. Xosanavongsa, C., Totel, E., Bettan, O.: Discovering correlations: a formal definition of causal dependency among heterogeneous events. In 2019 IEEE European Symposium on Security and Privacy (EuroS&P), pp. 340–355. IEEE (2019)
5. Xosanavongsa, C.: Heterogeneous event causal dependency definition for the detection and explanation of multi-step attacks (Doctoral dissertation, CentraleSupélec) (2020)
6. D'ausbourg, B.: Implementing secure dependencies over a network by designing a distributed security subsystem. In: Gollmann, D. (ed.) ESORICS 1994. LNCS, vol. 875, pp. 247–266. Springer, Heidelberg (1994). https://doi.org/10.1007/3-540-58618-0_68
7. Fowler, J., Zwaenepoel, W.: Causal distributed breakpoints. Presented at the (1990) Causal distributed breakpoints. In Proceedings of the Tenth International Conference on Distributed Computer Systems
8. Schwarz, R., Mattern, F.: Detecting causal relationships in distributed computations: In search of the holy grail. Distrib. Comput. **7**(3), 149–174 (1994)
9. Baldy, P., Dicky, H., Medina, R., Morvan, M., Vilarem, J.F.: Efficient reconstruction of the causal relationship in distributed systems. In Canada-France Conference on Parallel and Distributed Computing, pp. 101–113. Springer, Heidelberg (1994)

Evaluating the Effectiveness of ChatGPT for Analyzing Real-World Multi-File Cryptographic Vulnerabilities

Rezika Bouzid(✉) and Raphaël Khoury(✉)

Université du Québec en Outaouais, Gatineau, Qc, Canada
{bour71,raphael.khoury}@uqo.ca

Abstract. Large language models (LLMs), especially ChatGPT, have opened new avenues for detecting and mitigating software vulnerabilities. While this progress has sparked interest across the security community, the majority of existing studies still rely on simplified evaluation setups. Many studies use direct prompts that contain isolated code snippets, often using synthetic datasets with short, contrived examples or functions. Such conditions fail to reflect the complexity of real-world software systems, especially when vulnerabilities span multiple files. The automatic analysis of vulnerabilities distributed across multiple files remains largely unexplored in current research. This study contributes to filling this gap by exploring two complementary directions. First, we assess an enhanced version of single-file vulnerability analysis by incorporating explicit behavioral context into the prompts and applying this strategy to real-world vulnerabilities from operational open-source projects. Second, we investigate the relatively underexplored challenge of multi-file vulnerability analysis, where security issues arise from interactions across files. Our results indicate that ChatGPT performs significantly better on single-file vulnerabilities when given contextual prompts. However, it faces difficulties with multi-file vulnerabilities, often treating files independently. It is also prone to generating many false positive alerts.

Keywords: LLM for Secure Coding · Multi-File Vulnerabilities · Prompt Engineering

1 Introduction

Large language models (LLMs) have increasingly been employed to perform cybersecurity tasks, including the analysis of software vulnerabilities. However, most existing studies evaluate these models using synthetic vulnerabilities [6] [7]—artificially created for training or benchmarking purposes—which limits our understanding of their true effectiveness in real-world scenarios. In these studies, LLMs are typically evaluated on short code snippets with little to no contextual grounding. These evaluations often target a single security objective at a time—such as binary or CWE classification, line-level vulnerability detection, or

K. Adi et al. (Eds.): CRiSIS 2025, LNCS 16295, pp. 319–335, 2026.
https://doi.org/10.1007/978-3-032-20732-6_20

automated repair. Additionally, these setups are prone to a high false positive rate, as LLMs frequently exhibit a tendency to flag correct code as vulnerable. More specifically, to simplify evaluation, most existing studies restrict themselves to vulnerabilities located within a single file, relying on automated metrics that streamline scoring. Consequently, their applicability to realistic, multi-file scenarios remains underexplored. However, many real-world vulnerabilities arise from interactions between code modules or improper API use, not isolated files. This makes effective automated analysis across complex, connected code much more challenging.

To bridge the gap between simplified academic benchmarks and the complexity of real-world software vulnerabilities, this study investigates two approaches: (1) an enhanced single-file analysis method using structured prompts enriched with behavioral context, and (2) a multi-file analysis scenario that captures vulnerabilities spanning multiple files. Our goal is to assess how contextual and distributed information influences the capabilities of ChatGPT in realistic settings. This dual perspective aims to assess the capabilities of ChatGPT across several tasks related to software vulnerability analysis.

We further propose a novel conversational prompt engineering method, which replicates a security analysis framework developed at Microsoft. As detailed in *Designing Secure Software* by Loren Kohnfelder [2], this approach analyzes code using 4 guiding questions: (1) What does a particular fragment of code do?; (2) What could go wrong when performing such a task?; (3) How can these issues be addressed?; and (4) Has it been adequately addressed? Since our focus is on vulnerability analysis, our prompting strategy seeks to replicate the first three of these questions. We found that using this method improves the performance of the LLM at security tasks, as well as aids the analyst in rapidly ruling out false positives.

This evaluation is based on several aspects and leads to the following research questions:

- **RQ1:** Does providing a concise behavioral context within a structured prompt improve ChatGPT's ability to detect, prioritize, localize, and fix real-world vulnerabilities, along with proposing accurate explanation, in single-file vulnerability?
- **RQ2:** How well can ChatGPT analyze vulnerabilities that span multiple source files?

To answer these questions, this work introduces several novel contributions, as follows:

- We evaluate the ChatGPT's performance for several security-relevant coding tasks including vulnerability detection, vulnerability localization and patch creation using a dataset consisting of real-life vulnerabilities in large codebases. We contrast the performance of the model when evaluating single file and multi-file programs. We further evaluate the impact of providing the model with contextual information about the program's intended behavior.

- We further evaluate the use of a novel conversational prompt engineering method, which guides the model in a manner similar to a security analyst, using both vulnerable and benign programs.

The remainder of this paper is organized as follows: Sect. 2 describes the dataset and the design of the experiments. Section 3 explains the evaluation criteria. Section 4 details the results of the experiments. Section 5 provides a discussion of the main results and their implications. Section 6 reports on related works. Concluding remarks are given in Sect. 7.

2 Research Design

In the this section, we outline the methodology we employed to probe the strengths and limitations of ChatGPT for vulnerability analysis. Our approach combines two complementary strategies: a focused assessment of single-file vulnerabilities enriched with behavioral context to clarify code intent, and a broader evaluation across multi-file programs to explore the impact of distributed contextual information.

2.1 Description of the Dataset

We sought to test the effectiveness of ChatGPT when operating using a dataset composed of real-world scenarios, including both single- and multi-file codebases. To this end, we leveraged a carefully curated dataset from prior work [5], which comprises 30 cryptographic vulnerabilities for which both the vulnerable source code and corresponding patches are available through the National Vulnerability Database (NVD) [1]. This dataset includes every NVD vulnerability labeled as 'cryptographic flaw' for which source was available at the time of the dataset's creation.

We separated the vulnerabilities contained in this dataset into two groups according to whether they involved a single source file or multiple files. We also used the tokenizer provided by OpenAI[1] to remove from the dataset any program whose size may exceed the LLM's input token limit. Our final dataset consisted of 17 single-file CVEs and 12 multi-file CVEs written in C, C++, Erlang, Perl, JavaScript, Python, Go, Java and PHP.

For the single-file CVEs, an extra manual effort was necessary to identify the functional purpose of each code sample, which we refer to throughout the paper as *behavioral context*—defined as a brief natural language description of the intended functionality or goal of the code. This context was then incorporated in the prompts used in the experiments addressing RQ1. For example, the behavioral context for a password reset script might be: *"This code resets a user's password by generating a temporary one and emailing it."* Since this information is not explicitly included in the dataset, we inferred it through a close

[1] https://platform.openai.com/tokenizer.

examination of the provided documentation and by analyzing key technical indicators such as file headers, code comments, function names, and parameters, as well as NVD vulnerability descriptions.

2.2 Model Selection

For this study, we leverage GPT-4 Turbo [3], a variant of GPT-4 offered by OpenAI, via structured API calls. GPT-4 Turbo is designed to be faster and more cost-efficient than GPT-4, while sharing the same architectural foundation. It supports a context window of up to 128,000 tokens and allows up to 4,096 output tokens, making it particularly suitable for analyzing large, multi-file codebases. This model was trained up to December 2023, which likely means that the CVEs we selected for testing may have been included in its training data. We selected this model due to its enhanced ability to handle long-context prompts. The GPT models include a parameter called'temperature', which controls the randomness of the output. Lower values (such as 0) are recommended in the OpenAI documentation [4] for tasks requiring deterministic, structured, and repeatable outputs. To ensure consistent and reproducible results from the model, we configured the temperature parameter to 0 across all our experiments.

Direct Prompt

Role: You are a security analyst reviewing source code.

Analyze the following source code.

1. What vulnerabilities could be present in it?
2. If any of these vulnerabilities are present, on which lines are they located?
3. Propose a corrected version of those line(s).
4. Why does the fix resolve the problem?

`<code>` *(Each CVE corresponds to a single source file.)*

Fig. 1. Direct Prompt for Analyzing CVEs in Single-Source-File Programs

2.3 Prompt Engineering

To systematically evaluate the LLM's capabilities in vulnerability analysis, we designed three distinct prompt types, each tailored to a specific experimental setting. This design adopts a structured, expert-driven strategy in a conversational format, inspired by Microsoft's methodology as outlined in Designing Secure Software by Loren Kohnfelder [2]. This conversation with the LLM also helps eliminate false positives in the model's responses. The prompts used are shown in Figs. 1 to 3. The first prompt, referred to as the Direct Prompt, is shown in Fig. 1. This version serves as a baseline to evaluate the LLM's performance without any additional contextual information. To investigate whether including behavioral context improves the model's effectiveness in vulnerability analysis, we designed a second prompt, the Contextual Prompt, illustrated in Fig. 2. The last prompt, shown in Fig. 3, is the Cross-File Chain-of-Thought. It is specifically designed to support the analysis of vulnerabilities that span multiple source files. In this prompt, we clearly indicate that the files belong to the same software project, which provides the LLM with a unified context and enables it to reason more effectively about cross-file dependencies.

Contextual Prompt

Role: You are a security analyst reviewing source code.

This code {*insert here what the code does*}.

1. **What vulnerabilities could be present in it?**
2. **If any of these vulnerabilities are present, on which lines are they located?**
3. **Propose a corrected version of those line(s).**
4. **Why does the fix resolve the problem?**

<code> ***(Each CVE corresponds to a single source file.)***

Fig. 2. Conversational Prompt Augmented with Behavioral Context for Analyzing CVEs in Single-Source-File Programs

2.4 Experiments

The following three experiments detail our assessment of ChatGPT's performance in analyzing vulnerabilities, in alignment with our research questions.

- ***Experiment 1:*** This experiment evaluates ChatGPT's ability to analyze single-file vulnerabilities, without any additional guidance, using the prompt shown in Fig. 1. We retained the comments within the code to offer additional context and clarity, as the selected real-world CVEs fit within the token limit. This experiment includes a total of 17 cryptographic CVEs, and we evaluate both the vulnerable and patched versions separately.
- ***Experiment 2:*** This scenario replicates Experiment 1 but uses the prompt format shown in Fig. 2. It includes a concise behavioral context to assess whether providing such contextual information improves ChatGPT's performance.
- ***Experiment 3:*** This experiment consists of providing the LLM with real-world vulnerabilities that span multiple files. In each case, We supply the LLM with a set of related code files that together result in a vulnerability, using the prompt illustrated in Fig. 3. For this evaluation, we examine 12 different CVEs, each consisting of between 2 to 8.

Cross-File Chain of Thought Prompt

Role: You are a security analyst reviewing multiple source code files.
The following source code files belong to the same software project. They are contextually related and may interact with each other. Your task is to analyze security vulnerabilities that arise from how these files work together, rather than evaluating them in isolation.
Please follow these steps:
1. What vulnerabilities could emerge from the interaction between these files?

- **Briefly describe the issue.**

2. For each vulnerability found:

- **List the specific line(s) of code in the provided files that contribute to the issue.**
- **Propose corrected versions of the affected line(s) for each vulnerability.**
- **Why does the fix resolve the issue?**

`< file1 >, < file2 >,...`

Fig. 3. Chain of Thought Prompt for Multi-File Vulnerability Analysis With Explicit Project Context

3 Evaluation

We manually evaluate the LLM's responses to each CVE across five key dimensions. These include three core security tasks: (1) vulnerability detection, (2) localization of the vulnerable lines, and (3) remediation through proposed fixes. In addition, we assess the model's ability to (4) prioritize its findings and (5) provide a cogent explanation of how the proposed changes address the underlying issue. The analysis was applied to both vulnerable and correct code samples to capture a broader picture of the model's behavior.

To evaluate the prioritization task, we assessed the ranking precision, which reflects the model's ability to correctly prioritize the most critical vulnerabilities. Prioritization is expressed as a fraction (e.g., 2/4), indicating the position of the relevant issue correctly identified among the list of all issues reported by the LLM. A low rank (1–2) reflects good performance, while a high rank (3 or above, or missing) indicates the vulnerability was overlooked or poorly prioritized. Importantly, we intentionally avoided restricting the evaluation to only the top few results. Limiting the assessment—for example, to the top 3 findings—can introduce a serious bias: a genuine vulnerability identified in 4th or 5th position would be unfairly marked as a failure, while a model placing irrelevant findings at the top could be incorrectly deemed effective.

The results of Experiments 1, 2, and 3 are summarized in Tables 1, 2, and 3, respectively.To help interpret the model's effectiveness, we assign qualitative labels to each parameter being evaluated:

- **Localization** is marked as *"Yes"* if the LLM identifies the exact code location of the CVE's root cause, *"Partial"* if it points to the correct file or function but not the precise logic, and *"No"* if it only highlights unrelated lines or omits relevant code entirely. The criteria for vulnerability **detection** follow a similar *Yes(✓)/Partial(~)/No(✗)* hierarchy.
- **Fix** is marked as *"Correct"* if the LLM proposes a solution that addresses the CVE's root cause, *"Partial"* if the fix is related but insufficient or misaligned, and *"None"* if no relevant fix is provided (no fix is proposed or if the fix is unrelated to the CVE's root cause.).
- **Explanation** is marked as *"Correct"* if the LLM clearly explains how its proposed fix addresses the root cause of the vulnerability. *"Partial"* if it provides a related but incomplete or vague rationale, and *"Wrong"* if it gives an unrelated explanation, an incorrect one, or no explanation at all.

The final **Score** column indicates how many of the three core tasks—detection, localization, and fix—were successfully or partially handled by the LLM, reflecting an overall positive or negative performance.

Note: Each task is scored as 1 for correct, 0.5 for partial, and 0 for incorrect responses.

Table 1. Experiment 1 Results – Vulnerable Code without Declared Functional Context

CVE ID	Found	Rank	Loc.	Fix	Explain.	Score
CVE-2012-2417	✗	0/4	No	None	Wrong	○○○
CVE-2018-12520	✓	3/5	No	None	Wrong	●○○
CVE-2020-12735	✓	3/3	Yes	Correct	Correct	●●●
CVE-2020-28924	✗	0/2	No	None	Wrong	○○○
CVE-2021-41117	✗	0/8	No	None	Wrong	○○○
CVE-2019-10908	✓	2/4	Yes	Correct	Correct	●●●
CVE-2012-3458	✗	0/4	No	None	Wrong	○○○
CVE-2017-7526	✓	1/5	No	None	Wrong	●○○
CVE-2018-16870	✗	0/5	No	None	Wrong	○○○
CVE-2019-9155	✓	2/3	Yes	None	Wrong	●●○
CVE-2016-2053	✗	0/5	No	None	Wrong	○○○
CVE-2019-11578	✗	0/5	No	None	Wrong	○○○
CVE-2021-32738	✗	0/3	No	None	Wrong	○○○
CVE-2016-10530	✓	5/5	Partial	Partial	Correct	●◐◐
CVE-2014-5386	~	4/5	No	None	Wrong	◐○○
CVE-2015-8867	✗	0/5	No	None	Wrong	○○○
CVE-2018-19653	✗	0/4	No	None	Wrong	○○○
Overall(/17)	6.5	3	3.5	2.5	3	2

4 Results

This section summarizes ChatGPT's outputs from each experiment and presents our findings in response to each research question.

4.1 RQ1: Effect of Behavioral Context on Single-File CVE Analysis

Results on Vulnerable Codes. Based on the results from the two experimental settings, Experiment 1 (without context, summarized in Table 1) and Experiment 2 (with context, summarized in Table 2), we evaluate performance across five key dimensions: detection, prioritization, localization, remediation, and explanation of the proposed fix. This comparison highlights how contextual information influences the model's overall analytical effectiveness.

Table 2. Experiment 2 Results – Vulnerable Code with Declared Functional Context

CVE ID	Found	Rank	Loc.	Fix	Explain.	Score
CVE-2012-2417	✓	2/4	Yes	Correct	Correct	●●●
CVE-2018-12520	✓	1/1	No	None	Wrong	●○○
CVE-2020-12735	✓	1/2	Yes	Correct	Correct	●●●
CVE-2020-28924	✓	1/2	Yes	Correct	Correct	●●●
CVE-2021-41117	✗	0/6	No	None	Wrong	○○○
CVE-2019-10908	✓	1/1	Yes	Correct	Correct	●●●
CVE-2012-3458	✓	1/1	Yes	None	Wrong	●●○
CVE-2017-7526	✓	2/5	No	None	Wrong	●○○
CVE-2018-16870	✓	1/5	No	None	Wrong	●○○
CVE-2019-9155	✓	1/4	Yes	Partial	Correct	●●◐
CVE-2016-2053	✗	0/3	No	None	Wrong	○○○
CVE-2019-11578	✗	0/5	No	None	Wrong	○○○
CVE-2021-32738	✗	0/1	No	None	Wrong	○○○
CVE-2016-10530	✓	1/4	Partial	Partial	Correct	●◐◐
CVE-2014-5386	✗	0/5	No	None	Wrong	○○○
CVE-2015-8867	✓	5/8	Partial	None	Wrong	●◐○
CVE-2018-19653	✗	0/5	No	None	Wrong	○○○
Overall (/17)	11	10	7	5	6	5

Detection. Providing behavioral context significantly enhances ChatGPT's vulnerability detection capabilities: without it, the model detects only 6.5 out of 17 CVEs, whereas with context, detection rises to 11, as shown in Table 2. This substantial improvement indicates that understanding the intended behavior of the code helps the model better identify deviations and potential security flaws. Without context, ChatGPT frequently misses subtle or logic-based issues, suggesting that behavioral cues are essential for comprehensive vulnerability detection. For example, in the case of *CVE-2020-28924*, when provided with context, ChatGPT accurately identifies that the `Password` function relied on the insecure `math/rand` package instead of the cryptographically secure `crypto/rand`. In contrast, in its response when context was ommited, it falsely assumes that the secure package was already in use, entirely overlooking the vulnerability. As a result, it focuses on unrelated code (the `String` function), missing the actual vulnerability altogether.

While providing behavioral context generally improved ChatGPT's detection performance, *CVE-2014-5386* stands out as the sole exception. The core vulnerability lies in the use of a non-cryptographically secure RNG through `MCRYPT_RAND`, resulting in predictable initialization vectors (IVs). As shown in Table 1, without context, the model partially recognizes the insecure use of `rand()` for cryptographic purposes, but buries it as the fourth point in a list of five unrelated issues—demonstrating poor prioritization and lack of focus. In contrast, Table 2 shows that with context, ChatGPT entirely misses the vulnerability. While it discusses general cryptographic risks, such as deprecated APIs and weak randomness, it fails to identify or explain the deterministic IV issue stemming from `MCRYPT_RAND`, and proposes fixes for unrelated concerns only. This particular case illustrates that even with context, complex cryptographic flaws can remain elusive to the LLM.

Prioritization (Ranking). The presence of behavioral context drastically improves ChatGPT's ability to prioritize critical vulnerabilities. In the no-context setting in Table 1, only 3 out of 17 vulnerabilities were correctly placed among the top findings. With context in Table 2, this number jumped to 10.

In fact, in six cases, *(CVE-2020-12735, CVE-2019-10908, CVE-2018-12520, CVE-2019-9155, CVE-2017-7526, and CVE-2016-10530)* ChatGPT successfully detects the vulnerability in both settings, but ranks it significantly higher when behavioral context was provided. In the no-context scenario, these vulnerabilities were often buried among less relevant findings. In contrast, the contextual prompts led the model to correctly elevate them to the top positions. This result suggests that when the model understands the intended behavior of the program, it is better equipped to assess which flaws are most severe or relevant. Without this guidance, the model tends to surface superficial or less impactful issues first, leading to poor triage, and showing that understanding program intent enhances the model's ability to assess impact and prioritize accordingly.

Localization. Tables 1 and 2 illustrate the model's ability to locate the specific lines of code that are vulnerable across the 17 CVEs tested. In Table 1, without behavioral context, the model achieves a localization score of only 3.5 out of 17. With behavioral context (Table 2), this number increases to 7.

While this gain is more moderate than for detection or ranking, it is still meaningful. Context helps the model focus on the underlying faulty logic, making it more precise in identifying the exact lines of code that require fixing. The fact that localization didn't improve as drastically also suggests that line-level reasoning is more challenging and may require even deeper semantic understanding or iterative evaluation strategies.

Remediation. The accuracy of suggested fixes improves notably with the addition of behavioral context. As shown in Table 1, without context, the model achieves a total score of 2.5 out of 17 for the code correction task—where fully correct fixes receive one point and partially correct fixes receive half a point. When behavioral context is included (Table 2), this score increases to 5 out of 17, showing that aven a brief description of the intended code functionality helps the model generate more effective patches.

While the quantitative improvement may seem modest, the qualitative enhancements are significant. Contextual prompts helped the model better align fixes with both security objectives and the program's intended behavior, reducing vague or functionally incomplete patches. This is best illustrated with *CVE-2019-10908*, due to the insecure use of `RandomStringUtils.randomAlphanumeric(8)`, which relies upon a non-cryptographically secure PRNG (`java.util.Random`). Both responses suggested secure solutions, but the context-aware response, Table 2, was clearly superior: the LLM avoids distractions such as email validation and uses modern, idiomatic Java Streams for a more concise and maintainable fix. When behavioral context is provided,the model successfully identified the specific cryptographic vulnerability present, reports only that issue, accurately pinpointed the exact vulnerable line, and proposed a precise one-line fix using the Java Stream API and `SecureRandom.getInstanceStrong()`, producing a secure password from a custom ASCII range. This case shows a clear understanding of both the vulnerability and the correct mitigation strategy. In contrast, without context (Table 1), where the model lacked this level of precision, it still found the same issue but buried it among other less critical findings and relied on a more verbose helper class implementation.

In fact, the only case where we do not observe an improvement in the quality of the proposed fix is one where even without the context, the LLM easily provided a correct mitigation. The vulnerability, *CVE-2020-12735*, concerns the use of the `md5()` hash function to generate a password, resulting in a weak password with low entropy. Note that this is a syntactic vulnerability, easily uncovered even without a semantic-level understanding of the underlying code, and corrected by replacing the call to `md5()` with a call to a cryptographically secure random byte genokerator. For every case in which detecting or fixing the vulnerability required understanding of the underlying code however, providing context yeilded marked positive improvements in performance.

Aside from this case, the context-aware responses consistently demonstrates better structure, professionalism, and clarity—focusing immediately on the core vulnerability and presenting a well-justified, actionable fix. In contrast, the no-context output identifies the same issue but diluted its impact with unrelated observations and lacks a clear structure. Surrounding noise (other vulnerabilities) could make it less immediately actionable for a developer focused on addressing the password issue. Nonetheless, this security dimension remains challenging for the LLM overall. Despite improvements with context, the model still struggles to consistently produce accurate and reliable patches across all CVEs. It fails in 85.3% of cases without context, and in 70.6% of cases even when behavioral context is provided.

Explanation. The quality of the explanations of the proposed fixes provided by ChatGPT also improves significantly with the inclusion of behavioral context. Without context, as shown in Table 1, the model provides correct or relevant justifications for why the fix addresses the problem in only 3 out of 17 CVEs, often offering vague or partially accurate reasoning. When behavioral context is added, as illustrated in Table 2, this number increases to 6. In these enhanced responses, the model more consistently identifies the root cause, the attack vector, and the potential consequences of the vulnerability. Contextual cues enable the model to build a more accurate mental model of the code's behavior, allowing it not only to suggest a patch but also to explain why it resolves the issue. This explanatory capability plays a vital role in real-world adoption, as it enhances developer understanding and confidence in the model's suggestions.

Score. ChatGPT achieves a higher final score when provided with behavioral context (five positive outcomes) compared to the non-contextual scenario (two outcomes). While the overall results remain modest, the model demonstrates effectiveness in detecting vulnerabilities when behavioral context is included. However, it continues to struggle with localization and fix suggestion—two tasks that significantly contribute to the low global score and represent ongoing challenges that warrant further research efforts.

Results on Non-Vulnerable Codes. In order to assess whether the model can correctly recognize secure code and refrain from reporting vulnerabilities that have already been resolved or are unrelated, we repeated the same experiment using the already patched versions of the same 17 vulnerabilities.

1. **False Positives:** In all cases, ChatGPT flags issues, identifies their locations, proposes fixes, and provides explanations for its suggested solutions—even when the vulnerabilities have already been resolved—resulting in a high false positive rate. The only exception was observed in *CVE-2018-16870* (patched version without context), where ChatGPT reports five vulnerabilities without locating them and suggests a fix without any explanation. Notably, there is no instance in which the model explicitly acknowledges that the code is no longer vulnerable. This indicates that the model often struggles to distinguish secure code from insecure code.
2. **Repetition of Prior Explanation:** In some cases, the LLM repeats the same explanations and descriptions it had provided for the vulnerable versions. For example, when analyzing *CVE-2015-8867* (patched version with context), the model reports eight vulnerabilities—just as in the vulnerable version—with only minor variations of ordering and naming. This tendency to recycle prior analyses highlights the model's limited ability to validate code fixes effectively. Rather than demonstrating a deep understanding of the logic

behind security patches, the model often relies on surface-level code patterns. Its responses appear influenced by pattern repetition, memorization from earlier analyses of the vulnerable version, or by behavioral context provided in the prompt—where the LLM interprets what the code is doing and associates it with common vulnerabilities typically linked to that behavior. Likewise, when analyzing *CVE-2018-12520*, in which the code generates session IDs using a pseudorandom number generator, the model reports a *Predictable Session ID Generation* vulnerability, even though the issue is resolved. Similarly, with CVE-2019-10908, a code that involves password generation, the model wrongly flags issues related to how the password is handled or the security of the email transmission. The code actually performs these actions correctly.

Findng 1: Providing a concise behavioral context significantly improves ChatGPT's ability to detect, prioritize, localize, and remediate single-file vulnerabilities. It also enhances the accuracy of its explanations, aligning better with the real causes and security fixes. These findings highlight the critical role of structured contextual prompts in maximizing the effectiveness of LLM-based security analysis. However, despite these gains, localization and fix generation remain challenging tasks that affect the overall score. Additionally, when analyzing patched code, the model frequently generates false positives or reuses prior reasoning.

4.2 RQ2: Multi-File Vulnerability Analysis with ChatGPT

Table 3 presents the results of Experiment 3 on vulnerable codes. It summarizes ChatGPT's performance on vulnerabilities affecting multiple files, focusing on how the number of affected files correlates with its effectiveness across key dimensions—identification, localization, explanation, fix, and the quality of explanation—grouped by the file count per CVE.

In comparison to situations involving three or more files, ChatGPT typically performs better across all assessment dimensions when the CVEs only affect two files. Most notably, detection, prioritization, and localization are often successful or partially correct, with explanation and fix quality occasionally rated as correct. For example, in *CVE-2019-11808* it succeeds on all tasks, achieving a full score. However, performance begins to degrade even within the two-file group. For example, when treating *CVE-2022-1235*, ChatGPT fails on every tasks. This suggests that while two-file vulnerabilities are more manageable, challenges remain when code relationships are implicit or subtle. Additionally, once the number of affected files reaches three or more, ChatGPT's performance deteriorates markedly across all dimensions. In only one of the 3-files cases tested (*CVE-2022-1434*) did the model perform satisfactorily at the vulnerability detection task, and even in this case, it failed for the other tasks.

The decline in performance appears linked to increased context fragmentation, where relevant information is dispersed across multiple files. While ChatGPT can reason over small multi-file contexts, its grasp of inter-file dependencies

Table 3. Experiment 3 Results – Multi-File Vulnerability Analysis(On Vulnerable Code) *For brevity, CVE-2016-1000344&1000352 are abbreviated as CVE-2016-*.*

CVE ID	#F	Found	Rank	Loc.	Fix	Explain.	Score
CVE-2019-11808	2	✓	1/2	Yes	Correct	Correct	●●●
CVE-2013-1445	2	✓	1/2	Partial	None	Wrong	●◐○
CVE-2021-3538	2	✓	1/3	Partial	None	Wrong	●◐○
CVE-2022-1235	2	✗	0/3	No	None	Wrong	○○○
CVE-2022-1434	3	~	1/3	No	None	Wrong	◐○○
CVE-2011-0766	3	✗	0/3	No	None	Wrong	○○○
CVE-2016-*	3	✗	0/3	No	None	Wrong	○○○
CVE-2019-15075	4	✗	0/5	No	None	Wrong	○○○
CVE-2014-3570	4	✗	0/2	No	None	Wrong	○○○
CVE-2014-8275	4	✗	0/3	No	None	Wrong	○○○
CVE-2022-36045	5	✗	0/3	No	None	Wrong	○○○
CVE-2013-2548	8	✗	0/2	No	None	Wrong	○○○

weakens as complexity grows. *CVE-2014-8275* illustrates this limitation clearly. The actual flaw— a certificate fingerprint malleability— is a single cryptographic issue stemming from a lack of strict DER enforcement across four distinct files (`a_verify.c`, `dsa_asn1.c`, `ecs_vrf.c`, `x_all.c`). Each file contains a distinct line that fails to enforce a part of the required cryptographic signature or encoding validation, and all these lines together create the vulnerability. However, the model treats each file in isolation, reporting unrelated, generic C programming errors within each individual file, but failing to see the cryptographic flaw. Strangely, it pointed to the correct function name in one file but failed to recognize the actual issue, instead describing an unrelated problem while ignoring the impact of the other files in the vulnerability. Similarly, the analysis of *CVE-2019-15075* highlights the model's difficulty with multi-file vulnerabilities. Although the flaw involves key interactions across `config.php` (using the keys), `astpp-config.conf` (storing them), and `install.sh` (generating them), the model analyzed each file in isolation and reported unrelated issues, failing to recognize a systemic flaw tied to weak, hardcoded keys.

These results on vulnerable codes clearly demonstrate a negative correlation between the number of source files involved and the model's effectiveness. In addition, the model exhibits a 100% false positive rate across all cases when repeating Experiment 3 on the patched versions of the codes. There is not a single instance in which the model correctly identifies the absence of a vulnerability; instead, it consistently reports random, potential vulnerabilities, as also observed in the findings of Experiments 1 and 2.

Finding 2: ChatGPT struggles to analyze vulnerabilities that span multiple source files. While it performs reasonably well in two–file cases, its effectiveness declines sharply as the number of files present increases. It has a tendency to treat each file in isolation, failing to synthesize cross-file relationships–leading to incomplete or incorrect vulnerability analysis and a high number of false positives.

5 Discussion

Our findings demonstrate that providing behavioral context in prompts significantly enhances ChatGPT's performance in analyzing single-file vulnerabilities. In our experiments, contextual prompts exhibited substantial gains across all evaluation dimensions. Specifically, relative to the total possible score, detection improved by +26%, prioritization by +41%, localization by +20%, fix correctness by +14%, and its explanation quality by +17%, when compared to direct, context-free prompts.

However, despite designing chain-of-thought (CoT) prompts and clarifying that files belong to the same project, ChatGPT still struggled with multi-file vulnerabilities. It often treated each file independently and failed to reconstruct the implicit relationships required to understand systemic issues. For instance, in real-world cases such as *CVE-2014-8275* and *CVE-2019-15075*, it raised unrelated issues in individual files but failed to capture the cross-file interactions at the core of the vulnerability. This highlights the need for strategies that help LLMs understand multi-file context, such as leveraging call graphs, inter-file Abstract Syntax Tree (ASTs), or program dependency graphs.

Additionally, the model consistently exhibited a 100% false positive rate on the patched versions of all CVEs. In no case was it able to accurately recognize the absence of a vulnerability. Instead, it consistently reported arbitrary potential bugs, even in clean code. This points to a critical limitation in ChatGPT's capacity to distinguish between genuine and non-existent vulnerabilities. More specifically, as discussed in Sect. 4, our structured prompting strategy reveals deeper insights into the model's reasoning process when analyzing benign code. In contrast, simple binary classification prompts limit the model to yes/no answers and fail to uncover the nuanced thought process behind its predictions.

Besides that, our methodical prompting process guides the LLM to produce structured, step-by-step outputs—identifying, localizing, proposing fixes, and explaining why they resolve the issue. This approach provides analysts with clear, traceable reasoning and significantly enhances their ability to detect and eliminate false positives, even when reviewing vulnerable code, thereby improving the accuracy and efficiency of the overall review process. For instance, in *CVE-2015-8867* (Table 2), our structured prompt effectively exposes false positives by requiring a concrete fix and clear justification, making the model's misunderstanding easy to identify. Although the model correctly mentions the insecure `RAND_pseudo_bytes` function, it buries this critical issue among unrelated concerns. Nonetheless, for each of these other issues raised, the model could only provide vague explanations, as to the cause. It often failed to identify the line concerned, instead referencing unrelated code and could not suggest an adequate fix. This misalignment across localization, fix, and explanation demonstrates how structured prompting helps surface and filter out incorrect predictions.

Threats to Validity. Our data primarily focuses on cryptographic vulnerabilities and the performance of a single LLM, namely ChatGPT. As a result, it does not cover the complete range of vulnerability types or all relevant benchmarks. However, this choice allows for a controlled and in-depth evaluation without conflating differences across architectures and domain. Specifically, prior works [8–10] show that multiple LLMs tend to exhibit similar reasoning patterns and limitations, especially in security tasks. Additionally, our study provides a reusable evaluation framework, ensuring the methodology generalizes beyond the examined LLM. Moreover, it is likely that some of the CVEs selected for testing were part of the model's training data. However, our evaluation process was deliberately manual, enabling a detailed analysis of model performance on each CVE and capturing subtleties that large-scale, metric-driven approaches may overlook. This focused, qualitative methodology allowed for a careful selection of CVEs for in-depth testing. That being said, even if the model had encountered the code during training, its poor performance in the context-free setting suggests that prior exposure alone was insufficient for effective vulnerability analysis, and that it may have forgotten relevant details. Nevertheless, our framework is designed to be easily extensible, allowing for the inclusion of additional CVE scenarios and the evaluation of other models in the future, with token limits being the primary consideration.

6 Related Work

Several recent studies have investigated the use of LLMs in vulnerability analysis. While all aim to assess their effectiveness, the approaches differ across three key aspects: dataset selection, levels of granularity, and prompt design.

Dataset Selection. Some studies rely on synthetic datasets, such as Devign [11] and CrySL [12]. While useful for controlled experimentation, these synthetic cases often fail to reflect the complexity and contextual dependencies of real-world vulnerabilities, limiting their applicability. In contrast, other works use real-world CVE-based datasets such as CVEfixes [14] and Big-Vul [13], offering more realistic but challenging scenarios.

Levels of Granularity (Function, File, Repository). Most studies limit evaluation to function-level, which simplifies analysis but ignores interprocedural dependencies, or to single-file inputs. Few studies attempt multi-file analysis, but feeding entire repositories [15] which overwhelms the model with excessive and irrelevant context, degrading performance.

Prompt Design. Studies often use direct prompts, which are simple but fragile and offer limited insight [16]. More deliberate prompt engineering strategies have been proposed, such as semantics-guided prompting built on specialized CoT prompt [17]. Nonetheless, this strategy has mainly been tested on two single-file datasets—real and synthetic—forming a hybrid evaluation scenario, but its effectiveness in multi-file scenarios remains unclear.

Distinctively, our work addresses these limitations by combining real-world cryptographic vulnerability dataset with a prompt design inspired by professional auditing practices. We augment this prompt with behavioral context to enhance vulnerability analysis on single-file inputs. Additionally, we use it to evaluate the LLM's performance in multi-file scenarios by selectively providing only the relevant files that directly contribute to the vulnerability, avoiding context overload.

7 Conclusion

We perform a multi-task evaluation to assess ChatGPT's ability to detect, prioritize, localize, and repair real-world cryptographic software vulnerabilities, while also justifying its proposed fixes. The framework is driven by carefully designed prompts inspired by professional practices. Our research reveals that ChatGPT performs significantly better on single-file vulnerability analysis when provided with clear contextual information, compared to when behavioral context is absent. However, its performance drops in multi-file scenarios, where it struggles to integrate dispersed information—even when guided by structured prompts. Moreover, the model tends to generate a high rate of false positives, especially when analyzing benign code.

In future work, we aim to extend our behavioral context prompting strategy to each affected file in multi-file CVEs, as it has already proven effective in the single-file case. This will help determine whether improved performance in multi-file scenarios depends solely on prompt engineering or also on the model's internal reasoning capabilities.

Disclosure of Interests. The authors have no competing interests to declare that are relevant to the content of this article.

References

1. National Institute of Standards and Technology (NIST): National Vulnerability Database (NVD). https://nvd.nist.gov/, Accessed 25 June 2025
2. Kohnfelder, L.: Designing Secure Software: A Guide for Developers. No Starch Press, San Francisco (2021)
3. OpenAI, "GPT-4 Turbo," https://platform.openai.com/docs/models/gpt-4-turbo
4. OpenAI, "GPT Best Practices," https://platform.openai.com/docs/guides/gpt-best-practices, Accessed 25 June 2025

5. Khoury, R., Bolduc, J., Lafrenière-Nickopoulos, J., Odedele, A.-G.: Analysis of cryptographic CVEs: lessons learned and perspectives. In: Lal, C., Lanet, J.-L. (eds.) FPS 2023, LNCS, vol. 14334, pp. 208–218. Springer, Cham (2023)
6. Bakhshandeh, A., Keramatfar, A., Norouzi, A., Chekidehkhoun, M.M.: Using ChatGPT as a Static Application Security Testing Tool (2023)
7. Firouzi, E., Ghafari, M., Ebrahimi, M.: ChatGPT's potential in cryptography misuse detection: a comparative analysis with static analysis tools. In: Proceedings of the 18th ACM/IEEE International Symposium on Empirical Software Engineering and Measurement (ESEM 2024), pp. 582–588 (2024)
8. Khare, A., Dutta, S., Li, Z., Solko-Breslin, A., Alur, R., Naik, M.: Understanding the effectiveness of large language models in detecting security vulnerabilities. In: Proceedings of the 2025 IEEE Conference on Software Testing, Verification and Validation (ICST), pp. 103–114 (2025)
9. Ullah, S., Han, M., Pujar, S., Pearce, H., Coskun, A., Stringhini, G.: LLMs cannot reliably identify and reason about security vulnerabilities (yet?): a comprehensive evaluation, framework, and benchmarks. In: Proceedings of the 2024 IEEE Symposium on Security and Privacy (SP), pp. 862–880 (2024)
10. Lin, J., Mohaisen, D.: From large to mammoth: a comparative evaluation of large language models in vulnerability detection. In: Proceedings of the 2025 Network and Distributed System Security Symposium (NDSS) (2025)
11. Zhou, Y., Liu, S., Siow, J., Du, X., Liu, Y.: Devign: effective vulnerability identification by learning comprehensive program semantics via graph neural networks. In: NeurIPS (2019)
12. Krüger, S., Mainka, C., Schwenk, J.: CrySL: an extensible approach to validating the correct usage of cryptographic APIs. In: CCS (2018)
13. Fan, J., Li, Y., Wang, S., Nguyen, T.N.: A C/C++ code vulnerability dataset with code changes and CVE summaries. In: Proceedings of the 17th International Conference on Mining Software Repositories, ser. MSR '20. New York, NY, USA: Association for Computing Machinery, pp. 508–512 (2020)
14. Bhandari, G., Naseer, A., Moonen, L.: CVEfixes: automated collection of vulnerabilities and their fixes from open-source software. In: Proceedings of the 17th International Conference on Predictive Models and Data Analytics in Software Engineering (PROMISE '21), p. 10 (2021)
15. Li, Z., Dutta, S., Naik, M.: IRIS: LLM-assisted static analysis for detecting security vulnerabilities. In: International Conference on Learning Representations (ICLR 2025) (2025)
16. Farr, D., Talty, K., Farr, A., Stockdale, J., Cruickshank, I., West, J.: Expert-in-the-Loop systems with cross-domain and in-domain few-shot learning for software vulnerability detection. arXiv preprint arXiv:2506.10104 (2025)
17. Nong, Y., Aldeen, M., Cheng, L., Hu, H., Chen, F., Cai, H.: Chain-of-thought prompting of large language models for discovering and fixing software vulnerabilities. arXiv preprint arXiv:2402.17230 (2024)

Context-Aware Entity-Relation Extraction for Threat Intelligence Knowledge Graphs

Inoussa Mouiche(✉) and Sherif Saad

School of Computer Science, University of Windsor, ON, Canada
{mouiche,shsaad}@uwindsor.ca

Abstract. Cybersecurity Knowledge Graphs (CKGs) unify diverse Cyber Threat Intelligence (CTI) sources into structured, queryable formats, offering scalable solutions for automating proactive and real-time security responses. Their increasing adoption has significantly enhanced the workflow and decision-making efficiency of security professionals. However, constructing CKGs requires extracting entity–relation triples from unstructured CTI reports, a task hindered by complex report structure, domain-specific language, and semantic ambiguity. As a result, existing pipeline-based approaches often suffer from error propagation, reducing extraction accuracy and limiting generalizability. This paper introduces the Context-aware Threat Intelligence Knowledge Graph (CTiKG) framework, a pipeline architecture designed to accurately extract and classify threat entities and their relationships from CTI reports. CTiKG incorporates hybrid NLP models that leverage SecureBERT^{+} contextual embeddings and expert knowledge from a domain ontology to reduce misclassifications and mitigate cascading errors. Experiments on the DNRTI-AUG-STIX2 dataset, which comprises 21 entity types aligned with STIX 2.1, demonstrate significant improvements over state-of-the-art baselines, yielding 3–4% gains in NER and up to 8% in RE performance, based on precision, recall, and F1-score. Additional validation on DNRTI and STUCCO benchmarks confirms the framework's robustness and practical applicability. All datasets, including the curated DNRTI-AUG-STIX2, are released on GitHub to foster reproducibility and further research.

Keywords: Context-aware threat intelligence knowledge graphs · Cyber Threat Intelligence · Cyber Knowledge Graphs · Joint Extraction · Pipeline Extraction

1 Introduction

The rise of stealthy Advanced Persistent Threats (APTs) underscores the need for adaptive defense strategies. A recent breach disclosed by MITRE, affecting over 1,700 organizations, illustrates that no entity is immune to targeted cyberattacks [1,2]. To anticipate such threats, security teams rely on unstructured cyber threat intelligence (CTI) reports, which capture insights on threat actors, tactics,

K. Adi et al. (Eds.): CRiSIS 2025, LNCS 16295, pp. 336–352, 2026.
https://doi.org/10.1007/978-3-032-20732-6_21

and attack patterns. Cybersecurity Knowledge Graphs (CKGs) have emerged as a promising solution, transforming unstructured CTI into structured intelligence that supports automation, real-time analysis, and proactive defense [3,4]. By integrating diverse sources, CKGs enhance situational awareness, improve threat understanding, and enable predictive defense.

Constructing CKGs from CTI reports requires two NLP tasks: named entity recognition (NER) and relation extraction (RE). Joint extraction (JE) models integrate both tasks but often suffer from feature confusion and overlapping relations [5,6], while pipeline extraction (PE) allows modular optimization but is vulnerable to error propagation from entity to relation classification [8,9]. Both approaches struggle with the narrative complexity and language ambiguity of CTI, reducing the precision and generalizability of CKGs.

To address these issues, Mouiche and Saad [10] introduced TiKG, a pipeline framework leveraging SecureBERT [12] embeddings and a domain ontology. Despite strong performance, TiKG's NER component (a TDD-softmax classifier) can produce inconsistent BIO tags [13], and its RE model, based on a generic language model, struggles with cybersecurity-specific jargon. As a result, TiKG remains susceptible to error propagation, particularly on large and complex datasets. This paper extends TiKG with the following contributions:

- A novel NER architecture combining SecureBERT$^+$ [11] embeddings with a CRF layer, achieving up to a 4% F1 improvement across 21 entity categories.
- A new RE architecture, base-SecureBERT$^+$, which integrates domain-specific contextual embeddings and ontology-based error control, improving F1 by up to 8%.
- A comprehensive evaluation on the DNRTI-AUG-STIX2 dataset, with further validation on DNRTI [14] and STUCCO [15], demonstrating effectiveness and generalizability.
- The release of three benchmark datasets DNRTI-AUG-STIX2, DNRTI, and STUCCO on GitHub[1] to support reproducibility and future research.

Paper structure: Sect. 2 reviews related work, Sect. 3 presents the proposed framework and experiments, Sect. 4 discusses CKG construction, and Sect. 5 concludes with key findings and future directions.

2 Related Work

CTI-to-CKG extraction methods typically follow either pipeline (PE) or joint extraction (JE) paradigms.

2.1 Joint Extraction

JE unifies NER and RE in a single model to reduce error propagation and improve accuracy. Many approaches use multi-task learning with shared encoders

[1] https://github.com/imouiche/Threat-Intelligence-Knowledge-Graphs.

and transformer-based architectures. Examples include ERBTF [16], which combines relation and word embeddings; CyberRel [9,17] and CyberEntRel [8], which model JE as sequence labeling with BiGRU/CRF layers; and Liu et al. [18], who framed JE as a table-filling task with SecBERT. More recent models include CTI-TFN [19], a Fourier-based joint model, ITIRel [20] for overlapping IoT relations, and TIJERE [21], a data-centric JE framework.

JE models streamline extraction but lack flexibility; modifying one task often requires retraining the entire system. They also struggle with overlapping entities [5], feature confusion [7], and limited domain adaptation when relying on generic LMs [10].

This work instead extends the PE approach of TiKG [10], decoupling NER and RE for modular design. Each subtask leverages SecureBERT embeddings, with a domain ontology guiding entity–relation mapping to improve classification and CKG quality.

2.2 Pipeline Extraction

In PE, NER identifies entities, and RE generates relation triples. Studies adopting this paradigm include Gasmi et al. [22] (BiLSTM-CRF), HINT [23] (attention BiLSTM-CRF + heterogeneous graphs), Vulcan [24] (BERT-BiLSTM-CRF for ransomware), and STIXnet [25], which integrates regex, dependency parsing, and neural RE. Other methods include SVM-based vulnerability extraction [26], entity–coreference integration (EEMAP [27]), and OIE-based approaches like Open-CyKG [4].

Piplai et al. [28] structured a CKG using UCO 2.0, while our framework enhances TiKG [10] with SecureBERT^{+}-based NER/RE. These upgrades improve domain relevance, mitigate misclassification, and reduce error propagation. Evaluations on DNRTI-AUG-STIX2 and validation on DNRTI and STUCCO datasets show 3–4% higher NER F1 and 8% higher RE F1, establishing CTiKG as a robust, security-aware framework for threat analysis, profiling, and defense strategy development.

3 CTiKG: Context-Aware Threat Intelligence Knowledge Graph Framework

This section presents the proposed CTiKG framework, a novel CTI extraction pipeline for constructing CKGs, inspired by Mouiche and Saad [10]. As shown in Fig. 1, the framework comprises three main phases:

- **Phase 1: Data Collection and Processing**: Reports are crawled from CTI repositories (e.g., APT repository, MITRE ATT&CK, TrendMicro) and converted into plain-text using HTMLParser, PDFLib, and pdftotext. Preprocessing sanitizes text (e.g., obfuscating URLs and emails) to produce .txt files simulating raw inputs for the extraction pipeline.

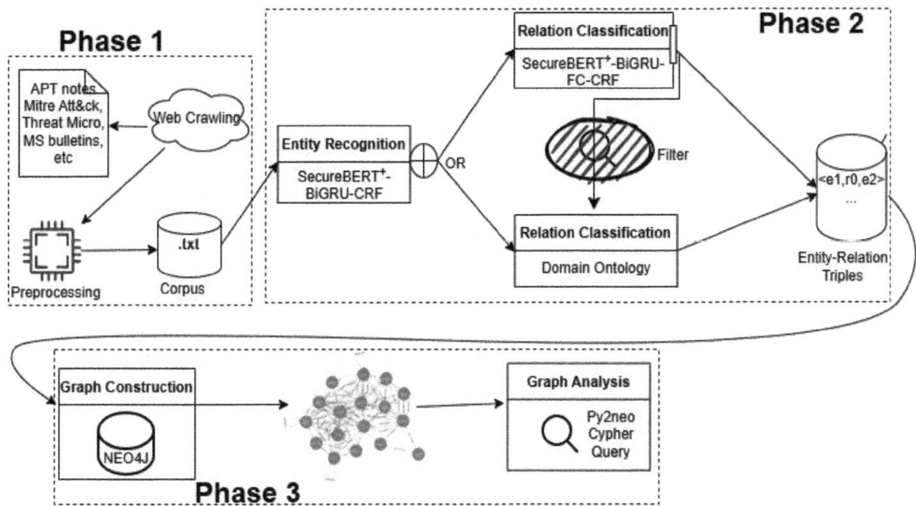

Fig. 1. Context-aware Threat Intelligence Knowledge Graph Framework: CTiKG.

- **Phase 2: Entity–Relation Extraction**: This phase extracts threat entities and their relationships from the processed text through two modules: *Entity Recognition* and *Relation Classification*. The former identifies and labels entities in the Phase 1 reports according to predefined categories, while the latter uses either a rule-based *Domain Ontology* or a hybrid method that combines SecureBERT$^+$-BiGRU-CRF with the ontology. For small to medium datasets, the ontology alone can generate reliable *Entity–Relation Triples*. For larger datasets, the hybrid method improves scalability and accuracy: the ML model predicts relations, and misclassified instances are corrected through the ontology.
- **Phase 3: Construction and Analysis of CTiKG**: This final phase builds and evaluates the knowledge graph using the entity-relation triples from Phase 2. Neo4j stores entities as nodes and relations as edges. The graph is populated and analyzed using the Neo4j graph data science library, which also enables query-based retrieval to assess the quality and effectiveness of the constructed CTiKG.

The proposed context-aware pipeline enhances the CTI workflow by transforming unstructured reports into a structured, queryable format that reveals hidden patterns and supports timely, informed decision-making for security stakeholders. The following sections detail the core components of the CTiKG framework and highlight the key enhancements introduced over the original TiKG model [10].

3.1 Entity Recognition

In pipeline extraction, errors in NER directly propagate to RE, reducing the quality of extracted triples and the resulting CKG. Ensuring high NER accuracy is therefore critical. In the TiKG framework [10], SecureBERT-BiLSTM-TDD was adopted for entity recognition: SecureBERT provided contextual embeddings, BiLSTM captured token dependencies, and the TDD layer performed token-level classification. However, since TDD predicts tokens independently with softmax, it often produces invalid spans (e.g., missing B-tags or misaligned I-sequences) [13], which introduce noise into RE and degrade relation classification. To address this limitation, we replace TDD with a CRF layer to enforce valid tag transitions and improve sequence-level consistency [29]. We also integrate SecureBERT$^+$ [11], a domain-adapted variant that improves contextual representation, and combine BiLSTM and BiGRU sequential modeling to further enhance dependency capture and robustness in CTI reports.

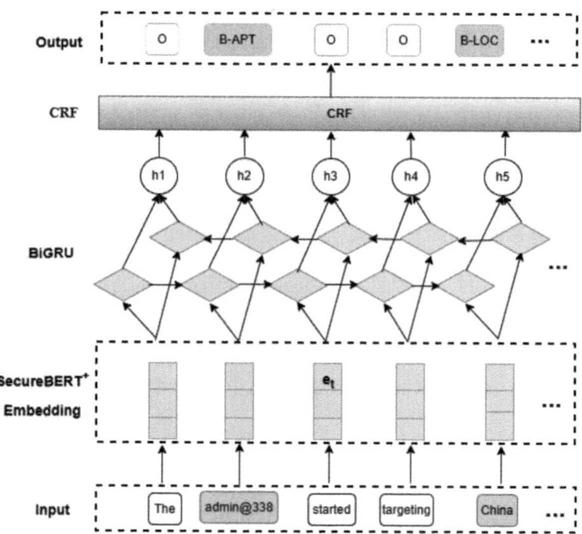

Fig. 2. NER model's archicteure (SecureBERT$^+$-BiGRU-CRF).

Figure 2 presents our hybrid model, which can be described as follows:

– **Input to SecureBERT$^+$ Embedding:**

$$\mathbf{e}_t = \text{SecureBERT}^+(\mathbf{x}_t) \quad \forall t \in \{1, \ldots, T\}, \tag{1}$$

Where $\mathbf{x}$ is the input sequence of length T, $\mathbf{x}_t$ represents the tth input tokens, and $\mathbf{e}_t$ is the corresponding embedding produced by SecureBERT$^+$.

- **SecureBERT$^+$ Embedding to BiGRU:**

$$\mathbf{h}_t = \text{BiGRU}(\mathbf{e}_t) \tag{2}$$

Here, $\mathbf{h}_t$ is the hidden state at time step t produced by the bidirectional GRU.

- **BiGRU to CRF Emissions:**

$$\mathbf{o}_t = \mathbf{W}\mathbf{h}_t + \mathbf{b} \tag{3}$$

where $\mathbf{W}$ is the weight matrix and $\mathbf{b}$ is the bias vector. $\mathbf{o}_t$ represents the emissions for the CRF layer.

- **CRF Layer:**

$$\mathbf{y} = \arg\max_{\mathbf{y}'} P(\mathbf{y}'|\mathbf{o}) \tag{4}$$

where $P(\mathbf{y}'|\mathbf{o})$ is the conditional probability of the label sequence $\mathbf{y}'$ given the emissions $\mathbf{o}$. In a CRF, the probability of a particular label sequence $\mathbf{y}$ given the emissions $\mathbf{o}$ is given by:

$$P(\mathbf{y}|\mathbf{o}) = \frac{\exp(\text{z}(\mathbf{o}, \mathbf{y}))}{\sum_{\mathbf{y}'} \exp(\text{z}(\mathbf{o}, \mathbf{y}'))} \tag{5}$$

where $\text{z}(\mathbf{o}, \mathbf{y})$ is given by:

$$\text{z}(\mathbf{o}, \mathbf{y}) = \sum_{t=1}^{T} \left(\mathbf{A}_{y_{t-1}, y_t} + \mathbf{o}_{t, y_t}\right) \tag{6}$$

Here, T is the length of the input sequence $\mathbf{x}$, $\mathbf{A}$ is the transition matrix, $\mathbf{A}_{y_{t-1}, y_t}$ represents the score of transitioning from label y_{t-1} to label y_t, and $\mathbf{o}_{t, y_t}$ is the emission score for label y_t at time step t. For the CRF, the loss function $\mathcal{L}$ is typically the negative log-likelihood given by:

$$\mathcal{L} = -\log P(\mathbf{y}|\mathbf{o}) = -\log\left(\frac{\exp(\text{z}(\mathbf{o}, \mathbf{y}))}{\sum_{\mathbf{y}'} \exp(\text{z}(\mathbf{o}, \mathbf{y}'))}\right) \tag{7}$$

where,

$$\sum_{\mathbf{y}'} \exp(\text{z}(\mathbf{o}, \mathbf{y}')) = \sum_{\mathbf{y}'} \exp\left(\sum_{t=1}^{T} \left(\mathbf{A}_{y'_{t-1}, y'_t} + \mathbf{o}_{t, y'_t}\right)\right) \tag{8}$$

The Eq. 8 is also called the partition function and normalizes the probability distribution over all possible label sequences $\mathbf{y}'$.

With the mathematical formulation established, we proceed to implement and evaluate the SecureBERT$^+$-BiGRU-CRF model, comparing its performance with existing extraction models in the literature.

3.2 NER Implementation

Datasets. This study uses DNRTI-AUG-STIX2, an augmented version of the DNRTI-STIX2 threat intelligence NER dataset recently released by [30]. DNRTI-STIX2 was designed to align with the STIX 2.1 standard [31], covering a diverse range of STIX domain and observable objects and making it well-suited for entity–relation extraction. Unlike earlier datasets with narrow coverage, it includes 21 entity categories distributed across 6,580 sentences (see Table 1). However, it suffers from severe class imbalance, with some categories having fewer than five instances. Prior work [32] suggests that at least 50 samples per class are needed for models to learn contextual features effectively. To mitigate this limitation, we applied targeted data augmentation to transform DNRTI-STIX2 into DNRTI-AUG-STIX2.

- **Data Augmentation (DA):** To increase representation of under-sampled classes, we annotated additional APT report sentences curated for CTiKG testing. A total of 1,367 sentences were manually labeled by three students (two master's and one PhD, all with security backgrounds) using the same 21 entity types and BIO tagging scheme as DNRTI-STIX2. Sentences were selected to ensure coverage of less frequent entity classes. Annotation guidelines were established through two calibration meetings, after which the dataset was divided (50% PhD, 25% each master's student). Conflicts were resolved by majority vote, with the PhD student's vote weighted at 50%. The resulting annotations were added to DNRTI-STIX2.
- **Data Consolidation (DC):** Rare classes were merged into broader categories. For example, SHA1, SHA2, and MD5 were consolidated into a single entity type, `HASH`, representing hash algorithms.

The results after applying DA and DC are shown in the last two columns of Table 1. This increased 1367 sentences and 2297 new vocabularies. Additionally, the number of entities was reduced from 21 to 19 due to merging SHA1, SHA2, and MD5 into a single HASH entity type. The resulting augmented dataset as DNRTI-AUG-STIX2 will be made available on our GitHub to support research in the field.
To scale the generalization and reproducibility, we validate our models on two additional open-source NER datasets: DNRTI [14] and STUCCO [15].

- DNRTI: This dataset contains 175,220 tokens in 6,592 sentences describing APT reports. It features 13 entity categories: HackOrg, OffAct, SamFile, SecTeam, Tool, Time, Purp, Area, Idus, Org, Way, Exp, and Features.
- STUCCO: This dataset contains CVE and NVD descriptions, totaling 680,764 tokens represented in 15,192 sentences. It encompasses 15 entity types: application, cveID, edition, file, function, hardware, method, OS, parameter, programming language, relevant term, update, vendor, and version.

Table 1. DNRTI-STIX2 transformed into DNRTI-AUG-STIX2 using Data Augmentation (DA) and Data Consolidation (DC).

DNRTI-STIX2		DNRTI-AUG-STIX2	
Entity Type	Count	Entity Type	Count
ACT	8871	ACT	9070
APT	5867	APT	5906
DOM	41	DOM	435
EMAIL	32	EMAIL	66
ENCR	41	ENCR	242
FILE	2105	FILE	2458
IDTY	5573	HASH	483
IP	14	IDTY	5845
LOC	3520	IP	229
MAL	3294	LOC	3615
MD5	5	MAL	3924
OS	242	OS	600
PROT	160	PROT	519
SECTEAM	1953	SECTEAM	2026
SHA1	2	TIME	3039
SHA2	6	TOOL	3898
TIME	2675	URL	100
TOOL	3062	VULID	803
URL	6	VULNAME	1312
VULID	747		
VULNAME	1243		
# of sentences	6580	# of sentences	**7947**
vocab_size	9444	vocab_size	**11741**
# of entity types	21	# of entity types	**19**

Training and Evaluation. For training and evaluation, we divided the dataset into training, validation, and testing sets with a split ratio of 70%, 15%, and 15% respectively. Table 2 provides the base model parameter settings, as reported in [10]. It is important to note that we used the same parameters for the RoBERTa base model as those used with SecureBERT variants.

To demonstrate the performance of our proposed NER models, we implemented other state-of-the-art approaches from scratch to serve as baselines. We employed standard metrics such as Precision (P), Recall (R), and F1-score (F1) for evaluation and comparison.

The performance comparison in Table 3 shows that the SecureBERT$^+$-BiGRU-CRF model consistently outperforms all other NER models across the

Table 2. NER Models' parameter settings.

parameters	SecureBERT	BERT	BiLSTM
batch size	8	8	16
dropout	0.2	0.2	0.2
epsilon	1e-8	1e-8	–
initial learning rate	5e-5	5e-5	5e-5
hidden layer size	128 × 2	128 × 2	100 × 2
embedding size	768	768	300
number of epochs	4	4	10
optimizer	AdamW	AdamW	AdamW

Table 3. NER models: Evaluation results, comparisons and validation across DNRTI-AUG-STIX2, DNRTI, and STUCCO datasets.

Models	DNRTI-AUG-STIX2			DNRTI			STUCCO		
	P	R	F1	P	R	F1	P	R	F1
BiLSTM-CRF	0.68	0.70	0.70	0.67	0.72	0.71	0.76	0.77	0.75
RoBERTa	0.80	0.83	0.81	0.81	0.85	0.83	0.93	0.94	0.93
BERT-BiLSTM-CRF [5,24]	0.80	0.85	0.83	0.82	0.84	0.83	0.95	0.96	0.95
BERT-BiGRU-CRF [9]	0.84	0.87	0.86	0.85	0.85	0.85	0.96	0.96	0.95
RoBERTa-BiLSTM-TDD+Att [10]	0.87	0.89	0.88	0.86	0.88	0.87	0.96	0.97	0.96
RoBERTa-BiGRU-CRF [4,8]	0.88	0.89	0.89	0.89	0.90	0.89	0.97	0.97	0.96
SecureBERT-BiLSTM-TDD+Att [10]	0.89	0.90	0.90	0.90	0.91	0.90	0.97	0.98	0.97
SecureBERT-BiLSTM-CRF	0.91	0.91	0.91	0.92	0.91	0.91	0.98	0.98	0.98
SecureBERT-BiGRU-CRF	**0.93**	**0.92**	**0.92**	**0.93**	**0.94**	**0.93**	**0.99**	**0.99**	**0.98**
SecureBERT^{+}-BiGRU-CRF	**0.93**	**0.94**	**0.93**	**0.94**	**0.95**	**0.94**	**0.99**	**0.99**	**0.98**

DNRTI-AUG-STIX2, DNRTI, and STUCCO datasets. It achieves the highest scores on all three datasets, with Precision (0.93), Recall (0.94), and F1-score (0.93) on DNRTI-AUG-STIX2, Precision (0.94), Recall (0.95), and F1-score (0.94) on DNRTI, and Precision (0.99), Recall (0.99), and F1-score (0.98) on STUCCO. These results confirm the superior performance and generalization capability of our proposed model in extracting cybersecurity-specific entities. The results also demonstrate that integrating a CRF layer over SecureBERT^{+} embeddings yields consistent improvements over earlier architectures such as SecureBERT-BiLSTM-TDD [10], achieving 3–4% higher precision, recall, and F1-scores. This enhancement can be attributed to the CRF's ability to model sequence-level dependencies and produce more coherent BIO tag sequences. Moreover, we observe that there is no significant performance gap between SecureBERT and its improved variant SecureBERT^{+} in the context of entity extraction. Despite SecureBERT^{+} achieving a 9% improvement in masked lan-

guage modeling [11], this gain does not directly translate into enhanced NER performance, suggesting that improvements at the pretraining level may not always yield proportional benefits for downstream tasks like NER.
All implemented models perform strongly on the STUCCO dataset. This is not only due to better class distribution but also because STUCCO's vulnerability descriptions exhibit consistent linguistic patterns, reducing ambiguity across entity types and improving model prediction accuracy.

3.3 Relation Extraction Model

The prior TiKG framework [10] relied on general-purpose language models pretrained on corpora such as Wikipedia and BooksCorpus. These models fail to capture cybersecurity-specific terminology and contextual nuances in APT reports. For example, terms like "APT28" or "Mimikatz" carry precise meanings only within the cybersecurity domain, yet generic models often misclassify their roles, leading to errors that degrade knowledge graph quality. To overcome this limitation, we adopt the same security-aware backbone used in our NER model, SecureBERT$^+$-BiGRU, ensuring consistency and domain-awareness across the pipeline. Unlike NER, relation types are independent and lack sequential dependencies, so we replace the CRF layer with a TDD layer, simplifying the architecture and enabling faster inference. This design significantly improves relation classification, yielding up to a 7% increase in F1 score compared to prior approaches. The resulting RE model architecture is illustrated in Fig. 3 and formally defined as follows:

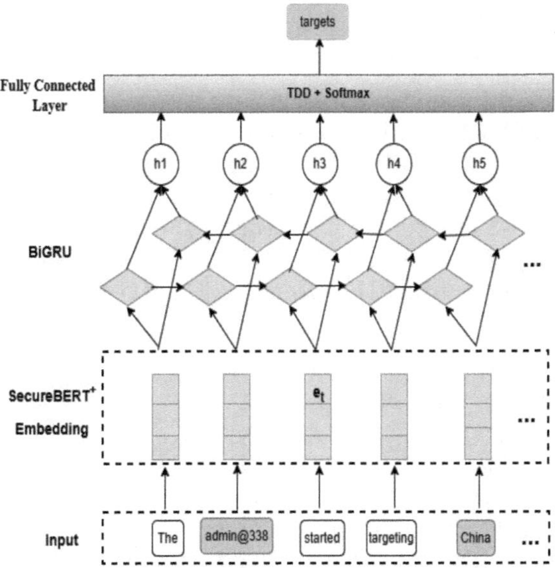

Fig. 3. SecureBERT$^+$-BiGRU-TDD relation extraction model.

- **Input to SecureBERT$^+$ Embedding:**

$$\mathbf{e}_t = \text{SecureBERT}^+(\mathbf{x}_t), \quad \forall t \in \{1, \dots, T\}, \tag{9}$$

 where $\mathbf{x} = (x_1, \dots, x_T)$ is the input token sequence, and $\mathbf{e}_t$ is the contextual embedding of token x_t produced by SecureBERT$^+$.
- **SecureBERT$^+$ Embedding to BiGRU:**

$$\mathbf{h}_t = \text{BiGRU}(\mathbf{e}_t), \tag{10}$$

 where $\mathbf{h}_t$ is the hidden state at time step t produced by the bidirectional GRU.
- **BiGRU to Fully Connected Layer (TDD):**

$$\mathbf{f}_t = \mathbf{W}_{\text{fc}}\mathbf{h}_t + \mathbf{b}_{\text{fc}}, \tag{11}$$

 where $\mathbf{W}_{\text{fc}}$ and $\mathbf{b}_{\text{fc}}$ are the parameters of the time-distributed dense layer, and $\mathbf{f}_t$ is the logit vector at time step t.
- **Softmax Output for Relation Classification:**

$$\hat{y}_t = \text{softmax}(\mathbf{f}_t), \tag{12}$$

 where $\hat{y}_t$ is the predicted probability distribution over relation labels for the entity pair at time step t.

Training and evaluating the relation extraction model requires an annotated dataset with relation labels. To support this, we introduce a domain ontology specifically designed for the DNRTI-AUG-STIX2 dataset. This ontology aids both in labeling the dataset and in post-processing model outputs, improving relation classification accuracy.

DNRTI-AUG-STIX2 Domain Ontology. Syed et al. [33] introduced the unified cyber ontology (UCO) 2.0 framework to standardize threat information representation. Inspired by this, we defined a domain-specific ontology tailored to the DNRTI-AUG-STIX2 dataset, capturing threat entities and their relationships. The ontology defines 15 relations to describe connections between entity pairs, improving the resulting CKG from the CTiKG framework:

- affiliatedWith: APT → APT
- associatedWith: (HASH, VULNAME, VULID) → (EMAIL, ACT, ENCR, DOM, URL, TOOL, OS, PROT)
- contains: (FILE, EMAIL) → (MAL, IP, URL)
- hasAttackLocation: (APT, MAL, ACT) → LOC
- hasAttackTime: (APT, MAL, ACT) → TIME
- hasLocation: (IDTY, SECTEAM) → LOC
- hasVulnerability: (IDTY, OS, URL, DOM, PROT, FILE) → (VULID, VULNAME)
- identifies: SECTEAM → (APT, MAL, VULNAME, VULID, ACT)

- identifiedBy: (APT, MAL, VULNAME, VULID, ACT) → SECTEAM
- monitors: SECTEAM → (IDTY, DOM, FILE)
- monitoredBy: (IDTY, LOC, FILE) → SECTEAM
- targets: (APT, MAL, ACT) → (IDTY, DOM, VULNAME, VULID, OS)
- targetedBy: (IDTY, DOM, VULNAME, VULID, OS, LOC) → (APT, MAL, ACT)
- uses: (APT, MAL, ACT) → (EMAIL, IP, URL, FILE, TOOL, HASH, ENCR, MAL, ACT)
- usedBy: (EMAIL, IP, URL, FILE, TOOL, HASH, ENCR, MAL, ACT) → (APT, MAL, ACT)

A sample schema is shown in Fig. 4, including 9 of 19 entity types and 12 of 16 relation types. We used this ontology to automatically assign relation types to entity pairs, discarding invalid ones. This enabled consistent, ontology-guided annotation of DNRTI-AUG-STIX2.

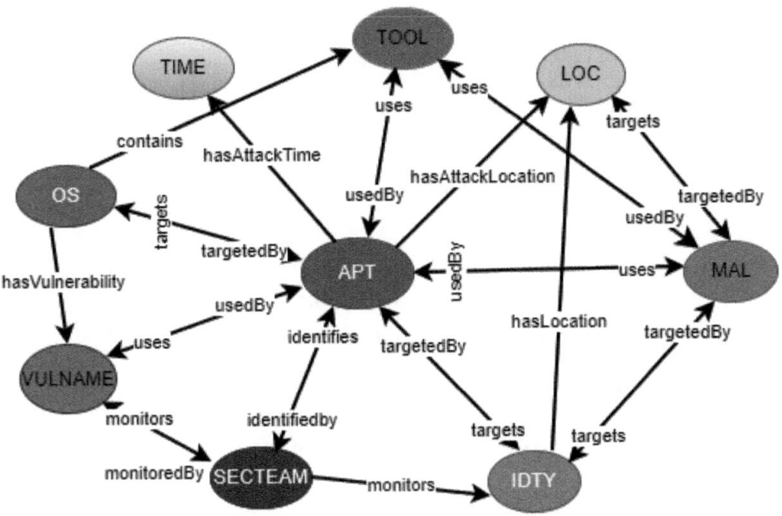

Fig. 4. A sample ontology schema containing entities (nodes) and 12 relation categories (edges).

Training and Evaluation. The DNRTI-AUG-STIX2 dataset was split into training, validation, and test sets (70:15:15). Default hyperparameters for each RE model are listed in Table 4, following [10]. We reimplemented several state-of-the-art RE approaches as baselines to benchmark our models.

Table 5 shows that SecureBERT^{+}-BiGRU-TDD achieved the best performance (Precision/Recall/F1 = 0.98), closely matched by SecureBERT-BiGRU-TDD. The added 9% MLM gain of SecureBERT^{+} provided no meaningful RE

Table 4. RE Models' hyper-parameter settings.

parameters	SecureBERT	BERT	BiLSTM	CNN
batch size	16	16	16	16
dropout	0.3	0.3	0.3	0.3
epsilon	1e-8	1e-8	1e-8	1e-8
initial learning rate	5e-5	5e-5	5e-5	5e-5
hidden layer size	100 × 2	100 × 2	100 × 2	-
embedding size	768	768	300	300
number of epochs	4	4	50	100
optimizer	AdamW	AdamW	AdamW	AdamW
window	–	–	–	3
pos_dim, pos_dist	–	–	–	5, 50

Table 5. RE models: Evaluation results and comparisons

Models	Precision	Recall	F1
Glove-CNN-TDD+Att [10]	0.84	0.84	0.84
BERT-BiLSTM-TDD+Att [10]	0.90	0.89	0.89
Glove-BiLSTM-TDD+Att [10]	0.91	0.91	0.91
RobERTa-BiGRU-CRF	0.94	0.94	0.94
RobERTa-BiGRU-TDD	0.95	0.94	0.94
SecureBERT-BiGRU-CRF	**0.97**	**0.97**	**0.97**
SecureBERT$^+$-BiGRU-CRF	**0.98**	**0.97**	**0.97**
SecureBERT$^+$-BiGRU-TDD	**0.98**	**0.98**	**0.98**

improvement. Similarly, CRF-based variants offered no advantage over TDD-only models, indicating that CRF layers add complexity without measurable benefit. Compared with RobERTa-BiGRU-CRF (F1 = 0.94) and Glove-BiLSTM-TDD+Att (F1 = 0.91), SecureBERT-based models show clear improvements in both precision and consistency. Overall, they outperform TiKG's RE module [10] by 6–8% across all metrics, validating the benefit of domain-specific contextual embeddings and streamlined architectures.

Figure 5 illustrates SecureBERT$^+$-BiGRU-TDD training dynamics, showing rapid loss reduction and stable validation trends, with F1 convergence near 0.96. This demonstrates effective learning and minimal overfitting. The early-stage divergence, characterized by a rapid decline in training loss but only a modest decrease in validation loss, indicates rapid model fitting with limited immediate generalization. However, both training and validation F1 scores continue to improve and converge around 0.96, confirming the model's ability to maintain high validation precision. Integrating these models into the TiKG pipeline yields

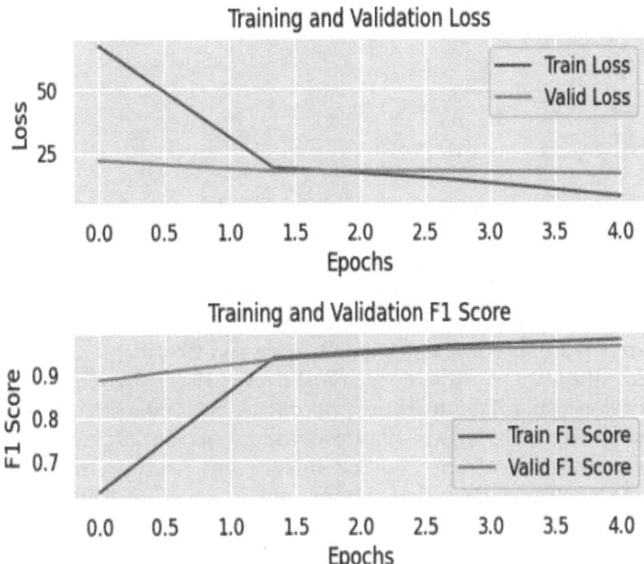

Fig. 5. SecureBERT$^+$-BiGRU-TDD: training and validation losses and F1 Scores.

CTiKG, a fully security-aware system with improved NER and RE, reducing error propagation and enhancing the reliability of the constructed CKG.

The knowledge graph construction and downstream analysis based on the proposed CTiKG framework follow a similar process to its predecessor, TiKG [10]. These aspects are left for future work, where a comparative study of both pipelines will assess their effectiveness in supporting threat prediction and countermeasure planning, ultimately aiding security analysts in timely and informed decision-making.

4 Conclusion

We presented CTiKG, a context-aware threat intelligence knowledge graph framework combining SecureBERT$^+$ embeddings with BiGRU and CRF architectures for accurate NER and RE. A domain ontology further guided entity-pair classification, ensuring coherent graph construction. Trained on DNRTI-AUG-STIX2, our models achieved up to 3–4% NER and 8% RE gains over prior work, including TiKG, with validation and robustness confirmed across DNRTI and STUCCO datasets. Future work will extend CTiKG to heterogeneous graphs integrating multiple CTI sources, expand datasets with recent reports, and design protocols to assess graph quality under realistic threat scenarios, advancing AI-driven threat intelligence for security analysts.

Disclaimer. The camera-ready version of this paper was partially edited using AI-assisted tools to meet conference page limits and formatting requirements. The authors remain fully responsible for the accuracy, validity, and integrity of the content presented.

References

1. MITRE: MITRE Response to Cyber Attack in One of Its R&D Networks. https://www.mitre.org/news-insights/news-release/mitre-response-cyber-attack-one-its-rd-networks. Accessed 02 June 2024
2. Crumpton, L., Clancy, C.: Advanced cyber threats impact even the most prepared. https://medium.com/mitre-engenuity/advanced-cyber-threats-impact-even-the-most-prepared-56444e980dc8. Accessed 02 June 2024
3. Pingle, A., Piplai, A., Mittal, S., Joshi, A., Holt, J., Zak, R.: RelExt: relation extraction using deep learning approaches for cybersecurity knowledge graph improvement. In: ASONAM '19: Proceedings of the 2019 IEEE/ACM International Conference on Advances in Social Networks Analysis and Mining, vol. 2, pp. 879–886, ACM, Vancouver, British Columbia, Canada (2020)
4. Sarhan, I., Spruit, M.: Open-CyKG: an open cyber threat intelligence knowledge graph. Knowl. Based Syst. **233** (2021). https://doi.org/10.1016/j.knosys.2021.107524
5. Zuo, J., Gao, Y., Li, X., Yuan, J.: An end-to-end entity and relation joint extraction model for cyber threat intelligence. In: 2022 the 7th International Conference on Big Data Analytics (ICBDA), pp. 204–209. IEEE, Guangzhou, China (2022). https://doi.org/10.1109/ICBDA55095.2022.9760342
6. Zhong, Z., Chen, D.: A frustratingly easy approach for entity and relation extraction. In Proceedings of the 2021 Conference of the North American Chapter of the Association for Computational Linguistics: Human Language Technologies, ACL, pp. 50–61 (2021)
7. Yan, Z., Jia, Z., Tu, K.: An empirical study of pipeline vs. joint approaches to entity and relation extraction. In: Proceedings of the 2nd Conference of the Asia-Pacific Chapter of the Association for Computational Linguistics and the 12th International Joint Conference on Natural Language Processing, ACL, pp. 437–443 (2022)
8. Ahmed, K., Khurshid, S., K., Hina, S.: CyberEntRel: joint extraction of cyber entities and relations using deep learning. Comput. Securi. **136** (2024). https://doi.org/10.1016/j.cose.2023.103579
9. Guo, Y., Liu, Z., Huang, C., Liu, J., Jing, W., Wang, Z., Wang, Y.: CyberRel: joint entity and relation extraction for cybersecurity concepts. In: Information and Communications Security: 23rd International Conference, ICICS 2021, pp. 447—463, Springer, Chongqing, China (2021). https://doi.org/10.1007/978-3-030-86890-1_25
10. Mouiche, I., Saad, S.: Entity and relation extractions for threat intelligence knowledge graphs. Comput. Secur., **148** (2025). https://doi.org/10.1016/j.cose.2024.104120
11. Hugging Face. https://huggingface.co/ehsanaghaei/SecureBERT_Plu, Accessed 25 Feb 2025
12. Aghaei, E., Niu, X., Shadid, W., Al-Shaer, E.: SecureBERT: a domain-specific language model for cybersecurity. Security and Privacy in Communication Networks, vol. 462 (2023) https://doi.org/10.1109/TrustCom50675.2020.00083

13. Lample, G., Ballesteros, M., Subramanian, S., Kawakami, K., Dyer, C.: Neural architectures for named entity recognition. In: Proceedings of NAACL-HLT (2016)
14. Wang, X. et al.: DNRTI: a large-scale dataset for named entity recognition in threat intelligence. In: 2020 IEEE 19th International Conference on Trust, Security and Privacy in Computing and Communications (TrustCom), pp. 1842–1848. IEEE, Guangzhou, China, (2020). https://doi.org/10.1109/TrustCom50675.2020.00252
15. Bridges, R.A., Jones, C.L., Iannacone, M.D., Goodall, J.R.: Automatic labeling for entity extraction in cyber security. In: The Third ASE International Conference on Cyber Security 2014 (2014)
16. Wang, X., Liu, Z., Liu, J.: Information extraction of cybersecurity concepts: an LSTM approach. Comput. Secur. **144** (2024)
17. Guo, Z., et al.: A framework for threat intelligence extraction and fusion. Comput. Secur. **132** (2024). https://doi.org/10.1016/j.cose.2023.103371
18. Liu, Y., Han, X., Zuo, W., Lv, H., Guo, J.: CTI-JE: a joint extraction framework of entities and relations in unstructured cyber threat intelligence. In: 27th International Conference on Computer Supported Cooperative Work in Design (CSCWD), pp. 2728–2733. IEEE, Tianjin, China (2024). https://doi.org/10.1109/CSCWD61410.2024.10580210
19. Lv, H., Han, X., Cui, H., Wang, P., Zuo, W., Zhou, Z.: Joint extraction of entities and relationships from cyber threat intelligence based on task-specific fourier network. In: 2024 International Joint Conference on Neural Networks (IJCNN), pp. 1–8, IEEE, Yokohama, Japan (2024). https://doi.org/10.1109/IJCNN60899.2024.10650942
20. Zhu, F., Cheng, Z., Li, P., Xu, H.: ITIRel: joint entity and relation extraction for internet of things threat intelligence. In: IEEE Internet of Things Journal, pp. 20867–20878 (2024). https://doi.org/10.1109/JIOT.2024.3373799
21. Mouiche, I., Saad, S.: TIJERE: a novel threat intelligence joint extraction model based on analyst expert knowledge. TechRxiv (2024). https://doi.org/10.36227/techrxiv.174286575.55673704/v1
22. Gasmi, H., Laval, J., Bouras, A.: Information extraction of cybersecurity concepts: an LSTM approach. Appl. Sci. **9** (2019)
23. Zhao, J., Yan, Q., Liu, X., Li, B., Zuo, G.: Cyber threat intelligence modeling based on heterogeneous graph convolutional network. In: In Proceedings of the 23rd International Symposium on Research in Attacks, Intrusions and Defenses (RAID 2020), pp. 241–256, USENIX, San Sebastian (2020)
24. Jo, H., Lee, Y., Shin, S.:Vulcan: automatic extraction and analysis of cyber threat intelligence from unstructured text. Comput. Secur. **120** (2022)
25. Marchiori, F., Conti, M., Verde, N., V.: STIXnet: a novel and modular solution for extracting all STIX objects in CTI reports. In: ARES '23: Proceedings of the 18th International Conference on Availability, Reliability, and Security (2023). https://doi.org/10.1145/3600160.3600182
26. Mulwad, V., Li, W., Joshi, A., Finin, T., Viswanathan, K.: Extracting information about security vulnerabilities from web text. In: 2011 IEEE/WIC/ACM International Conferences on Web Intelligence and Intelligent Agent Technology, Lyon, France, pp. 257–260 (2011). https://doi.org/10.1109/WI-IAT.2011.26
27. Li, Y., Guo, Y., Fang, C., Liu, Y., Chen, Q.: A novel threat intelligence information extraction system combining multiple models. Secur. Commun. Netw. (2022). https://doi.org/10.1155/2022/8477260
28. Piplai, A., Mittal, S., Joshi, A., Finin, T., Holt, J., Zak, R.: Creating cybersecurity knowledge graphs from malware after action reports. IEEE Access **8**, 211691–211703 (2020)

29. Lafferty, JJ., McCallum, A., Pereira, F.: Conditional random fields: probabilistic models for segmenting and labeling sequence data. In: ICML '01: Proceedings of the Eighteenth International Conference on Machine Learning, pp. 282–289 (2001)
30. Mouiche, I., Saad, S.: TI-NERmerger: semi-automated framework for integrating NER Datasets in cybersecurity. In: Proceedings of the 21st International Conference on Security and Cryptography, vol. 1, pp. 357–370, SciTePress, Dijon, France (2024)
31. OASIS OPEN. https://docs.oasis-open.org/cti/stix/v2.1/cs02/stix-v2.1-cs02.html. Accessed 10 Feb 2025
32. Pedregosa, F., Varoquaux, G., et al.: Scikit-learn: machine learning in Python. J. Mach. Learn. Res. **12**, 2825–2830 (2011)
33. Syed, Z., Padia, A., Finin, T., Mathews, L., Joshi, A.: UCO: a unified cybersecurity ontology. In: Proceedings of the AAAI Workshop on Artificial Intelligence for Cyber Security, pp. 195–202, AAAI Press (2016)

Toward Automated Security Risk Detection in Large Software Using Call Graph Analysis

Nicholas Pecka[1,2](✉), Lotfi Ben Othmane[1], and Renee Bryce[1]

[1] University of North Texas, Denton, TX, USA
[2] Red Hat, Kansas City, MO, USA
nicholaspecka@my.unt.edu

Abstract. Threat modeling plays a critical role in the identification and mitigation of security risks; however, manual approaches are often labor-intensive and prone to error. This paper investigates the automation of software threat modeling through the clustering of call graphs using density-based and community detection algorithms, followed by an analysis of the threats associated with the identified clusters. The proposed method was evaluated through a case study of the Splunk Forwarder Operator (SFO), wherein selected clustering metrics were applied to the software's call graph to assess pertinent code-density security weaknesses. The results demonstrate the viability of the approach and underscore its potential to facilitate systematic threat assessment. This work contributes to the advancement of scalable, semi-automated threat modeling frameworks tailored for modern cloud-native environments.

Keywords: Threat Modeling · Call Graph Analysis · Software Security · Graph Clustering · Heuristic Algorithms

1 Introduction

As the cyber landscape evolves, so does the attack surface of modern applications. A variety of tools exist to uncover vulnerabilities through static and dynamic analysis, but they rarely look beyond the application itself. These tools often ignore how an application interacts with its broader environment, namely deployed infrastructure, integrated components, and system-level dependencies, leading to overlooked threats or irrelevant findings.

Threat modeling employs a system-wide perspective, mapping data flows and interactions from end users to deployed components in order to assess threats applicable to the system. Although typically conducted during the design phase, threat modeling is often neglected after deployment. This presents a significant challenge, as software systems evolve continuously and an initial threat model can quickly become outdated. While vulnerability scanners may identify component-level issues, they rarely capture risks introduced at higher levels

K. Adi et al. (Eds.): CRiSIS 2025, LNCS 16295, pp. 353–362, 2026.
https://doi.org/10.1007/978-3-032-20732-6_22

of interaction. Moreover, even a single component update (particularly within complex systems) can invalidate an existing model.

Another challenge is that threat modeling remains largely manual and requires input from multiple stakeholders and domain experts. In large systems, no single person (or small group) can realistically maintain a complete, up-to-date model. This complexity often pushes threat modeling down the priority list once the software is in production.

This paper explores automating aspects of the threat modeling process through call graph analysis. Call graphs, generated from existing code, capture both current implementations and future changes. By applying clustering algorithms, we aim to detect structural patterns that signal potential risks. This approach can support threat modeling at scale, ease manual burdens, and enable models to remain relevant throughout the software lifecycle.

Our contributions are as follows:

1. Evaluation of clustering capabilities of Density-Based Spatial Clustering of Applications with Noise (DBSCAN) [1], Hybrid Density-Based Spatial Clustering of Applications with Noise (HDBSCAN) [2], Louvain [3], and Leiden [4].
2. Proposing an automated approach that applies clustering-based algorithms to call graphs, with heuristics for threat identification.
3. Evaluating the approach on the Splunk Forwarder Operator, a widely used logging agent in Red Hat OpenShift environments.

The remainder of this paper is organized as follows: Sect. 2 reviews related work; Sect. 3 describes the method; Sect. 4 presents results on the Splunk Forwarder Operator; Sect. 5 outlines threats to validity; and Sect. 6 concludes.

2 Related Work

Graph-based techniques and unsupervised learning have been widely applied in cybersecurity, particularly in malware analysis, network defense, and threat intelligence. Although these studies share methods with our work (such as clustering and structural graph analysis) their goals and domains differ. Here, we outline key contributions and how they relate to our focus on proactive, system-wide threat modeling with cluster-based detection.

Herranz-Oliveros et al. apply DBSCAN and HDBSCAN to study lateral movement in networks [5]. Their approach identifies pivot nodes attackers might exploit, offering relevant insights for threat modeling but not aimed at generating a full system model.

Gulbay and Demirici use the Leiden algorithm to analyze Advanced Persistent Threat (APT) reports [6], extracting actionable threat intelligence. Although this aligns with our interest in community detection, their work is reactive (responding to observed attacks), whereas threat modeling seeks to anticipate risks in advance.

Finally, traditional Static Application Security Testing (SAST) and Dynamic Application Security Testing (DAST) tools differ from threat modeling in scope.

SAST scans code for rule-based vulnerabilities, while DAST tests running applications. In contrast, threat modeling evaluates the entire system, components, integrations, and environment, revealing risks beyond code-level flaws.

3 Call Graph Analysis with Clustering Methods

To advance automated threat modeling, we turn to call graph analysis. Call graphs capture entry points, data flows, and sensitive interactions that are critical elements for identifying attack surfaces. They also reveal unused or legacy functions that could present hidden risks if left unmonitored. Visualizing these structures allows developers to verify code necessity, trace privileged actions, and better map security-critical pathways.

3.1 Clustering Approaches

We evaluated both density-based and graph-based clustering methods. DBSCAN [1] and Louvain [3] were briefly explored, but left to promote more robust alternatives. Consequently, our primary focus is on HDBSCAN [2] for density-based analysis and Leiden [4] for graph-based clustering, both of which demonstrated stronger performance on call graph data.

3.2 Density-Based Algorithms

Density-based clustering identifies regions of high connectivity while marking sparse nodes as noise, making it effective for anomaly detection. A common evaluation metric is the silhouette score [7], defined as:

$$silhouette = \frac{b - a}{\max(a, b)}$$

where a is the average distance from a point to others in the same cluster (intra-cluster distance) and b is the average distance from a point to those in the nearest neighboring cluster (where the nearest neighboring cluster is found by the smallest average distance of a cluster to the selected point). Scores near 1 indicate well-defined clusters, while scores near 0 or negative values suggest weak assignments or misclassifications. Averaging across all points yields a global measure of clustering quality, especially valuable when ground truth labels are unavailable.

While DBSCAN [1] provided a baseline, its reliance on a fixed ε value limited its utility in non-uniform call graphs.

HDBSCAN [2] removes this limitation by considering variable densities and forming a hierarchy of clusters. It introduces the concept of mutual reachability distance:

$$\text{mutual\_reachability}(a, b) = \max\{\text{core}_k(a),\ \text{core}_k(b),\ d(a, b)\}$$

where $d(a,b)$ is the distance between points a and b, $\text{core}_k(a)$ is the distance from a to its kth nearest neighbor, and k is the minimum number of neighbors defining a dense region. This transformation enables construction of a minimum spanning tree, from which stable clusters are extracted across density levels. For call graph analysis, this flexibility highlights dense, interconnected components while isolating sparse or anomalous regions (potential signals of risk).

3.3 Graph-Based Algorithms

Graph-based clustering identifies communities in which nodes are more densely connected internally than externally. The modularity metric [8] evaluates the quality of such partitions:

$$Q = \frac{1}{2m} \sum_{i,j} \left(A_{ij} - \frac{k_i k_j}{2m} \right) \delta(c_i, c_j)$$

where A_{ij} is the edge weight between nodes i and j, $k_i = \sum_j A_{ij}$ is the degree of node i, $m = \frac{1}{2} \sum_{i,j} A_{ij}$ is the total edge weight, c_i is the community of node i, and $\delta(c_i, c_j)$ is 1 if $c_i = c_j$ and 0 otherwise.

Louvain [9] was initially tested but produced inconsistent partitions for our dataset.

The Leiden method [4] improves upon Louvain by introducing a refinement phase that ensures each community is internally connected:

$$\forall u, v \in C_k,\ \exists \text{ a path } u \leftrightarrow v \text{ such that } (u,v) \in E(C_k)$$

This guarantees meaningful communities before aggregation, avoiding unstable or fragmented clusters. For call graphs, Leiden provides more reliable, convergent results, capturing trust boundaries and structural patterns critical for system-wide threat modeling.

4 Evaluation

4.1 Case Study: Splunk Forwarder Operator

The Splunk Forwarder Operator (SFO) [10] is a Red Hat [11] operator deployed by default on OpenShift [12] to collect logs from the cluster and forward them to an external Splunk instance [13]. Its widespread use across real-world customer clusters makes it an ideal case for evaluating automated threat modeling, as it encounters diverse runtime environments and integration patterns.

For analysis, we used `go-callvis` [14] to perform static analysis and generate a complete call graph from the operator's `main.go` file. This graph captures internal function calls and control flow, providing the structural representation necessary for clustering-based threat detection.

The call graph serves as input to the clustering algorithms (DBSCAN, HDBSCAN, Louvain, and Leiden), allowing us to assess how well each method isolates outliers, identifies modular structures, and highlights potential threats across the operator's architecture.

4.2 Algorithm Comparison Utilizing Call Graphs

To evaluate clustering algorithms on large-scale call graphs, we generated a graph from the `main.go` file of SFO using Go tooling, i.e., `go-callvis` The resulting graph comprised over 350,000 lines of call data, representing 39,024 nodes and 286,302 edges.

We applied DBSCAN, HDBSCAN, Louvain, and Leiden to assess their performance. Density-based methods were evaluated using the silhouette score, while graph-based methods used modularity. This comparison highlights the relative strengths of each approach and guides selection for deeper analysis.

DBSCAN struggled at this scale. The best configuration (`eps`=0.09, minimum sample size=5) produced 32 clusters in 2.64 s with a silhouette score of only 0.0227, indicating near-random clustering.

HDBSCAN addressed DBSCAN's limitations, handling noise and varying cluster density effectively. With a minimum cluster size of 8, it produced 180 clusters in 18.17 s with a silhouette score of 0.5087, demonstrating meaningful structure well above random behavior (see Fig. 1a).

Louvain generated 367 clusters in 6.45 s with a modularity score of 0.8090, successfully identifying modular structures in the call graph.

Leiden further improved on Louvain, producing 366 clusters in just 0.26 s with a slightly higher modularity of 0.8202. Its refinement phase produced higher quality clusters and drastically improved runtime, making it especially suitable for iterative or large-scale threat modeling (see Fig. 1b).

These results provide a clear basis for selecting HDBSCAN and Leiden for more detailed threat analysis in the following sections.

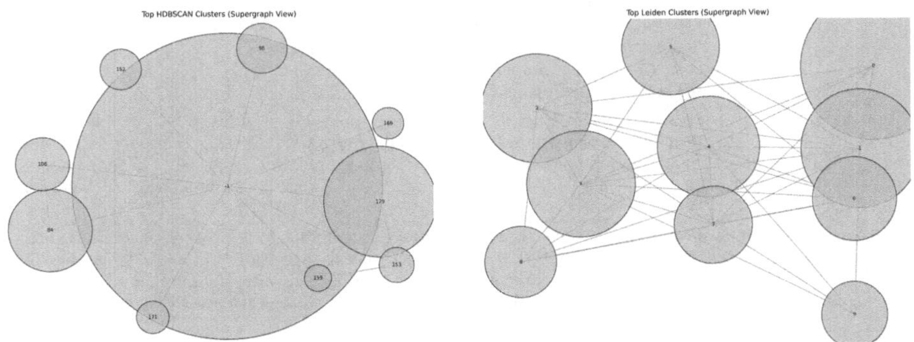

(a) Top 10 cluster illustration of HDBSCAN algorithm for SFO.

(b) Top 10 cluster illustration of Leiden algorithm for SFO.

Fig. 1. Comparison of top 10 clusters produced by HDBSCAN and Leiden algorithms for SFO.

4.3 Heuristics for Threat Identification

With the initial evaluation of clustering algorithms complete, we shift focus towards analyzing the clustering output for potential threat vectors. While the clustering results provide structure to an otherwise massive and complex graph, identifying security concerns within those structures requires additional analysis. To move from structural insights to actionable threat intelligence, we apply a set of heuristics designed to flag patterns commonly associated with insecure or suspicious behavior in software systems based on the MITRE corporations Common Weakness Enumeration (CWE) category system [15] relevant to software complexity. Table 1 provides the threats with a citation that inspired the heuristic, their detailed descriptions, and an explanation of how they are associated with CWEs.

Table 1. Threats related to software complexity and associated weaknesses.

Threat	Description	Associated Potential Weakness
Small clusters with many external connections (bridging) [16]	These clusters act as bridges between multiple larger clusters and may serve as entry points or intermediaries that cross trust boundaries.	This behavior aligns with CWE 668 [17]: Exposure of Resource to Wrong Sphere.
Large clusters with high incoming call volume (hotspots) [18], [19]	Clusters that receive a large number of incoming calls may act as critical processing units or bottlenecks. These can represent central services or APIs and could be likely targets for access control violations.	We associate this heuristic with CWE 284 [20]: Improper Access Control.
Dangling nodes [21]	Nodes that only connect to a single node in a different cluster and have no internal cluster connectivity may represent loosely controlled logic or misplaced code. The additional outlying logic could indicate a potential injection or code that wasn't properly cleaned up during the software development life cycle.	We associate this heuristic with CWE 94 [22]: Improper Control of Generation of Code ('Code Injection') or CWE - 1164 [23]: Irrelevant Code.
Hub nodes [24]	Individual nodes with an unusually high number of connections, either incoming or outgoing, could indicate points of aggregation, routing, or parsing.	These hubs often correlate with CWE 20 [25]: Improper Input Validation, especially if they process untrusted data without sufficient sanitization.
Weak clusters with low internal edge ratios [26]	Clusters that have more connections leaving than staying within may indicate poor encapsulation or broken modularity, often exposing internal data or logic externally.	Due to these we associate the heuristic with CWE 200 [27]: Exposure of Sensitive Information to an Unauthorized Actor.

We use this initial result to assess potential threats of the evaluated software. We plan to conduct a comprehensive literature review to identify the association between cluster types and potential threats, which will allow for exhaustive assessments of potential threats for large cloud-based software.

4.4 Findings and Observations

For the heuristic-driven threat detection analysis, we focused specifically on the output of the HDBSCAN and Leiden algorithms, given their strong performance in the previous sections clustering evaluation. For the scope of this paper, we examine the top three results for each heuristic applied to both algorithms. It is important to preface that the results of these heuristics are naturally correlated with quality metrics (silhouette score for HDBSCAN and modularity for Leiden) as discussed earlier. With additional parameter tuning, more precise or distinct findings may emerge, which we consider for future work.

HDBSCAN yielded actionable insights for *four out of the five* heuristics, as shown in Table 2. The heuristics flagged different clusters, each offering a lens into possible security concerns or tuning opportunities. For instance, both the *dangling node* and *hub node* heuristics each returned top results with similar neighbor or connection ratios, suggesting that some of these may be noise rather than clear signals. Expanding the evaluation to more candidates would help determine whether these clusters warrant investigation or are artifacts of imperfect partitioning.

Table 2. Heuristic results of associating the clusters generated using HDBSCAN and Leiden methods from SFO to software density-based CWE.

Heuristic	HDBSCAN	Leiden	Weakness
Bridging Clusters	0	0	CWE - 668
Hotspot Clusters	162	24	CWE - 284
Dangling Nodes	57	485	CWE - 123
Hub Nodes	80	217	CWE - 20
Weak Clusters	27	0	CWE -200
Total number of clusters	180	366	

More promising are the results from the *hotspot* heuristic. Cluster 179 was flagged with a significant call volume of 8,338, while the second highest, cluster 98, had 6,806. This level of disparity suggests a disproportionate concentration of traffic in a few clusters, which may warrant prioritization in security assessments.

The most compelling results came from the *weak cluster* heuristic. The top-ranked cluster (Cluster 152) had 458 nodes with an external-to-internal edge ratio of 687, whereas the next result, had only 24 nodes with a ratio of 120. This steep drop-off in both size and edge ratio indicates that Cluster 152 is significantly more exposed or loosely coupled and may represent a potential risk.

Leiden, on the other hand, reported findings for *three out of the five* heuristics (see Table 2). A noteworthy observation across multiple heuristics was the consistent appearance of the node `(reflect.Value).Call` [28]. This function surfaced as the top candidate in both the *dangling* and *hub* heuristics. It exhibited a connection split of 1,968 outgoing calls to different clusters out of a total of 3,447, while the second-ranked node had a mere 64/65 split. Furthermore, `(reflect.Value).Call` was identified as a hub across 23 clusters, compared to only 9 clusters for the second-ranked hub node.

This suggests poor cohesion and potential misuse or overuse of the `reflect` package. In Go, the `reflect` package enables runtime manipulation of types and values, which can bypass compile time checks, introduce runtime instability, and hinder debugging. Its ability to modify addressable values adds another layer of risk, particularly in a high-usage context like the one observed in this study. These characteristics may offer an attacker more flexibility and stealth, making this node a prime candidate for further investigation.

These heuristic findings represent the current endpoint of our research. They provide a filtered and structured view of potentially vulnerable areas in the application, setting the stage for deeper manual analysis in future work. Our next steps include evaluating the flagged clusters for specific vulnerabilities and validating these patterns against known security flaws.

5 Threats to Validity

This research is an early-stage exploration. Its limited scope may affect the generalization of our results.

First, the study relies on a single case—the SFO operator. While widely deployed, tuning clustering algorithms on this one application may introduce bias. Parameters and heuristics may not be generalized to other software systems with different architectures, sizes, or domain-specific behaviors.

Second, although HDBSCAN and Leiden showed promising results, we have not yet tested them on significantly larger or more fragmented call graphs. Future work should apply these methods across a broader set of applications and stress-test them under diverse structural conditions.

Finally, the heuristics for identifying potential threats are based on common vulnerability patterns (e.g., bridging, hotspots, weak cohesion) and CWE mappings. They have not been empirically validated or reviewed by experts to confirm their predictive value for real-world vulnerabilities. We plan to address this in future work.

Despite these limitations, the findings highlight a promising path forward. Future iterations will focus on refining algorithms, expanding validation, and improving practical applicability.

6 Conclusion

This paper explores automating threat modeling, with a long-term vision of building a fully automated pipeline. We evaluated four clustering algorithms,

DBSCAN, HDBSCAN, Louvain, and Leiden, on a large-scale call graph generated from the SFO, a production-grade operator widely used in OpenShift environments.

Comparing algorithms by their natural strengths (silhouette score for density-based methods, modularity for graph-based methods), we found HDBSCAN and Leiden to be the most effective. HDBSCAN produced meaningful clustering with a silhouette score of 0.5087 and 180 clusters, while Leiden achieved a modularity score of 0.8202 and outperformed Louvain in runtime.

Applying our heuristics revealed weaknesses such as poor cohesion, excessive external communication, and hub-like behavior. This helped surface critical nodes like `(reflect.Value).Call`, which might otherwise remain hidden in the complexity of the graph, demonstrating the value of combining clustering with targeted analysis.

Ultimately, this work bridges static program analysis with intelligent graph clustering, laying a foundation for scalable, automated threat modeling in real-world systems.

Acknowledgment. ChatGPT was used to check and improve the spelling and grammar of the paper and improve the flow of paragraphs of some sections.

References

1. Ester, M., Kriegel, H.-P., Sander, J., Xu, X.: A density-based algorithm for discovering clusters in large spatial databases with noise. In: Proceedings of the Second International Conference on Knowledge Discovery and Data Mining, KDD'96, pp. 226–231. AAAI Press (1996)
2. Malzer, C., Baum, M.: A hybrid approach to hierarchical density-based cluster selection. In: 2020 IEEE International Conference on Multisensor Fusion and Integration for Intelligent Systems (MFI), pp. 223–228. IEEE (2020)
3. neo4j. Louvain (2025). https://neo4j.com/docs/graph-data-science/current/algorithms/louvain/. Accessed Apr 2025
4. Traag, V.A., Waltman, L., van Eck, N.J.: From Louvain to Leiden: guaranteeing well-connected communities. Sci. Rep. **9**(1), 5233 (2019)
5. Herranz-Oliveros, D., Tejedor-Romero, M., Gimenez-Guzman, J., Cruz-Piris, L.: Unsupervised learning for lateral-movement-based threat mitigation in active directory attack graphs. Electronics **13**(10), 3944 (2024)
6. Gulbay, B., Demirci, M.: A framework for developing strategic cyber threat intelligence from advanced persistent threat analysis reports using graph-based algorithms (2024)
7. Rousseeuw, P.J.: Silhouettes: a graphical aid to the interpretation and validation of cluster analysis. J. Comput. Appl. Math. **20**, 53–65 (1987)
8. Newman, M.E.J.: Modularity and community structure in networks. Proc. Natl. Acad. Sci. **103**(23), 8577–8582 (2006)
9. Hu, B., Li, W., Huo, X., Liang, Y., Gao, M., Pei, P.: Improving louvain algorithm for community detection (2016)
10. Red Hat. splunk-forwarder-operator (2019). https://github.com/openshift/splunk-forwarder-operator. Accessed May 2025

11. Red Hat. Red hat (1994). https://www.redhat.com/en. Accessed Jan 2023
12. Red Hat. Openshift (2023). https://github.com/openshift. Accessed Feb 2023
13. Splunk. Splunk (2003). https://www.splunk.com/. Accessed May 2025
14. Ondrej Fabry. go-callvis (2016). https://github.com/ofabry/go-callvis. Accessed June 2025
15. MITRE. Common weakness enumeration (2006). https://cwe.mitre.org/. Accessed June 2025
16. Zhou, C., Zhang, M., Wang, X.: Community detection in software networks for vulnerability identification. Secur. Priv. **5**(1), e152 (2022)
17. MITRE. CWE-668: Exposure of Resource to Wrong Sphere (2008). https://cwe.mitre.org/data/definitions/668.html. Accessed June 2025
18. Cunha, C.R., Malvaso, V., Nicosia, V., Musolesi, M., Latora, V.: Complex networks vulnerability to module-based attacks. Sci. Rep. **5**, 13264 (2015)
19. Stergiopoulos, G., Kotzanikolaou, P., Gritzalis, D.: Time-based criticality metrics for attacker-controlled paths in critical infrastructures. In: Critical Information Infrastructures Security (CRITIS 2015), vol. 9578, Lecture Notes in Computer Science, pp. 98–109. Springer, Cham (2016)
20. MITRE. CWE-284: Improper Access Control (2006). https://cwe.mitre.org/data/definitions/284.html. Accessed June 2025
21. Alqahtani, A., Alazab, M., Awajan, A., Rubaiee, S., Khan, M.I., Jolfaei, A.: Graph-based machine learning methods for cyber threat detection: a comprehensive review. IEEE Access **11**, 112122–112149 (2023)
22. MITRE. CWE-94: Improper Control of Generation of Code ('Code Injection') (2006). https://cwe.mitre.org/data/definitions/94.html. Accessed June 2025
23. MITRE. CWE-1164: Irrelevant Code (2019). https://cwe.mitre.org/data/definitions/1164.html. Accessed June 2025
24. Darktrace Research. Using graph theory to identify critical nodes within computer networks (2023). Accessed June 2025
25. MITRE. CWE-20: Improper Input Validation (2006). https://cwe.mitre.org/data/definitions/20.html. Accessed June 2025
26. Sharma, C., Bedi, P., Kaur, P.: Multi-objective hyper-heuristic for software module clustering to improve modularity. Appl. Sci. **12**(11), 5649 (2022)
27. MITRE. CWE-200: Exposure of Sensitive Information to an Unauthorized Actor (2006). https://cwe.mitre.org/data/definitions/200.html. Accessed June 2025
28. go. reflect (2009). https://pkg.go.dev/reflect. Accessed June 2025

Advanced Attacks and Strategic Detection

SiamesePhish: An Advanced AI-powered URL Embedding Approach with Synthetic URLs for Phishing Detection

Austin Carthy, Nafiz Sadman(✉), and Farhana Zulkernine

School of Computing, Queen's University, Kingston, Canada
{austin.carthy,sadman.n,farhana.zulkernine}@queensu.ca

Abstract. Traditional approaches to phishing detection, such as URL blacklists, have limitations in detecting novel attacks and require time and regular updates of the list for verification processes. Machine learning (ML) models have emerged as an effective solution, but they are vulnerable to adversarial samples and concept drift. To address these challenges, we compare classification performance on URL embeddings generated by three URL detection BERT models: URLTran_BERT, *SiamesePhish* (ours), and SBERT. Our analysis demonstrates that *SiamesePhish* can outperform URLTran_BERT and SBERT with recall and ROC-AUC scores of 95.57% and 0.98, respectively. Since URLTran_BERT training data is not publicly available, we improve it further by training the model with AI-generated synthetic URLs.

Keywords: Phishing detection · Generative networks

1 Introduction

In 2025, breaches resulting from various phishing attacks cost an average of USD 5 million, as reported in the latest issue of Hoxhunt[1]. Consequently, safeguarding against phishing is crucial for everyone, including businesses and the general public. To prevent phishing attacks, researchers have proposed detecting fraudulent URLs [1–4,8,14–17] by cross checking with URL blacklists, which include a list of known phishing URLs. The blacklist website PhishTank[2] took over 13 h on average to verify a website as a phishing site in May 2017. There has been a shift towards detecting novel phishing URLs using Machine Learning (ML) and Artificial Neural Network (ANN) models. Early approaches to phishing detection employed machine learning models such as random forests and feature-based classifiers leveraging URL and HTML data, achieving around 92% accuracy, while later methods like RNNs relying solely on URLs improved performance to 98.7% [2,15]. More recently, pre-trained NLP transformer models

[1] https://hoxhunt.com/guide/phishing-trends-report.
[2] https://phishtank.org/.

K. Adi et al. (Eds.): CRiSIS 2025, LNCS 16295, pp. 365–375, 2026.
https://doi.org/10.1007/978-3-032-20732-6_23

have surpassed traditional deep learning architectures, setting new benchmarks in URL classification [8].

ML models are vulnerable to adversarial samples in URL phishing detection. These samples are created using heuristics and Generative Adversarial Networks (GAN) to replicate common attacks. The dynamic nature of URLs, including new phishing attacks, introduces concept drift, which can lead to performance degradation [7]. Concept drift also affects benign URLs, making it challenging to create a representative training dataset that can generalize to other benign datasets without performance degradation. Attackers continually adjust their adversarial URL creation techniques to evade detection by humans and classifiers. Research has shown that including adversarial samples in retraining ML models improves model resiliency [8]. Therefore, our contributions are as follows:

1. We present a novel URL embedding model, *SiamesePhish*, that leverages transformer models to learn URL embeddings for improved classification of benign and attack URLs. We compare the performance of Sentence-BERT (SBERT), *SiamesePhish*, and URLTran_BERT [8]. Our experiments demonstrate that the classification of URLs based on *SiamesePhish* URL embedding outperforms URLTran_BERT, achieving 95.57% in terms of recall and ROC AUC of 0.98, respectively, compared to 94.47% and 0.97 of URLTran_BERT.
2. To improve the robustness and generalization capability of URL classification models for phishing attack detection, we extend *SiamesePhish* to generate more effective URL embeddings. Through experiments, we provide evidence that the synthetic phishing URLs serve as valuable training samples, enhancing the benchmark model's accuracy from 99.744% to 99.801%, recall from 94.835% to 96.215%, ROC AUC score from 0.974 to 0.981, and TPR @ FPR 0.01% from 94.725% to 95.385%, on a test set with a 1:20 phishing to benign URL class imbalance ratio.

The rest of the paper is organized with a literature review in Sect. 2, especially focusing on transformer models. The methodology is discussed in Sect. 3 and the validation experiments are presented in Sect. 4. Section 5 concludes the paper and outlines future research directions.

2 Literature Review

While feature-based ML models [4,12,20] demonstrated promising results, the challenges associated with feature selection motivated researchers to explore alternative approaches, such as utilizing natural language models that focus solely on the URL texts. For instance, Bahnsen et al. [2] showed that a long short-term memory (LSTM) network analyzed on the URL characters outperforms a random forest model that analyzes 14 URL features for phishing URL detection. The authors reported an accuracy of 98.7622% and an ROC AUC score of 0.9991 for the LSTM model, compared to 93.4729% and 0.9845, respectively, of the random forest model.

Inspired by the success of CNN and multi-head self-attention (MHSA) networks, Xiao et al. combined these two networks for phishing detection [18]. The architecture embedded the input URLs into a matrix, which is duplicated and fed into two branches: the feature weight calculation branch and the feature branch. The authors reported an accuracy of 98.34%. This performance surpasses that of the CNN-LSTM model proposed by Bahsen et al. [2], which achieves an accuracy of 97.13% on the same dataset.

Encoder-based models like MPNet [13] unifies masked language model and permuted language modeling introduced by Yang et al. [19]. To pre-train the model on 160 GB of public data, Buu et al. [5] integrated fuzzy-logic calibration into a standard transformer encoder to improve stability and interpretability in phishing-URL detection. Transformers have achieved significant success in NLP tasks, especially, URLTran_BERT, which is used as the baseline model in this study. Maneriker et al. [8] drew inspiration from the success of transformer models and proposed the use of transformer encoder models for phishing URL detection. They proposed three models: URLTran_BERT, URLTran_RoBERTa, and URLTran_CustVoc. BERT, with its powerful language representation capabilities, proved to be very effective in this task.

3 Methodology

In this section, we elaborate our methodology to construct and train *SiamesePhish*. We compare URLTran_BERT [8] to a phishing URL classifier trained on URL embeddings produced by SBERT [11], and *SiamesePhish* across several datasets that contain benign URLs from CommonCrawl and phishing URLs from PhishTank. Since the training data plays a critical role in dictating model performance, we first present and analyze a set of phishing and benign URL datasets, and test the performance of URLTran_BERT, SBERT, and *SiamesePhish* to demonstrate the models do not transfer well on different datasets. Therefore, we generate synthetic data to retrain the models for improved detection.

3.1 Dataset

We used two PhishTank datasets, PhishOct2022 and PhishMar2023, all identified by download dates. For benign URLs, we randomly sampled Common Crawl's September/October 2022 crawl (CC-MAIN-2022-40; 20 of 300 Parquet files yielding over 28 million URLs, then split into 10 million for training and 10 million for testing) and January/February 2023 crawl (CC-MAIN-2023-06; 21 batches yielding 6 million URLs, split evenly), removing any URLs that overlapped with phishing sets or appeared in both publications[3]. Benign and phishing URL datasets extracted from PhishTank and Common Crawl are summarized in Table 1.

Synthetic URL Generation for Model Training: We employ the GPT-2 model, developed by Radford et al. [10], pretrained on the WebText dataset

[3] https://commoncrawl.org/the-data/.

Table 1. Phishing and benign URL datasets.

Class	Date	Split	Size	Name
Phish	Oct 2022	Train	100,000	PhishOct2022
	Mar 2023	Test	45,000	PhishMar2023
Benign	Sep 2022	Train	10,000,000	BenignSep2022Train
	Sep 2022	Test	10,000,000	BenignSep2022Test
	Jan 2023	Train	3,000,000	BenignJan2023Train
	Jan 2023	Test	3,000,000	BenignJan2023Test

and based of a transformer decoder architecture for URL generation. GPT-2 generates text by taking input text, calculating the next token distribution, and selecting a token from that distribution to append it to the input sequence.

3.2 SiamesePhish

We developed *SiamesePhish*, motivated by the Siamese network architecture of Sentence-BERT (SBERT) [11], to generate URL embeddings. The architecture of *SiamesePhish* consists of a BERT model with a mean-pooling layer on top, producing 768-dimensional embeddings by taking the final hidden layer [CLS] token embedding, followed by L2 normalization. The BERT model parameters used in *SiamesePhish* are the same as those employed in URLTran_BERT.

URLs behave like short sentences, so we employ a sentence-level embedding model rather than treating each token in isolation. We choose SBERT outperforms on both unsupervised and supervised semantic textual similarity benchmarks. We leverage SBERT's Siamese/Triplet architecture to produce fixed-size embeddings that place semantically similar URLs close together in the vector space, and we efficiently compare them using cosine or Euclidean distance. We used the 'all-mpnet-base-v2' version of the Sentence-Transformers[4] to implement SBERT, which has been trained on an extensive dataset of over a billion sentence pairs and yields 768-dimensional embeddings. This SBERT model uses a pre-trained mpnet-base model [13], which generates embeddings by incorporating a mean pooling layer and fine-tuning it through a contrastive learning objective. A batch

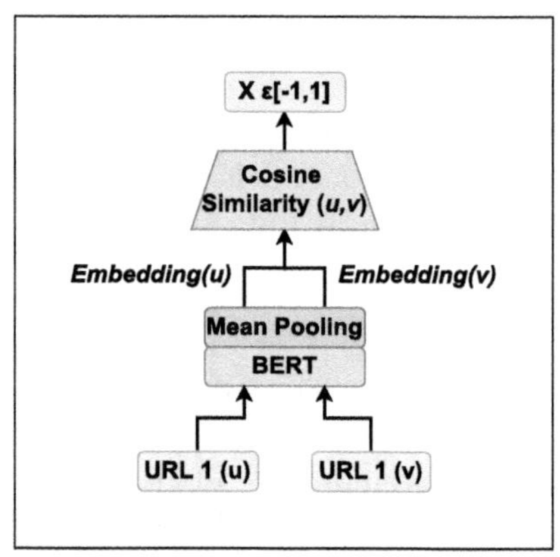

Fig. 1. *SiamesePhish* Architecture

[4] https://huggingface.co/sentence-transformers/all-mpnet-base-v2.

of N true sentence pairs is created to generate embeddings. The cosine similarity between each pair of sentence embeddings is then calculated, resulting in a similarity matrix of size NxN. The loss is calculated symmetrically over the similarity matrix using cross-entropy loss applied to the true pairs [9].

To train *SiamesePhish*, we generate random pairs of phishing and benign URLs, embed them, and compute a cosine similarity–based loss with targets of 1 for same-class pairs and -1 otherwise (Fig. 1). Training pairs are built from 5 million benign URLs (BenignSep2022Train) and an oversampled PhishOct2022 set, shuffled into 10 million URLs and batched in 64 with fixed pairing. For evaluation, 32,000 benign URLs (BenignSep2022Test) and 32,000 phishing URLs (PhishMar2023) form the test pairs. The model is assessed every 100,000 pairs, saving the best checkpoint, and is trained with Adam (learning rate of $2e^{-6}$).

3.3 URLTran_BERT

We implemented the model proposed by Maneriker et al. [8] to compare *SiamesePhish* with the URLTran_BERT, and followed a similar training procedure, since the authors did not publish the code of the model or their dataset. First, we downloaded a pre-trained BERT model from Huggingface and then fine-tuned it on our phishing and benign URL data using similar parameters as mentioned in the published work.

Fine-Tuning URLTran_BERT with Synthetic Data: Based on the observations that phishing detection models such as URLTran_BERT does not transfer well between different training and testing data, we hypothesize that training the phishing URL detection models on a more versatile set of URLs can improve the model performance. **Concept Drift** [7] occurs when the statistical properties of streaming data change over time, causing ML models to lose accuracy, a critical concern for phishing-URL detectors given the web's scale[5]. Therefore, we explore how to generate phishing URLs as there exists a limited set of phishing URLs. Our phishing URL generation algorithm is composed of three key steps as listed below:

1. ***Training Decoders***: To develop a decoder for URL generation, we use GPT-2 model pretrained on the WebText dataset and fine-tune it on 40GB URL data using the language modeling objective. We produce three distinct decoders: *OnlyPhishGPT2* trained on URLs from the PhishSep2022 set; *Benign10MGPT2* trained on URLs from the BenignSep2022Train set.; and *MixGPT2* trained Benign10MGPT2 on the PhishSep2022 set.
2. ***Extracting URLs***: We extract a portion of a real URL and then feed this as input to the decoder to generate the rest of the URL. We experiment with extracting from both phishing and benign URLs by splitting the URLs. A URL is composed of various components, including a scheme, a domain name, a port, a path to a file, parameters, and an anchor. To extract a portion of a URL for generation, we first remove URLs that do not have domains. Then

[5] https://hoxhunt.com/guide/phishing-trends-report.

we split the URL within the domain using the Python library 'tldextract'[6]. We experiment with splitting the URL at three different locations: the subdomain, domain, and top-level domain.
3. ***Generating URLs***: With a portion of a real URL as input to the decoder models, the next generated token is appended to the sequence. This is repeated until an end-of-string token is generated or the maximum length of the sequence is reached.

4 Validation

We perform experiments to evaluate the performance of URLTran_BERT, SBERT, and *SiamesePhish* on experimental datasets to observe the effect of concept drift. The experiments revealed that the models cannot generalize well on the phishing URLs, given the limited variety and the number of URLs. Thus, we generate synthetic phishing URLs using GANs to fine tune URLTran_BERT and re-evaluate its performance.

4.1 Evaluation of Models on Defined Datasets

We evaluate URLTran_BERT, an SBERT-based classifier, and the proposed *SiamesePhish* classifier using accuracy, precision, recall, ROC-AUC, and TPR at 0.01% FPR across four distinct phishing–benign dataset combinations (Table 2). URL embeddings from SBERT and *SiamesePhish* are classified using a fully connected linear NN (768→2), trained for five epochs with Adam and cross-entropy loss, applying learning rates of $1e^{-2}$ for SBERT and $1e^{-4}$ for *SiamesePhish*, while freezing the embedding layers.

Table 2. Phishing detection performance of URLTran_BERT, SBERT, and *SiamesePhish* on datasets D1–D4. 'Acc' stands for accuracy, and 'T@F' for the true positive rate at 0.01% false positive rate.

Model	D1		D2		D3		D4	
	Acc	T@F	Acc	T@F	Acc	T@F	Acc	T@F
URLTran_BERT	99.74%	**96.04%**	48.16%	3.50%	64.53%	0.42%	99.73%	**95.47%**
SBERT	97.64%	26.61%	96.96%	**10.59%**	97.26%	14.82%	97.50%	22.73%
SiamesePhish	99.71%	85.61%	84.97%	0%	98.70%	**33.17%**	98.35%	13.36%

Note: The same PhishOct2022 and PhishMar2023 are included in D1-D4. BenignSep2022Train and BenignSep2022Test in D1, BenignSep202Train and BenignJan2023Test in D2, BenignJan2023Train and BenignSep2022Test in D3, and BenignJan2023Train and BenignJan2023Test in D4.

[6] https://pypi.org/project/tldextract/.

Results and Discussion. In Table 2, we see that when the test benign URLs are from the same year as the training benign URLs (Dataset 1 and 4), URLTran_BERT and SiamesePhish both far exceed SBERT in detection accuracy (97–98% vs. 77%) with URLTran_BERT attaining the highest TPR@FPR 0.01 %, indicating fewer false negatives. However, for distinct benign train and test data from different years, URLTran_BERT performance collapses across accuracy, and TPR@FPR, confirming poor transfer under distribution shift. SBERT degrades only slightly in accuracy, demonstrating strong generalization while SiamesePhish degrades less than URLTran_BERT due to its contrastive pre-training (Table 3).

Table 3. Generated phishing URL datasets with 90,000 training samples. *Sub* refers to sub-domain, *Dom* refers to the main domain, and *Top* refers to top-level domain.

Decoder	Phish			Benign		
	Sub	Dom	Top	Sub	Dom	Top
OnlyPhishGPT2	OS_{Phish}	OD_{Phish}	OT_{Phish}	OS_{Benign}	OD_{Benign}	OT_{Benign}
MixGPT2	MS_{Phish}	MD_{Phish}	MT_{Phish}	MS_{Benign}	MD_{Benign}	MT_{Benign}
Benign10MGPT2	BS_{Phish}	BD_{Phish}	BT_{Phish}	BS_{Benign}	BD_{Benign}	BT_{Benign}

4.2 Evaluation of URLTran_BERT Trained on Synthetic URLs

As observed in the previous experiments, URLTran_BERT greatly degrades in performance due to differences in data distribution or concept drift observed in BenignSep2022 and BenignJan2023 train and test datasets. Therefore as explained in Sect. 3.3, we generate synthetic data by extending SiamesePhish to create three decoder models, and fine tune URLTran_BERT.

The generated URLs initially tended to be much longer than the original URLs possibly since a subset of URLs in the benignSep2022Train set were exceedingly long. To ensure that generated URLs are of similar length as their original inputs, we set the maximum token length of generated URLs equal to the original URL token length when tokenized with BERT's WordPiece tokenizer. In addition, we excluded URLs whose tokenized lengths were greater than 128 as URLTran_BERT takes inputs with a maximum length of 128 tokens.

We developed a baseline URLTran_BERT model by training it on a dataset consisting of 100,000 phishing URLs from the phishOct2022 set and 500,000 benign URLs from the BenignSep2022Train set. Consequently, the phishing to benign ratio in the training set was 1:5. The input URLs used to generate the phishing URLs were also included in training URLTran_BERT to ensure that no new generated data leaked into the training process. Next, the experimental URLTran_BERT was trained using the same real phishing and benign URLs, along with the generated URLs from the 18 different datasets. Two different class imbalance ratios were employed during training to examine the impact of generated URLs on performance: 1:5 as for the baseline model, and 1:2.63 with the new generated phishing URLs. We created a test and a validation data set by randomly sampling 5,000 and 100,000 URLs from the PhishMarch2023 and BeignSep2022Test sets respectively (1:20 class imbalance ratio). After each epoch, model performance was assessed on the validation set. The epoch with the highest TPR @ FPR 0.01% metric was selected as the best-performing epoch. This metric was chosen as it provides insight into how the model would perform in a production environment, where minimizing false positives is crucial. With the model parameters from the best-performing epoch, we tested it on the test data. The results using are shown in Table 4.

Table 4. URLTran_BERT results comparing Baseline vs Fine-tuned versions, across three decoders (OnlyPhishGPT2, MixGPT2, Benign10MGPT2), two class imbalance ratio (1:2.63, 1:5). 'Acc' stands for accuracy, and 'TPR@FPR with 0.01%' for the true positive rate at 0.01% FPR. Bold represents the state-of-the-art result while underlined values represent the second best.

Decoder	Ratio	Version	Acc	TPR@0.01%
All	All	Baseline	99.744	94.725
OnlyPhishGPT2	1:2.63	Fine-tuned (OS_Phish)	**99.798**	**95.155**
	1:5	Fine-tuned (OS_Benign)	**99.771**	**95.890**
MixGPT2	1:2.63	Fine-tuned (MS_Benign)	**99.801**	**95.385**
	1:5	Fine-tuned (MS_Phish)	**99.778**	**95.910**
Benign10MGPT2	1:2.63	Fine-tuned (BT_Phish)	99.707	88.960
	1:5	Fine-tuned (BT_Phish)	99.721	93.015

Results and Discussion. **OnlyPhishGPT2.** When the split location is the subdomain, the generated phishing URLs (from OS, MS, and BS datasets) achieve the best performance across all metrics except precision compared to the baseline model. For the training set class imbalance ratio of 1:5, we see improvements on all metrics using the subdomain split location. For other locations, we only observed improvements in precision and TPR @FPR 0.01% over the baseline. This suggests that the best-split location is the subdomain when using the OnlyPhishGPT2 decoder. This could be because the smaller input portion when using a subdomain split location in conjunction with top-P sampling leads to more variance in generated URLs than those with other split locations. The variance in the generated URLs then provides URLTran_BERT with more useful synthetic data as opposed to generated URLs that only deviate slightly from real phishing URLs. However, there are slight decrease in performances when using OnlyPhishingGPT2 with phishing URLs. Additionally, we see that when benign URLs are used as input to OnlyPhishGPT2, the generated URLs are mostly detrimental to performance if the split location is the domain or TLD.

This is because the generated URL has characteristics of a benign and phishing URL. But if the split location is the subdomain, there is a performance benefit because the input URL is so short that the decoder can generate almost all of the URLs and create a URL consistently like a phishing URL.

MixGPT2. The experiments with URLs generated using the MixGPT2 decoder have mixed results. Using phishing URLs as inputs show that there are improvements to almost all metrics for all three split locations. This shows that feeding phishing URLs to MixGPT2 produces samples with useful information. Comparing these results to those generated with OnlyPhishGPT2 and phishing URLs, we see that MixGPT2 is superior. This suggests that the combination of phishing and benign URLs used to train the decoder is more useful than just phishing URLs alone. However, when benign URLs are used as input to MixGPT2 and OnlyPhishGPT2, we see the same trend. Generated URLs with a subdomain split location achieve performance increases, but those with a domain or TLD split location see performance decreases.

Benign10MGPT2. Our experiments using generated phishing URLs produced with Benign10MGPT2 show almost no benefit except when the input URL is a portion of a phishing URL. This was expected as the generated URLs are similar to the benign URLs. However, we label them as phishing URLs and in turn, it lowers the accuracy of URLTran_BERT. This serves to illustrate that the inclusion of phishing URLs in the decoder training process is a key factor in creating useful synthetic phishing URLs. We can attribute the increases in recall and ROC AUC score to an increase in classifying URLs as phishing URLs with more false positives. This is demonstrated by the simultaneous decrease in precision. With generated phishing URLs from Benign10MGPT2, we should expect URLTran_BERT to predict more samples are phishing URLs because we labeled the generated URLs, which are similar to benign URLs as phishing URLs. Furthermore, we see that when using Benign10MGPT2 to generate phishing URLs, the performance decreases are less when phishing URLs are used as input and when the split location is further right in the URL. This is to be expected because the final generated URL will have more phishing-like components.

5 Conclusion

Our work introduces *SiamesePhish*, a SBERT-based architecture trained with a contrastive learning objective on URL pairs, and benchmarks it against URLTran_BERT and SBERT-derived classifiers. The experiments on four datasets demonstrate that phishing and benign URLs differ substantially over time, with URLTran_BERT excelling when benign URLs in training and testing sets overlap but struggling otherwise. While *SiamesePhish* trails URLTran_BERT in overall performance, it proves more resilient to distributional shifts, and SBERT-based classifiers provide consistent—though less robust—results. We also propose a novel strategy of generating phishing URLs using transformer decoders, showing that synthetic phishing URLs, especially those from MixGPT2 with subdomain splits, significantly improve detection. This contribution highlights the potential of generative augmentation in strengthening phishing detection systems, particularly when real-world phishing data is scarce.

One of the limitations of the study is that comparisons are restricted to URLTran_BERT, and more advanced models such as TransURL [6] have been proposed which needs to be explored. As part of our future work, we will explore which URL components or embedding dimensions drive classification performance, to encourage interpretability via SHAP, LIME, or Integrated Gradients.

Acknowledgments. The research is funded by *NSERC* Canada CREATE Cybersecurity program 528274 and Discovery Grant.

References

1. AlEroud, A., Karabatis, G.: Bypassing detection of URL-based phishing attacks using generative adversarial deep neural networks. In: The 6th IWSPA, p. 53–60. Association for Computing Machinery (2020)
2. Bahnsen, A.C., Bohorquez, E.C., Villegas, S., Vargas, J., González, F.A.: Classifying phishing URLs using recurrent neural networks. In: APWG, pp. 1–8 (2017)
3. Bu, S.J., Kim, H.J.: Learning disentangled representation of web address via convolutional-recurrent triplet network for classifying phishing URLS. In: ICEIC, pp. 1–4 (2021)
4. Butnaru, A., Mylonas, A., Pitropakis, N.: Towards lightweight URL-based phishing detection. Future Internet **6**, 154 (2021)
5. Buu, S.J., Cho, S.B.: A transformer network calibrated with fuzzy logic for phishing URL detection. Fuzzy Sets Syst., 109474 (2025)
6. Liu, R., et al.: TransURL: improving malicious URL detection with multi-layer transformer encoding and multi-scale pyramid features. Comput. Netw. **253**, 110707 (2024)
7. Lu, J., Liu, A., Dong, F., Gu, F., Gama, J., Zhang, G.: Learning under concept drift: a review. IEEE Tran. Knowl. Data Eng. (2018)
8. Maneriker, P., Stokes, J.W., Lazo, E.G., Carutasu, D., Tajaddodianfar, F., Gururajan, A.: URLTRAN: improving phishing URL detection using transformers (2021)
9. Radford, A., et al.: Learning transferable visual models from natural language supervision (2021)
10. Radford, A., Wu, J., Child, R., Luan, D., Amodei, D., Sutskever, I.: Language models are unsupervised multitask learners (2019)
11. Reimers, N., Gurevych, I.: Sentence-BERT: sentence embeddings using Siamese BERT-networks (2019)
12. Setu, J.H., Halder, N., Islam, A., Amin, M.A.: RSTHFS: a rough set theory-based hybrid feature selection method for phishing website classification. IEEE Access, 68820–68830 (2025)
13. Song, K., Tan, X., Qin, T., Lu, J., Liu, T.Y.: MPNet: masked and permuted pretraining for language understanding (2020)
14. Tajaddodianfar, F., Stokes, J.W., Gururajan, A.: Texception: a character/word-level deep learning model for phishing URL detection. In: ICASSP, pp. 2857–2861 (2020)

15. Tung, S.P., Wong, K.Y., Kuzminykh, I., Bakhshi, T., Ghita, B.: Using a machine learning model for malicious URL type detection. In: Internet of Things, Smart Spaces, and Next Generation Networks and Systems, pp. 493–505. Springer International Publishing (2022). https://doi.org/10.1007/978-3-030-97777-1_41
16. Wang, Z., Ren, X., Li, S., Wang, B., Zhang, J., Yang, T.: A malicious URL detection model based on convolutional neural network. Secur. Commun. Netw., 1–12 (2021)
17. Wei, W., Ke, Q., Nowak, J., Korytkowski, M., Scherer, R., Woźniak, M.: Accurate and fast URL phishing detector: a convolutional neural network approach. Comput. Netw. **178** (2020)
18. Xiao, X., Zhang, D., Hu, G., Jiang, Y., Xia, S.: CNN–MHSA: a convolutional neural network and multi-head self-attention combined approach for detecting phishing websites. Neural Netw., 303–312 (2020)
19. Yang, Z., Dai, Z., Yang, Y., Carbonell, J., Salakhutdinov, R., Le, Q.V.: XLNET: generalized autoregressive pretraining for language understanding (2020)
20. Zhang, Z., Wu, J., Lu, N., Shi, W., Liu, Z.: AdaptPUD: an accurate URL-based detection approach against tailored deceptive phishing websites. Comput. Netw., 111303 (2025)

Towards Lightweight On-Device Audio Deepfake Detection Using Squeezeformers

Ashkan Moradi[1,2(✉)], Yi Zhu[1,2], and Tiago H. Falk[1,2]

[1] Institut national de la recherche scientifique (INRS), Montreal, Canada
[2] INRS-UQO Joint Research Unit on Cybersecurity and Digital Trust, Gatineau, Canada
ashkan.moradi@inrs.ca

Abstract. The increasing threat of audio deepfakes necessitates detection mechanisms that can operate in real-time on resource-constrained edge devices. While large-scale systems, such as detectors based on speech foundation models, have demonstrated high accuracy, their computational and memory footprints make them ill-suited for on-device applications. This paper addresses this critical gap by investigating the key factors that influence the performance of lightweight deepfake detection models. We conduct a systematic comparison of model architectures, input feature choices, and data augmentation techniques, evaluating both deepfake detection accuracy and computational complexity across three datasets. Our findings show that with proper modeling choices, a lightweight model can achieve performance comparable to that of a much larger model while being approximately 100× smaller in size. This work provides actionable insights for developing efficient and effective audio deepfake detectors tailored for the constraints of edge computing.

Keywords: Audio Deepfake Detection · Lightweight · Edge Computing

1 Introduction

Although recent advancements in artificial intelligence have brought numerous benefits across domains such as healthcare, accessibility, and entertainment, they have also raised serious concerns, most notably is the rise of deepfakes (i.e., AI-generated content that convincingly mimics a human's face and/or voice). In the audio domain, deepfakes are created using techniques such as text-to-speech and voice conversion, enabling highly realistic voice synthesis. Unlike earlier methods, such as manual splicing or replay attacks, which often exhibited detectable artifacts, modern deepfake audio is far more natural and challenging to distinguish from genuine speech. While synthetic audio technologies can support positive applications like personalized speech tools, they also pose substantial risks [1,14,19,22]. Real-world cases have demonstrated this danger: for example, scammers used a voice deepfake to impersonate a German executive and

K. Adi et al. (Eds.): CRiSIS 2025, LNCS 16295, pp. 376–389, 2026.
https://doi.org/10.1007/978-3-032-20732-6_24

authorize a €220,000 bank transfer [15], and AI-generated robocalls mimicking President Biden targeted over 20,000 voters during the 2024 New Hampshire primary [29]. These incidents underscore the urgent need for reliable and generalizable detection systems to mitigate the growing threat of audio deepfakes.

Existing audio deepfake detection systems can broadly be categorized into two groups: foundation model-based approaches and lightweight models based on hand-crafted features. Foundation model-based methods leverage powerful self-supervised speech representations, such as Wav2vec2 [3], HuBERT [12], and WavLM [7], which are pre-trained on large-scale corpora, hence encompassing richer information compared to conventional speech features [42]. These representations are typically used as frontend encoders, followed by task-specific classification heads [21], and have shown strong performance, particularly in terms of generalizing to unseen attacks [32,34]. Notwithstanding, state-of-the-art models rely on large self-supervised learning (SSL) backbones [37] with more than $100M$ parameters [2,3,7,12,28]), which could bring computational demands that make them less suitable for real-time or resource-constrained scenarios.

On the other hand, lightweight models rely on hand-crafted acoustic features such as Mel-Frequency Cepstral Coefficients (MFCC), Linear-Frequency Cepstral Coefficients (LFCC), Gammatone Cepstral Coefficients (GTCC), and Constant-Q Cepstral Coefficients (CQCC), paired with efficient backend classifiers, such as Transformer models, Conformer models, RNN variants, and CNN-based architectures, just to name a few [6,26,30]. These models, however, while being more interpretable and easier to deploy, typically achieve lower performance levels compared to foundation model-based solutions. To fill this gap, in this work, we explore the possibility to obtain comparable performance as the large models while maintaining a small footprint. To this end, we performed a comprehensive evaluation on different modeling choices, with a specific focus on lightweight models. First, we experiment with a variety of knowledge-based input feature sets, namely MFCC and LFCC, as well as their combinations. Second, we investigate the impact of data augmentation techniques, such as speed perturbation (slow and fast), noise injection using MUSAN corpus [31], and reverberation with RIR simulations [17]. These augmentations aim to mimic the perturbations found in real-world audios. Finally, we compare two model architectures, namely Conformer [9] and Squeezeformer [16]. Conformer has demonstrated strong performance in modeling complex speech patterns [18] and has become the de facto backbone model for various downstream speech tasks, while Squeezeformer introduces architectural optimizations to reduce computational overhead [16]. These models were chosen to balance detection accuracy with computational efficiency, making them suitable for both high-performance and resource-constrained deployment scenarios.

In summary, our main contributions are summarized as follows:

1. We comprehensively evaluate the effects of input feature choices, training data augmentations, and model architectures on lightweight audio deepfake detection.

2. We show that with proper input feature and data augmentation combinations, a lightweight model can perform comparably to a large model while being 100× smaller.
3. We demonstrate that the Floating-Point Operations Per Second (FLOPS) can be further reduced when replacing Conformer with Squeezeformer, while maintaining similar performance on unseen data.

The remainder of this paper is structured as follows: Sect. 2 discusses related work in the field of audio deepfake detection. Section 3 presents our lightweight audio deepfake detection system. Section 4 outlines the datasets and baseline models. Section 5 presents experimental results and analysis. Finally, Sect. 6 concludes the paper and suggests directions for future work.

2 Related Work

Recent deepfake detection models rely on large SSL models like Wav2vec [3], HuBERT [12], and WavLM [7], which extract generalized speech embeddings from large-scale unlabeled corpora, and have demonstrated impressive performance on different deepfake dataset [10]. To further improve generalizability, fusion-based methods have been proposed. For example, Yang et al. [38] combined embeddings from HuBERT, XLS-R [2], and WavLM using multi-view feature selection to exploit their complementary strengths. Similarly, Liu et al. [20] combined XLS-R embeddings with formant dynamics to model bonafide speech patterns using one-class learning. However, these models are typically large in size, with parameter counts often exceeding 100M. For instance, Wav2vec2 large has $317.38M$ parameters, HuBERT large has $316.61M$, WavLM large has $316.62M$, and HuBERT-XL and Wav2vec-XLSR-1B reach $1B$ parameters [7]. Even the base versions of these models contain around $95M$ parameters [7], which is still considerably large for edge or real-time deployment. These SSL models demand substantial memory and compute resources, making them unsuitable for applications where latency, power consumption, and model footprint are tightly constrained. Some recent works have started to explore methods to reduce model size for on-device deployment. For example, Attentive Merging [24] selectively combines informative layers of WavLM to reduce computational overhead. Similarly, early-exit strategies [27] dynamically reduce inference time without significant accuracy loss. However, deploying large SSL-based models on edge devices still remains as a significant barrier.

Another type of pipeline that balances size and performance is to combine knowledge-based features with a discriminative backend classifier. Traditional acoustic features such as MFCC, LFCC, and other spectral and temporal descriptors have been commonly utilized. For instance, the work presented in [11] leverages classical cepstral (MFCC), spectral features (roll-off point, centroid, contrast, bandwidth), raw signal features (zero-crossing rate), and signal energy for deepfake audio detection tasks. Their findings underline that even relatively simple classical features can provide meaningful representations capable of detecting synthetic alterations in audio. Additionally, some studies have explored the use of biological and speech-pathological features, such as jitter, shimmer, glottal-to-noise excitation ratio, and harmonics-to-noise ratio, which are sensitive to subtle variations in human speech production and are difficult for generative models to replicate [5,8]. For instance, [5] demonstrates that segmental speech-pathological features can distinguish between bonafide and synthetic speech with high precision.

Meanwhile, the architectural backbone of detection systems has also evolved. Newer architectures such as Conformer have demonstrated strong performance by combining local convolution and global attention mechanisms. However, Conformer models are often computationally expensive. To address this, the Squeezeformer architecture [16] was introduced, offering a more efficient yet powerful hybrid design, enabling competitive performance with lower computational cost. Despite its success in automatic speech recognition, the use of squeezeformers in audio deepfake detection remains underexplored.

3 Proposed System

Our proposed audio deepfake detection system builds upon the HM-Conformer model introduced in [30]. The HM-Conformer model enhances detection performance by incorporating hierarchical pooling and multi-level classification token aggregation design. Specifically, it utilizes a hierarchical pooling strategy that processes input features at multiple levels of abstraction, combined with the aggregation of classification (CLS) tokens at each stage. This design enables the model to capture both local and global patterns in the speech signal, which is crucial for detecting subtle artifacts introduced by audio deepfake generation methods.

While the HM-Conformer has shown promising results in audio deepfake detection tasks, we observed potential areas for further improvement. First, the choice of model architecture could be modified for better efficiency. For example, we replace the original Conformer [9] model with the Squeezeformer model [16], which introduces several architectural optimizations (e.g., efficient depthwise separable subsampling) that reduce the number of floating-point operations per second (FLOPS) [16], making the model particularly attractive for edge devices. We observed that these modifications significantly reduce the computational overhead while maintaining, and in some cases improving, detection performance. The resulting model, which we refer to as HM-Squeezeformer, retains the core hierarchical CLS token aggregation strategy of the original HM-Conformer while taking advantage of Squeezeformer's computational efficiency and streamlined architecture. Additional to architectural changes, we ablate on the input feature choices to the detection models. While the original HM-Conformer relied on conventional spectral features such as LFCC [30], we further experiment with MFCC and the combination of LFCC and MFCC to explore the effects of input features on model performance.

3.1 Hierarchical Pooling Method

The hierarchical pooling component is introduced to progressively condense temporal information from each layer of the Conformer/Squeezeformer. The motivation stems from findings in image processing, where hierarchical pooling helps in capturing more abstract features layer by layer [25]. Here, pooling is applied after the 2nd and 4th Conformer/Squeezeformer blocks, reducing the length of the sequence tokens while preserving informative content. In [30], the authors experimented with various pooling strategies and found the most effective method to be max pooling. This observation is also consistent with prior research in the field [13,35], which demonstrated that pooling methods, particularly those that highlight the most salient or informative aspects of the extracted features, such as max pooling, are widely used in countermeasure systems and contribute significantly to detection performance. Based on these results, max pooling is adopted by our system.

3.2 Multi-level Classification Token Aggregation (MCA)

To complement hierarchical pooling, the MCA method was introduced [30], which injects learnable CLS tokens at multiple stages of the network (specifically, after the 2nd, 4th, and 6th Conformer/Squeezeformer blocks). These CLS tokens are designed to learn task-specific summaries of the sequence they are attached to. A CLS token at each block level is supervised with its own loss function, allowing different parts of the network to focus on different time scales and types of spoofing evidence. During inference, the CLS tokens and the global-level token embedding are passed through individual classifiers, and the final prediction is made using the most discriminative combination of these outputs.

3.3 Training Objective and Architecture Flow

For training both HM-Conformer and HM-SqueezeFormer, we employ the OC-Softmax [40] loss function for each embedding (CLS tokens extracted from each stage and the global-level token) promoting enhanced intra-class compactness and inter-class separability. As illustrated in Fig. 1, these embeddings are denoted as e1 through e5, corresponding to outputs from different levels of the hierarchical architecture. The final training objective is defined as a weighted sum of the individual loss terms from each embedding, with the best performance reported using a weight ratio of 4:3:2:1:1 across the stages.

3.4 Input Features

We compare five different input feature choices, namely LFCCs, 39-d MFCCs, 120-d MFCCs, LFCCs + 39-d MFCCs, and LFCCs + 120-d MFCCs. LFCC features were extracted using a window length of $20ms$, a hop size of $10ms$, and a 512-point FFT, with a linearly spaced triangular filter bank of 40 channels. Delta and delta-delta coefficients were also computed, resulting in a 120-dimensional

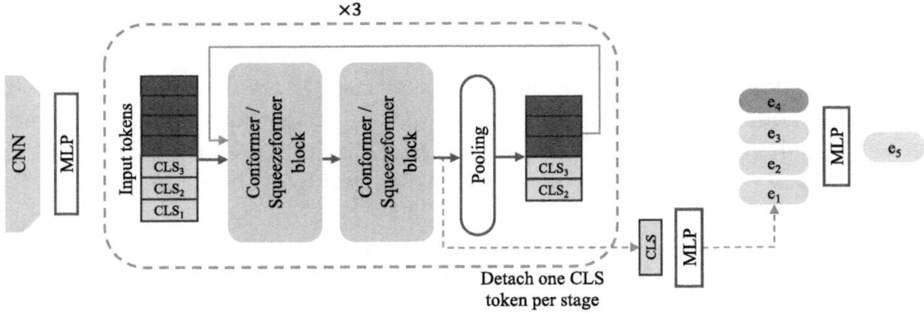

Fig. 1. Overview of the model architecture for Conformer and Squeezeformer. e1, e2, and e3 are intermediate CLS tokens from each stage, detached before their respective pooling layers. e4 is the global level token, extracted after the pooling layer of the last stage. e5 is the final aggregated embedding that is used to perform the audio deepfake detection task.

feature vector. The MFCC features were extracted using the same configuration (i.e., $20ms$ window, $10ms$ hop, and 512-point FFT) but employed a Mel-scale filter bank instead. Two MFCC setups were explored: a 13-d MFCC vector (augmented with delta and delta-delta features to form a 39-dimensional vector), and a 40-d MFCC vector (yielding a 120-dimensional vector after adding delta and delta-delta coefficients). These experiments aimed to determine whether MFCCs could serve as a competitive or complementary alternative to LFCCs. To further assess the complementarity between LFCCs and MFCCs, we performed feature-level fusion by concatenating MFCC and LFCC vectors. Two fusion schemes were evaluated: (1) a 159-d vector created by concatenating the 120-d LFCC with the 39-d MFCC, and (2) a 240-d vector formed by combining both 120-d LFCC and 120-d MFCC representations.

4 Experimental Setup

4.1 Datasets for Training and Evaluation

The ASVspoof 2019 [33] and ASVspoof 2021 [36] datasets are widely used benchmarks in the field of audio deepfake and anti-spoofing research. ASVspoof 2019 consists of two subsets: Logical Access (LA) and Physical Access (PA). The LA subset contains bonafide speech and spoofed samples generated by 17 different speech synthesis and voice conversion systems, while the PA subset focuses on replay attacks, simulating realistic scenarios through reverberation and acoustic variability [33]. In this study, we used both the training and development partitions of ASVspoof 2019 LA subset, totaling 151,098 samples (15,810 bonafide and 135,288 spoofed), to train our detection models. The dataset's class imbalance closely mirrors real-world conditions, challenging the model to learn robust discriminative features.

ASVspoof 2021 extends the 2019 version by adding a Deepfake (DF) subset, which focuses specifically on detecting speech generated by advanced deepfake techniques [36]. For evaluation, we used the DF evaluation partition to assess our model's generalization to unseen spoofing methods. While the original set includes 533,928 audio samples, technical limitations during data loading restricted us to 305,525 usable samples, consisting of 6,991 bonafide and 298,534 spoofed utterances.

The In-the-Wild (ITW) dataset [23] was introduced to evaluate the real-world generalization ability of audio deepfake detection models, particularly those trained on lab-controlled datasets. The ITW dataset consists of found audio recordings of public figures from online sources, simulating realistic deployment scenarios. It includes a total of 37.9 h of speech audio, divided into 20.7 h (11,816 samples) of genuine and 17.2 h (19,963 samples) of deepfake content [23].

Since our models are trained only on the ASVspoof2019 dataset, both the ASVspoof2021 and the ITW sets serve for cross-dataset evaluations. This setup directly tests the generalization capability of the proposed lightweight models to unseen spoofing methods. In particular, ITW contains diverse background noise and environmental variability, making it a challenging benchmark that closely resembles real-world deployment conditions.

4.2 Datasets for Data Augmentation

The RIR (Room Impulse Response) dataset provides a comprehensive set of room impulse responses and background noises collected from various acoustic environments [17]. By convolving these impulse responses with our training samples, we simulated realistic reverberant acoustic scenarios, mimicking the variations in speech recordings typically encountered in real-world environments. This augmentation effectively expands the diversity of acoustic conditions within our training data, enhancing our model's robustness against spoofing attempts in varied acoustic settings.

The MUSAN dataset comprises a collection of recordings organized into three distinct categories: music, speech, and noise [31]. We employed MUSAN primarily to introduce realistic background audio into our training samples. By mixing samples from these categories into our speech data at various signal-to-noise ratios, we further diversified the acoustic context of our training dataset.

4.3 Baseline Systems

We compare our lightweight models to a group of models that have demonstrated good performance on the employed datasets. The first baseline system relies on the combination of LFCC features with a HM-Conformer. The HM-Conformer model was re-trained using the hyperparameters originally proposed by the authors [30]. Data augmentation was performed via speed perturbation at factors of 0.9 and 1.1. Apart from the HM-Conformer baseline, we also include more recent models that use frozen self-supervised frontends coupled with lightweight attentive pooling-based backends. These include W2V-ASP

(Wav2vec2 + Attentive Statistics Pooling), WLM-ASP (WavLM + Attentive Statistics Pooling), and HUB-ASP (HuBERT + Attentive Statistics Pooling), which were introduced and evaluated in [41]. Each of these models incorporates a large SSL backbone with over 300 million parameters, which is 100 times larger than our lightweight models. Interested readers are encouraged to refer to [41] for more details.

4.4 Experimental Environment and Hyperparameters

All experiments were conducted on the Cedar cluster of Compute Canada [4]. Each job was allocated two NVIDIA P100 GPUs, 32 GB of system memory per node, and two compute nodes. The models were implemented in PyTorch 1.13.0 with CUDA 11.7. Training used the Adam optimizer with a fixed learning rate of $1e-6$. A batch size of 240 was employed, and models were trained for a maximum of 500 epochs, with early stopping triggered after 50 epochs without improvement on the validation set. For data augmentation, speed perturbation factors of 0.9 and 1.1 were applied. Additionally, background noise from the MUSAN corpus was injected at signal-to-noise ratios randomly sampled for each utterance: 0–15 dB for noise, 13–20 dB for speech, and 5–25 dB for music.

5 Experimental Results and Discussions

5.1 Effects of Input Features

We firstly compare the model performance obtained with different input feature sets. For a fair comparison between features, we ablated all feature choices with both HM-Conformer and HM-Squeezeformer models and report their performance in Table 1 using equal error rate (EER). We highlight the best performing feature set per model for a given dataset in bold. As can be seen, the 120-d MFCC is consistently shown as the top-performer on ASVspoof2021, as well as on ITW with the HM-Squeezeformer model. On the other hand, no significant improvement is seen when LFCCs are combined with MFCCs. Although better performance is obtained with HM-Conformer on ITW using 120-d LFCC + 39-d MFCC, such feature fusion is found sub-optimal elsewhere. A likely reason for the superior performance of the MFCCs is that mel-scale warping allocates greater resolution to the low–mid frequency bands where formant structure and other synthesis-related spectral artifacts are most pronounced, while down-weighting high-frequency regions that carry more noise and channel variability under mismatched conditions. Consistent with this, prior work has reported that low-frequency features perform better in detecting known attack types [39].

5.2 Effects of Data Augmentation

Next, we evaluate the effects of different data augmentation strategies. Based on results from Sect. 5.1, we select the 120-d MFCCs as the input features for this

Table 1. Comparison of different input features based on EER (%) obtained on ASVspoof2021 DF and ITW datasets. Best performing feature set per model architecture for each dataset is highlighted in bold.

Input Features	Model	ASVspoof2021	ITW
120-d LFCC	HM-Conformer	13.42	29.16
120-d MFCC		**12.97**	31.03
39-d MFCC		13.18	30.73
120-d LFCC + 39-d MFCC		13.85	**25.64**
120-d LFCC + 120-d MFCC		13.02	32.17
120-d LFCC	HM-Squeezeformer	16.70	33.62
120-d MFCC		**13.47**	**23.93**
39-d MFCC		16.71	30.37
120-d LFCC + 39-d MFCC		16.24	25.66
120-d LFCC + 120-d MFCC		14.21	30.62

ablation. The effectiveness of each augmentation strategy was evaluated individually and in combination. The results of these experiments are summarized in Table 2. As can be seen, for the HM-Conformer model, using MUSAN noise alone yields the lowest EER on both ASVspoof2021 and ITW, outperforming both RIR-only and combined augmentation strategies. A similar trend is observed for HM-Squeezeformer, where MUSAN also leads to the best performance on ITW, although the combined strategy remains competitive.

Table 2. Comparison of different data augmentation strategies based on EER(%) obtained on ASVspoof2021 DF and ITW. Best augmentation strategy per model for a given dataset is highlighted in bold.

Augmentation	Model	ASVspoof2021	ITW
Background Noise (MUSAN)	HM-Conformer	**10.97**	**23.67**
Reverberation (RIR)		13.10	29.51
Background Noise + Reverberation		11.63	24.83
Background Noise (MUSAN)	HM-Squeezeformer	14.78	**20.04**
Reverberation (RIR)		14.40	25.73
Background Noise + Reverberation		14.76	20.60

5.3 Comparison Between Lightweight and Large Models

After optimizing the input feature choice and augmentation strategy, we compare our best-performing lightweight models against the baseline ones. The results can be found in Table 3. The table presents the EER (%) achieved by our models and several baselines across both the ASVspoof2021 and ITW datasets. The first key observation is that our lightweight models achieve competitive performance relative to large SSL-based models, such as W2V-ASP, HUB-ASP, and WLM-ASP, which rely on over 300 million parameters. For instance, despite being significantly smaller, the HM-Squeezeformer achieves the best performance on the ITW dataset. Second, we compare the two lightweight variants (i.e., HM-Conformer and HM-Squeezeformer) to evaluate the trade-off between performance and efficiency. Based on the obtained results, HM-Squeezeformer outperforms HM-Conformer on the ITW dataset. Additionally, it reduces the FLOPS by approximately 40% (from 439M on Conformer to 269M on Squeezeformer), which highlights the HM-Squeezeformer's superior efficiency, particularly in resource-constrained scenarios.

Table 3. Comparison between baseline models and our lightweight models with optimized input features and augmentation methods based on EER (%) obtained on ASVspoof2021 DF and ITW. The SSL-based baselines (rows 2 to 4) contain over $300M$ parameters where $\approx 9M$ were trainable due to frozen SSL frontends. Best performing model for a given dataset is highlighted in bold. The second best is highlighted with underline.

Input Features	Augmentation	Model	ASVspoof2021	ITW	#Param
120-d LFCC	—	HM-Conformer [30]	13.42	29.16	$2.5M$
Raw waveform		W2V-ASP [41]	19.60	30.20	$300M$
Raw waveform		WLM-ASP [41]	**9.00**	25.40	$300M$
Raw waveform		HUB-ASP [41]	15.40	29.90	$300M$
120-d MFCC	MUSAN	HM-Conformer	<u>10.97</u>	<u>23.67</u>	$2.5M$
120-d MFCC		HM-Squeezeformer	14.78	**20.04**	$2M$

5.4 Discussion

Our comprehensive investigation highlights several key findings that advance the understanding and development of lightweight audio deepfake detection systems. First, regarding feature representations, the experiments in Table 1 demonstrate that 120-dimensional MFCCs consistently outperform LFCCs across both model architectures and evaluation datasets. This suggests that MFCCs are well-suited to capturing the subtle distortions introduced by spoofing methods. Interestingly, feature-level fusion between LFCC and MFCC did not universally lead to better results. While HM-Conformer saw marginal gains on ITW with 120-d LFCC + 39-d MFCC, such fusion was sub-optimal elsewhere, particularly when combining high-dimensional vectors like 120-d LFCC + 120-d MFCC. This may indicate that beyond a certain feature dimensionality, redundancy outweighs complementarity, leading to diminished returns.

Second, Table 2 shows the significant impact of data augmentation strategies. Among the tested augmentations, background noise injection using the MUSAN corpus consistently yielded the best results for both HM-Conformer and HM-Squeezeformer. Notably, it led to a substantial reduction in EER on ITW (e.g., from 31.03% to 23.67% with HM-Conformer). These findings underscore the effectiveness of noise-based augmentation in improving generalization to diverse acoustic conditions. It also highlights that carefully selected single augmentation strategy can sometimes be more beneficial than stacking multiple augmentation strategies.

Third, Table 3 presents a direct comparison between our lightweight models and large-scale SSL-based baselines. Although models like WavLM-ASP and HuBERT-ASP leverage over $300M$ parameters and pretrained representations, our proposed lightweight models perform comparably to, or even outperform, the SSL-based models. More impressively, HM-Squeezeformer achieves the best result on ITW (20.04% EER), despite having just 2M parameters. This finding is particularly important for real-world deployment, as the ITW dataset not only reflects practical conditions, but also serves as a cross-dataset evaluation with diverse and noisy recordings. Such performance gain, achieved without SSL pretraining, reveals the strong potential of carefully designed lightweight models when combined with the right features and augmentations.

It is worth noting that our training setup relies only on the LA partitions of ASVspoof2019, which include six spoofing systems [33], whereas our evaluation on ASVspoof2021-DF covers more than one hundred distinct attack algorithms [36]. Together with ITW, which introduces unconstrained and noisy real-world recordings, these experiments probe generalization under both attack diversity and mismatches in acoustics and channel conditions. The competitive results obtained suggest that the proposed models maintain robustness against advanced and previously unseen spoofing methods, even while operating with a reduced computational footprint.

In addition to performance, efficiency remains central to our study. The comparison between HM-Conformer and HM-Squeezeformer shows that the latter reduces model size by 20% (from $2.5M$ to $2M$ parameters) and FLOPS by 40% (from $439M$ to $269M$), while improving EER on ITW. This demonstrates that architectural choices, such as adopting time-reduction modules and utilizing standard Transformer-style blocks (as in Squeezeformer [16]), can lead to more efficient and generalizable detection systems without sacrificing the overall performance. Importantly, the reduction in number of FLOPS and parameters is indicative of potential reductions in inference latency and computational cost, which are critical for real-time, on-device deployment. Its strong performance on the unconstrained ITW dataset further confirms that efficiency does not come at the expense of robustness.

6 Conclusion and Future Work

In this study, we focus on lightweight deepfake speech detection models and investigate the impact of input features, augmentation methods, and model architectures on model performance. We show that with an optimized combination of these factors, a lightweight model (e.g., HM-Conformer) can achieve comparable performance with a SSL-based model while being 100 times smaller in size. We further demonstrate that with some architectural changes, e.g., replacing Conformer with Squeezeformer, the detection generalizability can be improved while halving the number of FLOPS. These findings demonstrate the potential of our proposed lightweight deepfake detectors for real-time and edge computing applications. As a next step, we plan to broaden our evaluation to datasets that feature more unseen attack types, real-world noisy environments, and multilingual utterances, thereby further validating the robustness and applicability of the proposed models. In parallel, we will also explore model compression techniques, such as pruning, quantization, and knowledge distillation, to further reduce the size of large SSL backbones and make them more suitable for edge applications.

Acknowledgments. The authors acknowledge funding from NSERC (RGPIN-2021-03246).

Disclosure of Interests. The authors have no competing interests to declare that are relevant to the content of this article.

References

1. Altuncu, E., Franqueira, V.N., Li, S.: Deepfake: definitions, performance metrics and standards, datasets, and a meta-review. Front. Big Data **7**, 1400024 (2024)
2. Babu, A., et al.: XLS-R: self-supervised cross-lingual speech representation learning at scale (2021). arXiv preprint arXiv:2111.09296
3. Baevski, A., Zhou, Y., Mohamed, A., Auli, M.: wav2vec 2.0: a framework for self-supervised learning of speech representations. Adv. Neural. Inf. Process. Syst. **33**, 12449–12460 (2020)
4. Baldwin, S.: Compute Canada: advancing computational research. In: Journal of Physics: Conference Series. vol. 341, p. 012001. IOP Publishing (2012)
5. Chaiwongyen, A., Duangpummet, S., Karnjana, J., Kongprawechnon, W., Unoki, M.: Potential of speech-pathological features for deepfake speech detection. IEEE Access (2024)
6. Chakravarty, N., Dua, M.: A lightweight feature extraction technique for deepfake audio detection. Multimedia Tools Appl. **83**(26), 67443–67467 (2024)
7. Chen, S., et al.: WavLM: large-scale self-supervised pre-training for full stack speech processing. IEEE J. Sel. Top. Sig. Process. **16**(6), 1505–1518 (2022)
8. Doan, T.P., Nguyen-Vu, L., Jung, S., Hong, K.: BTS-E: audio deepfake detection using breathing-talking-silence encoder. In: ICASSP 2023-2023 IEEE International Conference on Acoustics, Speech and Signal Processing (ICASSP), pp. 1–5. IEEE (2023)
9. Gulati, A., et al.: Conformer: convolution-augmented transformer for speech recognition (2020). arXiv preprint arXiv:2005.08100
10. Guo, Y., Huang, H., Chen, X., Zhao, H., Wang, Y.: Audio deepfake detection with self-supervised WavLM and multi-fusion attentive classifier. In: ICASSP 2024-2024 IEEE International Conference on Acoustics, Speech and Signal Processing (ICASSP), pp. 12702–12706. IEEE (2024)

11. Hamza, A., et al.: Deepfake audio detection via MFCC features using machine learning. IEEE Access **10**, 134018–134028 (2022)
12. Hsu, W.N., Bolte, B., Tsai, Y.H.H., Lakhotia, K., Salakhutdinov, R., Mohamed, A.: Hubert: self-supervised speech representation learning by masked prediction of hidden units. IEEE/ACM transactions on audio, speech, and language processing **29**, 3451–3460 (2021)
13. Jung, J.w., et al.: AASISIT-L: audio anti-spoofing using integrated spectro-temporal graph attention networks. In: ICASSP 2022-2022 IEEE international conference on acoustics, speech and signal processing (ICASSP), pp. 6367–6371. IEEE (2022)
14. Khanjani, Z., Watson, G., Janeja, V.P.: How deep are the fakes? focusing on audio deepfake: a survey (2021). arXiv preprint arXiv:2111.14203
15. Khanjani, Z., Watson, G., Janeja, V.P.: Audio deepfakes: a survey. Front. Big Data **5**, 1001063 (2023)
16. Kim, S., et al.: Squeezeformer: an efficient transformer for automatic speech recognition. Adv. Neural. Inf. Process. Syst. **35**, 9361–9373 (2022)
17. Ko, T., Peddinti, V., Povey, D., Seltzer, M.L., Khudanpur, S.: A study on data augmentation of reverberant speech for robust speech recognition. In: 2017 IEEE International Conference on Acoustics, Speech and Signal Processing (ICASSP), pp. 5220–5224. IEEE (2017)
18. Latif, S., Zaidi, A., Cuayahuitl, H., Shamshad, F., Shoukat, M., Qadir, J.: Transformers in speech processing: a survey (2023). arXiv preprint arXiv:2303.11607
19. Li, M., Ahmadiadli, Y., Zhang, X.P.: A survey on speech deepfake detection. ACM Comput. Surv. **57**(7), 1–38 (2025)
20. Liu, K., Wang, Y., Li, S., Shao, X.: Speech formants integration for generalized detection of synthetic speech spoofing attacks. In: Proceeding of INTERSPEECH 2024 (2024)
21. Liu, S., et al.: Audio self-supervised learning: a survey. Patterns **3**(12) (2022)
22. Mirsky, Y., Lee, W.: The creation and detection of deepfakes: a survey. ACM Comput. Surv. (CSUR) **54**(1), 1–41 (2021)
23. Müller, N.M., Czempin, P., Dieckmann, F., Froghyar, A., Böttinger, K.: Does audio deepfake detection generalize? Interspeech (2022)
24. Pan, Z., Liu, T., Sailor, H.B., Wang, Q.: Attentive merging of hidden embeddings from pre-trained speech model for anti-spoofing detection (2024). arXiv preprint arXiv:2406.10283
25. Pan, Z., Zhuang, B., Liu, J., He, H., Cai, J.: Scalable vision transformers with hierarchical pooling. In: Proceedings of the IEEE/CVF International Conference on Computer Vision, pp. 377–386 (2021)
26. Pham, L., Lam, P., Nguyen, T., Nguyen, H., Schindler, A.: Deepfake audio detection using spectrogram-based feature and ensemble of deep learning models. In: 2024 IEEE 5th International Symposium on the Internet of Sounds (IS2), pp. 1–5. IEEE (2024)
27. Pimentel, A., Zhu, Y., Guimarães, H.R., Falk, T.H.: Efficient audio deepfake detection using WavLM with early exiting. In: 2024 IEEE International Workshop on Information Forensics and Security (WIFS), pp. 1–6. IEEE (2024)
28. Radford, A., Kim, J.W., Xu, T., Brockman, G., McLeavey, C., Sutskever, I.: Robust speech recognition via large-scale weak supervision. In: International Conference on Machine Learning, pp. 28492–28518. PMLR (2023)
29. Rose, R., Cohen, M.: Political consultant behind fake biden AI robocall faces charges in new hampshire (2024). https://www.cnn.com/2024/05/23/politics/new-hampshire-ai-robocall-biden-charges/index.html. Accessed 30 June 2025

30. Shin, H.s., Heo, J., Kim, J.h., Lim, C.y., Kim, W., Yu, H.J.: HM-conformer: a conformer-based audio deepfake detection system with hierarchical pooling and multi-level classification token aggregation methods. In: ICASSP 2024-2024 IEEE International Conference on Acoustics, Speech and Signal Processing (ICASSP), pp. 10581–10585. IEEE (2024)
31. Snyder, D., Chen, G., Povey, D.: MUSAN: a music, speech, and noise corpus (2015). arXiv preprint arXiv:1510.08484
32. Tak, H., Todisco, M., Wang, X., Jung, J.w., Yamagishi, J., Evans, N.: Automatic speaker verification spoofing and deepfake detection using wav2vec 2.0 and data augmentation (2022). arXiv preprint arXiv:2202.12233
33. Todisco, M., et al.: ASVspoof 2019: future horizons in spoofed and fake audio detection (2019). arXiv preprint arXiv:1904.05441
34. Wang, C., et al.: fully automated end-to-end fake audio detection. In: Proceedings of the 1st International Workshop on Deepfake Detection for Audio Multimedia, pp. 27–33 (2022)
35. Wang, X., Yamagishi, J.: A comparative study on recent neural spoofing countermeasures for synthetic speech detection (2021). arXiv preprint arXiv:2103.11326
36. Yamagishi, J., et al.: ASVspoof 2021: accelerating progress in spoofed and deepfake speech detection (2021). arXiv preprint arXiv:2109.00537
37. Yang, S.w., et al.: A large-scale evaluation of speech foundation models. IEEE/ACM Trans. Audio Speech Lang. Process. **32**, pp. 2884–2899 (2024)
38. Yang, Y., et al.: A robust audio deepfake detection system via multi-view feature. In: ICASSP 2024-2024 IEEE International Conference on Acoustics, Speech and Signal Processing (ICASSP), pp. 13131–13135. IEEE (2024)
39. Zhang, B., Cui, H., Nguyen, V., Whitty, M.: Audio deepfake detection: what has been achieved and what lies ahead. Sensors (Basel, Switzerland) **25**(7), 1989 (2025)
40. Zhang, Y., Jiang, F., Duan, Z.: One-class learning towards synthetic voice spoofing detection. IEEE Signal Process. Lett. **28**, 937–941 (2021)
41. Zhu, Y., Koppisetti, S., Tran, T., Bharaj, G.: Slim: style-linguistics mismatch model for generalized audio deepfake detection. Adv. Neural. Inf. Process. Syst. **37**, 67901–67928 (2024)
42. Zhu, Y., Powar, S., Falk, T.H.: Characterizing the temporal dynamics of universal speech representations for generalizable deepfake detection. In: 2024 IEEE International Conference on Acoustics, Speech, and Signal Processing Workshops (ICASSPW), pp. 139–143. IEEE (2024)

Strategic Detection of APTs Through Federated Spatio-Temporal Graph Learning and Stackelberg Defense

Myria Bouhaddi(✉) and Kamel Adi

Computer Security Research Laboratory, University of Quebec in Outaouais, Gatineau, QC, Canada
{myria.bouhaddi,kamel.adi}@uqo.ca

Abstract. Existing Intrusion Detection Systems (IDS), including those based on Graph Neural Networks (GNNs), often suffer from high false positive rates and limited adaptability in distributed or federated environments. In this work, we introduce a novel federated intrusion detection architecture that combines spatio-temporal graph modeling, privacy-preserving local encoding, and strategic decision-making to effectively detect Advanced Persistent Threats (APTs). Our system extracts and obfuscates local provenance graphs on each device, then performs federated aggregation of encoded features without compromising data privacy. A Stackelberg game-theoretic module anticipates attacker behavior and dynamically adjusts detection thresholds through an equilibrium-based decision process. This architecture is coordinated by a federated orchestrator that consolidates distributed intelligence while preserving the confidentiality of sensitive information. As a result, our approach achieves a strong balance between privacy, adaptability, and detection accuracy. Experimental results on benchmark APT datasets demonstrate that our method outperforms existing baselines in terms of F1-score, robustness, and the privacy-utility trade-off, highlighting the benefits of unifying spatio-temporal learning, federated optimization, and adversarial reasoning in modern IDS frameworks.

Keywords: Intrusion Detection Systems · Spatio-Temporal Graph Neural Networks · Game Theory · Privacy-Preserving Federated Learning · Advanced Persistent Threats

1 Introduction

The growing reliance on digital infrastructure in critical sectors such as healthcare, energy, finance and public administration has significantly increased the volume and sensitivity of daily data processing [1]. Consequently, cyberattacks have become more frequent and sophisticated, with adversaries exploiting distributed environments, zero-day vulnerabilities, and advanced evasion tactics to

K. Adi et al. (Eds.): CRiSIS 2025, LNCS 16295, pp. 390–409, 2026.
https://doi.org/10.1007/978-3-032-20732-6_25

target high-value systems. The emergence of smart cities, Industry 4.0, and large-scale IoT deployments further broadens the attack surface, posing major challenges to cybersecurity. Once infiltrated, compromised systems can cause serious disruptions, from ransomware attacks in hospitals to surveillance breaches in military networks [10].

Among cyber threats, Advanced Persistent Threats (APTs) are particularly concerning due to their stealth, persistence, and targeted execution. Often orchestrated by state-sponsored or organized groups, APTs aim to maintain unauthorized access over long periods through multistage operations that involve compromise, lateral movement, escalation of privileges, and data exfiltration or sabotage [19]. Notable examples include the Dark Pink campaign, which covertly targeted military networks in Southeast Asia [12], and the SolarWinds supply chain attack, which remained undetected for months while harvesting sensitive data [11,20].

Detecting APTs is notoriously difficult. Unlike traditional cyberattacks that trigger immediate red flags, APTs often mimic normal user behavior, evolve over time, and evade detection by operating in multiple temporal layers. Their tactics leverage advanced obfuscation techniques, zero-day vulnerabilities, and social engineering strategies. In addition, their activity patterns tend to be contextual and relational, making them difficult to identify using static or signature-based detection methods. Detecting APTs requires analyzing subtle long-term changes in user behavior, network interactions, and data flows, something that exceeds the capabilities of most traditional Intrusion Detection Systems.

IDSs have historically relied on predefined rules, statistical thresholds, or anomaly detection to identify malicious activities in network traffic [6]. However, they often produce high false positive rates, lack temporal modeling, and are not well suited for distributed infrastructures such as IoT networks or edge environments. Even recent approaches using machine learning or Graph Neural Networks (GNNs) fall short in capturing the multistage, adaptive nature of APTs. Furthermore, their reliance on centralized learning raises significant concerns regarding privacy and scalability [27].

To address these challenges, we propose a strategic and distributed detection framework that integrates spatio-temporal graph modeling, federated learning, and adversarial reasoning. Our method captures the temporal evolution and structural patterns of network activities through spatio-temporal graph neural networks, enabling the identification of coordinated, multi-stage attacks. Furthermore, to improve robustness against evasive behaviors, the detection process is modeled as a Stackelberg game between an intelligent IDS and a strategic attacker, allowing the system to anticipate and counter adaptive tactics. Finally, to ensure scalability and privacy in distributed environments like IoT infrastructures, we adopt a lightweight federated learning approach, allowing nodes to collaboratively train detection models without sharing raw data. This multi-layered framework enables accurate, privacy-preserving, and adaptive threat detection, while remaining aligned with the scalability requirements of modern digital ecosystems.

The remainder of this paper is organized as follows. Section 2 presents the preliminaries, introducing the key concepts and definitions necessary to understand the present work. Section 3 reviews the related work, highlighting current limitations in APT detection, spatio-temporal GNNs, and privacy-preserving IDS architectures. Section 4 introduces our proposed detection architecture, including the spatio-temporal autoencoder, the game-theoretic formulation of the detection strategy, and the privacy-preserving learning process. Section 5 presents the experimental evaluation, comparing our approach with existing baselines in terms of detection accuracy, false positive rate, computational cost, and robustness to adaptive threats. Finally, Sect. 6 concludes the paper and outlines future research directions.

2 Preliminaries

This section introduces the key concepts underpinning our approach, including Advanced Persistent Threats, provenance graphs, Graph Neural Networks, and game theory, all of which are central to our proposed framework.

2.1 Advanced Persistent Threats

Advanced Persistent Threats are among the most critical and challenging forms of cyberattacks, characterized by their stealth, persistence, and strategic intent. Unlike opportunistic cyberattacks, APTs are often carried out by state-sponsored or highly organized threat actors, with the aim of infiltrating targeted systems and remaining undetected for extended periods. Their objectives include data exfiltration, espionage, sabotage, or long-term surveillance.

APTs typically progress through several coordinated stages that form a logical attack chain. The initial intrusion often involves exploiting system vulnerabilities or leveraging social engineering tactics such as phishing to gain unauthorized access. Once inside, attackers establish a foothold by deploying malware or installing backdoors to ensure continued access, even after system reboots. They then move laterally across the network, compromising additional systems in search of critical assets. To deepen control, they escalate privileges by exploiting misconfigurations or known vulnerabilities. This is followed by data exfiltration, where sensitive information is transferred to external servers, or by disruptive actions such as data corruption or service interruptions. Throughout the operation, attackers maintain persistence using sophisticated evasion techniques, including fileless malware, registry manipulation, and rootkits, allowing long-term undetected access.

The sophistication of APTs lies in their ability to mimic legitimate activity, dynamically adapt to detection attempts, and maintain a low profile through advanced obfuscation and stealth. Traditional signature-based Intrusion Detection Systems and rule-based models often fail to detect these attacks due to their multi-stage progression, temporal delay between stages, and polymorphic behavior. In addition, in modern infrastructures such as cloud-based environments and IoT systems, the attack surface is larger and more dynamic. This increases the difficulty of correlating distributed and time-dependent events, a key challenge that motivates the use of spatial-temporal graph-based models for APT detection.

2.2 Provenance Graphs

A provenance graph is a directed acyclic graph $G = (V, E)$ where nodes V represent system entities (for example, files, processes, IP addresses), and edges E encode the interactions between them, such as execution, read/write operations, or network connections. These graphs capture the historical sequence of system-level events, making them highly valuable for forensic analysis and intrusion detection. By modeling both data flows and control flows, they reveal hidden dependencies and behavioral patterns that are especially useful for identifying complex, multi-stage attacks such as APTs.

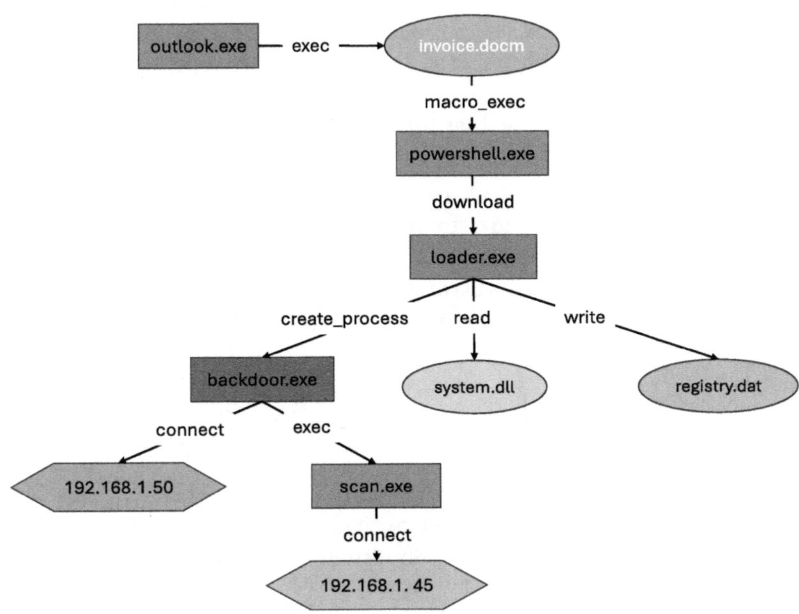

Fig. 1. Example of a provenance graph representing a multi-stage APT scenario.

The attack scenario depicted in Fig. 1 begins with a phishing email received through `outlook.exe`, which opens a malicious macro-enabled document `invoice.docm`. Upon macro execution, `powershell.exe` is launched, downloaded, and executed `loader.exe`. This loader initiates additional malicious processes such as `backdoor.exe` and `scan.exe`, reads local libraries like `system.dll`, and modifies sensitive files such as `registry.dat`. The network connections are then established with internal and external IP addresses (`192.168.1.45`, `192.168.1.50`) for command-and-control and reconnaissance purposes.

Each entity in the scenario (process, file, IP) is assigned to a node in the provenance graph, and each observed interaction becomes a directed edge labeled with the action type (e.g. *read*, *exec*, *connect*, *write*). The graph thus generated encodes the causal chain of events initiated by the attacker, offering a structured representation that is amenable to both rule-based and learning-based intrusion detection. This formal representation not only enhances the interpretability of system activity, but also facilitates the application of Graph Neural Networks, which we explore in the following subsection.

2.3 Graph Neural Networks

Graph Neural Networks are deep learning architectures specifically designed to operate on graph-structured data, where information is not arranged in regular grids (like images), but in the form of nodes and edges capturing complex relationships. In a graph $G = (V, E)$, each node $v \in V$ may represent an entity (e.g. process, file, IP address), and the edges $(i, j) \in E$ represent interactions or dependencies between entities.

Each node v is associated with an initial vector of characteristics x_v, and the GNNs learn hidden representations $h_v^{(l)}$ for each node in the layer l by aggregating features from its neighborhood. In the context of system provenance graphs, these characteristics may include, for example, the type of the node (process, file, IP), the number of connections, the access frequency, execution timestamps, or statistical indicators such as entropy or persistence time. A typical message-passing operation updates each node embedding as follows:

$$h_i^{(l+1)} = \sigma\left(W^{(l)} h_i^{(l)} + \sum_{j \in \mathcal{N}(i)} W_{\text{neigh}}^{(l)} h_j^{(l)}\right), \tag{1}$$

where $\mathcal{N}(i)$ denotes the neighbors of node i, $W^{(l)}$ and $W_{\text{neigh}}^{(l)}$ are learnable weight matrices, and σ is a non-linear activation function such as ReLU. This operation allows each node to iteratively integrate contextual information from its local structure.

The intuition behind this update is that the refined **embedding** combines its existing knowledge ($W^{(l)} h_i^{(l)}$) with the aggregated information of its neighbors ($\sum_{j \in \mathcal{N}(i)} W_{\text{neigh}}^{(l)} h_j^{(l)}$). This combined input is then non-linearly transformed.

This process unfolds across multiple layers: starting with initial features ($h_i^{(0)} = x_i$), each successive layer enables nodes to integrate information from an increasingly wider **neighborhood radius** (direct neighbors, then neighbors of neighbors, etc.). This iterative message passing allows GNNs to learn rich, context-aware node representations that capture both intrinsic node properties and structural patterns, vital for detecting complex, multi-stage APTs.

GNN variants such as Graph Convolutional Networks (GCNs), Graph Attention Networks (GATs), and Graph Autoencoders (GAEs) have been successfully used in tasks like node classification, link prediction, and anomaly detection.

Traditional GNNs consider static graphs, which are insufficient to model cyberattack dynamics where node behaviors and their interactions evolve over time. To address this, we use Spatio-Temporal GNNs (STGNNs), which combine spatial message passing with temporal modeling mechanisms.

These models are designed to capture two complementary dimensions: spatial dependencies, by applying graph convolutions over the network structure at each time step, and temporal dependencies, by aggregating node states across sequential time steps using mechanisms such as GRU, LSTM, temporal attention, or other recurrent layers.

A general update rule for an ST-GNN can be written as:

$$h_v^{(t)} = f\left(h_v^{(t-1)}, \mathrm{AGG}_{\mathrm{spatial}}\left(\{h_u^{(t-1)} : u \in \mathcal{N}(v)\}\right)\right), \tag{2}$$

where f integrates both temporal and spatial information.

Equation 2 defines the update rule for node v at time t, where $h_v^{(t)}$ denotes its latent representation. The function $\mathrm{AGG}_{\mathrm{spatial}}(\cdot)$ aggregates the embeddings of neighboring nodes $u \in \mathcal{N}(v)$ from the previous time step, and $f(\cdot)$ (for example, a GRU or MLP) integrates both spatial and temporal information to produce the updated state.

In our context, system activity is modeled as a time-evolving graph, where nodes (processes, files, IPs) interact over discrete time steps. To capture both structural and temporal patterns, we use a spatio-temporal graph autoencoder (ST-GNN-AE), which learns compact representations of local behaviors. This enables the detection of gradually evolving threats such as APTs while supporting privacy-preserving feature sharing in a federated setting.

2.4 Game Theory for Adversarial Detection

In adversarial settings such as cybersecurity, where attackers strategically adapt their behavior to evade detection, it is essential to model the interaction between defenders and attackers as a strategic process. Game theory provides a rigorous mathematical framework for analyzing such interactions between rational agents with conflicting goals.

We model the detection problem as a *Stackelberg game*, a type of leader-follower game in which the defender (IDS) commits to a strategy first, and the attacker observes this strategy and then optimizes their response. Let $\theta \in \Theta$ denote the detection strategy chosen by the IDS (the leader), and $a \in \mathcal{A}$ the attack strategy chosen by the adversary (the follower). The adversary solves:

$$a^*(\theta) = \arg\max_{a \in \mathcal{A}} U_A(\theta, a), \tag{3}$$

where U_A is the utility function of the attacker. Anticipating this response, the defender optimizes:

$$\theta^* = \arg\max_{\theta \in \Theta} U_D(\theta, a^*(\theta)), \tag{4}$$

where U_D is the utility of the defender. This bilevel optimization captures the sequential structure of the game and enables the defender to proactively select a strategy that is robust against the attacker's best response. This formulation enables the detection system to balance accuracy, computational cost, and adversarial robustness in a principled manner. By embedding this strategic reasoning into the model, we enhance its resilience in dynamic and hostile environments.

3 Related Work

The detection of Advanced Persistent Threats presents unique challenges due to their stealthy, multi-stage, and adaptive nature. In recent years, research has converged towards integrating *graph neural networks*, provenance-based modeling, and federated or distributed learning architectures to build more effective and scalable Intrusion Detection Systems. This section reviews the main contributions along the four major axes. GNN in cybersecurity, graph construction strategies, GNN-based APT detection models, and decentralized IDS frameworks.

Graph Neural Networks have shown promising capabilities in modeling complex dependencies among entities in network traffic. Compared to traditional rule-based or signature-based IDSs [13], GNNs can capture the latent structure of relationships between hosts, flows, and events, allowing detection of subtle APT behavior. Pujol-Perich et al. [18] demonstrate how GNNs, applied to flow-based graphs, can accurately detect attacks such as DDoS, port scans, and network scans. Several works have confirmed the efficacy of GNNs in cybersecurity. For example, Wang and Yu [22] highlight the utility of deep learning in structured graphs in the social, system, and provenance domains. Bilot et al. [4] further explore GNNs to model APT campaigns, showing their ability to detect stealthy and adaptive patterns. However, these methods are highly dependent on the quality and diversity of graph-based datasets. As noted by Liu and Jiang [16], many datasets remain outdated or anonymized, limiting their realism and impeding the generalizability of detection models.

The success of graph-based APT detection hinges on the nature of the graph representation. Graph generation methods can be categorized as *static* or *dynamic*. Static graphs represent a snapshot of the network at a specific time. Previous works [7,26] enrich static graphs by adding hyper-edges or hot encodings to improve structural expressiveness. Transformation techniques, such as edge-to-node conversion [28], are also used to optimize downstream node classification. For real-time detection, *the dynamic graphs* are essential. Snapshot-based techniques [15] divide data into discrete intervals, while sketch-based methods [17] reduce complexity by summarizing system behavior into lower-dimensional vectors. These dynamic representations allow for the modeling of temporal evolution and behavioral drift of APTs across time.

Numerous recent models leverage GNNs to detect APTs by learning graph representations at different granularities. MAGIC [14] uses a masked autoencoder with GAT and GCN layers to reconstruct edge-level representations from system logs. KAIROS [9] embeds temporal patterns in provenance graphs to identify new anomalies, while GCA [25] employs contrastive learning on attacker and benign subgraphs. Several architectures incorporate domain knowledge: GHUNTER [8] uses graph matching against known malicious patterns; ThreatRace [23] applies GraphSAGE for graph embedding; and XFedGraphHunter [21] uses a federated learning variant of GraphSAGE to scale across distributed environments. Despite their promise, GNN-based APT detectors still face challenges: high computational complexity, sensitivity to input noise, and reduced performance in early-stage or zero-day APT detection [3,9,14].

Most APT detection models are based on *centralized processing*, raising the issues of scalability, latency, and data privacy. To address this, Wu et al. [24] proposed PARADISE, a distributed IDS using Kafka servers to process logs in parallel. However, this approach remains vulnerable to bandwidth and privacy issues due to system-wide data aggregation. Federated learning presents a privacy-preserving alternative. FL allows clients to train local models while sharing only encrypted model updates with the server. Applied to APT detection, Son et al. [21] showed that FL-based GNNs reduce false positives and improve generalization to unseen attacks. In addition, FL mitigates the risks of data exposure and adapts better to heterogeneous client data, making it suitable for sensitive or large-scale environments [5].

4 Federated Spatio-Temporal Graph-Based Framework for APT Detection

This section presents our federated framework for detecting APTs, combining three key components: a local spatio-temporal graph autoencoder, a Stackelberg game-based defense strategy, and a privacy-preserving federated learning scheme. We begin with the threat model and then detail each component.

4.1 Threat Model

We consider a stealthy, multi-stage adversary operating in a federated environment, aiming to progressively compromise the network while evading detection and disrupting the global intrusion detection process. The attack begins with the compromise of one or more edge devices or local IDS agents through techniques such as firmware or software vulnerabilities exploitation or credential theft. Upon gaining access, the adversary escalates privileges and performs lateral movements across neighboring nodes by exploiting trust relationships or shared communication protocols. To remain stealthy, the attacker manipulates system logs, mimics benign behaviors, and subtly poisons local model updates during federated training, all while avoiding triggering detection mechanisms. The adversary may dynamically adapt its behavior to bypass threshold-based detection while subtly corrupting local contributions to mislead the global model. Figure 2 illustrates the progression and coordination of the attacker across the architecture layers.

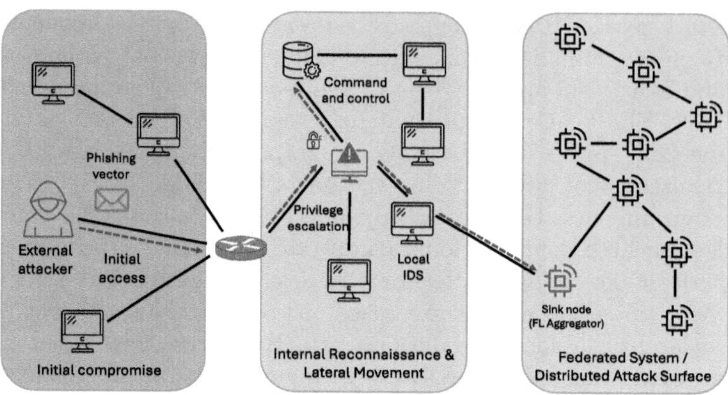

Fig. 2. Adversarial threat model in federated environments: the attacker progresses from initial access to lateral movement and remote coordination, aiming to remain stealthy while compromising detection.

The attacker exhibits a multi-phase capability, beginning with the initial compromise of vulnerable edge devices, followed by privilege escalation to gain full control over local systems. Once embedded, the attacker conducts lateral movements across the network, relying on stealth techniques such as log manipulation, process masquerading, and time-shifted activities to evade detection. Despite these evasive strategies, the attack induces subtle but detectable anomalies in the provenance graphs, such as irregular edge connections, unauthorized data flows, and temporal inconsistencies. Finally, the attack is remotely coordinated via covert command-and-control channels, allowing synchronized actions across compromised nodes while maintaining a low profile.

We assume no active Byzantine behavior or model poisoning at the server level. The cloud aggregator is considered *honest-but-curious*: it correctly follows the protocol, but may attempt to infer sensitive information from model updates. To protect against this, we integrate a lightweight privacy-preserving mechanism that ensures minimal leakage without degrading detection performance.

4.2 Overview of the Detection Framework

To detect advanced persistent threats in a distributed and privacy-aware environment, we propose a multi-phase detection framework that integrates spatio-temporal graph representation learning, federated collaboration, and game-theoretic decision-making. As illustrated in Fig. 3, the framework consists of six key components: (1) local data generation, (2) provenance graph construction, (3) feature extraction and obfuscation using a spatio-temporal graph autoencoder, (4) federated aggregation of local representations, (5) strategic defense modeled as a Stackelberg game between the IDS and the adversary, and (6) final decision making. Each phase is detailed in the following subsections.

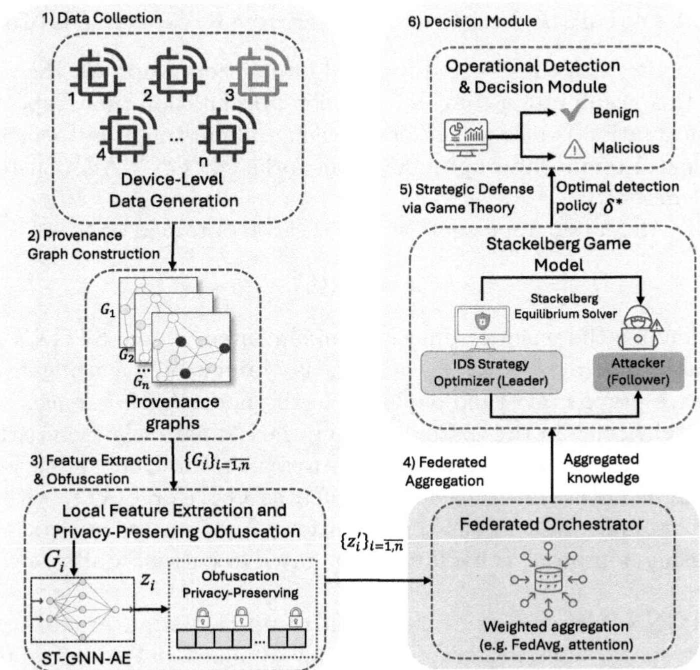

Fig. 3. Multi-Phase Detection Pipeline with Federated Aggregation and Strategic Defense.

4.3 Data Collection and Provenance Graph Construction

The detection process begins with the local collection of system events from devices distributed in the IoT environment. Each device (or node) continuously logs events such as process executions, file accesses, inter-process communications, or network connections. These raw events are transformed into provenance graphs that encode both the causal and temporal dependencies between system entities.

Formally, we define a dynamic provenance graph as $\mathcal{G} = (\mathcal{V}, \mathcal{E})$, where $\mathcal{V}$ is the set of nodes, each corresponding to a system object (e.g., a process, file or socket). $\mathcal{E}$ is the set of directed edges (u, v, t) that represents a causal interaction from node u to node v at time t. Each node $v \in \mathcal{V}$ is associated with a feature vector $\mathbf{x}_v \in \mathbb{R}^d$ describing its local attributes (e.g., type, privileges, usage statistics), and each edge can carry additional metadata such as the interaction type or timestamp. These dynamic graphs reflect the evolving behavior of the system and serve as the structural foundation for the following stage: spatio-temporal representation learning.

4.4 Local Feature Extraction and Privacy-Preserving Obfuscation

Once each node i has constructed its local interaction graph $\mathcal{G}_i$, the next step is to convert this graph into a compact vector representation that respects privacy. This transformation is performed locally using a lightweight autoencoder model based on spatio-temporal graph neural networks (STGNN-AE), customized for edge-level inference.

Formally, the latent representation $\mathbf{z}_i \in \mathbb{R}^d$ is obtained as

$$\mathbf{z}_i = f_\theta(\mathcal{G}_i),$$

where f_θ denotes the encoder function implemented by the STGNN-AE model and parameterized by θ. The encoder f_θ is trained offline using a dataset of representative graphs and then deployed to the nodes for inference.

The model f_θ uses both the topology and the temporal characteristics of $\mathcal{G}_i$. It combines spatial aggregation, which captures structural dependencies between nodes through message-passing layers (such as GCN or GAT), with temporal encoding techniques that model the evolution of node characteristics over time, typically using temporal convolutions or gated recurrent units (e.g., TCN or GRU).

The STGNN-AE consists of two main components: an **encoder** f_θ, which projects the spatio-temporal graph into a low-dimensional latent representation $\mathbf{z}_i$, and a **decoder** g_ϕ (used only during training), which reconstructs the input graph to help the model preserve essential structural and temporal features.

To support edge deployment, a lightweight encoder is used locally for inference, avoiding the transmission of raw graphs. Only the compressed vector $\mathbf{z}_i$ is forwarded to the obfuscation phase, preserving the privacy of the data.

4.5 Privacy-Preserving Obfuscation of Latent Representations

To preserve privacy, the latent vector $\mathbf{z}_i$ is immediately obfuscated to prevent leakage of sensitive or identifiable information before any further processing.

Formally, we define an obfuscation function $h_\phi : \mathbb{R}^d \rightarrow \mathbb{R}^d$, parameterized by ϕ, which transforms the original latent vector into an obfuscated embedding:

$$\mathbf{z}'_i = h_\phi(\mathbf{z}_i).$$

Latent Space Factorization. To achieve selective privacy protection, we first partition the latent space into two orthogonal subspaces.

$$\mathbf{z}_i = [\mathbf{z}_i^{\text{priv}} \parallel \mathbf{z}_i^{\text{util}}],$$

where:

- $\mathbf{z}_i^{\text{priv}} \in \mathbb{R}^{d_p}$ contains dimensions encoding sensitive attributes (e.g., user-specific behavior, identifiable device patterns),
- $\mathbf{z}_i^{\text{util}} \in \mathbb{R}^{d_u}$ encodes discriminative features necessary for downstream anomaly detection.

Obfuscation Strategies. The obfuscation is selectively applied to $\mathbf{z}_i^{\text{priv}}$ to reduce mutual information with any sensitive signal while preserving the detection utility.

$$\mathbf{z}_i' = \left[h_\phi(\mathbf{z}_i^{\text{priv}}) \parallel \mathbf{z}_i^{\text{util}}\right].$$

Several instantiations of h_ϕ are possible:

- **Gaussian Noise Injection**:

$$h_\phi(\mathbf{z}_i^{\text{priv}}) = \mathbf{z}_i^{\text{priv}} + \mathcal{N}(0, \sigma^2 I),$$

  where σ controls the trade-off between privacy and utility.
- **Differential Privacy Mechanism (Laplace)**:

$$h_\phi(\mathbf{z}_i^{\text{priv}}) = \mathbf{z}_i^{\text{priv}} + \text{Lap}(\lambda),$$

  where λ is calibrated according to the sensitivity Δ of the latent characteristic and the desired privacy budget ϵ.
- **Adversarial Obfuscation Networks**: learn h_ϕ by training a minimax model:

$$\min_\phi \max_\psi \mathbb{E}\left[\mathcal{L}_{\text{priv}}(D_\psi(h_\phi(\mathbf{z}_i^{\text{priv}})))\right],$$

  where D_ψ is a discriminator trying to infer private labels and h_ϕ aims to reduce this ability.

The obfuscation mechanism aims to minimize information leakage, that is:

$$I(\mathbf{z}_i'; \text{private data}) \approx 0$$

while preserving critical characteristics for anomaly detection, ensuring that $\mathbf{z}_i'$ remains as effective as $\mathbf{z}_i$ for classification. These obfuscated vectors $\mathbf{z}_i'$ are then securely transmitted to the central analyzer, enabling collaborative detection with strong privacy guarantees and minimal performance loss.

4.6 Stackelberg Game for Strategic Detection

Advanced adversaries do not act randomly; instead, they adapt their behavior in response to the detection strategies they face. This adversarial intelligence requires the defense mechanism to anticipate and strategically plan its actions. To capture this asymmetric interaction, we model the confrontation between the intrusion detection system and the attacker as a Stackelberg game, a leader-follower framework well-suited to sequential decision-making under strategic uncertainty.

Justification. Unlike standard detection schemes that rely on static thresholds or reactive policies, our Stackelberg game formulation enables the IDS to proactively shape its detection strategy while anticipating the attacker's optimal response. The attacker observes or infers the behavior of the defender (e.g., detection threshold) and adjusts their tactics accordingly, modifying the pace, stealth, or spread of the intrusion. By modeling this interaction, the IDS can optimize its strategy *in anticipation* of the best counter-move of the adversary, improving robustness in the face of intelligent threats.

Formally, we define our IDS-Attacker Stackelberg game as a triplet

$$\mathcal{SG} = (\{P_i\}_{i=1,2}, \{\mathcal{S}\}_{i=1,2}, \{\mathcal{U}\}_{i=1,2}), \tag{5}$$

where:

- $\{P_i\}_{i=1,2}$ is the set of players:
  - P_1 is the **defender** (IDS), acting as the leader. Select a detection configuration, such as a decision threshold τ, the aggressiveness of the defense, or a risk-privacy trade-off. The IDS first commits to its strategy.
  - P_2 is the **attacker**, considered as the follower. Observes or estimates the strategy of the defender and chooses an attack profile α that maximizes its success while minimizing detection. This may involve adjusting its stealth level, propagation speed, or timing.
- $\{\mathcal{S}_i\}_{i=1,2}$ is the set of strategy spaces:
  - The IDS selects $\tau \in \mathcal{T}$, which controls the sensitivity of detection (e.g., a lower threshold increases the true positive rate but may also raise false positives).
  - The attacker selects $\alpha \in \mathcal{A}$, representing its behavioral configuration (e.g., stealthiness, propagation speed, timing).
- $\{\mathcal{U}_i\}_{i=1,2}$ is the set of utility functions:
  - The IDS aims to maximize:

    $$\mathcal{U}_1(\tau, \alpha) = \mathrm{TPR}(\tau, \alpha) - \lambda \cdot \mathrm{FPR}(\tau) - \mu \cdot \mathrm{Cost}(\tau),$$

    where λ and μ control the trade-offs related to false alarms and operational burden.
  - The attacker aims to maximize:

    $$\mathcal{U}_2(\tau, \alpha) = \mathrm{Impact}(\alpha) - \gamma \cdot \mathrm{DetectionRate}(\tau, \alpha),$$

    where γ reflects the attacker's aversion to being detected.

Stackelberg Equilibrium. In equilibrium, the attacker responds optimally to any defense strategy.

$$\alpha^*(\tau) = \arg\max_{\alpha \in \mathcal{A}} U_{\mathrm{Attacker}}(\tau, \alpha),$$

and the IDS anticipates this response by solving:

$$\tau^* = \arg\max_{\tau \in \mathcal{T}} U_{\text{IDS}}(\tau, \alpha^*(\tau)).$$

The pair $(\tau^*, \alpha^*(\tau^*))$ defines the Stackelberg equilibrium, producing a robust detection policy that accounts for the adaptability of the adversary.

In our framework, the detection threshold τ is dynamically adjusted based on the inferred behavior of the attacker. For example, if the system observes signs of increased stealth or coordinated evasion, it can shift τ towards more aggressive detection, at the cost of raising alerts. In contrast, in benign phases, it can relax τ to conserve resources or reduce false alarms. This game-theoretic modulation enables strategic and context-aware decision-making beyond static or heuristic configurations.

5 Experimental Evaluation

This section presents the experimental validation of our framework using a real-world dataset. We aim to assess the detection performance, privacy-preserving capabilities, and strategic robustness of our approach in the detection of stealthy APT.

5.1 Dataset and Preprocessing

To evaluate the effectiveness of our proposed detection framework, we rely on publicly available datasets that simulate advanced persistent threat scenarios in realistic environments. Each dataset provides system-level provenance information, which we transform into spatio-temporal provenance graphs.

ATLAS Dataset. The ATLAS dataset [2] provides a collection of APT campaigns executed in a controlled environment, capturing detailed logs of benign and malicious activities across distributed nodes. Each event is time-stamped and linked to specific system entities (processes, files, network sockets). We parse these logs to build a sequence of dynamic provenance graphs $\mathcal{G}_i$, where each node represents a system object, and directed edges capture causal relationships (e.g. process spawning, file access, socket communication).

StreamSpot Dataset. StreamSpot is a benchmark dataset composed of synthetic provenance graphs that emulate benign and malicious executions. It includes labeled graphs derived from system audit logs, making it suitable for graph-based anomaly detection. We use StreamSpot to validate our model on lightweight graph representations in streaming settings.

CADETS Dataset. The CADETS dataset, part of the DARPA Transparent Computing Program, offers a rich set of provenance events from different operating systems and configurations. We extract subgraphs from labeled attack scenarios, focusing on temporal sequences that reflect stealthy adversarial behaviors.
For each dataset, we apply the following preprocessing pipeline.

1. Event logs are parsed into directed acyclic graphs (DAGs) preserving causal and temporal order.
2. Each node is represented by a feature vector $\mathbf{x}_v \in \mathbb{R}^d$ encoding its type (process, file, socket), access mode, and timestamp embedding.
3. Edges are annotated with interaction types and time deltas, supporting spatio-temporal reasoning.
4. Each dynamic graph $\mathcal{G}_i$ is extracted over a sliding window to form a sequence of temporal snapshots per device.
5. Labels (benign or malicious) are assigned at the graph level, based on ground truth or injected APT phases.

This representation enables direct integration into the STGNN-AE encoder and supports localized feature extraction, privacy-preserving obfuscation, and federated analysis.

5.2 Baselines and Comparison Methods

To assess the effectiveness of our proposed framework, we compare it with several state-of-the-art methods for graph-based anomaly detection and APT detection. The selected baselines include both centralized and federated approaches, as well as models that incorporate spatio-temporal and privacy-aware mechanisms.

GCN (Graph Convolutional Network). A standard GCN model trained on individual graphs for node or graph-level anomaly classification. It does not account for temporal dynamics or federated constraints, but serves as a strong baseline for structural anomaly detection.

STGCN (Spatio-Temporal GCN). A spatio-temporal variant of GCN designed to capture temporal dependencies in evolving graphs. It operates in a centralized setting and is trained on the full dataset, providing an upper bound on detection performance. However, this approach does not offer any privacy guarantees.

StreamSpot. A streaming-based anomaly detection method tailored to provenance graphs. StreamSpot computes compact sketches of incoming graph streams and compares them to reference profiles to detect deviations. It offers high efficiency, but does not incorporate learning-based representations or federated learning.

FedAvg-GCN. A federated version of GCN using the FedAvg algorithm for aggregation across distributed clients. This approach preserves privacy at the data level but lacks fine-grained temporal modeling and obfuscation mechanisms.

Ours (STGNN-AE + Obfuscation + Game-Based Defense). Our full model includes a local spatio-temporal graph autoencoder (STGNN-AE), a privacy-preserving obfuscation mechanism, and a dynamic decision-making strategy derived from a Stackelberg game formulation. This combination enables adaptive and privacy-aware detection of stealthy APT behaviors in federated settings.

All methods are trained and evaluated in identical settings using the same data splits and evaluation metrics described in the following subsection. The hyperparameters for each model are tuned using a validation set to ensure fair comparison.

5.3 Evaluation Metrics

To rigorously assess the performance of the proposed detection framework and its competitors, we employ several standard evaluation metrics widely used in anomaly detection and intrusion detection settings.

- *True Positive Rate/Recall:* measures the proportion of actual attacks correctly identified by the system.
- *False Positive Rate:* evaluates the proportion of benign instances incorrectly flagged as anomalies.
- *Precision:* indicates the fraction of predicted anomalies that are actual attacks.
- *F1-Score:* the harmonic mean of precision and recall, offering a balanced view of detection performance.
- *AUC-ROC (Area Under the Receiver Operating Characteristic Curve):* captures the trade-off between TPR and FPR in different threshold settings. A higher AUC indicates better separability between benign and malicious behaviors.
- *Privacy-Utility Trade-off:* in privacy-sensitive settings, we additionally report:
  - The degradation in detection performance due to obfuscation (drop in F1 or AUC).
  - The estimated mutual information $I(\tilde{\mathbf{z}}_i; \text{private data})$ as a proxy for privacy leakage (if measurable through synthetic or labeled private features).

All metrics are computed over multiple experimental runs with different random seeds to ensure statistical robustness. Mean values and standard deviations are reported for each metric.

5.4 Results and Analysis

The performance of our proposed approach is compared with the baseline models using the evaluation metrics described previously.

Table 1 reports the detection performance in terms of F1-score, AUC-ROC, precision, and recall. Our method consistently outperforms all baselines across all datasets, demonstrating its ability to detect stealthy and multi-stage intrusions with high accuracy. The improvement is particularly significant on ATLAS, where the adversary adopts adaptive and delayed strategies. This highlights the benefits of combining temporal provenance analysis, federated aggregation, and strategic decision-making.

Table 1. Detection performance comparison across datasets.

Method	F1-score	AUC-ROC	Precision	Recall
ATLAS Dataset				
GCN	0.76	0.81	0.75	0.77
STGCN	0.80	0.86	0.78	0.82
StreamSpot	0.72	0.78	0.71	0.73
FedAvg-GCN	0.85	0.90	0.84	0.86
Ours (Full Framework)	**0.91**	**0.96**	**0.90**	**0.92**
UNSW-NB15				
GCN	0.78	0.83	0.79	0.77
STGCN	0.81	0.86	0.82	0.80
StreamSpot	0.75	0.80	0.76	0.74
FedAvg-GCN	0.87	0.91	0.86	0.88
Ours (Full Framework)	**0.90**	**0.94**	**0.89**	**0.91**
CIC-IDS2017				
GCN	0.77	0.82	0.76	0.78
STGCN	0.82	0.87	0.83	0.81
StreamSpot	0.73	0.79	0.72	0.74
FedAvg-GCN	0.88	0.92	0.89	0.87
Ours (Full Framework)	**0.92**	**0.95**	**0.93**	**0.91**

To assess the impact of the privacy-preserving mechanism, we compare the detection performance with and without obfuscation of the latent representations. The results show that while a minor decrease (1- 2% in the F1 score is observed, overall detection capabilities remain robust. This confirms that the obfuscation scheme successfully hides sensitive patterns while retaining discriminative features (Table 2).

Table 2. Impact of the obfuscation mechanism on detection performance (ATLAS dataset).

Configuration	F1-score	Precision	Recall	AUC-ROC
Without Obfuscation	0.93	0.92	0.94	0.97
With Obfuscation	**0.91**	**0.90**	**0.92**	**0.96**

We evaluated the benefit of dynamic threshold selection through a Stackelberg game formulation by comparing our approach to fixed-threshold baselines. As illustrated in Fig. 4, our method adapts consistently to the evolving behavior of the attacker and maintains a higher F1 score while achieving a lower false positive rate. This advantage becomes particularly significant in the later stages of the attack, where the adversary adopts stealthier tactics to avoid detection.

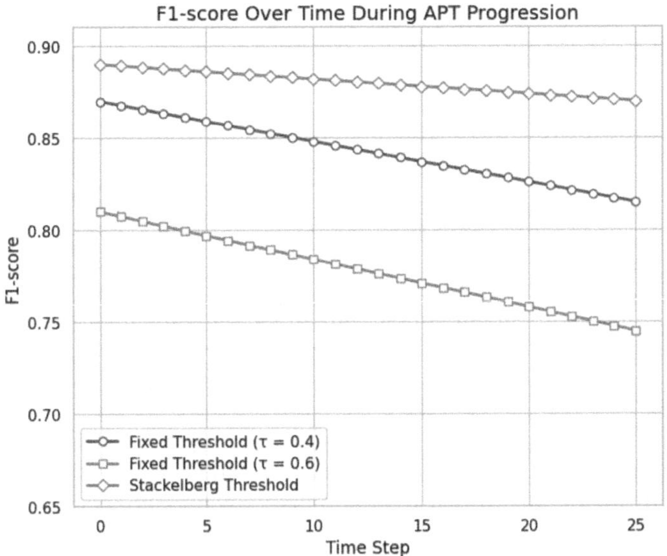

Fig. 4. F1-score over time during APT progression for different thresholding strategies. The Stackelberg-based approach outperforms static thresholds by dynamically adjusting to attacker behavior.

The gradual decline in the F1-score observed in all strategies reflects the increasing sophistication and obfuscation of the attacker during the progression of APT. The fixed thresholds ($\tau = 0.4$ and $\tau = 0.6$) do not adapt to this shifting behavior, leading to a pronounced drop in the detection performance. In contrast, Stackelberg-based IDS anticipates the adversary's optimal response and dynamically adjusts its detection strategy, resulting in a more resilient and stable detection rate over time. This demonstrates the practical utility of game-theoretic modeling in security-critical contexts where adversarial adaptation is inevitable. In summary, these results validate the practicality, accuracy, and privacy-preserving nature of the proposed strategic detection framework.

6 Conclusion

In this work, we presented a multi-phase framework for detecting stealthy and coordinated attacks in federated and distributed environments. Our approach leverages spatio-temporal representation learning to capture structural and behavioral patterns from local provenance graphs while ensuring data privacy through a dedicated obfuscation mechanism. To address the strategic nature of advanced adversaries, we introduced a Stackelberg game model between the IDS and the attacker, enabling dynamic adaptation of detection thresholds in response to adversarial behaviors. The proposed architecture combines local intelligence, sharing of privacy-preserving representations, and game-theoretic decision making to achieve resilient and adaptive intrusion detection. Our threat model captures realistic adversarial capabilities, including stealth propagation and remote orchestration, while the defense pipeline anticipates and mitigates these threats through coordinated learning and strategic reasoning.

References

1. AL-Aamri, A.S., Abdulghafor, R., Turaev, S., Al-Shaikhli, I., Zeki, A., Talib, S.: Machine learning for apt detection. Sustainability **15**(18), 13820 (2023)
2. Alsaheel, A., et al.: {ATLAS}: A sequence-based learning approach for attack investigation. In: 30th USENIX security symposium (USENIX security 21), pp. 3005–3022 (2021)
3. Altaf, T., Wang, X., Ni, W., Yu, G., Liu, R.P., Braun, R.: GNN-based network traffic analysis for the detection of sequential attacks in IoT. Electronics **13**(12), 2274 (2024)
4. Bilot, T., El Madhoun, N., Al Agha, K., Zouaoui, A.: Graph neural networks for intrusion detection: a survey. IEEe Access **11**, 49114–49139 (2023)
5. Bouhaddi, M., Adi, K.: Robust peer-to-peer machine learning against poisoning attacks (2025)
6. Bouhaddi, M., Radjef, M.S., Adi, K.: An efficient intrusion detection in resource-constrained mobile ad-hoc networks. Comput. Secur. **76**, 156–177 (2018)
7. Chang, L., Branco, P.: Graph-based solutions with residuals for intrusion detection: The modified e-graphsage and e-resgat algorithms. arXiv preprint arXiv:2111.13597 (2021)
8. Cheng, Z., et al.: Ghunter: a fast subgraph matching method for threat hunting. In: 2023 26th International Conference on Computer Supported Cooperative Work in Design (CSCWD), pp. 1014–1019. IEEE (2023)
9. Cheng, Z., Lv, Q., Liang, J., Wang, Y., Sun, D., Pasquier, T., Han, X.: Kairos: Practical intrusion detection and investigation using whole-system provenance. In: 2024 IEEE Symposium on Security and Privacy (SP), pp. 3533–3551. IEEE (2024)
10. Conti, M., Dehghantanha, A., Franke, K., Watson, S.: Internet of things security and forensics: Challenges and opportunities (2018)
11. FireEye: Highly evasive attacker leverages solarwinds supply chain to compromise multiple global victims with sunburst backdoor (2020), https://www.fireeye.com/blog/threat-research/2020/12/evasive-attacker-leverages-solarwinds-supply-chain-compromises.html, Accessed July 2025
12. Group-IB: Dark pink apt continues attacks on military, government, and religious organizations in apac and beyond (2023). https://www.group-ib.com/blog/dark-pink-apt/. Accessed July 2025
13. Han, X., Pasquier, T., Bates, A., Mickens, J., Seltzer, M.: Unicorn: Runtime provenance-based detector for advanced persistent threats. arXiv preprint arXiv:2001.01525 (2020)

14. Jia, Z., Xiong, Y., Nan, Y., Zhang, Y., Zhao, J., Wen, M.: {MAGIC}: Detecting advanced persistent threats via masked graph representation learning. In: 33rd USENIX Security Symposium (USENIX Security 24), pp. 5197–5214 (2024)
15. King, I.J., Huang, H.H.: Euler: Detecting network lateral movement via scalable temporal link prediction. ACM Trans. Priv. Secur. **26**(3), 1–36 (2023)
16. Liu, H., Jiang, R.: A causal graph-based approach for apt predictive analytics. Electronics **12**(8), 1849 (2023)
17. Paudel, R., Eberle, W.: Snapsketch: Graph representation approach for intrusion detection in a streaming graph. In: Proceedings of the 16th International Workshop on Mining and Learning with Graphs (MLG) (2020)
18. Pujol-Perich, D., Suárez-Varela, J., Cabellos-Aparicio, A., Barlet-Ros, P.: Unveiling the potential of graph neural networks for robust intrusion detection. ACM SIGMETRICS Perform. Eval. Rev. **49**(4), 111–117 (2022)
19. Rani, N., Saha, B., Shukla, S.K.: A comprehensive survey of advanced persistent threat attribution: Taxonomy, methods, challenges and open research problems. arXiv preprint arXiv:2409.11415 (2024)
20. SolarWinds: Solarwinds cyber incident report (2021). https://www.solarwinds.com/securityadvisory. Accessed July 2025
21. Son, N.D.H., Thi, H.T., Duy, P.T., Pham, V.H.: Xfedgraph-hunter: An interpretable federated learning framework for hunting advanced persistent threat in provenance graph. In: Meng, W., Yan, Z., Piuri, V. (eds.) International Conference on Information Security Practice and Experience, pp. 546–561. Springer (2023). https://doi.org/10.1007/978-981-99-7032-2_32
22. Wang, S., Yu, P.S.: Graph neural networks in anomaly detection. In: Wu, L., Cui, P., Pei, J., Zhao, L. (eds.) Graph neural networks: Foundations, frontiers, and applications, pp. 557–578. Springer, Cham (2022). https://doi.org/10.1007/978-981-16-6054-2_26
23. Wang, S., et al.: Threatrace: Detecting and tracing host-based threats in node level through provenance graph learning. IEEE Trans. Inf. Forensics Secur. **17**, 3972–3987 (2022)
24. Wu, Y., et al.: Paradise: real-time, generalized, and distributed provenance-based intrusion detection. IEEE Trans. Dependable Secure Comput. **20**(2), 1624–1640 (2022)
25. Ye, M., Men, S., Xie, L., Chen, B.: Detect advanced persistent threat in graph-level using competitive autoencoder. In: Proceedings of the 2023 2nd International Conference on Networks, Communications and Information Technology, pp. 28–34 (2023)
26. Zheng, J., Li, D.: Gcn-tc: Combining trace graph with statistical features for network traffic classification. In: ICC 2019-2019 IEEE International Conference on Communications (ICC), pp. 1–6. IEEE (2019)
27. Zhong, M., Lin, M., Zhang, C., Xu, Z.: A survey on graph neural networks for intrusion detection systems: methods, trends and challenges. Comput. Sec. **141**, 103821 (2024)
28. Zhu, H., Lu, J.: Graph-based intrusion detection system using general behavior learning. In: GLOBECOM 2022-2022 IEEE Global Communications Conference, pp. 2621–2626. IEEE (2022)

Security Governance, Compliance, and Adaptive Systems

Drift-RL: A Reinforcement Learning Framework for Simulating Textual Data Drift in Cybersecurity

Hadeer Ahmed[1(✉)], Issa Traore[1], Sherif Saad[2], and Mohammad Mamun[3]

[1] Department of Electrical and Computer Engineering, University of Victoria, British Columbia, Canada
{hsahmed,itraore}@ece.uvic.ca
[2] School of Computer Science, University of Windsor, Ontario, Canada
shsaad@uwindsor.ca
[3] National Research Council Canada, New Brunswick, Canada
mohammad.mamun@nrc-cnrc.gc.ca

Abstract. Data drift occurs when the distribution of input data changes over time, threatening the reliability of machine learning models in cybersecurity, where attackers constantly adapt their tactics and the data are constantly evolving. Most existing drift simulation methods are limited to numerical features and offer little support for text data or controlled drift dynamics. To address this gap, we present Drift-RL, a reinforcement learning framework that generates text datasets with four types of drift: sudden, gradual, incremental, and recurring. Drift simulation is framed as a sequential decision-making process in which an agent learns to apply specific text-augmentation methods to reproduce the desired pattern. The framework creates labeled datasets that make it easier to run consistent experiments and compare models fairly. We evaluated these datasets with drift-based metrics and external drift detection tools, which confirmed that the injected drift was present and followed the intended patterns.

Keywords: Drift · Augmentations · Reinforcement Learning · Cybersecurity · Textual data

1 Introduction

In artificial intelligence and machine learning, data drift refers to changes in the statistical properties of input data streams after a model has been deployed. Such shifts in the input distribution can cause predictive performance to deteriorate [7,17]. The issue is amplified in certain areas such as cybersecurity, where adversaries rapidly invent new attack variants, forcing detection models such as intrusion, phishing, or malware detectors to face patterns not seen during training. Furthermore, despite the vast amount of data available, cybersecurity

K. Adi et al. (Eds.): CRiSIS 2025, LNCS 16295, pp. 413–429, 2026.
https://doi.org/10.1007/978-3-032-20732-6_26

datasets, especially text-based ones, are often difficult to obtain or of poor quality (e.g., poorly labeled, unbalanced, or containing low-quality text). Studies show that overlooking the drift issue causes a massive drop in detection rates of up to 50% in real-world settings [11,20].

Drift also varies in the pattern in which it occurs [28]. Sudden drift triggers an abrupt shift in the data, for example, the sudden appearance of COVID-19 terminology in daily text on Twitter or articles discussing natural disasters. Gradual drift unfolds slowly and naturally over time as data changes. Recurring drift follows a periodic pattern; for example, articles discussing elections as election seasons come and go. Incremental drift occurs in a staircase-like pattern, where a shift is followed by a period of stabilization before another shift takes place. Currently available text-based cybersecurity datasets do not capture drift patterns of this kind. In addition, most existing drift simulation frameworks are designed for numerical data, focusing on shifts in feature distributions rather than changes in the input text. Studies that address drift mainly focus on after-the-fact solutions, such as adaptation and detection, rather than on simulating and benchmarking drift itself. This gap limits the ability to analyze how textual drift impacts model performance and to design methods specifically for text-based cybersecurity tasks.

To address this gap, we introduce **Drift-RL**, a reinforcement learning framework that simulates four types of drift patterns: sudden, gradual, incremental step, and recurring. The framework modifies text datasets so that these patterns emerge in a series of snapshots, giving researchers a practical way to generate controlled drift to study its effects or develop detection and adaptation methods. Unlike rule-based or purely synthetic methods, Drift-RL uses a reinforcement learning agent guided by a pattern-sensitive reward function, providing a controlled and systematic introduction of drift into text datasets.

Our main contributions are as follows:

- We introduce a framework to simulate textual data drift through augmentation and drift-aware scheduling.
- We formulate drift simulation as a sequential decision-making task, where an RL agent learns to apply transformations over time, enabling the generation of datasets that follow various temporal drift patterns.
- We design a drift scheduler and reward mechanism, both inspired by RL target tracking, to regulate drift timing and intensity.

The rest of this paper is organized as follows. Section 2 reviews related work. Section 3 introduces the drift simulation framework. Section 4 describes the experiments and the results. Section 5 concludes the paper.

2 Related Work

Most prior work has focused on detecting drift and adapting models to maintain accuracy. Müller et al. [18] showed that sentiment models trained on pre-COVID data lost more than 20% performance within 10 months, underscoring the need for continuous updates. Chadha et al. [3] investigated conversational topic drift by applying naive Bayes, logistic regression, and support vector machines, finding that a linear SVM achieved the highest precision of 86% for classifying drifted conversations. In the security domain, Angioni et al. [22] proposed SVM-CB for the detection of Android malware, which maintained a stable recall of 50âĂŞ60% compared to only 28.8% for the baseline SVM. Krawczyk et al. [13] improved online ensembles with abstaining classifiers that increased accuracy by 5 to 10%, while Klinkenberg et al. [12] adapted SVM training windows to lower error rates under drift.

Garca et al. [8] focused on the generation of artificial drifted datasets using four strategies: class swap, class shift, time slice removal, and adjective swap. Their benchmarks on Yelp and Airbnb reviews showed that such simulations help to test and improve the robustness of the model. Xu et al. [23] demonstrated that augmentation strategies that mimic drift patterns can improve robustness by up to 35% compared to static training. Belov et al. [1] proposed a generative AI method to simulate drift in text. Their approach employs LLM to inject drift at the sample level by altering adjectives, shortening the text length, or paraphrasing. Experimental comparisons showed that such injections based on LLM produce more diverse and realistic variations than rule-based manipulations, allowing more effective evaluation of drift detection and adaptation methods. Rabinovich et al. [21] simulated drift in short text streams by reshaping class distributions in the CLINC150 dataset. They did this by oversampling some of the data while undersampling or removing others, so that the relative frequency of the data changed over time. This approach provided clear drift points for evaluation, but only reflects shifts in label proportions rather than changes in the text itself. As a result, it does not capture more realistic forms of linguistic drift, such as new vocabulary, altered phrasing, or semantic changes that occur in natural language. Furthermore, there have also been commercial tools, such as Amazon SageMaker Model Monitor [19] and Fiddler AI [6], which provide options to simulate or detect drift in text data. These systems usually track numeric features extracted from the text, such as token counts, TF-IDF, or embedding vectors, rather than working directly on the text itself.

3 Methodology

In this section, we present our reinforcement learning framework for simulating data drift.

3.1 Preliminaries

Formally, drift generation is modeled as a sequential decision-making task. At each step, the RL agent applies augmentations to the dataset, and the scheduler determines how the drift intensity evolves over time.

The drift schedule is formalized as a discrete temporal sequence,

$$S = [s_1, s_2, \ldots, s_T],$$

where T denotes the total number of time steps in a simulation episode. Each element $s_t \in \mathbb{R}^+$ serves as a normalized drift modifier that adjusts the drift intensity according to the temporal dynamics of the selected pattern (e.g. gradual, sudden, incremental, recurring).

The relationship between the schedule factor and the target drift level is given by:

$$\tau_t = \text{base\_intensity} \times s_t, \tag{1}$$

where τ_t represents the desired drift level at time step t, and base_intensity is a global scaling parameter that controls the overall magnitude of drift transformations.

Drift Patterns

Gradual drift increases smoothly over time according to a power function:

$$s_t = \left(\frac{t+1}{T}\right)^{\alpha}$$

where $\alpha \in \mathbb{R}^+$ controls the rate of growth. Higher values of α produce slower initial growth and sharper late-stage increases.

Sudden drift remains inactive until a predefined step is reached, at which point a spike is applied:

$$s_t = \begin{cases} 0 & \text{if } t < t_s \\ \gamma & \text{if } t = t_s \end{cases}$$

where t_s is the point of onset of sudden drift and γ is the intensity factor of the spike.

Incremental step drift grows in discrete jumps at fixed intervals. The schedule forms a staircase pattern where each step increases the applied drift:

$$s_t = \min\left(\left\lfloor \frac{t}{\Delta} \right\rfloor, N\right) \cdot \text{base\_intensity}$$

where Δ is the interval between jumps, and N limits the maximum number of jumps. This pattern reflects environments with step-wise changes in distribution.

Recurring drift follows a cyclic on-off pattern, alternating between active and inactive phases. The schedule is constructed as a repeated binary cycle:

$$s_t = \begin{cases} 1 + \epsilon_t & \text{if } t \bmod L < L_{\text{on}} \\ 0 & \text{otherwise} \end{cases}$$

where L is the full cycle length, L_{on} is the number of active steps, and $\epsilon_t \sim \mathcal{N}(0, \sigma^2)$ is optional Gaussian noise added during the active phase to simulate instability.

3.2 Problem Formulation

We formulate the problem of generating controlled data drift as a Markov Decision Process (MDP), defined as $\mathcal{M} = \langle \mathcal{S}, \mathcal{A}, \mathcal{T}, \mathcal{R}, \gamma \rangle$. The components of the MDP are defined below.

State Representation. The state space $\mathcal{S}$ consists of 2D real-valued vectors:

$$s_t = \begin{bmatrix} \text{drift}_t \\ \text{target\_intensity}_t \end{bmatrix} \in \mathbb{R}^2, \tag{2}$$

where drift_t denotes the current drift magnitude and $\text{target\_intensity}_t$ is the expected drift level from the predefined schedule.

Action Space. The action space $\mathcal{A}$ comprises discrete transformation operations that the agent can apply at each step. These actions span multiple levels of text specificity:

$$\mathcal{A} = \{a_1, a_2, \dots, a_n\}, \tag{3}$$

where each action a_i corresponds to a predefined transformation that targets specific perturbations.

Transition Dynamics. The environment applies the selected action a_t to the current text batch:

$$\mathcal{B}_{t+1} \sim g(\mathcal{B}_t, a_t), \tag{4}$$

where g is the augmentation function, which varies depending on the selected action and the schedule context.

Discount Factor. We adopt a discount factor of $\gamma = 0.99$ to prioritize long-term drift strategies:

$$G_t = \sum_{k=0}^{T-t} \gamma^k R_{t+k+1}, \tag{5}$$

where G_t denotes the expected return at time t. A high discount factor ensures sustained focus on achieving drift alignment throughout the full simulation episode.

Drift Metrics. Drift is measured using the Jensen-Shannon Divergence (JSD) [4]:

$$\text{JSD}(P \| Q) = \tfrac{1}{2}\text{KL}(P \| M) + \tfrac{1}{2}\text{KL}(Q \| M), \quad M = \tfrac{1}{2}(P + Q), \tag{6}$$

where P and Q are probability vectors derived from count-based representations of the original and transformed text distributions.

Reward Function Design. The reward is designed to guide the agent to follow the planned trajectory (growth), remain close to the target (magnitude), and move in the correct direction (direction). We define the following core quantities:

$$d_t : \text{Observed drift at time step } t \tag{7}$$
$$\tau_t : \text{Target drift level at time step } t \tag{8}$$
$$\Delta d_t = d_t - d_{t-1} : \text{Change in observed drift} \tag{9}$$
$$\Delta \tau_t = \tau_t - d_{t-1} : \text{Target change relative to prior observation} \tag{10}$$

The observed drift d_t is calculated using JSD between the current and original text distributions after applying the action a_t.

The reward at each step is a weighted sum of three terms:

$$r_t = \alpha \cdot R_{\text{growth}} + \beta \cdot R_{\text{magnitude}} + \gamma \cdot R_{\text{direction}}, \tag{11}$$

with $\alpha = 0.5$, $\beta = 0.3$, and $\gamma = 0.2$. These terms encourage the agent to follow the target drift pattern.

Growth Term.

$$R_{\text{growth}} = \begin{cases} \min\left(\frac{\Delta d_t}{\Delta \tau_t}, 1.0\right) & \text{if } \Delta \tau_t > 0, \\ 1.0 & \text{otherwise,} \end{cases} \tag{12}$$

This term rewards the agent for adjusting the drift at the intended rate of change.

Magnitude Term.

$$R_{\text{magnitude}} = 1 - |\tau_t - d_t|, \tag{13}$$

This term penalizes deviation from the target drift level.

Direction Term.

$$R_{\text{direction}} = \begin{cases} +1.0 & \text{if } \operatorname{sign}(\Delta d_t) = \operatorname{sign}(\Delta \tau_t), \\ -1.0 & \text{otherwise.} \end{cases} \tag{14}$$

This term ensures that drift adjusts in the correct direction, ascending or descending according to the intended pattern.

In addition, there are two modifiers that complement the main reward terms. A plateau bonus, applied only in incremental drift, rewards the agent for keeping drift steady during flat segments. A transition penalty discourages low-drift actions during expected jumps. In periods when drift should remain unchanged, the agent is penalized for causing drift, yet not for performing cleanup actions, ensuring conformity with the intended schedule.

3.3 RL Agent Architecture and Actions

We use Proximal Policy Optimization (PPO) [24] for stable and efficient policy learning. The clipped objective of PPO helps improve the balance and stability, making it suitable for drift simulation. The agent is implemented with the standard `MlpPolicy` from Stable-Baselines3 [10], using actorâĂŞcritic networks (128 hidden units, `tanh` activations). Training uses a learning rate of 3×10^{-4}, 1,024 steps per update, a batch size of 64, and 4 epochs, for 100,000 timesteps per drift pattern.

Transformation Methods. To simulate drift, the agent alters the input text using the following methods:

- **Antonym Replacement:** Replaces words with their opposites (e.g., 'happy' → 'sad').
- **Synonym Replacement:** Substitutes words with close alternatives (e.g., 'quick' → 'fast').
- **Spelling Augmentation:** Injects typos to mimic user error (e.g., 'receive" → "recieve').
- **Key Term Substitution:** Replace a percentage of key terms in the dataset to alter semantics (e.g., 'vulnerability detected' → 'exploit detected').
- **Prompt-Based Generation:** Rewrites sentences using a LLaMA model guided by the original input.
- **Cleanup:** Restores text to its original form during OFF phases to preserve drift boundaries.

4 Evaluation

In this section, we evaluate Drift-RL's ability to generate controlled drifted datasets. To quantify distributional changes, we use the Wasserstein distance [26], the maximum mean difference (MMD) [9], and the adverse validation AUC [16], each capturing different aspects of drift for a comprehensive evaluation. We also employ three external validation tools: Alibi Detect [25], DataProfiler [2], and Evidently AI [5] to independently verify the presence of the induced drift.

We evaluated three cybersecurity datasets (Table 1): CWE Summary [14] for multiclass vulnerability classification, Phishing emails [15] for binary phishing detection, and Cybersecurity Attacks [27] for multilabel threat classification. Together, they cover diverse security domains and label structures. All datasets were pre-processed and individually sampled in 5,000 to 10,000 instances. We simulated each drift pattern on every dataset.

4.1 Results and Analysis

Performance Under Drift: Gradual Drift. As shown in Table 2, all three datasets exhibit a steadily increasing drift over time: the Wasserstein distance,

Table 1. Dataset Overview

Dataset	Size	Task
CWE Summary	6,000	CWE Codes
Phishing emails	10,000	Phishing vs Legit
Cyber Attacks	10,000+	Threat Types

Table 2. Drift Metrics Across The Datasets for Gradual Drift

Step	CWE Summary			Phishing emails			Cyber Attacks		
	Wass.	MMD	AUC	Wass.	MMD	AUC	Wass.	MMD	AUC
1	0.0000	0.0000	0.5000	1.0283	0.0007	0.3525	0.6829	0.0010	0.3321
2	0.1513	0.0032	0.1601	2.0567	0.0013	0.2050	1.3657	0.0020	0.1642
3	0.4001	0.0078	0.1948	5.0789	0.0029	0.2270	3.4056	0.0040	0.1884
4	0.6757	0.0127	0.2372	9.4967	0.0051	0.2592	6.3874	0.0070	0.2237
5	0.9792	0.0183	0.2956	14.1900	0.0075	0.2933	9.5552	0.0102	0.2613
6	1.3683	0.0243	0.3555	18.9049	0.0099	0.3277	12.7374	0.0134	0.2990
7	1.7451	0.0296	0.4221	23.6203	0.0122	0.3620	15.9202	0.0166	0.3367
8	2.1333	0.0352	0.4880	28.3358	0.0146	0.3964	19.1029	0.0198	0.3744
9	2.5220	0.0409	0.5581	33.0513	0.0170	0.4307	22.2856	0.0230	0.4121
10	2.8703	0.0457	0.6230	37.7667	0.0194	0.4651	25.4683	0.0262	0.4498
11	3.1800	0.0504	0.6751	42.4822	0.0218	0.4994	28.6510	0.0295	0.4876
12	3.4956	0.0544	0.7190	47.1976	0.0242	0.5338	31.8337	0.0327	0.5253
13	3.8073	0.0578	0.7515	51.9131	0.0266	0.5681	35.0164	0.0359	0.5630
14	4.1102	0.0612	0.7893	56.6286	0.0290	0.6025	38.1991	0.0391	0.6007
15	4.4192	0.0639	0.8211	61.3440	0.0313	0.6368	41.3819	0.0423	0.6384
16	4.5869	0.0657	0.8435	66.0589	0.0337	0.6712	44.5641	0.0455	0.6761
17	4.8181	0.0674	0.8609	70.7522	0.0361	0.7053	47.7319	0.0487	0.7137
18	5.0170	0.0691	0.8756	75.1700	0.0383	0.7375	50.7137	0.0517	0.7490
19	5.1683	0.0699	0.8808	78.1922	0.0399	0.7595	52.7536	0.0537	0.7732

the MMD, and the adversarial AUC increase at each step, indicating that the drift gradually accumulates. The CWE data set shows a slow and consistent increase in all metrics, while phishing emails and cyberattacks escalate more rapidly, as further confirmed in Figs. 1a through 1c. For CWE, Evidently AI reported a drift score of 0.79, DataProfiler measured an average change of 12.07% but did not flag it as significant, and Alibi Detect flagged the drift. For Cybersecurity Attacks, Evidently AI scored 0.97, DataProfiler found a 34.92% change, and Alibi Detect flagged the drift. For phishing emails, Evidently AI recorded a value of 0.80. DataProfiler observed an 11.1% change in the characteristics of the data but did not flag it as drift, whereas Alibi Detect maintained its detection of drift. These results can be seen in Table 3.

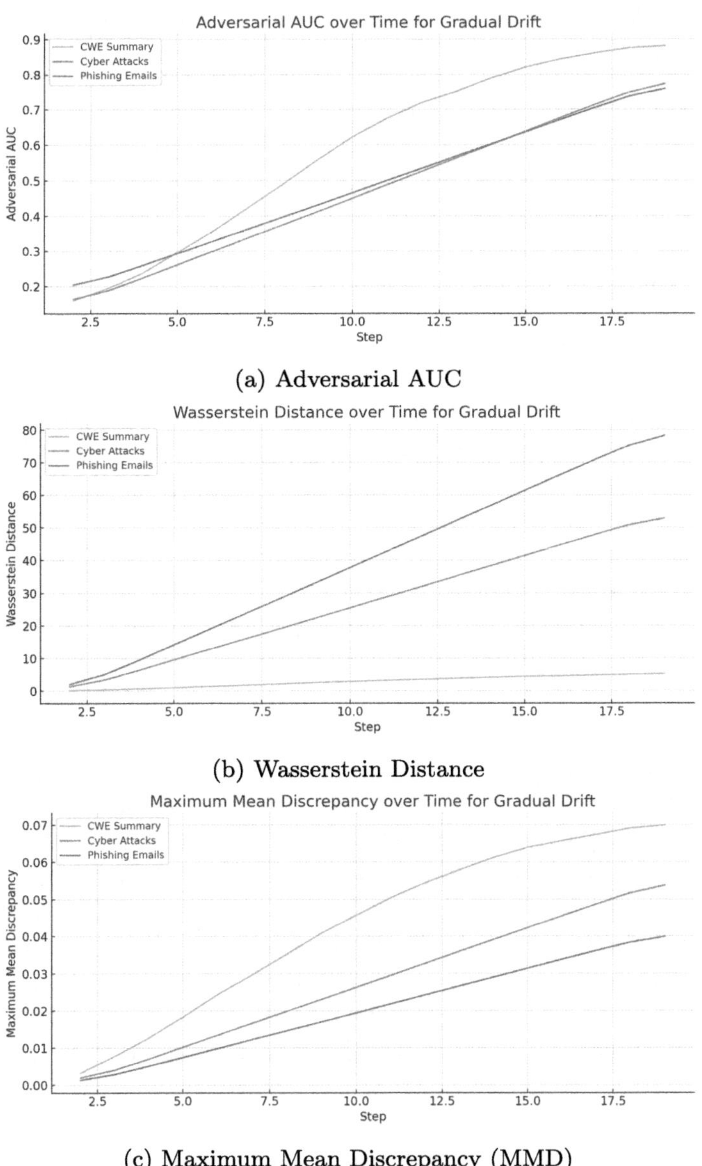

(a) Adversarial AUC

(b) Wasserstein Distance

(c) Maximum Mean Discrepancy (MMD)

Fig. 1. Comparison of drift metrics across datasets under gradual drift.

Performance Under Drift: Sudden Drift. As shown in Table 4, all three cybersecurity datasets exhibit a sharp and immediate change at step 5, consistent with a sudden drift pattern. The Wasserstein distance and the MMD stay near zero in the early steps, then jump sharply at step 5 and stabilize, reflecting a single disruption. The adversarial AUC follows the same pattern, remaining

Table 3. Drift Detection Results under Gradual Drift Scenario

Detection Result	CWE	Cyber Attacks	Phishing emails
Evidence AI Score	0.7	0.8	0.6
DataProfiler Drift Flag	No	Yes	No
DataProfiler Change (%)	12.07	34.92	11.10
Alibi Drift Detected	Yes	Yes	Yes

Table 4. Drift Metrics Across The Datasets for Sudden drift.

Step	CWE Summary			Phishing emails			Cyber Attacks		
	Wass.	MMD	AUC	Wass.	MMD	AUC	Wass.	MMD	AUC
1	0.0000	0.0000	0.5000	0.0000	0.0000	0.1889	0.0000	0.0000	0.1477
2	0.0000	0.0000	0.1790	0.0000	0.0000	0.1889	0.0000	0.0000	0.1477
3	0.0000	0.0000	0.1790	0.0000	0.0000	0.1889	0.0000	0.0000	0.1477
4	0.0000	0.0000	0.1790	0.0000	0.0000	0.1889	0.0000	0.0000	0.1477
5	55.9247	0.0910	0.8759	176.6758	0.0582	0.8687	160.5547	0.0972	0.8826
6	55.9247	0.0910	0.8759	176.6758	0.0582	0.8687	160.5547	0.0972	0.8826
7	55.9247	0.0910	0.8759	176.6758	0.0582	0.8687	160.5547	0.0972	0.8826
8	55.9247	0.0910	0.8759	176.6758	0.0582	0.8687	160.5547	0.0972	0.8826
9	55.9247	0.0910	0.8759	176.6758	0.0582	0.8687	160.5547	0.0972	0.8826
10	55.9247	0.0910	0.8759	176.6758	0.0582	0.8687	160.5547	0.0972	0.8826
11	55.9247	0.0910	0.8759	176.6758	0.0582	0.8687	160.5547	0.0972	0.8826
12	55.9247	0.0910	0.8759	176.6758	0.0582	0.8687	160.5547	0.0972	0.8826
13	55.9247	0.0910	0.8759	176.6758	0.0582	0.8687	160.5547	0.0972	0.8826
14	55.9247	0.0910	0.8759	176.6758	0.0582	0.8687	160.5547	0.0972	0.8826
15	55.9247	0.0910	0.8759	176.6758	0.0582	0.8687	160.5547	0.0972	0.8826
16	55.9247	0.0910	0.8759	176.6758	0.0582	0.8687	160.5547	0.0972	0.8826
17	55.9247	0.0910	0.8759	176.6758	0.0582	0.8687	160.5547	0.0972	0.8826
18	55.9247	0.0910	0.8759	176.6758	0.0582	0.8687	160.5547	0.0972	0.8826
19	55.9247	0.0910	0.8759	176.6758	0.0582	0.8687	160.5547	0.0972	0.8826

flat before step 5 and then rising sharply, indicating a sudden increase in drift detectability. This is also evident in Figs. 2a to 2c. Evidently AI, DataProfiler, and Alibi Detect consistently confirmed sudden drift (Table 5): CWE scored 0.82 with significant text changes, Cybersecurity Attacks 0.81 with shifts exceeding 50%, and phishing emails 0.78 with notable changes in data characteristics. All three datasets were flagged by Alibi Detect.

Performance Under Drift: Incremental Step Drift. Table 6 shows that all three cybersecurity datasets exhibit a stepwise drift pattern, consistent with incremental drift. The three metrics remain flat during the early steps and then

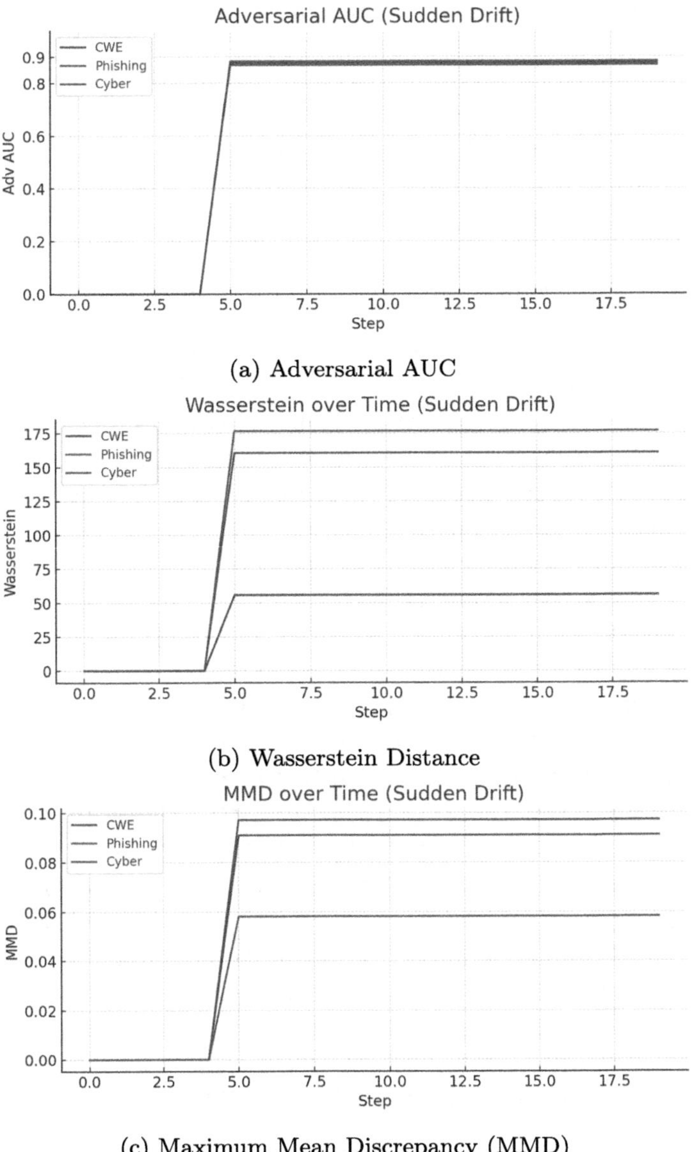

(a) Adversarial AUC

(b) Wasserstein Distance

(c) Maximum Mean Discrepancy (MMD)

Fig. 2. Comparison of drift metrics across datasets under sudden drift.

rise in distinct jumps at steps 6, 11, and 16, reflecting structured bursts of distributional change. The adversarial AUC follows the same trend, with low detectability until each drift point, followed by sharp increases. These results are further illustrated in Figs. 3a through 3c. Evidently AI, DataProfiler, and Alibi Detect all confirmed incremental drift (Table 7): CWE scored 0.60 with

Table 5. Drift Detection Summary (Sudden Scenario)

Method	CWE	CyberAttacks	Phishing
Evidence AI Score	0.83	0.90	0.81
Drift (DataProfiler)	Yes	Yes	Yes
Change % (DataProfiler)	21.74	52.59	31.10
Drift (Alibi)	Yes	Yes	Yes

Table 6. Drift Metrics Across The Datasets for Incremental step drift.

Step	CWE Summary			Phishing emails			Cyber Attacks		
	Wass.	MMD	AUC	Wass.	MMD	AUC	Wass.	MMD	AUC
0	0.0000	0.0000	0.5000	0.0000	0.0000	0.5000	0.0000	0.0000	0.5000
1	0.0000	0.0000	0.2401	0.0000	0.0000	0.1889	0.0000	0.0000	0.1477
2	0.0000	0.0000	0.2401	0.0000	0.0000	0.1889	0.0000	0.0000	0.1477
3	0.0000	0.0000	0.2401	0.0000	0.0000	0.1889	0.0000	0.0000	0.1477
4	0.0000	0.0000	0.2401	0.0000	0.0000	0.1889	0.0000	0.0000	0.1477
5	0.0000	0.0000	0.2401	0.0000	0.0000	0.1889	0.0000	0.0000	0.1477
6	51.1355	0.0577	0.5390	60.7626	0.0207	0.4761	53.3829	0.0351	0.4755
7	51.1355	0.0577	0.5390	60.7626	0.0207	0.4761	53.3829	0.0351	0.4755
8	51.1355	0.0577	0.5390	60.7626	0.0207	0.4761	53.3829	0.0351	0.4755
9	51.1355	0.0577	0.5390	60.7626	0.0207	0.4761	53.3829	0.0351	0.4755
10	51.1355	0.0577	0.5390	60.7626	0.0207	0.4761	53.3829	0.0351	0.4755
11	122.4382	0.1400	0.8499	142.7936	0.0481	0.7675	127.0762	0.0832	0.7787
12	122.4382	0.1400	0.8499	142.7936	0.0481	0.7675	127.0762	0.0832	0.7787
13	122.4382	0.1400	0.8499	142.7936	0.0481	0.7675	127.0762	0.0832	0.7787
14	122.4382	0.1400	0.8499	142.7936	0.0481	0.7675	127.0762	0.0832	0.7787
15	122.4382	0.1400	0.8499	142.7936	0.0481	0.7675	127.0762	0.0832	0.7787
16	165.3199	0.1883	0.9883	192.6660	0.0627	0.9091	172.4893	0.1131	0.9223
17	165.3199	0.1883	0.9883	192.6660	0.0627	0.9091	172.4893	0.1131	0.9223
18	165.3199	0.1883	0.9883	192.6660	0.0627	0.9091	172.4893	0.1131	0.9223
19	165.3199	0.1883	0.9883	192.6660	0.0627	0.9091	172.4893	0.1131	0.9223

a 20.99% change, Cybersecurity Attacks above 0.80 with 57.39%, and phishing emails above 0.80 with 35.78%. All three datasets were flagged by Alibi Detect.

Performance Under Drift: Recurring Drift. Table 8 shows recurring drift across all datasets, with metrics spiking at regular intervals before returning to zero, indicating periodic shifts between drift and stability. These results are further illustrated in Figs. 4a through 4c. Evidently AI, DataProfiler, and Alibi Detect consistently confirmed recurring drift (Table 9): CWE scored 0.70 with

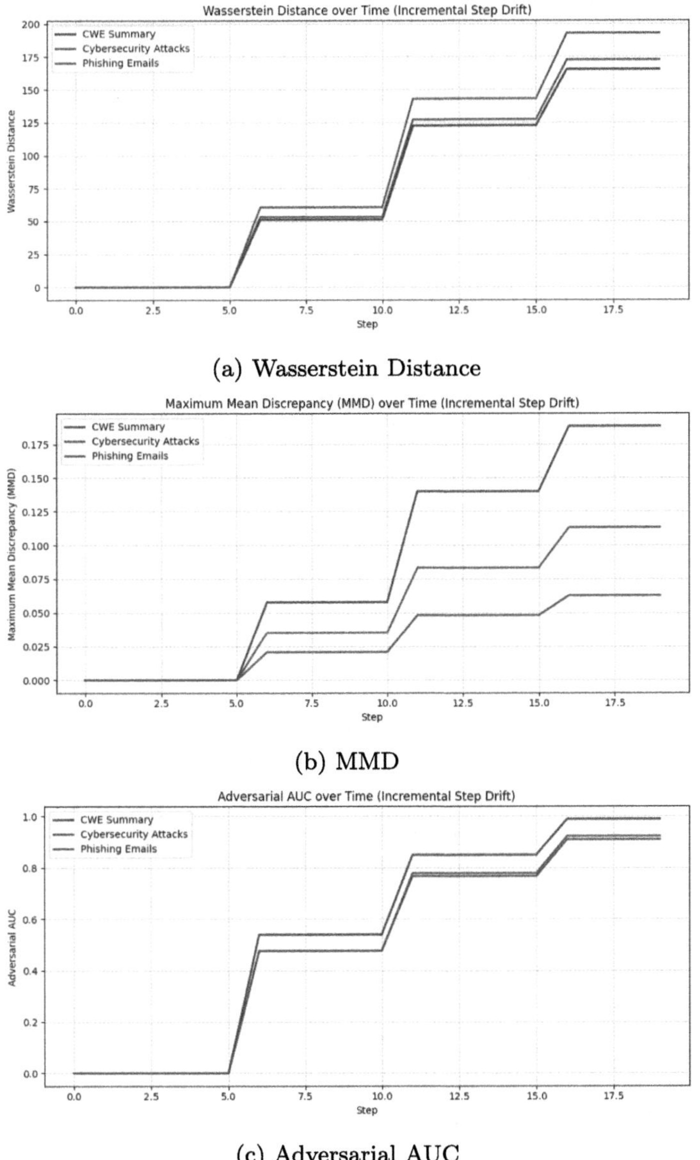

(a) Wasserstein Distance

(b) MMD

(c) Adversarial AUC

Fig. 3. Evaluation metrics for incremental step drift across cybersecurity datasets.

a 15.99% change, Cybersecurity Attacks 0.82 with 20.10%, and phishing emails 0.80 with 20.78%. All three datasets were flagged by Alibi Detect.

Table 7. Drift Detection Summary (Incremental Scenario)

Method	CWE	CyberAttacks	Phishing
Evidence AI Score	0.60	0.80	0.82
Drift (DataProfiler)	Yes	Yes	Yes
Change % (DataProfiler)	20.99	57.39	35.78
Drift (Alibi)	Yes	Yes	Yes

Table 8. Drift Metrics Across The Datasets for Recurring drift metrics.

Step	CWE Summary			Phishing emails			Cyber Attacks		
	Wass.	MMD	AUC	Wass.	MMD	AUC	Wass.	MMD	AUC
0	0.0000	0.0000	0.5000	0.0000	0.0000	0.5000	0.0000	0.0000	0.5000
1	5.4020	0.0115	0.2685	59.5649	0.0213	0.4688	70.9605	0.0507	0.5731
2	10.9012	0.0216	0.3652	100.4407	0.0350	0.6311	113.8412	0.0801	0.7431
3	0.0000	0.0000	0.1790	0.0000	0.0000	0.1889	0.0000	0.0000	0.1477
4	0.0000	0.0000	0.1790	0.0000	0.0000	0.1889	0.0000	0.0000	0.1477
5	5.4074	0.0114	0.2730	58.8580	0.0217	0.4727	72.0270	0.0502	0.5616
6	10.1483	0.0202	0.3667	99.6270	0.0351	0.6363	114.7194	0.0788	0.7373
7	0.0000	0.0000	0.1790	0.0000	0.0000	0.1889	0.0000	0.0000	0.1477
8	0.0000	0.0000	0.1790	0.0000	0.0000	0.1889	0.0000	0.0000	0.1477
9	5.4466	0.0125	0.2879	60.2124	0.0216	0.4580	70.2040	0.0504	0.5658
10	10.1229	0.0213	0.3645	102.1264	0.0351	0.6243	112.6207	0.0801	0.7267
11	0.0000	0.0000	0.1790	0.0000	0.0000	0.1889	0.0000	0.0000	0.1477
12	0.0000	0.0000	0.1790	0.0000	0.0000	0.1889	0.0000	0.0000	0.1477
13	5.3237	0.0114	0.2757	60.7494	0.0211	0.4664	72.2420	0.0513	0.5653
14	10.8641	0.0209	0.3677	104.0777	0.0341	0.6362	115.7924	0.0815	0.7331
15	0.0000	0.0000	0.1790	0.0000	0.0000	0.1889	0.0000	0.0000	0.1477
16	0.0000	0.0000	0.1790	0.0000	0.0000	0.1889	0.0000	0.0000	0.1477
17	5.0404	0.0124	0.2779	59.2644	0.0206	0.4607	72.9696	0.0501	0.5502
18	10.9002	0.0216	0.3674	101.1763	0.0336	0.6257	116.0365	0.0809	0.7267
19	0.0000	0.0000	0.1790	0.0000	0.0000	0.1889	0.0000	0.0000	0.1477

Table 9. Drift Detection Summary (Recurring Scenario)

Method	CWE	CyberAttacks	Phishing
Evidence AI Score	0.70	0.80	0.82
Drift (DataProfiler)	Yes	Yes	Yes
Change % (DataProfiler)	15.99	20.39	20.78
Drift (Alibi)	Yes	Yes	Yes

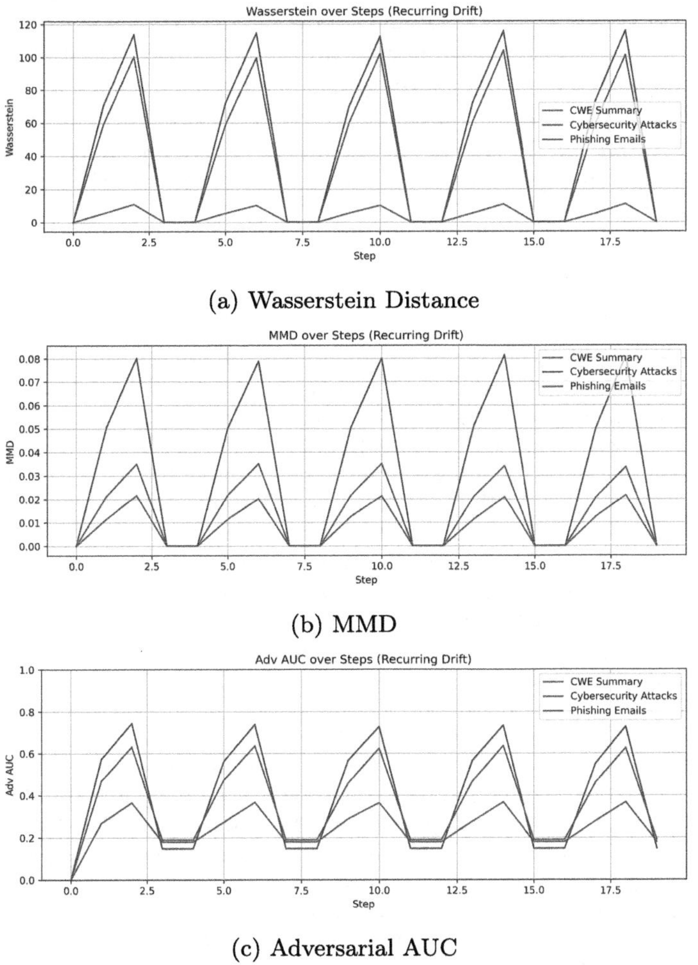

(a) Wasserstein Distance

(b) MMD

(c) Adversarial AUC

Fig. 4. Evaluation metrics for recurring drift across cybersecurity datasets.

5 Conclusion

Overall, Drift-RL demonstrates its ability to generate text datasets with four types of drift: sudden, gradual, incremental, and recurring. Our evaluation with multiple drift metrics and three external detection tools confirms that the induced drift is both present and reproducible. The metric values not only increase consistently with time but also mirror the shapes of the intended patterns when plotted, indicating that the generated datasets faithfully embed the desired drift dynamics. Moreover, the magnitude of the metric responses reflects the nature of each pattern: strong spikes in sudden drift correspond to large, abrupt shifts, while the smaller, smoother increases in gradual drift correspond to subtle changes over time. Our results also show that drift manifests itself differently across domains. CWE summaries evolve smoothly, while phishing emails and threat reports exhibit more abrupt and unpredictable changes. Even under identical transformations, the magnitude of drift varies across datasets, underscoring the role of dataset characteristics. For future work, we plan to make Drift-RL adaptive to dataset-specific characteristics, evaluate it on live data streams, and extend its functionality for integration into MLOps pipelines to support real-world deployment.

References

1. Belov, B., Panfilov, P.: Generative ai-based approach to concept drift generation in streaming text data. WSEAS Trans. Inf. Sci. Appl. **22**(2B), 11–20 (2025). https://doi.org/10.37394/23209.2025.22.2Boris. https://wseas.com/journals/isa/2025/a045109-001(2025).pdf
2. Capital One Engineering team: Dataprofiler: Python library for data analysis, profiling, monitoring, and PII/NPI detection (2019). https://github.com/capitalone/DataProfiler. Accessed 04 July 2025
3. Chadha, C., Gupta, V., Gupta, D., Khanna, A.: Classifying text using machine learning models and determining conversation drift. In: AIP Conference Proceedings, vol. 2919. AIP Publishing (2024)
4. Endres, D.M., Schindelin, J.E.: A new metric for probability distributions. IEEE Trans. Inf. Theory **49**(7), 1858–1860 (2003). https://doi.org/10.1109/TIT.2003.813506
5. Evidently AI team: Evidently: ML LLM evaluation, testing, and monitoring framework (2025). https://github.com/evidentlyai/evidently. Accessed 04 July 2025
6. Fiddler Labs, Inc.: Fiddler AI: Responsible ai observability platform for drift detection and simulation (2025). https://www.fiddler.ai. Commercial platform providing AI observability, including model monitoring, drift detection, explainability, and fairness metrics. Accessed 17 Sept 2025
7. Gama, J., Žliobaitė, I., Bifet, A., Pechenizkiy, M., Bouchachia, A.: A survey on concept drift adaptation. ACM Comput. Surv. **46**(4), Article 44, 37 p (2014). https://doi.org/10.1145/2523813
8. Garcia, C.M., Koerich, A.L., Britto Jr, A.D.S., Barddal, J.P.: Methods for generating drift in text streams. arXiv preprint arXiv:2403.12328 (2024)
9. Gretton, A., Borgwardt, K.M., Rasch, M.J., Schölkopf, B., Smola, A.: A kernel two-sample test. J. Mach. Learn. Res. **13**(25), 723–773 (2012). http://jmlr.org/papers/v13/gretton12a.html
10. Hill, A., Raffin, A., Ernestus, M., Gleave, A., Kanervisto, A., Dormann, N.: Stable baselines (2018). https://github.com/hill-a/stable-baselines
11. Jordaney, R., et al.: Transcend: detecting concept drift in malware classification models. In: 26th USENIX Security Symposium (USENIX Security 2017), pp. 625–642. USENIX Association, Vancouver, BC (2017). https://www.usenix.org/conference/usenixsecurity17/technical-sessions/presentation/jordaney
12. Klinkenberg, R., Joachims, T.: Detecting concept drift with support vector machines. In: ICML, pp. 487–494 (2000)
13. Krawczyk, B., Cano, A.: Online ensemble learning with abstaining classifiers for drifting and noisy data streams. Appl. Soft Comput. **68**, 677–692 (2018)

14. Kronser, A.: CVE (common vulnerabilities and exposures) dataset. Kaggle dataset (2018–2020). https://www.kaggle.com/datasets/andrewkronser/cve-common-vulnerabilities-and-exposures
15. Liu, Z.: Phishing Email Dataset (2024). https://huggingface.co/datasets/zefang-liu/phishing-email-dataset. Accessed 01 July 2025
16. Lopez-Paz, D., Oquab, M.: Revisiting classifier two-sample tests. In: 5th International Conference on Learning Representations (ICLR 2017). OpenReview.net, Toulon, France (2017). https://openreview.net/forum?id=SJkXfE5xx
17. Lu, J., Liu, A., Dong, F., Gu, F., Li, J., Zhang, G.: Learning under concept drift: a review. IEEE Trans. Knowl. Data Eng. **31**(12), 2346–2363 (2019). https://doi.org/10.1109/TKDE.2018.2876857
18. Müller, M., Salathé, M.: Addressing machine learning concept drift reveals declining vaccine sentiment during the covid-19 pandemic. arXiv preprint arXiv:2012.02197 (2020)
19. Nigenda, D., et al.: Amazon sagemaker model monitor: a system for real-time insights into deployed machine learning models. arXiv preprint arXiv:2111.13657, pp. 1–12 (2021). https://doi.org/10.48550/arXiv.2111.13657, https://arxiv.org/abs/2111.13657, arXiv preprint arXiv:2111.13657, version v1
20. Pendlebury, F., Pierazzi, F., Jordaney, R., Kinder, J., Cavallaro, L.: Tesseract: eliminating experimental bias in malware classification across space and time. arXiv preprint arXiv:1807.07838 (2018). https://arxiv.org/abs/1807.07838
21. Rabinovich, E., Vetzler, M., Ackerman, S., Anaby-Tavor, A.: Reliable and interpretable drift detection in streams of short texts. In: Proceedings of the 61st Annual Meeting of the Association for Computational Linguistics (Volume 5: Industry Track), pp. 438–446. Association for Computational Linguistics (2023). https://doi.org/10.18653/v1/2023.acl-industry.42. https://aclanthology.org/2023.acl-industry.42
22. Rathore, H., Sahay, S.K., Nikam, P., Sewak, M.: Robust android malware detection system against adversarial attacks using q-learning. Inf. Syst. Front. **23**, 867–882 (2021)
23. Rebuffi, S., Gowal, S., Calian, D.A., Stimberg, F., Wiles, O., Mann, T.A.: Data augmentation can improve robustness. CoRR abs/2111.05328 (2021). https://arxiv.org/abs/2111.05328
24. Schulman, J., Wolski, F., Dhariwal, P., Radford, A., Klimov, O.: Proximal policy optimization algorithms. arXiv preprint arXiv:1707.06347 (2017)
25. Van Looveren, A., et al.: Alibi detect: algorithms for outlier, adversarial and drift detection (2019). https://github.com/SeldonIO/alibi-detect
26. Villani, C.: Optimal Transport: Old and New, Grundlehren der mathematischen Wissenschaften, vol. 338. Springer, Heidelberg (2009). https://doi.org/10.1007/978-3-540-71050-9
27. vinitvek: Cybersecurity Attacks dataset (2024). https://huggingface.co/datasets/vinitvek/cybersecurityattacks. Accessed 01 July 2025
28. Webb, G.I., Hyde, R., Cao, H., Nguyen, H.L., Petitjean, F.: Characterizing concept drift. Data Min. Knowl. Disc. **30**(4), 964–994 (2016). https://doi.org/10.1007/s10618-015-0448-4

Role Mining in RBAC for Preserving Confidentiality

Franck Fotso Kuate[1(✉)], Omer Nguena Timo[3], and Florent Avellaneda[1,2]

[1] Université du Québec à Montréal (UQAM), Montréal, Canada
fotso_kuate.franck_arnaud@courrier.uqam.ca, florent.avellaneda@uqam.ca
[2] Centre de Recherche de l'Institut Universitaire de Gériatrie de Montréal, Montréal, Canada
[3] Université du Québec en Outaouais (UQO), Saint-Jérôme, Canada
omer.nguena-timo@uqo.ca

Abstract. The CIA triad—Confidentiality, Integrity, and Availability—is a fundamental foundation for information system security, serving as an overarching model for system and data protection. But achieving the mutual fulfillment of the three principles at the same time is a significant challenge. Role-Based Access Control (RBAC) is a widely used and easy-to-manage permission management approach that does not inherently guarantee CIA triad compliance, which can lead to the introduction of security vulnerabilities in access control frameworks. Role Mining is the critical optimization issue, particularly when CIA triad properties are required to be maintained at the same time, as this step minimizes policy administration and maintenance complexity without relaxing tight security constraints. In this work, we define the minimum role extraction problem within the context of confidentiality demands and suggest a formal modeling solution using propositional logic and the solution provided by Boolean Satisfiability (SAT) solvers, leveraging the computational efficiency of SAT solvers known for solving combinatorial optimization problems. Empirical testing on industrial-sized access matrices proves the feasibility and the scalability of the methodology presented, thereby validating its applicability in real-world small and medium enterprise settings plagued with complex permission arrangements.

Keywords: Role-Based Access Control · Role mining problem · Confidentiality · Information flow control · Access control matrix · sparsity · SAT Solver

1 Introduction

Role-Based Access Control (RBAC) [23] assigns roles to users and associates permissions with roles, simplifying policy design compared to Access Control Matrices (ACM). Rising digitalization, along with advances in Internet of Things (IoT), and Cloud services is driving the growth of the adoption of RBAC [27] and the development of embedded systems with limited users and resources [10].

K. Adi et al. (Eds.): CRiSIS 2025, LNCS 16295, pp. 430–448, 2026.
https://doi.org/10.1007/978-3-032-20732-6_27

RBAC reduces administrative complexity by minimizing the number of roles. Read/write permissions induce information flows between users and resources, and poorly designed policies may violate confidentiality, integrity, or availability. Our goal is to derive a role-minimal RBAC policy from an ACM while preserving key security properties, with a focus on confidentiality.

Confidentiality refers to the principle of protecting information from unauthorized access or disclosure [4]. It ensures that sensitive information—such as that held by high-privilege users or storage resource units—is not exposed to unauthorized users, such as low-privilege users. Confidentiality can be enforced by analysing [18,21] or controlling the flow of information, i.e., by ensuring that information only flows along allowed paths [9,14,17,18,22].

Pure RBAC, ACL, and DAC models do not inherently enforce confidentiality, integrity, or availability, unlike lattice-based models such as MAC, Bell-LaPadula [4], or Biba [5], which control information flow via fixed security labels and a lattice structure [9,24]. Despite RBAC's weakness in flow control, it remains favored in practice for its flexibility and administrative simplicity [17,20,28]. Recent work explores integrating RBAC with information flow control [18,22], especially in role mining [8].

Role mining - automatically discovering roles from ACMs - helps organizations create cleaner, more secure, and easier-to-manage RBAC systems by simplifying access control through role abstraction. The approaches in [15,30] aim to discover a minimal set of roles that preserves the original dense ACM, without considering information flow. A dense access control matrix explicitly grants or denies every permission for every user - or implicitly assumes that ungranted permissions are denied - whereas a sparse access control matrix may leave undefined the status (granted or denied) of some permissions, i.e., neither granted nor denied. The approach in [22] discovers roles compatible with a Bell-LaPadula policy, which already accounts for information flow. The minimality of the role set is not addressed. The work also analyzes RBAC policies to detect indirect information flows - those occurring over multiple reads and writes - and their underlying causes. While the authors suggest that this information can help administrators refine RBAC policies, no automatic refinement mechanism is proposed. The work in [18] analyze a dense ACM policy and an initial compatible RBAC policy for building a new RBAC policy that reveals indirect flow in the initial policy. The new RBAC is expected having fewer roles than the original, however the minimality of the number of role is not discussed.

Sparsity in the access control matrix enables scalable, flexible, and modular policy design by allowing certain permissions to remain undefined—neither explicitly granted nor denied—until further refinement. These undefined entries can later be interpreted based on the desired security posture: under strong security settings and the principle of least privilege, they are typically treated as denied; under weaker settings, they may be treated as granted. This choice influences the complexity of the resulting RBAC policy, as strong security may increase the number of roles due to finer access distinctions. However, in systems concerned with information-flow properties, resolving undefined permissions requires careful, non-trivial decisions to preserve security guarantees, which may in turn reduce the number of roles needed by avoiding over-specification. Sparsity in the ACM is analogous to the "floating label" concept from [16], enabling dynamic declassification or surclassification of entities in lattice-based access control models. To the best of our knowledge, constraining role mining with information flow properties and resolution of sparsity has received little attention, despite its clear practical relevance and applicability to real-world security policies.

This paper introduces and investigates four variants of the role mining problem aimed at preserving fine-grained confidentiality: **Check-NoLk-0**, **RMP-NoLk-1** to **RMP-NoLk-3**. We propose SAT-based solutions by encoding role mining and information flow properties as SAT formulas, enabling the use of efficient SAT solvers to derive role-minimal RBAC policies equivalent to a given ACM. We evaluate the scalability of our approach on industrial-scale ACMs.

The remainder of the paper is organized as follows. The next section introduces preliminary concepts and motivates our work. In Sect. 3, we define the confidentiality checking problem and formulate three role mining problems aimed at preserving a confidentiality property. Section 4 presents a SAT-based approach for checking confidentiality in security policies expressed as sparse access control matrices. In Sect. 5, we propose methods to solve the three role mining problems. An empirical evaluation of our approaches is provided in Sect. 6. Related work is discussed in Sect. 7, and Sect. 8 concludes the paper and outlines directions for future research.

2 Preliminaries

2.1 Access Control Matrix

An access control matrix specifies whether the operations a subject wishes to perform on objects are granted, denied, or left undefined. Let Sub be a finite set of subjects (users), Obj be a finite set of objects (resources) and Op be a finite set of operations or Rights.

Definition 1 (Dense and sparse access control matrix). *An access control matrix (ACM) is a total function* $M : Sub \times Obj \times Op \to \{deny = 0, grant = 1, undef = \llcorner\!\lrcorner\}$. *Given* $i \in Sub$, $j \in Obj$ *and* $o \in Op$, *we denote* $M^o_{i,j}$ *as a shorthand for* $M(i, j, o)$. M *is dense if* $M^o_{i,j} \neq undef$ *for every* $i \in Sub$, $j \in Obj$ *and* $o \in Op$; *otherwise* M *is sparse.*

An *access* is a pair in $Op \times Obj$, controlled by entries in the access control matrix M. Each entry corresponds to an access control *rule* as $\{grant, deny, undef\} \times Op \times Obj$. A *permission* grants access, a *prohibition* denies it, and *undefined* indicates no explicit rule.

Our definition of the access control matrix extends [12,25] by allowing undefined accesses. Their interpretation—granted or denied—varies across security models. Strong models (e.g., military) deny them by default, while weaker ones (e.g., public systems) may grant them. Intermediate cases require analysis, which is the focus of our work.

2.2 Information Flow Control

Information Flow Control (IFC) ensures that information flows only along permitted paths according to a security policy. Policies are often defined using a partial order on security labels (e.g., `TopSecret` $\geq$ `Confidential` $\geq$ `Public`). The Bell-LaPadula model [4] enforces confidentiality via *No Read Up* (NRU) and *No Write Down* (NWD), preventing unauthorized reads and leaks.

Lattice-based access control (LBAC) models use a function $\lambda : Sub \cup Obj \rightarrow Lab$ assigning a security label in Lab to every entity in $Sub \cup Obj$, which permits formalization of the definition of confidentiality and generalize the Bell-LaPadula Models.

The NRU, NWD, NRD, and NWU rules assume all entities have defined security labels. In practice, some entities may have undefined labels, requiring generalizations of these rules to analyze information flows involving such entities. Confidentiality is violated if information flows from a higher (e.g., `Secret`) to a lower (e.g., `Public`) level—either directly (as captured by the classic rules) or indirectly via intermediate entities. The core challenge is to assess whether undefined labels permit flows that breach confidentiality. A *strong* security hypothesis treats undefined labels as low, while a *weak* one treats them as high. A more flexible approach allows selective assignment, reducing violations—this forms a label engineering problem [7,16].

2.3 Role-Based Access Control

Role-Based Access Control (RBAC) addresses challenges of the ACM, where access rules are defined per subject-object pair. As systems scale, maintaining such rules becomes difficult. RBAC simplifies policy design by associating access with roles, aligning with organizational structures and easing enforcement of least privilege.

Definition 2 (RBAC configuration).
A basic RBAC configuration is a tuple $Conf = (Sub, Obj, Op, Roles, f_A, f_B)$*, where:*

- *Sub and Obj are finite sets of subjects and objects,*
- *$Roles$ is a finite set of roles,*
- *$f_A : Sub \rightarrow 2^{Roles}$ maps each subject to a set of roles,*
- *$f_B : Roles \rightarrow 2^{Op \times Obj}$ maps each role to a set of permissions.*

An RBAC configuration defines only positive rules; permissions not assigned to a role are implicitly *prohibitions*. Similarly, $r \notin f_A(s)$ means subject s does not have role r. The functions f_A and f_B can be represented by dense Boolean matrices user-role assignment A and role-permission assignment B. We denote these as A and B to simplify notation. Matrix A is $m \times k$ and matrix B is $k \times n \times |Op|$, where $m = |Sub|$, $k = |Roles|$, and $n = |Obj|$. Hence, an RBAC configuration is represented as $(Sub, Obj, Op, Roles, A, B)$ with A and B replacing f_A and f_B.

2.4 A Short Introduction to SAT and MaxSAT

Let $V = \{v_1, v_2, \cdots v_n\}$ be a finite set of Boolean variables. A literal l_i for v_i is either v_i or $\neg v_i$. A clause is a disjunction of literals of the form $(l_{i_1} \vee l_{i_2} \vee \cdots \vee l_{i_k})$ with $i_j \in [1..n]$. A Boolean formula in conjunctive normal form (CNF) is a conjunction of clauses. Given a CNF formula ψ, the Boolean Satisfiability Problem (SAT) asks whether there exists an assignment of truth values to the variables that makes ψ true. Such an assignment is called a model of ψ. Modern SAT solvers [11] efficiently handle tens to hundreds of thousands of variables, depending on the problem's structure. If variables represent ACM entries and ψ is a constraint on them, a model of ψ defines an ACM satisfying ψ. This mechanism helps derive an RBAC configuration compatible with the ACM.

MaxSAT [2] distinguishes between hard and soft clauses, and asks whether there exists an assignment that satisfies all hard clauses and the maximum possible number of soft clauses. This property allows estimating the minimal number of ACM entries to modify to satisfy a constraint, by representing each entry as a soft clause.

SAT is NP-complete, and MaxSAT is NP-hard. While both are theoretically exponential, SAT solvers often exhibit near-polynomial performance in practice; MaxSAT solvers are slightly less efficient but still practical.

3 Role Mining Problems for Preserving Confidentiality

The Basic Role Mining Problem (RMP) [13] consists of finding an RBAC configuration with a minimal set of roles from a given dense access control matrix (ACM) M that preserves the original subject-access-rule assignments. The objective is to minimize the number of roles generated. Formally, Basic-RMP can be stated as finding an RBAC configuration $(Sub, Obj, Op, Roles, A, B)$ from a dense ACM M by minimizing the number of roles $k = |Roles|$ such that $M = A \circ B$, where $\circ$ denotes Boolean matrix multiplication defined as

$$(A \circ B)_{i,j} = \bigvee_{l=1}^{k} (A_{i,l} \wedge B_{l,j}) \tag{1}$$

The Basic-RMP requires an exact match between $A \circ B$ and M. Variants like the δ-approximate RMP, Minimum-Noise RMP, and Edge RMP [19] relax this. The δ-approximate RMP allows up to δ mismatches while minimizing roles. The Edge RMP minimizes the total non-zero entries in A and B. Other variants constrain the number of roles per subject or permissions per role.

To the best of our knowledge, existing role mining approaches—such as the Basic-RMP and its variants—have largely overlooked two important aspects discussed in previous sections: the sparsity of the initial access control matrix (ACM) and the preservation of key information flow security properties, particularly those defined by the CIA triad (confidentiality, integrity, and availability). This observation also applies to access control models that can combine labels with ACM or RBAC to support richer security policies based on information flow.

Addressing the challenge of preserving confidentiality in RMP, our work considers a simple, yet interesting vision, where labels are unavailable and the security properties are expressed in terms of forbidden information flow between entities.

The following definitions relate sparse ACMs, dense ACMs, and RBAC configurations.

Definition 3 (Compatibility between sparse and dense ACMs). *A dense ACM M' is compatible with a sparse ACM M if M' defines (set to grant or deny) every undefined entry of M.*

Definition 4 (Compatibility between an RBAC configuration and a sparse ACM). *An RBAC configuration $conf = (Sub, Obj, Op, Roles, A, B)$ is compatible with a sparse ACM M if $A \circ B$ is compatible with M.*

Definition 5 (Satisfaction of an information flow property P).
Sparse ACM M satisfies a property P if there is a dense matrix M' compatible with M such that the information flow induced by M' satisfies P.
RBAC configuration $Conf = (Sub, Obj, Op, Roles, A, B)$ satisfies a property P if $A \circ B$ satisfies P.

Definition 6 (Mutant of a sparse ACM). *A sparse ACM M' is a mutant of M if M' is obtained by changing defined entries of M.*

We introduce a fine-grained confidentiality property C_{i_1,j,i_2} over specific entities, which can be composed to define medium- and coarse-grained dataflow properties.

Property $\boldsymbol{C_{i_1,j,i_2}}$: If subject i_1 has (direct or indirect) write access to object j, then subject i_2 must not have (direct or indirect) read access to the information stored in j.

An indirect access occurs via a sequence of read-write operations across multiple entities. Property C_{i_1,j,i_2} prevents information flow from i_1 to i_2 via sensitive object j, assuming that such a flow would violate security clearances and constitute a leak through j.

Property $\boldsymbol{NoLk_{i_1,i_2}}$: We study the medium-grained property $\boldsymbol{NoLk_{i_1,i_2}} := \bigwedge_{j=1}^{n} C_{i_1,j,i_2}$, which states that none of the n objects allows information leak from subject i_1 to subject i_2.

For readability, subscripts i_1, i_2 are omitted when clear from context. We address the following problems, given two subjects i_1 and i_2:

Check-NoLk-0: Check whether a sparse ACM M satisfies property $NoLk_{i_1,i_2}$.

RMP-NoLk-1: Given a sparse ACM M and an integer k, find an RBAC configuration with k roles that satisfies $NoLk_{i_1,i_2}$ and is compatible with M.

RMP-NoLk-2: Find an RBAC configuration with a minimal number of roles that satisfies $NoLk_{i_1,i_2}$ and is compatible with a given sparse access control matrix M.

RMP-NoLk-3: Given a sparse ACM M that does not necessarily satisfy $NoLk_{i_1,i_2}$, find an RBAC configuration with a minimal number of roles, compatible with a minimal mutant M' of M, such that the configuration satisfies property NoLk.

We tackle these four interdependent problems of increasing complexity using SAT-based encodings. **Check-NoLk-0** introduces key concepts reused throughout. **RMP-NoLk-1** serves as the foundation for **RMP-NoLk-2**, both extending Basic-RMP to sparse ACMs while preserving confidentiality. **RMP-NoLk-3** handles cases where **RMP-NoLk-2** is unsatisfiable by minimally overriding access rules to restore feasibility. Although selectively overriding some rules while preserving others is practically relevant, it is beyond this work's scope.

4 A SAT-Based Approach for Checking Property NoLk

We encode **Check-NoLk-0** as a SAT problem. Although dense ACMs allow polynomial-time solutions, we use SAT encoding to support RMP with property NoLk. This approach suits sparse ACMs, efficiently inferring undefined entries during the construction of compatible RBAC configurations. Let M be a sparse ACM over subjects Sub, objects Obj, and operations $Op = \{r = read, w = write\}$, with $m = |Sub|$ and $n = |Obj|$. Each entry $M^o_{i,j} \in \{0 = deny, 1 = grant, \_ = undef\}$ represents the permission of subject i on object j for operation $o \in \{r, w\}$.

Abbreviation: $\bigwedge_{i,j=1,1}^{m,n} \varphi_{i,j}$ abbreviates $\bigwedge_{i=1}^{m} \bigwedge_{j=1}^{n} \varphi_{i,j}$ for readability.

The SAT encoding of **Check-NoLk-0** consists in introducing boolean variables, encoding indirect flow relations, and property NoLk. We introduce **information flow boolean variables:** $F^o_{i,j} \in \{0, 1\}$ where $F^o_{i,j} = 1$ captures whether subject i can access object j for reading (i.e., $o = r$) or writing (i.e., $o = w$), either directly through role assignments or transitively through information flow paths. The encoding result is the formula $\psi_{Check-NoLk}$ defined by

$$\psi_{Check-NoLk} := canflow \wedge \psi_{NoLk} \tag{2}$$

where, $\psi_{NoLk} := \bigwedge_{j=1}^{n}(F^w_{i_1,j} \Rightarrow \neg F^r_{i_2,j})$ ensures $NoLk_{i_1,i_2}$ and the formula *canflow* build indirect flow between every pair of entities.

The values of each variable $F^r_{i,j}$ occurring in ψ_{NoLk} is 1 when $M^r_{i,j} = 1$ or there is a indirect flow from j to i and this indirect flow will be determined when the solver will resolve formula *canflow*. The value of each variable $F^w_{i,j}$ occurring in ψ_{NoLk} is exactly the value of $M^w_{i,j}$ except when $M^w_{i,j}$ is undefined and in this case its value will be inferred by the solver if property $NoLk_{i_1,i_2}$ can be violated.

Our definition of *canflow* is as follows:

$$\mathit{canflow} := \bigwedge_{i,j=1,1}^{m,n} (C^r_{i,j} \wedge C^w_{i,j}) \wedge \bigwedge_{i_1,i_2=1,1}^{m,m} \bigwedge_{j_1,j_2=1,1}^{n,n} \mathit{canflow}(j_1, i_1, j_2, i_2) \quad (3)$$

The formula $\mathit{canflow}(j_1, i_1, j_2, i_2)$ allows setting $F^r_{i_2,j_1} = 1$ whenever subject i_2 can indirectly read information from resource j_1. This occurs when a subject i_1 can read j_1 and write to an object j_2 that i_2 can read, either directly or indirectly. It is defined as follows:

$$\mathit{canflow}(j_1, i_1, j_2, i_2) := (F^r_{i_1,j_1} \wedge F^w_{i_1,j_2} \wedge F^r_{i_2,j_2}) \Rightarrow F^r_{i_2,j_1} \quad (4)$$

The formula $(C^r_{i,j} \wedge C^w_{i,j})$ allows setting as indirect flow every direct flow induced by read and write permissions defined in M. $C^r_{i,j}$ and $C^w_{i,j}$ are unitary clauses defined as follows:

$$C^w_{i,j} := \begin{cases} F^w_{i,j} & \text{if } M^w_{i,j} = 1 \\ \neg F^w_{i,j} & \text{if } M^w_{i,j} = 0 \\ \top & \text{if } M^w_{i,j} = \llcorner\!\lrcorner \end{cases} \quad (5)$$

$$C^r_{i,j} := \begin{cases} F^r_{i,j} & \text{if } M^r_{i,j} = 1 \\ \top & \text{if } M^r_{i,j} = 0 \text{ or } M^r_{i,j} = \llcorner\!\lrcorner \end{cases} \quad (6)$$

When $M^r_{i,j} = 0$ or $M^r_{i,j} = \llcorner\!\lrcorner$, we set $C^r_{i,j} = \top$ (i.e., *True*) to enable information flow analysis through indirect paths. This allows the detection of indirect information propagation from object j to subject i via intermediate objects and subjects, even when direct read access is denied. This propagation is computed with the conjunctions of $\mathit{canflow}(j_1, i_1, j_2, i_2)$ in Eq. 3.

Lemma 1 follows directly from the construction of $\psi_{Check-NoLk}$ and it ensures that a solution to **Check-NoLk-0** can be obtained by constructing and solving the formula $\psi_{Check-NoLk}$. we omit the formal proof for the sake of readability.

Lemma 1 (Correctness of Confidentiality Checking). *The formula $\psi_{Check-NoLk}$ is satisfiable if and only if the sparse ACM M satisfies the fine-grained confidentiality property $NoLk_{i_1,i_2}$.*

The formula $\psi_{Check-NoLk}$ is a conjunction of Horn clauses, and thus its satisfiability can be determined in linear time. The empirical evaluation in Sect. 6 demonstrates the practical scalability of our approach on industrial-sized ACM, validating the theoretical efficiency considerations.

5 SAT-Based Approach for Role Mining Preserving Confidentiality

This section addresses the confidentiality-preserving role mining problems **RMP-NoLk-1** to **RMP-NoLk-4**, defined in Sect. 3. Our SAT-based approach builds on prior work in Boolean matrix factorization [3], extended to incorporate security constraints that introduce new reasoning challenges and practical considerations in the security domain.

5.1 Solving RMP-NoLk-1 and RMP-NoLk-2

Recall that **RMP-NoLk-1** seeks an RBAC configuration with k roles satisfying Property NoLk and compatible with a sparse ACM M. **RMP-NoLk-2** extends this by additionally minimizing the number of roles. Our search-based solution to **RMP-NoLk-2** reduces the problem to a sequence of **RMP-NoLk-1** instances, starting with one role and incrementally increasing the number up to $\min(|Sub|, |Obj|)$.

Before solving **RMP-NoLk-1**, we illustrate how enforcing confidentiality alters the RBAC configuration. Consider the sparse ACM in Fig. 1 with two subjects and two objects. Subject 1 can read object 2; other accesses are undefined. If undefined entries may be set to either 1 (grant) or 0 (deny), the basic RMP admits an optimal solution with a single role—assuming all undefined entries are grants. However, enforcing confidentiality requires at least two roles. A compatible RBAC is defined by the subject-role assignment matrix A and role-permission assignment B in Fig. 2 and Fig. 3 (Fig. 4).

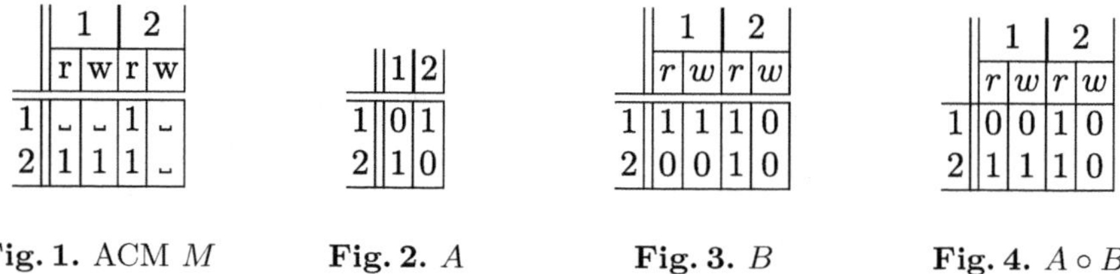

	1		2	
	r	w	r	w
1	␣	␣	1	␣
2	1	1	1	␣

Fig. 1. ACM M

	1	2
1	0	1
2	1	0

Fig. 2. A

	1		2	
	r	w	r	w
1	1	1	1	0
2	0	0	1	0

Fig. 3. B

	1		2	
	r	w	r	w
1	0	0	1	0
2	1	1	1	0

Fig. 4. $A \circ B$

Our solution to **RMP-NoLk-1** combines solving the Basic RMP with the satisfaction of property NoLk. The encoding consists of three main components: (1) Boolean variables, (2) Basic RMP constraints, (3) information flow constraints and (4) confidentiality constraints.

Boolean Variables:

- **Subject-assignment variables:** $A_{i,l} \in \{0,1\}$ where $A_{i,l} = 1$ indicates whether subject i is assigned to role l.
- **Role-assignment variables:** $B^r_{l,j}, B^w_{l,j} \in \{0,1\}$ represent read and write permissions of role l on objects j, respectively.

- **Information flow variables:** $F^r_{i,j}, F^w_{i,j} \in \{0,1\}$ where $F^o_{i,j} = 0$ means i cannot access object j for reading or writing, either directly or indirectly.

Basic-RMP Constraints:
Equation 1 can be rewritten with two equations: $M^r_{i,j} = \bigvee_{l=1}^{k}(A_{i,l} \wedge B^r_{l,j})$ and $M^w_{i,j} = \bigvee_{l=1}^{k}(A_{i,l} \wedge B^w_{l,j})$. Therefore solving the basic RPM problem– i.e., finding an RBAC configuration with k roles compatible with a sparse M– consists in finding values for variables $A_{i,l}$, $B^r_{l,j}$ and $B^w_{l,j}$ for matrices A and B such that $A \circ B$ is compatible with M. Compatibility is required because of sparsity.

The encoding of the Basic-RMP for a sparse ACM M includes two types of constraints on $A_{i,l}$ and $B^o_{l,j}$, based on the value of $M^o_{i,j}$ for $o \in \{r, w\}$:

1. A *permission constraint (**isOne**)* is introduced whenever $M^o_{i,j} = 1$ for enforcing at least one role to granting the access: $\bigvee_{l=1}^{k}(A_{i,l} \wedge B^o_{l,j})$. This latter constraint is rewritten into the equivalent constraint in disjunctive normal form appearing in Eq. 7.

$$isOne^o_{i,j}(k) := \bigwedge_{l=1}^{k}(Z^o_{i,j,l} \Rightarrow A_{i,l}) \wedge \bigwedge_{l=1}^{k}(Z^o_{i,j,l} \Rightarrow B^o_{l,j}) \wedge \bigvee_{l=1}^{k} Z^o_{i,j,l} \quad (7)$$

where each introduced **auxiliary variables** $Z^o_{i,j,l} \in \{0,1\}$ indicates whether role l contributes to granting permission $o \in \{r, w\}$ to subject i on object j. At least one $Z^o_{i,j,l}$ should be true –i.e., at least one role must permit granting the access– which is specified with $\bigvee_{l=1}^{k} Z^o_{i,j,l}$ in Eq. 7. These auxiliary variables are introduced to build formulas in conjunctive normal form, so as to respect the format of formulas given as inputs to SAT-solvers. We recall that $a \Rightarrow b$ is equivalent to $\neg a \vee b$ is a clause in conjunctive normal form.
2. A *prohibition constraint (**isZero**)* is introduced whenever $M^o_{i,j} = 0$ for enforcing every role prevent access of i to j.

$$isZero^o_{i,j}(k) := \bigwedge_{l=1}^{k} \neg(A_{i,l} \wedge B^o_{l,j}) \quad \text{equivalent to CNF} \quad isZero^o_{i,j}(k) := \bigwedge_{l=1}^{k}(\neg A_{i,l} \vee \neg B^o_{l,j}) \quad (8)$$

3. *Undefined entry handling* : For entries where $M^o_{i,j} = undef$, the values of variables $A_{i,l}$ and $B_{l,j}$ for $l = 1, \ldots, k$ are left unconstrained and can be determined later to satisfy the confidentiality property. Therefore, no explicit constraints are imposed.

Let us define

$$\psi_{Basic-RMP}(k) := \bigwedge_{i,j,o \text{ s.t } M^o_{i,j}=1} isOne^o_{i,j}(k) \wedge \bigwedge_{i,j,o \text{ s.t } M^o_{i,j}=0} isZero^o_{i,j}(k) \quad (9)$$

The following lemma provides a solution to the basic RMP.

Lemma 2. *Given a sparse ACM M and an integer k, an RBAC configuration with k roles exists if and only if the formula $\psi_{Basic\text{-}RMP}$ is satisfiable. Furthermore, any solution to $\psi_{Basic\text{-}RMP}$ defines the dense subject-role assignment matrix A and role-permission assignment matrix B of an RBAC configuration compatible with M.*

Information Flow Constraints: We encode the existence of direct and indirect information flows induced by the Basic RMP solution matrices A and B. Since $\psi_{\text{Basic-RMP}}$ yields dense matrices A and B with $A \circ B$ compatible with the initial sparse ACM M, analyzing information flow directly from $A \circ B$ provides a more efficient encoding than first computing $A \circ B$ and then applying the method from Sect. 4.

- *Direct flow constraints:*These constraints establish the direct relationship between role assignments and access permissions. For each subject i, each *object* j and each role l we introduce the direct information flow constraint:

$$directflow_{i,j,l} := (A_{i,l} \wedge B^r_{l,j} \Rightarrow F^r_{i,j}) \wedge (A_{i,l} \wedge B^w_{l,j} \Rightarrow F^w_{i,j}) \tag{10}$$

- *Indirect flow constraints ($canflow_{rmp}$):* These constraints capture the propagation: "if subject i reads object j and writes to object k, and subject l reads object k, then subject l can indirectly access information from object i".

$$canflow_{rmp} := \bigwedge_{i_1,i_2=1,1}^{m,m} \bigwedge_{j_1,j_2=1,1}^{n,n} canflow(j_1, i_1, j_2, i_2) \tag{11}$$

where $canflow(j, i, k, l)$ is defined in Eq. 4.

Let us define

$$\psi_{flow}(k) := \bigwedge_{i,j,l=1,1,1}^{m,n,k} directflow_{i,j,l} \wedge canflow_{rmp} \tag{12}$$

Lemma 3. *Information can flow from subject i to object j or from object j to subject i w.r.t an RBAC configuration having k role and compatible with a sparse ACM M if $\psi_{flow}(k) \wedge (F^w_{i,j} \vee F^r_{i,j})$ is satisfiable.*

Confidentiality Constraint:

$$\psi_{NoLk} := \bigwedge_{j=1}^{n} F^w_{i_1,j} \Rightarrow \neg F^r_{i_2,j} \quad \text{with} \quad n = |Obj| \tag{13}$$

where i_1 and i_2 are the specific subjects in the definition of property $NoLk_{i_1,i_2}$.

Complete SAT Formula for RMP-NoLk-1: The complete solution of formula **RMP-NoLk-1** is given by the following lemma the proof of which derives Lemma 2, Lemma 3 and Eq. 13.

Lemma 4. *Given a sparse ACM M and an integer k, there exists an RBAC configuration with k roles and compatible with M that satisfies property NoLk if the formula* $\psi_{RMP\text{-}NoLk\text{-}1}(k) := \psi_{Basic-RMP}(k) \wedge \psi_{flow}(k) \wedge \psi_{NoLk}$ *is satisfiable. Moreover a solution of* $\psi_{RMP\text{-}NoLk\text{-}1}(k)$ *defines the dense subject-assignment matrix A and the dense role-assignment matrix B for the compatible RBAC configuration.*

Solving RMP-NoLk-2 **RMP-NoLk-2** extends **RMP-NoLk-1** by seeking the minimal number of roles that satisfies both compatibility with M and property $NoLk_{i_1,i_2}$.

RMP-NoLk-2 is mathematically formulated as follows:

$$k^* = \arg \min_{k \leq min(m,n)} [\psi_{\text{RMP-NoLk-1}}(k) = True] \tag{14}$$

The proposed solution to **RMP-NoLk-2** using an incremental search approach is presented in Algorithm 1. The algorithm performs a sequential search for the minimal number of roles k such that RMP-NoLk-1 is satisfiable. The search terminates at the first value of k for which a solution exists, ensuring optimality in terms of role count. The worst-case complexity is $O(min(m,n) \times T_{\text{SAT}})$, where T_{SAT} represents the time complexity of the underlying SAT solver. In practice, modern SAT solvers exhibit excellent performance on structured instances, making this approach viable for industrial-scale problems.

Algorithm 1: Solving RMP-NoLk-2

Require: Sparse ACM $M : Sub \times Obj \times \{r, w\} \rightarrow \{0, 1, \llcorner\!\lrcorner\}$, subjects $i_1, i_2 \in Sub$, object $j \in Obj$ for property $NoLk$
Ensure: RBAC configuration $(Sub, Obj, \{r, w\}, Roles, A, B)$ with minimal number of roles, or $\emptyset$ if none exists

```
1: // First check if M can satisfy property NoLk
2: if ¬SAT(ψ_{Check−NoLk}) then
3:     return ∅                                   {M cannot satisfy NoLk}
4: end if
5: // Search for minimal number of roles
6: for k = 1 to min(|Sub|, |Obj|) do
7:     Construct ψ_{RMP−NoLk−1}(k)
8:     model ← SAT(ψ_{RMP−NoLk−1}(k))
9:     if model ≠ null then
10:        (A, B) ← ExtractSolution(model)
11:        return (Sub, Obj, {r, w}, {1, 2, ···, k}, A, B)   {Optimal solution found}
12:    end if
13: end for
14: return ∅                                      {No solution exists}
```

Since **RMP-NoLk-1** and **RMP-NoLk-2** are novel, no baseline solutions exist for efficiency comparison.

5.2 Solving RMP-NoLk-3

Given a sparse ACM M that may not satisfy property NoLk, Problem **RMP-NoLk-3** seeks an RBAC configuration $Conf = (Sub, Obj, \{r, w\}, Roles, A, B)$ that is compatible with a minimal mutant M' of M, satisfies property NoLk, and minimizes $|Roles|$. This describes practical cases where M violates property NoLk, and the goal is to minimally modify M to enforce confidentiality and enable a compatible RBAC configuration.

Mutant M' is created by applying a mutation operation called a *read permission override*, which degrades a read permission to a prohibition by changing $M^r_{i,j}$ from 1 to 0. Permission overrides adhere to the principle of least privilege by restricting access rights, thereby supporting confidentiality (property $NoLk_{i_1,i_2}$) and preventing information leaks. For simplicity, we focus only on read permission overrides, though write permission overrides can be handled similarly using our proposed approach. The minimality of a mutant is determined by the number of degraded read permissions.

MaxSAT Formulation for RMP-NoLk-3. The MaxSAT encoding allows us to jointly find a minimal modification of M and a compatible RBAC role-minimal configuration, avoiding costly exhaustive enumeration of each and every mutant. It extends **RMP-NoLk-1** with *override variables* $R^r_{i,j} \in \{0, 1\}$, where $R^r_{i,j} = 1$ indicates a read permission in $M^r_{i,j} = 1$ is overridden and becomes $M^r_{i,j} = 0$. $R^r_{i,j} = 0$ indicates a read permission in M is retained. The formulation combines soft constraints minimizing overrides with hard constraints for defining RBAC configuration satisfying $NoLk_{i_1,i_2}$ and compatible with the mutant correctness and confidentiality. Formally,

$$\psi_{\text{RMP-NoLk-3}}(k) := \psi_{\text{hard}}(k) \wedge \psi_{\text{soft}} \quad \text{where :} \tag{15}$$

1. **Soft constraints**: $\psi_{\text{soft}} := \bigwedge_{i,j=1,1}^{m,n} \neg R^r_{i,j}$. It consists of unit clauses $\neg R^r_{i,j}$, and maximizing their satisfaction corresponds to maximizing the number of variables $R^r_{i,j}$ set to 0, which is equivalent to minimizing the number of variables set to 1, i.e., the number of overridden permissions.
2. **Hard constraints**: $\psi_{\text{hard}}(k) := \psi_{\text{Basic-RMP-Ovrd}}(k) \wedge \psi_{\text{flow}}(k) \wedge \psi_{NoLk}$ where,
   - ψ_{flow} is the **information flow constraints** defined in Eq. 12.
   - ψ_{NoLk} is the **confidentiality constraints** defined in Eq. 13
   - $\psi_{\text{Basic-RMP-Ovrd}}(k)$ encoding the Basic RMP constraints with overiddes is defined by:

$$\begin{aligned}\psi_{Basic\text{-}RMP\text{-}Ovrd}(k) := & \bigwedge_{i,j \text{ s.t } M^w_{i,j}=1} isOne^w_{i,j}(k) \wedge \bigwedge_{i,j,o \text{ s.t } M^o_{i,j}=0} isZero^o_{i,j}(k) \\ & \wedge \\ & \bigwedge_{i,j \text{ s.t } M^r_{i,j}=1} (R^r_{i,j} \Rightarrow isZero^r_{i,j}(k)) \wedge \bigwedge_{i,j \text{ s.t } M^r_{i,j}=1} (\neg R^r_{i,j} \Rightarrow isOne^r_{i,j}(k))\end{aligned} \tag{16}$$

$\psi_{\text{Basic-RMP-Ovrd}}(k)$ is an adaptation of $\psi_{\text{Basic-RMP}}$ to handle permission overrides. If $R^r_{i,j}$ is True (i.e. its value is 1), then $M^r_{i,j}$ becomes 0 and the constraint $isZero^r_{i,j}(k)$ holds; otherwise, $\neg R^r_{i,j}$ is true, $M^r_{i,j}$ retains its value 1, and the constraint $isOne^r_{i,j}(k)$ holds.

Lemma 5. *Given a sparse ACM M that does not necessarily satisfy property NoLk, there is an RBAC configuration with k roles compatible with a mutant M' of M if $\psi_{Basic\text{-}RMP\text{-}Ovrd}(k)$ is satisfiable. Moreover model of $\psi_{Basic\text{-}RMP\text{-}Ovrd}(k)$ determines the RBAC configuration.*

Lemma 6 (Solution for RMP-NoLk-3). *Given a sparse ACM M that does not necessarily satisfy property NoLk, there is an RBAC configuration with k roles compatible with a mutant M' of M if $\psi_{Basic\text{-}RMP\text{-}Ovrd}(k)$ is satisfiable. Moreover every model of $\psi_{Basic\text{-}RMP\text{-}Ovrd}(k)$ determines a desired RBAC configuration.*

RMP-NoLk-3 is mathematically formulated as follows:

$$k^* = \arg \min_{k \leq min(m,n)} [\psi_{\text{RMP}-\text{NoLk}-3}(k) = True] \tag{17}$$

Our algorithm for solving **RMP-NoLk-3** follows the same structure as Algorithm 1, but uses $\psi_{\text{RMP}-\text{NoLk}-3}(k)$ instead of $\psi_{\text{RMP}-\text{NoLk}-2}(k)$ and relies on MaxSAT solvers instead of SAT solvers.

6 Empirical Evaluation of the Proposed Approaches

Our empirical evaluation assesses scalability and performance across varying problem dimensions, focusing on the impact of the number of roles k and the practical applicability of our SAT-based approaches to enterprise-scale access control.

6.1 Experimental Protocol

For each problem dimension (with m subjects, n objects) and a number of roles k, we conducted 23 independent experiments, each consisting of:

1. generating a sparse synthetic ACM M with a compatible random RBAC configuration.
2. solving each of the four problems using M and recording the resolution time.

A timeout of 10 min was set for each experiment, with dashes (-) in the results tables indicating instances where the solver could not find a solution within this limit. We report the median resolution time over the 23 experiments. Summary of results for selected problem dimensions are shown in Table 1. To analyze scalability with respect to the number of roles, we estimate execution times for increasing k. Results are presented in Fig. 5. All resolution times are reported in milliseconds.

Algorithm 2 randomly generates two dense RBAC matrices A and B for k roles, then derives a sparse ACM M by setting 20% of the entries in the dense ACM $A \circ B$ to be undefined. A 20% sparsity simulates realistic enterprise settings where permissions are selectively granted. This generation ensures each sparse ACM is compatible with an RBAC configuration, enabling meaningful evaluation of **Check-NoLk-0** and **RMP-NoLk-1** to **RMP-NoLk-3** resolution times.

Algorithm 2: Matrix Generation Protocol

Require: Number of users m, resources n, roles k
Ensure: Sparse ACM M
1: Generate randomly dense subject-assignment matrix A for m subjects and k roles
2: Generate randomly dense permission-assignment matrix B for k roles and n objects
3: Compute dense ACM $M_{dense} = A \circ B$
4: Select 20% of entries from M_{dense} uniformly at random
5: Set selected entries in M_{dense} to undef to create M
6: **return** M

The experiments span five problem dimensions of increasing scale: $(10, 10)$, $(20, 20)$, $(40, 40)$, $(80, 80)$, and $(100, 100)$. For each dimension, we vary the number of roles k from 1 to 10, conducting 23 experiments per setting. The problem dimensions correspond to the number of users and files in information system of the huge numbers of existing small and medium enterprises [1].

All experiments were conducted on a MacBook Pro M2 8 core ($4 \times 3, 49GHz$, $4 \times 2, 42GHz$) with 32 GB RAM using python-sat v0.1.7.dev22 with MiniSat v2.2.1 and RC2 solver.

6.2 Result Analysis and Impact

Experimental results in Table 1 and Fig. 5 **show Check-NoLk-0** scales efficiently across all tested dimensions with sub-second resolution times, validating the polynomial-time complexity of our Horn clause encoding. For the role mining problems (**RMP-NoLk-1** to **RMP-NoLk-3**), computation times increase significantly with problem size, particularly beyond 40×40 dimensions. Notably, several instances for dimensions 80×80 and 100×100 exceeded the 10 min timeout, especially for **RMP-NoLk-3** with higher role counts. Figure 5 reveals that computational complexity grows non-linearly with the number of roles k, with **RMP-NoLk-3** showing the steepest increase due to the additional overhead of permission override optimization.

Results in Fig. 5 show that computation time increases with problem size. In particular, for the optimization problem **RMP-NoLk-3**, a higher number of roles results in longer computation time.

Results in Table 1 show that the proposed approaches scale well for embedded and IoT systems with tiny file systems managing a limited number of users and resources. Examples include handheld terminals used in military or medical contexts [10], which typically support around 30 users and up to 100 small files. Another example is a digital door access control system for a building with dimensions $(20, 50)$.

Table 1. Summary table - Median times by problem and configuration (ms)

Problem	(10×10)	(20×20)	(40×40)	(80×80)	(100×100)
Check-NoLk-0	0.09	1.20	0.02	0.21	0.12
RMP-NoLk-1	0.15	2.05	59.41	2085.00	4540.00
RMP-NoLk-2	0.16	4.60	270.23	3315.00	2800.00
RMP-NoLk-3	0.55	6.47	168.14	4300.00	12760.00

7 Related Work

Categories of approaches used for solving the basic Role Mining Problem (RMP) include clustering-based methods, graph-based techniques, heuristic and metaheuristic algorithms, probabilistic and Bayesian approaches, and SAT/SMT or ILP-based formulations [13]. Among these, SAT/SMT and ILP-based approaches—which often formulate RMP as a Boolean matrix factorization problem—are particularly well-suited for confidentiality-preserving RBAC. They allow fine-grained and precise (non-approximate) control over the permissions granted in a solution, offer modular and reusable encodings, leverage the efficiency of modern SAT solvers, and scale to small- and medium-sized real-world systems.

In our recent work [2,3], we developed a SAT-based framework for Boolean matrix factorization and designed an efficient MaxSAT solver. The present contribution builds on that foundation and adapts it to the role mining problem in flow-secure RBAC systems.

The studies in [6,26] explore RMP variants with cardinality constraints on the number of roles per user and permissions per role. These constraints are useful for maintainability but do not address information-flow properties as we do. Nonetheless, our MaxSAT-based solution to **RMP-NoLk-3** is modular and can be extended to incorporate both cardinality and confidentiality constraints.

The notion of sparse cells we use is conceptually related to the "floating label" mechanism in [7,16], which supports dynamic (de)classification of subjects and objects. In our setting, sparse cells enable dynamic permission granting or revocation based on specified security properties.

Previous works such as [22,24] have motivated the need for information-flow control in RBAC by proposing configurations that enforce the Bell-LaPadula

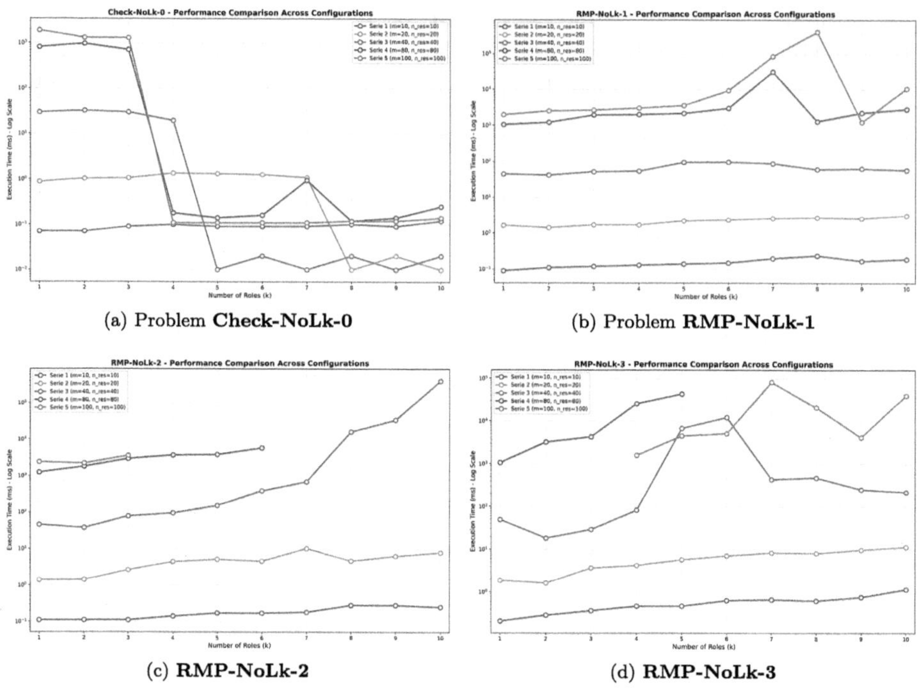

(a) Problem **Check-NoLk-0**

(b) Problem **RMP-NoLk-1**

(c) **RMP-NoLk-2**

(d) **RMP-NoLk-3**

Fig. 5. Computation times for increasing value of the number of roles and problem dimensions. Blue curves = (10, 10), yellow curves = (20, 20), green curves = (40, 40), red curves = (80, 80) and magenta curves = (100, 100). (Color figure online)

model via security labels. These approaches assume pre-defined labels for subjects and objects and perform flow analysis on existing RBAC policies. In contrast, our work jointly performs role mining and flow-preserving RBAC construction from an input ACM, using a reusable SAT-based framework.

Finally, [17,29] establish a correspondence between Denning's syntactic and semantic label models, and enforce information flow security via preorders induced by read/write permissions. Unlike those works, we do not assume an existing RBAC policy; instead, we synthesize one from scratch to simultaneously minimize roles and enforce information-flow confidentiality.

8 Conclusion

In our effort to engineer RBAC models with confidentiality preservation in mind, we introduced and solved four variants of the role mining problem—**Check-NoLk-0** and **RMP-NoLk-1** to **RMP-NoLk-3**—each ensuring a representative confidentiality property. The proposed logical and modular approach is promising, as it can be extended to other information flow properties such as integrity and availability. It also allows customization to organization-specific confidentiality goals by adjusting the Boolean encoding of the property while retaining the general framework.

Experiments show that the approach scales well to small embedded and IoT systems with typical subject counts and few objects, such as handheld terminals used in military or medical contexts.

Future work includes enhancing the encoding to support larger RBAC configurations and extending the approach to preserve all three CIA Triad properties—confidentiality, integrity, and availability—during maintenance operations, such as the addition of subjects or objects.

References

1. Anderer, S., Scheuermann, B., Mostaghim, S., Bauerle, P., Beil, M.: Rmplib: a library of benchmarks for the role mining problem. In: Proceedings of the 26th ACM Symposium on Access Control Models and Technologies, pp. 3–13 (2021)
2. Avellaneda, F.: Evalmaxsat 2023. MaxSAT Evaluation 2022: Solver and Benchmark Descriptions, pp. 12–13 (2023)
3. Avellaneda, F., Villemaire, R.: Undercover boolean matrix factorization with maxsat. In: Proceedings of the AAAI Conference on Artificial Intelligence, vol. 36, pp. 3672–3681 (2022)
4. Bell, D.E., La Padula, L.J.: Secure computer system: unified exposition and multics interpretation (1976)
5. Biba, K.J., et al.: Integrity considerations for secure computer systems (1977)
6. Blundo, C., Cimato, S.: Role mining under user-distribution cardinality constraint. J. Inf. Secur. Appl. **78**, 103611 (2023)
7. Boulares, S., Adi, K., Logrippo, L.: Information flow-based security levels assessment for access control systems. In: Benyoucef, M., Weiss, M., Mili, H. (eds.) MCETECH 2015. LNBIP, vol. 209, pp. 105–121. Springer, Cham (2015). https://doi.org/10.1007/978-3-319-17957-5_7
8. Coyne, E.J.: Role engineering. In: Proceedings of the first ACM Workshop on Role-Based Access Control, pp. 4–es (1996)
9. Denning, D.E.: A lattice model of secure information flow. Commun. ACM **19**(5), 236–243 (1976)
10. DIResearch: Global handheld terminal competitive landscape professional research report 2025. Market research report (2025). https://www.dirmarketresearch.com/en/reports/handheld-terminal-1734533615339282432
11. Froleyks, N., Heule, M., Iser, M., Järvisalo, M., Suda, M.: Sat competition 2020. Artif. Intell. **301**, 103572 (2021)
12. Harrison, M.A., Ruzzo, W.L., Ullman, J.D.: Protection in operating systems. Commun. ACM **19**(8), 461–471 (1976)
13. Jia, J., Guan, J., Wang, L.: Role mining: survey and suggestion on role mining in access control. In: International Symposium on Mobile Internet Security, pp. 34–50. Springer (2019)
14. Kozyri, E., Chong, S., Myers, A.C., et al.: Expressing information flow properties. Found. Trends® Priv. Secur. **3**(1), 1–102 (2022)
15. Kumar, C.A.: Designing role-based access control using formal concept analysis. Secur. Commun. Netw. **6**(3), 373–383 (2013)

16. Kumar, N.N., Shyamasundar, R.: Realizing purpose-based privacy policies succinctly via information-flow labels. In: 2014 IEEE Fourth International Conference on Big Data and Cloud Computing, pp. 753–760. IEEE (2014)
17. Kumar, N.N., Shyamasundar, R.: A complete generative label model for lattice-based access control models. In: International Conference on Software Engineering and Formal Methods, pp. 35–53. Springer (2017)
18. Logrippo, L.: Data flow security in role-based access control. J. Inf. Secur. Appl. **90**, 103997 (2025)
19. Mitra, B., Sural, S., Vaidya, J., Atluri, V.: A survey of role mining. ACM Comput. Surv. (CSUR) **48**(4), 1–37 (2016)
20. Nyanchama, M., Osborn, S.: The role graph model and conflict of interest. ACM Trans. Inf. Syst. Secur. (TISSEC) **2**(1), 3–33 (1999)
21. Osborn, S.L.: Information flow analysis of an RBAC system. In: Proceedings of the Seventh ACM Symposium on Access Control Models and Technologies, pp. 163–168 (2002)
22. Radhika, B.S., Kumar, N.V.N., Shyamasundar, R.K.: Towards unifying RBAC with information flow control. In: Proceedings of the 26th ACM Symposium on Access Control Models and Technologies, pp. 45–54 (2021)
23. Sandhu, R.: Role hierarchies and constraints for lattice-based access controls. In: Bertino, E., Kurth, H., Martella, G., Montolivo, E. (eds.) ESORICS 1996. LNCS, vol. 1146, pp. 65–79. Springer, Heidelberg (1996). https://doi.org/10.1007/3-540-61770-1_28
24. Sandhu, R.S.: Lattice-based access control models. Computer **26**(11), 9–19 (1993)
25. Saunders, G., Hitchens, M., Varadharajan, V.: Role-based access control and the access control matrix. ACM SIGOPS Oper. Syst. Rev. **35**(4), 6–20 (2001)
26. Sun, W., Yuan, X., Su, H.: Role-engineering optimization with user-oriented cardinality constraints in role-based access control. Int. J. Netw. Secur. **23**(5), 845–855 (2021)
27. The Brainy Insights: Role-based access control market size by model type (constrained RBAC, hierarchical RBAC, and core RBAC), and by organization size (small and medium enterprises and large enterprises), regions, global industry analysis, share, growth, trends, and forecast 2023 to 2032. Market research report (2024). https://www.thebrainyinsights.com/report/role-based-access-control-market-13919
28. Tripunitara, M.V., Li, N.: A theory for comparing the expressive power of access control models. J. Comput. Secur. **15**(2), 231–272 (2007)
29. Tuval, N., Gudes, E.: Resolving information flow conflicts in RBAC systems. In: Damiani, E., Liu, P. (eds.) DBSec 2006. LNCS, vol. 4127, pp. 148–162. Springer, Heidelberg (2006). https://doi.org/10.1007/11805588_11
30. Vaidya, J., Atluri, V., Guo, Q.: The role mining problem: a formal perspective. ACM Trans. Inf. Syst. Secur. (TISSEC) **13**(3), 1–31 (2010)

The Impacts of (Anti)Encryption Laws on Secure Technology Development: A Case Study of Australia

Md Mehedi Hassan Onik(✉)

Deakin Cyber Research and Innovation Centre, Deakin University, Geelong, VIC 3216, Australia
m.onik@deakin.edu.au

Abstract. The 'Going Dark' debate—concern over encryption limiting law enforcement and intelligence agencies' (LEIAs') access to evidence—centres on tension between 'encryption-weakening' and 'encryption-strengthening' policies. In response, governments are increasingly mandating technical industry assistance (TIA) through (anti)encryption laws that require surveillance capabilities in digital products. However, how technology companies navigate the resulting challenges and cybersecurity implications remains underexplored. Focusing on TIA provisions of Australia's Assistance and Access Act 2018 (AA2018), this study addresses this gap by drawing on 35 interviews with tech professionals working in Australia. Preliminary findings suggest that while participants are generally willing to assist LEIAs, legal obligations complicate secure software development practices. Participants reported navigating the law with technical, legal, professional, and psychological considerations in mind. Mandated weakening of encryption was reported to increase attack surfaces, introduce hidden vulnerabilities, compromise supply chain security, and undermine privacy. Beyond technical risks, broader harms were also identified, including damage to product integrity and business trust, and negative impacts on staff reputation and productivity. This study calls for more transparent encryption laws and recommends legal reforms that safeguard fair usage of encryption and essential cybersecurity practices.

Keywords: Encryption policy · Cybersecurity risks · Government surveillance · Lawful hacking · Trust and accountability

1 Introduction and Background

Technology users, governments, law enforcement and intelligence agencies (LEIAs), civil liberties advocates, and tech companies continue to debate the need to balance data privacy, national security, cybersecurity, and encryption. While fair use of encryption protects security and privacy, it can also shield criminal activity—a concern known as the 'Going Dark' debate [1].

K. Adi et al. (Eds.): CRiSIS 2025, LNCS 16295, pp. 449–464, 2026.
https://doi.org/10.1007/978-3-032-20732-6_28

Thus, to weaken the ubiquitous encryption shield and to assist LEIAs, governments have increasingly introduced (anti)encryption laws[1] [2]. Under these laws, LEIAs can request technical industry assistance (TIA)[2] from tech companies to access decrypted evidence. Such provisions often require the secret development of surveillance mechanisms (e.g., backdoors) within encrypted services, even as many jurisdictions pursue counter-laws that strengthen encryption [3]. This creates a paradox: governments demand stronger cybersecurity, while pressing companies to weaken it to comply with TIA or similar provisions.

The increasing use of lawful backdoors poses significant risks to cybersecurity and could have catastrophic consequences for society. For instance, in 2025, Apple Inc. stopped offering end-to-end encryption (E2EE) to UK-based iCloud users in response to TIA mandating the Investigatory Powers Act 2016 of the UK. While similar laws exist in 'Five Eyes' nations [3], the European Commission is also targeting E2EE [4]. Meanwhile, scholars have recognised encrypted communication as a basic human right for personal data privacy; yet, these laws enable surveillance of law-abiding citizens, highlighting the need for further legal reform [5,6]. It was particularly argued that TIA endangers global trade and economic stability [7], with Budish et al., [8] projecting losses of up to USD 180 billion for U.S. tech firms following the post-2013 'Snowden effect'. Walker-Munro [9] and Davis [10] have found that Australia's vital (anti)encryption law, the Assistance and Access Act of 2018 (AA2018)[3], lacks the legal ability to retrieve evidence effectively and is often in technical dispute with other laws.

However, what has been missing from the discussion of the implications of the (anti)encryption policy is a recognition of the legal implications for the cybersecurity of products. While it has been amply demonstrated that (anti)encryption laws harm *civil liberties rights* [11], *economic and political stability* [12], and *national reputation and security* [3], an underexplored dimension is how tech companies navigate TIAs while maintaining secure product development practices.

Existing studies focus on legal impacts, offering limited industry feedback on commercial aspects [7], and paying little attention to technical implications [10,13]. So it remains unclear: Are tech companies risking their product security by complying with TIA? If so, how? In the absence of sufficient scholarly analysis, legislators continue to pass encryption laws without balancing human rights, the rule of law, cybersecurity, and business growth. This article builds upon existing scholarship and re-examines the regulatory burden associated with TIA provision and provides further empirical insight. Thus motivated, this study asks:

---

[1] (Anti)Encryption Laws allow access to encrypted data, potentially weakening or bypassing encryption for legal evidence collection from digital sources.

[2] Technical Industry Assistance (TIA), as used in this paper, refers to technical cooperation and capability development powers granted to LEIAs under AA2018. Comparable measures in other jurisdictions may be referred to as lawful access, exceptional access, or lawful interception capabilities.

[3] Telecommunications and Other Legislation Amendment (Assistance and Access) Act 2018, available at https://www.legislation.gov.au/C2018A00148/latest/text.

RQ1. What challenges do Australian tech companies face when complying with the obligations of TIA?
RQ2. To what extent and how do TIA policies impact – (a) products' cybersecurity and risk management practices; (b) products' integrity, competitiveness and growth; and (c) staff's work environment and productivity?

To answer these questions, this study draws on 35 in-depth interviews with tech professionals in Australia, from a total of 45 conducted after the initial submission of this paper. Specifically, it focuses on the AA2018, particularly the voluntary Technical Assistance Request (TAR), compulsory Technical Assistance Notice (TAN), and compulsory Technical Capability Notice (TCN) under Part 15 (Industry Assistance). These TIA obligations are often marked as *vague* [12] (p.11), *controversial* [11] (p.1), and *dangerous powers to crack encrypted communications* [14] (para 1). This paper uses *TIA* or *TIA provisions* to denote encryption policies requiring weak encryption or cybersecurity from vendors.

Building on these concerns, section (317E(1)(a–j)) of the AA2018 lists *acts or things* that companies are compelled to perform, including *removing one or more forms of electronic protection such as encryption and authentication*, as defined in (317E(1)(a)) and 317B. Studies suggest this could *circumvent encryption* [7] (p.10) by requiring the delivery of *encryption keys or passwords* [11] (p. 233). Similarly, under Section (317E(1)(b)), companies are required to provide *technical information*—such as *encryption key, WiFi location, source code, technical changes, network or service design plans, configuration of network and encryption schemes* [15] (p. 3). Likewise, Sect. 317E (1)(c-f) allows LEIAs to *modify, install, or test software* to access encrypted services [13,15]. Finally, Section (317(1)(J)) and (317ZF(1)) prohibit *unauthorised disclosure of [TIA]*, or, *imprisonment for 5 years.*

However, the law also emphasises in section 317ZG of AA2018 and its explanatory documents explicitly stress that the law prohibits *implementing or building Systemic weakness/vulnerabilities, so-called 'backdoors'* that make providers' *encrypted systems less effective or weaken cybersecurity* [10] (page 5). However, this prohibition applies only to *systemic weaknesses* that affect *a whole class of technology* [10] (page 6). Thus, critics note that the terms "systemic weakness" and "systemic vulnerability" are poorly defined, leaving scope for targeted access mechanisms that may still operate as or facilitate backdoors [3,9,10,13].

Consequently, (anti)encryption laws have significantly expanded the surveillance powers of LEIAs. Reports of Australian Federal Police raids on News Corp [16], ABC News [17], and encrypted App developers [18] highlight how LEIAs can now undermine encryption right. These developments raise questions about technical impacts of such powers, warranting further empirical analysis.

Therefore, an empirical study on the impacts of TIAs on cybersecurity is critical. First, with 72% of companies relying on encryption [19], this study gives empirical evidence on the risks associated with weakening it. Second, as encryption underpins integrity [20], the study shows how weakening its standards tarnishes trust and marketability. Third, since a positive work culture is crucial for secure software development [21], our findings also reveal how secret TIA obligations hinder staff's ability to uphold security practices, impacting the work ethics, productivity, and mental health.

2 Research Method and Flow

This work studies the challenges faced by tech companies in Australia in responding to (anti)encryption laws, using a qualitative case study method. To get an in-depth understanding of the perceptions of individuals within tech firms, semi-structured one-on-one interviews were conducted with experts in cybersecurity, risk management, and executive roles (see the interview guide in Appendix A and participant details in Table 1, Appendix B). Each 45-min interview focuses on questions tailored to the staff's expertise. Questions were asked mainly on three themes: cybersecurity questions were asked to technical experts, policy ones to CEOs and managers, and work environment questions to all staff. Special emphasis was placed on AA2018's TIA provision. Audio-recorded interview transcripts are being analysed using a reflexive thematic analysis approach. Figure 1 depicts the overall research flow.

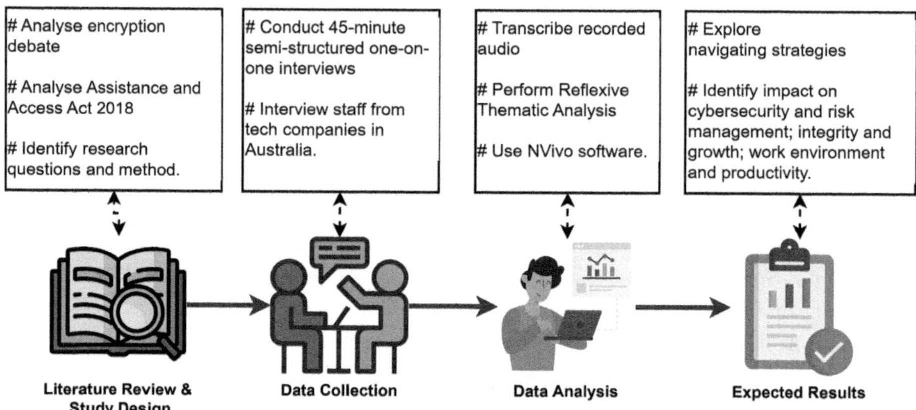

Fig. 1. Overall research flow and approach.

Human ethics approval was obtained from Deakin University (Faculty of Science, Engineering and Built Environment (SEBE), Human Ethics Advisory Group (HEAG) SEBE-2024–28) in September 2024, in accordance with the National Statement on Ethical Conduct in Human Research 2023. As the secrecy provision of encryption laws often restricts direct sharing of experiences, potential scenarios and views were shaped by professional, legal and ethical bindings.

This is an ongoing work. At the time of writing this paper (May 2025), the analysis was based on 35 interviews. Data collection was later completed with

45 participants (August 2025), a carefully balanced sample size that ensured data saturation, alignment with the study timeline, consistency with relevant literature [22], and sufficient depth to explore research questions [23]. Thus, this paper only presents preliminary findings based on the researcher's initial familiarisation with transcripts, field notes, and common patterns observed during the first 35 interviews. Findings and definite themes will evolve as the thematic analysis progresses.

3 Industry Perspectives and Implications

3.1 RQ1: What Challenges Do Australian Tech Companies Face When Complying with the Obligations of TIA?

Approximately 65% of tech professionals were familiar with the TIA provision under AA2018 and criticised it as an added legal burden and workload that conflicts with secure software development practices, while the rest learned about it through this research. It was observed by at least 70% of the participants that the cybersecurity guidelines of the Australian Signals Directorate's (ASD) directly conflict with the legal demands of the TIAs. Around 90% of staff confirmed that the highest level of authentication and authorisation can only be ensured by a fair application of encryption, and concluded that a sub-standard version would seriously damage product security. Thus, 70% of the staff would refuse to change product design and security standards just to comply with TIA obligations. They preferred maintaining 'security and privacy by design' over creating surveillance capabilities. However, at least 30% of staff expressed willingness to deliver specific user data to LEIAs, subject to the availability of a valid warrant and company approval.

Since the data is meant to be stored securely and only shared with the entities who have signed the contract, it shouldn't be shared or be shown to any third party. In case of sensitive details, it [data] need to be masked or hidden and only the high level structure needs to be shown [to LEIAs]. - P34, Technical Manager at Threat Intelligence.

Hidden capabilities in software were identified as a major barrier to maintaining customer satisfaction and trust, with concerns raised about product integrity. Around 60% of experts opposed the secrecy provision and argued that risky technical modifications should be transparent. Since LEIAs would not fully protect companies or staff if modifications are exposed or lead to data breaches, experts advised protecting reputations by disclosing legal backdoors to the customers.

To navigate challenges, staff adopted varied approaches influenced by legal, technical, professional, and emotional factors. Around 30% prioritised work terms, crime prevention, national security, and financial security, and would comply with TIAs without hesitation. Other 70%, however, prioritised privacy, integrity, ethics, and reputation, and would directly refuse TIAs.

Consulting a company or personal lawyer was mentioned more than 80% of the time. However, concerns were raised about lawyers' limited technical knowledge and the secrecy provision. Still, approximately 60% of staff agreed that their

TIA-related action must be decided according to the company policy. They preferred to discuss with experienced technical managers or executives, hoping to receive technically and legally feasible guidance.

We have a strong legal team and you know that, um, corporate affairs, so I believe if the [IA] requests come, we can raise with them and they can take it. -P26, Principal Network Security Architect.

TIA was perceived as technically misaligned with software industry practices. First, 80% of staff said that standard practices of code auditing, testing, and version controlling before production make secret deployment of backdoors impractical. Second, even if 60% of staff were willing to assist LEIAs, the nature of technologies - E2EE, multi-factor authentication, full disk encryption, single sign-on, active directory services, and access management - often makes it technically impossible to develop TIA. Third, targeting the staff was also opposed by about 80%, arguing that only executives can authorise crucial technical changes.

Having examined the challenges tech companies face in responding to TIA provisions (RQ1), the next section (RQ2) explores how these challenges affect cybersecurity (a), integrity (b), and work environment (c).

3.2 RQ2. (a) To What Extent and How Do TIA Policies Impact Products' Cybersecurity and Risk Management Practices?

Insecure Technology Development Led to Increased Attack Surface: At least 80% of participants argued that revelation of encryption keys, disclosure of source code, execution of external codes, exposure of algorithms, and granting of additional privileges to LEIAs were seen as threats to core cybersecurity practices - such as secure coding, testing, patching, and maintaining code integrity. A regional chief information security officer of one of the top global tech giants opposed TIA, referencing the company's security development lifecycle principles, and argued that software design and coding should be naturally secure and come with least privilege (P08). Almost 60% of experts recognised that the mismanagement of backdoors by LEIAs would compromise innovation, undermine product integrity, and introduce cyber threat. Referring to the Salt-Typhoon attack, which exploited legal backdoors within U.S. telecommunication and internet providers in 2024, a CEO stated that TIA undermines core cybersecurity posture and puts Australia's tech sector at a similar risk (P24).

Deliberately created lawful backdoors would broaden the attack surface. Risk management gets challenging, especially when added capabilities and compromised security features cannot be strictly confined to intended users, timeframes, or specific cases. Moreover, TIA places additional strain on small and medium-sized enterprises' (SMEs) cybersecurity teams, which often run with limited resources and cyber experts, as predicted by at least 50% of the experts.

Privacy, which often coexists with security and protects user trust [24], would be compromised by TIA. At least 60% of experts warned that constant government surveillance on software poses a threat to data privacy. TIAs were often categorised as a surveillance tool, with participants questioning why, instead of targeting specific user, LEIAs demand tools capable of spying on everyone.

It [TIA] is for mass surveillance purposes. It has nothing to do with security of society or anything like that. – P29, Founder and Security Researcher.

Hidden Vulnerabilities and Supply Chain Risks: Secret capabilities in software sold to third parties risk the entire supply chain by introducing hidden vulnerabilities. As the secrecy provision restricts transparency and limits technical oversight, embedded security flaws would remain unknown to external developers and clients, according to around 50% of participants. Likewise, code cloning, the practice of duplicating useful code snippets, would be riskier due to the potential presence of backdoors. TIA obstructs coordinated vulnerability management by external bodies in open-source projects, which in turn amplifies systemic risk.

We will ask them [Seller] to remediate that issue [backdoor] and give us the better version [of software] until that obviously we won't compromise our security and we will immediately put some [legal] procedures or maybe some sort of a restriction [ban]. – P02, Technical Lead.

Unfair Usage of Encryption Resulting in Distrust on the Internet: TIAs prohibit fair use of encryption and authentication tools. The removal of electronic protections and sharing of technical information, as permitted by section 317E(1)(a)) and 317E(1), were identified as commonly cited barriers that obstruct the development of a strong security culture. It was argued by at least 65% experts that unauthorised sharing of encryption keys compromises trusted key distribution models—a fundamental pillar of the internet's security architecture. For instance, allowing a ghost user within an encrypted chat by compromising the key distribution tool undermines trust in E2EE altogether. Around 20% of participants mentioned that unfair use of encryption undermines confidentiality and integrity in the CIA (confidentiality, integrity, and availability) triad. Losing confidence in this trust-based internet model risks business reputation.

3.3 RQ2. (b) To What Extent and How Do TIA Policies Impact Products' Integrity, Competitiveness and Growth?

Compromised Product Security and Its Impact on Competitiveness: Around 70% of participants expressed that TIAs initially lower products' cybersecurity standards, then their integrity and acceptability, and later products' marketability and growth. As customers usually avoid software that compromises privacy, sales teams are failing to market Australian tech products. Alternatively, foreign competitors benefit from stronger privacy and lighter surveillance laws.

But for us in Australia, when we will release our projects and products. I think that would make us less competitive than those who are in European Union or something like in US. – P01, CEO.

Overhead Financial Costs of Building and Maintaining Capabilities: TIAs impose a significant financial burden despite limited government compensation. First, weakened security soar data breach risks, potentially leading to lawsuits and fines. TIA was found to be incompatible with the GDPR (General Data Protection Regulation) and the HIPAA (Health Insurance Portability and Accountability Act). Second, executing TIA would require extra hours, and approximately 70% of executives recognised it would reduce the workforce available for core development and service. Third, added highly skilled cybersecurity staff would be needed to manage backdoors, increasing financial strain. Around 50% of staff even prioritised backdoor management over building them. Finally, retaining staff who are aware of the hidden backdoors could add extra costs.

It's [building backdoor] another layer of expertise they [tech companies] need, it means more cost for the business. -P26, Principal Network Security Architect

Overhead Reputation Costs of Building and Maintaining Capabilities: TIA undermine customer trust in products and damages companies' reputations, according to around 75% of participants. The risk of clients discovering hidden backdoors capabilities puts customer relationships in constant jeopardy. Given the interconnected nature of the software supply chain, selling products with embedded backdoors poses serious risks to vendors. To protect the quality of encrypted services, around 20% of the companies suggested outsourcing to jurisdictions with more supportive legal environments - an option that brings additional systemic CapEx (Capital Expenditure). Such outsourcing would also risk business environment, gross domestic product (GDP), and job security.

It's hard to articulate how disruptive it has been, to be honest. I mean, the amount of work and effort it takes to have set up the new company, to move the IP [intellectual property] across to, to move employees across. And then strategising for future people that we might bring across, and now we have this hybridised format where there are some still some people in Australia and some people overseas, and we're working across time zones, whereas we didn't have to before so much. So it has been a huge hit. – P19, CEO and President

3.4 RQ2. (c) To What Extent and How Do TIA Policies Impact Staff's Work Environment and Productivity?

Accusation of Insider Threat and Career Damage: Participants expressed concern about severe career damage if TIA implementation involvement were exposed. Given how tech companies operate, hidden capabilities would eventually be revealed - either internally or within the supply chain. As the secrecy provision prohibits disclosing TIA-related information, around 75% of developers feared being viewed as insider threats. Also, professional relationships with colleagues and management would deteriorate notably. Staff feared losing their job and worried about not receiving a positive reference due to their TIA-related actions that might contradict company policy. At least 20% of experts would leave the tech industry or Australia to avoid this legal burden.

Yeah, that and the general reputation in the industry would be damaged. So, no other employer will be keen on hiring that person since they have been known to carry out things without informing the correct management. – P34, Technical Account Manager at Threat Intelligence.

Psychological, Emotional, and Legal Burden Reduces Productivity: Violating customer privacy and acting against company interests would cause stress and ethical discomfort, as stated by at least 80%. While a few staff viewed TIAs as a professional obligation, most found it difficult to accept that their actions might compromise product security, breach customer data privacy, and damage company's reputation. They expressed concern about being unable to cope with the potential legal outcomes, both emotionally and financially. Staff worried about privacy, and stated that they were trained to code for the benefit of humanity, not to enable lawful surveillance. Although at least 35% of the staff expressed reluctance to comply with the TIA, they ultimately have no choice but to follow the law to avoid potential legal consequences.

If we are really concern about our customers' privacy and customers' betterment, then we will not really comply with their [LEIAs] request and instead take a legal route. – P21, Lead Software Developer

These burdens reduce productivity. Software development requires peace of mind, but contributing to hidden capabilities creates stress and inefficiency.

Most of the time it's [IA policies] something that creates uncertainty and anxiety in the day to day among the team and for team culture and morale. – P19, CEO and President

4 Discussion And Consideration

The ubiquitous use of encryption that hides evidence [25] certainly demand extensive legal actions [2]. Thus, governments have pushed for additional (anti)encryption laws, often by ignoring tech companies' outcries due to limited research highlighting cybersecurity impacts. This study observed that privacy [15], technical adaptability [10,13], and commercial [7,26] issues surrounding these laws largely arise from the government's ignorance of cybersecurity implications.

By delivering vital empirical evidence, this study adds knowledge to the 'Going Dark' debate. A *ripple effect* was observed, where compromised cybersecurity led to *downstream impacts* on product integrity, competitiveness, and the work environment (Fig. 2). To navigate this debate, tech experts suggested that the laws should be transparent, technically practical, and supportive of secure development practices. While at least 40% of participants urged disclosure of such legal assistance in customer terms and conditions (T&C), about 20% also recommended a trusted third-party auditor to oversee the entire TIA, thereby increasing trust between the LEIA and the tech company.

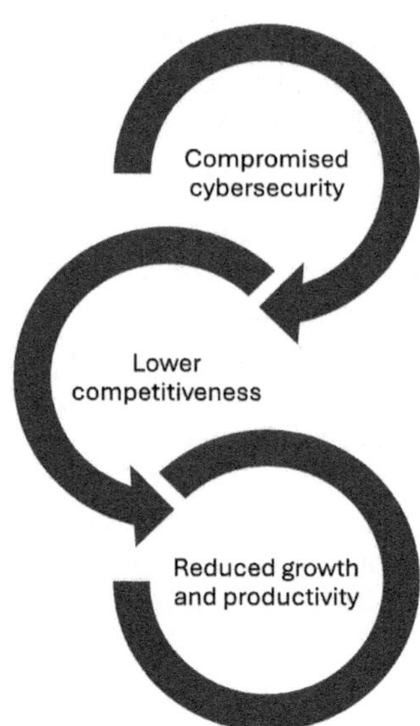

Fig. 2. The ripple effect of Technical Industry Assistance (TIA).

Although the primary rationale for incorporating surveillance capabilities with encryption is to access criminal evidence [25], this is frequently pursued in a disproportionate way [26]. To protect participants' rights, this study did not assess whether they had direct experience with TIA requests. However, they technically argued that so-called *mandatory backdoors* are often unreliable for evidence and pose risks that may outweigh potential benefits, indicating policymakers' technical limitations [9]. Given the ineffectiveness of the presently demanded TIA capabilities, about 20%-30% of participants expressed conditional support for a manageable and trackable backdoor or relevant capabilities to assist LEIAs when evidence was otherwise difficult to obtain.

Moreover, a lack of technical understanding among policymakers, combined with a surveillance-driven mindset among LEIAs, creates various challenges within the broader encryption debate: First, while scholars have argued that (anti)encryption policies compromise privacy [3,28], surveillance tends to grow significantly when trust in encryption cannot be ensured [6]. It is understood that customers are likely to distrust software if trustworthy encryption is not guaranteed during development. Second, despite a significant rise in technology-based policing, continued upskilling of LEIAs is widely recommended [29]. Particularly, cracking encryption to access evidence requires advanced hacking skills. Instead, LEIAs are found to demand weaker encryption to conceal their technical inability. As one founder and CEO stated, LEIAs *want to make their job easier*, characterising them as *lazy* and *not technical* (P32).

They [LEIAs and policy makers] don't understand the technology. They just think that there needs to be a solution; so there must be one. – P23, CEO.

Finally, building on insights from [30], who identified concerns around unintended consequences and ethical dilemmas among developers, our study found that forced implementation of capabilities can lead to a range of negative outcomes. These include ethical dilemmas, remorse, mental health issues, misunderstandings, and reduced productivity. Participants noted that non-executive tech experts should not be subject to direct or indirect TIA obligations.

As governments and LEIAs increasingly rely on TIAs, our study makes the following recommendations acknowledging the role of tech companies in encryption debate: First, the study endorses the need for greater knowledge and awareness among tech staff and policymakers. While policymakers must recognise the importance of fair encryption, tech companies also need to demonstrate potential cybersecurity risks to executives and provide secure alternatives to LEIAs.

Second, this study urges the reform of legal discrepancies that allow policymakers to overlook security risks faced by tech companies due to TIA. Comparatively weaker privacy laws [31] are often inadequate in the face of expanding digital surveillance laws [3]. While the AA2018 states it is not an (anti)encryption Act, participants observed that TIA requirements under Part 15 contradict this. Existing cybersecurity guidelines are still at the policy level instead of being legally enforced. To counter encryption-weakening laws, privacy and cybersecurity uplifting policies need to be better supported.

Third, more accountability is required regarding the operation of TIA. Rather than merely publishing application numerals, AA2018's TIA annual report should publicly disclose examples of its usage, how industries responded, and what measures were taken to prevent cybersecurity breaches. Such detailed reporting would enable tech companies to demonstrate to customers how TIAs can be implemented securely [32].

Finally, transparency in the supply chain is essential to protect reputation. If customers were to discover surveillance-enabling hidden capabilities, it would be impossible to regain their trust. Thus, it is suggested that products' terms and conditions (T&Cs) should disclose the reasons for including lawful hidden backdoors in advance, similar to Apple Inc.'s recent disclaimer regarding iCloud's E2EE ban in the UK mandated by the IPA2016. However, AA2018's secrecy provision, which impede such transparency, require legal reform.

I think the best strategy would be 100% transparent, being transparent 100% to all the stakeholders. - P01, CEO

Limitations: This study is limited by the lack of direct implementation experience related to TIA aiding (anti)encryption laws and evidence collection through them. Due to legal protections, experiences of participants associated with these policies are presented only in general and technical terms. Future research could also incorporate customer feedback on TIA aiding (anti)encryption laws.

5 Conclusions

There are growing global concerns about how regulations impact cybersecurity practices [33]. While regulating encryption has provided new ways to access encrypted evidence, it has also increased cybersecurity and state surveillance risks. Preliminary results accumulated so far, after an initial review of 35 interviews with tech staff, reflect that Australian policymakers prioritise national security over essential cybersecurity practices by enacting laws that facilitate surveillance abilities. At least 85% of participants identified TIA laws as backdoor facilitating and cybersecurity-weakening surveillance laws. It was found that TIA aiding (anti)encryption laws directly diminish cybersecurity, increase threat vectors, and risk privacy. Also, initial cybersecurity issues were found to impact product integrity and business growth by at least 70% of staff. Likewise, hidden implementation of TIAs was observed to harm secure work environment and reduce productivity by 80% of experts.

These findings can serve as a starting point to highlight key cybersecurity issues and drive necessary policy reform about the 'Going Dark' debate. Current encryption policies should enable companies to inform their users about the TIA, clearly define legal parameters to ensure that access is restricted to specific data only, and offer adequate legal and financial protection for experts and companies that implement the TIA. This would protect and support not only broader national security objectives but also the security of tech products. As critical infrastructure increasingly depends on technology, protecting its cybersecurity is not just a technical imperative; it is a matter of national security [34].

Acknowledgments. I am sincerely grateful to anonymous research participants who voluntarily shared their experiences and insights for this study. I also express my gratitude to my supervisory team, A/Prof. Diarmaid Harkin and A/Prof. Zubair Baig, for their guidance and encouragement throughout this study. This research was supported by the Deakin University Postgraduate Research Scholarship (DUPR-0000018830).

Disclosure of Interests. The authors have no competing interests to declare that are relevant to the content of this article.

A Appendices

A.1 Appendix A: Sample Interview Guide and Themes (Each One-on-One Interview Last Around 45 Min)

1. Are you familiar with (anti)encryption policies? If yes, what is your understanding of these laws? (Generic)
2. Could you provide more details about the best cybersecurity practices you and your company follow within your products and services? (Generic)
3. Does the demand from (anti)encryption laws contradict your regular cybersecurity practice? (Cybersecurity)
4. How do the threat vector or attack surface changes with backdoor inclusion? Any added tasks for the threat monitoring team? (Cybersecurity)

5. How would you handle TIA a situation? Are you ready to change your product design to comply with such legal issues? (Cybersecurity)
6. To what extent could these (anti)encryption laws initially impact your security practices and gradually affect product integrity? (Integrity and growth)
7. Any potential impact on user trust in your security & privacy standard, since you're complying Australian (anti)encryption laws? (Integrity and growth)
8. If your hidden backdoor is discovered by your customer or clients within your product's supply chain, what will be their reaction? (Integrity and growth)
9. With such burdens, have you experienced or predicted any impact on your relationship with colleagues or the employers? (work environment)
10. If your action hampers trust, privacy, and security of your product, will it eventually betray your customers? To what extent will it impact your work ethics? Any aftereffects on your productivity? (work environment)

A.2 Appendix B: Participants List and Company Details

Table 1. Participants list and Company details.

Sl Number	Role	Company Type
P01	CEO	privacy and security
P02	Technical Lead	commercial bank
P03	Data Engineer	software, web, and App
P04	Data Analytics	software, web, and App
P05	Software Engineer	software, web, and App
P06	Security Consultant – GRC	cybersecurity insurance
P07	System Admin and Head of IT	educational technology and IT
P08	Regional Chief Cyber Security Officer	operating system and cloud
P09	Business Analyst	medical and healthcare tech
P010	Software and ML Engineer	agricultural technology
P011	Inventory and Store Software Manager	laptop producer and IT service
P012	CEO	software, web, and App startup
P013	Product Manager	IT audit, and consultancy
P014	Software Automation Engineer	aeronautical technology
P015	Product Manager	software, web, and App
P016	Software Developer	IT service and educational tech
P017	Software Developer	IT service and educational tech
P018	IT Support Officer	IT service and educational tech
P019	President and CEO	encrypted messaging App
P020	CEO	cybersecurity and Risk Management
P021	Lead Software Developer	payment software and App
P022	Security Practice Lead	search engine and email

continued)

Table 1. (*continued*)

Sl Number	Role	Company Type
P023	CEO	cybersecurity and Risk Management
P024	Co-Founder and CEO	cybersecurity threat intelligence
P025	Cyber Security Engineer	rail and transportation technology
P026	Principal Network Security Architect	internet, IT, and telecommunication
P027	Chief Information Officer	software, web, and App
P028	Senior Business Analyst Fraud	internet, IT, and telecommunication
P029	Founder and Security Researcher	cybersecurity and risk management
P030	Data Analyst	software, web, and App
P031	Director	software, web, and App
P032	Founder and CEO	cyber threat intelligence
P033	Founder & Director	software, web, and App
P034	Technical Manager at Threat Intelligence	cybersecurity and risk management
P035	Dev Tester and Developer	software, web, and App

References

1. Liguori, C.: Exploring lawful hacking as a possible answer to the "Going Dark" debate. Mich. Tech. L. Rev. **26**, 317 (2019)
2. Abelson, H., et al.: Bugs in our pockets: the risks of client-side scanning. J. Cybersecur. **10**(1), tyad020 (2024)
3. Mann, M., Daly, A., Molnar, A.: Regulatory arbitrage and transnational surveillance: Australia's extraterritorial assistance to access encrypted communications. Internet Policy Rev. **9**(3) (2020)
4. The Record. https://therecord.media/european-commission-takes-aim-encryption-europol-fbi-proposal Accessed 12 Mar 2025
5. Van Daalen, O.L.: The right to encryption: privacy as preventing unlawful access. Comput. Law Secur. Rev. **49**, 105804 (2023)
6. Dizon, M.A.C.: The value of trust in encryption: impact and implications on technology law and policy. IEEE Trans. Technol. Soc. **4**(4), 343–351 (2023)
7. Barker, G.R., Lehr, W., Loney, M., Sicker, D.: The economic impact of laws that weaken encryption. ANU College Law Res. Paper **21**(42) (2021)
8. Budish, R.H., Burkert, H., Gasser, U.: Encryption policy and its international impacts: a framework for understanding extraterritorial ripple effects. Hoover Institution Essay 1804 (2018)
9. Walker-Munro, B.: A shot in the dark: Australia's proposed encryption laws and the disruption calculus. Adel. L. Rev. **40**, 783 (2019)
10. Davis, P.A.E.: Decrypting Australia's 'Anti-Encryption'legislation: The meaning and effect of the 'systemic weakness' limitation. Comput. Law Secur. Rev. **44**, 105659 (2022)
11. Thresher, K.: Deciphering Australia's encryption laws: a human rights approach. Australian J. Hum. Rights **28**, 225–248 (2022)

12. Hardy, K.: Australia's encryption laws: practical need or political strategy? Internet Pol. Rev. **9**, 1–16 (2020)
13. Farlow, H., Edwards, B.M.: Shining a light on 'going dark': a framework to guide the co-design and communication of decryption laws based on the passage of the Telecommunications and Other Legislation (Assistance and Access) Bill 2018. Comput. Law Secur. Rev. **46**, 105726 (2022)
14. Aljazeera. https://www.aljazeera.com/news/2022/4/5/australias-dangerous-encryption-law-in-works-in-2015-document. Accessed 12 Mar 2025
15. Hutchinson, M.: Unintended consequences and Australia's assistance and access act 2018-Is Australia creating a technology base human rights problem? Int'l. In-House Counsel J. **12**, 1 (2019)
16. The Guardian. https://www.theguardian.com/australia-news/2020/apr/15/high-court-rules-afp-warrant-for-raid-on-news-corp-journalists-home-was-invalid. Accessed 12 Mar 2025
17. ABC News. https://www.abc.net.au/news/2019-07-15/abc-raids-australian-federal-police-press-freedom/11309810 Accessed 12 Mar 2025
18. The Guardian. https://www.theguardian.com/australia-news/2024/nov/05/session-encrypted-messaging-app-developer-moves-out-of-australia-police-visit-switzerland. Accessed 12 Mar 2025
19. Statista Research Department. https://www.statista.com/statistics/529768/worldwide-enterprise-encryption-use-by-industry/. Accessed 12 Mar 2025
20. Tam, T., Rao, A., Hall, J.: The good, the bad and the missing: a narrative review of cyber-security implications for Australian small businesses. Comput. Secur. **109**, 102385 (2021)
21. Kalhoro, S., Rehman, M., Ponnusamy, V., Shaikh, F.B.: Extracting key factors of cyber hygiene behaviour among software engineers: a systematic literature review. IEEE Access **9**, 99339–99363 (2021)
22. Albrechtsen, E.: A qualitative study of users' view on information security. Comput. Secur. **26**, 276–289 (2007)
23. Marshall, B., Cardon, P., Poddar, A., Fontenot, R.: Does sample size matter in qualitative research?: a review of qualitative interviews in IS research. J. Comput. Inf. Syst. **54**, 11–22 (2013)
24. Aquilina, K.: Public security versus privacy in technology law: a balancing act? Comput. Law Secur. Rev. **26**, 130–143 (2010)
25. Pisaric, M.: Communications encryption as an investigative obstacle. J. Crimin. Crim. L. **60**, 61 (2022)
26. McGarrity, N., Hardy, K.: Digital surveillance and access to encrypted communications in Australia. Common Law World Rev. **49**, 160–181 (2020)
27. Maxwell, F.: When good is not good enough: evaluating the proportionality and necessity of the Australian government hacking warrants. Curr. Issues Crim. Just. **34**, 136–154 (2022)
28. Gill, L., Israel, T., Parsons, C.: Shining a light on the encryption debate: a Canadian field guide. Citizen Lab and the Samuelson-Glushko Canadian Internet Policy and Public Interest Clinic (2018)
29. Joh, E.E.: The consequences of automating and deskilling the police. UCLA L. Rev. Discourse **67**, 133 (2019)
30. Ramulu, H.S., Schmitt, H., Wermke, D., Acar, Y.: Security and privacy software creators' perspectives on unintended consequences. In: 33rd USENIX Security Symposium (USENIX Security 24), pp. 3259–3276 (2024)
31. Daly, A.: Privacy in automation: an appraisal of the emerging Australian approach. Comput. Law Secur. Rev. **33**, 836–846 (2017)

32. Setty, S.: Surveillance, secrecy, and the search for meaningful accountability. Stan. J. Int'l L. **51**, 69 (2015)
33. Mishra, A., Alzoubi, Y.I., Anwar, M.J., Gill, A.Q.: Attributes impacting cybersecurity policy development: an evidence from seven nations. Comput. Secur. **120**, 102820 (2022)
34. Nissenbaum, H.: Where computer security meets national security. Ethics Inf. Technol. **7**, 61–73 (2005)

Author Index

K. Adi et al. (Eds.): CRiSIS 2025, LNCS 16295, pp. 465–466, 2026.
https://doi.org/10.1007/978-3-032-20732-6

GPSR Compliance

The European Union's (EU) General Product Safety Regulation (GPSR) is a set of rules that requires consumer products to be safe and our obligations to ensure this.

If you have any concerns about our products, you can contact us on ProductSafety@springernature.com

In case Publisher is established outside the EU, the EU authorized representative is:

Springer Nature Customer Service Center GmbH
Europaplatz 3
69115 Heidelberg, Germany

Batch number: 10425590

Printed by Printforce, the Netherlands